From Renaissance Monarchy to Absolute Monarchy

FRENCH KINGS, NOBLES, & ESTATES

J. Russell Major

The Johns Hopkins University Press

BALTIMORE & LONDON

The Johns Hopkins Paperbacks edition, 1997
06 05 04 03 02 01 00 99 98 97   5 4 3 2 1

THE JOHNS HOPKINS UNIVERSITY PRESS
2715 NORTH CHARLES STREET
BALTIMORE, MARYLAND 21218-4319
THE JOHNS HOPKINS PRESS LTD., LONDON

Frontispiece: The Estates General of 1614. From Pierre Chaunu, *La civilisation de l'Europe classique* (Paris, 1966). The original is in the Bibliothèque Nationale, Cabinet des estampes.

ISBN 0-8018-4776-1
ISBN 0-8018-5631-0 (pbk.)

Library of Congress Cataloging-in-Publication Data will be found at the end of this book.

A catalog record for this book is available from the British Library.

For Blair

FOR WHOM NOTHING WAS IMPOSSIBLE

Contents

ACKNOWLEDGMENTS ix

INTRODUCTION xiii

ONE   *The Establishment of the Renaissance Monarchy*   3

TWO   *The Flowering of the Renaissance Monarchy*   23

THREE   *The Late Medieval–Renaissance Nobility*   57

FOUR   *The Wars of Religion*   107

FIVE   *Henry IV*   130

SIX   *The Reprieve, 1610–1620*   181

SEVEN   *France Finds a King, 1620–1624*   205

EIGHT   *Richelieu and Marillac, 1624–1629*   220

NINE   *Marillac and the Provincial Estates*   236

TEN   *The Triumph of Richelieu and Mazarin*   261

ELEVEN   *The Nobility*   304

TWELVE   *Louis XIV*   335

THIRTEEN   *Kings, Nobles, and Estates in Retrospect*   367

ABBREVIATIONS 377

NOTES 379

BIBLIOGRAPHY 413

INDEX 435

Acknowledgments

There is no greater pleasure than finishing a book, not only because it gives one an opportunity to turn to something new, but also because it provides a chance to thank the people and the institutions who have made it all possible. As this book is intended to be a synthesis of the forty-five years I have devoted to studying the history of France, my debts are indeed numerous. I begin by recalling the memory of my parents and secondary school teachers, who first instilled in me a love of history. To the Virginia Military Institute I am indebted for a disciplined way of life and for the requirement that students write more papers, both long and short, than are required at even the most prestigious colleges today. At Princeton University I had the good fortune to study under Jinks Harbison, who inspired in me an interest in the age of the Renaissance and Reformation, and Joe Strayer, who showed me the importance of institutional history. To Joe Mathews I am grateful for the guidance he gave me in the early stages of my career, and for the atmosphere he created during the ten years he served as chairman of the Emory history department. By his leadership and his example he made Emory a delightful and fruitful place for a historian to work.

Neither this book nor much else that I have done during the past forty-five years would have been possible without the generous support of a number of foundations. I would like to express my appreciation for two Guggenheim Fellowships, two Social Science Research Council Fellowships, two memberships at the Institute for Advanced Study at Princeton, a Fulbright Research Fellowship, a National Endowment for the Humanities Senior Fellowship, and seven sabbatical leaves and several research grants from Emory University. The support provided by these sources enabled me to travel to the archives and libraries in my early career and gave me the leisure to think and write in recent years.

I have profited greatly from my graduate students. They provided intellectual stimulation when they were in the seminar room and great satisfaction as I watch their careers. The reader will find their books and articles frequently cited in this study. To the American Historical Review *and the Yale University Press I wish to express my thanks for giving me permission to reproduce or* condense portions of my work that they so capably published. I am also indebted to many French and American archivists and librarians for their knowledgeable and courteous assistance. Of those who have helped me at Emory, I would especially like to single out Marella Walker. When I joined the faculty in 1949, Emory was just beginning the transition from a small liberal arts college with several professional schools attached to a research university. The college library could not have had much over 100,000 volumes, and it was almost devoid of foreign-language materials. From this inauspicious beginning, Marella managed by working far more than the prescribed number of hours to transform our holdings in late medieval and early modern French history into a splendid collection. It has been years since I have had to travel for my research.

I am indebted to the many secretaries who have transcribed my almost illegible hand into typescript. In this instance I would especially like to thank Patsy Stockbridge, who not only produced this book but in its final stages has patiently tried to introduce me to the mysteries of the computer, which she herself has so completely mastered. William Beik kindly read the introduction, and I benefited from his comments on the third chapter and those of the other members of James Allen Vann Seminar of Emory University. To my colleague Susan Socolow I am grateful for devoting many hours of her valuable time to demonstrating to me the map-making potential of the computer. To Dan Costello I owe my thanks for doing most of the work on the map in this book, and to Jeff Young credit should go for bringing it to completion. Peter Dreyer has provided the most careful job of copyediting that I have yet experienced. We have not always agreed, but it is already clear to me that this will be a better book because of his endeavors.

And finally I wish to thank my wife. We were married while I was still in the army in World War II and have enjoyed the entire academic experience together. It began at 11 Dickinson Place at Princeton, where we shared a tiny kitchen and all other facilities with five other families. It progressed to a voyage to Europe in 1952 with four children aged six and under, and it was capped the following summer by a three-month tour of the French provincial archives in a four-passenger Ford Victoria with all our luggage tied on the roof and a child in her lap. The six of us lived on $15 a day by staying in one-roof Guide Michelin hotels without private baths and cooking our food in city parks. Our next long expedition included camping for over three months in the Bois de Boulogne and many more months wandering through the beautiful French countryside. To anyone but Blair such traveling with four small children on a limited budget would have been impossible. But without these expeditions *neither this book nor much else could have been accomplished. It is therefore most fitting that I should affectionately dedicate the volume that pulls together all that I have done to the one who has shared the glorious adventure with me from the very start.*

Introduction

This is the last book on French history that I shall ever write. I began my research forty-five years ago and want to turn to something entirely different. In the circumstances, I would like to give an account of how my interpretation of late medieval–Renaissance–early modern France developed, and how it interacted with existing interpretations by other historians.

When I began my graduate study at Princeton on March 1, 1946, the middle class, the bourgeoisie, were still considered the great heroes, the prime movers of the historical process. Even Marxist historians, following the lead of their founder, gave them grudging admiration. The books I read in course after course had a common theme: the rise of the middle class, who, in alliance with the kings, suppressed the great feudal nobility and created the absolute monarchy. The principal author of this interpretation was Augustin Thierry. Thierry was born in Blois in 1795. After brief careers as a teacher, the secretary to the social scientist Saint-Simon, and a newspaper correspondent, he turned to history. His *Histoire de la conquête de l'Angleterre par les Normands* was published in 1825 and brought him wide recognition. Although Thierry became blind the following year and was in generally failing health, other works followed in which he formed his interpretation of the evolution of the French state and society. In 1836 he was assigned the task of collecting documents for a multivolume series on the history of the third estate. Three volumes appeared during his lifetime, and a fourth was published some years after his death in 1856.[1] Numerous manuscripts still lie in the Bibliothèque nationale awaiting their publisher.[2] They bear elegant testimony of the devotion of the blind historian and his assistants to the project. It was as an introduction to this monumental series that Thierry wrote his "Essai sur l'histoire de la formation et des progrès du tiers état," which originally appeared in the *Revue des Deux Mondes* in 1846. It was reprinted in an expanded form in the first volume of the documents, as a separate volume in 1853, and in an English translation in 1859.[3]

Thierry dreamed of a unified, centralized France in which all citizens were free and subject to the same laws, a dream he thought had been achieved briefly in 1789 and again in the July Monarchy of Louis Philippe. He believed that after the disappearance of the Roman Empire, the inhabitants of France were divided into two main groups, the Gauls, who became the ancestors of the third estate, and their conquerors, the Franks, who were the antecedents of the nobility. The history of France, then, became the story of how these peoples of such diverse origins and social, economic, and legal status were welded together into a single nation. Thierry found that "during the period of six centuries, from the twelfth to the eighteenth, the history of the Third Estate and that of the kings are indissolubly bound together in such a manner that . . . one is . . . the counterpart of the other. From the accession of Louis the Fat to the death of Louis XIV, each decisive epoch in the progress of the different classes of the common man in liberty, prosperity, enlightenment, and social importance corresponds, in the series of the reigns, to the name of a great king or a great minister. The eighteenth century alone was an exception to this law of our national development; it introduced distrust and prepared a fatal divorce between the Third Estate and the crown."[4]

Thierry thought that the clergy and the nobility were the great enemies of equality and national unity. He was generally at a loss to find any constructive role for them in the unfolding historical process. Indeed, for the most part they were obstructive. The best Thierry could do for the nobility was to say that "chivalry belonged to them with all that there is of military valor, glory, and honor around that name. They knew how to die, it was their boast, and in this lay their legitimate pride."[5]

Thierry recognized that the third estate was not a monolithic class. There were peasants, artisans, and mere laborers as well as the bourgeoisie. He sought to maintain the essential unity of the order by insisting that although the middle class was the upper class of the third estate, it was "continually augmented by the accession of the inferior classes." With this slight gesture toward the less fortunate, he proceeded to declare that the third estate "drew its strength and spirit from two different sources: the one complex and municipal, the commercial classes; the other simple and central, the class of the royal judicial and financial officers, whose number and power rapidly increased, and who, with rare exceptions, all sprang from the common people." When these offices were made hereditary early in the seventeenth century, their owners "began to imbibe the spirit of independence and pride, and high opinion of self, that were formerly the attributes of gentlemen." Nevertheless, Thierry persisted in the belief that these nobles of the robe remained part of the third estate. The spirit of the urban corporations "was liberal, but narrow and immobile, attached to its local immunities, to its hereditary rights, to the independent and privileged existence of the municipalities and communes. The spirit of the judicial and administrative corporations [on the other hand] recognized only one law, that of the state, only one liberty, that of the prince, only one interest, that of order under one absolute guardianship, and their reasoning did not regard the privileges of the common people with more favor than those of the nobility."[6]

Thus the bourgeoisie, "the nucleus of the third estate," had two segments, which appeared to be moving in opposite directions. The royal magistrates continued to advance, but the leaders of the municipalities were subjected to ever more stringent control. "The privilege of a free and quasi-sovereign community, which had protected the rebirth and first developments of the civil order, was treated in the same manner as the feudal privileges, and passed like them under the level of royal authority, of which every encroachment was then a step toward civilization and toward national unity. But while the nobility lost, and its losses were irreparable, the losses of the bourgeoisie were so only in appearance; if the beaten road was closed to them, new and broader paths were immediately opened. *The continued elevation of the third estate is the predominant fact and the law of our history*" (emphasis added).[7]

Thierry's interpretation quickly became orthodox.[8] Historians set their research in the framework of an alliance between the bourgeoisie and the crown that led to the overthrow of a decadent, economically declining aristocracy and the establishment of the absolute monarchy, a step that was necessary before national unity could be achieved. There was a tendency for each historian to see the critical, decisive change taking place in his own period, whether it was the Middle Ages, the Renaissance, or the seventeenth century. It mattered not that the evidence, sometimes collected with great effort, did not snugly fit into the scheme Thierry had devised; the author simply crafted his conclusions to fit the reigning orthodoxy. Even the great Gustave Dupont-Ferrier, who knew the archives of the late Middle Ages better than any other historian before or since his time, did not escape the net. In his monumental study *Les Officiers royaux des bailliages et sénéchaussées et les institutions monarchiques locales en France à la fin du moyen âge*, he pointed to the administrative disorders, the ignorance of Parisian officials of local conditions, the confusion of boundaries, and the overlapping jurisdictions. When it came time to prepare a map of the bailiwicks and seneschalsies, he refused to draw linear boundaries. Instead, he made a line from each local seat to the smaller towns and villages that he could prove were dependent on it. Yet, in stating his conclusions, Dupont-Ferrier declared that France was fast becoming a centralized, unified, absolute monarchy. He found the motivating force behind this development primarily in the councils of the bailiwicks, which were dominated by the third estate. It is not surprising that this is the weakest part of the book. Dupont-Ferrier never demonstrated exactly how the councils functioned, and the importance he attached to them has not withstood the test of later investigations. Nevertheless, his work had a profound influence on younger students of administrative history. Some of their studies were purely descriptive, but when they sought to place their work in a larger perspective, they chose the scheme devised by Thierry and Dupont-Ferrier. Republican historians who specialized in the seventeenth century accepted the theory that an absolute monarchy had been necessary to strip noble, province, and town of their special privileges so that all Frenchmen would become as one. To them the centralized absolute monarchy was a necessary stage that led to the Revolution of 1789 and eventually to the creation of the Third Republic.

Marxist historians could accept the above scheme with some obvious adjustments. Like Thierry they saw the state and society moving toward a preconceived goal, in which the bourgeoisie's overthrow of the aristocracy was a necessary early step. Boris Porchnev departed from the scheme by insisting that members of the bourgeoisie who purchased offices became feudalized and thereby joined the aristocracy, but his compatriot A. D. Lublinskaya also found a place for a rising bourgeoisie in the early seventeenth century.[9]

I do not know to what extent English historians were influenced by Thierry, but the theory of a rising middle class and a declining aristocracy became as firmly implanted in their country as in France. The great academic statesman and Tudor historian A. F. Pollard combined all the existing clichés in a series of lectures he gave early in the twentieth century. The growth of commerce and industry, he declared, led to the emergence of the middle class. With its assistance the new monarchies were born, the British Empire later came into being, and everything he regarded as good received an assist. "Where you had no middle class, you had no Renaissance and no Reformation," he confidently asserted.[10] At the same time the decline of the manorial system, the invention of gunpowder, the growth of nationalism, the emergence of the absolute monarchies, and so forth, led to the decline of the nobility. So popular was Pollard's synthesis that it reappeared over a half-century later in a paperback edition. The theory of a rising middle class allied to the new monarchs and a declining aristocracy was so much a part of historians' vision that it became almost universally accepted.

In 1932, Georges Pagès published a provocative article in which he argued that "venality of offices contributed powerfully in old France to the rise of the inferior classes and the renewal of the leading classes." The abuses and mismanagement of these officials provoked many complaints. "But it is nonetheless true that through them all bourgeois, even the smallest, were associated in the exercise and profits of public power. And this is why the entire bourgeoisie was interested in supporting the absolute monarchy, which it aided with its money." In return, the monarchy "abandoned to it little by little the honor and the benefit of administering the kingdom in its name." Richelieu recognized the faults of venality, but he also saw that it had become a political and social necessity. Eventually, the monarchy sought to recover its authority by employing intendants, who, although of bourgeois origin, were nobles. In consequence, "their interests coincided narrowly with those of the nobility. Is it astonishing that the bourgeoisie, which continued to enrich itself and was the most enlightened class in the country, but which saw itself dispossessed of its share of public power, became irritated, and that its loyalty, once so strong, gave way to disaffection?"[11] In this way Pagès accounted for the alliance between the monarchy and the bourgeoisie and explained why the bourgeoisie abandoned the monarchy in 1789.

In a footnote to his article, Pagès mentioned that his student Roland Mousnier was studying venality of office. Mousnier, who was to become the ablest and most prolific of Pagès's students, published his monumental study *La Vénalité des offices sous Henri IV et Louis XIII* in 1945. From that time on, there could never be any doubt of the central place that venality of offices would hold in the history of early modern France. Meanwhile, Dupont-Ferrier, with his *La Formation de l'état français et l'unité française*, and Pagès, with his *La Monarchie d'ancien régime en France*, both first published in the interwar years, did much to cement their interpretations, and indirectly those of Thierry, on historical thought. Together they covered the history of France from its origins until the eighteenth century. Brief, concise, interpretative, and resting firmly on the monograph literature of that time, they deserve to be compared favorably, or almost favorably, with Marc Bloch's better-known *Les Caractères originaux de l'histoire rurale française*, which was first published at about the same time. Bloch, incidentally, shared the prevailing belief in the economic backwardness of the nobility. These studies were admirable in many respects, but they erred in grossly overrating the power of the monarchy, in underrating the role of the nobility, and in equating the nobility of the robe with the bourgeoisie. Nevertheless, they reflected the standard interpretation when I began research on my doctoral dissertation on the Estates General of 1560 in the fall of 1947.

My study of this meeting of the Estates General led me to at least two important conclusions. First, the crown often looked upon the Estates General as an instrument to enhance its ability to govern rather than as a natural enemy. Second, to secure the necessary cooperation the crown bargained on an equal basis with the deputies. There was a genuine give-and-take, and to secure the support of the elite, the crown was willing to make surprising concessions, such as to offer to let the estates collect any taxes they were willing to vote. Further research between then and 1962 pointed to the inherent weaknesses of the Renaissance monarchy that were overcome only when the king won the support of the leading elements of society. Of these elements the most important were the nobles, who enjoyed a dynamic resurgence in the century before the Wars of Religion.[12]

I then turned my attention to how the Renaissance monarchy was transformed into an absolute monarchy.[13] I chose the provincial estates as the most likely vehicle for this investigation, and I worked in France from June 1961 through August 1962 collecting material for this study. The first summer was spent exploiting the depositories in Paris, and the remainder of my time was devoted to the departmental and municipal archives. The biggest lesson I learned from this experience was that the history of France could not be written from the viewpoint of Paris alone. The historian gets a quite different perspective if he also views the scene from the provinces. The final step was to discover how the nobility met the many challenges that threatened their position as leaders of society.[14]

The original goal of this book was to try to persuade my fellow historians: first, that my interpretation of the Renaissance monarchy was correct, and that the role that Richelieu and some other statesmen played in altering its character needed to be reevaluated; and second, that the theory, devised by Thierry and updated by later scholars, that the driving force in French history was an alliance between the kings and the bourgeoisie was incorrect, and that the most dynamic element in the society of that day was, in fact, the nobility. This no longer seems necessary; there has been a remarkable change in most historians' perspectives during the past decade or so.

Few historians, if any, would now argue that the nobility underwent a crisis during the sixteenth century. Led by James B. Wood, Jean-Marie Constant, Amanda Eurich, and William A. Weary, a number of scholars have demonstrated that the nobles of this or that locality or this or that family more than held their own.[15] Françoise Autrand, Donna Bohanan, and Jonathan DeWald, among others, have shown that the family origins of many nobles of the robe lay in the *noblesse de race*.[16] The robe and sword can no longer be so sharply separated, although the reason for the friction between the two has not been fully explained, as John Salmon has shown.[17] The vertical ties among the aristocracy have also been explored. P. S. Lewis has given us several excellent articles on indentures in the late Middle Ages, Robert Harding has written a splendid book on the provincial governors and how they functioned, a number of scholars have contributed to a study of clientage dedicated to the dean of early modern historians, Roland Mousnier, and Sharon Kettering has given us an excellent book and a number of articles that make clientage in the late sixteenth and seventeenth centuries better known than in any other era.[18] Arlette Jouanna, Ellery Schalk, and Kristen Neuschel have explored the noble mind, and Mack Holt, Mark Motley, Jouanna, and Constant have done much to explain noble behavior and even to justify noble rebellions.[19]

The changes in our conception of the state have been less revolutionary, but a host of scholars too numerous to name have written biographies and institutional studies that have added greatly to our knowledge. It has always been understood that the definition of absolutism employed by French historians differs somewhat from that used in this country. To Mousnier, for example, the absolute monarchy was *tempérée*—that is, limited in some respects—and he has recognized that the people played a role in the government.[20] Differences between the most recent and the older scholarship are perhaps as much a matter of definition, emphasis, and degree, as of substance. That there are real differences in substance is nonetheless true. In two impeccable studies, Albert N. Hamscher has shown that even Louis XIV catered to the financial and social interests of the *parlementaires* and sought to limit the number of *évocations* that so angered them.[21] In a widely acclaimed book, which has been hailed as a model for such studies, William Beik has demonstrated how much the elites of Languedoc received in return for their cooperation with the crown.[22] Roger Mettam has even questioned whether Louis XIV's monarchy should be considered absolutist, and he has insisted that the high aristocracy remained a very influential element in society.[23]

Thomas S. Kuhn has suggested that scientists develop conceptual boxes, or paradigms, into which they fit each new discovery.[24] When discrepancies are discovered, they make adjustments until a point is reached in which the paradigm becomes excessively complex, and each new correction causes further discrepancies. At this point, a new paradigm becomes necessary. Although Kuhn was careful to limit his argument to the world of science, something of the sort appears to have happened to the study of the state and the motivating forces in society. Thierry, and even Dupont-Ferrier and Pagès, are all but forgotten, and Roland Mousnier, the greatest historian educated in their school, has abandoned his earlier position. In one of his most recent works, he has declared that "what seems clear is that there is no economic determination of the social and no social determination of the political (contrary to the hypothesis I held when I began my work), but rather a complex and sometimes subtle interaction of mutual influences and reciprocal reactions."[25]

In the midst of this disarray, and building on the work of hundreds of other scholars as well as my own, I have decided to slant this book more toward trying to establish a new synthesis than attempting to answer my critics. The essence of my argument is this. The monarchy that emerged after the Hundred Years War was *inherently* weak, because its army and bureaucracy were pitifully small, and the former was controlled by the nobility. The kings were always short of funds and had to rely on expedients, because nobles, royal officials, and some towns—that is, those best able to pay—avoided most taxes. Hence kings had to cater to the desires of their subjects. They recognized their privileges, created provincial sovereign courts, codified local customs instead of developing a common law for the entire kingdom, and used provincial estates rather than the Estates General to consent to taxation where consent was necessary. Provinces, towns, and villages were left largely to their own devices. As a result, they increased their capacity to govern themselves. The growth of the bureaucracies of the provincial estates was especially noteworthy. To hold this decentralized monarchy together, kings sought to use the clientage systems that their great nobles had developed. An able and popular king who used his patronage wisely could bind the great nobles to his side, and through them the nobles of middle and lesser rank. Francis I, who did so, was a strong king by any standard. The danger occurred when kings were incapable of winning the support of the great nobles, because these nobles were able and often willing to use their clientage networks against the crown and to their own advantage.

The Wars of Religion revealed the inherent weakness of the system. Only gradually, and with occasional setbacks, was the monarchy transformed during the seventy-five years that followed. In studying these changes, I have stressed two themes. The first is the relations between the kings and their ministers on the one hand and the local notables on the other. Here I have concentrated on the provincial estates, as their activities provide the most revealing evidence. I have emphasized the seventeenth century, because if it can be clearly demonstrated that there was genuine bargaining then, it will more readily be accepted that the same situation existed in the earlier period, and extensive proof will not be necessary. Also, it was in the seventeenth century that notable changes began to take place that transformed the Renaissance monarchy into an absolute monarchy. By *absolute monarchy* I mean one in which there were no theoretical limitations on the king's authority other than those imposed by divine, natural, and a few fundamental laws, and in which the king controlled the vertical ties necessary to hold society together and had an obedient army and bureaucracy of sufficient size to enable him to impose his will under ordinary circumstances. Louis XIV achieved such a monarchy in the 1670s, but he had to purchase the cooperation of the leaders of society and cater to many interests to achieve this position, and there was subversive resistance to his rule.

The second theme of this book is the nobility. Nobles undoubtedly faced many challenges as they emerged from the Hundred Years War, but I believe that they were able to adjust to meet the changing circumstances in nearly every respect. In studying how they did so, I have laid stress on the vertical ties that bound the greater and lesser members of their order together. It was through these ties that they remained the dominant class, and it was by using them that Renaissance monarchs were able to govern. The emergence of a robe nobility created a problem for the historian. Legally, they were nobles; intermarriages, although rare, took place often enough for nearly all sword nobles to have ancestors or relatives in the robe, and some families had members who followed both careers, yet there was a rivalry between the two. In chapters 11 and 12, I have tried to suggest a solution to this problem and to show how Louis XIV established reasonably effective control over his kingdom. His reign marks a logical terminal point for this study.

The Kings of France, 1226–1589, and Some of Their Relatives

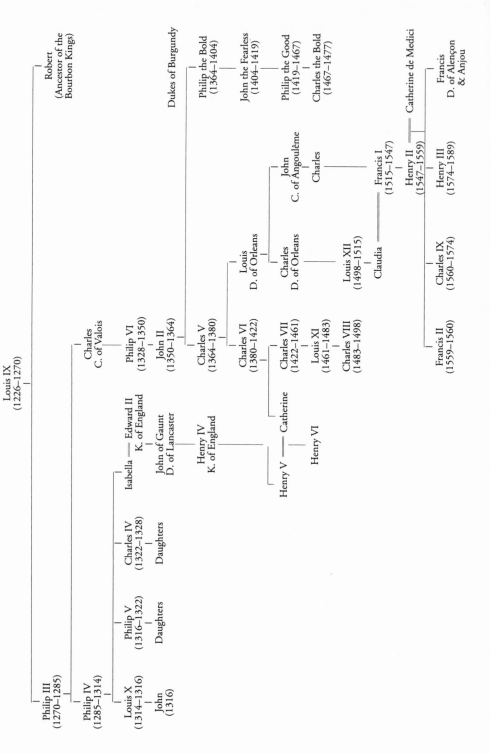

FROM RENAISSANCE MONARCHY TO ABSOLUTE MONARCHY

France in 1601

Estates vote and collect taxes		Estates occasionally discuss taxes
Estates vote, Elus collect taxes		Estates rarely meet for any purpose
Estates often vote taxes for own use		Provincial boundaries

1. Labourd	7. Bigorre	13. Limousin	19. Bugey
2. Navarre	8. Nébouzan	14. Marche	20. Gex
3. Soule	9. Foix	15. Forez	21. Touraine
4. Béarn	10. Saintonge	16. Lyonnais	22. Bourbonnais
5. Marsan	11. Angoumois	17. Beaujolais	23. Nivernais
6. Gavardan	12. Périgord	18. Bresse	24. Boulonnais

I

The Establishment of the Renaissance Monarchy

In late February 1429, a young girl pulled her horse up in front of a hostelry in the little town of Chinon. Her eyes must have turned upward toward the castle at the top of a steep hill, for it was here that her dauphin, Charles, resided with his court. She could not obtain an audience for that night, but when she succeeded several days later, she readily identified him as he mixed among his courtiers. By some means, she quickly gained Charles's confidence and was sent to Orléans, where her presence helped inspire the troops to raise the siege. Other victories followed, and soon Charles was crowned at Rheims. The maid had achieved the goal that the voices of the archangel Michael, St. Margaret, and St. Catherine had set for her. Soon she was to be captured, tried by an ecclesiastical court, and burned at the stake. But according to the long-held interpretation, she had so inspired Charles that he gradually gained a degree of self-confidence and drove the English back to their island kingdom. So much for the beautiful and tragic tale of Joan of Arc and the role she played in the recovery of France.

One look at Jean Fouquet's portrait of Charles lends credence to the traditional view of him as a rather stupid, weak man subject to the influence of court favorites and ever-willing to abandon a faithful servant if the forces of the moment so dictated. His bloated face, large fat nose, tiny eyes, and vague expression all suggest a less than average man; one who could hardly have earned the sobriquet "the very victorious" without a considerable amount of luck and the aid of able, more inspirational leaders. Nevertheless, a recent biographer suggests that Charles learned at an early age to play one court faction off against another and so to retain a degree of independence. It has even been suggested that there was a dynamic element in his early administration as he rushed from one town to another to hold the provincial estates.[1] The distinction between the young Charles and the old Charles becomes blurred, and the role of Joan as his inspirer and confidence-giver fades. Probably the revisionists are too kind to Charles, but it was during his reign that the Renaissance monarchy took form.

CHARLES VII, LOUIS XI, AND THE ESTATES

Charles was born on February 22, 1403. As the third son of the insane king Charles VI and his queen, Isabella of Bavaria, he was not a likely candidate for the throne, but the deaths of his brothers elevated him to the position of dauphin several months after his fourteenth birthday. These were stirring times for the unpromising young prince. In 1337, Edward III of England had laid claim to the throne of France on the grounds that he was the grandson of Philip IV, while Philip VI, who then reigned in France, was but a nephew. Edward's claim had, however, been through his mother, who enjoyed a questionable reputation, while Philip VI had been firmly ensconced on the French throne for nine years. A long and sporadic war ensued, which was not completely resolved for over a century. In spite of several spectacular English successes, Philip VI's grandson, Charles V, was able to drive the invaders from much of their hereditary territory in France by his death in 1380. For a generation, internal affairs preoccupied the English, and Charles VI enjoyed a relatively peaceful reign notwithstanding, first, his youth and, later, his periods of insanity.[2]

Then Henry V of England renewed the war. In 1415, he routed the French army at Agincourt, and he soon began to conquer Normandy with an eye on the French throne. The members of the royal family had cooperated with each other in the 1370s and 1380s, but they had been replaced by a new generation. Instead of brothers governing the great feudal appanages, there were now first cousins in control, and a bitter rivalry sprang up among them. In 1407, John the Fearless, duke of Burgundy, had had his first cousin, Louis, duke of Orléans, assassinated. Posing as a reformer, he had won some public support in spite of his crime. The Armagnac faction rallied to the Orléanist cause, but in May 1418 the Burgundians were able to seize Paris and the mad king. The dauphin, Charles, escaped to the south. John's triumph was short-lived, for he was treacherously murdered by the Armagnacs the following year, in circumstances that gravely implicated the dauphin. Feeling compelled to avenge his father, John's son and successor, Philip the Good, made an alliance with England. Any chance of expelling the English came to an end, and France was doomed to years of civil war.

Gradually France became divided into at least four parts. The English governed Normandy and Guyenne, provinces they regarded as hereditary possessions, with only token acknowledgment of the suzerainty of the Paris government, and Philip of Burgundy assumed similar privileges in his hereditary lands. What remained of the territory under their control was administered by officials from Paris, who for the most part were Burgundian appointees. South of the Loire River, the cause of the dauphin was generally favored, but the magnates who controlled much of the region often went their individual ways. As the central administration remained at Paris, the dauphin had to establish comparable institutions to help govern the provinces he controlled. A *parlement* to deal with judicial matters and a court of aides to handle the *aides,* or sales taxes, were established in Poitiers, and a chamber of accounts to deal with the *taille* and other direct taxes was set up at Bourges. Bourges became as much of a capital as the roving dauphin was to have during the years that France was divided.

The leaders of the various segments into which France was split had to advocate popular measures in order to win adherents, or at least not to drive lukewarm supporters into another camp. At the same time, the costs of competing administrations and of the war increased the need for additional funds. The obvious solution was to persuade the people to give more financial assistance—that is, to consent to taxation.

The medieval ideal had been for a king to support himself and his government from the income of the royal domain and the aid that his vassals were supposed to provide in return for their fiefs. By the late thirteenth century, the crown could no longer support itself from these resources, even in time of peace. To supplement their income, the late Capetian and early Valois kings taxed the clergy, sought to extend their feudal dues beyond their immediate vassals to their other subjects, extracted forced loans, debased the currency, and milked the Jews of all they could. In time of war, they declared that an urgent necessity existed, a situation that, in accordance with Roman-canonical principle, justified levying a war subsidy. The idea that a representative assembly might vote a tax, and that its vote was binding on its constituency, was still in its infancy in France.

This was not because there was no tradition of holding assemblies of important people. The Franks, Merovingians, and Carolingians had held frequent meetings, but it was the rise of feudalism that provided a firmer base for the development of institutionalized assemblies. A lord might require his vassals to give him aid and counsel. To avail himself of these services, he had to summon them to meetings. Soon meetings were being held by kings, by great nobles in their domains, and occasionally by royal officials in this or that bailiwick or province. The composition of these assemblies depended largely on the purposes for which they were held. Often only nobles, or prelates, or burghers were summoned. Some assemblies drew members from all three orders and from nearly every corner of France. They later became known as Estates Generals. Others were composed of leaders from two or more provinces and will be referred to as central assemblies. The most frequently convoked and important of these central assemblies drew deputies from the portions of northern and central France under the dauphin's control and were called the estates of Languedoil. A smaller, but comparable, institution was the estates of Languedoc to the south. There were assemblies of duchies, counties, and dioceses that were born in the summons of feudal magnates and prelates. There were local assemblies convoked by bailiffs and seneschals. In some places there were assemblies of small towns and villages summoned by the magistrates of larger towns. These assemblies dealt with taxation and a host of other matters, but when the Hundred Years War broke out in 1337, they had not yet firmly established the right to consent to taxes, and many had not yet been born.

The war brought the need for greatly increased revenue. When the Estates General met in Paris in 1347 following the defeat at Crécy, a substantial levy was agreed upon with the understanding that local assemblies would determine the nature of the tax in each locality and elect tax collectors, called *élus*. Unfortunately, the Black Death struck soon thereafter and killed many of the tax collectors and taxpayers alike. As a result, the crown received only a small percentage of the anticipated revenue, and the disorganized government reverted to negotiating with local assemblies when consent to taxation was needed.

There was strong resistance to taxation, but King John's defeat and capture at the battle of Poitiers in 1356 caused the situation to change abruptly. In the absence of the king, his teenage son, Charles, assumed the direction of the state. Meetings of the three estates of Languedoil and Languedoc became frequent, and there was at least a chance that they would become a permanent part of the institutional structure. The perilous plight of the country left no doubt of the necessity to tax. To the time-honored doctrine of evident necessity was added the equally accepted obligation to pay the ransom of a captive lord. Out of this double duty, a permanent system of taxation emerged. Unfortunately, anti-royal factions won control of the three estates of Languedoil in

1356–59, and this led Charles and his advisers to turn against represent-ative assemblies. When he reestablished the position of the monarchy in the 1360s, there was little room for such institutions in their thinking. The marriage of taxation and representative assemblies did not take place, and Charles, who became king in 1364, was gradually able to stifle the large assemblies of the estates and the smaller local ones in his domain.

The élus retained their name, but they became royal appointees rather than elected officials, and collected taxes as the king commanded. Even the long reign of Charles VI did not bring forth a revival of the demand for consent to taxation, this despite the fact that he was a minor when he came to the throne and was periodically insane from 1392 until his death thirty years later. The explanation for this curious fact is not to be found in the desperate state of the kingdom. Charles V had expelled the English from most of France, and they did not again pose a serious threat until 1415. Rather it was Charles's decision to let the great nobles keep about a third of the taxes collected from their lands. The weaker Charles VI often let them keep it all. It has been estimated that a third or more of the royal taxes fell into other hands. With the magnates' own financial position depending heavily on the king's capacity to tax, it is little wonder that they did not present a united front against such exactions. Since they had large clienteles both within and without the royal government who profited from their largess, the forces favoring heavy taxes were almost irresistible.

When the dauphin began to set up his government south of the Loire River in 1418, the various types of representative assemblies that had briefly been so active in the fourteenth century were thus moribund, and nobles had become accustomed to plundering the royal treasury. The small repute the estates then enjoyed as tax-consenting institutions is clearly revealed in the treaty of Troyes of May 1420. By its terms, Charles VI recognized the victorious Henry V as his heir, and the dauphin was removed from the line of succession because of his presumed complicity in the murder of John the Fearless. The three estates of both kingdoms were to swear to uphold the treaty, and no agreement was to be reached with the so-called dauphin without the consent of both assemblies. Henry undertook to seek the "advice and consent" of the estates of both kingdoms in his efforts to prevent future discords between the two realms, but when it came to taxation, he engaged himself only not "to impose any impositions or exactions on our [Charles's] subjects without reasonable and necessary cause, nor otherwise than for the public good of the said kingdom of France."[3] The consent of the estates was necessary to ensure the acceptance and implementation of the treaty, but on taxation the monarch would go no further than to reiterate the old doctrine that the goods of subjects should not be taken except in case of evident necessity and for the public good.

The dauphin Charles netted a profit by grossly debasing the currency, but it was not enough.[4] His hold on southern France was far too tenuous for him to uphold the traditional practice of taxing without consent. He needed every ounce of public support he could get. Following his flight from Paris, he immediately began to convoke the estates of several provinces together or individually to consent to taxation. In 1421, he took the bold step of summoning nearly all the lands that recognized his authority to an Estates General. By this act, he inaugurated a fifteen-year experiment in which there were meetings of the Estates General or of the estates of Languedoil on an average of about once a year. Occasionally, as in 1422, 1429, and 1430, there were no such meetings, but in some other years there were more than one. At these meetings Charles nearly always asked for financial assistance, but he was generally voted less than he requested. The proportion of this sum to be paid by each participating jurisdiction was then established. The final step was to collect the promised money, and it is here that no pattern can be established. In some provinces the consent of the central assembly sufficed; in others it was necessary to negotiate with the provincial estates before any money could be collected.

In 1435, Charles made peace with Philip the Good of Burgundy, and thereafter the ultimate defeat of the English was nearly assured. The following year, the three estates of Languedoil met in Poitiers, voted a taille of 200,000 livres, and revived the aides to run for three years. After that time had elapsed, Charles continued to collect the aides in Languedoil without the consent of central, provincial, or local assemblies, on the pretext that they had been granted in perpetuity. In 1437, he began determining the amount of the taille in Languedoil without consulting the central assembly, but where it was customary, he continued to summon the local estates to vote their share.

In 1439 and again in 1440, Charles convoked the Estates General to advise on whether he should make peace. At the first meeting, the deputies voted a taille of 100,000 livres, in addition to a levy of 300,000 Charles had imposed on his own authority earlier in the year. A feudal uprising led Charles to cancel the meeting scheduled for 1440. There-after, he held no central assemblies of the three estates during his reign, but he continued to convoke meetings of a single order, such as the clergy, and to hold various types of consultative assemblies, which were devoid of representative elements.

Charles's abandonment of central assemblies did not mean that he levied the taille at will. The provincial and local estates continued to meet in most parts of France where they had been summoned to approve their share of taxes voted in central assemblies. Instead of haggling over whether they should contribute their full share of a tax set in a central assembly, the new policy meant that these assemblies were asked to consent to their share of a tax set by the king and council alone. Languedoc and Rouergue had always opposed central assemblies, and some other regions, such as Dauphiné, had never participated in them. Small wonder they made little or no protest over their abandonment.

The apparent losers were the inhabitants of areas where the local estates had not habitually been assembled to approve taxes voted in central assemblies, for they now lost whatever right they had had to determine how much they would contribute. Included were the inhabitants of Maine, Anjou, Berry, Orléanais, Touraine, Poitou, Saintonge, and Lyonnais, who had long recognized Charles, and also those in the newly conquered provinces of the Ile-de-France, Champagne, and southern Picardy. The people in these regions quietly accepted this change in policy because their estates had not become sufficiently established to be regarded as essential to the preservation of their privileges and to the maintenance of low taxes. Indeed, the *généralités* (tax jurisdictions) of Normandy and Languedoc, where the provincial estates were strong, were more heavily taxed than the généralités of Languedoil and Outre-Seine, where active estates were rare.

Those who were in the best position to protest—that is, the nobles, clergy, royal officials, and bourgeois oligarchies of the larger towns—had escaped most royal taxes by the end of the reign of Charles VI and had no strong personal interest in the matter. Philippe de Commynes said that the nobility permitted Charles VII to tax without the consent of the estates because of the pensions he gave them, and in 1429 the count of Foix admitted that the crown granted the large towns in Languedoc remission of taxes so that they would be more willing to vote for taxes when the estates met—taxes that would fall heavily on the smaller towns and communities that were less able to defend themselves. Indeed, towns such as Lyons and Poitiers believed that they could fare as well or better in direct negotiations with the crown than when they acted through the local estates. The principal losers were the inhabitants of the small towns and villages, and they rarely participated in the estates. Thus those who lost by the implementation of the new policy were those who were not in a position to offer effective protests, even if they had had the wisdom to do so.

It is not difficult to explain why Charles embarked on this new course. He had revived the estates in the desperate days of his youth, but now that he was well on the way to reconquering his kingdom, he was anxious to revert to his father's policies. The central assemblies had served him well. At their meetings they had always voted him a substantial portion of the money that he had requested, and in some parts of France this had sufficed for him to collect the tax without further negotiations with provincial estates. Even where the provincial estates also had to be convoked, the fact that his needs had been established by a central assembly must have had some propaganda value when negotiations began. Charles had no reason to fear central assemblies. At no time had they sought to take control of the government as those in the 1350s had done. On the other hand, they were time-consuming and costly to hold, and their complaints were often irritating. Some of his subjects were outspoken in their opposition to their use. Hence, after 1439, when central assemblies were no longer necessary to him, he ceased to convoke them regularly, but he and his Valois successors continued to turn to them occasionally when it appeared to their advantage to do so. Provincial estates were even more time-consuming and expensive because there were so many of them. Where local sentiment in their favor was weak, Charles ceased to employ them in tax matters, although if an occasion arose when one of them could be of use, he had no hesitation in calling a meeting.

By the early 1440s, Charles felt that he was in a position to attack some of the best-established local and provincial estates. In 1443, he told the three estates of Languedoc, which had refused to vote him all that he had requested, that he had had enough of such assemblies. However, a few generous, well-placed bribes sufficed to win the estates friends at court, who persuaded the weak-willed king to relent.

The estates in central France were less fortunate. Since 1445, they had been asked to consent to two direct taxes. One, the *taille des gens de guerre*, was designated for the support of permanent garrisons established in each province that year. The other taille was assigned to support the general war effort and other government activities. By 1452, the war was seemingly at an end. The garrisons could be reduced and the second taille abandoned altogether, because the reconquest of Normandy and Guyenne during the preceding two years had brought additional revenues to the crown. Seeing his opportunity, Charles directed the élus in Haute- and Basse-Auvergne to collect the taille without convoking the estates. In Haut- and Bas-Limousin, La Marche, and Périgord, where there had hitherto been no élus, they were established to assume the duties of apportioning the taxes that had formerly been performed by royal commissioners and officials these assemblies elected. Once more annual consent to taxes by the estates was dispensed with. There was little or no protest, because people were more pleased by a 30 percent reduction in taxes than they were angered by the loss of the right to consent to those taxes that remained.

Although seriously weakened, the estates in central France did not die suddenly. The feudal lords of Auvergne, Bourbonnais, Forez, and La Marche continued to summon their respective estates to grant them financial assistance. These estates and those of Limousin also assembled to look after their own needs and upon occasion to perform some service for the crown. However, since the élus had become essential elements in the tax-collecting process, it was necessary for these estates to obtain royal approval to assess taxes to benefit their feudal overlord and themselves. The estates of Auvergne, Forez, and Périgord remained active during the sixteenth century, and the king himself occasionally made use of the estates of Haut- and Bas-Limousin and Haute- and Basse-Marche for tax purposes.

The estates of Normandy refused to vote all the money Charles requested to support the army in 1450–51. In retaliation, he took advantage of the presence of élus in the province and ordered them to collect taxes in the years that followed without convoking the estates. Then, for some reason, he reversed himself in 1458 and specifically promised not to levy taxes in the future without the consent of the three estates, thereby ensuring that they enjoyed a healthy existence.

The situation is more obscure in Guyenne, where the estates of the seneschalsy of Bordeaux had been active under the English, and there had been occasional meetings of those of the whole duchy. Both assemblies had negotiated with Charles VII in 1451, and in return for their submission, Charles granted terms that seemed to ensure a prominent role for the estates and the autonomy of the province. In the accord, Charles swore that the inhabitants would not be compelled to pay any taxes, that a sovereign court would be created at Bordeaux, and that money would be minted in that city "with the advice and deliberation of the officers and people of the three estates of the said province."[5]

Apparently the pledge concerning taxation was quickly violated, and the Bordelais invited the English to return in 1452. Once more Charles drove the English from the region, and this time he was in a position to impose his terms on the Bordelais. He abrogated their right to have a sovereign court and placed the province in the jurisdiction of the parlement of Paris. In addition, he established the aides and levied them by royal decree, but conspicuous by its absence was his failure to mention the estates or the taille.[6]

Can we assume, as has nearly always been done, that the estates ceased to exist and that the taille was henceforth levied by royal fiat? If this was Charles's intention, why did he not include the taille with the aides as a tax that he would directly control? These are troublesome questions, and before one makes the traditional assumption that the estates were abandoned, and that henceforth Charles levied the taille at will, one must explain how the taille was apportioned and collected. As far as is known, Charles appointed élus only in Lannes and Périgord, but the estates continued to function in both seneschalsies in spite of the presence of royal tax officials. Elsewhere in Guyenne, including Bordelais, we must assume that the estates or their officers apportioned and supervised the collection of taxes. There is evidence that they did so in some of the seneschalsies during Charles's reign, and there is proof that they did so in all of those without élus during the reign of Francis I. In Dauphiné, also, the estates continued to be active in the years following the Hundred Years War.

Thus Charles VII, unlike Charles V, did not establish a relatively uniform tax administration after defeating the English, although his victory was far more complete. Part of the reason for his failure to do so must be attributed to his personal weakness. It was easy to rid himself of the central assemblies, because there was little demand for them, but where the provincial or local estates had responded strongly to his occasional efforts to curtail their activities, he ultimately acquiesced to their desires. Perhaps by this time the estates in southern France and Normandy had become so important in people's minds that he would have had difficulty in destroying them even if he had had the energy to try. Certainly, with each passing year it became more difficult to alter the characteristics that the Renaissance monarchy had assumed. Perhaps Louis XI (1461–83) had the last real chance to do so until after the Wars of Religion.

On the surface, Louis seems an ideal candidate to have changed the direction the monarchy was taking. He was a man of tremendous energy and one of the few Valois kings who had a truly original mind; moreover, he was both able and willing to grasp new ideas, and he was determined to be obeyed. One is entranced at finding him suggest that a system of uniform weights and measures and a common law be established, that internal tolls be removed, and that the nobility be permitted to engage in trade, as in Italy. But he never consistently pursued these policies and on his death left the existing order as entrenched, or indeed more entrenched, than before. Except perhaps during the first couple of years of his reign, he was relatively consistent in his desire to break the power of those over-mighty subjects whom he did not trust, but to do so he had to seek the support of other nobles. By his death, these nobles were stronger than before. In 1464, he told the Milanese ambassador that he wanted peace with England so that "he could keep himself from being put into subjection by the barons of his realm."[7] Seven years later, he suggested to another Milanese envoy that France and Milan reduce Savoy to the mode and form of the French monarchy so that its duke could impose taxes in the French fashion.[8]

Louis's efforts to achieve his objectives were marred by a lack of intellectual stability. At times he was impetuous and acted without considering the implications and dangers of a move. On other occasions he was unduly cautious. More serious were his defects in character. He was cunning, deceitful, and cruel, and he surrounded himself by people of like caliber. His chancellor was a man whom Charles VII had removed from parlement because of his corruption. Once in office, the new chancellor utilized his position to sell justice. Louis's most famous adviser, Philippe de Commynes, had deserted his Burgundian master in search of more lucrative rewards. Louis even included in his entourage a cleric who had forged a papal bull permitting the count of Armagnac to marry his sister. To retain the loyalty of this motley crew, Louis showered land, offices, and money on them to a degree hitherto unknown in French history. To some extent he was successful, but neither he nor his servants were of a sort to inspire respect or confidence.

At first Louis reversed his father's policies and sought popularity by instituting tax reforms and giving the estates a greater role in tax administration. He offered to permit the provincial estates to choose any tax they desired to replace the aides and taille. The élus were to be abolished, and the estates were to appoint the necessary officials to levy and collect taxes. Where there were no provincial estates, Louis directed his officials to determine the least objectionable form of tax; but instead of waiting for them to reach a decision, he abolished the aides in the countryside and compensated himself for his loss by increasing the taille. Many towns were exempted from the taille, and some of them were relieved from part of the aides as well. Indeed, Louis seemingly shared the popular dislike of the latter tax to such a degree that he abolished the court of aides. Bordeaux was forgiven its rebellion in 1452 and granted exemption from all aides, tailles, and other subsidies. "At the request of the people of the three estates of our *pays* and duchy of Guyenne, and especially of our town of Bordeaux and the *pays* of Bordelais," Louis established a parlement in that city.[9] When it became necessary in 1463 to impose an additional tax to repay the mortgage the duke of Burgundy held on some towns in the Somme region, he turned to the estates. There were regional assemblies at Montferrand for eastern Languedoil, at Tours for western Languedoil, and at Troyes for Champagne and the surrounding region. In addition, the local estates met in Périgord, Lannes, and the Somme region itself.

Unexplainedly, Louis soon abandoned most of these reforms except those dealing with Guyenne. Perhaps he had come to realize that the suppression of the élus and the court of aides would seriously weaken the monarchy, perhaps he tired of haggling with the estates over how large the new, single tax should be, or perhaps the estates themselves became disillusioned. Whatever the reasons, the tax machinery that his ancestors had so laboriously constructed was operating in full force again by 1464.

Louis loved to consult his most important and best-informed subjects from each of the estates. His avowed goal was to receive their advice, but the loquacious king often used them as a forum to test his own ideas. Those he summoned reflected the purpose of the meeting. When military matters were under consideration, he convoked the "captains and people of war."[10] When ecclesiastical concerns were foremost, he called the "archbishops, bishops, abbots, prelates, and other notable clerics."[11] When trade, industry, or monetary problems occupied his mind, he summoned the deputies of the more important towns. Occasionally, members of two estates met together, but only in 1468 did Louis hold a meeting of the Estates General. In February of that year, he asked about seventy towns to elect deputies from the clergy and third estate to meet at Tours, and he sent individual summons to leading nobles and prelates. The purpose of the brief meeting was to win popular support for his decision not to permit his younger brother to have the wealthy and strategically located duchy of Normandy as an appanage. It was a brilliant success.[12]

Louis suppressed the estates of Artois when he seized the county following the death of Charles the Bold, but in general he was willing to employ such institutions. No other king, however, was more insistent that he be given all that he demanded. At first the size of his levies were not unreasonable. As late as 1469, the taille was set at 1.2 million livres, only 150,000 more than it had been at the beginning of his reign. But then the amount skyrocketed. By 1471, it reached 1.9 million livres; it peaked in 1481 at 4.6 million livres. Since the size of the aides and gabelle remained at about 700,000 livres, this meant that Louis's tax revenue grew from about 1.75 million livres in 1461 to over 5 million in 1483, nearly a threefold increase. It is easy to see where all this money went. Louis nearly doubled the size of his army and employed several thousand Swiss mercenaries. As early as 1470, 35 percent of his net income went to pensions given to those whose services he wanted or whose loyalty he sought to ensure. Even his court cost half again as much as that of his father, who had not himself been noted for his frugality when he had the wherewithal. It might seem that since so many great fiefs reverted to the crown, the revenue from the domain would have grown enough to alleviate the burden on the people. However, at the close of Louis's reign, the domain brought only 100,000 livres annually, because he gave away nearly all the lands that came into his possession, keeping only the titles of duke of Burgundy or count of Provence for himself. Perhaps the best proof of the wasteful character of his administration is that following his death, the taille was reduced to about a third of what it had been in 1481.

Too often Louis has been seen as the creator of an absolute national monarchy, but to accomplish such a feat, it was not enough to impose his will in an arbitrary fashion and extract vast sums from his poorer subjects. It was necessary to create an effective administrative machine and to win the support of substantial segments of the population so that the new system would be perpetuated after his death. Louis did none of these things. His permanent administrative innovations were few. As Martin Wolfe has observed, "Although Louis XI is famous for his high-handed use of the fiscal system, he changed it hardly at all."[13] He won few genuine supporters for his method of government. Even the townsmen, whom he had favored in his tax policies at the expense of the peasants and to whom he had made numerous concessions, were not sorry at his passing, because he had also handled them roughly upon occasion. When the Estates General met at Tours in January 1484, those who attended devoted most of their efforts to undoing his work and returning to the policies of his father. Louis XI had made Charles VII a popular king, a feat that the poor dauphin of Joan of Arc could never have accomplished for himself.

This meeting of the Estates General is important institutionally, because for the first time the three estates were asked to meet in bailiwick and seneschalsy assemblies to elect deputies to the Estates General. Previously nobles and prelates had been summoned individually, and monasteries, chapters, and towns had elected deputies.[14] Henceforth historians have considered only assemblies in which the new electoral procedure was used as Estates Generals, a questionable practice, since at times the crown reverted to the earlier procedure of summoning individual members of the first two estates and asking the towns to elect deputies. At the meeting in 1484, two matters were discussed that would have profoundly influenced the history of representative assemblies in France if they had been implemented. First, the deputies voted a taille for two years and asked for authority to name officers to participate in its division among the various jurisdictions. At the end of the two-year period, they wanted to meet again to consider the tax question. The chancellor accepted these conditions, but when the period elapsed, the crown proceeded to set the amount of the taille and to apportion it without consulting the Estates General. Second, a suggestion was made that the élus be abolished and that provincial estates be established in all of France to consent to taxes. Some royal councillors succeeded in persuading the deputies from areas where there were estates not to support this proposal, since they themselves already had this privilege. As a result of this selfish particularism, no article was included in the *cahier* to this effect, and the nature of the Renaissance monarchy was not significantly altered by this brief revival of the Estates General.[15]

CONSENT AND EVIDENT NECESSITY

The monarchy that Charles VII had established gradually hardened as the years went by. Its fiscal and judicial structure became so set that even the Wars of Religion left it intact. One thing was abundantly clear: there was to be no national or central assembly to give consent to taxation, although consultative assemblies of various types were frequently held and royal ordonnances stipulated that they had been issued upon the advice of many prominent persons. Some parts of France were to have representative assemblies that regularly voted taxes for the crown's and for their own use. Other areas were to have estates that voted taxes for local needs and protested exactions that the crown imposed by fiat. Still other areas were to have estates that occasionally dealt with tax matters. And, finally, in some parts of France, the estates met only on rare occasions when there was need to ratify a treaty, to redact the custom, or to elect deputies to the Estates General.[16]

With the role of the estates in taxation varying so much from one part of France to another, it is not surprising that no clearly defined, generally accepted theory of consent developed. After the decline of the idea of consent to taxation during the reigns of Charles V and Charles VI, it was revived in the 1420s because of the weak position in which Charles VII found himself. In his letters of convocation, he clearly accepted the concept of consent by asking that deputies be given full power "to consent" to what would be decided, although his chancellery never developed a rigid formula for making this request. In seeking to impose a tax voted by the estates of Languedoil, he did not hesitate to point out that those who had attended had "consented" to the levy. Even after a central assembly had given its approval, he was careful to tell the commissioners whom he sent to hold the provincial estates to ask those assembled "to consent" to their share. Charles also began to give formal recognition of the right of provinces to consent to taxation. Languedoc won this distinction in 1428 and Normandy in 1458. In 1438 Charles referred to Haut-Limousin as though its inhabitants had long had this privilege.

Further evidence of the growth of the idea of consent to taxation may be found in the argument that a royal official made before the court of aides that "no *aides* or subsidies would be imposed in the future without summoning the three estates."[17] In 1442 some feudal magnates thought it worthwhile to complain about taxes being levied without calling "the princes, prelates, barons and people of the three estates of the kingdom."[18] A few historians and memoir writers picked up the theme, especially after the close of the Hundred Years War had apparently removed the necessity for a standing army and the attendant taxation. One official reported seeing a book predicting that the three estates would eventually be driven to take over the administration of taxes. Thomas Basin argued that the need for an army had ended with the coming of peace, and that the troops should be disbanded because they oppressed the people. Philippe de Commynes repeatedly stated that neither the king of France nor any other monarch had the right to tax without consent, and he was sharply critical of Louis XI's tax policy.

Others who were less vocal, but no less influential, held the contrary view. Commynes reported that around 1484 there were some people "of low estate and little virtue who had said then and several times since that it is the crime of lese majesty to speak of assembling the estates, because it would diminish the authority of the king."[19] Perhaps some kings felt less strongly on the subject, but Charles VII dispensed with the practice of convoking the Estates General after 1440 and rejected a proposal by some magnates that it be revived. He sought the consent of only the well-established provincial and local estates, some of which specifically had the right to agree to taxation. In making financial requests to the estates, Charles and his successors invariably offered justification for their needs, but what if the estates failed to vote the desired amount, or if unforeseen needs made it advisable to increase taxes after the estates met? Such circumstances rarely occurred in Charles's reign after the close of the Hundred Years War, because he was able to reduce taxes at that time and to avoid significant increases thereafter. Louis XI was somewhat less fortunate and much more extravagant. When he was fearful that the estates of Dauphiné would not vote the desired amount in 1465, he instructed his commissioners to use force. When additional funds were needed immediately from Languedoc, he ordered that the tax be collected without waiting to call the estates. Louis justified these acts on grounds of necessity, which he, like so many of his predecessors, believed took precedence over privilege. The concept of privilege itself he never attacked. Indeed, at the beginning of his reign, he confirmed the privileges of towns, provinces, and other groups without hesitation, and during his regime, he was generous in granting new privileges, especially to the towns. When Lorenzo de Medici asked permission to send a galley to Languedoc, Louis regretfully refused to give permission until he had "informed the three estates of my province of Languedoc in order to obtain their consent, because through the privileges that I have granted them no foreign galleys can visit or land in the said *pays*."[20]

The doctrine of evident necessity was invoked by some members of the council during the Estates General of 1484. Strong reaction against the heavy fiscal exactions of Louis XI had led to an insistence on the part of the deputies that they determine the amount of the taille. When they refused to agree to as much as the council thought necessary, some councillors and other royal officials accused the Norman deputies of protecting subjects "from paying to the prince as much as the needs of the state require . . . which is contrary to the laws of nations. . . . We believe that you have the pretension of writing the constitution of an imaginary monarchy and of suppressing our ancient laws." And then they added, "we do not doubt that the king has the right to take the goods of his subjects in order to provide for the dangers and the needs of the state. Otherwise, of what good is it to have a king if one deprives him of the power to bring opponents and disaffected persons to their senses?"[21]

The doctrine of evident necessity was thus opposed to the right of consent. The deputies in 1484 succeeded in winning a reduction of the taille to a third of its former amount, eloquent testimony of the extravagance of Louis XI. It is not surprising, however, that the crown did not see fit to convoke the Estates General again, and consent to taxes at the national level ceased. Locally, the issue remained, and the question was whether future monarchs would invoke the doctrine of evident necessity so frequently that it would reduce the privilege of consenting to taxes to a farce, or whether they would use it only in grave emergencies when there was not time to call a special session of the estates and no way to find money from other sources. The answer was soon given. In May 1485 when the government found that it needed an additional 463,500 livres, it called special sessions of the various provincial estates to ask them to consent to their shares. This became the normal practice of the Renaissance monarchs until well into the reign of Henry III.

THE DECENTRALIZATION OF THE MONARCHY

Before and during the early stages of the Hundred Years War, it had seemed probable that France would become a relatively centralized state with sovereign judicial courts, centralized financial institutions located in Paris, and one, or more likely two, representative institutions to give consent to taxes that everyone paid. During the course of the prolonged struggle, however, vast areas virtually escaped from the control of Paris, and local institutions sprang into being, or if they already existed, became more firmly established. Sometimes these institutions were created by a great noble to administer his duchy or county, in which case they were often modeled after those of the crown. Others were created by royal officials far removed from Paris, or were the outgrowth of leagues formed around a bishop or important town for protection against marauding troops. During the course of the war, a standing army supported by annual taxation came into being, and most people developed a sense of loyalty to the reigning dynasty and enough of a national spirit to dislike outsiders, although not always enough to love their fellow Frenchmen. But these favorable developments, which have so often been stressed by historians, were countered by contrary provincial forces. Provincial institutions became firmly entrenched, and strong provincial loyalties developed in many parts of France that countered the growth in national feeling. Nobles, clerics, royal officials, and many towns took advantage of the crown's weakness to escape taxation. Thus, as we have seen, when Renaissance monarchs sought consent to taxation, they did so at the provincial level, and the bulk of the burden fell on those least able to pay, a situation that left the crown strapped for money from that time until the Revolution.[22]

In a similar manner the Renaissance monarchs decentralized their judicial institutions. As their territory expanded, medieval monarchs had tried to maintain the essential unity of their justice and administration by establishing temporary sovereign courts in the distant provinces called grand jours. These courts were composed partially or entirely of members of the parlement of Paris. Thus unity was preserved, and people were spared the burden of carrying their appeals to Paris. Even Aquitaine and Burgundy, in spite of their powerful dukes, and Languedoc, with its separate law, language, and culture, had in theory, and generally in practice, always been kept under the jurisdiction of the parlement of Paris. It was, therefore, a marked reversal of medieval policy when Charles issued an ordinance creating a parlement at Toulouse in March 1420. He professed to take this step because of the great distance and the perils of travel between Languedoc and Poitiers, where he had established his own parlement during the Anglo-Burgundian occupation of Paris. He might have added with greater truth that he did so because he wanted to ensure the loyalty of the south, whose inhabitants had been on the verge of throwing in their lot with the Burgundians some months before. By 1428, this threat had been removed, and over the protests of the estates of Languedoc, he merged the parlement at Toulouse with that of Poitiers, although the distance and probably the dangers of travel were no less. With the return of parlement to Paris in 1436, the estates of Languedoc once more pressed for a separate parlement. Charles initially gave way, but then sought a compromise when the parlement of Paris argued that there should be only one parlement for the kingdom. Continued solicitations by the estates eventually had their effect, however, and in 1444 a parlement once more opened its doors at Toulouse to those who sought sovereign justice.

It is clear that Languedoc wanted its own sovereign court, and that members of the parlement of Paris were opposed to reducing their jurisdiction by creating what some called a two-headed monster. But what of Charles? Why did he break with medieval tradition and create a second parlement, which was to survive until the Revolution? His initial step in 1420 may have been an act of desperation necessitated by his precarious position, but by 1444 he could have ignored the estates of Languedoc had he so desired. He and his more immediate advisers were less interested than the Parisian sovereign courts in creating a centralized state. They also had a better idea of what was necessary to establish a stable regime. In an age of relatively small and questionably loyal armies and bureaucracies, the key to monarchical authority lay not in geographic and administrative centralization but in winning the acquiescence of the vocal elements of the population to the regime. By creating a parlement at Toulouse, Charles bound the inhabitants of Languedoc more closely to the crown.

In 1437, even before he definitely committed himself to creating a second parlement, Charles had ordered that a court of aides be established at Montpellier for Languedoc and part of Guyenne because of the distance of this region from Paris and the dangers of travel. After the reconquest of Normandy in 1450, he preserved the Exchequer, from which evolved the Norman judicial and financial sovereign courts. Neither distance nor danger can explain the failure to incorporate Normandy fully into the Parisian administrative system. Charles acted as he did solely because of his desire to placate the Normans, who had enjoyed considerable autonomy under the English. Guyenne had also been semiautonomous, and at the request of its estates, Charles was prepared to establish a parlement at Bordeaux in 1451. Even the decision of the Bordelais to invite the English to return the following year did not sour him so much on the idea of local autonomy as to prevent him from instituting a grand jours there. Finally, in 1453, the dauphin, Louis, transformed the Conseil delphinal into a parlement at Grenoble for Dauphiné, and three years later Charles gave his approval to this act. The monarchy had therefore taken a firm course in the direction of decentralization when Charles died in 1461.

Charles VII, who was caught between the desires of the provincial estates and the advice of his sovereign courts, had hesitated before destroying the judicial unity of his state. A weak, indecisive man, he had moved cautiously. Louis XI, on the other hand, was more given to precipitous actions than to lingering doubts. Soon after becoming king, he gave Guyenne its parlement, and at some point during his reign, he established a second court of aides, this time seated in Caen, in Normandy. The death of Charles the Bold offered Louis his biggest opportunity to put his institutional concepts into practice, because both the duchy and county of Burgundy then came into his hands. He recognized the right of the estates of the duchy to consent to taxation and transformed the ducal judicial and administrative organs of government into a parlement and a chamber of accounts. In response to the request of the estates, he also promised to give the county of Burgundy a parlement.

The process of decentralization was also furthered in other ways. Charles divided the older part of the royal domain into four sections, each with a treasurer, but he retained a central chamber of the treasury at Paris. As time passed these sections, called *généralités,* were subdivided. New généralités were created when feudal dependencies escheated to the crown. In 1454, Charles decided to hold local assemblies of the estates to codify the customs in the various provinces and bailiwicks. Once these customs were definitely established and put into writing, it became virtually impossible for a common law to develop for the entire country by any means short of revolution. Charles even turned over to the diocesan clergy the responsibility of electing bishops, but in the long run these positions were too valuable to let escape, and bishoprics became among the most valuable gifts at the disposal of his successors.

II

The Flowering of the Renaissance Monarchy

THE VALOIS KINGS, 1483–1562[1]

The form the monarchy had begun to take during the reign of Charles VII was consolidated during those of Charles VIII and especially Louis XII. Charles VIII was a sickly, slightly deformed child of mediocre intelligence when he came to the throne, and for nearly a decade the government was in the hands of his able older sister, Anne de Beaujeu, and her husband. When he did take over the government, Charles made concessions to the English, Spanish, and the Habsburgs to ensure peace on France's borders and then, in 1494, departed for Italy in an effort to make good a dynastic claim to Naples, which has generally been regarded as utter folly by modern historians. On the domestic scene, however, Charles was relatively successful. The taille had to be increased, but in only one year did it exceed three million livres, a figure below what his father had assessed during the last seven years he had ruled.[1]

Charles did not hold any full meetings of the Estates General after 1484, but in July 1495, during his absence in Italy, Pierre de Beaujeu, now duke of Bourbon and his lieutenant general of the kingdom, convoked an assembly at Moulins. Present were great nobles, prelates, members of several sovereign courts, and deputies from the towns. Charles himself summoned the deputies of the towns and other leading elements of the population to meetings to discuss problems related to taxation and the currency. He also adopted the practice of sitting with the parlement of Paris on important occasions, and he continued the custom of using the estates to swear to uphold important treaties.[2]

In 1498, the kindly, popular Charles died suddenly, and his cousin Louis, duke of Orléans, came to the throne. A combination of hardship and self-indulgence had aged the new monarch more than his thirty-five years warranted. In spite of his poor health, he managed to carry on the

23

war Charles had begun in Italy with initial success and to provide France with the most efficient government it enjoyed during the Renaissance. Louis made every effort to keep taxes low. The taille fluctuated at around two million livres until 1512, when military reverses compelled him to increase it. He is supposed to have forgone the customary gift on his joyous accession to the throne and to have halted the collection of a special tax to suppress a revolt in Genoa when the uprising petered out, an honest act that had few precedents in history. Although Louis made no move to revive the Estates General to consider tax matters, both he and Charles VIII held frequent consultative assemblies, and both respected the right of provincial estates to consent to taxes where this right existed. Other privileges were also honored, laws were enforced, and the kingdom enjoyed unparalleled tranquility and prosperity.

The idea of provincial sovereign courts was so embedded in the minds of French kings and those of their advisers that when the estates of Burgundy wanted to abolish their new parlement as an economy in 1484, Charles assumed the burden of paying its judges. As governor of Normandy, Louis had become aware that the practice of holding meetings of the Exchequer for a month or so every year or two was inadequate to provide justice. On becoming king, he therefore summoned some Normans to Paris, where he offered to give them a parlement. "The king is your debtor, he owes you justice,"[3] Louis's chancellor declared several times in his presence. After establishing the court in Normandy in 1499, Louis made a similar present to Provence two years later.

Did Charles VIII and Louis XII create provincial sovereign courts because of their weakness? Obviously not. On several occasions they took the initiative in establishing and preserving these institutions. In fact, by accepting, nay, even encouraging, provincial autonomy and by respecting the privileges of their subjects, Charles and Louis strengthened the monarchy. People with little historical association with the crown, like those of Dauphiné and Provence, and those who had been devoted to their dukes, like the Burgundians, learned to become loyal subjects. In an age when the crown had neither an adequate army nor a bureaucracy to compel obedience, this accomplishment was of the highest importance. Louis, especially, came to be considered an ideal monarch. Named "the father of his people" during a meeting of the estates in 1506, he was rightfully famous for his efforts to spare his subjects from taxes, to render them justice, and to provide them with security. Small wonder his praises were sung throughout the sixteenth century. Even after Henry IV had made his great contribution, there were still cries for a return to the days of Louis XII. His role, like that of Louis IX, was more to make the monarchy beloved than to change its character. Louis XII was never a candidate for sainthood—a man who divorced a saintly wife and called a schismatic council to suspend the pope could hardly hope for such an honor—but his contribution to the monarchy, like that of his godly predecessor, nonetheless exceeded that of the currently much-admired activist kings, whose harsh measures brought reactions from their people.

Louis XII died early in 1515, worrying, it is said, that "this big boy"—his son-in-law and successor, Francis I—would "spoil everything."[4] His concern was at least partly justified. Expenses mounted. Francis continued his predecessors' costly war in Italy and spent far more on his châteaux and his court. Pensions multiplied; Swiss, Germans, and England's Henry VIII shared in the royal largess. To meet these demands, the taille was gradually increased from about 2.4 million to 5.3 million livres during the course of the reign, and the *gabelle* (salt tax) was tripled in northern and central France. Still this was not enough, and Francis sought to tap those who usually escaped. Sometimes he won papal permission to levy *décimes* on the clergy, but most often he turned to assemblies of the individual dioceses to obtain consent. When these sources proved inadequate, he sought the assistance of the closed towns.

In 1516 Francis negotiated the Concordat of Bologna with the pope. By its provisions, most bishops and abbots were no longer to be elected, and the administrative autonomy of the Gallican church was set aside. Instead, Francis was to nominate the prelates, and the pope was to approve them if they met canonical requirements. Francis and his predecessors had had considerable influence over ecclesiastical appointments prior to 1516, but the Concordat nevertheless enhanced the crown's power over the church. The agreement was intensely unpopular in France because of the loss of liberty to Rome and the strong probability that various papal exactions would be revived. To overcome these objections, Francis sought support for the Concordat in several enlarged meetings of his council, which included ecclesiastics and members of the sovereign courts. Twice in 1517 he appeared before the parlement of Paris with some great nobles, leading clergymen, and representatives of the University of Paris to ask that the Concordat be registered. Parlement procrastinated and only gave in under duress in March 1518.[5]

It had long been customary to have estates, towns, sovereign courts, and other notable persons swear to uphold important treaties. As we have seen, such groups were involved in the Treaty of Troyes in 1420, and they played important roles in the century that followed. In 1506, Louis XII had given a new twist to this practice by using a request by the three estates as an excuse to break the marriage contract between his daughter, Claude, and the future emperor, Charles V, so that she could marry the heir to the French throne, Francis himself. Francis was therefore well aware of the use of the estates and other groups both to swear to uphold treaties and to break them. He made good use of this information in 1515, 1516, and especially after his capture in the battle of Pavia in 1525. Before setting out for Italy in that year, he had named his mother, Louise of Savoy, regent. That astute woman quickly realized the weakness of her position and enlarged her council to include fifteen or sixteen great nobles and prelates, members of the parlements of Paris, Rouen, and Bordeaux, and for a time several deputies of the town of Paris. There was talk of holding the Estates General, but Louise opposed this move for fear that those assembled would challenge her authority, although Francis had specifically empowered her to hold the estates and considered ordering from captivity that the deputies be summoned. Louise purchased an alliance with England, and the estates of Normandy and Languedoc were asked to swear to uphold the treaty along with the parlements and some towns. Francis was finally released in return for agreeing to surrender Burgundy and Auxonne to Charles and other concessions. As guarantees he promised to have the treaty ratified by the Estates General, parlements, and other groups, and to surrender his two sons as hostages.

After Francis was freed, he used the advice of an enlarged meeting of his council at Cognac, the expressed desire of the estates of Burgundy and Auxonne, and the doctrine of the inalienability of the royal domain as excuses to break his word.[6] To further justify his conduct and to prepare for a heavy tax to be used either to carry on the war or to ransom his children, Francis held an assembly at Paris in December 1527. Present were some two hundred persons, including nobles, prelates, members of the various parlements, and municipal officials from Paris. At length Charles agreed to be content with a ransom, and it became necessary to negotiate with the clergy, nobility, towns, and provincial estates to obtain the needed sums. When John II had fallen into the hands of the English in 1356, nobles, like others, had been assessed without consent, but their privileges had become so firmly entrenched by the 1520s that Francis held local or provincial assemblies to seek their consent, although ransoming a lord was among the most accepted obligations of a vassal. In one such meeting, he told the nobility of the Ile-de-France that he did not want them to pay the taille; he explained, "I am a gentleman; it is the principal title I bear and the one I esteem the most. As a gentleman and your king, I speak to you as gentlemen. I pray you . . . to offer me such gifts and presents that will enable me to know the love and affection you bear me." In response, the nobles of the Ile-de-France offered a tenth of the revenue from their fiefs.[7]

In spite of these efforts, Francis was faced with constant deficits. To meet his needs, he turned to expedients. He sold part of the domain, the crown's jewels, and those of the church. More serious for the future, he began to create needless offices to sell and established the *parties casuelles* to handle the transactions. When borrowing was necessary, Francis could either turn to foreign bankers, who charged exorbitant rates, or demand that his officials, wealthy burghers, or some other group loan him the required sum. If the latter method was used, Francis usually paid no interest, for usury was a sin, and it was the duty of his subjects to provide money in emergencies. It was therefore advantageous for king and subjects alike to have the city of Paris borrow the needed money against its credit and pay interest at the relatively modest rate of $8^1/_2$ percent, which was guaranteed by taxes designated for this purpose. The merchant received interest, and the king paid lower rates than he would have to foreigners. In this fashion, the *rentes sur l'hôtel de ville* were born, and a class of persons partly supported by monetary investments came into being.

The immediate importance of these revenue-raising innovations should not be exaggerated. The number of offices Francis created was limited, and his borrowing was surprisingly restricted. During his thirty-two-year reign, his revenue merely doubled, growing at an average annual rate of less than 2.2 percent. A slow rise in prices largely justified this increase, and a generally prosperous economy would have enabled the nation to carry the burden easily if the well-to-do had paid their share of taxes.

Francis's other innovations were also less striking than they have sometimes been depicted as being. In 1523, he created a special treasury at Paris to which royal revenue not needed for authorized local expenses was sent. Previously, each financial jurisdiction had retained the money it collected until it was moved on royal order to a place where it was needed or turned over to creditors who presented the proper papers. This experiment with a centralized treasury was abandoned because it was not successful, and in 1542, Francis divided the country into seventeen généralités, which became the principal units for fiscal administration.

The treasurers were told to reside in their respective généralités rather than in Paris, and the financial system became more decentralized than before.

Francis's experiment with a more centralized fiscal administration was motivated by the desire to develop a war chest, not by any impulse toward centralization for its own sake. Indeed, he continued the practice of creating sovereign courts in the new territories that he added to the crown. When he confiscated the principality of Dombes from the duke of Bourbon in 1523, he gave the inhabitants a parlement. Brittany and Savoy also received parlements, and chambers of accounts were established at Montpellier, Rouen, and Turin.

Francis saw as little need for the Estates General as he did for centralized courts, and no meetings were convoked during his reign. He did hold an assembly of the towns in 1516 to discuss the currency problem, and another in March of the following year for the avowed purpose of advising on how to enrich the kingdom. Actually, the crown wanted the deputies' cooperation in instituting a rigid mercantilist policy. When the deputies refused, they were accused of being motivated only by self-interest, and the assemblies of the towns were abandoned as being useless. Nevertheless, Francis's dislike of central assemblies should not be exaggerated. In 1515 and again in 1523, he specifically gave his mother the authority to convoke the Estates General when he appointed her regent. In addition, he accepted the existence of the provincial and local estates, recognized their right to give consent to taxation, and generally respected their privileges. When he took the principality of Dombes from the duke of Bourbon, he promised the inhabitants that they would have to pay only those taxes that they consented to in their estates, and he made a similar guarantee to the Bretons when their duchy was finally reunited with the crown. His decision to tax the clergy regularly led to assemblies of the first estate to give consent, especially at the diocesan level. At times Francis made sounds as though he wanted to alter the nature of the Renaissance monarchy. In 1519, he declared "that the administration of the revenue would be carried on throughout [the kingdom] in a uniform manner," and he expressed a desire in 1542 that his laws be applied to all his subjects "without any diversity, division or particularity . . . so that there will be a common clarity and light."[8] In the end, however, he gave in to the particularistic forces. The nature of the monarchy inaugurated by Charles VII was not significantly altered. Glamorous and powerful as Francis seemed to his contemporaries, one can only agree with Roger Doucet that he had "neither the strength of mind nor the steadfast will to apply himself to a systematic transformation of society and institutions."[9]

Henry II (1547–59) seemed even less likely to make fundamental changes than his father, but a number of important innovations took place immediately after Francis's death. It is uncertain to whom these changes should be attributed. Most likely they were suggested by unknown persons in the administration, but when he became king, Henry was quick to act on ideas once planted in his ear. Perhaps the most important change that took place was the appointment on April 1, 1547, the day after Francis's death, of four secretaries of state, each of whom was to handle the administrative correspondence with the provinces in a given part of France and, strangely enough, the foreign policy with the adjoining states. France was thus to have four secretaries of the interior, all of whom also served as foreign secretaries. This arrangement reflected the clerical nature of the positions, but the secretaries were nevertheless of great importance in the administration of the kingdom.

On April 12, still less than two weeks after he had come to the throne, Henry created the post of controller general, with the duty of verifying the receipts and expenses of the government. Sometimes several persons held this office; at other times only one person performed its duties. Officials called superintendents of finances or intendants of finances were assigned the controller's functions, but briefly under Henry IV and permanently after 1661 the controller general replaced the chancellor as the most important person in the royal administration.

Henry was also responsible for laying the groundwork for the subsequent rise of the intendants. These officials developed out of the councils of the governors. The governors were great nobles whose training was primarily that of soldiers. As virtual viceroys in their governments, they were as much in need of the advice of experts as was the king. First in Italy, where governors served in Piedmont, Corsica, and Sienna, and then in France itself, the practice developed of appointing commissioners to their councils to deal with judicial and financial affairs. In the following century, these comissioners became the intendants of the provinces and of the army.[10]

Henry continued the costly war in Italy and made little effort to curb the expenses of the court or the size of pensions. Prices in the 1550s rose more sharply than in the earlier period and explain much of the increased cost of government. Henry therefore borrowed heavily in Lyons and Italy and issued new *rentes* on the hôtel de ville of Paris. He also increased the taille and created offices to sell. Among the latter were judgeships in the presidial courts he created in 1552. These courts were inserted between the bailiwick courts and the parlements and given final jurisdiction over minor criminal and civil cases. Their establishment angered the parlements because it reduced their competence and further decentralized the judicial system.

Another potential source of revenue was to raise the gabelle in southwestern France to the same level as in the north. Francis I had begun to move in this direction in 1537 but had initially desisted when he met strong protests. When he and his son renewed the effort in the 1540s, there were revolts, the last of which was brutally suppressed. The government then sought an accommodation, and in return for substantial sums, it first reduced and finally, in 1554, abolished the gabelle in southwestern France. Negotiations leading to these agreements caused increased activity of the estates in Guyenne and a revival of those along its northern border. Regional assemblies of Poitou, Saintonge, Angoumois, Haut- and Bas-Limousin, Haute- and Basse-Marche, and La Rochelle, where the estates had not been active in tax matters for generations, were frequently held. Périgord and, less often, other parts of Guyenne participated.

In 1549, Henry created one important new tax, the *taillon*, in response to complaints that underpaid troops were living off the countryside. The taillon, which was collected after the fashion of the taille, was designated to augment substantially the military's pay; in return, soldiers were forbidden to require food, lodging, and other services from the inhabitants.

In spite of new and higher taxes, increased borrowing, and other expedients, Henry's financial situation steadily deteriorated. The crisis came in August 1557, when the French army was defeated by the Spanish at Saint-Quentin. Paris itself was threatened, and there was a desperate need for an enlarged army. Henry sought contributions from the closed towns, but they proved uncooperative. He then turned to a central assembly to explain his desperate needs to his subjects. In composition the assembly in Paris in January 1558 was somewhat similar to those of Charles VII: members of the first two orders were generally individually summoned and the towns rather than the bailiwicks deputed for the third estate. Here the crown asked for a loan of six million livres, one-third of which was to come from the clergy and the remainder from the closed towns. At first there was resistance, but the news of the capture of Calais created sufficient enthusiasm to persuade those present to acquiesce to the royal desires. There remained the slow and sometimes painful task of negotiating the details of the loan with the individual towns.

The peace that followed did no more than slow the decline in the fiscal position of the crown, and the accidental death of Henry II in 1559 led to the reigns in turn of his three sons, none of whom combined the intelligence, energy, and will to rule effectively. In desperation the government turned again to a central assembly in 1560. This time those who attended were elected in bailiwick assemblies, as for the estates of 1484. It soon became evident that the three estates would make no financial concessions, on the grounds that their constituents had not authorized them to do so. At the closing meeting, the chancellor, Michel de L'Hôpital, therefore asked each estate for a special six-year contribution and offered to permit them to name a committee to oversee its assessment. In short, he proposed to return to the days of the captivity of John II, when the privileged paid taxes and the estates participated in their collection.

The Estates General of 1560 was followed by a meeting at Pontoise the following year, in which the deputies were to be empowered to respond to the crown's financial proposals. The third estate was willing to offer only its goodwill, and the nobility proved no more generous, but both estates expressed their willingness to see the crown solve its financial problems at the expense of the church. Thoroughly alarmed, the clergy signed the contract of Poissy, which provided the king with a substantial sum for a period of years. In return, they were given the right to assess and collect the tax and to have syndics to defend their interests. Furthermore, their willingness to make financial concessions led to regular meetings of their order from that time until the Revolution.

If the secular orders had proved equally generous, might not the Estates General, even at this late date, have become an integral part of the government? One can never know, but it is certain that the secular estates gained little by their refusal to cooperate, because in September 1561 the crown imposed a wine tax on them anyway. This tax was submitted to the provincial and local estates for consideration and was the last new levy imposed before the outbreak of the Wars of Religion the following year. But before considering that costly series of conflicts, it is necessary to explore how the Renaissance state was administered.

THE ADMINISTRATION OF THE RENAISSANCE MONARCHY

A generation ago the eminent Italian historian Federico Chabod depicted the essence of the Renaissance state as being "the formation of a 'corps of officials'—of what we call a bureaucracy, which is active and powerful and constitutes the 'structure' of the State."[11] The number of royal officials did increase during the Renaissance, and they did gradually become conscious of themselves as a corps or order in society, but we must not exaggerate the size of this bureaucracy or its ability to administer the kingdom. Roland Mousnier has calculated that in 1515 there were at least 4,041 royal officials in France—one for each 115 square kilometers, or one for each 4,700 inhabitants. Even after we make allowances for the fact that officials were then expected to employ whatever assistants and clerks they needed to perform their duties, it is apparent that by modern standards the crown had a pitifully small number of officials to enforce its policies.

By the Wars of Religion, these assistants and clerks had themselves become royal officials, who purchased their offices, and such newly constituted officials doubtless accounted for much of the numerical growth in the bureaucracy that took place during the half century after 1515. We would probably not be far from the truth if we thought in terms of there being one official to every 1,500 to 2,000 inhabitants during the period under consideration.[12] In 1980, by way of contrast, there was roughly one official for every twenty inhabitants and about five officials for each square kilometer.

Furthermore, in spite of the coffee break, the eight-hour day, and the weekend, the official of our day can do many times more work in a month than his sixteenth-century predecessor. The computer, the typewriter, the telephone, the duplicating machine, and a host of other labor-saving devices had yet to be invented, and the state made only limited use of the printing press. When the crown wanted to send a directive to France's hundred odd bailiwicks and seneschalsies, it was necessary for the chancellery clerks laboriously to copy each one in turn. As a result, communications were brief and far between. Only four letters to Montpellier and two to Bordeaux survive for the thirty-seven years between 1461 and 1498. Towns nearer Paris received more attention, but even the important banking and commercial city of Lyons received only 101 letters—fewer than three a year, although still more than the combined total of the surviving letters to the towns of Languedoil, Burgundy, and Normandy.[13] Once a letter was written, it could be days, even weeks, before it reached its destination. There are instances of a courier aided by relays going ninety miles in a day, but between thirty and forty-five miles was normal, depending on the terrain and weather. It took about nine days for a message to get from Paris to Bordeaux, twelve days to get to Toulouse, and fifteen days to Carcassonne. Even Poitiers was six days away.[14]

The royal army was as inadequate as the bureaucracy. In 1445, Charles VII created a standing army of 1,500 lances of six men each, four of whom were combatants. Three years later, he added an infantry militia of 16,000 men. The official size of these forces fluctuated in the years that followed, and the units were rarely kept up to strength, but the peacetime army generally consisted of about 20,000 men. During wars, it was augmented for the most part by foreign mercenaries. A professional army was not as superior to the military capacity of civilians as it is today, and it was plagued by slow transportation and communication. Every castle contained armor and other weapons, and towns were walled and often well supplied with artillery. Troyes marched 3,875 men before the duke of Orléans in 1544, and Amiens boasted 3,000 men in 1597. Although the king could defeat any single nobleman and capture any but the best-fortified towns, it was cheaper and easier to seek the cooperation of noble and burgher alike. Certainly an army of 20,000 men was not enough to hold a nation of 15,000,000 people and 130,000 square miles in subjection.[15] The people of France were therefore left to their own devices. What government there was lay largely in their hands. There were thriving institutions at the provincial, bailiwick, town, and village levels. Of these none was more important in much of France than the provincial and local estates.

We have seen how the medieval estates had been discontinued by Charles V in those parts of France directly under his control. With his small bureaucracy, he left government largely in the hands of the towns, nobles, and villages. Charles VII had revived the estates during the desperate early years of his reign, but once he had seemed assured of victory over the English, he abandoned the central assemblies. As the Hundred Years War drew to a close, he ceased to convoke the estates in Picardy, Ile-de-France, Champagne, and the Loire Valley, provinces long in the royal domain, unplagued by strong provincial loyalties, and close to the watchful eyes of king and council. Here the estates of the bailiwick rarely met in the sixteenth century except to elect deputies to the Estates General and to redact and reform the customary law. They never developed bureaucracies or played significant roles in local government.[16] At the other extreme, there were parts of France where provincial loyalties were strong, and the estates gradually became the principal administrative organs of the government, with their own well-established procedures and bureaucracies.[17] One reason the crown wrote so few letters to the cities in southern France was that there the estates rather than the towns were the principal organs of government. But before the provincial estates could become important units, the territory under their jurisdiction had to be determined, their relation to local estates, nobles, towns, and other jurisdictions defined, their memberships stabilized, their privileges formally or informally recognized, their bureaucracies developed, and executive committees established to look after their interests when they were not in session.

There was an ad hoc quality about the estates during the reign of Charles VII, but steps were soon taken to turn them into stable, well-defined institutions. In Languedoc, meetings of the estates of the seneschalsies were virtually terminated, and those of the dioceses were subordinated to the provincial estates. In Dauphiné, the semiautonomous towns, bishops, nobles, and owners of allodial property were brought more fully within the body politic. Not until around the middle of the fifteenth century did the Valois dukes of Burgundy abandon the smaller estates in the lands adjacent to their duchy and begin to try to consolidate their territories. The estates of Auxerre, Bar-sur-Seine, Autun, and the other former royal enclaves were allowed to die, and representatives from these localities were incorporated into the estates of the duchy. Even then the process was incomplete; not until 1668 was the county of Auxonne absorbed, Charolais did not suffer a similar fate until 1751, and Mâconnais retained its estates until the Revolution. In Provence, the assemblies of the smaller territorial jurisdictions had to be subordinated to the provincial estates, but the powerful towns of Marseilles and Arles were able to maintain their autonomous position. The parlement of Brittany, like that of England, performed political and administrative, as well as judicial functions, and it was only near the close of the ducal period that the assembly of the estates emerged as a separate institution.

The English monarchs were more favorably disposed toward representative assemblies than were Charles V and Charles VI. Henry V revived the estates of the duchy of Normandy in 1420, and insofar as local assemblies were allowed to exist thereafter, they were kept in a strictly subordinate capacity. In Guyenne, the English influence was less permanent. The three estates of the duchy were probably their creation, and one of the earliest promises in France to seek consent for taxation was made by the Black Prince in 1368. The fluctuating boundaries of the duchy, followed by Charles VII's suppression of its privileges after the rebellion in 1452, prevented the estates from establishing their position. Hence the estates of the seneschalsies and *recettes,* not those of the region, became the tax-consenting bodies. Some of these institutions can be traced well back into the fourteenth century, but others appeared relatively late. Only one meeting of the three estates of Agenais has been found before 1436, and the estates of Périgord may not have assembled before 1378. The three estates of Comminges first met in 1412, but they were rarely convoked until the county passed into royal hands at the close of the century. The estates of Béarn emerged only in 1391. The earliest-known meeting of the estates of the seneschalsy of Lyons was in 1418 and of Beaujolais in 1420.

The fifteenth century did not see an end to the creation of representative institutions. The estates of Guyenne, revived by Louis XI and occasionally utilized by Francis I, began to meet frequently and became a permanent part of the institutional structure of the region just before the Wars of Religion. The conquest of most of Navarre by the Spanish gave the French claimant an opportunity to dispense with the estates in what remained, but he chose to create a new assembly in 1523. The first known meeting of the government of Lyonnais was in 1556. The estates of Poitou, Saintonge, Angoumois, Haut- and Bas-Limousin, Haute- and Basse-Marche, and the town and government of La Rochelle were revived around the middle of the century to deal with the gabelle, although they soon became moribund again. When the duchy of Savoy fell to Francis I, he preserved the estates, and the popular demand for new estates continued throughout the century.

The composition of the medieval assemblies varied widely from one meeting to another. In some instances, large numbers attended, but only five clergymen, four nobles, and the representatives of thirteen towns took part in the first known assembly of the duchy of Burgundy in 1352. With the advent of frequent meetings during the last three-quarters of the fifteenth century, a degree of order began to be introduced concerning who was summoned to the various provincial estates. But even then the composition of the estates continued to change. By the 1480s, there was a near consensus that the number of voting members of the third estate in Languedoc should equal that of the other two orders combined, but another generation elapsed before the composition of the clergy became fixed, and as late as 1612, it was necessary to redefine the membership of the nobility. Yet the composition of the three estates of Languedoc was the most specifically regulated of all. Around 1500, the nobility and clergy ceased to participate regularly in the estates of Haute- and Basse-Auvergne, Agenais, and Condomois, and the assemblies of the towns replaced those of the three estates. In Provence it was not until the 1580s that the assemblies of the communities came to be convoked more frequently than those of the three estates. By the time this happened, nobles in some other provinces were displaying more interest in participating, and there were pressures to increase the suffrage.

The members of the third estate, who paid most of the taxes, nearly always displayed the greatest interest in representative assemblies. As a result, the smaller towns and villages that were excluded exerted pressure during the Renaissance to participate. In Normandy and Haute-Auvergne, they were accommodated by the creation of electoral assemblies of the viscounties and provostships, which they could attend without much expense. In Languedoc, diocesan assemblies, to which some of them sent deputies, were formed to apportion taxes. In Guyenne, some of the smaller communities were included in most of the estates of the seneschalsies. Where they were not, there were sometimes subordinate assemblies of *collectes,* valleys, counties, and viscounties in which they took part. But their voices in these localities were heard only weakly. More fortunate were the inhabitants of the valleys of the Alps in Dauphiné and of the Pyrenees, who had their own representative institutions, through which they might depute to larger assemblies.

These modest efforts to give a role to the mass of the country people were not duplicated in all of France. In some regions the leading towns were determined to dominate the third estate completely. Here the smaller towns and villages often banded together to prevent the urban centers from shifting part of the tax burden intended for them onto the countryside, and to make the burghers pay taxes on the rural lands they held. First perhaps in Lyonnais, then in Dauphiné, Basse-Auvergne, Velay, and Périgord, they formed their own assemblies and elected syndics to defend their rights. Thus, although by 1500 the estates were beginning to take form, demands that their composition be changed continued to be made throughout the sixteenth century.

While the estates were being created or revived and were taking form during the Renaissance, they were also receiving recognition for their privileges and developing procedures that enabled them to function more independently of the crown. After threatening the very existence of the estates of Languedoc, Charles VII relented in 1443. He suppressed the élus and promised to retain the institution with all its privileges. Francis I, that supposedly absolute monarch, pledged that neither he nor his successors would levy taxes or create offices in Languedoc without the consent of the estates. He also granted the deputies the privilege of being free from arrest while traveling to and from the estates and while they were in session. They in turn sought to safeguard their position by refusing to permit royal officials to serve as deputies or officers of the estates and by taking oaths to keep their deliberations secret. Henry II forbade parlement to interfere in their affairs in 1555, and they adopted the secret ballot in 1559.

Charles VII also considered terminating the three estates of Normandy, and actually collected taxes there for five years without consulting them, but he reversed his position in 1458 and included in his confirmation of the Norman charter a promise not to tax without the consent of the three estates. His grandson, Charles VIII, gave the three estates of Agenais permission to meet whenever they desired. Dauphiné, Burgundy, Provence, and Brittany already had estates when they were acquired by the French crown. In each instance the reigning monarch promised to respect their privileges at the time of the reunion. Louis XI detailed the Burgundian privileges in a more specific fashion than ever before when he took possession of the duchy in 1477. He even promised the deputies to the estates that they would be free from arrest during their travels and deliberations. The three estates of Provence had won the right to consent to taxation from their count in 1437, and in 1538 royal officials were forbidden to serve as deputies. The dukes of Brittany had often levied taxes without consulting their parlement, which doubled as their estates, but after the reunion with France, first Charles VIII and later Louis XII and Francis I promised not to levy taxes without the consent of the three estates. These kings designated the estates as custodians of the privileges of the province. Among the privileges that the three estates claimed was the right to consent to the creation of offices and the installation of garrisons. Louis XII even promised that new laws would not be applied to Brittany without their consent.

During the Renaissance, the estates also began to appoint syndics and to develop permanent bureaucracies, acts that leave no doubt that they had become legal corporations. The medieval estates had appointed officials to collect a single specified tax, after which their offices lapsed. Furthermore, whatever progress the estates then made toward the creation of bureaucracies was terminated when Charles V discontinued the practice of convoking them. Thus it was only in the latter part of Charles VII's reign, when it had become clear that taxation would be annual, and the estates would meet regularly, that they established bureaucracies. The three estates of Languedoc did not appoint a permanent clerk until 1455, a syndic until 1480, and a treasurer to administer the money allocated for their use until 1522. As their administrative role increased, they felt the need to expand the bureaucracy and to create an archives to preserve their records, which they did in 1486. The seneschalsies also had syndics, and the dioceses developed their own bureaucracies. In the 1380s, the crown had asserted its authority to appoint diocesan receivers, and it was not until 1419 that the three estates of Velay regained a voice in naming this official. Only in the middle third of the century did they, and apparently the estates of the other dioceses, assume full control over the appointment of these officers. A little earlier, in the 1420s, they began to name syndics.

Because the provincial estates in Guyenne did not become a permanent institution until the eve of the Wars of Religion, and even then did not supplant the estates of the seneschalsies, the deputies never developed a full-fledged bureaucracy. They apparently had a clerk for a brief period in 1544, and in 1562 they appointed a receiver on orders of the king. On the seneschalsy level, however, considerable growth took place. Nearly all of these estates had syndics: Rouergue by 1478, Agenais by 1486, Comminges by 1520, Quercy by 1551, and Périgord by 1552. Quercy boasted a clerk by 1447 and eventually added an assistant clerk, two more syndics, and four tax assessors. Comminges had a treasurer, a clerk, and an archivist, and the three estates of Périgord were electing a committee to act for them between sessions by 1544. The bishops of Cahors and Rodez played important roles in looking after the interests of the estates between meetings in Quercy and Rouergue, respectively, and the municipal officials of Bordeaux, Agen, and Condom performed similar services for Bordelais, Agenais, and Condomois.

The Normans were much slower in developing a bureaucracy. The *procureur* of Rouen appears to have acted as the syndic and archivist of the estates until 1569, when a full-time syndic was appointed. Probably not until 1578 did the estates have a treasurer, and not until 1609 a clerk who did not double as a royal official. The Burgundians moved more rapidly. In 1438 they increased their influence over the appointment of the members of the chamber of the élus, their chief administrative organ, at the expense of their duke, and in 1476 they obtained from him the right to appoint the clerk. Thereafter, the bureaucracy continued to grow, and in 1584 the estates began to appoint a committee known as the *alcades* to investigate the activities of the chamber of the élus near the close of their term of office.

During the first quarter of the fifteenth century, the counts of Provence replaced the tax collectors appointed by the estates with their own officials and refused to permit the estates to appoint a committee to look after their interests between meetings. However, this trend was reversed, and in 1437 the right of the three estates to consent to taxation was recognized in a written document. In 1480, they obtained the long-sought permanent committee, and after the reunion with France in 1481, they continued to strengthen their position. In 1538, they began to appoint an agent to handle legal cases, in 1544, they secured the right to name a treasurer, and in 1582, they began to have an agent in Paris. The three estates of Brittany were relatively new and underdeveloped at the time of the reunion with France, but their administrative role increased rapidly under the Valois kings. By 1526, they had a syndic, a treasurer, and a clerk, and by 1534, they were taking steps to establish an archives. The three estates of Béarn enjoyed a strong position during the last third of the fifteenth century, when they also began to have a syndic, secretaries, auditors to watch over the viscount's fiscal administration, a treasurer, and an abbreviated assembly that could be quickly summoned in an emergency.

Only in Dauphiné did the estates violate the general chronology developed above. Because of their relatively precarious hold over this newly acquired fief, the Valois kings continued to use the estates to obtain consent for taxation between the 1360s and 1420, when they did not convoke them in France. As a result, the three estates matured more rapidly. Before this period closed, they had a procureur, tax collectors, a treasurer, and a rudimentary archives, and their bureaucracy continued to grow thereafter.

As the estates could be in session only for a small part of each year, the need arose to have an individual or a group of individuals to look after their interests when they were disbanded. The bishops of Cahors assumed this role for the estates of Quercy, and to a lesser extent the bishop of Rodez did so for Rouergue. Where only towns and villages were assembled, the officials of the capital assumed leadership. Thus the officials of Agen acted for Agenais, of Bordeaux for Bordelais, of Condom for Condomois, of Laplume for Bruilhois, of Villefranche for Beaujolais, of Clermont for Basse-Auvergne, of St. Flour for Haute-Auvergne, and so on. In other places, such as Languedoc the syndics appeared to suffice. More common were the practices of establishing executive committees and abbreviated forms of the estates that could be quickly summoned. Thus Dauphiné had its *assemblées des commis des états,* which consisted of the *consuls* of eight (later ten) leading towns and a smaller representation from the other orders. Burgundy had its chamber of the élus composed of representatives of the clergy, nobility, and the towns as well as royal officials. Provence opted for the *procureurs du pays*, presided over by the archbishop of Aix or his vicar-general and consisting of the three *consuls* and the *asseseur* of Aix. When important matters arose, the procureurs du pays expanded into the *procureurs du pays nés et joints,* which included two elected members of the clergy and two of the nobility, as well as two deputies from the towns. Périgord had its *définiteurs,* consisting of six deputies from each estate, and Béarn opted for an *abrégé des états* made up of three clergymen, four nobles, and fourteen representatives of the towns and villages. Little Navarre was content to summon in emergencies those who had attended the previous meeting of the estates, thereby removing the delay that would be caused by new elections. The estates of Brittany resisted the move to develop an abbreviated form of the estates for fear that it would be less able to resist the crown's demands for additional taxes, but found it necessary to appoint standing committees to treat with royal officials between sessions.

The growth of bureaucracies was paralleled by an increase in the functions of the estates. Indeed, it was the demand for increased services by the estates that led to the growing number of offices. To the crown, at least, the most important function of the estates was to vote, apportion, and collect taxes. To the populace, their most important duty was to reduce the rapacious demands from Paris. Shortly after the estates opened, royal commissioners would present the king's fiscal requests. The estates usually offered less if more than the customary appropriation was demanded. Negotiations followed and did not cease until the estates had voted enough for the commissioners to believe that the minimum needs of the crown were being met, although the final figure might fall considerably below the amount originally requested. In return, the estates extracted a number of concessions on other matters. It remained to see whether the crown would accept the hard-won agreement between the commissioners and the estates. Deputies were sent to court for this purpose. To increase their chances of success, the estates almost invariably voted presents for their governor, the royal commissioners, the secretary of state responsible for their province, and other influential persons. Thus the governor and other royal officials were as much the agents of the estates as they were of the crown. Well might the estates of Languedoc refer to Anne de Montmorency as their "governor and protector."[18]

The estates also levied taxes to support projects of local interest, and there was hardly any form of human activity that escaped their attention. They voted money to build roads, bridges, and canals, to establish postal services, and to support other activities that would help the economy. They raised and equipped armies, built and repaired fortifications, and constructed buildings for public purposes. The estates of Languedoc sought to increase the faculty at the University of Toulouse on one occasion and tried to prevent the faculty from cutting so many classes on another. The three estates at Quercy went further, providing support for a university at Cahors, two colleges, and six elementary schools. In 1555, they even tried to entice the eminent law professor Jacques Cujas to their university's faculty. Sponsored research was not unknown. A member of the medical faculty of Montpellier won financial recognition for his efforts to grow plants that had medicinal value, and historians were occasionally supported in local history projects.[19]

The estates voted and usually collected taxes in 52.4 percent of France. In another 8.2 percent of the country, the estates met regularly, had permanent officials, voted taxes for their own purposes, and prepared remonstrances to the king when they thought they were being taxed too heavily or had other complaints. In another 12.6 percent, the estates occasionally met to deal with tax matters. Only in the remaining 26.9 percent of France was the role of the estates largely limited to electing deputies to the Estates General, redacting customs, and ratifying treaties during the sixteenth century. These duties alone, however, led to about a dozen meetings in each jurisdiction between 1483 and 1651, and occasionally there were assemblies for other purposes, as in Touraine in 1464, 1466, and 1468.

The Valois kings were not always pleased with the rapidly growing administrative role of the estates, although it was the estates' resistance to taxes that bothered them the most. Charles VII appointed élus to replace the tax collectors for the estates in Lannes and in parts of central France. Louis XI sometimes violated the very privileges he had just granted by taxing without consent, and he also attempted to limit the amount that the estates of Languedoc could levy for their own use. Thereafter kings seem to have been more receptive to the growing role of the estates. Francis I was probably motivated by a desire to profit from the sale of offices when he created élus in Guyenne and Languedoc in 1519 and in Guyenne again in 1544. In any case, he quickly abandoned the scheme when offered suitable compensation by the estates, as did his son, Henry II, after he had created élus in Burgundy in 1555. Francis I attempted to reduce the expenses of the estates of Dauphiné and Provence and to curb their activities to some extent, but his efforts failed. He lacked the persistence to do battle with the estates even if he had the desire.

The argument that representative government increased in France at the provincial level during the Renaissance is hardly revolutionary. Henri Prentout, one of the few historians to undertake a serious study of one of the important provincial estates during this period, stoutly maintained that not only the Norman estates but also those of the other provinces held their own. He based his argument primarily on the fact that they continued to consent to taxation. Henri Gilles saw the estates of Languedoc's control over taxation weakening under Louis XI, but recognized that this diminution was paralleled by their growing administrative role. Barthélemy Pocquet declared that the assembly of the estates was "the great institution that gave Brittany a real vitality and unique character."[20] Charles Higounet went further: "In the course of the sixteenth century, it was the estates of Comminges that really administered the province."[21]

The same phenomenon took place in one of the few surviving feudal principalities. "The beginning of the sixteenth century," Danielle Oppetit-Perné recently declared, "marked the shift from the viscount's direct administration of the viscounty [of Turenne] to that of the estates."[22] Henri Drouot insisted that as that century drew to a close, the Burgundian estates "still enjoyed a more extended prestige than parlement." To their activities in the defense of the province, he largely attributed the development of a Burgundian consciousness. "To these estates," he insisted, "the Burgundy of the sixteenth century owed in great part its existence."[23]

With local historians often insisting that the estates fared very well during the sixteenth century, we are faced with the problem of why those who have generalized from their works have nearly always insisted that the estates were a medieval phenomenon, and that their role declined sharply during the Renaissance. Roger Doucet, the most widely read of these authors, recognized that the estates became "one of the essential elements of provincial life in the middle of the fifteenth century because by that time royal taxes had become permanent, and it was necessary to convoke assemblies annually to consent to them." He then demonstrated that only after this had happened did the estates attain "their full development and regular activity." At this point, while admitting the growing administrative role of the estates, he insisted on their decadence: "The sixteenth century saw the provincial estates flower with respect to their administrative organs, but with respect to their political activities, they were only ghosts without vitality."[24]

In his critique of the provincial estates, Doucet distinguished too sharply between administrative and political activity, and he compounded this error by assuming that the latter was much more important. Actually, it was largely through their administrative role that the estates made themselves necessary to the crown and to the inhabitants of their respective provinces. Furthermore, their petitions, which kings often granted unless they would cause financial loss, strongly influenced legislation. What seems to have troubled Doucet and others of like mind was that the crown raised taxes higher and higher during the Renaissance, and a large proportion of these levies were voted by the estates. In other words, historians who have insisted that the Renaissance estates were decadent have relied very heavily on their conception of the estates' role in taxation.

It is unquestionably true that taxes rose during the Renaissance and that the estates nearly always voted traditional sums without serious debate, but if these facts alone are considered, erroneous conclusions will be reached. Population growth, territorial expansion, the rise in national income, and above all inflation must be given their due weight. Unhappily, there are no precise data for all of France for any of these factors. Even surviving statistics on royal taxes are nearly always based on what the king asked for, not on what he received, or on what was taken from the people. Towns, provincial estates, the clergy, and others often prevailed upon the king to take less than he desired. After a tax had been set, a village might get it reduced or even cancelled if its crops were destroyed, and entire provinces sometimes obtained a remission when they were preyed upon by marauding troops. On the other hand, if the king found that he had underestimated his needs, he often imposed increments on the inhabitants of this or that province or on his kingdom as a whole. Sometimes governors or other local officials imposed taxes in emergencies. Dauphiné especially suffered on this score because it lay in the path of the armies sent to Italy. When all factors are considered, the buying power of the crown's tax revenue was probably lower on the eve of the Wars of Religion than it had been during the last years of Louis XI, although the real gross national product was rising. As late as 1580–90, taxes consumed only 6.2 percent of the gross agricultural produce of Languedoc. It has been estimated that even if we take as a base the beginning of the reign of Francis I, when taxes were relatively low, the crown's revenue grew no faster than the income of the people during the remainder of the century. In 1581, a contemporary observed that the real income of the crown had fallen. Indeed, Renaissance France must have been a taxpayers' paradise for all save the peasantry.

The continual demands that Francis I and other monarchs made on their subjects must be interpreted as efforts to maintain their purchasing power during an inflationary age and not as callous exploitation of the people. Their failure to achieve greater success drove them to such expedients as creating offices to sell and borrowing heavily. Also, the willingness of the estates to vote increasingly higher taxes must be related to the fact that the money they gave bought less. They frequently refused to appropriate all the crown requested, and in 1560, they voted less in real terms than they had nearly a century before. This is not to say that royal taxation caused no suffering, for not all Frenchmen shared in the general prosperity, and the tax burden was not equitably distributed. The burghers, and especially the nobles, paid less than their share, although they were becoming more prosperous. The real wages of urban workers fell, but the taxes they paid may have done likewise. There were more of them to pay, and municipal governments provided some protection. The number of peasants also increased, but the amount of land they owned actually declined, and with it their principal source of income. The provincial estates limited tax increases, but not enough to save the peasants, who had to eke out a living on plots that became smaller with each generation.

The towns, like the provincial estates, also enjoyed an enviable role during the Renaissance. Charles VII showered privileges upon them in return for their support during the Hundred Years War. Automatic ennoblement of their officials and exemption from taxes were among the rewards he sometimes granted. Furthermore, he gave municipal charters to some towns that had not previously enjoyed them and generally refrained from excessive interference in their internal affairs. In many respects, Louis XI went further, for he sought to strengthen the towns so that they could play a more significant role in the administration and defense of the kingdom. He readily gave them permission to tax their citizens and increased their privileges, powers, and duties. At a time when he was increasing the fiscal burden on the population as a whole, he actually reduced the taxes on their inhabitants because he wanted "to see his *bonnes villes* autonomous, assured of steady resources, capable of maintaining public order within their confines, and pretty free in their behaviour vis-à-vis his officers if not vis-à-vis himself."[25] The towns often shirked the additional responsibilities that he sought to impose on them, such as providing for their own security and supplying his armies with food. To see that they did not do so, Louis frequently interfered in their internal affairs and tampered with their elections. Upon his death, the meddling largely ceased, but the privileges he had granted were confirmed by his successors.

Far from witnessing the decadence of towns, the sixteenth century was a time of growth. Not since the thirteenth century had they enjoyed such a rapid increase in wealth and population. Important urban centers like Rennes, Nantes, Clermont, Bellac, and Saumur that had failed to obtain constitutions at an earlier date now received them, as did a host of lesser places. By midcentury, at least eighty towns, and probably many more, had won exemption from the taille. The crown repeatedly negotiated for more revenue, but its partial success should not be interpreted as an indication of municipal weakness. In terms of real money, the towns paid less as time went on, and this is doubly true if their increased wealth and population are considered. Francis I and Henry II might occasionally audit municipal accounts and interfere in municipal elections, but it is surprising how much they left the towns to their own devices. Of the 35,502 acts that emerged from the chancellery of the former, only 6 percent concerned the towns. The great majority of these granted the towns further privileges rather than restrained their activities. Henry even forbad his officials to hold municipal offices for fear that they would become more enamored of their new constituents' devotion to local autonomy than of his service. The limited inroads kings did make into municipal autonomy during the first half of the sixteenth century were more than compensated for by the number of new towns that were given charters and old towns that won additional privileges. In the Wars of Religion, the privileged towns, now more numerous than ever before, were able to regain whatever independence they had lost to the crown, but a few of them did fall under the influence of governors or local magnates. The *échevins* of Rouen actually began to refer to their city as a "republic," and in 1564 they suggested that they keep a permanent agent at court, as the clergy had begun to do.

The enviable position of the towns during these wars and their ability to transfer their responsibilities to others were not lost on contemporaries. The Huguenot soldier and author François de La Noue wrote that "the great cities extracted all the profits that they could, chattered about their privileges, and threw all the charges and burdens on the poor country people." Another observer charged that "following the example of Paris, every town is a republic that furnishes no more than it pleases, contributes to public expenses as it wishes, and receives neither garrisons nor governors except on such conditions as it desires."[26] Modern historians have often agreed. Georges Tholin declared that "the Agenaise republic was still half-independent." More recently, Bernard Chevalier found that between 1400 and 1600, and more especially between 1480 and 1550, municipal autonomy was in "its full brilliance," and François Lebrun entitled a chapter in a history of Angers, "L'Autonomie municipale, 1475–1657."[27]

The varied and essential activities of the municipal governments need hardly be stressed. They levied and collected taxes for their own needs and those of the king. When he requested too much, they usually sent deputies to court to negotiate reductions. Town governments were active in regulating economic matters, enforcing law and order, and rendering justice. They built fortifications, purchased artillery and munitions, and raised troops for their defense and occasionally to take the offensive. In the fields of health, education, and welfare, they were much more active than were the provincial estates. They frequently financed and controlled primary and secondary schools and occasionally assisted universities. In short, in many respects the role of municipal governments was larger during the Renaissance than today, for their military and fiscal duties were then much greater, and they performed most of the functions of their modern counterparts.

Spectacular as the growth of towns was during the Renaissance, the vast majority of the population continued to reside in villages, but here, too, people displayed a growing capacity for self-government. During the late Middle Ages, the seigneur gradually ceased to play a direct role in the administration of the village. For himself, or more correctly for his agents, he reserved only the administration of justice, the imposition of feudal obligations, and the management of his own lands. In his place emerged the assembly of the community, which was attended by the heads of households, including women in some instances. With the advent of a permanent system of taxation, it fell to this assembly to elect officials to apportion and collect the impositions. Since villages were recognized as corporations with legal personalities by the close of the fourteenth century, their assemblies elected syndics to represent them in disputes. Gradually the syndic was transformed from being a temporary official designated to perform a single task into a permanent official charged with administering the village. During this same period, the parish priest ceased to manage the property of the church, and the laity began to elect *marguilliers*, or church wardens, to perform this duty.

These village and parish officials managed the common lands, repaired the church and other public buildings, and performed a host of other duties in addition to collecting taxes and defending local interests against king, seigneur, curé, town, and other villages. Some villages even sought to provide primary education and rudimentary care of the sick. As their local role increased, they began to play a larger part in national and provincial affairs. In 1483, the deputies of the villages were rarely asked to participate in the bailiwick assemblies to elect deputies to the Estates General, but during the sixteenth century, they were increasingly summoned to such meetings, as well as to assemblies to redact the customs and for other purposes. By the time elections to the Estates General were held during the Fronde, they were being called upon to participate almost everywhere, except in provinces in which there were strong provincial estates that sought to retain the traditionally limited suffrage. In such regions, the villages often organized their own assemblies and elected syndics to serve as their spokesmen. Towns and villages thus came to play greater roles in the government during the Renaissance, although within the towns themselves the suffrage often became more restricted.

THE RENAISSANCE MONARCHY IN POLITICAL THOUGHT

The people, then, increased their role in the government of France during the Renaissance. The provincial estates that had emerged around 1350 had been laid to rest in the last third of the century, only to be reborn again during the reign of Charles VII. In the intervening period, Charles V and Charles VI came nearer to enjoying "absolutist" tax power than any other kings in French history. Are we then to say that the monarchy reached its peak in the reign of the mad Charles VI and then slowly declined during the Renaissance before the rising tide of popular government? Are we to argue that Francis I was but pale image of that rarely lucid monarch? Of course not. There can be no doubt that Charles was a weak king and that Francis was a strong one. Our seeming paradox will be resolved only if we accept the proposition that *the growth of self-government paralleled the growth of monarchical government.* Liberals in the nineteenth century assumed that the two must be in conflict with each other, that the one could not wax unless the other waned, but this was not the assumption of the Renaissance man. In practice and in theory, he saw the strength of the state as dependent on cooperation between the king and the people.[28]

Even Machiavelli, that disillusioned cynic who so often counseled cruelty and deceit, was careful to add that "it is well to seem merciful, faithful, humane, sincere, religious, and also to be so." "The prince," in short, "must . . . avoid those things which will make him hated or despised." Only then could he be truly strong. "Therefore the best fortress is to be found in the love of the people, for although you may have fortresses they will not save you if you are hated by the people."[29] Erasmus, so different in nearly every respect, was equally certain that a king's strength depended less on his army than on whether he had gained the love of his subjects. "He does not lose his prerogatives, who rules as a Christian should," he informed the future emperor Charles V. "The following arguments will make this clear. First, those are not really yours whom you oppress in slavery. . . . But they are really yours who yield obedience to you willingly and of their own accord. Secondly, when you hold people bound to you through fear, you do not possess them even half. You have their physical bodies, but their spirits are estranged from you. But when Christian love unites the people and their prince, then everything is yours that your position demands, for a good prince does not demand anything for which service to his country does not call."[30]

Claude de Seyssel, Thomas More, and many others shared similar views. So commonplace was the belief during the Renaissance that the strength of a state was dependent upon the support of the people that it survived the early stages of seventeenth-century absolutism and sometimes assumed strange forms. Cardinal Mazarin, who did so little to please the French people during the many years he governed them, and who came within an ace of losing his post because of this oversight, informed his ambassador to England in 1646 that it would be less damaging to France if "the king of Great Britain was reestablished in his traditional authority, although we were certain that [his state] would be our enemy, than if it became a republic . . . in the uncertainty whether it would be a friend or a foe of this crown."[31] His justification for preferring a definite to a possible enemy across the English Channel was based on the premise that there a king could not tax enough to support a war without provoking the resistance of his subjects, but that "in a free state, as a republic," the people would pay as much as was necessary to obtain their objective because taxes would be voluntary and the objective would be set with the unanimous consent of all.[32]

No Valois king was so patriotic as to establish a republic in order to make France stronger, but they were surprisingly willing to permit provincial estates and other popular institutions to increase their roles, and they occasionally encouraged them to do so. When he ascended the throne, Louis XI attempted to reform the tax structure. Where there were provincial estates, he planned to replace the taille and aides by a single tax designed to yield an equal amount but levied as the estates desired and collected by their officials. Where royal tax officials had been established, they were to be discharged. In Normandy, Languedoc, Dauphiné, and perhaps elsewhere, steps were actually taken to implement his plan, but they were soon halted, in the case of Normandy, at least, at the request of the three estates themselves. Again, in 1561, the crown offered to permit the deputies at the Estates General to appoint a committee to supervise the collection of taxes as part of an unsuccessful effort to win their support for additional levies. Some months later, the clergy proved more cooperative, and in return for a substantial sum, they were allowed to establish their own tax-collecting machinery and to assemble periodically thereafter. Between the close of the Hundred Years War and the outbreak of the Wars of Religion, the crown rarely sought to check the ever-expanding bureaucracies and functions of the provincial estates. When it did move, it achieved only temporary success.

We must therefore abandon the liberal assumption that the kings and the estates were natural adversaries. Rather their roles can be more aptly compared with those of the president and Congress of the United States. Disagreements between the two are frequent, and at times one tries to dominate, but each accepts the existence of the other and makes no effort to destroy it. The idea that the estates could govern a territorial state, as opposed to a city-state, without a king was not invented until the creation of the Dutch republic near the close of the Renaissance; until then, kings rarely saw reason to fear representative institutions. Since their bureaucracies were small by modern standards and sometimes disobedient, they found it useful to utilize the officials of the estates and other popular institutions. Furthermore, the modest size of their armies made it advisable for them to rule by persuasion rather than by force.

The idea that a king's power depended upon the support of the people was reflected in the role royalists assigned to the estates. During the Council of Fontainebleau on the eve of the Wars of Religion, Charles de Marillac, archbishop of Vienne, advocated convoking the Estates General to win popular support for the crown's policies. In the years he had served as an ambassador, he had observed the functioning of the English Parliament and many continental assemblies. He was also well aware that the great Conciliar theorists had insisted that royal power was derived from the people. In a long speech, he expressed his conviction "that there are two . . . pillars . . . upon which are based the security of the king's estate: the integrity of religion and the benevolence of the people.

If they are strong, it is not necessary to fear that obedience be lost. . . . There is no difference between a king and a tyrant except that the king reigns with the benevolence and consent of the people, and the tyrant by force." In the Estates General, the king could win the support of the people by hearing and remedying their complaints and by explaining why his financial difficulties required additional taxation. The estates, Marillac declared, "are to establish the authority of the king, and not to diminish it, because [the people] will propose only just things that do not transgress his will. . . . They will hear his wishes, and since they are such good people, they will refuse him nothing." Only two centuries before, during the reign of King John, the estates sought to reduce the role of the crown. The situation was not as bad now as it had been then, because France was at peace and the king was not a captive. The best way to ruin the designs of troublemakers "and to satisfy the people is to have the estates hear how business is treated and money spent, how necessities have reduced us so that we are unable to satisfy all those who have requests; how we desire to reform the church, to hear and care for all the afflicted, relieve the oppressed, and to approve every good work."[33]

Marillac's recommendation was adopted without any recorded dissent. When the Estates General met at Orléans a few months later, Chancellor L'Hôpital adopted the same position in his opening address, as did Chancellor Biragues in the Estates General of 1576. Henry III himself informed the Estates General of 1588 "that holding the estates is a remedy . . . to reaffirm the legitimate authority of the sovereign rather than to disturb or diminish it." During the same meeting, the duke of Nevers declared that "the Estates General was established for the grandeur of the prince, the increase of the state and the relief of the people."[34] Many political theorists concurred, and Henry VIII merely voiced a commonly accepted Renaissance belief when he declared to the Commons in 1543, "We at no time stand so highly in our estate royal as in time of Parliament wherein we as head and you as members are conjoined and knit together in one body politic."[35]

This is not the place to explore in detail the role of the estates in the political thought of the Renaissance, but it might be suggested that an investigation of this subject should be divided into two parts. The first part should consist of a study of the opinions of jurists who wrote under the influence of Roman law and declared that their kings were "absolute." In the early sixteenth century, their adulation of their ruler reached its height. They called him "the vicar of Christ in his kingdom," "the king of kings," and "a second sun on earth." He was, one of them declared, "like a corporeal God."[36] Nonetheless, these jurists remained constitutionalists. Most of them were connected with the parlement of Paris or lived within its jurisdiction, where there were few provincial estates to trouble their ideas of monarchical power. It served their interests as well as their convictions to exalt their sovereign over feudal magnates and the vast array of semiautonomous corporative institutions, but when the crown began to intervene too much, it was another matter. As early as 1481, Cosme Guymier was likening parlement to the Roman senate, and the claims of the parlementarians grew in the century that followed. Even those who eulogized the king to excess, like Barthélemy de Chasseneuz, declared, or came very close to declaring, that the king could not set aside the custom. He and his successors came equally near to denying that the king could compel parlement to register a decree by a *lettre de jussion*. Indeed, in the early seventeenth century, Bernard De la Roche-Flavin specifically made such a claim.

There were also those scholarly theorists who derived their inspiration more from practical experience in government or from history and French customary law. They believed that all power originated with the king, or that it had been granted to him in perpetuity by the people, but that in either case there were definite checks on his power. To Claude de Seyssel, these checks consisted of the obligation to obey the fundamental laws of the state, to submit to the religious obligation to be just and to the legal obligation to respect the privileges of provinces, towns, and social classes, and to give heed to the parlements, the guardians of the law. Seyssel's successors retained his emphasis on the sovereign courts and frequently stressed the role of the Estates General as well. Indeed, there was a notable increase in the discussion of the duties of the estates during the latter part of the sixteenth century. The growth of self-government in Renaissance France was thus paralleled by a growing emphasis by theorists on institutional checks on the crown. "Hence," Julian Franklin has declared, "looking back at the entire period from the end of the fifteenth century to 1572, we may conclude that the dominant trend of political ideas was favourable to constitutionalism."[37]

In the 1570s, critics of royal authority became more numerous, and theories of resistance became more fully developed. In reaction, the crown's defenders became more extreme. Nevertheless, some royalists continued to adhere to the older concept of a mixed or limited monarchy in which the king and his subjects cooperated in governing in accordance with the law. In what was probably the assembly of the estates of Clermont-en-Beauvaisis to elect deputies to the Estates General of 1588,

Louis Le Caron, the lieutenant of the bailiwick and a famous jurist, reiterated the Renaissance concepts of cooperation and of the supremacy of the law: "The difference between a prince and a tyrant is that the prince governs with advice, in accordance to the law, a people who voluntarily obey him, and the tyrant rules, in accordance to his pleasure, a people who are compelled to obey him." He then informed his listeners: "I believe that the opinion of Polybius is correct, that of the three kinds of government . . . , to wit monarchy, aristocracy and democracy, one cannot exist alone. Rather the three together, organized and limited, form a true republic. Still, one of them dominates and surpasses the others, who are only its aids or members. So it is in France, where there is a king who has sovereign power, yet he governs with the advice of the peers of France, who are the ancient and natural councillors of the kingdom, through whom is represented aristocracy; and the people . . . who are summoned by the king to be heard concerning the most important affairs of the kingdom . . . , through whom is revealed a form of democracy."[38]

Most fiscal officials who wrote books about taxation worked within the jurisdiction of the chamber of accounts of Paris, where provincial estates were rare. Those who were exposed to the estates, however, usually discussed the problem of consent to taxation. Jean Combes, who was born in Riom in 1512 and served first as *lieutenant particular* of Auvergne and then as president of the court of aides in Clermont, published a treatise on the taille in 1576. As the son of an official and later an official himself at Riom, he was jealous of the échevins of Clermont and disapproved of their right to convoke assemblies of the good towns. It is not surprising, therefore, that he ignored this institution, or that he called the king absolute and thought that everyone should aid him in case of urgent necessity. Nevertheless, he believed that the king should obtain the consent of the estates for taxation under normal circumstances, and he stressed the mutual friendship between the king and his subjects.[39]

Jean Hennequin came from Champagne, where there were no assemblies, but he became acquainted with Norman fiscal practices. After insisting that the early Valois kings had promised not to levy taxes without the consent of the estates, aside from cases of necessity, he confessed that this practice was no longer followed except in a few provinces, such as Normandy, where the three estates were held every year. They had, however, only traces of their former liberties, because they were expected to vote what the king wanted, whether the country was at peace or at war.[40] Years later, René-Laurent La Barre, the president of a Norman élection, declared that "the fundamental laws of the kingdom neither permit nor authorize anyone, not even the kings, to raise armies or to levy taxes without the deliberation of the public and the consent of the estates, the three orders of the kingdom being for this gathered together and assembled." He recognized, of course, that this situation no longer existed for France as a whole, but he called attention to the continued activities of the estates in Burgundy, Normandy, and Auvergne.[41]

The second part of an investigation of political thought concerning the estates should concentrate on the ideas of people who did not write political treatises and rarely read those who did. Here there are few contemporary studies, but the available evidence suggests that there was a widespread belief that ultimate authority still rested with the people. Surprisingly, such beliefs were upon occasion turned to good advantage by the crown.

When Louis XI died in 1483, he intended that his daughter, Anne de Beaujeu, and her husband, Pierre, should have the care of his minor son, Charles, and the governance of the kingdom until he came of age. Their position was quickly challenged by Louis, duke of Orléans, Charles's nearest male relative, and by a host of magnates. An Estates General was summoned, and in the debate over how the council should be consti- tuted, Philippe Pot, seigneur de La Roche and a client of the Beaujeus, who had been elected at their behest, made an eloquent speech designed to strengthen their position by appealing to the popular belief that power was derived from the people.

> Kingship is a dignity, he declared, and not an heredity, and as such it does not pass to the nearest relatives in the way in which a patrimony passes to its natural guardians. If, then, the commonwealth is not to be bereft of government, the care of it must devolve upon the Estates General of the realm, whose duty it is, not to administer it themselves, but to entrust its administration to worthy hands.
>
> History and tradition tell us the kings were originally created by the votes of the sovereign people, and the prince is placed where he is, not that he may pursue his own advantage, but that he may strive unselfishly for the welfare of the nation. The ruler who falls short of this ideal is a tyrant and a wolf, and is no true shepherd of his flock. Have you not often read that the commonwealth is the people's common concern? Now if it be their concern, how should they neglect it and not care for it? Or how should flatterers attribute sovereign power to the prince, seeing that he exists merely by the people's will? And so I come to the question under discussion, namely, to the problem which arises when a king by infancy or otherwise is incapable of

personal rule. Now we are agreed that the commonwealth is the people's; that our king cannot himself govern it; and that it must be entrusted to the care and ministry of others. If then, as I maintain, this care devolves neither upon any one prince, nor upon several princes, nor upon all of them together, it must of necessity return to the people from whom it came, and the people must resume a power which is their own, the more so since it is they alone who suffer from the evils of a long interregnum or a bad regency. I do not suggest that the right of government is taken from the sovereign. I argue only that government and guardianship, not rights and property, are for the time being transferred by law to the people and their representatives; and by the people I mean all subjects of the crown, of what rank soever they be. If, then, you will regard yourselves as the deputies of all the estates of the realm and the depositaries of the aspirations of them all, you cannot avoid the conclusion that the main object of your convocation is to direct the government by your counsels in the vacancy which has arisen through the minority of our sovereign.[42]

Pot's speech was well-received, but the influence of the magnates on the deputies was so great that in the end they refused to name the council, thereby leaving the councillors chosen by the magnates after Louis's death in office. The Beaujeus had lost in their imaginative bid to control the council, but the idea that the people were the ultimate authority refused to die. Claude de Bauffremont, the speaker of the nobility, informed Henry III in the meeting of the Estates General of 1576 that the nobility "placed the crown on the head of the first King."[43] The historian and jurist François Hotman was not as out of touch with the thinking of many Frenchmen as some have thought when he published *Francogallia* in 1573. In this book he argued that some regions of ancient Gaul were ruled by councils of the nobility and that others were kingdoms. These "kingdoms were not hereditary but conferred by the people on someone who had a reputation for justice; and, in the second place, the kings did not possess an unlimited, free and uncontrolled authority, but were so circumscribed by specific laws that they were no less under the authority and power of the people than the people were under theirs."[44] Hotman supposed that there was a council for all of Gaul in addition to these regional states. The Romans conquered Gaul, but during the third century, the Franks, assisted by the Gauls, began the long, slow process of driving them from the land. Together they elected Childeric the first king of Francogallia. During the centuries that followed, kings were elected and, when necessary, deposed by the council. Hotman conceded that the council, which he associated with the Estates General, had usually elected the king from the same family, and that from the time of the Capetians, there had been a gradual erosion of the ancient constitution, but he held that it had not been fully subverted until the reign of Louis XI.

Theodore Bèza, Philippe du Plessis Mornay, and other Huguenot writers accepted the concept of an ancient constitution and the right to elect and depose kings when the need arose, although the central thrust of their arguments often differed from that of Hotman. The pamphleteers of the Catholic League adhered to somewhat similar views and almost put their theory into practice by electing a king in 1592–93. They had no need to borrow their ideas from their Huguenot rivals, however, for there was an ample base in the popular political thought of the times on which they could build. Statements concerning the constitutional importance of the Estates General persisted until the Fronde, when they were reiterated by Claude Joly and a number of pamphleteers, before becoming less commonplace during the personal reign of Louis XIV.

The writers thus far discussed dealt primarily with the Estates General and the central government. It has rarely been recognized that somewhat similar theories evolved concerning the role of the provincial estates. Pierre de Saint-Julien, for example, traced the estates of Burgundy back to the ancient Gauls. Born of a noble Burgundian family, his love of history caused him to enter the clergy, although he was the eldest of sixteen children. The deanship of Chalon-sur-Saône was given to him, along with other rich benefices, but his greatest pleasures were derived from his controversial historical investigations and his election to the office of élu of the estates of Burgundy in 1566.

Saint-Julien argued that the Burgundians were Gauls, whose society had consisted of druids, soldiers, and plebeians, from whom emerged the three estates. The various regions of Gaul had had local assemblies, and there was also an Estates General, which elected a sovereign magistrate for a one-year term. Saint-Julien recognized that the French monarchy had long ago become hereditary and that the Burgundian estates had lost some of their ancient authority, but he nevertheless insisted that these estates were the envy of their less fortunate neighbors and that their élus enjoyed a position comparable to that of the tribunes of Rome. "It would be better," he wrote, "for Burgundy to have lost the title of first peerage of France than the Estates." The estates of such provinces as Burgundy, Languedoc, Dauphiné, and Brittany "are the foundation of their liberties and the true tie that holds the men who are in the same government in society and friendship."[45]

In no place did Saint-Julien cite Hotman, and neither did he list him in his bibliography. His inspiration appears to have come from his own study of history, his practical experience as an official of the Burgundian estates, and the general climate of opinion of his day. Indeed, he completed the draft of the section of his book on the estates prior to the massacre of Saint Batholemew, and almost certainly owed little or nothing to Hotman and other Protestants, whose religious beliefs he strongly opposed.[46] In the end, he joined the Catholic League, and he is the probable author of a pamphlet arguing that France was an elective rather than a hereditary monarchy.

That there was a widespread belief in the antiquity of the estates is suggested by a Catholic League manifesto published in 1576, which advocated that "the ancient rights, preeminences, franchises, and liberties of the provinces and estates of this kingdom be restored as they were at the time of King Clovis, the first Christian king."[47] Not to be outdone, the syndic of the Haute-Marche of Rouergue traced the history of the estates of Rouergue from the time of Julius Caesar down to the reign of Henry IV.[48] Jean Savaron, a noted jurist and future deputy to the Estates General of 1614, insisted that the estates of Auvergne dated back to the time of the druids and Romans.[49] Nor were such legends to die quietly with the advent of royal absolutism. During the reign of Louis XIV, the first president of the parlement of Dijon could still speak of the provincial estates at the time of the Gauls and of the very great antiquity of the Burgundian assembly.[50] The three estates of Navarre laid claim to less age but were more accurate when they informed Louis XIV in their *cahier* in 1672 that their first king "was the creation and the creature of his subjects; they drew him from their midst and put him at their head in order to fight the Moors; they submitted to his domination in order to conserve their goods and their liberty."[51] A century later, Jean Albisson, a lawyer and official of the estates of Languedoc who was eventually to serve the First Republic, found the origins of that institution in the municipal regimes established by the Romans.[52] Thus, from the Middle Ages until the Revolution, some Frenchmen believed that the provincial estates were older than the monarchy itself, and they occasionally voiced the logical implications of this premise.

III

The Late Medieval-Renaissance Nobility

During the Hundred Years War and the years that followed, French kings had to cater to their subjects' desires to win their support. They had to accept a multitude of sovereign courts and provincial estates in lieu of a single court to administer justice and an Estates General to give consent to taxation, if consent had to be given at all. They had permitted provincial estates, towns, and villages to develop or retain existing administrative structures and bureaucracies that enabled them to govern themselves. They had encouraged the codification of local customs instead of trying to create a common law. They had accepted the growth of provincial loyalties, which had become as cemented in the minds of the people in many parts of France as any sense of national identity or purpose. In short, at the very time when they appeared to be creating a united kingdom by driving out the English, they were permitting the formation of centrifugal forces that threatened to keep the nation forever divided. To counter this tendency, they had to establish vertical ties that reached from themselves through the greater to the lesser members of society. Neither the standing army created in 1445 nor the royal bureaucracy was large enough or loyal enough to impose the king's will. This was doubly true in an age of slow transportation and communication, and in the absence of all the mechanical instruments used by a bureaucracy today, except pen and paper.

From the days of Augustin Thierry until quite recently, historians have insisted that kings found the support they needed in an alliance with the third estate and with officials drawn from that segment of society. It is doubtful, however, whether the idea of doing this ever crossed a king's mind. They knew that as single individuals they needed assistance to control their many millions of subjects, but from the first they turned primarily to the nobility. It was with the upper nobility that they had been raised, and it was with them that they shared a common culture and set of values. The question was whether the nobles were prepared to meet the challenge. They were always divided into jealous, quarreling factions, and during the late Middle Ages and the Renaissance, they were confronted by additional problems. Wars and plagues had decimated their numbers. High labor costs followed by the inflation of the sixteenth century threatened their economic position, the invention of gunpowder raised the question of their military usefulness, and the advent of the Renaissance caused many to wonder if they could meet the educational requirements of the new age. Through these centuries there was also a question of whether meaningful vertical ties could be constructed to counter the disintegrating forces in society. The lord-vassal relationship was clearly in a state of decline. What, if anything, could be found to take its place?

THE NOBILITY DEFINED

A noble is someone who is accepted as being noble by the society in which he lives. The criteria varied by time and place during the Middle Ages. Under the Carolingians, birth was the principal component. Following the breakup of their empire, military prowess became more of a factor. Ennoblement by the king or a powerful noble was an accepted avenue to this status during the Hundred Years War. It was only in the course of the sixteenth century that recognition of one's noble status by the crown became the principal, indeed the only, standard that could be legally applied. But when our study begins, the criteria were in a state of flux.

There is no question but that the son of a noble who followed a noble way of life was considered a noble. But what if the status of the father were in doubt, and of what did a noble way of life consist? It is in the borderline cases that the most intriguing evidence can be found. An interesting dispute concerning the status of an innkeeper of noble descent came to trial in Dauphiné in 1408. Twenty-one persons including two ecclesiastics, eleven nobles, and eight commoners were asked what a noble was. Only one believed that nobility depended on birth. The remainder thought that it was a way of life. There was less agreement as to what a noble way of life comprised. Sixteen, including all the ecclesiastics and commoners, believed that it consisted of living off revenues and not working. Interestingly, only six of the eleven nobles agreed. Five of the twenty-one said that a noble should not engage in usury or trade. Only eleven saw nobility as being closely tied to a career in arms, and among these were only five of the eleven nobles consulted.[1] Dauphiné, of course, may not have been typical of France; indeed, it was not then technically a part of France. Nonetheless, the responses of those consulted reveal some of the contemporary confusion as to what a noble was and how he should live.

This confusion persisted until the close of the Middle Ages and took a different turn in France than in England. In France, as in most continental countries, knights, who were not usually nobles, and the hereditary aristocracy merged into the same class in the eleventh, twelfth, and thirteenth centuries.[2] All the children of this merger were considered nobles. In England, on the other hand, knights and squires were gradually excluded from the nobility, and only the eldest son of a noble was regarded as a noble. As a result, in England there were only a handful of nobles in the sixteenth century but in France there were thousands.

THE CATASTROPHES

The Hundred Years War commenced in 1337, and it was followed a decade later by the appearance of the Black Death. Between the plundering raids of undisciplined soldiers and the ravages of disease, the population was sharply reduced. Before the war began, the population had apparently outstripped the capacity of Frenchmen to produce enough food, especially in years of poor harvest. There were some instances of famine and many more of malnutrition, a situation that must have enhanced the deadliness of the plague when it came. Perhaps 40 percent of the population died between 1347 and 1350, but the war continued and the plague returned again and again. There were periods of modest recovery as between c. 1380 and c. 1410, but when Charles VII ascended the throne in 1422, France was in the worst crisis. By midcentury, Provence had lost nearly 60 percent of its hearths and Dauphiné two-thirds of hers. Burgundy, the Paris basin, and Normandy appear to have suffered as much. The France of 1450 may have had little more than 40 percent of the inhabitants of the France of 1340. If in 1340 there were 18,000,000 people living within the boundaries of the France of 1559, there may have been as few as 8,000,000 in 1450.[3]

The prevailing opinion is that the demographic collapse contributed to economic collapse of the nobility. The scarcity of labor compelled landlords to lower rents both in money and in kind, to reduce seigneurial dues, and to increase wages in order to attract and retain tillers of the soil. At the same time, declining demand reduced the price of the agricultural products nobles had to sell. The result was a golden age for peasants and hard times for the lords of the manor. If nobles tried to retrieve their fortunes by resisting the economic trend toward higher wages and lower rents, they were brought into conflict with the peasants. They might have remained financially solvent if they had curtailed their expenses, but most historians believe that they did not. The war, extravagance, and pious gifts conspired to keep their expenses high. The manorial system weakened, the role of the seigneur declined, and the village community became the principal force in administering the countryside.[4]

We should not, however, exaggerate the economic difficulties of the nobility during the first half of the fifteenth century. A few in isolated parts of the realm managed to escape the destructivenesss of the war. Some nobles profited from the demise of numerous relatives to increase the size of their estates through inheritance. Still others managed to turn the war to their advantage by plunder, ransoms, and military pay. But the greatest new source of revenue was the king himself. Charles V had permitted some magnates to take about a third of the royal taxes collected from their lands, but his son, the mad Charles VI, was in a weaker position. He sometimes let them take it all. It has been estimated that from 700,000 to 1,000,000 livres found their way into the hands of the magnates out of a total royal tax revenue of from 2,000,000 to 2,400,000 livres. And this was not all. Many nobles received substantial pensions from the crown in addition to the salaries for the positions they held. A segment of the nobility thus lived in great wealth, and the Valois princes became generous patrons of the arts.[5]

A further advantage was seized by the nobility. It was during the latter half of the fourteenth century that royal taxation became permanent in France, but the nobles slowly managed to escape its clutches. In the early days of the Hundred Years War, it seemed unlikely that they would be so fortunate. In 1356–58, they were actually taxed more heavily than the burghers, but thereafter the crown sought their support and shifted more of the tax burden onto the towns. Nevertheless, for many years nobles continued to be subject to taxation unless they were personally serving in the army. The details of how and when the nobility as a whole escaped direct taxes are far from clear. As late as 1404, Charles VI was still insisting that everyone, including members of the royal family, was to pay, except nobles frequenting arms, clergymen, who were to pay another tax, and paupers. Powerful pressure groups quickly won exemptions from this and other levies. Before the close of the Hundred Years War, the nobility as a whole in northern and central France had been exempted from the taille, a direct tax on income from land. In the south, where the taille was said to be *réele,* they paid on their income from the non-noble land they held, but not on the noble land. Royal officials won similar exemptions, albeit more slowly, and many towns were excused from some taxes. The privileged also largely escaped the aides, or sales taxes. Thus the strong and wealthy—those best able to pay—were for the most part removed from the tax roles. It was the fact that they did not have to pay themselves, and that part of the money collected from those less fortunate eventually fell into their hands, that led to the nobility's willingness to permit the crown to exploit the peasantry. In most parts of France, nobles lost interest in the provincial and local estates. Only a small proportion of them came, and in a few places, including parts of Guyenne and Auvergne, they ceased to attend altogether.[6]

The military role of vassals also declined. In the formative period of feudalism, kings and magnates had given fiefs to nobles in return for aid and counsel. As time passed, women and children, who were unable to provide the required services, were permitted to inherit fiefs. Other vassals were often too old, sickly, or otherwise incapable of performing military service. The feudal array was undisciplined and ill-trained. Ultimately, the French kings, like their English adversaries, had to employ professional soldiers, although in desperation they occasionally summoned men to the feudal levy well into the seventeenth century. In seeking a substitute for their vassals, kings and great nobles turned to a contractual relationship formalized by an indenture.

THE INDENTURE

The indenture was a written contract. It might be for a limited duration or it might be a lifetime arrangement. The former was known as a *lettre de retenue* in France and became one of the principal means of enrolling professional soldiers during the Hundred Years War. It was the indenture for life that became one of the most important vertical ties that held the aristocracy together. In its more permanent form the indenture was a natural outgrowth from the fief-rente, which had appeared in the late eleventh century. By then the money economy had developed enough for a king or great noble to pay a vassal an annual income rather than providing for his support by granting him a fief. The indenture surfaced in France in the fourteenth century. It differed from the fief-rente only in the fact that homage was not performed; the oath of fealty was retained. By obtaining large sums from the crown, great nobles could afford to use fief-rentes and indentures to increase the number of their followers. It was through this means that some of the revenue the great nobles extracted from the crown trickled down to the lesser nobility. For this reason, both the dukes and those simple seigneurs who had direct or indirect access to the royal trough favored taxation. Those who were excluded or believed that they got less than their share talked of protecting the poor people from the fiscal exactions of the crown.[7]

The traditional feudal relationship persisted, of course. The king and great nobles continued to require aid and counsel of their vassals. They also placed reliance on their military contribution during the early stages of the Hundred Years War, with disastrous results. Nevertheless, as late as 1465, the duke of Bourbon sought the assistance of his vassals when he revolted, and the dukes of Burgundy relied heavily on theirs until they created a standing army in 1471. In spite of these survivals of the past, the vassal's political and social role was gradually usurped by the indentured retainer or client, who was often a professional soldier.[8]

From the viewpoint of the lord, fief-rentes and indentures presented many advantages over the traditional form of vassalage. The number of traditional vassals one could have was limited by the number of fiefs one could give. The domiciles of one's vassals were limited to the areas where one owned fiefs to award. Indentured retainers and holders of fief-rentes, on the other hand, could be seated in faraway regions where a lord had political interests but no fiefs, or they could be placed in the royal bureaucracy, where they could keep their lord well informed and become his tools to influence and even direct the government. Thus the Burgundian dukes found retainers in Flanders and the western portion of the Empire who helped them secure a rich inheritance and spread their influence. Louis, duke of Orléans, also sought followers by awarding fief-rentes and indentures in the Empire to offset Burgundian influence, and he packed the government of his demented brother, Charles VI, with his henchmen. The Burgundian duke, John the Fearless, countered by having Louis assassinated and replacing the Orléanist officials with his own. The fief-rente and the indenture thus proved more flexible instruments for aggrandizement than traditional vassalage.[9] A further advantage was that they were usually awarded only for life, and the lord was not obligated to replace the deceased father with his heir if he or she were undesirable. The landed fief did not disappear, however. The vassal might become nearly useless from a military and political point of view, but the lord continued to derive some revenue from his fiefholders, and his fiefholders regarded their land as an inheritable property right. As a result, this aspect of feudalism persisted until the Revolution. The fief-rente, on the other hand, devoid as it was of landed property rights, was to slowly disappear, as will be indicated later.

Ties between the greater and lesser nobility did not cease, however, and indentures or less formal arrangements, most commonly called patron-client relationships, became the order of the day. Any monetary recompense a client received from his patron was referred to as a pension, or if he performed specific duties, as a wage. No period in the history of clientage is so poorly known, but it is obvious that clientage and pensions grew out of the fief-rente and indenture. As far back as the thirteenth century, the payments made by English kings to foreign ecclesiastics who held fief-rentes were referred to as pensions. The term *pension* was also employed to designate grants to those who had not done homage.[10] This confusion in terminology is clearly revealed in Burgundian fiscal records. Here the term *pension à vie* was used to designate both feudal and nonfeudal grants for life, and *pension à volenté* was employed for grants that could be revoked by the duke. In 1420, the treasurer of Duke Philip the Good paid Pierre Lauwart the pension à vie he had given him in return for his "good services," but it was stipulated that "he become the man of my said lord and render him faith and homage in promising to serve him against all commers except the king of England and his liege lord."[11] The number of fief-rentes had long been declining, and there is no hint that homage was required in the vast majority of the lifetime pensions fifteenth-century dukes awarded. Hereditary fief-rentes were even rarer, but they persisted generation after generation until the dukes compensated the heirs, or until the heirs themselves ceased to exist. The dukes had clearly come to prefer pensions à volenté, which they could revoke if their clients ceased to perform in a loyal and efficient fashion.[12]

The term *pension* was also employed to designate annual payments in both feudal and nonfeudal contracts in other parts of France. Thus, in 1404, Louis, duke of Orléans, received faith and homage from Waleran de Luxembourg in return for a pension of 6,000 livres. John, duke of Brittany, on the other hand, was content to require only that Raoul de Kersaliou swear on the Holy Gospels to serve him faithfully when he granted him an annual pension of 1,200 livres in 1380, and Gaston IV, count of Foix, accepted a similar guarantee when he awarded a pension of 300 moutons d'or to the seigneur of Estissac in 1439. A written contract and an oath of fealty on the Gospels characterized all three contracts, and the word *pension* was used, but homage was performed only in the first. It was a fief-rente, whereas the other two contracts were indentures. As the Middle Ages faded in these far-flung areas, however, both homage and written contracts apparently disappeared, or all but disappeared, as they had in the domains of the Burgundian dukes. The pension remained.[13]

The record of thousands of homages to the French kings survive, but only a tiny handful of those for the sixteenth century were fief-rentes. These fief-rentes survived because they were either hereditary or newly created to satisfy special family needs. Thus, in 1467, Pierre Ferrebouc did homage for 100 sous per year derived from the rent of four adjoining houses in Lagny-sur-Marne. His son repeated the act when he inherited in 1470. In 1536, this modest income passed to a nephew who was a curé in Lagny, and from him it went to the abbot and monks of the monastery of Saint-Pierre de Lagny, who did homage for it by proxy in 1555.[14]

Of more interest is the use of the fief-rente for the benefit of a vassal's family. On December 10, 1498, Jean de Saint-Benôit did homage for the seigneurie of Jouy-le-Comte, less sixteen livres, which he had inherited from his father. That same day his mother did homage for a newly constituted fief-rente of sixteen livres derived from this seigneurie. Why the widow was provided for in this fashion rather than through a family arrangement we can only guess. In 1527, Francis I created a fief-rente of 300 livres for the benefit of the widow of one of his gentlemen and her minor son. Again, in 1528, he established a fief-rente of 300 livres for Michel Gorgias, a younger son who had just married. The income was to be derived from his parents' seigneurie of Lévignen. And in 1537, Francis provided a fief-rente of 258 livres derived from two seigneuries for the benefit of the widow and children of his late secretary Guillaume Courtin. Why Francis chose to provide for the widows and children of his faithful servants with feudalized pensions rather than simple pensions can only be a matter of speculation, but his actions and those of the Saint-Benôit family prove that many persons were still aware of the fief-rente, even though its use was declining.[15]

To explain why indentures were preferred to fief-rentes, one must recognize that the only significant difference between the two was that with the latter homage was performed; with the former it was not. A logical hypothesis would therefore be that homage was the factor determining the change. The ritual of homage varied somewhat as to time and place, but in its most common form the vassal, without sword, belt, or spurs, knelt bareheaded and placed his joined hands between those of his lord. In this position he declared that he became the lord's man in return for a specified fief. The lord then raised the vassal, kissed him on the mouth, and said that he took him as his man. Fealty consisted of the vassal taking an oath of fidelity, most frequently upon the Gospels. This ceremony was born at a time when the kiss was used by members of the same sex or by different sexes as a sign of welcome, of reconciliation, and on a guest's departure. It was also used to confirm an agreement, such as the gift of a piece of property, the renunciation of a disputed claim, or the making of a marriage alliance. It is not surprising, therefore, to see it employed in homage as a mark of mutual fidelity.

There is overwhelming evidence that by the sixteenth century the ceremony of homage had become unpopular, and determined efforts were made to modify it when the customs of the various parts of France were redacted and reformed. To Charles Du Moulin, a distinguished jurist who published a very influential treatise in 1539, the kiss was "indecent, nay, reprehensible." Kneeling before a noble was ridiculous. One only knelt before a prince. Women presented a special problem. Sir Thomas Littleton, an English jurist who wrote in law French around 1475, took offense at a woman having to say, "I become your woman; for it is not fitting that a woman should say that she will become a woman to any man, but to her husband when she is married."[16] Many French jurists quoted him with approval, and Littleton was eventually translated into modern French. To the later French jurist Gaspard Thaumas de la Thaumassière, the ceremony was a "ridiculous and superfluous formality." It would suffice if the vassal took the oath "cap in hand."[17] Still another referred to the ritual as "kids' stuff, the sort of thing that is done in a theater."[18]

The unpopularity of the ceremony of homage must be attributed to a change in social mores that can be traced back to the late thirteenth century, when a change in the attitude toward kissing can be detected. In the ancient world, homosexuality had been widely accepted, and it was not until the late twelfth century that the church began to make a concerted effort to stamp out homosexual practices. Whether this change was caused by the slow implementation of the Gregorian reforms or some other factor is difficult to determine, but by 1300, homosexuality was condemned by church and state alike. Kissing by members of the same sex, which had once served as a sign of peace, reconciliation, and agreement, now became associated with homosexuality. The kiss of peace that had been exchanged at church between members of the same sex just before communion was abandoned. Homosexuality was among the alleged misdeeds for which the Templars were brought to trial. Most significant of all, kisses ceased to be used to seal the various types of contracts. Under these circumstances, it is not surprising that homage, or at least the kissing part of the ritual, also came under attack. Homage was, of course, just a special kind of contract.

Kneeling was also decried. When the ceremony of homage began to evolve, vassals had usually been ordinary freemen, or even serfs. They did not object to kneeling humbly before their lord, but by the close of the thirteenth century a virtual revolution had occurred. The typical vassal was now a noble fully conscious of his dignity and worth. The prestige of the monarchy had become so great that only the greatest of magnates objected to kneeling before a king, but for one noble to kneel before another was, as an eighteenth-century jurist put it, "ridiculous."

In Normandy and perhaps elsewhere, the great nobles tried to preserve the practice. It inflated their egos to have people kneel before them. However, the preponderant opinion was to reduce the practice as far as the law allowed. In some places, the redacted or revised sixteenth-century customs specified that only one knee need be placed on the ground, and others failed to describe the ritual, thereby leaving lord and vassal to their own devices. It therefore seems probable that the shift from the fief-rente to the indenture was brought about by growing dislike of the homage ritual. Property and seigneurial revenue were involved when landed fiefs were awarded or changed hands. Hence, homage was preserved in such cases, but the traditional ritual was often modified to satisfy opponents of the ceremony.

Although more and more lords abandoned the fief-rente for the indenture during the fourteenth and fifteenth centuries, this did not mean that they wanted or anticipated less loyalty under the new system than under the old. The indenture was generally written on parchment. A copy retained by the lord was sealed and signed by the client, and a copy retained by the client was sealed and signed by the lord. The typical indenture of the late fourteenth century stated that the client swore on the Holy Gospels to serve his lord faithfully and well against everyone except the king and perhaps some other person or persons. The lord in return promised to protect, succor, and aid the client. Often he agreed to pay the client a specified sum. No termination date for the arrangement was usually specified, but it was understood that it was for life, unless, of course, both parties agreed to abrogate it.[19]

The few fifteenth-century indentures that have been found tend to be less specific. In 1429, Gilles de Rais signed and sealed an indenture on parchment in which he swore to serve Georges de La Trémoille with all his strength until death because of past favors and future expectations.

No specific rewards were promised, and no specific services were stipulated. Service and good lordship were understood by both parties. Rais served his lord faithfully, and La Trémoille obtained the post of marshal of France for him three months after signing the indenture. Even the allusion to future expectations was dropped in 1451 when Gailhard de Durefort swore "to serve, succor, and aid" Charles d'Albret and his children for life against everyone except the king and the dauphin.[20]

The great noble used his clients much as he used his vassals. He expected them to accompany him into battle and on his journeys to court. They were to fight under his banner, and when at court they were to wear his livery or at least his device. Always they were to come with a suitable number of followers, depending on their rank. The lord might travel with an entourage of several hundred; to go about with only a handful of attendants would lower his dignity and perhaps endanger his person. In return, the great lord was prepared to do much for his clients. He often employed them in his household and made them commanders of his châteaux. Through his influence at court, he obtained positions for them and their children in the government, the army, and the church. He protected them in troubled times, and if they fell foul of the law, he overawed the judges and saw to it that they went unharmed. The taxes, salary, and pension he received from the king, added to his own resources, often enabled him to reward them handsomely.

The fact that indentures supplanted the fief-rente by the middle of the fifteenth century indicates that the lords had found that a written contract coupled with an oath on the Gospels provided as much assurance of loyalty as the oath of homage. Certainly the authors of the various late medieval treatises that dealt with how a noble should behave drew no distinction as to the degree of loyalty a vassal and a client owed his lord. Honoré Bonet, probably the most widely read of these authors, insisted in *The Tree of Battles* that a knight "should be willing to die to keep the oath of his faith to his lord. I say the same of the knight in receipt of wages from the king or other lord, for since he has pledged to him his faith and oath he must die in defense of him and his honour." Knights "should keep the oath which they have made to their lord to whom they belong, and to whom they have sworn and promised to do all that he shall command for the defense of his land, according to what is laid down by the laws." "If a knight quits his lord in time of peace, whilst in receipt of wages, he should be condemned to go henceforth not mounted, but on foot like a sergeant."[21] In time of war, he should be executed.

The indenture system has been given the pejorative name "bastard feudalism" on the assumption that it was inferior to traditional feudalism. In actual fact, it was traditional feudalism that was in a state of decay, and indentures were invented in part to serve as a new way to tie the greater and lesser nobility together. Indeed, around 1389, Philippe de Mézières indicated that royal officials could do homage to a great noble for land without putting their loyalty in doubt, but that it would be improper to enter into alliances with him, because the nonfeudal contract was more binding than the feudal one. The dukes of Brittany agreed. They appear to have used indentures to strengthen their fading ties with their vassals. Homage was not enough to ensure loyalty; a written contract was needed.[22]

The weakness of feudal ties is also revealed by the efforts of kings and great nobles to tie their vassals more closely to their sides by creating orders of chivalry. In 1351, King John introduced chivalric orders into France by establishing the Order of the Star, and his unknightly descendant Louis XI brought the raft of medieval creations to an end when he founded the Order of St. Michael in 1469. In the intervening period, a number of great nobles created their own orders, the most famous being Philip the Good of Burgundy's Golden Fleece (1431) and René of Anjou's Croissant (1448). These orders undoubtedly were designed to serve a number of purposes: to defend the true religion, to protect noble ladies, to sponsor tournaments, and so on, but in the minds of most of their creators one of the greatest was to bind their vassals more closely to them and to seek outside supporters. They put great stress on loyalty to the commander of the order and to one's sovereign lord, who was often one and the same person. Disloyalty and flight from the battlefield after the banners had been unfurled led to disgrace and expulsion from the order. The Burgundian dukes and René of Anjou found their order useful in drawing together the high nobility of their far-flung domains. Occasionally, a non-vassal would be inducted in the hope of attracting support from the outside, just as the fief-rente and clientage were used, but this was a secondary purpose of the orders. Only three of the thirty-two knights who were members of René's Croissant in 1453 were not his vassals. So much were these orders like clientage that the collar or other insignia of the members was often identical to the livery clients wore.[23] Thus, in spite of many signs of decadence, nobles were actively seeking solutions to their problem as the Hundred Years War drew to a close.

THE NOBILITY AND THE DEMOGRAPHIC REVOLUTION

Between 1340 and 1450, disease and wars cost France over half its population, but during the hundred years that followed, it fully recovered from these losses, and by 1560 the number of inhabitants rivaled that of the early fourteenth century. The causes of this growth are not far to seek. The period was one of relative peace and order. Revolts were few, and the center of warlike activity was transferred to Italy. The low level of population during the early part of the period meant that there were high wages and ample food for the mass of the people. The plague returned less frequently and was less virulent; or, at least, the better-fed population was more able to withstand the assaults of disease. After the death of Louis XI, the state even restrained its demands for taxes, and levies grew at about the same rate as the price of grain. Finally, relative prosperity led to earlier marriages and more childbearing years.[24] In Rheims in 1422, the average bride was only 15 or 16 years of age at her first marriage. As the population grew, economic conditions became less favorable. Between 1450 and 1550, the age of a bride at her first marriage at Dijon crept up from 20.5 years to 21.5, still substantially below the 25 years that was commonplace during the seventeenth century.[25]

The population growth was not uniform. It began earlier in some places than in others, and at times it was relatively stagnant. The rate of increase over the century averaged about 0.7 percent per year, only half the speed with which the U.S. population grew between 1930 and 1980, and a fourth that of some underdeveloped countries today. Nevertheless, it was enough to alter the picture of the French countryside. From being underpopulated in 1460, France had become overpopulated a century later, and the change had profound economic and social consequences.[26]

But did the nobles' demographic pattern follow the downward trend of the rest of the population between 1340 and 1450, and did the nobility enjoy the same natural growth thereafter? Or was a massive infusion from the lower classes necessary to maintain the same proportion of nobles to the total population? There are few precise data to enable one to answer these questions, but what is known makes it clear that a powerful infusion of new blood was necessary.

A study of the marriage patterns of the upper and middle nobility reveals surprising consistency from the fourteenth through the sixteenth centuries. About two-thirds of the men and three-fourths of the women married. The average couple had 4.5 children prior to 1500 and a fraction more during the sixteenth century. This should have enabled the important noble families to have nearly kept pace with the population as a whole. English ducal families more or less held their own numerically during the same period.[27]

Local studies of the French nobility that include the less important families, however, suggest a different story. In addition to the demographic hazards of war and disease that threatened the entire population, nobles faced economic ones, which forced many of them to abandon their way of life. For example, five villages in Provence boasted thirty-eight nobles in 1377, of whom seventeen were not living as nobles, presumably for economic reasons. By 1427–31, these same villages contained twenty-two nobles, and by 1458 there were only six. The number then began to increase, and by 1474 there were twelve.[28]

The county of Forez provides a larger and equally devastating example. Out of 215 noble lineages recorded in the thirteenth century, 66 disappeared before 1300. Between 1300 and 1400, 80 of the remaining 149 families became extinct in the male line. Thirty-eight more died out by 1500, leaving only 31 lineages of the original 215 to carry on their family names.[29] No doubt some of the surviving lineages had prospered demographically and produced two or more nuclear families, but they could hardly have matched the general population growth after 1450. This fact can be illustrated from data taken from the élection of Bayeux. Here there were 163 male lineages in 1462, but by 1540 the number had shrunk to 104, a decline of 57 percent. The number of nuclear noble families only shrank from 211 to 172, a decline of 23 percent, but the population as a whole nearly doubled during these years.[30]

A number of factors explain the nobility's difficulty in reproducing itself even at a time when the population as a whole was growing. In the first place, nobility was transmitted in the male line. The children of a noblewoman who married a commoner were nearly everywhere considered commoners. A higher percentage of the upper nobility chose military or ecclesiastical careers than any other component of society. The resulting violent deaths and celibacy took a heavy toll. Finally, there was the economic factor. Few nobles were formerly stripped of their status because they engaged in trade, but it is probable that many of the lower nobility were so poor that they dropped all pretense of living nobly and swelled the ranks of the artisans or peasantry. It is worthy of note that in the Beauce, a well-endowed agricultural region a little to the southwest of Paris, families with two or three fiefs were less likely to disappear than those with only one.[31]

The proportion of the total population who were of old noble families therefore declined during the years of catastrophe. Even when the population as a whole began to rise after 1450, the nobility had difficulty reproducing itself. If the nobles were to increase or even maintain their proportion of the total population, they would have to admit new families into their ranks, and this they did in great numbers. In the Beauce, only 19 percent of the fiefs in 1500 were owned by families whose nobility dated back a century or more. Fifty-one percent of the fiefs were owned by new nobles; 22 percent by commoners, who doubtless anticipated assimilation into the second estate; and 7 percent by outsiders.[32] Of a group of 108 noble Provencal families in 1550, only 33 had attained that status by the beginning of the fifteenth century.[33] In 1668, only 28 percent of the Breton nobility had medieval origins, but over half had become nobles during the great numerical reconstruction prior to the Wars of Religion.[34] In neighboring Savoy, which was not then a part of France, 263 families were ennobled during the fifteenth and sixteenth centuries.[35]

The most rapid way to become a noble was to obtain letters of ennoblement. Before the close of the thirteenth century, French monarchs were trying to establish a monopoly on the right to ennoble by denying this privilege to the great nobles, but two hundred years elapsed before they prevailed. The Valois dukes of Burgundy ennobled about a hundred commoners between 1371 and 1476, and Jean V, duke of Brittany, matched their record between 1426 and 1432. John II, Charles V, and Charles VI issued at least 959 letters of ennoblement between 1350 and 1421. Their successors were less generous. Between 1420 and 1560, the crown issued only an average of 6 letters of ennoblement per year in the jurisdiction of the chamber of accounts of Paris. A majority of these ennoblements were for services rendered, but a significant minority of the letters record the amount the recipients paid for the honor. In Normandy, the kings were less restrained. Between 1460 and 1670, they issued over 1,300 letters, for the most part after 1560.[36] Letters of ennoblement, however, accounted for only a small percentage of those who swelled the ranks of the nobility. Large numbers were accepted as nobles by prescription. The heir of a burgher or wealthy peasant who purchased a fief and adopted a noble way of life, which might include a campaign or two, was accepted by other nobles after several generations. He was subject to a tax called the *franc fief,* but it was rarely collected, and many towns won exemptions for all their citizens. In 1470, Louis XI freed non-noble fief owners in the entire duchy of Normandy from the tax in return for 47,250 livres, and concessions were made in some other provinces. There was often local resistance to ennoblements, because in northern and central France, nobles escaped the taille, and commoners had to make up the difference. In 1555, Henry II forbad anyone to assume the status of a noble illegally, but hundreds, indeed thousands, must already have slipped into the ranks of the nobility. There was a general tightening during the last half of the sixteenth century. Ordonnances against illegal assumption of nobility were repeated several times, searches for false nobles became more frequent, and ennoblement by prescription became rarer.[37]

A new way to achieve nobility that partially compensated the aspiring lower classes for the loss of other avenues to the second estate gradually came into being, ennoblement by office. Kings had long ennobled individual officeholders in return for their services, but in December 1372, Charles V inaugurated the practice of collective ennoblements, decreeing that the mayor, échevins, and councillors of Poitiers and their successors would henceforth be nobles. The following month he granted similar privileges to the municipal officials of La Rochelle. The purpose of these ennoblements was to reward the officials of the frontier towns for their loyalty during the English wars and, more important, to ensure their future loyalty. Municipal officials of Toulouse were ennobled in 1420. Louis XI, ever favorable to the towns, added seven to the list. Between his death in 1483 and the Wars of Religion, only three more towns were so favored. Louis XIV ennobled the officials of a like number of towns, the last being Paris, which was so honored in 1706. These *noblesse de cloche,* as they were called, added fewer numbers to the ranks of the nobility than one might suspect. Many, especially in later years, were already nobles when they took office, and there was a tendency for the same individuals and families to hold office year after year. Furthermore, Louis XIV managed to restrict their privileges.[38]

More important in the long run was the growing practice of ennobling royal officials. By the dawn of the fifteenth century, the great offices of the crown—constable, chancellor, grand chamberlain, marshal of France, and so on—were considered ennobling, but nearly all the occupants of these positions were nobles when they took office, except the chancellor and the keeper of the seals. The secretaries of the king, the secretaries and councillors of state, and other groups of officials were added to this list during the late fifteenth and sixteenth centuries. All these posts brought immediate ennoblement to the occupants. Another category of offices, which included members of sovereign courts, gave gradual ennoblement. Holders of these positions had noble privileges while they performed their duties, but they became permanent nobles with the power of transmitting their nobility to their descendants only after they had held office for twenty years. In addition, certain military posts ennobled, such as membership in the royal guards, governorships, and captaincies of companies.[39]

It is impossible to arrive at precise figures as to the relative importance of the various types of ennoblement in the whole of France, but there have been studies for a few areas. In the Beauce, 125 families were ennobled between 1400 and 1560. Of these, 22 owed their advancement to the ownership of fiefs, 16 to military service, 14 to offices, and 1 to ennoblement by the king. The most striking change during these years was that only 3 families were ennobled through office during the fifteenth century but 11 were between 1500 and 1560, a development that points to the predominant role officeholding was to play in ennoblement in the late sixteenth and seventeenth centuries. There is no precise information as to how 72 of these 125 families became nobles. Probably they were ennobled simply by living nobly and in time being accepted as nobles by their neighbors.[40]

Data concerning other parts of France point to somewhat different conclusions. Of 108 noble families in Provence in 1550, 33 had held that status from time immemorial and 54 had been ennobled after 1400 as a result of holding office or by an act of the sovereign granting ennoblement or permission to own a fief. The remaining 21 were ennobled by prescription. Of these, 18 owed their rise to the ownership of a fief, 1 to his military prowess, and 2 to social visibility, achieved through municipal offices and marriage alliances.[41] Of the 68 families in the élection of Bayeux who were ennobled between 1463 and 1540, 41 were elevated by letter, 15 by prescription, and 12 for unknown reasons. Some of the new nobles held offices that would have ennobled them in time, but they seem to have preferred the immediate but more expensive route to the second estate of obtaining royal letters.[42]

The most surprising part of the above data is the small number of the Beauce nobility who were ennobled by royal letter when compared with their counterparts in Bayeux and Provence. Perhaps part of the discrepancy can be attributed to the destruction of most of the records of the Paris Chamber of Accounts in a fire in the eighteenth century. It is here that royal letters of ennoblement for the Beauce would have been preserved. In their absence, we are forced to rely primarily on copies made from the chamber's records prior to the fire. Our data, in short, may be incomplete. Still there were almost certainly wide regional variations.

The noble population as a whole was thus reconstituted between 1450 and 1560, a little by natural growth but for the most part by the elevation of commoners. But what was the fate of the titled nobility during the age of demographic catastrophes and the period of reconstruction that followed? A study of the counts is most revealing. In 1327, there were thirty-nine lay counts in France exclusive of the king, and in 1422, when Charles VII came to the throne, there were the same number. This appearance of stability, however, hides significant changes. During the period, fifteen new counties had been created, five had been elevated to duchies, and still others had reverted to the king. More significant, the thirty-nine lay counts of 1327 represented twenty-three dynasties. Of these, only eight survived to 1422. Fifteen new comital dynasties had had to be created during these pest-ridden and war-torn years to retain the same number of counts. Or to express it another way, sixty nobles had to be elevated to maintain the number of counts that had existed before the troubles began. In spite of forty-two creations between 1422 and 1515, the number of lay counts exclusive of the king stood at thirty-one at the latter date, a loss of six in just under a century. The kings did not follow a conscious policy of creating new counts to replace lines that had become extinct. Rather, the number of nobles they promoted to this rank was related to their need to win support. Philip VI and John II accounted for thirty-one creations during their troubled reigns, but the victorious Charles V was responsible for only five. When Charles VII was seeking support from every possible quarter between 1422 and 1429, he created a new count on an average of once a year, but during the last decade of his reign, with the English defeated, he elevated not a single one. Louis XI proved as generous with promotions as he was with pensions, but Charles VIII and Louis XII created only five counts each.[43]

A study of the peerage is also revealing. Of the six original lay peerages of France, only two survived the Hundred Years War. One of these, the duchy of Burgundy, escheated to the crown in 1477, and the other, the county of Flanders, passed to the Habsburgs and was officially recognized as no longer being under French sovereignty in the early sixteenth century. The lay peerage, therefore, had to be reconstituted from scratch. Philip IV began the process by creating three peerages in 1297, and by 1498, thirty-three more dukes, counts, and barons had been awarded this dignity. Nevertheless, as of 1505 there were only nine lay peers.[44] At this point what British historians have called an inflation of honors began. Between 1505 and 1588, the crown erected seventy new peerages, twice the number created during the preceding two centuries.

As a result, in spite of the extinction of many lineages, the number of lay peers reached forty by 1588.[45] In addition, there were twelve new counties, twelve new marquisates, twenty-six new duchies, and five new principalities.[46] At the beginning of the century, there were important nobles who were designated only as sire or seigneur; by its end there were few who were not called at least viscount or count. The nobility, both great and small, had had to be reconstituted with new blood, and the number of titles its members came to enjoy far exceeded anything the Middle Ages had ever known.

THE ECONOMIC RECONSTRUCTION

There is little doubt that the typical noble was in financial difficulty when the Hundred Years War drew to a close. The decline in population had created a scarcity of labor. Peasants could be found to till the soil only if favorable terms were offered. Land rents had to be lowered and wages raised. At the same time, the smaller population meant reduced demand for agricultural products and lower prices. Then, too, castles and manor houses had been destroyed in many parts of France, livestock had been stolen, fences destroyed, and fields trampled down. Peasants' huts could be rebuilt quickly, but a noble's home took longer, and years were needed to replenish the livestock so necessary for fertilizer, food, and labor. There was an obvious need for frugality, but some nobles persisted in an extravagant way of life. Those who failed to draw revenue from the royal trough, or who had not profited from ransoms or plunder during the war were apt to be in serious financial straits. Yet in the long run the future had never been brighter.[47]

The extinction of many noble families meant that those that survived had more land than ever before. Abandoned peasant holdings could often be incorporated into the demesne. In the county of Bigorre, for example, there were forty fiefs in 1313 but only eighteen in 1429. Twelve fiefs had disappeared because the villages on which they depended had ceased to exist, although the land, of course, remained. Ten fiefs had been acquired by six of the eighteen surviving seigneurs. For a time these eighteen seigneurs were in a difficult economic position, but they possessed what forty had shared a century before. In a generation or two population increases would reverse the economic vice in which their families were held. More peasants meant cheaper labor and higher land rents. More people in town and country led to higher food prices. At first the improvement in the economic status of the typical noble was barely discernible, but by the dawn of the sixteenth century it began to pick up momentum. The rising fortunes of the nobility can best be studied in the vast surviving records of the house of Foix-Navarre-Albret.

With the exception of the Valois dukes of Burgundy, no French noble family accumulated as many fiefs during the late Middle Ages as did the house of Foix. Through marriage, purchase, and war, the family acquired one lordship after another in southern France, including the kingdom of Navarre and the independent viscounty of Béarn. The problem of the counts of Foix was not to provide for a multitude of children in each generation but to produce an adult male heir. The demographic disasters of their age were both a splendid opportunity to acquire more land and a serious threat to their existence. At length the Foix family, too, failed to produce a son, and in 1484 the daughter of the house married Jean d'Albret, heir to extensive lands in the southwest.

The family owed its fiscal success during the Renaissance largely to Henri II d'Albret (1517–55). Henri did not need the bourgeoisie to tell him how to manage his estates. His grandmother's ancestors, the counts of Foix, had had their treasurers keep detailed records of their receipts and expenses as far back as the fourteenth century. For administrative supervision, Henri turned to the crown for a model. In 1520, he established a chamber of accounts at Pau to audit the records of the financial officials in his numerous domains and to perform other duties. In 1527, he reduced its jurisdiction by creating a chamber of accounts at Nérac to supervise Albret, Armagnac, Périgord, Limousin, Rouergue, Foix, and other French fiefs. The chamber of accounts at Pau retained responsibility for Béarn, Navarre, and Bigorre. Henri d'Albret divided his counties, viscounties, and other domains among a number of treasurers, each of whom administered one or more of these jurisdictions. Each treasurer collected the money due from his jurisdiction, paid local expenses, and periodically turned over the surplus to a general treasurer. The accounts of all of the treasurers and of the officials who expended sums to support the royal household were verified annually by the appropriate chamber of accounts.

The best surviving series of accounts is that for the independent viscounty of Béarn. Here, after deducting their expenses, the stewards (*baylies*) and notaries turned over the sums they collected from the individual subordinate jurisdictions to the treasurer of Béarn. Mills were leased for six years, but the tolls were farmed for more limited periods or collected by local officials. Careful management brought ever-increasing revenue, until Béarn itself was invaded during the Wars of Religion. Officials were evidently proud of their achievement, for one of them recorded in 1539 that revenue from the domain had been increased by 2,000 écus "without doing an injustice to anyone." Gross receipts that in 1530–31 had stood at 12,856 Béarnais écus reached 38,461 écus in 1564–65, a threefold increase in thirty-four years (see table 3.1).

Table 3.1. The Revenues of Béarn Contrasted with Paris and Toulouse Prices, 1526–1567

Period	Paris Wheat Indices[a]	Toulouse Wheat Indices[b]	Toulouse Wine Indices[c]	Fiscal Year[d]	Béarn Domain Indices[e]	Béarn Domain Receipts[e]
1526–35	1.00	1.00	1.00	1530–31	1.00	12,856
1533–37	0.83	0.73	0.72	1534–35	1.07	13,797
1538–42	0.97	1.01	0.96	1539–40	1.59	20,388
1543–47	1.41	0.87	1.10	1544–45	1.68	21,644
1548–52	1.39	0.83	0.62	1550–51	1.78	22,907
1553–57	1.21	1.44	0.76	1554–55	1.97	25,347
1558–62	1.76	1.25	0.88	1561–62	2.31	29,678
1563–67	2.60	2.07	1.41	1564–65	2.99	38,461

[a]Calculated August through July; derived from Micheline Baulant and Jean Meuvret, Prix des céréales extraits de la mercuriale de Paris, 1520–1698 (Paris, 1960), 1: 243.

[b]Calculated for the calendar year; derived from Georges Frêche and Geneviève Frêche, Les Prix des grains, des vins, et des légumes à Toulouse, 1486–1868 (Paris, 1967), 85–87.

[c]Calculated for the calendar year for local red wine; ibid., 118–21.

[d]The Béarn receipts are for the fiscal year, November 1–October 31. Data from AD, Pyrénées atlantique, B 225, B 229, B 234, B 238, B 242, B 246, B 251, and B 254.

[e]In Béarnais écus (1 écu = roughly 1.35 livres tournois, a parity retained throughout most of the period; Charles Dartigue-Peyrou, La Vicomté de Béarn sous le règne d'Henri d'Albret, 1517–1555 [Paris, 1934], 299–302). The figures are for gross receipts in money; payments in kind have been omitted because they were relatively stable and came to less than 2 percent of the gross receipts.

Receipts from the Albret domains in Périgord and Limousin increased from 10,566 livres in 1550–51 to 16,762 livres in 1573–74. The treasurers of the southern fiefs—except those of Béarn, Navarre, and Foix—turned over 65,952 livres to the treasurer of the royal household in 1556 and 85,039 livres in 1560. The total receipts from Navarre, Béarn, and the domains in France in the jurisdictions of the parlements of Toulouse and Bordeaux increased from 151,247 livres in 1557–58 to 191,520 in 1564. There were, of course, occasional exceptions to the general upward trend prior to the most destructive stage of the Wars of Religion. Much of the domain in Navarre yielded fixed monetary payments, and an exceptionally high proportion of the receipts were derived from tolls. The result was a relatively static situation there, except when a rebellion reduced the receipts in 1568, or when the provincial estates gave more or less than their customary amount. Receipts from Armagnac appear to have stabilized, at least temporarily, before the Wars of Religion began. In 1555–56, the various subordinate jurisdictions turned over 20,793 livres to the treasurer of the county; in 1562–63, they surrendered 20,744.

The Albrets neither directly exploited the domain nor relied heavily on the growing practice of turning their land over to sharecroppers. The payments they received in kind were of little importance. They preferred monetary leases, and since these were nearly always for three years, their value leaped upward with the demand for land; land rents rose even faster than grain prices. The Albrets broke up their domain into segments small enough to permit aspiring peasants to compete for leases, a practice that led to more competitive bidding than there would have been had they catered to the affluent. In 1531, those interested in leasing domain lands in the viscounty of Lautrec were summoned to Carcassonne, but by 1549 the Albrets had realized that competition for farms would be greater if the auctions were held in various parts of the viscounty itself. The viscounty was therefore divided into eleven parts, and the approach of Albret agents to this or that segment of the domain was widely advertised. The domain in the viscounty of Fézenzaguet was divided into a dozen or so segments before it was leased. Even so, two, and more often three or four, persons had to join together to make a successful bid in 1562, and doubtless in other years. With rare exceptions, the bidders were men without any form of title, not even that of judge, notary, or bourgeois of a small town. It is striking that only one group that obtained a parcel of the domain in 1562 did so again in 1565. Had the demand for land forced rents so high that the lessees of 1562 could not or would not compete three years later? It seems likely that they had, for nearly every parcel of the domain was leased for more in 1565 than it was in 1562. In several instances, the rent more than doubled.

Furthermore, only part of a great noble's income came from his domain. Unless he was in disgrace, he held lucrative royal offices and often received pensions and other gifts. These sums usually do not appear in the accounts of the receipts of the domain, but they were an important part of the total income. In 1546, Henry d'Albret drew 36,375 livres from the crown for his service as governor and in other capacities. This sum amounted to 48.4 percent of his income, and it does not include the pension the king gave his wife.[48]

The critical question, however, is not whether a noble's income increased, but rather whether it rose as rapidly as the price of the goods and services that he bought—that is, whether his real income increased. Prevailing scholarly opinion is that it did not, but in France and elsewhere this opinion has been based primarily on a comparison of noble income and grain prices, a practice that entails serious problems. In the first place, scholars have generally derived their price indices from the Paris grain market, although prices at Paris rose more rapidly than at Toulouse and probably in most other places in France. Nevertheless, gross receipts from the domain in Béarn increased more rapidly than wheat prices at Paris as well as at Toulouse, the nearest locality for which grain indices are available. In the second place, prices in general rose more slowly than grain prices. Local wine in Toulouse actually sold for less in 1558–62 than it had in 1526–35. Clearly, we must consider what a noble purchased with his income (see table 3.1).

The requirements of great nobles like the Albrets differed from those of typical country gentlemen. A gentleman counted himself lucky if he owned a fief or two. He probably produced nearly all of the food his household consumed, either by direct exploitation of all or part of his domain, through sharecropping, or from dues paid him in kind. Guillaume de Murol, an Auvergne noble of the early fifteenth century, for example, produced all or nearly all of the grain he and his household of about twenty consumed. Furthermore, the bread they ate represented only 22.7 percent of what they spent on food, which in turn was only a little more than 60 percent of their overall expenses in money and in kind. Even if Guillaume had had to buy his bread, it would have come to less than 14 percent of his total expenses. About a century and a half later, the sire de Gouberville also grew his grain and baked his bread. Only on special occasions did he purchase a higher-quality bread from a baker. Bread was an infinitesimal part of his expenses. Over half of his expenditures between 1549 and 1563 were for clothes, fabrics, and wages (see table 3.2). Available indices suggest that industrial prices rose less than half as rapidly as grain prices, and that the wages of skilled workers rose more slowly still.[49] Gouberville also spent significant amounts on meat and game, travel, and legal expenses, but the prices of such things certainly did not keep pace with grain (table 3.2). Very likely, during most of the sixteenth century, the cost of living index for the typical country gentleman rose about half as fast as grain prices. If this is true, the country gentlemen prospered during these years.

The practice of great nobles traveling from one estate to another and to and from court with retinues that might run to several hundred made it impossible for them to supply their own food. They were not, however, thrown entirely on the mercies of the marketplace. Rather, they made contracts with merchant-purveyors to provide food and wine at a fixed

Table 3.2. The Sire de Gouberville's Average Annual Expenses, 1549–1563

Category	Cost		Percentage
	Livres	Sous	
Clothes	51	5	28.3
Fruits and Sugar	0	15	0.4
Meat and Game	19	13	10.9
Fish	1	12	0.9
Spices and Salt	1	2	0.6
Beer for the Harvesters	0	6	0.2
Bread for the Harvesters	0	10	0.3
Candles	3	2	1.7
Legal Expenses	29	18	16.5
Travel Expenses	28	12	15.8
Wages	44	1	24.4
Total	180	16	100.00

SOURCE: Emmanuel Le Roy Ladurie, Introduction to *Un Sire de Gouberville, gentilhomme campagnard au Cotentin de 1553 à 1562*, ed. A. Tollemer (Paris, 1972), xliii.

price wherever they might be. The amount the Albrets agreed to pay remained surprisingly stable in spite of the rise in prices. The purveyors sought to fulfill their contracts by browbeating local merchants and peasants and by requisitioning goods at reduced prices. The three estates of Béarn complained bitterly of this practice. When inflation was at its worst, the Albrets relented somewhat and compensated their hard-pressed purveyors more fully. Nevertheless, they appear to have paid less than the market price for their provisions. Their expenditure for food generally came to from 30 to 50 percent of their household expenses. Household expenses were only a small part of the Albret outlay, however, especially during the Wars of Religion. Expenses for food were therefore only a minor part of the family's total expenses. The other big household expense was for wages. Here, the Albrets tended once more to ignore inflation and to pay those who served them the same amount, or but little more, near the end of the century as at the beginning. Their chamberlain, for example, was paid 556 livres in 1518 and 600 in 1587. Those in favor might be given an additional office or a pension, but most were less fortunate. Furthermore, when hard pressed the Albrets were capable of reducing the size of their household and of forgoing paying the salaries of some of those on their roles.[50]

Formulating a cost-of-living index for the Albrets or any other great noble family is difficult. They bought some food, but food was a small part of their total expenses. They had many servants, but they made no attempt to increase their salaries commensurately with inflation. Their costs rose, but the average price of the things they bought probably increased no more than half as rapidly as grain prices. If this is true, the Albrets would obviously have prospered throughout the century had peace been preserved. From their accounts, we see that, as their revenue increased in the peaceful years, they permitted themselves more luxuries and greater display. When they entered the Wars of Religion, they reduced needless expenses and devoted more of their resources to the military effort. When in 1572 it looked as though the marriage between Henry of Navarre and Marguerite of Valois would ensure a period of peace, Jeanne, Henry's mother, spent 32,133 livres on jewels and other things for the wedding, although she had to borrow at least part of the money to make these purchases. But jewels were not a useless luxury. They could be transformed into cash if the war were renewed more quickly than parts of the domain could be alienated. She had mortgaged her jewels before, and doubtless her son made good use of them in the years ahead.

Some may argue that the Albrets' ability to increase their revenues was atypical. It is true that, as sovereigns of Béarn and Navarre, they had the right to coin money and to ask the estates for donations. But they farmed the right to make coins for ever-increasing amounts, which paralleled the general growth of their revenues, and the donations of the estates of Béarn were not included in the domainal revenue. Granted, in Foix and Armagnac, where the estates occasionally voted the Albrets a donation, and in Navarre, where they regularly did so, the sums collected were incorporated into the domainal revenue, but only in these lands did the sources of their income differ significantly from those enjoyed by other great nobles. Others may argue that Henry d'Albret was an exception, because in his later years he resided on his estates and took an interest in making them efficient, and that his daughter Jeanne and granddaughter Catherine (who served as Henry of Navarre's regent after 1577) were captives of the so-called Protestant ethic. Fiscal responsibility came naturally to them, and as women they had fewer expenses than men. The financial practices of other noble families must therefore be considered.

The finest extant records of any other family are those of the La Trémoilles, and these records have been carefully studied by William A. Weary. The La Trémoilles had no more need to wait for the bourgeoisie to invade the countryside and teach them how to administer their estates than did the house of Foix-Navarre-Albret. During the lordship of Georges de La Trémoille, who is best known for his violence and intrigues during the days of Joan of Arc, a detailed memorandum was prepared on how the family's extensive estates should be managed. Special attention was paid to bookkeeping and the preservation of records. A century later, one of Georges's descendants, François de La Trémoille, an equally vigorous administrator, extracted every possible sou from his tenants and even prepared his own legal briefs. "Through marriage, purchase, and law-suit" such men managed to increase the number of their estates. In 1486, the family owned thirteen; in 1550, they had thirty-five.

The La Trémoille family usually leased their land for three years, which provided them with ample opportunities to raise rents to accommodate inflation. They also made use of sharecroppers. The results were striking. The average annual seigneurial income was 8,200 livres in 1486–96; by 1525–41 it had risen to 26,200 livres. Furthermore, the average salary and gifts the family annually received from the crown increased from 3,000 livres in 1486–88 to 18,200 livres in 1508–10. The La Trémoille fortunes occasionally took a turn for the worse, as, for example, when François had to provide for five sons and give dowries to two daughters. But, aided by several profitable marriages and, above all, by efficient administration, the general trend of the family fortune was upward. In 1500, the family's revenues were the equivalent of 220 kilograms of silver; in the 1530s, of 600 kilograms. A division of the estate and the Wars of Religion led to a drop to 430 kilograms in 1619, but a recovery followed. In 1679, the family income was the equivalent of 585 kilograms of silver, and in 1709, of 710 kilograms.[51]

The Montmorency, whose origins dated back to the tenth century, provide a third example of how a noble family could achieve great wealth. During the Middle Ages, their rise to wealth and power was relatively slow but surprisingly steady. The groundwork was laid for spectacular growth during the reigns of Francis I and Henry II, the golden age of the French nobility. In 1522–23, Guillaume de Montmorency enjoyed an income of 10,617 livres from his landed estates. In 1560–61, his son, Anne, now duke, peer, governor of Languedoc, and constable of France, drew 106,420 livres from the same source, and the latter figure does not include some 20,000 livres from usufructs. This twelvefold increase was obtained in part from increased income from existing family estates and in part from the acquisition of more land. During the period under consideration, revenue from the fief of Montmorency grew from 2,000 to 15,500 livres; from Chantilly from 2,200 to 8,400; from Damville from 1,090 to 4,500, and from Villiers from 104 to 4,300.[52] The money to purchase the new land was derived from the salaries and pensions Anne received from the crown, gifts from the estates of Languedoc and, no doubt, other institutions whose interests he furthered at court, investments in land, rentes (municipal bonds), and other sources. "Given the Constable's prolonged domination at court," Mark Greengrass observes, "royal favour counted for less than one might imagine in direct ways (alienations of royal demesne, pensions and gifts), and rather more in indirect ones (influence on legal decisions, providing a valuable liquidity for purchases, access to a property market, etc.). The Constable demonstrated that stealth and steady application, complemented by the work of loyal and efficient estate stewards, could accomplish more than swift accumulation of patrimony with the inevitable political and legal repercussions."[53]

The Albrets, La Trémoilles, and Montmorencies were among the richest nobles in France. As such, they could and did employ a number of able men to handle their affairs. Great nobles might thus have prospered even had they been guilty of all of the follies historians have attributed to them. We must ask, therefore, how well nobles with less far-flung estates and fewer servants coped with inflation and war.

The Gascon fief of Auzan provided its lords with 15,000 livres in 1454 and 86,000 livres in 1614. The barony of Sully-sur-Loire brought its owners increased revenues at least until 1545. In Normandy, the demand for land led to a threefold increase in rent for parcels at Dèville-lès-Rouen between 1480 and 1510, and from an eight- to tenfold increase at Hautot-sur-Dieppe between 1480 and 1550. The Norman counts of Tancarville rented their marshlands for grazing in 1459 for 340 livres per year. In 1498, they received 550 livres; in 1515, 900 livres; in 1521, 1,450 livres. Although leases were for nine or twelve years, the rents from their land grew from 110 livres per year in 1506 to 550 livres in 1554, after which the first War of Religion likely caused the drop to 493 livres in 1563. The total revenue from the county grew less rapidly because seigneurial dues stabilized; nevertheless, it increased from about 2,200 livres in 1460 to an average of 7,000 livres annually between 1540 and 1550, more than enough to compensate for inflation, but not sufficient to fully restore the prosperity the counts had enjoyed before the English invasion in 1415.[54] Around 1400, the Norman barons of Neubourg were making the most of their resources, but their income toppled following the English conquest in 1418. The yield from their fiefs, which stood at 739 livres in 1405–6, fell to 264 livres in 1444–45. The expulsion of the English was followed by a slow recovery, initially made possible by an increased emphasis on livestock. Scanty surviving evidence elsewhere suggests that seigneurial revenue increased at least until the latter half of the sixteenth century.

In the vicinity of Paris, nobles who owned vast estates and those who held court positions or received royal pensions managed to retain, or even increase, their holdings after the Hundred Years War. The scant surviving evidence suggests that they also increased their purchasing power, but not to the extent that their financial position of the first half of the fourteenth century was fully restored. Lesser royal officials—that is, those in the sovereign courts and in finance—did penetrate the countryside and purchase some of the fiefs of the poorer gentlemen. The merchant, however, rarely participated in this process; in other words, there was no "bourgeois conquest of the soil."[55] At Lyons, where merchants rather than royal officials predominated, much of the land was owned by the church. This prevented commoners from acquiring fiefs until after 1525, when the lands of the constable of Bourbon and, later, some church property were put on the market. Local noblemen, who were neither wealthy nor numerous, were unable to compete. Wealthy citizens of Tours began to purchase fiefs in earnest after 1470 and especially after 1490. By 1520, they had acquired at least 233, but these acquisitions were not sufficient to involve a massive transfer of property except perhaps in the neighborhood of the town itself.[56]

In regions more removed from large bureaucratic or commercial centers, nobles appear to have held their own. In the élection of Bayeux, the owners of 215 fiefs are known in 1503 and in 1552. Seventy-four percent of these fiefs were owned by old nobles in the former year and 73 percent in the latter. New nobles—that is, those who had held that status for less than a century—increased their holdings from 12 to 17 percent. The percentage owned by nonresident nobles, commoners, and unidentifiable persons actually declined from 15 to 10 percent. In terms of income from fiefs, old nobles increased their share from 52 to 60 percent between 1552 and 1562.[57]

A similar situation existed in the Beauce in spite of the proximity of the middle-sized towns of Chartres and Orléans and the presence of Paris less than two days ride away. Here old noble families usually owned twice as many seigneuries and more land than new noble families. They succeeded in increasing their income through careful management of their estates.[58] "Thus," Jean-Marie Constant has declared, "the gentleman of Beauce, far from neglecting his lands, exploited them methodically. He does not seem to have been touched, as has traditionally been asserted, by the crisis of noble revenue of the sixteenth century."[59]

Furthermore, nobles did not derive all their agricultural income from fiefs. Many began to acquire peasant land after the Hundred Years War. In the Gâtine of Poitou, they took the lead in buying scattered parcels in order to form more consolidated farms, which they rented to sharecroppers on five-year leases. The Norman family of Maignart purchased a small estate of only eight hectares in 1503, but by 1552 it had grown to thirty-three hectares, and by 1583 to fifty-four hectares. In the region in Brittany around Vannes, the middle and especially the lesser nobility purchased peasant land in large quantities from about 1490. They brought new land under cultivation and built mills and manor houses. As elsewhere, these nobles, for the most part of old families, far outstripped the merchants in the acquisition of both noble and common land.[60]

The nobles' purchases of peasant holdings created a serious problem in provinces where the taille was *personnelle,* because such property was withdrawn from the tax digest, and the difference was made up by increasing the burden on the remaining peasant holdings. In Dauphiné, where the villagers were able to produce a legal argument that the nobility and other privileged groups should pay the taille on the common land that they owned, an exceptionally bitter dispute arose. During Henry IV's reign, the villagers gathered data to prove that from one-half to two-thirds of the taxable land had passed into the hands of those who claimed to be exempt. Perhaps the peasants' figures should not be fully trusted, but the king's council recognized that they had a legitimate complaint.

As might be anticipated, in provinces where the taille was *réelle,* the privileged sometimes sought to have it declared personnelle so that they would not be taxed on the non-noble land they had acquired. The effort to redefine the taille surfaced in Agenais, Condomois, Provence, Languedoc, and probably elsewhere. In general, the effort failed because of the strength of tradition and the crown's realization that reducing the number of taxable acres was not in its interest. What the nobles were unable to accomplish by royal decrees or judicial decisions, they sometimes achieved by more devious means. In Comminges, they managed to get some of the common parcels of land they held classified as noble in the tax digest in spite of the watchful eyes of tax officials.[61]

Of course there were a few nobles who combined stupidity with bad luck to thwart the upward economic trend. The dukes of Nevers, for example, committed every folly that historians have long attributed to the nobility as a whole. Expensive entertainment, gambling, large dowries, and conspicuous consumption were coupled with participation in foreign wars when no domestic conflicts were available. Even biology appeared to be their enemy, for in 1564 the male line became extinct. At this point Charles IX stepped in and appointed commissioners to straighten out the family finances. He also permitted the title and property to devolve on a daughter married to an Italian noble. To provide for the bride's younger sisters, substantial properties had to be sold in 1566. Nevertheless, the family were able to retain their status as great nobles during the Wars of Religion. The nobility as a class lost little by their misfortunes, for other nobles purchased most of the Nevers estates that were put on the market.[62]

We have focused on the nobles' agricultural income, but it must also be remembered that many of them profited greatly from the crown and the church, as well as from rentes and investments in mining, glassmaking, and commerce. Their prosperity was achieved by their ability to take advantage of the new demographic and economic circumstances. They and their employees adopted improved methods of accounting and exploiting the soil before there was significant bourgeois penetration of the countryside. Nobles increased their agricultural income as rapidly or more rapidly than grain prices by using short-term leases, usually of three to six years. Such leases rose quickly in response to the growing peasant demand for land that was sparked by the demographic explosion. Since the price of the goods and services they purchased grew much more slowly than grain prices, they very likely doubled their purchasing power during the century before the Wars of Religion.

INHERITANCE STRATEGIES AND MARRIAGE LAWS

Although demographic and economic trends forced the typical noble's income upward more rapidly than prices during the century before the Wars of Religion, too many children could bring even a frugal and businesslike family to the brink of disaster. Thus, although Francis de La Trémoille was able to add substantially to the family estates, his death in 1542 provoked a crisis, because he left five sons and three daughters to be provided for, only one of whom opted for the church.[63] Gaspard de Saulx-Tavannes urged his fellow nobles to "marry few daughters for that is the ruin of a noble house," but the royal governors provided dowries for nearly two-thirds of their female offspring.[64] The solution most noble families sought lay, not in imposing chastity upon their children, but in the laws of inheritance and family property.

In England, a combination of primogeniture and entails did much to preserve the property of noble lineages. French customary law in northern and central France, on the other hand, limited how far parents could go in favoring the eldest son. Property was classified as personal (*meubles*) and real (*immeubles*). Real property in turn was divided into *propres*, which were inherited and belonged to the lineage, and *acquêts*, which consisted of the goods a person had acquired. The disposition of propres among the heirs was determined by the custom of the jurisdiction and could not be altered by a parent's will. Included were land, buildings, rentes, and offices when they became inheritable. The customs varied widely. That of Anjou decreed that if a noble estate amounted to 1,000 livres and there were three sons, 700 livres would go to the eldest son and the remainder would be divided equally between the other two sons. In Paris, the eldest son's share was 550 livres, and in Poitiers, 400 livres, with the remainder being divided equally in both cases. In Perche, the 1,000 livres was evenly divided among the three sons. A testator was usually free to dispose of his personal property and acquêts as he saw fit.[65] From these sources, he could provide dowries for daughters, supplement the portions of younger sons, or further advantage his eldest son. Whatever course he took, it is clear that if he had more than one child, the family's economic status would decline on his death unless he had either acquired enough wealth to compensate for the portion of his younger children or his eldest son made an advantageous marriage.

Younger children were not always happy with the inheritance laws, and a modest effort was made to improve their position when the customs of Maine and Anjou were redacted in 1508. In these two jurisdictions, the eldest son received two-thirds of the propres and the younger children shared the remaining third during their lifetimes, but on their deaths, their third reverted to the lineage rather than going to their own children. Spokesmen for the younger children were not so foolish as to seek an equal division of the inheritance; all they tried to achieve was the hereditary ownership of their third, but even this was denied to them. Indeed, primogeniture seemingly became increasingly popular among the jurists who wrote on the subject as the sixteenth century progressed.[66]

In southern France, Roman law had a profound influence. In accordance with its provisions, children divided the estate equally, a situation that would have decimated family fortunes quickly had not Roman law also granted a father the right to bequeath his property as he chose. Justinian slightly curtailed parental authority by a proviso that the younger children must receive something, but left open the possibility that a father might greatly favor one child. Until the close of the thirteenth century, parents rarely used this authority, and estates were generally divided equally among all the children. At this point, a powerful movement to reform family law began, which was reflected to some extent in the customs that were redacted, and especially in wills, family and marriage pacts, and entails. An influence from the north was clearly felt, and the newly redacted custom of Bordeaux insisted that the principal fief go to the eldest son, and that the unity of the fief be preserved. Younger children were to receive something, but no specific percentage of the family's goods was assigned to them. Wills and family pacts were also used to preserve the prestige of the lineage. Amanieu VII d'Albret, for example, inherited a greatly expanded domain, but he decided on a most unequal division of property between his three sons and four daughters. He provided dowries for the latter when they married but insisted that they renounce any further claims upon his estate, a practice that was to become commonplace everywhere in France. After persuading his sons to recognize his right to dispose of his property as he saw fit, he named his eldest son his universal heir and gave his other sons lesser fiefs provided that they did homage to their eldest brother. This practice became a family compact and was soon declared to be the custom of the jurisdiction in which the Albrets' principal seat was located. In this manner, the once obscure Albrets were able to achieve and retain such prestige that one of their number was to marry into the house of Foix-Navarre, and his great-grandson was to become Henry IV of France.[67]

It was not enough for the would-be founder of a dynasty to ensure that most of his estates were inherited by his eldest son; he also had to make certain that future generations continued the practice of giving preference to a single heir, and that none of these favored descendants squandered their patrimony. The inventive noble mind did not fail to meet the challenge. As early as 1121, a seigneur of Montpellier prescribed in his will the beneficiary of his estate after his heir had died. The practice became increasingly popular, first in the south and then in the north, first among the leading nobles and then among the nobility at large, until by the sixteenth century entailing an estate from one generation to another had spread throughout France, except in provinces where the customary law did not permit the practice, such as Auvergne, Brittany, and Normandy. There was widespread opposition to entails, not only on the part of younger sons, daughters, and heirs, who lost the right to dispose of their inheritance as they saw fit, but also on the part of creditors, who could not seize the estate of a debtor who merely held a lifetime use. Furthermore, would-be purchasers of land were denied the opportunity to obtain entailed estates. As a result, efforts were made to limit the number of times the creator of an entail could tie up an estate. In 1561, the ordonnance of Orléans restricted new entails to two degrees after their institution, and in 1566 entails created prior to 1561 were limited to four degrees. Furthermore, an entail did not prevent younger children from obtaining their legal share of an estate as prescribed by custom. In some places, daughters who had renounced all claims on an estate upon receiving a settlement were permitted to lodge claims after their parents' deaths if they had been seriously disadvantaged. Entails in France thus never achieved the importance they enjoyed in England or even Castile, but they nevertheless helped to preserve the status of many noble families.[68]

The relatively limited role of entails in France was partially compensated for by *retrait lignager,* the right to buy from the purchaser at the sale price, plus costs, the propres, and in some provinces the acquêts, that a relative had sold. This, as Montesquieu later said, made it possible for a noble family to regain "the lands that the prodigality of a relative had alienated." Indeed, when a noble found it necessary to sell land, he often reserved the right to buy it back. Like the royal domain, lineage property could not be permanently alienated. Retrait lignager appeared in Auch in the eleventh century and slowly spread elsewhere in France. By the sixteenth century, it was part of the law of most of the country.[69]

The choice of a spouse also played an important part in a family's strategy for advancement, and indeed sometimes for survival. Noble parents married their children to those who would bring their families political, social, and financial advantages. In planning the family strategy, French parents had one great advantage over their English counterparts. Their kings did not claim minor children of their deceased tenants in chief as their wards, to be disposed of in marriage as they saw fit. In England, wards were valuable prizes, who were literally bought and sold with little regard for the wishes of the deceased parents or their own desires. French parents had only to fear that their children would marry foolishly after their deaths or contract alliances without their permission during their lives. They could do little to prevent the former, and Antoine d'Argenton's ancestors must have turned over in their graves when he married a well-born woman without wealth "for his pleasure," despite the fact that his once-powerful barony was in financial straits. The greater fear on the part of parents, however, was that their children would marry clandestinely. To prevent this mishap, a concerted effort was made to strengthen parental authority in the sixteenth century.[70]

Under church law prior to the Council of Trent, a marriage could be contracted without either a priest, witnesses, or written records. A couple had only to make a binding pledge to take each other as man and wife. Elopements and secret marriages were frequent enough to alarm parents, and a determined effort was launched to increase parental authority and bring clandestine marriages to an end. In 1556, an assembly of the estates of the government of Lyonnais came out against such unions, and in February 1557, a royal edict forbad children to marry without their parents' consent. If they did so before the husband was over thirty and the bride over twenty-five, they were to be disinherited, and those who assisted the errant couple were to be punished. The French delegation to the final session of the Council of Trent sought to make church law conform more closely to that of France. They failed in their effort to have secret marriages declared invalid, but after much debate, they did succeed in requiring that a priest and at least two witnesses be present and that a registry of marriages be kept by parish priests. Secrecy was thus ended, but parental desires could still be thwarted. The Ordonnance of Blois (1579) therefore further strengthened the laws against clandestine marriages, as did subsequent legislation.[71]

THE NOBILITY AND THE ARMY

It has often been asserted that the mounted, armored noble was made obsolete by the technological developments of the late Middle Ages. The longbow, the crossbow, and finally firearms made his exposed position on a horse precarious, and well-trained pikemen blunted the effect of his wild cavalry charges. Artillery battered down his castle walls, and, finally, the establishment of standing armies gave kings the power to compel his obedience. In a series of pitched battles during the first half of the fourteenth century, infantrymen with their missiles and pikes proved their superiority. The mounted man-at-arms had seemingly become an anachronism. But as so often happened in other fields of endeavor, the nobility managed to adapt to the changed circumstances and remain the dominant class in warfare.

Around 1350, plate armor designed with glancing surfaces to deflect missiles and blows from lances and other weapons began to replace mail armor. Horses were provided with armor, and around 1400, a higher quality of iron and steel began to be produced. Sturdier horses were imported and a conscious effort was made to breed warhorses capable of carrying the heavy loads required. After the mid fifteenth century, ways were even found to reduce the weight of the armor without reducing the protection provided. By 1480, the weight of the armor for the horse and a 140-pound man was only 126 pounds. If another 30 pounds were added for arms, saddle, and so forth, the total weight on the horse came to only 296 pounds, about the same amount a cavalry horse was expected to carry four centuries later. New techniques of fighting with lances were developed. The improved methods of defense and offense actually led to an increase in the importance of cavalry during the latter half of the fifteenth century. Firearms became more important around the close of the Middle Ages, but it was not until 1567 that they completely replaced the crossbow in the French army. By then the mounted man-at-arms had been supplanted by the infantry as the principal branch of service, but the nobility had already become accustomed to fighting on foot if need be.[72]

Artillery was effectively used to batter down town and castle walls during the closing years of the Hundred Years War, but this did not necessarily doom the nobility. They too purchased cannons, which could be used when they besieged their foes. Cannon were also excellent weapons for defense, and means were found to mount them so that they could blast the besiegers. At first castles were provided with taller and thicker walls, but around the close of the fifteenth century, the ultimate solution to the invention of artillery was found in Italy in the form of low, very thick walls with angle bastions that served as platforms for artillery and permitted the defenders to cover all the walls with flanking fire. The earliest fortification of this new style in what is now France was commenced by Henry d'Albret at Navarrenx in the heart of his viscounty of Béarn. Other great nobles rarely followed his example, however, because they found better ways to maintain their position. Their Renaissance châteaux were designed more for beauty, elegance, and courtly life than for defense. A way to forestall artillery had been discovered, but the nobility did not feel the need to use it.[73]

Much has been made of the creation of a standing army in 1445. Actually, there was ample precedent for this step. French kings, and indeed the high nobility, had long had their guards and garrisons. Charles V maintained a number of companies from 1369 until the end of his reign, but they were disbanded during the financial troubles that followed his son's ascension to the throne. Charles VII did not in fact create a standing army from scratch; rather he incorporated a select number of the existing bands that had been fighting the English and preying on the inhabitants. These bands had been employed by great nobles and captained by men of less exalted rank who owed their positions to their military prowess. As the captains, who were at first drawn for the most part from the nobility of middle rank, determined the composition of their troops, they emerged collectively as the controlling force in the new army. As time passed, more and more dukes and counts sought and obtained command of companies, so that by the close of the Middle Ages, the high nobility exercised considerable influence over the component parts of the new army. It belonged, in a sense, as much to them as to the king. Charles could have established a more purely mercenary force made up of foreign troops if his goal had been to weaken the French nobility, but he seemingly had no desire to do so. The selected native companies sufficed to drive out the English and to suppress the disorderly bands that Charles had not seen fit to convert into royal troops. Over some protest, he retained this army after the recovery of France and the restoration of peace.

The initial force consisted of 1,500 *lances,* each composed of a heavily armed mounted man-at-arms, two mounted archers, and three other men, only one of whom was a combatant. These lances were organized into *compagnies d'ordonnance* under the command of a great noble. The typical company consisted of from fifty to a hundred lances, but they were rarely kept up to strength. The number of lances was soon increased; for a time Louis XI maintained about 4,000. In addition, there were infantry and other categories of troops. The army as a whole fluctuated between 14,000 and 25,000 men in the last half of the fifteenth century. Louis XI built up a large force, including foreign mercenaries, during the latter part of his reign, but there was a sharp cutback in the size of the army following his death, which was only gradually reversed. This royal army was far larger than that of any great noble, including the duke of Burgundy, and it surpassed that of any neighboring country. It was clearly capable of defeating any individual noble or town in the kingdom, but even assuming it remained loyal to the king, it was not strong enough to subjugate the population as a whole or the nobility collectively. Towns were walled and possessed militias and often cannon. Nobles kept their castles well supplied with arms. When they served with or against the king, they furnished their own mounts, armor, and weapons. Even with the rapid transportation and communication of today and the immense superiority of the arms and training of the modern soldier over the civilian population, a force of from 14,000 to 25,000 men could not subject a population of 15,000,000. Indeed, the United States was unable to pacify South Vietnam, a country only a third of the size of the France of 1500, with a modern army twenty times as large.[74]

THE PATRON-CLIENT RELATIONSHIP

By the close of the Hundred Years War, the military value of the lord-vassal relationship had largely dissipated, but the tie between lord and vassal was so involved with property rights that it survived until the Revolution. Kings almost never undertook to receive homage personally and delegated the duty to subordinates. Even Henry, duke of Montmorency and Damville and admiral of France, rated no more than the chancellor when he rendered homage for a host of fiefs in 1614. Loyalty continued to be prized, and it was largely in the hope of ensuring that valuable commodity that Louis XI, the most unknightly of kings, created the order of Saint Michael in 1469 and always insisted on elaborate oaths. He placed little stock in the homage ritual, however, and permitted the duke of Brittany to take the oath acknowledging his lordship standing, and with his sword at his side.[75] When Louis restored Jean, count of Armagnac, to his ancestral acres, he made him sign a document in which he stated: "I swear and promise by the faith and oath of my body, on my honor, by the Baptism through which I have been brought from the depths, on the peril and damnation of my soul, on the holy Gospel of God, and on the holy relics of the chapel of the Palace at Paris . . . that I will serve and obey my lord the king always and forever, and against everyone, living and dead."[76] During Louis's reign, great nobles continued to make written alliances with each other that were sealed with oaths almost as elaborate as the one Louis required of Armagnac, and they were careful to extract pledges of loyalty from their officials. Louis's brother, Charles, for example, required the three estates of Quercy to promise "to serve him against all comers, the person of the king excepted."[77]

As the fifteenth century drew to a close, the magnates ceased to rebel. Written alliances between them became unnecessary and such documents passed from the scene until the Wars of Religion. Magnates still sought faithful followers, however, and sometimes extracted oaths to provide further assurance, but a new order based on peaceful service and rewards gradually became the principal vertical tie between the greater and lesser nobility. The famous treason trial of Marshal Gié, which took place between 1504 and 1506, provides convenient evidence of how the old and new conceptions of the bonds among the aristocracy were intermixed in these transitional years.

Gié was the younger son of a junior branch of the powerful Rohan family of Brittany. His father had died when he was quite young, and he had been raised by his maternal grandfather at the French court. His exceptional ability had led to his rapid advancement, and favors were heaped upon him by Louis XI, Charles VIII, and finally Louis XII. Then, at the height of his influence, he was accused of treason. At that time the queen, Anne of Brittany, had persuaded Louis XII to promise to marry their eldest daughter, Claude, to the future emperor, Charles V, a union that would have delivered Brittany and the extensive Orléans lands into the hands of the Habsburgs and left an imperiled France to Francis, count of Angoulême, upon Louis's death. Gié strongly opposed this arrangement and advocated that Francis and Claude be married, thereby assuring the Breton and Orléans inheritance for the crown of France. In 1504, Louis became gravely ill. He recovered, but soon thereafter Gié's enemies accused him of having plotted to seize Anne and Claude and to marry the latter to Francis in the event of the king's death. In three respects, the voluminous records of the long trial that ensued are very revealing of the vertical ties among the aristocracy. First, the judges went to considerable length to explore the possible feudal ties between Gié and the dukes of Brittany, presumably to discredit him as a false vassal, as though a noble was not free to prefer to serve the king rather than a feudal lord. There is no doubt where Anne stood on this question. She disliked having her Breton nobles entering royal service and probably encouraged this line of questioning. Second, the judges were much troubled by a special oath Gié was reported to have administered to the guards designated to protect Francis in the château of Amboise, where he resided. The king had charged Gié with the responsibility of guarding the young count, but the judges had been informed that Gié had required the soldiers to swear on the Holy Sacrament in the château's chapel to serve him, or in his absence his lieutenant, "toward all and against everyone." Apparently the judges accepted the fact that a great noble might require a loyalty oath of his servants, but Gié's reported failure to name the king as an exception caused concern. Third, the judges explored a charge that Gié had placed his followers in Francis's entourage and had given them key positions in the reorganization of the royal infantry. Gié was hardly the inventor of this practice, and it was to be developed into an art as the sixteenth century progressed.[78] After a long trial, Gié was found innocent of the more serious charges, but he was stripped of his offices.

The Gié trial was one of the rare instances in which the crown showed much concern about a great noble's relation with his clients. Occasionally it was thought necessary to curb acts of violence. The swarm of clients who accompanied the court to the meetings of the Estates General of

Tours in 1468 and 1484 led the government to take special precautions, and the town officials were directed to arrest all unruly persons, including the people of the king and the princes. In 1547, Henry II began his reign by trying to assure that murderers and assassins were punished, whether they were gentlemen or commoners. Francis II began his by forbidding anyone to carry pistols or arquebuses, and Charles IX responded favorably to a complaint of the third estate at Orléans that gentlemen protected their followers who had committed crimes, but for some reason the Ordonnance of Orléans, which followed, contained nothing specific on this score. The truth was that the crown quickly found means to make use of the patron-client relationship and only tried to curb its worst excesses prior to the Wars of Religion.[79]

It must be remembered that the royal bureaucracy and army were quite small, communication was slow, and many of the provinces had long traditions of independence. To hold the country together, kings had long found it expedient to work through the high aristocracy, who in turn worked through their clients and indirectly through their clients' clients. In the Middle Ages, kings had functioned through a system of vassalage, which had eventually been supplemented in part by indentures and other nonfeudal arrangements. Now, when nearly all of the great fiefs had escheated to the crown, the governors who replaced the dukes became the principal agents on whom the crown leaned. These governors rarely resided in their governments. They were usually at court or in Italy serving in the army, but they kept watchful eyes on their governments, which were important sources of their wealth and power. They placed their clients in the military units they commanded and used their influence to find positions for them in the church and the judicial, administrative, and financial branches of the royal bureaucracy. There were also positions in their own entourages both for gentlemen who became their *fidèles* and for lawyers, administrators, and members of their elaborate households. Their influence through their clients extended into the royal bureaucracy at Paris and down to the smallest levels of their governments. Kings, who could win the loyalty of their greatest nobles by distributing patronage and other favors judiciously, found that through these nobles they could penetrate into the provinces and still lower reaches of the government.[80]

There was a reverse flow as well. Towns, provincial estates, and individuals turned to the governors and other high officials when they wanted to obtain some royal favor. Governors frequently intervened to get taxes lowered, for which they were handsomely rewarded by the estates and towns, and the individuals they assisted often became their clients. It was not unknown for an aspiring provincial to seek the favor of rival court factions, such as the Guise and the Montmorency. Like the feudal system it supplanted, the system was of necessity flexible, for a client might be caught between two quarrelsome patrons, just as a vassal sometimes had to choose between two lords from whom he held fiefs. Yet the system worked if there was a reasonably capable king at the head of the clientage pyramid, and there were no deep internal divisions to rend the body politic. Such were the happy circumstances between the beginning of the last decade of the fifteenth century and the close of the sixth decade of the century that followed.

It is probable that only a small segment of the nobility participated in any clientage system. With peace there was less need for a strong local protector than there had been during the wars and rebellions of the earlier period. Only the more ambitious country gentlemen aspired to positions in the army, the church, or the bureaucracy. The typical noble was content to remain at home and mind his estates. In an emergency he might turn to a local magnate and hope that his long negligence would be overlooked. The sire de Gouberville seems to have been remarkably free of the Norman power structure, an independence he doubtless regretted when he set off for the court in 1555 in search of an important position in the *eaux et forêts*. On his way he obtained letters of introduction from his brother-in-law, a lieutenant general in Bayeux, hardly a man to have influence at court. At Blois he was willing to bribe, pay for services, and give a substantial sum for the office itself. He saw the king and powerful courtiers at a distance, but never spoke with anyone of importance who was interested in his cause. With no patron at court or even a feudal lord who could be approached—he held his fiefs directly from the crown—he was shunted from one place to another. Finally, after an absence of forty-three days and an expenditure of over a hundred livres, he returned home empty-handed.[81]

THE CAREERS OF THE NOBILITY

Gouberville held a minor office before his journey to Blois, but his principal interest had always been his estates. In this he was typical of the French nobility, whose commonest occupation was landowning. A few had many fiefs, totaling thousands of acres, which were managed by a host of officials, whom they supervised. Others, like Gouberville, had to be content with a fief or two, or perhaps much less, which they very likely exploited themselves. In the journal he kept daily, we find him supervising the harvest, recording income and expenses, and performing the other chores of a landed proprietor. As the village leader, he also served his poorer neighbors as doctor, lawyer, judge, and arbitrator of disputes. Peasants looked to him for every sort of assistance.[82]

The real question nobles faced was whether they should seek an additional career, even though it might take them away from their estates for a good part of the year. It has been presumed that the natural career choice for a young noble was the army. Since the thirteenth century, it had been customary to divide society into those who prayed, those who fought, and those who worked. Those who fought became equated with the nobility, and this served as a justification for their preferred tax status after royal levies became annual affairs, for did they not serve with their blood? Even in time of war, however, only a small percentage of the nobles were in the army. When Charles VIII invaded Italy in 1494, a little over half his troops were Swiss and Italian mercenaries. The French component consisted of between 6,000 and 7,200 horse and from 4,000 to 4,800 foot soldiers. Of these, from 1,700 to 2,100 were nobles. If we add 900 more to account for the royal guard, troops remaining in France, and those in the navy and other branches of the service, we arrive at a total of 2,600 to 3,000 nobles in military service at this critical time. As there were from 30,000 to 40,000 noble families in France, it becomes apparent that there was only one noble soldier for every 10 to 15 noble families, and this ratio did not alter significantly in the two generations that followed.[83]

Local studies confirm these figures. In the élection of Bayeux, only 8 percent of the noble, fief-owning heads of family were in military service when the ban and arrière-ban was convoked in 1552 and 1562. In the region around Chartres, the Beauce, only 32 of 719 nobles—that is, less than 5 percent—opted for careers in the military and the royal household. The popularity of military careers varied widely from one district to another, but for France as a whole only between 10 and 15 percent appear to have followed military careers even during the Wars of Religion. Wealthy nobles were more likely to have military careers than poor ones. New nobles were more apt to serve than old ones, and in the Beauce, at least, oldest sons more often had military careers than younger sons. Of course, there were many nobles who cannot be said to have followed military careers, but who served briefly in the ban and arrière ban or participated in a campaign or two. Still, it is probable that well over half of the nobility never engaged in any sort of military activity in their entire lives. One reason for the failure to choose a military career was the expense involved. Gaspard de Saulx, seigneur de Tavannes, marshal of France, recommended that gentlemen who lacked great wealth rear only one son for the army, and Nicolas de Brichanteau de Beauvais-Nangis complained that he lacked the money and the friends at court to achieve his ambitions. Nevertheless, there were opportunities for poorer nobles to enter the service as men-at-arms or archers. One cannot escape the conclusion that notwithstanding the vast literature to the contrary, most nobles had no great desire to pursue military careers.[84]

A second career option of the nobility was the church. Prior to the Concordat of Bologna in 1516, archbishops and bishops were theoretically elected by the cathedral chapter, but in actual practice great nobles, popes, and especially kings were able to exert a profound influence. Under Louis XII, the last king before the Concordat, 93 of the newly appointed prelates were sons of nobles, 6 were sons of commoners, 18 were foreigners, and 18 were Frenchmen of unknown origins. Royal nomination replaced election in accordance with the terms of the Concordat, but under Francis I the proportion of noble to non-noble new prelates remained almost identical. Francis did display a greater preference for princes of the blood and the old nobility as opposed to nobles of more recent origin, and he appointed more foreigners to further his foreign policy, but on the whole the Concordat made less difference than one might have thought.[85] Of the 243 prelates appointed between 1516 and 1559, 133 were from very old noble families, 7 were from families ennobled over a century before, 35 were from families ennobled more recently, and 6 were commoners. Of the remainder, 48 were foreigners and 14 were of undetermined social origins.[86] Clearly, nobles wanted high ecclesiastical offices, and kings were anxious to satisfy their craving. The number of prelacies in the kingdom, however, varied from 113 to 116, hardly enough to satisfy 30,000 or 40,000 noble families. Of course, there were other positions in the church open to the nobility, including some lucrative abbeys, but the more attractive opportunities were gobbled up by the great nobles. Between 1500 and 1560, only 24 of 719 noblemen in the Beauce entered the church, and women were even less attracted by this option. Of 480 noblewomen, only 7 gave their lives to the church.[87]

A third option open to the nobility was to obtain a judicial or administrative position under the crown. The nobility had long performed judicial and administrative duties in their fiefs, and they were naturally appointed to the more important positions in the royal government when the kings began to create a bureaucracy in the late thirteenth and early fourteenth centuries. Of the 422 members of the parlement of Paris between 1345 and 1454 whose social origins are known, 58.1 percent were nobles and 10.9 percent were *anoblis*.[88] The nobility especially sought to become chatelains, captains, bailiffs, and seneschals, but a significant number won judicial and financial positions. According to one calculation, nearly two-thirds of all government officials between 1450 and 1515 were nobles (see table 3.3).

Table 3.3. Noble and Non-Noble Officeholders in the Bailiwicks and Seneschalsies

Office	1340–1450					1450–1515				
	Nobles	%	Non-Nobles	%	Total	Nobles	%	Non-Nobles	%	Total
Viscount	183	100	0	0	183	112	100	0	0	112
Chatelain	2,108	78	601	22	2,709	934	82	212	18	1,146
Governor	197	88	27	12	224	250	92	22	8	272
Captain	2,414	87	365	13	2,779	1,592	98	27	2	1,619
Provost	59	14	352	86	411	297	81	70	19	367
Bailiff	557	73	206	27	763	437	84	81	16	518
Seneschal	279	70	118	30	397	379	87	59	13	43
Lieutenant general	177	53	157	47	334	220	84	43	16	263
Viguier	214	27	565	73	779	122	32	260	68	382
Gens de justice	179	8	2,133	92	2,312	615	27	1,633	73	2,248
Gens de finance	67	7	915	93	982	282	30	650	70	932
Total	6,434	54	5,439	46	11,873	5,240	63	3,057	37	8,297

SOURCE: Etienne Dravasa, *"Vivre noblement": Recherches sur la dérogeance de noblesse du XIVe au XVIe siècles* (Bordeaux, 1965), 133.

It should be noted, however, that many of these officials employed assistants, who were not then considered royal officials, but later became so when the crown found that such posts could be sold to its profit. New positions also were created, and by 1560 the proportion of the bureaucracy that was of noble birth was much smaller than it had been at the beginning of the century. Under any circumstances, however, the bureaucracy was too small to provide employment for many nobles. Only 23 of 719 nobles in the Beauce served their king in judicial or administrative capacities between 1500 and 1560. Indeed, a bare 11 percent of the Beauce nobility found employment in the military, the royal household, the bureaucracy, and the church. In other regions of France, the nobility may have been more energetic in seeking careers, and there were limited opportunities for other forms of employment, such as service in a great noble's household, wholesale trade, law, and medicine, but it is probable that not more than one noble in five had a regular occupation other than that of landowner.[89]

THE EDUCATION OF THE NOBILITY

The careers nobles could aspire to depended on their education. In the late Middle Ages their education was for the most part adequate for the available posts. There were few positions that required more than modest learning, and there were enough nobles who met the existing standards to satisfy the limited demand. Over 5 percent of the students who attended the universities of Avignon, Cahors, Montpellier, and Toulouse between 1378 and 1403 were nobles. None were children of the high nobility, but thirty or forty came from baronial families such as the Lévis, Noailles, and Rochechouart. The great majority, however, were drawn from the lesser nobility. Law was the favorite subject; 195 chose to specialize in canon law and 114 in civil law; only 2 chose theology, and none opted for medicine. Clearly the church and the high administration were the goals of these students. Four became cardinals and at least twenty-four bishops. A few of the less ambitious turned to academe. Had our sample been from northern universities, one would expect a higher percentage to have sought careers as laymen, for it was easier for a northerner to penetrate the bureaucracy, while southerners had better access to ecclesiastical preferment when the papal court was in Avignon. Every one of the thirty-eight members of the parlement of Paris in 1345 whose background is known was a noble, and all but seven were from old noble families. Doubtless the remaining fifty-eight members included commoners, but during the Middle Ages, when the judges filled vacancies by election, and there were no strict educational requirements, the nobility played a prominent role.[90]

Thus in the late Middle Ages, nobles as a whole were considered qualified for their chosen careers. A son born into a lesser noble family was apt to receive his early education at home or in one of the *petites écoles* that were beginning to appear in large numbers. Although of a family of modest importance, Guillaume de Murol was sent far away to school in the 1360s, and the account books he kept attest to his education and his interest in his estates. He was, however, more fortunate than most, because he had a cardinal for an uncle. Once a basic education was achieved, noble youths were often placed in the household of a great noble or even the king, where they learned to joust, hunt, and engage in other manly arts. If designated for a military career, they were assigned to experienced captains and learned in much the same manner as apprentices in lesser trades. Great noble families employed tutors for the academic side of children's education and relied on the experienced members of their households to teach riding, fencing, and the like. They had officials to keep their accounts, but where evidence has survived, it seems clear that they were able and willing to keep a watchful eye on the progress of their estates.[91]

Humanists were soon to heap scorn on the education of the French nobility, but their criteria consisted primarily of a knowledge of the classics. It is true that what most nobles knew of antiquity was derived from translations, but some of them had broader cultural interests than their critics. Charles V assembled a great library, and many of his Valois cousins were collectors of works of art. They were quite capable of writing about things that interested them, of tournaments, of hunting, and of falconry. Some nobles were talented authors, and Charles d'Orléans was among the greatest writers of his age.

In the late fifteenth and early sixteenth centuries, the situation began to change in regard to judicial offices. The number of university-trained lawyers multiplied, but the number of available appointments to office shrank in spite of a modest increase in the size of the bureaucracy. Many appointments had previously been for a limited period of time, but now they became for life, and fathers often resigned their positions in favor of their sons or other relatives. The smaller turnover in offices was accompanied by a requirement in the ordonnance of March 1499 that appointees to the coveted post of lieutenant general of a bailiwick have a doctor's or a *licence en droit* degree. Both developments threatened the position of the old nobility. It was not that nobles ceased to hold offices; rather, it was that most officials who were nobles had recently achieved that status. Of the twenty-seven nobles who held important offices in the bailiwick of Senlis between 1500 and 1550, only nine at the most were of the old nobility.

The failure of most nobles to keep pace with the growing educational requirements for judicial office should not be interpreted to mean that nobles took no interest in the education of their children. About one fourth of the students from the bailiwick of Senlis studying in the Faculty of Arts at Paris were nobles, a percentage that was not surpassed by the merchants. Indeed, about 10 percent of the Faculty of Arts' student body were nobles, but after receiving the arts degree it was necessary to study for six additional years to obtain a licence en droit. Providing this education was beyond the means of the poorer nobility even in the early sixteenth century, and educational costs skyrocketed as the century progressed. As a result, nobles who desired judicial office often could not afford the required education, and nobles with the necessary means aspired to more prestigious careers in the army or at court.[92]

The advent of printing and the impact of the Renaissance led to a pedagogical revolution. New educational institutions appeared at every level, and nobles availed themselves of the opportunity to give their children better educations than they themselves had received. As a result, nobles usually obtained all the education they needed to pursue the nonjudicial careers to which they aspired. Literacy was almost universal, and arithmetic manuals included problems concerning the pay of soldiers and the like that were designed to interest noble youths in this practical subject. Wealthy nobles were sufficiently educated to supervise those they employed to manage their estates, and most lords of only a seigneurie or two apparently knew enough to keep account of their own affairs. The education nobles received varied greatly from one to another. Philippe Duplessis-Mornay knew a half-dozen ancient and modern languages counting his own and spoke with authority on history, law, political theory, and theology, while François de La Trémoille could prepare his own legal briefs. On the other hand, Constable Anne de Montmorency was reputed to be barely literate. However, in spite of his faulty education from the bookish point of view, Montmorency was a patron of the arts, and he had enough practical knowledge to advance himself and his family more than the other two, although it cannot be said that France profited from his successes as much as he did.

Nobles continued to receive part of their education at home and at court or in some great noble's household, but more than before they also obtained their formal education in colleges and broadened themselves in foreign travel. In spite of the criticism often leveled at French nobles that they preferred arms to letters, they continued to produce such great literary figures as Philippe de Commynes, Marguerite d'Angoulême, and Joachim du Bellay. Many combined pen and sword. Between 1494 and 1550, French nobles produced more military treatises than the Italians and nearly twice as many as the Spanish, Portuguese, English, Dutch, and Germans combined. Well might a recent student argue that nobles adapted themselves to the new circumstances and developed an educational system that enabled them to maintain their military and political predominance. Of the desirable positions, only law-related offices escaped them in large numbers.[93]

THE ROBE AND THE SWORD

Many historians have found in a conflict between the nobility of the sword and the nobility of the robe one of the central themes of early modern French history. That there was a dispute by the latter half of the sixteenth century cannot be denied. The problem is to explain how and why it developed. As has been indicated, only a small percentage of the traditional nobility pursued careers in arms, and they certainly had no monopoly on the martial arts. Furthermore, in its formative period, the nobility had made up a large proportion of the bureaucracy. Indeed, a significant number of royal officials were still descended from the old nobility in the male or female line when the Wars of Religion began.

The concept of a robe nobility probably first emerged in the parlement of Paris. Sixty-nine percent of its members between 1345 and 1454 whose backgrounds can be identified were nobles or anoblis. Most of them served for many years and some were followed by their sons. As time passed, their ties to their feudal lords and patrons dimmed, and the idea that they were servants of the king took hold. Social origins became blurred: members who were commoners were ennobled, sons replaced fathers, and intermarriages took place. At first noble members were called *chevaliers,* but as a sense of unity developed, all councillors regardless of their origins were referred to as *maîtres.* Some sons of members opted for military careers, and twenty-four relatives of *parlementaires* fell at Agincourt in 1415. Under these circumstances, it is not surprising that the members of parlement developed an esprit de corps and came to be considered nobles as a group. They won the privileges of the *noblesse de race,* including the all-important fiscal ones. To Françoise Autrand, this process had taken place by 1454. Actually, it was much slower, but a start was made toward the creation of a self-conscious robe.[94]

In 1479, Louis XI took the important step of excusing the members of the parlement and chamber of accounts of Paris from serving in the ban and arrière-ban as required of the traditional nobility who owned fiefs. In doing so, he separated the bureaucratic nobility from the rest of their order. Louis's goal was to placate these high officials, not to create a separate nobility, but intentional or not, this and later acts freeing noble officials from military service furthered the establishment of a new nobility by the close of the fifteenth century.[95] These nobles were often descended from the noblesse de race, but they served the king as officials rather than as soldiers in the rare instances when the ban and arrière-ban were summoned. Those who were born commoners were considered nobles while they held office, but if they resigned, they lost their status.

Only gradually during the sixteenth century did the custom develop of giving permanent ennoblement to those who held office for twenty or more years, and legislation recognizing that the descendants of those so ennobled were nobles was not enacted until 1600.

A liberal proportion of the membership of the provincial sovereign courts were also nobles during the Middle Ages, and this facilitated the development of a robe nobility centered on these institutions. Officers of the royal household were accepted as nobles at an early date, as were those of the chancellery from 1485. As time passed, the four secretaries of state, the secretaries of the king and other high officials were ennobled upon appointment to office, and were granted exemptions from the ban and arrière ban. Offices at the bailiwick and seneschalsy level did not ennoble, although some who held these posts were nobles in their own right and were considered part of the robe when the concept of such a category of nobles developed.[96]

The deliberations and the cahier of the Estates General of 1484 provide no evidence that those who attended thought in terms of a robe and a sword nobility. The deputies of the three estates asked in the name of national security that French rather than foreign nobles be given command of frontier fortresses and the great offices of the crown, and they had no trouble in agreeing that useless offices be abolished and the sale of offices forbidden.[97] The three estates of Languedoc had so little animosity toward the robe in 1506 that they asked that the number of councillors in the parlement of Toulouse be increased, but Claude de Seyssel's reference to the *robe longue que de robe courte* in 1515 indicates the existence of a robe nobility in some people's minds.[98] He still thought in terms of cooperation rather than rivalry, but perhaps some friction is suggested by a petition prepared two years later by Breton nobles asking that merchants and wealthy farmers be forbidden to purchase fiefs and judicial offices.

This relatively peaceful relationship began to be altered when Francis I's fiscal requirements led him to turn to the sale of offices as a regular source of income. In 1522 he systemized the practice. Soon nearly all offices were sold through the parties casuelles, and offices came close to becoming hereditary property rights. To raise more money, Francis created more offices, and his successors were not loathe to follow his example. There has not been sufficient research to determine exactly what the impact of this expansion was and when and where it took place. The percentage of the councillors belonging to the traditional nobility who entered the parlement of Paris had begun to decline before the parties casuelles was created, and between 1483 and 1515 they numbered just over 10 percent. Although nobles who held no offices managed to obtain from 13 to 22 percent of the new positions in the parlement of Rouen between 1539 and 1638, it seems clear that the great majority of the posts created after 1522 went to commoners.[99] The result was a steady growth in assertiveness on the part of the robe and a growing irritation on the part of the traditional nobility at seeing positions they felt to be rightfully theirs being taken by upstarts swollen with pride.

The assembly that met in Paris in January 1558 reflected the rise of the robe to a self-conscious status. To the traditional prelates, nobles, and deputies of the towns, six presidents of the parlement of Paris and one president from each of the other seven parlements were added. After the orators of the clergy and the nobility spoke, and before the deputy of the towns was given the floor, the first president of the parlement of Paris was called upon to speak "for the order of justice." The crown again seemingly recognized the officers as a fourth estate when it ordered that a tax be levied on Burgundy to pay the expenses of the president of the parlement of Dijon to the "general convocation of the four estates."[100]

But France was too tradition-bound to accept the idea of a fourth estate composed of the officers of justice and perhaps other high officials. When a full meeting of the Estates General was held in 1560, the deputies were divided into three estates, and the royal officials who were elected as deputies became a minority in the third estate, where their influence was limited. The nobility elected Jacques de Silly, count of Rochefort, to present their views before the king in the closing ceremony. In a brief but scholarly address, Rochefort pointed out that Aristotle had identified four types of nobility: of birth, of civil office, of war, and of intellectual accomplishments. Of these, only the first were true nobles, and the remainder were sources of disorders and misery. In coming out squarely for a nobility based on birth and in opposition to ennoblement by any type of office or intellectual accomplishment, Rochefort brought into the open the noblesse de race's growing irritation at the pretensions of the robe. His harangue caused a sensation. André Devyver has asserted that "it marked in actual fact a turning point in social history."[101] To justify an aristocracy of birth, some nobles and their scholarly sympathizers soon concocted the myth that the nobility were descendants of Frankish conquerors of France. Members of the robe countered by claiming that they were as good or better than the nobles of the sword.

The nobility was too divided over political and religious issues in 1560 to agree on a single cahier. In the end, most of the deputies adhered to one of three cahiers that were prepared. These cahiers were similar when it came to the bureaucracy. There was a universal demand that the sale of offices cease and that the number of positions be reduced. Often the nobles urged that judicial officials be elected. They asked that all positions in the army and royal household be reserved for them, as well as some positions in the parlements and other sovereign courts. They wanted royal officials to cease interfering in the affairs of the great fiefs. Perhaps nowhere did they reveal their consciousness of their separation from the nobles of the robe more than in their frequent practice of referring to themselves as "gentlemen" rather than simply as nobles, as they had usually done in 1484. Expressions such as *gentilshommes de robbe courte portant épée* leave no doubt that they wanted to distance themselves from the nobles of the long robe. When the estates met again the following year at Pontoise, the nobility prepared a single cahier, which repeated the above demands and added a new one of their own— that judicial officers serve for three-year terms rather than for life. In all these goals, except in their desire for preferential treatment, the nobles were joined by the other estates. The robe had few friends.[102]

Meanwhile, the pretensions of the parlementaires had been growing by leaps and bounds. During the meeting of the estates at Pontoise in 1561, a new quarrel arose between the nobility, aided by the third estate, and the parlement of Paris. The crown had prepared an ordonnance based on the cahiers of the Estates General of Orléans, which had met the preceding year, and had sent it to parlement to be registered. The judges, who disliked some of the provisions of the ordonnance, procrastinated, with the obvious intent of making changes once the estates had closed. The deputies refused to consider the crown's financial needs until the ordonnance had been registered unchanged. The financially pinched crown did all it could to make the parlement comply, but the judges insisted on considering each article with care. In the end, the crown forced the parlement to register the ordonnance, and the secular estates offered the king the goods of the clergy, but not their own. To avoid having their own cahiers pass through the hands of parlement, the deputies at Pontoise asked that they be sent with the royal replies to the various governments to be displayed. The secular estates thus proclaimed that ordonnances based on their cahiers were not subject to parlement's scrutiny, and the judges insisted that they had the obligation and right to review all legislation. The lines of conflict between robe and sword were thus drawn by the time the Wars of Religion began.[103]

IV

The Wars of Religion

In July 1559, Henry II was accidentally killed in a tournament held in honor of his daughter's marriage to Philip II of Spain. His successor, the fifteen-year-old Francis II, was a weak, unhealthy lad heavily influenced by his beautiful wife, the ill-fated Mary, Queen of Scots, who in turn was guided by her Guise uncles. When Francis died in December 1560, the throne passed to Charles IX, a minor. His mother, Catherine de Medici, became regent and continued to be the principal directing force in the government after the weak-willed Charles came of age. Charles in turn died in May 1574, while still in his twenties, and was succeeded by his brother, Henry III. Henry was more intelligent than his immediate predecessors and some of his policies foreshadowed those of his more successful successors, but his unstable character and lack of leadership qualities prevented him from attracting the necessary support to the monarchy. After a trouble-filled reign of fifteen years, he was assassinated in July 1589, and the Valois dynasty came to an end.[1]

With such monarchs as heads of state, it is scarcely surprising that France soon found itself in chaos. Calvin had begun to send missionaries to France in 1555, and by 1559 they had won so many converts that they secretly held a national synod in Paris. The following year Admiral Coligny publicly proclaimed that there were 2,150 Protestant churches and communities in the country. To many it appeared likely that within a year or two France would become predominantly Calvinist. What made the Calvinists so dangerous was not only their splendid organization at the local, provincial, and national levels and their dedicated missionary spirit but also their close ties to the nobility. From the late 1550s on, increasingly large numbers of nobles joined the new faith. Threatened as the early Protestant churches were, they put themselves under the protection of sympathetic local magnates. Soon Louis, prince of Condé, became the leader and protector of the movement at the national level. Although a man of relatively limited means when one considers his exalted birth, he was able to attract a large number of adherents. Thus part of the warrior class of the nation became allied with a dynamic religious movement.

In the meantime, a Catholic revival was taking place, characterized in part by an escatological anguish that, as Denis Crouzet has suggested, "was intensified by signs from heaven, astrological forecasts, and predictions by panic-stricken mendicants."[2] Some Catholic nobles who had fought in the Italian wars imbibed its spirit and were more than ready to embark on a crusade against the heretics.

Some of the nobles who joined Condé were sincere converts to the new faith, but many, like the young prince himself, were motivated more by ambition, greed, the desire for fame, and the love of adventure than by religious zeal. A somewhat similar mixture of zealots and self-seekers rallied behind the duke of Guise and other Catholic leaders. Unhappily, the crown was unable to satisfy the demands of these restless spirits. Henry II and Philip II had terminated the Italian wars in 1559 as much because of their mutual bankruptcies as from a desire to exterminate heresy in their domains. As a result, there were numerous unemployed soldiers and a limited amount of patronage to dispense. The series of internal conflicts that wrecked France between 1562 and 1598 became nearly as much a struggle to control royal patronage as a quarrel between two religions.

KINGS, PATRONS, AND CLIENTS

During these years of intermittent warfare, the kings sought to patch the disintegrating body politic.[3] Since their army and bureaucracy were inadequate, and the vertical ties of vassalage had long ago ceased to be of political or military significance, they sought cooperation by reinvigorating the system of clientage. Unhappily, with the restoration of peace in 1559 and the near bankruptcy of the crown, there were fewer material rewards to distribute. During the brief reign of Frances II, the Guise were dominant and distributed what largess there was to their followers. The number of their would-be clients swelled, and the excluded Bourbon and Montmorency factions were disgruntled. Indeed, the Guise monopoly of patronage was one of the causes of the Conspiracy of Amboise, which was designed to remove them from power. Upon the accession of Charles IX, Catherine de Medici assumed the regency, and with it the control of crown patronage. Her goal was to keep the leaders of the factions under her watchful eye and to divide the limited patronage more evenly. The Guise, disgruntled at their loss of a monopoly of power, left the court, and there was not sufficient money to pay long overdue pensions. Even the wages of the troops fell into arrears.

The crown tried to compensate for the lack of material rewards by giving honorary ones. When the Order of St. Michael was created in 1469, the number of knights was limited to thirty-six. By 1559, this figure had been increased to seventy. Only then did the inflation of honors begin in earnest. "This morning," Catherine de Medici wrote in 1563, "we created only thirty-two knights of the Order, because there was nothing else to give them."[4] Soon there were to be thousands. Titles also cost nothing to give. Between 1550 and 1599, forty-three new peerages and numerous lesser titles were created. Ennoblements were disadvantageous in the long run because of the tax exemptions involved, but the crown took the short-run view, and many commoners entered the second estate. The chamber of accounts at Paris alone registered 310 ennoblements between 1550 and 1600.[5]

When Henry III came to the throne in 1574, he carried the inflation of honors to new heights. At one point he was prepared to sell one thousand letters of ennoblement, and higher titles were dispersed with abandon. His most important innovation was to try to create a loyal force to counter the Guise and Bourbon factions. To do so, he heaped wealth, titles, and offices on a handful of young nobles of middling or lesser rank who possessed undoubted courage. Of these the most famous were Anne de Joyeuse and Jean Louis de Nogaret de La Valette. Henry made both of them provincial governors, army commanders, and dukes, the latter with the title of Epernon. Since their wealth and power was derived almost entirely from the limited resources of the crown, they were not able to muster sufficient strength to counter either the Guise or the Bourbons effectively, and the favors showered upon them angered the older nobility. Hence their elevation did more harm to the royal cause than good. To protect his person, Henry appointed forty-five guardsmen of unquestioned loyalty. It was to them that he turned when he had the duke of Guise assassinated in 1588. Since membership in the Order of St. Michael had become so commonplace that it was no longer considered much of an honor, Henry created the Saint-Esprit, a new and more select chivalric order in December 1578, and made loyalty to himself and the Catholic church the principal criteria for membership. Only twenty-six knights were initiated into the order at the first installation, and the numbers were held in check thereafter. In an elaborate rite, each new knight was required to swear that: "I will guard, defend and support with all my power the honor, quarrels and rights of your royal majesty toward all and against all. In time of war I will proceed to your suite equipped with horses and arms as required by the statutes of this order: and in time of peace . . . when it pleases you to summon me to serve you against anyone . . . without exception until death."[6] The record of the Guise was not such that they were admitted at first, but after a period of loyalty, they were initiated at a later date. How well they kept this elaborate oath is well known.

Henry's inability to hold the loyalty of his over-mighty subjects and the bitter religious strife left governors, towns, and local royal officials largely to their own devices. The governors, on whom the maintenance of order largely depended, had been directed to reside in their governments in 1560. They still had their clients, through whom they had effectively governed from the court or the army in Italy prior to the religious troubles, but there were fewer rewards they could obtain for them from the crown, and even the number of positions in the companies of ordonnance were reduced, because foreign mercenaries could be hired for half, or even less than half, the price. To meet the challenge, governors sought the cooperation of the sovereign courts, municipal officials, and above all one of the two competing religions. Protestants at an early date had placed themselves under the protection of this or that local magnate who was sympathetic to their cause. Soon these magnates were drawing on Protestants for troops and money. They worked through the highly developed Protestant organization of political assemblies at the local, provincial, and even the national level. In Languedoc, Protestants in the provincial estates broke away to form their own assembly. Catholic governors sought the adherence of their co-religionists. In the later phases of the wars, they often formed councils composed of ecclesiastical, royal, and municipal officials, town governors, and nobles to assist in governing. A few governors sought the cooperation of moderate Catholics (*politiques*) and Protestants. Their efforts prevented total anarchy, but in many parts of France, plundering troops wreaked havoc even in periods of nominal peace.

Governors and other great nobles continued to seek their clients from among their kinsmen and neighbors as before. A few were already their vassals, but clientage was valued as an additional tie, since many vassals gave no thought to providing their lords with aid and counsel. Governors often provided clients with positions in their households or in other aspects of their service. They also used their influence to find positions for them in the royal judiciary and bureaucracy, the municipalities, the clergy, and, of course, their companies of ordonnance. If they lacked effective ties with a parlement or other important institutions in their jurisdiction, they sought clients from among its officials. Some Catholics entered the service of Catholic lords, and some Protestants sought out Calvinist magnates. Religious parties were thus no barrier to the clientage system, but rather possible sources of recruits. The duke of Guise had clients in the sovereign courts of Paris who followed him into the Catholic League, but the Paris governing body known as the Sixteen became his clients only because of his ultra-Catholic stance. On the other hand, there were a few Catholics who served Protestant lords, and the reverse was equally true. Nevertheless, because of the strength of the political and religious animosities and the willingness of many clients to put their own interests above those of their lords, the clientage system was insufficient to maintain order. The reduced patronage available to the governors made some of them more than willing to shift masters if they felt slighted, and a governor who was relieved of his post lost many of his followers, as the duke of Epernon discovered when he was replaced as governor of Provence in 1595. A governor could rally adequate support only when his government was threatened by an approaching army, and it was clearly in the interest of noble, judge, and burgher to come to his assistance.

The breakdown in the ties of loyalty is clearly reflected by the emphasis on elaborate oaths that great nobles required of their allies and followers. When Condé raised his standards of rebellion at Orléans in 1562, the nobles who responded to his call swore not only to obey him but also "to hold ourselves in readiness as far as we are able in money, arms, horses, and other required things, . . . to accompany him wherever he commands, and to render him faithful service."[7] That same year the Protestants of the estates of Languedoc chose the count of Crussol as their leader, and in an elaborate oath, which was to be repeated by the individual town councils, swore to serve him "to the last drop of their blood." He in his turn vowed to protect their religion and their interests.[8] Catholics followed a similar course. They even turned to the confraternities to bind their co-religionists together, and the members of the various Catholic leagues invariably took long and elaborate oaths. In Auvergne, they swore in God's name to recognize "only one holy Catholic, apostolic, and Roman church, under the obedience of which we wish to live and die." To preserve their church, their king, and their laws, they undertook that they "would always be ready to march with arms and the best possible equipment under the command of the king or under the duke of Anjou his brother."[9]

Kristen Neuschel has noted that many nobles who pledged themselves to follow Condé in 1562 departed from his ranks when it was to their advantage to do so. Indeed, the very extravagant language of these oaths suggest that they were desperate efforts to retain loyalty rather than the perfunctory rituals that characterize oaths of office and allegiance today. In this they had a degree of success, for there were those who remained faithful under the most adverse circumstances. Those less conscientious often hesitated before abandoning their lord. In October 1588, Henry III required the great nobles, members of his council, and deputies to the Estates General to take an oath of allegiance to him. Before the Parisian deputies felt free to turn against him following the assassination of the duke of Guise, they took the precaution of consulting the faculty of theology in Paris.[10]

THE ESTATES

The weakening of clientage ties made it necessary for kings to turn once more to national assemblies in the hope of holding the body politic together. The meetings of 1558, 1560, and 1561 were followed by an Assembly of Notables at Moulins in 1566. Here great nobles and prelates were joined by members of the various parlements and other officials to produce an ordonnance designed to reform justice and correct the abuses that had led to so many complaints. The judicial nature of the meeting probably explains the absence of the deputies of the towns, but burghers were in attendance at the assembly of the estates of Paris in 1575, when the king's finances were the subject of discussion, just as they had been in 1558. The year 1576 saw a full meeting of the Estates General at Blois. In 1583 there was another Assembly of Notables at St. Germain, with tax reform as one of its principal objectives, and 1588 witnessed the famous meeting of the Estates General at Blois. To top off the royally convoked assemblies, the deputies of the towns were invited to join individually summoned nobles, prelates, and officials at Rouen in 1596. These numerous meetings reveal how willing the desperate kings were to seek the support of their subjects, although the Estates Generals proved uncontrollable, and the lengthy reforming ordonnances produced by some of the assemblies were poorly enforced. Perhaps the Rouen meeting of 1596 contributed most toward the pacification of the kingdom, but even it accomplished so little that the crown may not have considered it worth the effort. Then, too, there was the Estates General of Paris that met on the summons of the League in 1593 to elect a Catholic king. From 1561 on, there were also periodic meetings of the Catholic clergy, and the Protestants organized a system of political assemblies.

During this period of religious wars and frequent consultations at the national level, the theory that the monarchy had been created by the people, and that power should be shared with the people, as represented in the assemblies of the estates, won wide acceptance. This theory of a mixed monarchy was especially popular among the middle nobility. It was these nobles who represented their order in the Estates General and played leading roles in most of the provincial estates. They claimed the right to consent to taxation, to influence legislation, and to hold public office. At no point did they doubt that they acted for the public good. A few members of the lower nobility who took an active interest in public affairs concurred, but the position of the great nobility was more ambiguous. Their most common goal was to sit on the right side of the king and guide him in the governance of the realm. In this capacity they expected to share the royal bounty and to sprinkle their clients through-out the army, the church, and the royal administration. The trouble was that only one noble could sit at the king's right hand, and there was a perpetual rivalry among the magnates as to who this person should be. He who was successful was usually content with the status quo; it was the excluded magnates who sought meetings of the Estates General and claimed the right to revolt in the name of the public good. Rare was the great noble who, like Henry, duke of Guise, seems to have had a sincere belief in the mixed monarchy, and who had the ability to win the support of most of the towns and the deputies of the third estate.[11]

The nobility were too divided to prepare a common cahier in the Estates General of 1560, but in their first article, their deputies from Champagne asked the king "to communicate more often with his subjects" by holding the estates in each province every five years and the Estates General every ten years. Some months later, at Pontoise, the nobles were better organized and produced a single, hard-hitting docu-ment in which they asked that the Estates General be held every two years and that the estates of the bailiwicks and seneschalsies meet every October 15 without waiting for royal directives. Should a king accede to the throne before the age of twenty, the first prince of the blood was to summon the Estates General within three months to establish the government. If he failed to do so, each bailiwick and seneschalsy was to elect three deputies without orders from higher authority to assemble at Paris on the fifteenth of the fourth month after the accession to constitute the government. In addition to demanding the right to determine the membership of the royal council, the nobility insisted that the Estates General consent to taxes, interest-bearing loans, declarations of war, and many other things. The better-organized deputies of the third estate at Orléans prepared a single cahier in which they asked that the Estates General meet every five years, a time period they reduced to two years at Pontoise in 1561. The secular estates as a whole, however, were more interested in avoiding taxation in the two meetings than they were in winning a larger role for the Estates General. L'Hopital had offered to permit them to collect any taxes they consented to, but they refused. The clergy were more circumspect in the privileges they claimed, but they granted the crown a large sum to pay its debts, and enjoyed periodic assemblies from that time until the Revolution.[12]

The deputies of the clergy and nobility who assembled at Blois in 1576 sought meetings of the Estates General every five years. The third estate advocated meetings every decade. There was general agreement that there should be consent to taxation and that the role of local royal tax officials should be reduced or abolished, their duties being assumed by the estates, elected syndics, or municipal officials. The provincial estates, in turn, sought to ensure that the petitions of the Estates General would be enacted after the deputies had disbanded.[13] In 1588, the deputies generally repeated the demands of their predecessors concerning consent to taxation and a greater role for provincial and local estates, but for some reason they failed to insist that the Estates General meet periodically. Perhaps they realized that if they made good their demand for consent, the crown would have to convoke the estates as frequently as they desired. The very fact that the deputies had to repeat the same requests in meeting after meeting suggests that even when kings granted their petitions, civil dissension was so great that reforms could not be enforced.[14]

This activity at the national level was paralleled by a multiplication in the number of meetings at the provincial and local levels. The gradual breakdown of royal authority, however, made it as difficult for these estates to be effective as it did for the Estates General and the Assembly of Notables. In their efforts to cope with the situation, the provincial and local estates displayed considerable ingenuity and imagination, but their willingness to innovate brought only limited success. The time and severity of the challenge to these estates varied from one region to another. From the beginning there were strong Protestant minorities in Languedoc and Dauphiné who quickly developed their own system of self-government at the expense of the authority of the estates, as well as of the king. For the most part, however, the estates survived the 1560s and part of the 1570s without excessive strains being placed on their positions. In Burgundy, Brittany, Languedoc, and even in Normandy and Dauphiné, the king convoked special sessions of the estates on one or more occasions when it became necessary to levy additional taxes, or when some other matter was in dispute. In Auvergne and Guyenne, where the échevins of the capital town frequently had the right to convoke the third estate, meetings were especially numerous.[15]

The difficulty arose when an unfriendly army threatened a province, and there was no time to indulge in the slow and cumbersome process of convoking the estates and holding the necessary elections. To meet this situation, smaller meetings were developed that could be assembled with relative rapidity. The three estates of Brittany and those of some other provinces were reluctant to see their authority fragmented, but the need for speed was so great that they had no alternative. During this period the assembly of the communities was created in Provence, and meetings of the twelve principal towns in Agenais began to be substituted occasionally for full assemblies of the third estate. Sometimes permanent committees of the estates, such as the commis des états of Dauphiné, or the officers of the estates, such as chamber of the élus of Burgundy, were called upon to act. At times the initiative to hold a meeting was taken by the king or an officer of the estates, but most often it was the royal governor who wanted some sort of an authorization to levy a tax to defend his government. Legal levies were easier to collect than those imposed by fiat, and this was especially true where the tax-collecting machinery was in the hands of the estates. The three estates often protested when they were bypassed, and the committees and officers grumbled, but they had little choice but to cooperate. An invading army or even an unpaid friendly garrison posed more of a threat to them than the collection of a few thousand livres without the consent of the full estates.

The forced loans the crown sought should not be considered taxes, because they were generally repaid without interest from future levies, but even in the early days of the wars there were instances when taxes were levied without a pretense of obtaining some form of consent. In 1562 and 1571, Charles IX attempted to impose levies on the Breton towns and in 1574 Catherine de Medici taxed Normandy without the consent of their respective estates. These acts were clear infractions of their privileges, unless one is willing to accept the crown's argument that "urgent necessity" took precedence over the rights of subjects. Henry III found it necessary to act arbitrarily more often. In 1584 he bypassed the estates of Languedoc and went directly to the dioceses for a tax, and in 1587 he ordered that 120,000 livres be imposed on the towns and *bourgs* of Brittany in spite of the fact that the estates had refused to authorize the levy. Henry was a desperate man and was soon to risk everything by having the duke of Guise assassinated, but even he generally preferred to raise money by forced loans, the sale of offices and patents of nobility, and taxes imposed in the routine fashion.

Actually the estates' control over taxation was threatened more often by the governors, the Huguenots, and the League than by the crown. A governor was responsible for the defense of his government. When it was threatened, he often failed to wait for the next meeting of the estates or to obtain the king's permission to tax. Rather, he turned to a quickly assembled abbreviated form of the estates or to their officers or permanent committee and demanded the needed funds. If consent was not granted, he sometimes acted unilaterally, but on the whole the need was so obvious that those consulted generally granted at least part of what was asked. In divided Dauphiné, governors sometimes sought a semblance of legality by turning to parlement. From the first the Huguenots appropriated royal taxes in the regions they controlled. Their commanders negotiated for funds with towns held by members of their faith and took what they wanted from the Catholic localities they seized. When the Catholic League completely broke with Henry III after the assassination of the duke of Guise, its leaders behaved in a similar fashion.

It will never be possible to write an accurate history of taxation during this confused period, but it is clear that from the standpoint of the crown, the growing confusion spelt financial disaster. Receipts during the early wars fell below what they had been during the reign of Henry II, while rising prices and military expenses created increasing demands on the treasury, which were met in part by extensive borrowing. The crown sought huge increases in taxes during the later stages of the wars, but growing difficulties in collection prevented the government from achieving the necessary revenue. Our figures are more accurate for the amount the crown sought than for the amount it received. The difficulties the crown faced are best revealed by the valuable surviving records concerning the gifts the Assemblies of the Clergy voted for the years 1568 through 1578. In the dioceses controlled by the Protestants or where war raged, little or nothing was collected. Provinces lately added to the crown were less likely to contribute than the older royal possessions in northern

France. In a peaceful year like 1572, which followed another year of calm, 90 percent of the required amount found its way into the royal treasury, but in troubled 1578 barely half did so. In the latter year, because of disillusionment with the crown, strongly Catholic and peaceful Brittany gave only about half its share, despite the fact that the Assembly of the Clergy had voted the tax and the Catholic hierarchy preferred their king to his Protestant adversaries, notwithstanding his faults. How much worse tax collection must have been when demands were made on rebellious Protestants, lukewarm Catholics, and the taxable population as a whole.[16]

That there was a wide discrepancy between the amount the royal treasury received and the taxes collected is clearly revealed by careful studies made of Dauphiné. There, as elsewhere, local treasurers were authorized to use the money collected to meet local expenses, including such items as salaries, supplies for troops, road and building repairs, and a host of other things. To cite an extreme case, 154,018 écus were levied on Dauphiné in 1581, but only 7,500 écus reached the royal treasury in Paris. In addition to the huge sums siphoned off legally, large amounts found their way into the hands of rebellious armies and powerful persons. Dauphiné had provincial estates whose consent was theoretically necessary before a tax could be collected, but the governor and the parlement of Grenoble sometimes bypassed the estates and ordered that a tax be levied to meet emergencies. As a result, although the sums the crown received were insufficient, the people were heavily taxed and towns and villages were frequently forced to borrow large sums to meet fiscal demands.[17]

THE TOWNS AND THE SOVEREIGN COURTS

The population of France at least doubled during the century before the Wars of Religion, and the numerical growth of the towns almost certainly exceeded that of the countryside. Commerce, industry, and banking shot forward rapidly, and the wealth of the towns grew apace. It was but natural that the crown would seek to direct some of this new wealth into its pockets. The privileges of many of these towns included exemption from the taille. Extraordinary measures were required to tap their resources. Special levies and gifts were demanded, and wealthy burghers were occasionally tapped for forced loans. To win compliance, if not willing cooperation, it was sometimes necessary to interfere in the internal workings of the towns, even to the point of tampering with the election of their magistrates or reducing their number, so that they could be more easily controlled. Yet when all is said and done, at the outbreak of the religious wars, the towns had lost little of their independence vis-à-vis the crown, and they were wealthier and more populous than ever before.

The religious wars saw an end to the general growth of the towns' size and prosperity. An unstable period ensued, in which this or that town enjoyed periods of advance and times of adversity. The cost of protecting their walls increased, as did royal demands for money. To tighten his control over the more important towns, Charles IX even directed in 1564 that they choose two persons for each municipal office, from whom he would select the one to serve.[18] This directive appears to have remained a dead letter, but the quest for the towns' financial resources persisted. By the time the wars ceased, the typical town was less prosperous and more indebted than it had been forty years before. During the conflict many towns were able to compensate for these losses by regaining what little independence they had lost since the Middle Ages. They might be as flooded by acts of the king's council and decrees of the parlement as before, but now they were in a position to ignore directives that displeased them. They were protected by sturdy walls defended by their militias. Only a numerous army equipped with artillery could batter down their fortifications and fight its way through the breach. Many towns had artillery of their own to keep the attackers at bay. If they were willing to incur the expense, they could replace their tall medieval walls with low, thick angular bastions that could withstand artillery fire. Many towns emerged as true republics—independent city-states—whether they supported the Catholic cause, like Marseilles, or gave their allegiance to Geneva, like La Rochelle.[19] Royal officials and other rival authorities within a town often fell under the control of the town hall. The disgruntled could only flee to safety. The principal threat came from provincial governors and the captains and garrisons of the châteaux within the town's walls, but the governors had difficulty controlling important towns, except where they usually resided, and the garrisons were too small vis-à-vis the urban militias to impose their wills, except in the smaller localities, or where the burghers themselves were divided.

A noble's château could be transformed into a château fort that could protect its owner from marauding troops, but it was almost useless when confronted with an army equipped with artillery. Theoretically, like towns, nobles could construct low, angular bastions that could withstand cannonballs, but they almost never went to the expense of doing so. Nor did they normally have sufficient men to defend the walls against armies of any size. Thus the wars became a struggle characterized by the siege of towns, punctuated by occasional pitched battles. In a perverted way, the wars enabled the towns to enjoy their last golden age of independence. Under these circumstances, factions and social classes struggled to control the town governments.

There have been attempts to explain the history of the towns during the Wars of Religion in economic and social terms, but with no great success. The social determinism that is so popular among historians today may offer partial explanations of the events in this or that town, but the varying aspirations of individual men were more important determinants of the historical process.

The first great split that occurred within the towns was between Catholics and Protestants. Studies made to date do not suggest that there was a significant correlation between any particular economic status or occupation and those who became Protestants. The holders of high judicial offices were fearful of joining the new religion in Rouen, but in Paris and Toulouse they were more inclined to do so than the population as a whole. Perhaps there was a tendency for persons who were literate, or who were engaged in one of the newer trades, such as printing, to become Protestants, but the Protestant stronghold in the Cévennes was not a likely center of the print culture at the time of conversion. The textile workers of Amiens and the shoemakers of Nîmes, members of two of the oldest trades, who converted in large numbers, were not noted for their literacy or independence of mind. Then there is the almost unasked but equally important question of why many people chose to remain Catholic. Here Mack Holt has demonstrated that the winegrowers of Dijon and elsewhere remained loyal to the traditional faith.

Local leadership, or the lack of it on the part of the authorities, the chance course of events, and a number of other factors must have determined why this or that town remained Catholic or became Protestant. When the Protestants moved too rapidly or were soon confronted by strong opposition, as at Lyons, Rouen, and Toulouse, they were ousted from their position of power. Those towns where the Protestants won and maintained predominance became virtually independent city-states. In wartime they ignored royal directives, and in periods of peace they gave them little more than lip service. Only Protestant governors and military commanders sometimes infringed upon their independence.[20]

The second great split that occurred within the towns was between those who supported the Catholic League, and the Catholics known as politiques, who remained loyal to the king. Although this division within the Catholic ranks did not reach serious proportions until the Parisians raised barricades in May 1588, and became widespread only after the assassination of the duke of Guise on December 23 of that year, the sociopolitical background to the dispute dates back to an earlier era.

During the Middle Ages and early sixteenth century, the bourgeois oligarchies strengthened their control over the towns. General assemblies of the inhabitants became rare; artisans and laborers were often excluded from the government. Then, around midcentury, royal officials and lawyers began to compete with merchants for the control of the municipalities. In October 1547, almost before it had become a serious problem, Henry II issued an edict forbidding this practice. He gave the merchants' greater experience and efficiency in municipal affairs as an excuse, but he may well have been fearful that his officials would become more loyal to the towns that elected them than to himself. Although the edict was widely publicized, it seemed almost to stimulate the very process it was designed to prevent. Toulouse took the trouble to have itself declared an exception, but most of the towns simply ignored the royal directive. The lure of municipal office was too strong. In some towns, office brought automatic ennoblement; in all towns, it brought additional power, wealth, and prestige. In some municipalities, a bitter struggle ensued; in others, most often the smaller localities, the merchants gave way with little protest. Often it was difficult to draw clear social lines between the contestants, because officials, lawyers, and merchants were frequently related.[21]

As the century progressed, more and more sons of merchants chose legal careers and dreamed of offices that would bring more prestige and economic security than merchants could hope to enjoy, especially during the turmoil of civil war. Henri Drouot has found that the number of lawyers in Burgundy increased fivefold between 1500 and 1587, but the number of royal officials only doubled. Even these few positions were largely preempted by the sons and kinsmen of occupants who resigned their offices in favor of their relatives. Lawyers in smaller towns sought positions in the bailiwick and presidial courts, but in spite of new creations, there were not enough to meet the demand. Drouot found the nucleus of the League in the disappointed aspirations of these lawyers. They and their allies used the League to seize the municipal offices that had thus far escaped them and thereby satisfy their political and social aspirations, which had been blocked by the urban elite. Royalist members of the sovereign courts fled, leaving the Leaguers free from the crown's control, and largely from that of the sovereign courts, which had so often meddled in municipal affairs. Paris approximately fits the Burgundian pattern, but recent research indicates that the parlement of Rouen did not close its doors to newcomers, and in Angers, Rennes, and Nantes the League drew from all social classes.[22]

Although social conflict was an aspect of the League in various localities, it is doubtful whether a single definition of that conflict can be devised to fit all or even most of the League towns. It must also be remembered that the composition of the League changed from one period to another. If one must seek common denominators to explain the urban League, especially in its more radical phase, it is to be found, first, in the increased devotion to the church that accompanied the Catholic Reformation; second, in the widespread disgust with the corrupt royal court and its grasping, venal officials; third, in the desire for a purified monarchy that governed in conjunction with the Estates General; and fourth, but by no means least, in a return to the municipal autonomy and civic spirit of an earlier age when officials were chosen by a fairly widespread electorate. The civic guards of the individual towns, composed as they largely were of middle-level burghers, may have served as breeding grounds for this revived civic spirit. In its presence and in the desire for municipal autonomy, the League and Protestant towns discovered a common ground. As has so often been the case, a radical movement found its inspiration in an idealized version of the past and not in dreams of a new future.[23]

In their quest for municipal autonomy, the Leaguers did not lose sight of France as a whole. The Parisians established a General Council of the Holy Union designed to aid the duke of Mayenne in governing France. The capital cities of the various provinces were encouraged to create similar organizations to provide leadership for the smaller towns. Some bailiwick seats followed their example. A few clergy and nobles were usually included in these councils, but the towns themselves remained dominant. The experiment reveals once more how resourceful Renaissance Frenchmen were in improvising means to govern themselves. The whole apparatus may be compared with the national and provincial political assemblies created by the Huguenots, but in its brief life of about five years, it proved less effective. Provincial capitals were no more disposed to follow the lead of Paris than they had been that of the crown, and lesser towns often acted independently of provincial capitals.

The split between the League and the Catholic royalists had a profound effect on the sovereign courts. The gradual breakdown of royal authority that had begun soon after the sudden death of Henry II enabled the courts to increase their political role as measured by the boldness of the acts they promulgated. They stepped into the vacuum created by the weakening position of the crown, and the provincial governors turned to them when they wanted to clothe their actions with more legal façades. The problem was that their directives were ignored as often as those of the crown and the provincial estates. Protestant, League, and even royal armies did much as they pleased, and governors, nobles, towns, and villages were not averse to going their own way. When the League took possession of Paris and eventually all the provincial capitals except Bordeaux and Rennes, pro-royalist judges in the sovereign courts became increasingly uncomfortable. After the assassination of the duke of Guise at the close of 1588, many of them sought safety in flight. In March 1589, Henry III established a royalist parlement at Tours to rival the League-controlled court at Paris. Similar parlements at Carcassonne, Flavigny, Pertuis, and Romans soon followed to compete with the League courts that remained at Toulouse, Dijon, Aix, and Grenoble. When Rennes kept faith with the royalist cause, pro-League members of its parlement formed the nucleus of a rival court set up at Nantes. Other sovereign courts suffered fates similar to the parlements. Subjects were left with a choice of which of two courts to obey, when they saw the need to pay attention to the decrees of either.[24] Only the royalist parlement at Bordeaux remained intact, but the Protestants held so much of its jurisdiction that its authority was no more recognized than that of its sister institutions. Cognizant of its weak position, this parlement informed Henry IV in 1590 that "your authority is scarcely recognized [meaning also its own], your justice is without force, your good subjects in various places are defenseless, the majority of your people are crushed."[25]

The breakdown of authority in the countryside was even more severe than in the towns. Communities of the inhabitants and villages had no walls to protect their citizens from marauding troops. If forewarned, they might seek the protection of a nearby town or castle, leaving their homes, livestock, and crops at the mercy of the invaders. They were also less able to defend themselves from tax collectors. Legal and illegal taxes were heaped upon them by king, governor, provincial officials, and armies, whether Catholic or Protestant. The villagers and small townsmen did what they could. Their existence as corporate entities had already been established, and they took advantage of this fact to press for lower taxes. In Dauphiné and other places, they created assemblies, to which they sent their syndics to deliberate on how best to defend their interests.

These assemblies, and sometimes individual villages, dispatched deputies to the king and council and to the sovereign courts to plead for lower taxes and other considerations. Between 1560 and 1614, they increased their representation in the bailiwick assemblies that chose deputies to the Estates General, and with difficulty they sometimes managed to win a greater voice in the provincial estates. In spite of their efforts, their position worsened in the later stages of the Wars of Religion. When they could pay no more taxes, they borrowed to meet the demand placed upon them. By the close of the wars, the village of Gigors owed 5,000 écus; Châteauneuf-de-Mazenc, 15,000; St-Paul-Trois-Châteaux, 14,000; and Livron, 12,000. Thus, at the very moment when the smaller towns and villages achieved political maturity, they became fiscally insolvent. Being insolvent, they became vulnerable to the assaults of their creditors and of royal officials, who eventually felt obliged to straighten out their financial affairs.[26]

THE WARS AND NOBLE INCOME

During the first six decades of the sixteenth century, the rapid growth in population resulted in increased grain prices and land rents. As landowners, the nobility profited immensely. On average their purchasing power at least doubled. The advent of the Wars of Religion marked a pronounced change. The population stabilized, and plundering troops destroyed crops and the livestock so necessary for food, labor, and fertilizer. As a result, crop yields fell and food prices continued to rise.[27]

The receipts of Jeanne d'Albret and her son, the future Henry IV, from Béarn give a clue as to how the nobility fared in these changed circumstances. On March 28, 1569, the baron of Terride led a Catholic army into Béarn. Pau quickly fell, and soon nearly all of Béarn was in his hands. He reorganized the government to ensure Catholic control, confiscated the goods of the Protestants who had fled, and held a meeting of the estates to vote money to support his regime. Jeanne countered by commissioning the count of Montgomery to reconquer her lands, and by August 22, he had regained possession of Béarn. Thereafter, the viscounty escaped direct involvement in the wars. As table 4.1 indicates, domainal revenue continued to increase faster than the prices of wheat and wine in nearby Toulouse and compared favorably with those of distant Paris, which were unnaturally inflated because the city was semi-besieged from 1589 until its capitulation in 1594. The one bad year was 1568–69, when revenue dropped sharply because of Terride's invasion. Table 4.1 suggests that seigneurial purchasing power increased during the wars, although less rapidly than before, provided that plundering troops caused no losses and no lands were alienated.[28]

Table 4.1. The Revenues of Béarn Contrasted with Paris and Toulouse Prices

Period	Paris Wheat Indices[a]	Toulouse Wheat Indices[b]	Toulouse Wine Indices[c]	Fiscal Year[d]	Béarn Domain Indices[e]	Béarn Domain Receipts[e]
1526–35	1.00	1.00	1.00	1530–31	1.00	12,856
1563–67	2.60	2.07	1.41	1564–65	2.99	38,461
1568–72	2.60	1.95	0.72	1568–69	1.96	25,238
1573–77	3.56	3.13	1.40	1575–76	3.31	42,500
1578–82	2.47	2.55	0.91	1579–80	3.24	41,648
1583–87	4.45	2.86	0.94	1584–85	5.00	64,249
1588–92	7.67	3.35	1.98	1589–90	7.09	91,067
1593–97	6.12	3.87	1.23	1594–95	6.19	79,594
1598–1602	3.23	3.08	1.23	1600	7.86	101,040

[a]Calculated August through July; derived from Micheline Baulant and Jean Meuvret, *Prix des céréales extraits de la mercuriale de Paris, 1520–1698* (Paris, 1960), 1: 243.

[b]Calculated for the calendar year; derived from Georges Frêche and Geneviève Frêche, *Les Prix des grains, des vins, et des légumes à Toulouse, 1486–1868* (Paris, 1967), 85–87.

[c]Calculated for the calendar year for local red wine; ibid., 118–21.

[d]The Béarn receipts are for the fiscal year, November 1–October 31. In 1600 the treasurer used the calendar year, but local officials continued to follow the earlier practice. Data from AD, Pyrénées atlantique, B 225, B 254, B 257, B 262, B 265, B 271, B 279, B 286, and B 294.

[e]In Béarnais écus (1 écu = roughly 1.35 livres tournois, a parity retained throughout most of the period; Charles Dartigue-Peyrou, *La Vicomté de Béarn sous le règne d'Henri d'Albret, 1517–1555* [Paris, 1934], 299–302). The figures are for gross receipts in money; payments in kind have been omitted because they were relatively stable and came to less than 2 percent of the gross receipts. Accounting methods caused the receipts for 1589–90, 1594–95, and 1600 to be inflated.

The county of Armagnac was plundered in 1562–63 and almost regularly from 1569 through the 1580s: domainal receipts showed little growth during these years, and the lords' purchasing power clearly declined. Near the close of the decade, there was a precipitous drop in revenue from 24,966 livres in 1583–84 to 7,818 livres in 1588–89. The discouraged peasants of Armagnac and other Bourbon lands had had enough. Instead of crowds competing for the once much-prized land, only a few came to the auctions. No one bid for some farms, and others offered ridiculously low amounts. Bourbon agents made every effort to make the terms of the leases more attractive, and they occasionally reduced their length from three years to one in the hope of finding bidders who would gamble on one year of local peace but not on three. The usual requirement of a down payment upon assuming a lease was often omitted, and certain manorial rights were assigned to the lessees rather than being retained by the Bourbons as before. It had long been the custom to grant lessees rebates if they suffered heavy losses from hail, drought, or other natural disasters. At first the Bourbons were equally willing to grant rebates to those who had suffered from plundering troops, but now demands for such concessions soared. In Armagnac, the rebates granted rose from 738 livres in 1574–75 to 3,872 livres in 1587–88, and 7,713 livres were pending at the latter date as opposed to 22 livres in 1574–75. At length the hard-pressed Bourbon agents were forced to make some leases "without any hope of a rebate." One of the few areas where they leased their rights for significant amounts in kind rather than for money were the mills in the barony of Nérac. The wheat thus received was sold by a merchant of Toulouse. At first their revenue grew rapidly, but by 1585–86 substantial rebates were necessary, and by 1594–95 the Bourbons received little more than a third of what they had gotten a few years before, despite higher wheat prices. Faced with the financial demands of the war and lower purchasing power, the Bourbons sold trees from their extensive forests and alienated some of their lands. In choosing the latter, they always selected fiefs exposed to plundering troops and not those in relatively well-protected Béarn, where custom forbad the practice anyway.[29]

Unfortunately, only the house of Foix-Navarre-Albret has left account books that enable us to estimate its income from domain after domain, year after year, but scattered records do survive for a number of noble families. The landed estates of the Constable Anne de Montmorency produced a revenue of 106,420 livres in 1560–61 and 138,465 livres in 1563–64 following the first War of Religion. Unfortunately, the Montmorency revenues after the Constable's death await their historian. The middle-sized barony of Pont-St.-Pierre produced real income in increasing amounts from the early sixteenth century. By 1571–72, it stood at more than ten times what it had been in 1506–7. Then the wars began to take their toll, and the revenue fell by more than a half. In the Caux region of Normandy, seigneurial revenue ceased to increase just before the wars and dropped precipitously as a result of the military operations in the area in 1562–64 and again in 1589–93. In the Beauce region around Chartres, domaine revenue remained relatively stable from the 1560s through most of the 1580s, only to drop drastically from then until the end of the century. Because of inflation, it should be added, a stable income meant declining purchasing power.[30]

The religious wars did enable the nobility to lay the groundwork for increased revenue from land once peace had been restored. Pillaging troops and higher taxes forced impoverished peasants to sell their land

faster than ever before, and nobles as well as officials and burghers profited from this opportunity. Once in the hands of a privileged person, the
land ceased to be taxed if he exploited it himself, except in the south, but
even there nobles were often able to obtain lower assessments on their
common land. Peasants were loud in their complaints, and by the close of
the century, their lawyers in Dauphiné claimed with some exaggeration
that nobles and other exempt persons had acquired a third or more of the
best land in every village. In addition, the wars caused the crown to
persuade the clergy to alienate part of their land and goods on one
occasion after another to pay royal debts. In 1569, the nobility acquired
26.9 percent of these alienations in the twenty-two dioceses in northeast-
ern France, which included the great bureaucratic and merchant towns of
Paris and Lyons. In the diocese of Périgueux, further from the center of
activity, they made the bulk of the purchases.[31]

Many nobles drew income from a number of sources other than land.
The high nobility often received substantial salaries as governors, army
officers, members of the royal household, and holders of other positions.
They also were sometimes awarded parts of the royal domain, gifts, and
pensions. If they were fortunate enough to be governors, they were the
recipients of the largess of provincial estates, towns, and other bodies
seeking to profit from their influence at court. Then, too, there were the
profits of war. Plunder, ransoms, and the seizure of royal taxes made some
nobles very rich. Less lucrative, but nevertheless rewarding, was the
interest nobles drew on the sums they had loaned the crown. War and
office made it possible for Matignon to increase his revenue tenfold
during the twelve years he was the lieutenant governor of Guyenne.
Alfonso d'Ornano, a Corsican, came to France to seek his fortune and left
his family well established in the new land. The future duke of Sully
garnered about 60,000 livres from ransoms and pillaging between 1576
and 1591, and by 1610 his profits from war reached 330,000. Gaspard de
Saulx-Tavannes is reported to have seized 60,000 livres in the sack of
Mâcon. Most fortunate of all was François de Bonne, who enjoyed only
a few hundred livres a year in rent when the wars began but by 1610 had
an annual income of 121,699 livres. Soon he was to become duke of
Lesdiguières and constable of France.[32]

But only a tiny fraction of the second estate profited from royal largess
or military plunder. Of the 1,036 nobles living in the Beauce
between 1560 and 1600, only 5.98 percent served in the military and the
royal household. If you add to these those who held other offices or who
entered the church, the total would come to only 12.53 percent. Some

royal largess trickled down to other nobles who were clients of the local magnates, but the great majority of the Beauce nobility were dependent on their own resources. Of course, neither the Beauce nor any other region in France can be said to be typical, but it is likely that those who lived much further from Paris had even less contact with the bounty of the king.[33]

Noble expenses were as much a determinant of financial status as noble income. Not surprisingly, the general trend was upward, because of rising prices and the war costs of those who participated. Yet there were some sudden shifts. Jeanne d'Albret's household costs rose from 17,294 livres in 1556 to 27,982 livres in 1565, but when Terride's invasion of Béarn in 1569 sharply reduced her income, she curtailed her expenses by reducing the size of her household and sometimes neglecting to pay those who remained. Following her death, her son greatly increased the size of the household, but even he was willing to reduce or suspend payment of its members when military expenses claimed his funds. Then, too, great noble families did not necessarily pay the same prices for food as lesser inhabitants. By midcentury it had become customary for them to employ merchant-purveyors to provide the food and other items necessary for their households as they meandered about the countryside. The contract Jeanne d'Albret made in 1564 stipulated the price that was to be paid for each kind of food over the next four years. Only if wars or inflation caused the purveyors to suffer "great, evident or notorious losses" were they to be permitted to petition for additional compensation. Under such circumstances, the prices of about 150 different kinds of meat and fish remained relatively stable between 1538 and 1584. The price paid for bread increased by only a fourth between 1571 and 1586 in spite of a more rapid rise in grain prices. In any case, bread took up only about 15 percent of their food budget. The lion's share—about 60 percent—went for meat and fish.

No doubt the purveyors were able to browbeat some minor merchants and farmers into selling at less than the market price, but they also extracted bonuses and other concessions from the Bourbons themselves to compensate for the higher costs they did pay. Food costs did increase. Between 1579 and 1587, Henry of Navarre's expenditure for food grew from 80,768 livres to 115,582 livres, but the number of those who fed at his table also swelled as he moved from rebellious noble to heir to the throne.[34] The Foix-Navarre-Albrets thus handled their revenues and controlled their expenses with reasonable success. By modern middle-class standards, they were sometimes guilty of conspicuous consumption, but they kept their follies within bounds. A degree of magnificence was essential to enhance their power. Their way of life contributed in at least a small way to their rise to the throne of France. If they had been more parsimonious, they would have had fewer clients to assist them.

The Nevers were also a very wealthy family before the Wars of Religion began, but they managed their affairs less well than the Albrets. One member of the family paid a ransom of 125,000 livres, and another failed to produce a male heir, but was saddled with large dowries for his daughters. They alienated many of their estates and had to be saved several times from financial disaster by the king. In return they sometimes paid the king's foreign mercenaries and their own companies from their purse. They had to borrow to do so and also to loan the king hundreds of thousands of livres. In spite of their problems, the Nevers were still one of the wealthiest families in the kingdom when the religious wars drew to a close, albeit nearly a third of their revenue went to pay the interest on their debts.[35]

Louis de Lusignan enjoyed a less exalted status, but through royal favor and occasional assists from the rival houses of Guise and Montmorency, he managed to amass a considerable fortune both before and during the religious wars. Unfortunately, his son, Guy, was a less successful courtier and received few of the profits of royal favor. For a time he served the Catholic League and he even became a spy for Philip II of Spain. A large part of Louis's acquisitions went to his daughters, and Guy gambled away part of the family wealth that fell into his hands. The family was in a state of decline as the wars drew to a close, and it never revived after peace was restored.[36]

But the Albrets, Nevers, and Lusignans were great noble families who derived much of their wealth from the crown. What of the typical minor noble who had no ties at court and rarely a patron who did? Few of them pursued active military careers, thus both avoiding paying ransoms and missing out on the spoils of pillage. Instead, they stayed home and hoped that their houses and farms would escape plunder, whether by Protestant or Catholic troops. When danger drew near, they very likely fled to the forest or to some walled town for safety. There are few data indicative of their economic fate, but it is significant that in the Beauce both old and new nobles slightly increased the number of fiefs they owned between 1560 and 1600, despite the fact that their revenue per acre seems to have declined during the last decade of the Wars of Religion. In the élection of Bayeux, the nobility owned 88 percent of the fiefs on the eve of the wars, and 88 percent in 1597 at their close. During this same period, the old nobility increased its share of fiefs at the expense of the new nobility from 57 to 63 percent.[37] These figures suggest that although most nobles probably lost economically during the wars, peasant, burgher, and officeholder did likewise, and that if there was a slight change in the nobility's relative position, it was for the better. Furthermore, there were a few nobles, such as Epernon and Joyeuse, who profited greatly from royal favor and others, such as Monluc and Lesdiguières, who made fortunes from the wars themselves.

Perhaps the greatest significance of the Valois phase of the Wars of Religion was the breakdown of royal authority and the reduced effectiveness of governors, parlements, and other officials and institutions. There was little change in the relative position of the various groups of which society was composed, but the political collapse paved the way for Henry IV to rebuild his government on a somewhat different basis.

V

Henry IV

When the Jacobin monk Jacques Clément struck down Henry III on August 1, 1589, the allied royal and Huguenot armies appeared on the verge of capturing Paris. But Henry's death completely altered this prospect. His successor by hereditary right, Henry of Navarre, was unacceptable to many Catholics because of his Protestant faith. In a partially unsuccessful effort to retain his Catholic troops, Henry offered so many concessions that some Protestants became disgruntled and departed for their homes. Soon his once-powerful army had dwindled from 40,000 to a mere 22,000. Spain intervened and the Catholic League convoked the Estates General to elect a king. Under these circumstances, Henry despaired of conquering his kingdom. Finally, in May 1593, he decided to gamble that a change in religion would win enough Catholics to his cause to compensate for any defections among the Protestants. His abjuration, which took place in July, brought him more Catholic support than he had dared hoped, and by the summer of 1596, only Mercoeur, among the great League chiefs, had failed to make his peace. Spain remained a stubborn and dangerous foe, but Henry now held so much of France that he decided to attempt to restore financial and administrative order to his kingdom.

THE FINANCIAL PROBLEMS

Henry's position was critical.[1] His debts, including the alienated royal domain, stood somewhere near 300 million livres, but his unalienated annual income was only in the vicinity of 6.9 million livres, less than 30 percent of his annual expenses. It was not that the French paid so few taxes but rather that so much of what was paid did not reach the king. Governors, provincial estates, and towns levied taxes without royal consent, and part of what was legally collected found its way into the hands of the great nobles and municipal officers, as well as those of royal officials, who were notoriously corrupt. To obtain the money to carry on the war, Henry borrowed wherever he could, alienated what remained of his domain, created unneeded offices, and sold patents of nobility. These expedients brought him into frequent conflict with the sovereign courts, who sought to prevent such measures by refusing to register his decrees. When they did so, he usually overrode their opposition, but not without incurring their anger. In January 1596, the first president of the parlement of Dijon boldly informed Henry that the officers of his sovereign courts were "a barrier between the crown and the people designed to defend the latter from taxes and extraordinary burdens."[2]

Henry was also often thwarted by the great nobles who controlled much of his army and, through their clients, part of the royal bureaucracy. To retain the loyalty of his followers and to win the allegiance of the League chiefs, he had to promise governorships, offices, and large sums of money. He usually gave them less than they wanted, but the fact remains that he regained his kingdom more through bribes than by force of arms. Towns and provincial estates had become accustomed to pursuing semi-independent courses, and Henry usually found it expedient to recognize their privileges. By the summer of 1596, when nearly all of France save Brittany recognized him as king, he was on the verge of bankruptcy.

The big problem that faced Henry was what form the restored monarchy should take. Should he try to reconstitute the Renaissance monarchy, with its privileged estates and towns, and its magnates with their numerous clients scattered throughout the bureaucracy and the countryside? Or should he embark on a new course and slowly undermine the position of the magnates and corporate groups so that a new, more centralized, more absolute monarchy could emerge? It is doubtful whether Henry ever thought specifically in these terms. His approach to government was pragmatic rather than theoretical. He wanted to establish his dynasty firmly on the throne, and he wanted to be obeyed. To secure these objectives and to provide for his pleasures, he knew that he had to improve his financial position. Beyond this he may not have gone very far, but he found at least two ministers who were capable of visualizing all aspects of his government and projecting coherent plans for the restoration of the monarchy. The first of these ministers was Pomponne de Bellièvre (1529–1607), and the second was a Protestant noble, Maximilian de Béthune, baron of Rosny and later duke of Sully (1560–1641).

The elderly Bellièvre could call upon vast experience to formulate his plan. He had been a bailiwick lieutenant general, a member of parlement, a diplomat, a royal councillor, a superintendent of finances, and an intendant in Lyons. He saw the need for a strong monarchy and concurred with those who believed that kingship was a divinely ordained institution, and that the estates, sovereign courts, municipal governments, and other constituted bodies derived their authority from the crown. On the other hand, he was equally firm in his belief that the king was under the law, that the rights and privileges of the various constituted bodies should be respected, and that through consultation the vocal elements of the population could be persuaded to support needed reforms, even at some cost to themselves.

As a member of the council of finances in the winter of 1595–96, Bellièvre was constantly called upon to provide Henry with money to support the war. The difficulties he encountered pointed to the need for a new approach to royal finances. He prepared a plan that offered some hope of fiscal solvency and persuaded Henry to summon an Assembly of Notables to consider his proposals. To balance the budget, Bellièvre recommended that the king's personal and household expenses be reduced, and that the amounts spent on pensions, the military, and the bureaucracy be cut substantially. He also urged that the interest on rentes be lowered. The total savings from these measures would come to 11,580,000 livres, but a deficit of 6,420,000 livres would still remain. Additional revenue was clearly mandatory, and this was especially true because Bellièvre felt that it was necessary to reduce the taille by 3 million livres in order to relieve the hard-pressed peasants. It could be secured, he thought, by more efficient tax collection and a levy on goods brought into towns.

Bellièvre's proposals were bold indeed. Reducing household expenses, pensions, and the military establishment would hurt the nobility. Cutting the number and salary of royal officials would antagonize that vocal class. Lower interest rates on rentes and transfer of part of the tax burden from the countryside to the towns would antagonize urban communities. As if this were not enough, Bellièvre also struck a blow at the court aristocracy, and, through it, at the patron-client relationship, by recommending that taxes yielding nearly half the royal revenue be placed under a specially created *conseil du bon ordre* and devoted exclusively to paying salaries, rentes, and other contractual obligations. The remaining revenues were to continue to be administered by the council of finances and used for the royal household, the military, and related expenses.

Bellièvre hoped thus to reduce courtiers' influence in financial affairs by removing nearly half of the royal revenue from their grasp, and at the same time to establish the credit of the monarchy by ensuring that salaries and debts were paid.[3]

It was one thing to prepare a plan that would lead to financial solvency and another to win the backing necessary for its implementation, especially when its provisions would injure the most influential classes in the kingdom. To prepare public opinion to accept his suggestions, Bellièvre therefore arranged for an Assembly of Notables to meet in Rouen on November 4. The notables refused to recommend a reduction of the interest on rentes but were finally persuaded to accept a 5 percent sales tax on merchandise sold in towns, known as the *sol pour livre,* or *pancarte.* This was not expected to yield enough to enable the crown to reduce the taille, and the notables sought to relieve the peasantry by recommending that some of the exemptions to the taille be curtailed, and that the undertaxed provincial estates pay more. Like Bellièvre, the notables wanted revenues divided into two parts, one of which was to be assigned to meet the contractual obligations of the crown, but they did not suggest that a semi-independent conseil du bon ordre be created to administer it. Before they disbanded, however, Henry told the notables that he could not accept such a rigorous division of his revenue, because he needed more flexibility to meet his obligations. Finally, the notables stressed economy, efficiency, and honesty in government. They asked that the sale of offices cease, that salaries be cut 10 percent, and that the bureaucracy, royal household, and military establishment be reduced. As a further economy they recommended that the provincial and diocesan estates be held every third year rather than annually in Languedoc. To ensure honesty, they urged that the accounts of royal tax officials and those of the estates, towns, and communities be audited.

Bellièvre was thus successful in persuading the notables to adopt most of a program that was essentially a restoration of the Renaissance monarchy, albeit a more honest, frugal, and efficient one. Henry's objectives are more difficult to define. He took a direct hand only in persuading the notables to accept the pancarte and in pressing Achille de Harlay, the first president of the parlement of Paris, to obtain a declaration from them that royal officials should not become involved in the affairs of the princes and other seigneurs. This declaration, if enforced, would have greatly reduced the influence of the nobility on the government and seriously curtailed their ability to extract money from the royal treasury, to tax illegally, and to escape punishment for their misdeeds.

The key to the future of France lay less in how fully the notables accepted Bellièvre's proposals than in how well the king and his council implemented them. For about six months, the progress made must have exceeded Bellièvre's expectations. Steps were taken to weaken the venal system of officeholding and reduce the size of the bureaucracy. The patron-client system was attacked, and royal officials were forbidden to accept positions in the households of the princes. The burden of taxation was shifted somewhat from the country to the towns by the establishment of the pancarte and the reduction of the taille by 10 percent. Most surprising of all, pressure from the town and parlement of Paris did finally lead Henry to divide his revenue into two parts and create a conseil du bon ordre, or *conseil particulier,* as he called it, to administer the portion dedicated to meeting the contractual obligations of the crown. Finally, a chamber of justice was established to investigate and punish those guilty of financial malpractices.

When the Spanish captured Amiens on March 11, 1597, and threatened Paris itself, it soon became apparent that Bellièvre's reform program was not compatible with the increased financial needs of the crown. New offices had to be created to sell, the conseil particulier had to be abandoned because Henry could not afford such a rigorous division of his income, and the chamber of justice was abolished in return for a substantial gift from the financial officials. The greatest casualty was Bellièvre himself. His fall was not sudden, but his belief that "one must act gently and after due thought"[4] produced less money than Sully's harsh, brusque approach. Gradually, Henry came to rely more on the younger man in monetary matters. By June 1598, following the end of the war with Spain, Sully was the acknowledged leader of the financial administration, and soon the office of superintendent of finances was revived for his benefit. Bellièvre did not immediately lose the confidence of his sovereign, however. He was elevated to the chancellorship in 1599 and continued to influence the government until Henry took the seals from him in the early winter of 1604–5.

Sully paid Bellièvre the compliment of borrowing some aspects of his program. He sought to make the fiscal administration honest and efficient. He dispatched commissioners to the provinces to audit accounts, and on several occasions the chamber of justice was reconstituted. He tried to make the towns bear more of the costs of government by increasing the gabelles and other sales taxes and by slashing the taille, which fell so heavily on the countryside. He even managed to reduce the interest rate of the rentes in spite of considerable opposition. By 1600, the budget was balanced again, and by the time of Henry's assassination in 1610, a substantial portion of the crown's debts had been repaid, much of the domain had been redeemed, and a large treasure had been stored in the Bastille for emergencies. To accomplish this miracle, Sully had acted ruthlessly. He had canceled much of the debt owed to the Swiss and to French officials and merchants. He had showed little regard for duly constituted bodies and had often ignored the protests of the sovereign courts. Although he eventually succumbed to pressure and abandoned the pancarte, he insisted that the estates help pay the king's debts and redeem his domain.

Neither ruthlessness nor heavy fiscal demands inevitably lead to absolutism, however. For France to become absolute, it was necessary for the crown either to establish firm control over the estates and other duly constituted bodies or to appoint royal officials to assume their tax-collecting and other administrative duties, a step that would ultimately lead to their disappearance. Henry had had considerable experience in dealing with the provincial estates before coming to the throne. His ancestral lands of Bigorre, Nébouzan, Foix, Soule, Béarn, and Navarre had had active estates, with whom he had negotiated since his mother's death in 1572, and as governor of Guyenne he had dealt with the numerous assemblies of that vast region. It was there that his policy toward the estates first began to be revealed.

THE ESTATES IN GUYENNE

There were assemblies of the estates in the ten seneschalsies that composed the government of Guyenne.[5] In eight of them, agents of these estates collected the taxes, while in the other two, Périgord and Bordelais, this duty was performed by royal officials called élus. In addition, there was an assembly of the entire government of Guyenne, in which the deputies of the seneschalsies dealt with their common problems, but it was the seneschalsy and not the government estates that normally gave consent to taxation. Henry was reluctant to convoke any of these assemblies before order was restored. As he told his lieutenant general in Guyenne in April 1595: "The time is not right to hold such assemblies, which ordinarily do more to free my subjects from expenses than to assist and aid me in my affairs, because no one now looks further than his individual welfare. Therefore, I want you to skip this assembly if possible and postpone it to a more opportune time."[6] Thus instructed, the lieutenant general managed to stave off until January 1596 a request of the town of Bordeaux that the estates of Guyenne be held. Once Henry's authority had been restored, however, the estates were frequently convoked and displayed no hesitancy in voting less than the amount he requested. Rouergue, for example, could be persuaded to grant only 180,000 of the 396,000 livres that he sought in 1596.

At first Henry attributed his financial difficulties to the dishonesty and inefficiency of his own officials, but as he fell more and more under Sully's influence in financial affairs, he began to think differently. By the waning months of 1597, he had begun to place equal blame on the officials of the estates and towns. That November, his Council of Finance forbad the *consuls* in Guyenne to levy taxes without royal permission and directed that their records be verified by the seneschals of their respective jurisdictions. In July 1598, the council struck at the related problem of the failure of the estates to levy all the taxes ordered by the crown, and they were instructed to do so at once. In anticipation that the estates would appeal to the sovereign courts to intercede, the parlements of Bordeaux and Toulouse were forbidden to take any action that would cause a delay. Then in August 1598, Henry directed that commissioners be sent to most of the généralités of France to ensure that the taille was apportioned and collected in a fair, honest, and efficient manner. The man chosen to head the commission to Guyenne was Michel de Marillac, then a maître des requêtes and later, as keeper of the seals, the most implacable and dangerous foe the provincial estates ever had.

After visiting many of the seneschalsies in Guyenne and holding the estates, Marillac returned to Paris, where he wrote an unfavorable report. This led to the assignment of a treasurer at Bordeaux to investigate the activities and procedures of the estates. The treasurer found that the estates were needlessly burdening the people with the costs of their frequent meetings, which they often held on their own initiative, and by the sums they levied to support their own activities. He issued directions that struck severe blows at the independent position the estates had enjoyed. The length of their sessions, the number of deputies who could attend, and their daily remuneration were strictly limited. Meetings were to be called only with the express permission of the king, and a limit was set on the amount that could be voted to support their legitimate activities. Sully and the king's council backed up his recommendations and also ordered that the debts incurred by the various estates be verified.

Commissioners were dispatched to perform this duty. The very strength of the opposition these measures evoked suggests the guilt of many local officials. The *consuls* of Agen, for example, warned their counterparts in other towns in Guyenne in 1602 that the commissioners had no respect for their traditional methods of bookkeeping and would arbitrarily condemn them to pay large fines. The estates of Guyenne and of the seneschalsies met frequently and managed to get the order sending out the commissioners temporarily revoked in December. Then, in January 1603, the most severe blow of all fell. An edict was issued creating élections in the eight seneschalsies where they did not then exist. Royal tax collectors were to replace those of the estates. Henceforth, the king would have servants who could collect taxes without the consent of the estates, and who could refuse to collect taxes the estates voted for their own purposes.

The estates did not despair. The crown had created élections in all or part of Guyenne four or five times before, and on each occasion they had succeeded in having the offending edict revoked by giving the king a special gift or reimbursing those who had purchased the offices. They had simply to do so again. First, they asked their sympathetic lieutenant general, Marshal Alphonse d'Ornano, to use his influence at court on their behalf and to arrange for the estates of Guyenne to meet; next, they sent deputies to the sovereign courts to persuade them to delay implementation of the king's edicts in order to provide time for the deputies sent to Paris to get them revoked. Money and presents were showered on Ornano and others to ensure their cooperation. A few minor victories were won, but the establishment of the élections drew ever nearer. Finally, in the winter of 1604–5, deputies from the various seneschalsies converged on Paris, the most active of their number being Julien de Camberfore, sieur de Selves, the first *consul* of Agen.

Selves quickly contacted the king, who referred him to Sully and his council. There followed a ten-month battle between the powerful minister and the resourceful, outspoken defender of municipal liberties. Their frequent engagements are clearly revealed by Selves's numerous letters to the *consuls* of Agen, letters that also give specific information about Sully's intentions regarding the provincial estates, not just in Guyenne but in all of France. Neither Sully nor Selves were intellectuals. Sully gave no learned explanations of royal prerogative such as those with which James I was then regaling the elected representatives of the English people, and Selves made no comments on the concept of popular sovereignty, which had lately found some defenders in France. Sully justified his acts in terms of the corruption of the estates and the welfare of the people, Selves in terms of tradition and privilege.

The contest between the two men was not as uneven as it may initially seem. Selves was not important nationally, but before going to Paris, he had had the forethought to obtain favorable letters from Ornano to the king and to other influential persons. A spokesman for traditional privileges and procedures, he found supporters in the council itself, where Bellièvre had not been alone in advocating making the old system of government work. To counter Selves, Sully had to retain the support of the king and a majority of the council, some of whom were susceptible to being influenced by the gratifications the deputies from Guyenne were sure to offer. His proud demeanor and fiery temper had won him many enemies, and their numbers were augmented by his firm opposition to the graft and corruption that had lined the pockets of courtiers and officials for so long. During the early months of 1605, he once more thought that he was on the verge of disgrace. Under such circumstances he called upon all his resources to meet the threat from Guyenne.

Sully's first line of defense was to try to discourage or frighten the deputies so that they would not present their petitions to the council. He gave Selves several audiences a week during the early months of his mission. The élections were necessary, he insisted, because of the heavy tax burden the estates imposed on the people. These taxes were unfairly distributed, the *consuls* and syndics exempted themselves from paying them, and much of the money that was collected was squandered on deputations and other activities rather than going to the purse of the king. He refused to authorize payment to the deputies for their mission, charged them with peculation, and on one occasion threatened to throw Selves into the Bastille on the grounds that powers of attorney given him were faulty. If Selves's charges are correct, he even tampered with their correspondence with their constituents in Guyenne.

During the course of his conversations with Selves, Sully revealed some of his plans for the reorganization of France. Guyenne was not to be the only pays d'états in which élections were to be established. The king, he declared, "wants the taille to be levied in all of France in the same fashion."[7] Languedoc, Dauphiné, and Provence were earmarked for élections. Royal tax officials were to replace those of the estates and they were to supervise the towns and villages carefully. Henceforth, the king could levy whatever tax he pleased, and the estates would be allowed to die, because the funds they voted for their own use would be levied by the élus only if they were authorized to do so. Gone would be the power to offer handsome presents to important persons in return for their assistance in winning concessions at court. As small a matter as sending a deputation to Paris could be undertaken only with the crown's concurrence. This would not be often, Selves early concluded, for "those who come here for the welfare of the people are hardly welcome." "There is nothing so odious here," he wrote, "as syndics and deputies."

From the first, Selves clearly realized the threat that the establishment of the élus posed for the towns and estates. In moments when he despaired of success, he punctuated his letters with remarks like, "[They want] to abolish the privileges of the towns in order to be able to do as they please, and remove the means of complaining"; "Adieu, liberties! privileges! *Consular* offices will not longer have their luster or power"; "They have created *élus* in order to reduce the authority of the *consulat*. . . . If we do not take care, we shall be *consuls* only to have the streets cleaned."

Selves was not a man to accept defeat without a struggle. Upon his arrival in Paris, he had sought interviews with the leading members of the council. Unfortunately, one potential ally, Bellièvre, was of little use, because the king had decided to take the seals from him and give them to Brulart de Sillery, who took the oath as keeper of the seals on January 5, 1605. The aging Bellièvre was left the title of chancellor but ceased to be influential in the government. Denied this potential source of support, Selves quickly found others. On December 21, he reported that Sillery himself, Forget de Fresnes, the secretary of state for Guyenne, Villeroy, the influential secretary for foreign affairs, and other councillors did not believe it obligatory to establish élections in Guyenne, but they added that it would be necessary to fight Sully. Gilles de Maupeou, on the other hand, handled him as roughly as did Sully.

Selves's instructions had been to secure the revocation of the edict creating the élus on the grounds that Agenais and other seneschalsies in Guyenne had paid a substantial sum in 1582 in return for the crown's abolishing the élections forever. This was true, but Selves was not so naive as to believe that justice alone would prevail at the court of Henry IV. It was necessary to offer the king a sufficient sum to reimburse him for the loss of the revenue he anticipated from the sale of offices in the new élections. Unfortunately, the estates of Guyenne were not allowed to meet to authorize such an offer. Soon after his arrival in Paris, Selves had reported that no one except Sully and Maupeou thought that it was necessary to have élus in Guyenne. He repeated this on March 3, just five days before the letters Ornano had sent to the king and the councillors won him and several other deputies a hearing before the council. Sully, who had wanted to send them away without replying to their petition, left the room in anger when it was decided to admit them in deference to the marshal. With Sully gone, the audience went well, but Selves clearly anticipated the unfavorable reply that was handed down on March 10. He reported back that day that the majority of the councillors were favorable to the estates' position but that Sully "is so absolute that no one resists him."

Selves knew Sully would now want to proceed to establish the élections, but he still did not despair. He and several other deputies from Guyenne adopted a plan so secret that it was decided that one of their number should go in person to Guyenne to win the support of their constituents. They dared not write about it because of "the perfidity of the world and the interception of letters." Part of this plan was to obtain permission for the estates of Guyenne to meet and offer the king a substantial sum of money in return for abandoning the élections. But there had to be something more involved, because there was no reason to keep this a secret. Indeed, the possibility of a financial offer must have been suggested informally to the council, because on March 22, Selves reported that it had been discussed on three occasions, but Sully had been opposed. Certainly the secret was important to Selves, because he constantly urged the *consulat* at Agen to adopt the plan. The key to the secret can almost certainly be found in his letter of April 22, in which he told of a deputy who had been sent to protest to the king and council about the tyrannies of the new tax farmers of the river commerce. Sully had received him "as lovingly as he did us" and wanted to send him away without being heard. The king, however, fearing some disturbance, had given reasonable satisfaction. "Use this information," Selves hinted. The *consuls* in Guyenne, then, were to see to it that there was enough unrest to cause Henry to intervene personally rather than leave the decision to his brutal and inflexible minister. The deputies won Ornano's support, and the activities of the nobility and the Protestants were sufficiently threatening to cause the government grave concern. Finally, there was the need to win as much support at court as possible, and when all was ready, to find means to bypass Sully and go directly to the king. Among those enlisted were Ornano, the seneschal of Guyenne, Forget de Fresne, the secretary of state for Guyenne, and the relatively obscure Nicolas de Netz, a councillor in the Court of Aides. Probably all of them expected some sort of reward, but no one was as blunt as Netz. "Send a well-filled purse," Selves wrote on September 12, ". . . to pay M. de Netz, because he has frankly told us that he will do nothing without money."

By the middle of June, Selves believed he was in a position to act. He had apparently received authority to make the king a concrete offer, although probably only in the name of Agenais, whose estates had met in April. Sully had gone to Châtellerault to attend a Protestant assembly, and Henry's latest mistress, the countess of Moret, had agreed to act as go-between with her lover (for which service, Selves noted, it was necessary to give her a "fine present"). About three weeks later, Selves reported that he was awaiting the king's decision concerning the élus through the intercession "of one of his friends. If this fails there is no hope." However, Henry was unwilling to make a decision in Sully's absence, and when the minister returned near the end of August, he was as intransigent as before. By that time the estates of Agenais, discouraged, had voted to recall Selves, but the intrepid deputy followed the court in its wanderings until late October, hoping somehow to alter the decision of the crown.

Henry had had a choice. He could make a handsome profit by accepting Selves's offer and abandoning the idea of creating élections, or he could persist in his original determination and make an immediate profit by selling the new offices. If he chose the latter, he would incur the burden of paying the élus' salaries indefinitely and the risk of provoking an uprising in an already troubled region. Acting on Sully's advice, and apparently against that of the majority of his council, he chose the less profitable and more dangerous course. Surely his goal and that of his minister must have been to undermine the estates and towns so that their own authority could be more fully implemented. In doing so, they took a step toward creating an absolute state, a step that Sully had declared would be followed by others as the provincial estates fell one by one before the élus.

The estates, of course, could continue to function with élus collecting the taxes provided the crown was well disposed toward representative assemblies. The estates of Normandy had flourished under such conditions during most of the sixteenth century. In the government of Guyenne, the seneschalsies of Bordelais and Périgord already had élections. The three estates of the former had lost the right to consent to taxation long before the Wars of Religion. Several types of assemblies did survive there, but their role was to protest the taxes the crown ordered levied and to observe the division of taxes by the élus. The three estates of Périgord and their officials, on the other hand, had continued to be active. An important meeting was held in 1595, in which three syndics were chosen to serve three-year terms in succession and a committee of eighteen was selected to act for the three estates for nine years when they were not in session. This was the customary practice, and with so large a committee, the three estates sometimes went nine years without a meeting. Henry expressed his satisfaction with the 1595 meeting and obviously intended to continue to hold the estates. By 1604, however, when the mandate given the syndics and the committee had expired, Sully had caught his master's ear and permission to hold the estates was denied. Henceforth, the three estates met only to elect deputies to the Estates General.

THE ESTATES OF BRESSE, BUGEY, AND GEX

During the summer of 1600, France seized Bresse, Bugey, and Gex from Savoy, and in doing so won a narrow salient extending to the environs of Geneva that cut one of the main Spanish routes from Italy to the Low Countries. The Savoyard dukes had had an elaborate system of representative institutions in their lands. There had been assemblies in which participants came from all parts of their domain, but their more common practice had been to hold separate meetings for those who dwelt on the Italian and French sides of the Alps. In addition, the three estates of Bresse and Bugey sometimes deliberated together and sometimes apart. Meetings of the individual estates were frequently held in both provinces, the syndics of Bourg having the right to convoke the third estate of Bresse if they obtained permission from the local ducal official. The very wealth of alternative forms of representation was probably detrimental to the survival of these assemblies, because the loyalty of the inhabitants was not centered in any one institution. The French had preserved the system between 1536 and 1559, when they controlled the region, but the able, autocratic duke Emmanuel Philibert began to reduce the power of the estates when he resumed control over the area in 1559. After 1563, meetings of the three estates of Bresse and Bugey became rare, and the size of the tax was set by the duke. Nevertheless, the nobles and clergy continued to elect syndics to represent their respective orders, and the municipal officials of Bourg continued to summon the communities to protest the size of the tax and other matters, to vote and levy additional sums for local use, and to divide the assessments among the various localities. Assemblies of the three estates and of the individual estates of Gex also continued to function. In the three territories, the taille was actually collected by the officials of the individual communities. Hence

Henry inherited a system in which he determined the size of the taille but was dependent on local officials to collect it, a situation that made delays and protests commonplace. This was especially true because additional taxes could be added by the third estate for such local purposes as bribing the governors and other royal officials to support their cause.[8]

The situation was not likely to please Henry. Hardly had the success of the Savoyan campaign become apparent than he assigned Sully the task of integrating the new territories into the financial administration of the kingdom. Sully treated the local authorities brutally, increased the taille, but refused to permit them to levy taxes for their own use, and interfered in municipal elections. On February 20, 1601, he placed the capstone on his plan by presenting a decree to the council of finances creating élections in Bresse, Bugey, and Gex. With their duties sharply curtailed, the estates would probably have died had not the three territories been attached to Burgundy. When the triennial meeting of the estates of the duchy was held, it became customary for them to send deputies to Dijon to present their cahiers to the governor.

THE GREAT PAYS D'ETATS

Henry and Sully had attacked the estates in Guyenne in part because more tax abuses were alleged against them than against their counterparts in other parts of France. There were both unfavorable reports by royal officials like Michel de Marillac and complaints by residents. In 1552, a nobleman who served as syndic of the villages of Comminges had gone so far as to try to have an élection created there. Equally significant, the estates in Guyenne were weaker than those in most other parts of France. The provincial assembly never established its supremacy over those of the seneschalsies, and the nobility and clergy were relatively inactive in most jurisdictions. Similarly, the estates in Bresse, Bugey, and Gex were weak when they were incorporated into France because of the absolutist tendencies of the Savoyard dukes and the failure of the first two orders to participate fully. Hence Henry and Sully were able to impose élections on both regions in spite of numerous protests and delaying tactics on the part of the estates. But what of the great pays d'états? We have seen that Sully told Selves, the intrepid deputy from Agen, that he intended to establish élections in them as well, but their stronger position made it more dangerous for him to take this step. We turn first to the estates of Languedoc.[9]

The three estates of the entire province of Languedoc met together for the first time following the wars in the spring of 1599. At this meeting, Henry sought a special appropriation of 300,000 livres per year for five or six years to pay his debts, but the estates were only willing to vote half that sum for a period of four years, and then only if Henry made a number of concessions. In 1603 the estates renewed the grant conditionally for another four years, but earlier they had displayed their independence by refusing to give Henry a wedding present.

Until this point, the three estates had held their own against the crown; both sides had made concessions, and more often than not the government had accepted less than it had asked for. The estates owed their success to both the influence of their friends and the preference of most of the king's councillors for compromise rather than confrontation. Gratifications were regularly voted for their governor, Montmorency, who usually resided at Chantilly or at court, for their lieutenant governor, Ventadour, who acted for him in Languedoc, and for other influential persons. By 1604, however, Sully, who had earlier curried favor with the constable, had won a paramount position on the council of finances and was in a position to join battle with the powerful Montmorency family. The contest was over whether Languedoc should remain a partially self-governing province in return for making an annual contribution to the royal treasury, or whether its provincial and diocesan estates and its towns should be weakened by a series of measures culminating in the establishment of élus.

The dangers of the new situation that confronted the three estates became apparent when their deputies at court reported back in the fall of 1604, just before Selves began his ill-fated mission to defend Agenais. On November 18, a syndic who had been a member of the delegation informed the estates that Sully and the council had refused to approve the concessions that the king's commissioners had made in return for the renewal of a tax of 150,000 livres for four years. In so doing they had technically voided the tax, but on the 23d, Ventadour told the estates that they would have to continue the levy. Persuasion, not resistance, appeared to him the safer policy, especially as he may have had reason to be optimistic about the chances of success. He almost certainly knew that after the syndic had been rebuffed by the council, he had gone to Montmorency to plead for his assistance. Probably Montmorency in turn had presented the case to the king, for when the bishop of Carcassonne spoke to him on the subject, Henry expressed his regret that the province had not been given satisfaction and instructed him to see Sully. When he did so, he found the minister much more accommodating, for causes one may easily guess.

Sully thus had to wait for a more opportune moment to strike. There is no reason to doubt that his ultimate objective was to create élus as he had told Selves. To do so two preliminary steps were necessary. First, the power of the three estates to tax would have to be limited, so that they could not afford large delegations that spent months at court intriguing with and sometimes bribing influential persons. Second, royal officials would have to inspect the books of the estates, dioceses, and towns to gather evidence of corruption. Only if evidence of dishonesty was uncovered could he hope to persuade the king to adopt his plan over Montmorency's and Ventadour's objections. With the élus established, the king could impose what taxes he liked without waiting for the consent of the estates, as he did in Normandy. If the estates proved troublesome, he could cease to convoke them altogether, as he had done in Périgord.

When the estates opened in November 1607, one of the syndics reported that the chamber of accounts insisted on examining the diocesan and municipal tax records and had imprisoned a *consul* from Narbonne and a diocesan official from Nîmes. Violations of the promises the crown had made in 1599 and 1604 in return for the special 150,000 livres each year were soon revealed. A large delegation was elected to go to court, and Ventadour himself proceeded to Paris, where he and Montmorency gave the deputation all the assistance they could. By the terms of the decrees of March 6, 1608, the chamber of accounts was to audit diocesan and communal records of money collected for local use. Unless special permission was obtained, severe limits were placed on the amount that could be levied for local purposes. Disgruntled, the three estates suggested that the king forgo his special 150,000 livres, but voted Montmorency and Ventadour 18,000 each, and the former's son 6,000. Sully was almost certainly behind the crown's moves, and his hand can be seen even more clearly in an edict of March 15, 1608, harshly forbidding the estates to levy any money at all for their own support unless they collected 18,000 livres to construct a bridge at Toulouse, a project in which he was very interested.

Meanwhile, the battle over auditing the diocesan and communal books by the chamber of accounts continued. The estates of 1608–9 accused officers of the chamber of stealing documents from their archives, and a deputy from Toulouse charged that the chamber had calumniously informed the king that the estates were misappropriating public funds. It was altogether impractical, the deputy argued, for any court to verify the records of six thousand communities annually, especially as a majority of the *consuls* could not read or write and did not keep records in account books. Indeed, in some areas, any records that existed were made by notching sticks. The chamber had arrested municipal officials, broken down the doors of the houses of the *consuls*, seized records from the communal archives, and violently handled everyone in the dioceses and towns with provincial responsibilities. Thoroughly aroused, the three estates sent a deputation to court and opened direct negotiations with the chamber.

During the interval between this meeting of the three estates and the one that opened in 1610, Sully continued his efforts to curtail the expenses of the estates, towns, and dioceses. Decrees in September required the commissioners to the estates of Languedoc to see to it that the diocesan estates limited their expenses to those set by the council in 1608. They also renewed the order forbidding the provincial and diocesan estates and the towns to levy any tax or to borrow money at interest without permission. In November, the council created three receivers of extraordinary revenue in each diocese in Languedoc, a measure that aroused the opposition of the three estates, because it meant that taxes levied for their own use as well as royal taxes would be turned over to royal officials rather than to their own.

After considerable negotiation, the estates that assembled in January 1610 reached an accord with the chamber of accounts. In doing so, they owed much to Montmorency and Ventadour, who persuaded Henry to support them rather than Sully. The estates had lost a little ground during the preceding years, but once the quarrel with the chamber of accounts was settled, partially to their satisfaction, their grievances consisted primarily of the substitution of royal receivers for their own tax collectors and the limitation placed on their daily stipends for attending the estates, both matters that were set right during the months that followed.

Sully had made a determined effort to break the power of the provincial and diocesan estates of Languedoc, but on critical issues he and the council of finances had often been overruled by the king. The cause of Henry's leniency is not difficult to find, for when he had acted, it had been at Montmorency's behest. The relations between the two men have never been fully explored. Henry undoubtedly owed his throne to the constable more than to any other man, but he was ever more generous in buying the submission of his enemies than in rewarding his friends. More important was the bond of friendship and mutual respect that existed between the two men. Both had been born into great noble families and had demonstrated their abilities as soldiers, diplomats, statesmen, and leaders of factions. Both had engaging personal character-istics that won the loyalty of those who served them, and both shared the faults of their class. Henry is reported to have said that if ever the Bourbons died out, no family in Europe was worthier of the crown of France than the Montmorencys.

Henry probably trusted Montmorency as much as he did any other great noble capable of causing serious trouble. He had designated Montmorency's son to succeed his father as governor, although by doing so he turned Languedoc into a virtual hereditary possession of that house. Nevertheless, Henry knew that there were limits to any man's loyalty. To interfere in Languedoc too much against Montmorency's wishes could lead to a serious revolt, for the constable had the wealth, ability, and prestige to bring together a more formidable coalition of nobles than anyone else in France, and he could count on the support of the bulk of the clergy and burghers in his government. Cardinal Richelieu, who had one or more frank conversations with Sully, reported that Henry was well aware of the financial abuses of the estates and the powerful position of the governor, but that he had not dared to establish the élus there as he would have liked to have done. In addition to Henry's relations with Montmorency, events in France and in Europe influenced his treatment of Languedoc. The approaching war with Spain in 1610 probably contributed to Henry's reversal of Sully's policy at that time. Another possible factor was Condé's flight to Flanders with his wife to remove her from Henry's attentions. The teenage princess was Montmorency's daughter, and the amorous, aging king needed her father's assistance in persuading her to return.

Although the three estates of Languedoc owed their good fortune primarily to the influence of their governor and to events elsewhere in France and in Europe, they themselves were not without credit. There was little friction between the three orders, and they joined together in defending their provincial privileges. Complaints against the nobility and clergy centered on their failure to attend the sessions. Those who did so functioned effectively with the deputies of the towns and dioceses. Bishops who undertook missions to court sometimes refused payment for their services, a rare virtue at this time. It was to the unity of prelate, noble, and townsmen, the well-organized procedures of the provincial assembly, and the clearly subordinate position of the diocesan estates that the people of Languedoc owed their strong position against outside interference.

Peace did not return to Provence until 1595, and it was only at the close of that year that the estates met united as before the war. Henry and Sully treated the province with unaccustomed consideration. They created fewer venal offices, launched fewer investigations, and made more modest demands for increased taxation there than elsewhere. The Provençals did not hesitate to oppose the royal will when the occasion warranted, but at times they thought that they could afford to be gracious, as when they made a contribution to help Henry defray his marriage expenses. They escaped Henry's and Sully's none-too-delicate attentions in part because of the undeserved popularity that the young duke of Guise, their governor, enjoyed with former members of the League. More important, however, were Henry's doubts about their loyalty. The estates had invited the duke of Savoy to intervene during the religious wars, and the duke had been well received in many quarters. Soon after order was restored, war had broken out with Savoy in 1600. Once more it became advisable not to test the loyalty of the Provençals too strongly. Disturbing reports continued to flow into Paris even after the Savoyard problem had been settled. Some nobles met secretly at night during estates in January 1606, one informer wrote, and in 1609 he added the disturbing news that President Coriolis of the parlement of Aix, a man who had done much to persuade the Provençals to invite the duke of Savoy to intervene during the religious wars, was openly leading the opposition in the estates.

There is no reason to doubt that Sully ultimately intended to establish élus in Provence, as he had told Selves, but he evidently preferred to attack the liberties of one province at a time. Guyenne had fallen before he began to undermine the estates of Languedoc, and Languedoc was no doubt to fall before Provence had its turn. By 1609, however, the approaching war with Spain made it inadvisable to tamper with the privileges of a frontier province of such questionable loyalty, and Henry's death the following year removed any chance that a concerted effort would be made to undermine the estates.

The three estates of Provence also deserve some credit for their success. There had been indications during the later stage of the Wars of Religion that their meetings might be superseded by the assembly of the communities, which consisted of the *procureurs nés et joints* and the deputies of the towns with direct representation in the estates. This was because the assembly could gather on shorter notice, but after 1600, when a state of relative calm had been restored, the three estates reassumed their traditional role, and the assembly of the communities was rarely convoked during the remainder of the reign. In spite of bickering about what contributions the clergy and nobility should make, there was sincere cooperation between the orders. The three estates deliberated together, and many of their decisions were recorded as being unanimous. The *procureurs du pays nés* served as permanent executives for the estates, and there were a number of salaried officials to do their bidding. Perhaps the estates' greatest weakness was their failure to integrate the important towns of Arles and Marseilles fully into the province.

Once peace had been restored in Dauphiné, the quarrel between the third estate and the privileged orders over whether the latter should pay the taille was resumed. The spokesmen for the third estate attacked on three fronts. First, they produced a series of pamphlets defending their cause. Second, they gathered information designed to show that the privileged had acquired so much common land that the tax burden on what remained was unbearable. Third, they made one appeal to the king's council after another seeking redress for their grievances. The general theme of their argument was that by a statute of 1341, their feudal overlord had granted all his subjects immunity from taxation, and that the king of France had confirmed this privilege when he had acquired the province. Of course, the estates could make a free gift to the crown, but the burden of such generosity should fall on all the inhabitants, and not just the third estate.

The nobles and privileged officials were also active. At times the sovereign courts went out of their way to injure the third estate. They set aside delays Henry granted in paying taxes and in repaying loans, and they largely ignored an edict he issued revoking ennoblements that had taken place during the preceding twenty years. The nobles also began to hold separate assemblies frequently. They had occasionally met alone in the sixteenth century, but the quarrel with the third estate made such meetings more routine. They also created a council of the nobility dominated by ennobled jurists to carry on the battle with the third estate. It met often and, with the permission of a favorably disposed governor or parlement, convoked provincial assemblies, to which the nobles of each bailiwick and seneschalsy elected deputies. The three estates continued to meet at least once a year, but whereas formerly they had usually deliberated together, voted by head, and taken extreme care to present a united front to the crown, they now began to deliberate and vote apart.

Henry and his council were anxious to have the contestants resolve their own difficulties, but their efforts to promote a compromise ended in failure. In a meeting of the estates at Grenoble in the winter of 1601, the third estate decided neither to vote nor to levy any more taxes until the question of who was to pay the taille was settled. Henry and his advisers were compelled by this to conclude that the three estates would never reach a compromise, and that they must impose a solution. When Henry and his councillors acted in April 1602, they sided with the nobility and royal officials. They had tried to effect a compromise and had avoided making a decision as long as they could, but when they recognized that an agreement could not be reached, it became a question of whether the nobility and high officials or the towns and villages could more safely be alienated. Given this choice, they naturally favored the former, but they did so reluctantly. In August 1597, Sillery had written Bellièvre a letter in which he said that the third estate was "truly worthy of compassion," but he had also pointed out that a decision favorable to it would have dire consequences.[10] By the terms of the decree, nobles and important royal officials were to continue to be exempted from paying the taille on the non-noble land they owned. Their leaseholders and sharecroppers were to pay, and they themselves were to help meet a few local expenses, such as the repair of roads and bridges, but that was all. The council did revoke ennoblements during the past twenty years and ordered that a search for false nobles be made, but the crown's right to create new nobles was affirmed.

The leaders of the third estate, although disappointed, did not desist in their efforts to improve the lot of the people. They attacked the vague aspects of the ruling, such as the definition of which officials were exempt from the taille. They sought to have the taille divided more equitably within their order, to expose false nobles, and to prevent new ennoblements. They tried to shift part of the tax burden from the taille to levies on the sale of wine and salt that would fall in part on the privileged. They also sought to exclude the privileged from participating in the fiscal administration. Differences among the towns continued to exist, and the relations between the towns and the villages were often tense. One factor that contributed to the latter development was the emergence of Claude Brosse as the syndic of the villages.

Brosse was the chatelain of an important noble family and styled himself seigneur of Serizin when he served as a deputy in the Estates General of 1614, but he was probably born into the third estate and early in his career espoused the peasants' cause. Around 1599, he was elected syndic of the villages and in that capacity participated in the efforts of the third estate to make the nobles contribute that had led to the decree of 1602. A man of exceptional energy, courage, and, during his early years,

devotion to his adopted cause, he was to persist in his attempt to reduce
the tax burden on the peasants, and, when the prospects of success were
more promising, to have the taille declared réelle in Dauphiné. As a result
of his efforts, he incurred the enmity of the nobility of the robe and of the
sword. To protect him from the parlement of Grenoble, the king's council
had to assume jurisdiction over cases concerning him, and in 1608 it
authorized him to carry a pistol to defend himself.

When the interests of the towns and the villages coincided, Brosse
worked with the influential burghers, but when they failed to do so, he
did not hesitate to attack them just as he did the nobles. One of the most
serious problems that confronted the villages was that they were deeply in
debt. Many of Brosse's appearances before the council were directed at
verifying and reducing both these debts and the interest rates charged.
Another of Brosse's objectives was to obtain a greater voice for the villages
in the deliberations of the province. In 1606, he complained to the king
that in the meetings of the commis, the villages had only one vote to the
ten of the leading towns, although only a tenth of the units of taxation lay
behind their walls. He asked that the villages and the towns each have five
votes and complained about the underrepresentation of the former in the
estates as well. Here the council sidestepped the request by referring the
matter to an investigatory commission then in Dauphiné.

During the Wars of Religion, taxes had often been levied without the
consent of the estates, just as in other parts of France. What was nearly
unique about Dauphiné was that the government continued this practice
after peace had been restored. This undoubtedly threatened the position
of the three estates, but its motivation was to obtain the necessary
revenue to govern the province and not, for the moment at least, to
destroy the representative assembly. The quarrel between the orders had
been so bitter that the third estate had often refused to approve any levy
unless the other estates contributed. The government was therefore
virtually compelled to order that the needed sums be collected anyway
and justified its action in terms of the widely accepted doctrine of urgent
necessity. Its goal through 1602, and probably thereafter, was not to
destroy the estates but to reconcile the differences among the orders so
that they could agree on what each should pay. Dauphiné was on Sully's
list of provinces to receive élections, but he took no steps to implement
his design. Indeed, he interfered less in Dauphiné than in most other
provinces.

Henry received very little revenue from Dauphiné. In the decade that
began in January 1600, there were three years in which the Dauphinois

paid only 720 livres into his treasury, and the maximum amount was a mere 37,888 livres. Dauphiné's taxes were spent in Dauphiné. Thus when an order was issued in Henry's name to levy a tax without the consent of the estates, it was to meet local needs, including the support of troops in the province, and not to line the king's pockets. This raises the question of who was responsible for most of the illegal taxes. The answer appears to be the duke of Lesdiguières. From the time he had become the leader of the Protestant movement in Dauphiné, he had often taxed his co-religionists and everyone else under his control without consent. He was named lieutenant governor shortly after order was restored, and it was only subsequently that it was difficult to justify taxes in terms of "urgent necessity," although the practice of ordering levies without the consent of the estates became commonplace at about this time. Sometimes Lesdiguières sought the king's permission or turned to a sympathetic sovereign court before imposing a tax, but he was widely believed to have acted unilaterally on many occasions. In the process he acquired a considerable fortune, with which he supported his clients and a small private army and embarked on an ambitious building program in Grenoble and elsewhere.

In spite of his financial exploitation of the people and his decision to throw his weight behind the nobility in the quarrel concerning the taille, Lesdiguières was not an unmitigated misfortune for Dauphiné. A man of great determination and exceptional administrative ability, he obtained such a firm hold over the province that neither Henry nor Sully thought it prudent to interfere more than necessary. Catholics and Protestants were made to live together in peace. When provincial deputations were sent to Paris, Lesdiguières dispatched letters supporting their cause, except in those rare instances when he himself was at court and could further their interests in person. When Henry was assassinated in 1610, Dauphiné was still semiautonomous, although its privileges were sometimes violated, especially in fiscal matters. However, its body politic was too divided to be capable of defending itself once its powerful protector and exploiter departed from the scene.

Organized resistance ceased in Burgundy around the close of the summer of 1595, and the reunited estates met at Dijon in January of the following year. Here they devoted most of their energies to trying to obtain a reduction in taxes. The duke of Biron, their governor, became so angered at their recalcitrance that he accused the bishop of Autun of being a better Spaniard than royal servant. Opponents of the wine tax, he declared, were serving their own interests rather than the public good and should be shut up in a cage for two or three years. In spite of this explosion, Biron proved to be a strong supporter of the estates, and the estates in return rewarded him generously for his endeavors. Together they managed to win sharp reductions in taxation and other concessions. Even an effort to audit their accounts proved less threatening than elsewhere, because the crown dispatched President Jeannin, a loyal Burgundian, to perform this task.

Meanwhile, Sully was laying plans to launch an attack on the privileges of the estates. Rumors of his plans reached Burgundy, and shortly before the estates that opened in June 1605, Jean de Souvert, a lawyer employed by the estates, published a long pamphlet in which he stressed that the most important privilege of the province was the right to have the estates, but he hinted that this privilege was threatened. Taxes too often escaped the direct control of the estates, he charged, and those collected were unwisely spent.

It is likely that the difficulty experienced in installing élus in Guyenne caused Sully to delay his attack on Burgundy, but he did not give up all of his aggressive designs. Soon after the estates had ended, he had a directive sent to the chamber of the élus in his capacity of *grand-voyer* telling them to levy a tax to repair some roads. Later, presumably at his instigation, the chamber of accounts at Dijon sought to examine the tax records of the estates since 1596, but the chamber of the élus refused to surrender the necessary documents. The worst blow fell in March 1608. The three-year grants made in the preceding assembly of the estates had expired, and the meeting for that year had not yet been held. Faced with this situation, the council directed the chamber of the élus to impose the tax for the garrison anyway.

When the estates finally opened in September 1608, those who attended were more in a mood to curtail taxes than to submit to further royal interference. They asked to be relieved of all obligation to support the garrison, protested the creation of some new offices as being contrary to their privileges, and refused to establish a fund to repair roads and bridges. Henry was voted the usual 50,000 livres, and with it came the obligation to hear the complaints of the deputies of the estates. He received them courteously, but he became angry because of their constant references to their privileges. Provinces with estates, he charged, had always deceived him. They never kept their promises. As for their privileges, "The finest privilege the people could have was to be in the good graces of their king."[11] This last thought pleased him so much that he repeated it, and the deputies departed after being told that they were like little children who asked for sugar after reciting a verse.

Henry also attacked the privileges of Dijon during the last two years of his reign by insisting that he choose its mayor from a list of the three candidates who had received the most votes. This posed a serious threat to the estates as well, because the mayor had a seat in the chamber of the élus. If he became a royal appointee, the king would control half the voting strength in that important committee.

Brittany was the last province in France to be pacified. In 1596 and again in 1597, the royalist estates had offered substantial sums to Henry if he came to Brittany at the head of an army to defeat Mercoeur, the leader of the Catholic League there, and drive the Spanish from a toehold they held in the province. When Henry finally appeared in the spring of 1598, he came with his court, not his army. He had delayed until after he reached an agreement with Mercoeur and was nearing a peace with Spain. He nevertheless sought the sum promised to support his army and a commitment from the estates to pay his Brittany-related debts, including the substantial sums he had offered the League chiefs for making peace. As he was willing to make some concessions in return, the estates voted, in addition to the customary taxes, 2.4 million livres, to be raised over a period of years by a tax on wine and salt. In 1602, 1603, and again in 1604, Henry sought to add to this burden by asking the Bretons to vote funds to redeem the alienated royal domain in the province, but the estates refused.

The Bretons' ability to block Henry's repeated efforts to have them redeem the domain must be attributed in part to the fact that unlike other provinces, they controlled the farming of indirect taxes on wine, salt, and other products. Furthermore, the money collected by the farmer of these taxes was turned over to the treasurer of the estates, not to an official of the crown, a procedure that circumvented royal efforts to misuse the funds collected. Indeed, royal fiscal officials were almost nonexistent in Brittany. The province had neither élus nor a bureau of finances. Sully was evidently tempted to correct this last deficiency, for he included among a number of fiscal proposals he considered presenting to Henry in 1604 the establishment of a bureau of finances in Brittany. Whether Sully intended this to be the first step in putting a royal fiscal administration in Brittany to replace that of the estates, or whether it should be considered merely an excuse to create more offices to sell cannot be determined, but other actions by Sully during this period suggest the former. In any case, Henry did not act on the suggestion, perhaps because the estates did offer "to negotiate" with his representatives on the subject of the domain when they met in 1605. By that time, Henry's Breton debts had been paid by the tax on wine voted in 1598, and in return for a number of concessions, the deputies agreed to continue the tax for two years at a rate estimated to yield 400,000 livres annually. This sum was designated to begin redeeming the domain in Brittany, whose value was set at 4,722,094 livres. In 1608, Henry sought a nine-year commitment to pay off the 3.6 million livres still owed on the domain, and after some haggling, the estates agreed, in the understanding that they would control how it was collected.

In spite of several setbacks, the three estates emerged at the close of the reign in good condition. The Bretons owed their success to their well-defined privileges, which took the form of a written contract with the crown, and their strong feeling of provincial loyalty (although not separatism, as has sometimes been argued). Furthermore, the estates and the sovereign courts usually cooperated to maintain their respective privileges and those of the province as a whole. Within the estates, the three orders generally worked together. Their leadership was good, and they were willing to spend generously to win influential friends.

THE ESTATES IN THE HEREDITARY LANDS

When Henry became king, a problem arose concerning the relationship between Béarn and Navarre, which he had ruled as a sovereign prince, and France.[12] There was also need to reconsider the position of Foix, Bigorre, and the other fiefs that he had governed as a vassal of his Valois sovereigns. Henry was under considerable pressure from his French subjects to incorporate these hereditary lands into the royal domain. Until he did so, there was always a chance that they would be inherited by a woman who was more closely related than the nearest male heir, who alone could inherit the crown of France. This situation left open the possibility that these strategically located territories on the borders of Spain might one day escape French control, and, through the marriage of a Navarre heiress, even pass into the hands of the Spanish Habsburgs. Nevertheless, it was only in 1607, three years after his only sister had died, that Henry incorporated the fiefs that he had held from the Valois kings into the royal domain, but at the same time he reaffirmed the independent status of Béarn and Navarre.

The Béarnais had retained the independence they so much desired, because Henry's interests coincided with their own, but on the religious issue, he proved more difficult, because he needed the support of the French Catholics and the pope. His decision to rejoin the Catholic church in 1593 raised the question of whether as a Catholic monarch he could long permit laws against his faith to remain in force in a land he ruled. At length in 1599, one year after he had granted concessions to French Protestants in the Edict of Nantes, he ordered that part of the confiscated possessions of the Catholic church be restored in Béarn, and that Catholics be permitted to worship in twelve parishes.

La Force, the governor, was at court in 1599 when Henry decided to remove most of the restrictions on the Béarnais Catholics. The clever monarch made sure that this staunch Protestant saw the necessity of making concessions in view of the need to get the strongly Catholic French parlements to accept the Edict of Nantes. When La Force returned to Pau, he was thus prepared to push the edict on the mass through the estates and conseil souverain, which served as the Béarnais parlement. The estates caused him little trouble, because the Catholics persuaded their fellow deputies that if the edict were accepted, they would make no further demands. The conseil souverain, however, proved more difficult; only after making remonstrances to the king did it register the decree in August 1599, with reservations. In spite of their promise to the estates, the Catholics sought to persuade the king to return all the former property of the church and to permit the celebration of their rites throughout the viscounty.

The Protestants countered in 1606 by including anti-Catholic provisions in the cahier and refusing to vote Henry the customary donation until he had satisfied their grievances. Henry was furious and told La Force in no uncertain terms that withholding taxes was no way to win concessions from him. The Catholics were instructed to name deputies to court to present their case alongside the Protestant delegation the estates had elected. La Force himself was also summoned.

La Force delayed going to court as long as he could in order to give the king's anger time to cool. When he finally arrived, he assumed the role of the defender of his government by mollifying the anger of the king before the deputies were heard. This time the Protestant majority won a significant concession, a grant of 6,000 livres annually from the royal purse to support their educational establishment. Nevertheless, when the estates next met, they voted to pay the Protestant deputies at court but not the Catholic bishops who had represented the minority religion. The Catholics appealed to Henry, and he ruled that since the estates had paid the Protestant deputies, they should also pay the Catholic ones. The

Protestants protested plans to admit the two bishops to the conseil souverain and to introduce Jesuits into the viscounty. The exasperated monarch forbad the estates to deal with religious matters and bluntly told the bishops that it would be better if they devoted their energies to the people of their dioceses rather than traveling to and from court with their protests. The Catholic offensive subsided, and the last two years of Henry's reign passed relatively quietly in Béarn. Henry had certainly used pressure to restore Catholicism, but the essential privileges of his subjects remained intact when he fell before the assassin in 1610.

The situation in Navarre was quite different from that in Béarn in one respect, for here the majority of the people continued to adhere to the Catholic faith in spite of the efforts of Jeanne d'Albret to convert them. Henry was far less doctrinaire than his mother and did not pursue her efforts in this respect prior to his return to Rome. In his youth his principal concern was to extract all he could from his Catholic Navarrese subjects to help support the Protestant cause or, more accurately, his own aspirations in France. His decision to have his sister, Catherine, and then La Force, both Protestants, act as his viceroys in Navarre as well as his governors in Béarn may have caused some concern, but after his reconversion to Catholicism in 1593, the Navarrese must have rested more securely.

Henry's treatment of his fiefs of the French crown in tax matters can be investigated only for the viscounty of Bigorre. As a frontier province, Bigorre claimed to be exempt from the taille and other direct taxes, but its estates graciously bestowed a donation upon their sovereign each year. In 1589, the year Henry became king, they extended themselves by giving him 9,000 livres and his sister and heir 3,000. From then until 1610, they voted him varying amounts, which dropped as low as 1,500 livres in 1602. The fluctuation in the size of the gifts during this period suggests that despite persuasion and threats, the three estates were the final determinant of the amount they gave. In April 1610, the council of finance altered this situation by decreeing that henceforth Bigorre would make an annual donation of 7,000 livres, of which they could retain 300 to pay the salaries of those who participated in their meetings.

It is difficult to escape the conclusion that Henry favored the inhabitants of these hereditary lands. They were relatively lightly taxed. Béarn and Navarre were permitted to retain their independent status, and royal officials in Languedoc were prevented from interfering in the affairs of those fiefs that were adjacent. Even the ubiquitous Sully left them to their own devices, and they were spared the horde of investigators from

Paris that so troubled the officials of the estates and towns elsewhere in France. Henry's moderation must be attributed primarily to a sentimental devotion to the land of his birth and to the people who had supported him during the Wars of Religion, although gratitude was not generally his strongest trait. He also may have believed that he could not extract enough additional money from these relatively poor lands to make it financially expedient to risk having to suppress a rebellion, which would almost certainly take place if he applied too much pressure on the estates or trampled on their privileges. Only the religious issue led to serious conflicts with the estates in the hereditary lands, and this issue appeared well on the way to being settled when he was assassinated in 1610, leaving the position of the estates intact.

THE PROVINCIAL ESTATES IN THE PAYS D'ELECTIONS

The estates in provinces where there were royal tax collectors were in a weaker position to resist the fiscal demands of the crown than those in regions where agents of the estates performed this duty. Nowhere was this truer than in Normandy, which had long contributed more to the crown than any other region of comparable size. Henry did not even begin to hold annual meetings of the Norman estates until December 1597. Prior to that year he had often imposed the desired taxes without consulting the estates. When he did hold the estates and those present voted less than the amount requested, he followed the practice of his predecessor and ordered that the élus levy the entire sum anyway. The end of the religious wars brought some reduction in taxation, but Henry continued to collect the amount he requested whether the estates voted the entire sum or not. The estates pled each year for lower taxes until 1607, when they abandoned the effort and threw themselves on the mercy of the king, with no better results than before.[13]

The weakness of the Norman estates must be attributed largely to the existence of the élus, but the failure of the leading nobles and prelates to participate actively, and their own unwillingness to vote large sums for their governors, the royal commissioners who held the estates, and other influential persons were contributing factors. In 1609, their ineffectiveness was clearly revealed in their complaint that the crown's replies to their cahiers of 1608 were "a pure extract from [their replies to] the cahiers of the preceding year."[14] The royal councillors had evidently given no consideration to their new requests or reconsidered their old ones.

The return of peace to Basse-Auvergne in 1594 brought no end to the activities of the towns. In that year the assembly of the nineteen good towns was convoked no fewer than seven times, and on two occasions the deputies of four towns met. The year 1595 was hardly less active. Included in the agenda was one meeting of the three estates. By 1596, the expense of having so many meetings was becoming intolerable, and it was decided to hold assemblies of the nineteen towns only twice a year. In case of emergency, the seven towns nearest to Clermont were to be consulted. Admirable as this resolution was, it was adhered to more in the breach than in the observance. A year during the remainder of Henry's reign in which there were not three or four full assemblies of the towns was exceptional.

The frequency of these meetings was undoubtedly owing in part to the right of the échevins of Clermont to convoke the towns, a right they exercised whenever they saw fit. At first it may seem surprising that Henry did not take away this privilege, but his own position was too precarious to attack the liberty of his subjects unless they provided him with some excuse. Clermont had been loyal during the perilous years; he now had no reason to curtail its privileges. But he did keep a careful eye on the activities of the assemblies. Basse-Auvergne, like other provinces, was visited by numerous commissioners to verify accounts and report on what they saw. Local inhabitants were also called into service. In 1590, Henry wrote a Protestant gentleman, who had been in his service prior to his ascension to the throne, to tell him "to attend the assembly of the estates of the province . . . in order to propose on my behalf and to put in deliberation what it seems to me to be necessary."[15] Manipulation more than force appears to have been the weapon designated for Basse-Auvergne.

The royalists in Forez were so outnumbered that they do not appear to have held assemblies at the height of the Catholic League's sway. After Henry's conversion, however, they became stronger, and early in 1595 the bailiff was able to summon the three estates to advise on measures to reestablish order. Separate meetings were thereafter held for the secular estates; there were about a dozen assemblies of the thirteen good towns during the remaining fifteen years of Henry's reign. At these meetings, the deputies devoted most of their efforts to the problems of arrears in taxes, the payment of debts, and the dismantling of fortifications. There were the usual protests about new taxes, the usual efforts to make the privileged orders contribute, and the usual deputations to court. From the council, on the other hand, came the usual decrees ordering that financial records be made available to and verified by designated royal officials. At times the towns acted in conjunction with the syndic of the *plat pays* of Lyonnais and the deputies of the third estate of Beaujolais. The nobles met less frequently, but they apparently had a syndic and a committee to look after their interests.

After a decade or more of struggle, what had Henry and Sully accomplished? In the provinces where the élus were already established, they took what money they needed. The estates, if any, were permitted to function provided they were not too troublesome or too costly. Only the three estates of Périgord were terminated, although most of the remainder had been weakened. But what of Sully's statement that Henry wanted the taille "to be levied in all of France in the same fashion"?[16] By the end of the reign, the élus were functioning in the newly conquered provinces of Bresse, Bugey, and Gex, and in all of Guyenne. Languedoc and Burgundy had been threatened, but they and the other provinces whose officials had collected taxes had escaped the élections. The pragmatic Henry had checked his imperious minister for fear that his measures would provoke too much opposition. Indeed, one wonders whether Henry fully shared Sully's goal of a France in which there were élus to collect taxes in every province. An adequate revenue, not uniformity, may have been his goal.

In one area Sully did infringe on the privileges of even these estates. In 1599, he was appointed to the newly created post of grand-voyer, with responsibility for building and maintaining roads, bridges, and canals throughout the kingdom. Slowly his authority was extended, and by 1605 he was in a position to act effectively. That year the amount devoted to transportation facilities jumped from a few thousand livres to over a half million, and from 1607 through 1610 an average of about a million livres was spent annually. Prior to Sully's time, the money devoted to construction and repairs had been furnished by those who used the facilities or by nearby landowners or towns, but under his direction an attempt was made to draw on the resources of the entire kingdom to support the construction of a transportation system based on the needs of the nation as a whole. The result was a major move toward a more centralized administration, which brought the crown into conflict with the provincial estates and other local authorities.

Where the provincial estates were weak, as in Normandy, Sully simply ordered that taxes be levied, despite complaints from the Norman estates. Where the estates were strong, however, serious clashes sometimes occurred. In 1608, Sully forbad the estates of Languedoc to levy any taxes for their own support unless they at the same time collected 18,000 livres to construct a bridge at Toulouse. When the estates of Brittany refused to act on a transportation request, he angrily ordered his agents to make the necessary repairs anyway and pay for them by assessing the neighboring parishes, this despite the fact that the estates had not approved the levy. On the whole, however, the strong provincial estates successfully resisted the overzealous minister, and Sully's role as grand-voyer is significant because it provides additional examples of his willingness to override the privileges of duly constituted bodies when they prevented him from obtaining his objectives. Well might he tell the English ambassador that "his master had placed him in office to encrease his revenue, and not to deliver justice."[17]

THE CONSTITUTED BODIES

Henry's relations with the towns were hardly less important than those with the provincial estates.[18] In general, he dealt with three types of towns. First, there were a handful of Protestant towns that had been allied to his cause even before he inherited the throne; second, there were some Catholic towns that had recognized him as king shortly after the death of Henry III; and finally, there were the League towns that accepted him as king only after he had abjured the Protestant faith in 1593. As the loyalty of the first two categories of towns was not in doubt, Henry was at first content to leave them alone except in a few instances, as in the case of royalist, Catholic Bordeaux, where there was already a tradition of the crown choosing the mayor. More serious was the problem of the League cities, whose towering walls and rabid citizenry presented a serious threat. To secure their recognition, Henry confirmed their privileges and even hinted that he might extend them. "I have forgotten the past, and intend to conserve the privileges, franchises, and liberties of the town of Amiens, and even augment them if I am able," he declared during his royal entry into Amiens in August 1594; this to the citizens of the League capital in Picardy.[19]

Once Henry had won recognition from the bulk of his kingdom, he felt that he was in a position to adopt a more aggressive policy. Soon after Lyons submitted in February 1594, he dispatched Bellièvre to that city to bring it firmly under royal control. Bellièvre's family had come from Lyons, but even with these ties, it took him many months to arrive at a solution. One problem was that Lyons had a huge debt. It had become customary for the incoming mayor and échevins to assume personal responsibility for the debt upon taking office. This practice made it necessary for a large number of wealthy persons to serve; only if ex-Leaguers were included could enough candidates be found. Henry solved the problem by forbidding further borrowing and arranging for the debt to be gradually liquidated by municipal taxes. He thereby made a large *échevinage* composed in part of ex-Leaguers unnecessary. Then, in December 1595, he ordered that the mayor and twelve échevins be replaced by a provost of the merchants and four échevins. By reducing the number of officials, he made it easier to control their actions and perhaps added something to the efficiency of the city government. To ensure a loyal regime, he named the provost and two of the échevins. He promised that in the future there would be free elections, but he nevertheless continued to interfere. Lyons's municipal government thus became identical to that of Paris, and it became one of the models for reforming the regimes of other cities, including Abbeville, Amiens, and Limoges.[20]

There were other ways Henry intervened to ensure cooperative municipal officials. If he was satisfied with someone's loyalty, he sometimes ordered that that person remain in office for another term. This occurred in Amiens, Dijon, Paris, and Marseilles. Sometimes he directed that three candidates for each office be elected, and he chose the one who was actually to serve, as happened in Nantes and Dijon. His choice frequently fell on royal officials, some of whom were his clients. Of the forty-one Lyons échevins between 1595 and 1610, twenty-four were royal officials. Of the approximate fifty-eight échevins who served in Orléans between 1598 and 1610, at least sixteen were royal officials.[21] Protestant and Catholic royalist towns fared somewhat better than League ones, but when there was considerable internal bickering or riots, as occurred in Limoges in 1602, Henry was capable of decisive action. Limoges found the number of its *consuls* reduced from twelve to six and its suffrage sharply curtailed. Occasionally, a town balked when he interfered in its elections. In 1599, for example, Nantes refused to elect the man Henry had designated to be mayor and dispatched a deputy to court with a list of three names that would be acceptable to them. To accept the crown's candidate, they complained, left them with "no liberty." Angered, Henry shot back a letter declaring, "I will be obeyed in this. If not, I will find both reason and means to make myself obeyed."[22]

In the first decade or so of the reign, Henry was primarily concerned with ensuring that the municipal officials would be loyal, but during the last decade, electoral intrigues and fraud claimed his attention. Alarming stories of this sort reached his ears from Poitiers, Lyons, Dijon, Marseilles, and Troyes. To combat these evils, Henry introduced the secret ballot at Poitiers, an oath by newly elected officers that they had won honestly at

Dijon, and a requirement that the names of the three candidates who had received the most votes in the mayor's election at Troyes be sent to him. He seemed to generalize this last solution in 1600 when he declared that "as in the majority of other good towns of the realm, . . . we very expressly move, order, and enjoin that before the declaration and nomination of the mayor . . . you will send me the name of three councillors who have the greatest number of votes."[23] He would choose the one to serve.

Sully was thoroughly convinced that municipal governments were rife with waste and fraud. Local officials overtaxed most inhabitants but undertaxed themselves and their friends. Large sums were spent on deputations, municipal activities, and luxurious banquets that would be better devoted to the king's service. Sully was thus determined to audit municipal accounts, just as he sought to do those of the estates. Also, the towns had fallen deeply into debt during the wars, and he was anxious to have these debts verified before they were paid. Once more he suspected fraud, inasmuch as many of the municipal creditors were also leading citizens—indeed, officers of the towns. Since it might alleviate their debts, municipal officials were not necessarily opposed to having them verified—that is, if they themselves were not the creditors. They invariably fought investigations of income and expenditures, on the other hand, because they regarded these as violations of municipal privileges and a threat to their position. The result was frequent clashes between Sully and the towns.

When a town dispatched deputies to plead its cause before the king's council, Sully was likely to subject them to brutal treatment. On March 29, 1601, a deputy from Lyons reported to his municipal government that any hope of the success of his mission rested upon the kindness of the king, because Sully had "either conceived a special hatred against this town or else he treats all the others in a similar fashion. He has dealt us a blow so astonishing that it is unbelievable. The chancellor [Bellièvre], who listens to us, dares not say a word in the council because Sully has assumed so much authority." When a question concerning custom duties arose, Sully "lost his temper and said that the town of Lyons is worthless to the king. . . . It costs him a hundred thousand écus a year. Its inhabitants are mutinous and seditious and do not want to receive the *pancarte*. . . . They have torn it down where it has been posted. . . . The king is no longer obligated to adhere to what he has granted." When an effort was made to answer Sully's charges before the council, he would not listen and shouted that most of the taxes that had been collected there had been appropriated by those who were in charge of them.[24]

Yet one must not exaggerate the progress that Henry made in obtaining control over the towns. By imposing his choice of municipal officials, he increased the chances that they would be loyal to him, but in doing so he saddled himself with urban bureaucracies that had limited influence on their fellow citizens. Even if they so desired, they were in too weak a position to impose unpopular measures. As a result, royal directives were sometimes ignored, and delaying tactics were often employed. The pancarte, a 5 percent tax on goods brought into towns, was, for example, a source of constant complaint. It never yielded more than a small fraction of the anticipated revenue, a fact that in itself suggests noncooperation, and in November 1602 it was abolished. To recover part of his losses, Henry increased the taille by 400,000 livres. Once more the towns had succeeded in shifting more of the burden of taxation onto the countryside.

Henry's reconciliation with the Catholic church was too subject to suspicion for him to dare to undermine the position of the Assembly of the Clergy. He did, however, need the financial support of the church. When he assembled the ecclesiastical deputies in Paris early in November 1595, less than a month after he was reconciled with the pope, he had Bellièvre try to persuade them to renew a contract to furnish financial assistance to the crown for the next ten years and to do something about the arrears due under the previous contract. For some time the clergy refused to renew the contract, but in the end a compromise was reached in which they agreed to pay 1.3 million livres per year for ten years in return for favorable responses to many of their demands.

In 1600, Henry attempted to extract a special grant of 600,000 livres from the clergy for his forthcoming marriage and other expenses, but in the end he had to be content with about half of the amount he requested. In 1605, he persuaded the clergy to renew their contract for another ten years and to give him 300,000 livres and his wife 100,000 because she had given France a dauphin. In 1608, Henry again asked the clergy for a special grant of 400,000 livres, and they again accorded it to him. As Henry felt himself more securely seated upon the throne, his aspirations vis-à-vis the church thus grew from simple renewal of the ten-year grant in 1595 to occasional requests for relatively small additional sums, but at no time did he risk offending the clergy in the manner he did many of his other subjects.

One incident reflects the consideration with which Henry and Sully treated the clergy, by whom they were suspect, as opposed to the way they dealt with the provincial estates and the towns. In the course of the

Assembly of the Clergy in 1605, a deputation headed by the archbishop of Tours was appointed to visit Sully. Sully received them with "all the kindness and courtesy they could desire," and when they took their leave he thanked them "with words so courteous that one could imagine nothing more gracious."[25] Perhaps it is suggestive of Sully's reputation for bellicose rudeness that the clerk thought it worthwhile to include these remarks in his journal of the assembly, but it does point to the determination of Henry and even Sully to give no offense to the clergy, although they might try to milk them a little now and then.

If the Catholic church was a source of income to Henry, the Protestants were an expense. Although they made up only 6 or 7 percent of the population, Henry knew that he would have difficulty mustering sufficient force to compel their obedience. He therefore granted the Protestants many concessions by the Edict of Nantes when their loyalty became suspect following his conversion to Catholicism. During the remainder of his reign, however, he attempted to weaken their political organization and to convert their leaders to Catholicism to make them less of a threat.

Henry's conversion led the Protestants to divide France into ten provinces, each of which was to have a council composed of the local dukes and lieutenant generals and from five to seven members elected by the provincial assembly. Among its duties were to provide for the defense of the province and to determine the tax that was to be paid by each church. The provincial assemblies were to consist of a noble, a pastor, and a magistrate elected by each colloquy in the jurisdiction. At the summit of this edifice, there was to be a general or national assembly, consisting of one deputy chosen from each of the provincial assemblies and the Protestant dukes and lieutenant generals. It was thought that the general assembly would meet once or twice a year, but from the spring of 1596 until May 1601, it was in almost continuous session.

The general assembly negotiated the Edict of Nantes, by whose terms Protestants were given freedom of conscience, the privilege of worshipping in designated places, the right to hold public office, and other concessions that were to be perpetual. It is the secret clauses of the edict, however, which were guaranteed for only eight years, that are of the most interest. In these clauses, Protestants were permitted to have about a hundred places of security, some of them very strongly fortified. To provide garrisons for these places, Henry promised an annual subsidy, not to exceed 540,000 livres. The need to keep such articles secret to avoid arousing the ire of the Catholics is readily understandable, but the eight-year limitation Henry placed upon his promise suggests that he intended to do away with the part of the bargain that guaranteed the Protestants an independent political and military existence. Henry did, indeed, quickly reduce the promised support for Protestant garrisons and displayed considerable reluctance to permit Protestants to hold political assemblies. The fact remains, however, that he created, or rather legalized, the existence of a Protestant state within a state.

In article 83 of the Edict of Nantes, Henry forbad the political assemblies in the provinces to meet, but to persuade the general assembly that had opened in 1596 to disband in 1601, he relaxed this rule and also permitted the Protestants to elect one or two deputies to represent their church at court. There were some precedents for the latter concession, but at this point the practice became standardized. Henry had to permit a general assembly to meet at Sainte-Foy in October 1601 to elect and instruct these deputies, but thereafter he felt strong enough to place additional restraints on the political activities of the Protestants. Only reluctantly did he permit a general assembly to meet at Châtellerault in 1605 to choose new deputies. The conditions he established for this meeting included the approval of a new procedure for choosing the deputies so that no further political assemblies would be necessary. The destruction of the political assemblies was to coincide with that of the provincial estates of Guyenne, but Henry was too cautious to alarm the Protestants so much that they rebelled. To give them a sense of security while he destroyed their political organization, he extended their right to hold the places of security he had granted them in the secret clauses of the Edict of Nantes until 1610.

Henry wanted the Protestants to shift the duty of electing their permanent representatives to court to the nonpolitical and less represent-ative synods so as to avoid the necessity of summoning political assemblies for this purpose in the future, but they resisted his efforts. After considerable agitation, they obtained permission to hold another political assembly in October 1608, at Jargeau, where they insisted on empowering their deputies for only two years and on hearing Henry's replies to their cahier before they disbanded. Sully, who informally represented Henry at the meeting, advised that some concessions be made—he was more sympathetic to the desires of the Protestants than he was to those of the provincial estates—and in the end they obtained part of what they wanted.

Henry was equally cautious in his dealings with the sovereign courts. On the eve and during the early stages of the Wars of Religion,

Chancellor L'Hôpital had done his best to check their ambitions and to attack the venality so dear to officeholders, but this had only made matters worse. Henry was determined not to make the same mistake, although the judges in parlement sorely tried his patience. Initially, his problem with them centered primarily in their reluctance to register his edicts on taxation, the creation of offices, alienations of the royal domain, and other matters, nearly all of which were designed to produce money to carry on the war. He explained his needs, he flattered, and occasionally he threatened, but the judges always took their time, oblivious of the military situation. "I love you as much as a king can love," he once told a deputation of judges. "My words are not of two colors. What I say is in my heart."[26] But almost in the same breath, he threatened them with a lit de justice. Parlement even balked at registering the pancarte, which had been approved by the Assembly of Notables. Yet in spite of constant provocations, Henry held only one lit de justice, on May 21, 1597, to enforce his will. He did this only after numerous letters to parlement and interviews with delegations of judges had brought no action. On one occasion, he repeatedly yelled, "I am the king! I shall be obeyed!"[27] Even the lit de justice did not bring total victory. The clerk failed to record the offending edicts in the register as directed, but the offices Henry wanted created were apparently sold anyway to support the war effort. We would have heard from him again if this were not the case.[28]

The coming of peace in 1598 reduced, but did not entirely remove, Henry's conflict with the parlement of Paris over financial matters. In 1604, for example, parlement balked at registering an edict creating offices despite five *lettres de jussion*, but Henry commenced to sell the offices before the judges finally gave in. Religious problems now proved more important causes of friction, however, and Henry had difficulty getting the Paris and provincial parlements to register the Edict of Nantes and the chambre de l'edict, which provided for some Protestant judges to participate in cases that involved their co-religionists. The judges also resisted Henry's decision to readmit the Jesuits in 1603, because they feared the Society's justification of tyrannicide and ultramontane position. In these matters, as in others, Henry finally got his way, but only after long delays and making some minor concessions. When one considers his desperate financial needs and the importance of making a satisfactory religious settlement, one can only be surprised at his restraint.

Henry had dealt directly with parlement himself, and the legally minded members of his chancellery influenced his decisions, but during the last decade or so of his reign, he left dealing with the financial sovereign courts largely to Sully. One need not be surprised to find that they fared less well than the parlements. Since nearly all royal financial offices were venal, it was very difficult to control their actions. Sully quickly came to the conclusion that most fiscal officials, including those in the sovereign courts, were dishonest, inefficient, and disobedient. He therefore gathered around himself a group of men whom he used to verify the accounts of the Parisian courts and officials, as well as those in the provinces. He even gained access to the archives of the chamber of accounts and, with Henry's backing, had one of his creatures appointed to that court. Sully's vigilance corrected many of the abuses both in Paris and the provinces. To further this work, a chamber of justice was created to investigate financial officials, including those who served in the sovereign courts. Although the chamber was composed in part of members of those bodies, they were dependent directly on the king and council, and in their activities they assumed many of the duties of the courts themselves. As a result, offers of substantial sums were soon forthcoming from the financial community in return for suppressing the chamber. The greedy king and his minister accepted, only to create a new chamber soon thereafter. In all, four such chambers were created during the reign. When functioning, they gave the crown greater control over the confused financial administration and centralized more power in Paris. Indeed, Sully seems to have contemplated subordinating the provincial chambers of accounts and bureaux of finances to those at Paris. A passion for uniformity and centralization is clearly in evidence in his administration. A shift from the traditional government through the chancellery to government through financial administration was beginning to take place, only to be cut short by Henry's sudden death. The revolutionary change was to be renewed a half-century later.[29]

JEAN BODIN AND THE
RISE OF ABSOLUTIST POLITICAL THOUGHT

Henry and Sully's hesitant absolutist moves were paralleled by a tendency to a more absolutist political theory. In the sixteenth century, there had been general agreement that power had originally belonged to the people, and the great debate was over whether the people had permanently surrendered their power when government was constituted, or whether they could resume their authority if subjected to an evil king. The former group, acting under the influence of Roman law, had grown more numerous during the first half of the century, but the French legal historians' discovery of their own ancient constitution had led to a revival of constitutionalism and a renewed analysis of the role of the estates, parlements, towns, and other corporate groups, and of the laws and customs of society. First the Protestants and then the Catholics had taken this body of knowledge and developed it into theories of resistance, which eventually became fully secular in their content. The concept of a mixed monarchy with divided sovereignty became very much in vogue. Unfortunately, the development of this constitutional theory was paralleled, or indeed largely provoked, by the religious wars. It was only natural, therefore, that some theorists began to believe that royal authority needed to be strengthened to reduce disorders. The key figure in this development was Jean Bodin.

When Bodin published his *Methodus ad facilem historiarum cognitionem* in 1566, he believed, as Julian Franklin has said, that "the civilized and proper form of sovereignty was supremacy within the law."[30] He was still confident of France's future as late as 1572, but the worsening situation soon led him to embark on a long political treatise designed to strengthen the position of the king and to crush the emerging Huguenot theory of mixed sovereignty. "Sovereignty," Bodin now declared, "is the absolute and perpetual power of a commonwealth . . . that is to say, the greatest power to command."[31]

Sovereignty could be exercised by a king, an aristocracy, or the people through the estates, but Bodin much preferred the first solution. All institutions were subordinate to the sovereign, and none of them had any independent authority. "But someone will say," he postulated, "that there could be a commonwealth in which the people appointed officials, controlled expenditures, and granted pardons, which are three marks of sovereignty; and the nobility made laws, determined on peace and war, and decided on taxes, which are also marks of sovereignty; and in addition in which there was a royal magistrate above them all to whom all the people in general and individually rendered faith and liege homage and who judged in the last resort and from whose judgment there was no appeal." Such a state, Bodin admitted, would have elements of democracy, aristocracy, and monarchy because sovereignty would be divided, but he insisted that "no such state has ever been found or could even be imagined, since the attributes of sovereignty are indivisible."[32]

Although Bodin insisted that France was a pure monarchy and that neither the estates nor any other institution had independent authority, he thought representative assemblies and other popular institutions served a useful purpose. Like most other royalist theorists of his day, he saw the Estates General as an institution that increased the authority of the king. "We conclude, therefore," he wrote, "that the sovereignty of the monarch is neither altered nor diminished by the presence of the estates. On the contrary, his majesty is much greater and more illustrious seeing that all his people acknowledge him as their sovereign."[33] Corporations, communities, and provincial estates were equally valuable to the sovereign, Bodin thought, although he admitted that tyrants feared assemblies of their subjects and sought to destroy them: "Nevertheless, the just monarchy has no more assured foundation than the estates of the people and corporate groups, because if it is necessary to levy taxes, assemble troops, or defend the state against enemies, it cannot be better done than by the estates of the people of every province, town, and community."[34] Bodin, who had studied law in Toulouse, then enumerated many of the advantages of holding the provincial estates and gave some specific examples of the activities of those of Languedoc.

To enable the king to cope with the growing disorders in France, Bodin assigned him the sole power to make human law and denied that the magnates, sovereign courts, and estates had any independent legislative authority. Nevertheless, he was not an absolutist. The king, he asserted, was under divine and natural law. These intangible concepts would not in themselves have provided much protection had he not insisted that property was a natural right, and that therefore "there is no prince in the world who has the power to levy taxes on the people at his pleasure, any more than he can take their goods." At this point, however, Bodin weakened his position by accepting the medieval doctrine that "if the necessity is urgent, the prince should not wait for the estates to assemble or the people to consent, since their safety depends on his foresight and diligence."[35] Bodin also placed the king under fundamental law and argued that he was bound by the contracts he had made, a proviso that offered some protection for provincial privileges.

In spite of Bodin's reservations, he was attacked by a Genevan for having given the king too much power. Angrily he responded in the preface to the 1578 edition of *Les Six Livres de la république* that he had been

the very first, even in the most perilous times, to refute unhesitatingly the opinions of those who write of enlarging the rights of the treasury and of the royal prerogative, on the ground that these men grant to kings an unlimited power, superior to divine and natural law. But what could be more in the interest of the people than what I have had the courage to write: that not even to kings is it lawful to levy taxes without the fullest consent of the citizens? Or of what importance is my other statement: that princes are more stringently bound by divine and natural law than those subject to their rule? Or that princes are bound by their covenants exactly as other citizens are? Yet nearly all the masters of legal science have taught the contrary. But when I perceived on every side that subjects were arming themselves against their princes; that books were being brought out openly, like firebrands to set Commonweals ablaze, in which we are taught that the princes sent by providence to the human race must be thrust out of their kingdoms under a pretense of tyranny, and that kings must be chosen not by their lineage, but by the will of the people; and finally that these doctrines were weakening the foundations not of this realm only but of all states; then I denied that it was the function of a good man or of a good citizen to offer violence to his prince for any reason.[36]

Bodin had indeed tried to provide a theoretical framework to increase the king's power so that he could cope with the civil disorders of the day and at the same time preserve the right of the estates to consent to taxation and to participate in the government. However, his acceptance of "urgent necessity" left a loophole that permitted the king to bypass the estates to obtain additional funds whenever the need arose, and his insistence on the omnipotent and indivisible nature of sovereignty imperiled their administrative role. Later theorists were to remove the safeguards that Bodin had erected. Property, in the minds of many, ceased to be a natural right and therefore could be appropriated by the king at his good pleasure. The administrative role of the estates that Bodin had praised became abhorrent. Since the estates had no independent authority to perform these functions, their work could be terminated by royal command. Gradually the theory of the divine right of kingship was joined with Bodin's theory of legislative sovereignty, and by the close of Henry IV's reign there were those who argued that "what the king wills, so wills the law."[37] The theory of absolutism began to be taught in the universities to the exclusion of the idea that power had once resided with the people. The University of Paris, once the home of the Conciliarists and then of Jacques Almain and John Major, became a center for the propagation of the absolutist theory to future lawyers and theologians for the remainder of the old regime. It is symbolic that the Renaissance funeral ceremony, with its ceremonial interregnum between the death of one king and the coronation of his successor, was not observed in 1610. The ritualistic separation of the royal dignity from the royal person was soon abandoned, and the principle that "the king never dies" became sanctified.[38]

HENRY IV, THE SWORD, THE ROBE, AND CLIENTAGE

Henry and Sully realized that it was not enough to weaken the people's instruments of self-government and to check the independent actions and corruption of royal officials. It was also necessary to create a force to counter the independent power of the subjects they feared the most: the great nobles. During the sixteenth century, the position of the nobles had steadily improved. The demographic expansion plus new creations had increased their numbers. Rising food prices, the purchase of crown, peasant, and church lands, short-term leases, and the development of the sharecropping system had strengthened their economic position, and the emergence of the patron-client relationship had enabled them to replace the decaying feudal system with a new, more flexible means of dominating society and government. Magnates had come to control the king's council, and their clients were placed in the sovereign courts, bureaucracy, army, and church. As governors, the magnates had become the most important single factor in the provinces, where they maintained their positions through the aid they received from clients serving in the estates, the local courts, the bureaucracy, and their guards. Henry could not have won his throne without their assistance, but they made him pay handsomely for their services. Once in power, he was constantly troubled by noble conspiracies. To sit securely and peaceably on his throne, he saw that it was necessary to modify the social as well as the institutional structure of his kingdom.

As in his dealings with institutions, Henry proceeded cautiously, but his plan was obvious: he would place more reliance on the men of the robe and less on those of the sword. The senior magistrates had generally been uncomfortable with the Catholic League, and once he had become a Catholic, they flocked to his standard without waiting for the generous bribes the nobility had insisted upon. Furthermore, they had no power base of their own from which to launch an assault upon the crown. Hence Henry named them in greater numbers to his council than he did the traditional nobility. Sully, of course, became his principal adviser, and he was careful to solicit the opinions of Montmorency and a few other magnates; nevertheless, his appointments reveal a marked shift toward the robe—toward men like Villeroy and Jeannin. Especially noteworthy was the appointment of eighty-eight members of the parlement of Paris to high administrative positions between 1596 and 1622.[39] Henry often named lesser royal officials to municipal offices when he had a chance, as we have seen. In doing so, he reversed the policy of his predecessors, who had feared that these officials would become more the servants of the towns than of the crown.

Henry also broke the nobility's monopoly on high positions in the church. Of the 295 Frenchmen (whose social origins can be determined) who were made bishops between 1515 and 1588, 207 were members of the noblesse de race. On the other hand, barely over half (49) of Henry's 96 identifiable French appointees were members of the old nobility. The remainder were new nobles, for the most part of the robe, and a full dozen were commoners.[40] As a further gesture toward high royal officials, Henry lumped them with the nobility of the sword in March 1600 when he "forbad anyone to take the title of *écuyer* and to insert themselves in the corps of the *noblesse* if they are not descended from a grandfather and a father who followed the profession of arms or *served the public in honorable offices* [emphasis added] that by the laws and customs of the kingdom can commence to give nobility to posterity."[41] As the decree implies, it was already customary for some offices to ennoble in time, but this was the first case of the practice being given legal sanction.

These acts clearly show Henry's desire to achieve a more balanced society by upgrading the more important judges and officials, but the power base of the great nobles lay less in their personal presence on the council and high ecclesiastical preferments than in the patron-client relationship around which their class was organized. From the time Henry believed victory was within his grasp, he had worried about the power the magnates wielded through their clients both among the nobility and in the officer corps. One danger was that Mayenne, as chief of the Catholic League, would insist on negotiating a settlement in the name of all of his supporters. Peace could be restored more rapidly and at less expense in this fashion, but Mayenne would enjoy the position of patron or factional chief of a substantial part of the French nobility and of some of the bureaucracy. As such, he would constitute an intolerable threat to the monarchy. Hence Henry sought to detach the lesser League leaders one by one until the point was reached in which Mayenne could speak only for his immediate family and clients. In March 1594, he criticized Sully for not quickly concluding arrangements for the submission of the seigneur de Villars, who held a large part of Normandy. It was better, he argued, to spend twice as much dealing separately with each individual than to achieve the same results "in a general treaty made with a single chief." In July the following year, when Mayenne's price for his submission seemed exorbitant, Henry complained that "such demands are very suspicious and make me believe that the duke of Mayenne wishes to remain a chief of party in order to have the means to agitate again when he wishes. I do not want this in my kingdom, and I hope with God's help to prevent it."[42]

Mayenne had been largely isolated when he came to terms, but Henry's concern about clientage remained. In 1596, we find him pressing the first president of the parlement of Paris to support an effort to obtain a declaration from the Assembly of Notables that royal officials should not become involved in the affairs of princes and other seigneurs. He was successful, and in their recommendations the notables asked that judicial officials be forbidden to mix in the affairs of princes and lords, to accept positions in their entourages, or to receive pensions or salaries from them. Hardly had the assembly ended before Henry issued a decree to this effect.[43] Later, in 1599, Gilles de Maupeou, a close associate of Sully's, was dispatched to Brittany to reform the chamber of accounts. In the edict that resulted, Henry forbad officers of the chamber "to take any office, salary, pension, or gift from princes, seigneurs, and other persons, or to undertake any mission or solicitation in their behalf on pain of being deprived of their offices and arbitrarily fined." Furthermore, when they accepted their positions, they were to "take an oath to observe the contents of the above."[44]

It was with these concerns in mind that after over two years of debate within his council, Henry issued an edict in December 1604 creating the *paulette,* or *droit annuel,* which provided that nearly all royal officials could resign or bequeath their positions to any qualified person they pleased in return for an annual payment of a sixtieth part of the value of their office. Henry thus made his already venal, semihereditary bureaucracy hereditary. Bellièvre had put forth persuasive arguments against this move. By making offices hereditary, he insisted, deserving people would be denied positions, the quality of the bureaucracy would be lowered, hopes of reducing its size would cease, and royal control would be reduced, because its members would no longer be subject to dismissal or hopeful of advancement.

Bellièvre's thoughtful arguments did have some effect. Henry was clearly impressed by the possibility that he might not be able to control such a well-entrenched bureaucracy, and a Parisian diarist shared these fears, a fact that suggests that many ordinary citizens were of the same opinion. It was probably for this reason that Henry exempted a few high officials, including the first presidents of the sovereign courts, from the provisions of the paulette and limited the concession to the remainder to a period of nine years. Officers would thus know that if they failed to cooperate, the paulette might not be renewed. Furthermore, Henry, and more certainly Sully, had a contempt for the men of the robe, and they may have blamed part of the sovereign courts' resistance to their measures on the backing they received from the magnates and the provincial estates. Remove the magnates' influence from the bureaucracy and undermine the estates. Then the spineless lawyers and bureaucrats would become more amenable to the royal will, whether their positions were hereditary or not.

The question remains, why did Henry gamble on the paulette? One motive was obviously money. Sully anticipated that the measure would net an additional 400,000 livres annually. Although his financial position was better than it had been, and Sully had begun to amass a surplus in the Bastille, Henry was still heavily in debt, and there were constant demands on the treasury. A second motive was to please the bureaucracy. Prior to the paulette, bureaucrats could resign their offices in favor of an heir or someone else, but this was valid only if one did so at least forty days before one's death, an event not always easy to anticipate. As long as the forty-day rule remained in effect, an investment in an office was not safe. With the paulette, it was. The paulette was one more measure that Henry approved to win the support of important judges and officials as a counter to the power of the magnates. It should be coupled with his decision to give nearly half the bishoprics to such families and to legalize the custom of ennobling officeholders.

Henry and Sully also had a third motive. If offices became hereditary, the magnates would have fewer opportunities to place their clients in the bureaucracy. As we have seen, Henry was worried about this practice, and the Biron conspiracy had just failed, but only after again revealing the threat of clientage. Sully told Richelieu that the principal purpose of the paulette was to reduce the great nobles' influence in the bureaucracy. In the heyday of the League, the duke of Guise especially had owed much of his power to the support of his clients in the royal administration. Impressed, Richelieu advised Louis XIII "that the suppression of the sale and heritability of offices would conform with both reason and all concepts of good government, but the inevitable abuses which would result from the distribution of appointments on the simple basis of the king's wishes and consequently on the favor or cunning of those most influential with him, makes the present system more tolerable than the appointive one which formerly prevailed."[45] By 1614, the paulette was being publicly defended as an attack on clientage, and the usually well informed Jacques-Auguste de Thou attributed the paulette in part to the king's desire to escape the importunities of avaricious courtiers seeking offices for their clients.[46]

Although Henry wanted to reduce the magnates' influence in the royal bureaucracy, he was not opposed to clientage per se. Indeed, he relied on the clientage networks of his governors and lieutenant generals to establish and maintain order in the provinces. Before he could entrust this delicate task to them, however, it was necessary to relieve them of some of the pretensions they had developed during the religious wars. Prodded by a group of magnates, the youthful and stupid duke of Montpensier had the gall to approach Henry with the proposition that the governments be made hereditary property, for which the holders would render simple liege homage. In return they would furnish a well-equipped army when required. Henry tactfully but firmly rejected this amazing suggestion, which, if accepted, would have returned the monarchy to the days before Philip Augustus. He was equally unsympathetic to Biron's proposal that he be given Périgord in full sovereignty. Where League governors had established firm bases in their governments, as Mercoeur had in Brittany and Mayenne in Burgundy, they were replaced. The young duke of Guise was given Provence rather than one of the governments that members of the house of Lorraine had previously held, but once such obvious precautions had been taken, Henry set about doing all he could to restore the authority of his governors. When, in 1597, the estates of Haute-Auvergne sent a deputation to court to plead for lower taxes, Henry gave his council instructions to give as favorable a response as possible. Their new governor had interceded, and Henry wanted him to seem an effective spokesman on their behalf at court so that he would be better obeyed.[47]

Henry apparently assumed that the governors would spend most of their time in their governments, as they had during the religious wars. In general, he believed that nobles should reside on their estates.[48] The lure of Paris, however, drew them to that city. Henry himself lived there far more than his Valois predecessors had done. With the court in the capital, Paris became an almost irresistible attraction, and great nobles who did not already have hotels in the city began to acquire them. The city became the center of culture and boasted a more lively social life than any country seat could hope to offer. There court patronage was dispensed and marriage alliances could most conveniently be arranged. There legal business could best be conducted and loans negotiated with bankers, who shifted the center of their operations from Lyons to the capital. The great nobles' move to Paris was a gradual one, and a few continued to prefer the provinces, where they could be lords and masters. Lesdiguières built a fortified residence in Dauphiné, which he is reported to have stocked with equipment for three thousand horse and ten thousand foot soldiers, and Epernon built a huge château on the banks of the Garonne. Nevertheless, every major governor who was appointed between 1605 and 1650 had a residence in Paris, and it became the principal abode of most. This shift eventually loosened the ties between the magnates and the country gentlemen from whom they had once derived so much strength.

Other changes also tended to weaken the vertical ties that had held society together. The paulette made many offices hereditary, and the venal positions that did become available became too expensive for the average noble to purchase. Magnates continued to use their influence to obtain the offices that remained at the disposal of the king, but there were fewer such opportunities than before. Even the captaincies of châteaux and forts became less plentiful as one by one many of those in the interior were abolished. Then, too, whereas the sons of important provincial nobles had once received their educations while serving as pages in great noble households, they now began to send them to the new academies and colleges. Once lord and vassal, noble and client, had known each other well and were often close friends. Now they became bare acquaintances.[49]

It must be stressed that these changes were only beginning to take place during Henry's reign, and the clientage system only slowly weakened. If social changes were so slow as to be barely perceptible, administrative changes were not. Perhaps more than any of their predecessors, Henry and Sully used special officials to implement their wills. Some were maîtres de requêtes or royal councillors; others were councillors in the parlements or treasurers in the bureau of finances in various généralités. To them should be added the lieutenants Sully sent out in his capacity of grand-voyer and grand master of the artillery, who were more active than even the agents of the king. Some of these men were given commissions with wide powers and remained in one region for several years. Others were given specific tasks, such as to audit accounts, reform the estates, construct or repair transportation facilities, or supervise the farming of the salt tax in a given region. They were clearly the ancestors of the future intendants, but no one considered them rivals of the governors at this time. A few were actually the clients of governors, and some were appointed at the governor's request. The low position they were assumed to occupy is suggested by the fact that they shared much less significantly in the largess of the estates than did the governors.

Henry did try to curb the worst offenses of his governors and military commanders. Through his council, he issued repeated edicts during the Wars of Religion forbidding them to seize his revenues or levy taxes without his permission, but as late as 1598, Sully had to persuade a timorous council to halt a tax of some 180,000 livres that the powerful, ill-tempered duke of Epernon had imposed on his government on his own authority. With the restoration of peace, and under Sully's vigorous administration, the number of such abuses was reduced, and the magnates were denied one source of income. Henry was not guilty, however, of leaving them to their own resources. During the quieter years of his reign, he devoted about 15 percent of his budget to pensions, and there were other forms of largess as well.[50]

It apparently never occurred to Henry to increase the size of his army so that he could impose his will on his people. Indeed, as soon as his war with the League and Spain had ended, he drastically reduced the number of men under arms. In Brittany, for example, there were a dozen garrisons in 1599, whose combined strength totaled only 400 men, this despite the fact that Bretons were among the most provincially minded people in France and the bulk of them had recognized Henry as king only the year before. By 1608, even this paltry figure had been reduced to 300 men. To strengthen his control over the few troops he did have, Henry reduced the appointive powers of the colonel general of the infantry. It is probable that he intended to let this position and that of constable remain vacant when the current occupants died.

The artillery was the one important area in which military changes were made that may actually have contributed to the rise of absolutism. In 1599, Sully was appointed grand master of this important arm, and he was soon making full use of his new post. Most of his plans were directed toward being prepared for foreign wars, and it was largely owing to his efforts that campaigns against Savoy and Sedan were terminated so quickly. He also had a political motive: to keep artillery out of the hands of potential rebels. In 1605, Henry declared that "to us alone belongs the right to possess artillery,"[51] but Sully had long since begun to implement this policy. Supplies of powder and ball were stored in border arsenals, but most of the cannon were kept in Paris under Sully's watchful eye. From here they could be dispatched to the nearby northeast frontier in case of need. To further his plan, Sully did his best to make his guns more mobile. One reason Biron's conspiracy failed so miserably was that Sully had withdrawn the artillery from his government of Burgundy and had horses and men ready in Paris and Lyons to bring the royal guns into action if the situation so required. In 1603, Ornano assured Henry that cannon could be quietly withdrawn from Catholic towns and châteaux in Guyenne, and he noted, perhaps disapprovingly, that those in Protestant strongholds were not to be touched. It was not by the expensive process of creating a large army that Henry planned to impose his will, but rather by removing the capacity of his subjects to offer effective resistance to his limited forces.

Too much significance has been attached to the destruction of the châteaux-forts after the Wars of Religion. Very few of them had the thick, low, wide-angle bastions necessary to withstand artillery fire and to mount guns to keep the enemy at bay. They were no threat to an army equipped with artillery and therefore no danger to the monarchy itself. However, a château-fort that fell into the hands of malcontents or brigands could serve as a base for murder, rape, and pillage, especially because local officials who were without artillery had difficulty mounting effective sieges. In the Estates General of 1588, the nobility asked that the owners of fortified places guard them more carefully, and the other estates petitioned for their demolition. In 1590, the royalist estates of Burgundy told one noble lady to drive the thieves from her châteaux, who were plundering the countryside, and asked that some fortresses be dismantled. In 1593, the League estates of Burgundy forbad anyone to construct fortifications or make cannon, and they renewed an earlier injunction that proprietors of châteaux guard them at their own cost or dismantle them. Thus whether royalist or Leaguer, whether clergyman, noble, burgher, or peasant, Frenchmen wanted the châteaux guarded or dismantled. The provincial estates frequently moved more rapidly in this direction than the crown, and the only debate was over who should pay the costs of demolition.

The efforts of the crown to halt the practice of dueling should not be regarded as an attempt to weaken the nobility; rather, they were designed to preserve members of that class from self-destruction. During the Estates General of 1588, the nobles themselves asked that the death penalty be imposed on duelists. In April 1602, Henry published an edict forbidding anyone to issue a challenge, accept a challenge, or serve as a second in a duel. Soldier that he was, however, he found one excuse or another to pardon those who disobeyed his decree. Little wonder he had to issue another edict on the same subject in June 1609, in which he admitted that his earlier attempt to curb this form of violence had failed. This time he attempted to find a judicial means of settling affairs of honor, and among the possible punishments for infraction of his rule were loss of office, pension, and revenue. A nobleman, it seems, could more properly fear such penalties than the loss of his life.

One of Sully's accomplishments that certainly contributed to the strengthening of the monarchy was his successful effort to make it financially solvent. In 1596, expenses were three times income. By 1600, the budget was balanced, and by 1610, a surplus of 15 million livres had been amassed. Furthermore, foreign and domestic debts had been reduced and steps had been taken to redeem the domain by 1625.

More controversial were Henry and Sully's attacks on the provincial estates, towns, Protestant political assemblies, and, to a lesser extent, the sovereign courts. But except for destroying the estates of Périgord, establishing élus in Guyenne, Bresse, Bugey, and Gex, and interfering in some municipal elections, they made little headway toward undermining the duly constituted corporate bodies that stood in the way of an unimpeded exercise of royal authority. What they did accomplish was enough to make their goals apparent, however, and to alienate many influential groups. The establishment of a hereditary bureaucracy weakened the influence of the magnates, but it strengthened the capacity of royal officials to resist the crown. Contemporaries clearly recognized the evils of the system, and it was unpopular in many circles.

Sully envisioned a centralized, absolute monarchy in which the provinces would be administered in a uniform manner. It is doubtful whether Henry sought more than a secure seat on his throne and ample revenue to govern effectively and pursue his pleasures. When the deputies who came to court talked of their privileges, he became infuriated, but he often held Sully in check when he sought to undermine those very privileges. Perhaps Henry feared the opposition that the enactment of Sully's proposals would cause, or perhaps he did not fully share his minister's goals. In either case, and in spite of his great accomplishments, there was intense dissatisfaction in many circles at the time of his assassination. With his death the question became one of what direction the inevitable reaction would take and how far it would go.

VI

The Reprieve, 1610–1620

MARIE DE MEDICI AND VILLEROY

When Henry IV was assassinated on May 14, 1610, he left as his heir a child who had not yet celebrated his ninth birthday. A regency was clearly necessary, and the queen mother, Marie de Medici, was quickly installed in this office. Marie was then about thirty-six years old. The daughter of a grand duke of Tuscany and an Austrian Habsburg, she inherited her physical traits from her mother. Tall, blonde, and handsome, until she added the countless pounds that Reubens was to paint, she had proved a satisfactory wife to Henry in one key respect. In less than ten years of marriage, she had borne him six children, including two sons who were to survive to manhood. On the other hand, although honorable and loyal, she was jealous, quarrelsome, and rather stupid. She loved power, because it placed her in the center of things and provided the money to support her extravagances, but she had little concept of how to govern and had to follow the directions of her advisers.[1]

The magnates flocked to court with their numerous clients to render homage to their new king and see what profit they could win in the new state of affairs. Marie admitted them to an enlarged council but retained Henry's four principal advisers—Sully, Brûlart de Sillery, Jeannin, and Villeroy—in an inner council that continued to exercise the primary role in the governance of the kingdom. She had little love for Sully, but she recognized his financial ability and anticipated that his presence in the inner council would reassure the Huguenots. It was necessary to have a good fiscal administration to keep the money flowing from the provinces to Paris, so that the court rather than the officials in the country could profit from royal taxes. However, Sully made many enemies because of his overbearing manner and his insistence on economy. Villeroy plotted to remove him from office, and soon Sully was faced with a choice of resigning or exercising his office in accordance with the desires of the dominant clique at court. On January 26, 1611, he chose the former course and withdrew to his estates.

Sully's departure left Villeroy the undisputed leader of the inner council. For over fifty years he had served the crown, for the most part as secretary for foreign affairs, but now at sixty-seven he was to have the dominant voice in domestic matters as well. Like Bellièvre, he believed that the provincial estates, municipal governments, and other duly constituted bodies derived their authority from the king and should serve as instruments of his policy. For this reason he had no objection to using them when the situation warranted. This emphasis on royal authority should not be interpreted as meaning that Villeroy was an advocate of absolutism. He believed that kings were bound by their own laws in theory and forced to take into consideration the aspirations of their more powerful subjects in practice.

In a memorandum he prepared for Marie de Medici in 1611, Villeroy faced the realities of governing during a minority. In his view, France was still a personal, rather than a bureaucratic, monarchy, in which nearly everything depended upon the king's ability to isolate and placate the magnates, whom he regarded as the most important forces in the kingdom. He began by saying that those who formed leagues against the sovereign should be punished, but then quickly added that "inasmuch as it is difficult and dangerous to chastise the magnates, the queen must use the following means to weaken them."[2] Condé must be prevented from assuming a position of authority in the council and from making alliances with the other magnates. The magnates should be kept divided by playing on their mutual jealousies, and the nobility should be placated by pensions. Ties should be established with the princes' ministers and favorites and with others who could prevent them from executing their evil designs. In direct opposition to the tactics later used by Louis XIV, Villeroy suggested that the magnates (except Condé) be sent to their individual governments so that they would have more difficulty in forming alliances than if they remained at court. Negotiations should be commenced with the Huguenots to ascertain their designs, and care should be taken to prevent them from joining Condé. Pensions should be given to influential seigneurs in the provinces, and they should be forbidden to follow the princes. Requests that princes made for their clients should be refused, and these clients should be directed to address themselves directly to the queen mother, so that she would receive credit for any favors granted. Agents should be placed in the princes' entourages to report on their activities, and the governors of citadels and towns should be won to her cause in provinces whose governors were united against her service. The royal guards and cavalry companies should be enlarged—not to discourage revolts but to provide employment for the nobility. In this way, Villeroy sought to keep the magnates divided and isolate the prince of Condé, who as first prince of the blood had some claims to being named lieutenant general of the kingdom. Every effort was to be made to use the crown's patronage to build up a large clientele and to make the clients of the princes beholden directly to the queen mother for any favors they received.

Absent from Villeroy's reasoning was any fear of the other elements of the population. "The disease is not, thank God, with the people of the country or of the towns, or with the parlements, the ecclesiastics, or all the nobility."[3] Such persons, he implied, could be counted on to remain loyal provided that they were permitted to enjoy their traditional privileges without undue royal interference and without increases in taxation. Marie de Medici did not wait to receive Villeroy's memorandum before increasing the pensions and household expenses of the royal family to the profit of the aristocracy, and she was careful not to increase taxes.

Villeroy had been fearful that the Protestants would become involved in the magnates' plots and was therefore anxious to preserve Henry's religious settlement, staunch Catholic though he was. The Protestants nevertheless became alarmed at a proposal to marry Louis to a Spanish princess and one of his sisters to the heir to the Spanish throne. With Sully's departure from court, they no longer had a member of their faith in the inner council of the government. It was with growing concern that their deputies assembled at Saumur in the spring and summer of 1611. To calm their fears, Marie extended the time for which they could have places of security for another five years and promised to continue to provide financial support, but this was not enough, and those present took steps to strengthen their political and military organization.

The magnates also remained dissatisfied, and in January 1614, Condé turned from conspiracy to open revolt. Among his demands was that the Estates General be convoked. In March, Villeroy addressed another memorandum to the queen mother, in which he argued that the outcome of a trial of strength was so uncertain that it was advisable to make handsome gifts to Condé and his supporters. To minimize the danger that they would win additional support, he recommended that the government renew the promises it had made to the Protestants and summon the Estates General to undertake a general reformation of the kingdom. Matters such as the retrenchment of venality of offices and the abolition of the paulette should be considered. Marie followed Villeroy's advice, and by the terms of the Treaty of Sainte-Menehould (May 1614) she gave Condé and his allies generous rewards. On February 22, she had had to withdraw half of the five million livres Henry and Sully had stored in the Bastille, and by August it was all gone. The hoard her son had inherited had been dissipated, but bloody civil wars had been avoided.

THE ESTATES GENERAL AND THE ASSEMBLY OF NOTABLES

As part of the agreement with Condé, Marie convoked the Estates General. She probably had no objection to doing so. Villeroy and most other Renaissance statesmen approved of assemblies, provided they were held under circumstances favorable to the crown. To make certain that this would be the case, Marie embarked on a tour of the western provinces with her son to quell discontent and ensure that deputies favorable to her cause were elected. Rohan warned Condé that the queen mother would control the estates, because "those on whom you count will abandon your cause." "Fear and hope are the two great factors which influence the members of these assemblies; you are neither in a position to promise them much or to frighten them."[4] Condé appears to have arrived at the same conclusion, for he declared that it would be unnecessary to hold the Estates General, but Marie, confident, persisted in her plan. She held a lit de justice at which Louis, now in his fourteenth year, was declared to have reached his majority. He in turn named her his chief of council, and together they participated in the opening of the estates in Paris on October 27.

Marie's confidence proved justified. Condé soon found that he had very little influence in the estates, but Marie herself had to watch the deliberations carefully to be certain that the deputies did not unite behind a common program. Early in the session, the clergy proposed to the other two orders that when they were in agreement on a matter of general interest, they should immediately submit a joint petition to the king so that he could respond before their departure. If this were done, the lengthy cahiers each estate had submitted in previous meetings just before returning to their homes would be transformed into individual "bills" approved by the three "houses" and submitted to the king in council for immediate action. Marie and her advisers saw the danger and summoned deputies from each of the estates to inform them that the traditional procedures would be followed. Opposition to the clergy's proposal had already appeared among the third estate, where numerous Gallicans thought that it was a trick to win their cooperation for securing the publication of the decrees of the Council of Trent and the establishment of the Inquisition in France. Under these circumstances, they readily accepted Marie's decision. Another possible danger the Estates General posed for the crown passed, and thereafter when the three estates dealt with controversial problems, they often had difficulty reaching agreement.

The first important clash occurred over the related questions of venality of offices and the paulette. Since the institution of the latter, the price of offices had skyrocketed, because making them hereditary had removed the danger that premature death would lead to the loss of the investment. The nobility regarded offices as their due and saw no reason to pay inflated prices for them, even when they could afford to do so. Hence they asked that many positions be reserved wholly or in part for their order and that steps be taken to abolish the paulette. The clergy concurred, thereby putting the deputies of the third estate in a difficult position. Most of them had been elected in bailiwick assemblies in which the burghers and the deputies of the villages were the most numerous elements. Both opposed venality and had often instructed their deputations to the Estates General to have the practice abolished. In many instances, however, they had chosen royal officials to be their representatives, because they were usually the best-known local notables and were more willing to attend than busy merchants and farmers. As a result, deputies of the third estate were often caught in a position in which their mandates made it necessary for them to assist the nobility and clergy in their effort to abolish venality, but to do so would transform their offices from a form of property into insecure salaried positions.

To escape from this dilemma, the deputies of the third estate coupled their request for the abolition of venality with a plea that the taille be reduced by 4 million livres. Since the acceptance of the two proposals would cost the crown 5.6 million livres annually, they recommended that pensions be cut by a comparable amount. As this figure was about the size of the budget for pensions, acceptance of the proposal would mean the virtual abolition of this valuable addition to the nobles' income. The nobles, therefore, insisted that the proposals be treated separately, although they were willing to accept a reduction in the amount spent on pensions. A bitter quarrel ensued, which was carried on in pamphlets as well as in the debates of the estates. As we have seen, Villeroy had recommended that the nobles be placated in the matter of the offices before the estates met. It is not surprising, therefore, that on March 24, after the formal closing of the estates, the chancellor informed those deputies who were still in Paris that the king would reduce pensions and suppress the paulette and venality of offices.

Preliminary moves against the paulette had already led to strong remonstrances from the sovereign courts. The reaction of the members of the parlement of Paris to this blow was rapid. On March 28, they invited the princes, dukes, and officers of the crown to meet with them to discuss affairs of state. The king forbad the meeting, but agitation in the sovereign courts continued even after the crown postponed the abolition of venality until January 1, 1618.

The second clash was between the deputies of the clergy and those of the third estate. The latter attributed the assassination of Henry IV largely to Jesuit and other ultramontane theorists who stressed the ultimate authority of the pope and justified tyrannicide. To counter this position, the third estate proposed as the first article of its cahier that the king promulgate in the estates a fundamental law stating that since he "holds his crown from God alone, there is no power whatever on earth, whether spiritual or temporal, which has any rights over his kingdom."[5] In response to this proposal, Cardinal Perron made a famous speech in the chamber of the third estate in which he condemned the doctrine of tyrannicide but insisted that subjects were justified in rebelling if a king violated his oath to live and die as a Catholic or sought to introduce an alien doctrine into his kingdom. If such a situation arose, the church could absolve subjects from their oath of allegiance. Perron chided the deputies of the third estate for interfering in matters of faith, and the clergy, aided by the nobility, begged the king to forbid them to do so.

The third estates' advocacy of this article should not be construed to mean that they favored absolutism. In other parts of the cahier, they asked that the Estates General be convoked every ten years and that municipal officials be freely elected, a reference no doubt to the interference of Henry and his governors in such matters. They were also anxious that local institutions be granted authority to levy taxes to support their activities without having to obtain the crown's approval. "Each seneschalsy and diocese," they argued, should be permitted "to impose upon itself for its affairs, by the general consent and deliberation of the deputies, an amount up to 3,000 livres, and . . . episcopal and presidial towns should be permitted to impose for their affairs, with the advice and consent of their inhabitants, 1,500 livres, and other royal towns, 600 livres, small towns, 300 livres, and parishes, 50 livres."[6]

The nobility requested that their order and the clergy be authorized to meet in each province once every three years to elect syndics to look after their respective affairs. They apparently thought that the third estate already had this privilege. If this article had been implemented, they would have been organized on a corporate basis in every province in the kingdom with a permanent elected official to defend their interests. The élus, the nobles argued, should be suppressed throughout France, but the third estate should not be permitted to levy any taxes, except those of the king, without their consent and that of the local clergy. To ensure the independence of the provincial and local estates, the nobles also requested that judicial officers not be permitted to attend unless the bailiff or seneschal could not be present. If this situation arose, the role of the lieutenant of the bailiwick was to be limited to reading the royal letter and making known the king's intentions. The clergy, already so well organized at the diocesan and national level, had no need to make such requests.

One of the most interesting facets of the cahiers was the attitude of the nobility to the patron-client relationship. Instead of defending or at least ignoring the system, the nobles made proposals that would have undermined it had they been implemented. For example, to prevent magnates from using royal patronage to enlarge the number of their clients, they requested "that no pensions, offices, or other gifts be given in the future through the intercession of the princes and seigneurs of your kingdom, so that those who have them will be bound entirely to your majesty."[7] To prevent magnates from using their own resources to expand their influence to the bureaucracy, they asked that royal officials be forbidden to receive pensions and other presents from them. Judicial officers ought to be specially forbidden to become involved in the magnates' affairs, because it would divert them from rendering justice.

It seems clear that most of the deputies of the nobility preferred to be beholden directly to the king for any favors they might receive. To have to bind themselves to a prince to receive a royal office or a pension might lead to their being required to follow their patron down the dangerous road to rebellion. It should be borne in mind that the great magnates themselves did not sit in the estates. Those who served belonged to the leading local families. Many were bailiffs, officers in the army, gentlemen of the king's chamber, members of his household or the conseil d'état, and the like. They were not, then, potential dispensers of patronage on a large scale, but they were either already beneficiaries of royal largess or sufficiently prominent that they might reasonably hope to become so.

Their cahiers reveal that it lay within the power of the king to assume direct control over royal patronage, as Villeroy had suggested, bypass the magnates, and dispense his favors directly to them. They in turn would become his majesty's loyal clients and hold the countryside in his obedience. It is strange that so many years were to elapse before this was done on a large scale.

Marie did nothing to implement the desires of the estates. Her failure to act proved costly. The parlement of Paris was not placated by the decision to postpone the abolition of the paulette until January 1618. On May 22, it boldly assumed a political role by demanding that many of the reforms advocated by the estates be enacted. Concurring, Condé again raised the banner of revolt. This time the Protestants in Languedoc, Guyenne, and Poitou lent some assistance. Once more Villeroy counseled negotiations and once more, this time in May 1616, Condé made peace in return for huge gifts for himself and his fellow nobles, albeit little enough for his Protestant allies, who were fast learning the wisdom of not tying their fortunes to the magnates.

That spring and summer, Villeroy and the other leading advisers of Henry IV were dismissed. They were all in their seventies, but the main reason for their downfall was not their age but the desire of Concino Concini, Marie's Italian favorite, to have men in the ministry who were more devoted to his service. Claude Barbin, the intendant of Marie's household, assumed responsibility for finances in May. Claude Mangot, the first president of the parlement of Bordeaux, became first a secretary and then in November, keeper of the seals. At the same time, Armand du Plessis, bishop of Luçon, and future cardinal of Richelieu, was made secretary for foreign affairs and war.

The new ministers did not have to wait for the appointment of Richelieu to embark on a bolder course than their predecessors. On September 1, they had Condé arrested. The dukes of Nevers, Mayenne, Bouillon, and other allies of Condé raised the standard of revolt, but this time instead of negotiating, the government dispatched three armies in their direction. Unfortunately, the new ministers neglected to note the growing animosity of the neglected young king, now in his sixteenth year, and the influence that Charles d'Albert, seigneur de Luynes, his falconer, exercised over him. Encouraged by Luynes and others, Louis had Concini murdered on April 24, 1617. Barbin and his ministers were dismissed, and Marie de Medici lost her leading role in the government. Luynes became the new favorite, and Villeroy was recalled with the other aging ministers of Henry IV. The magnates who professed to be fighting to rid

France of the foreign favorite seized the opportunity to make peace, although without such generous gifts as before.

The problems that confronted Villeroy and his colleagues when they returned to office were identical to those they had faced before they were ousted, except that the time that had elapsed made their solution more imperative. The cahiers of the deputies to the Estates General of 1614 still had not been acted upon. Failure to do so gave the magnates the excuse to rebel in the name of reform. This was especially true because, in May 1616, Condé had been promised that an edict based on the cahiers would be published within three months. Then there was the paulette, which was scheduled to expire at the end of the year, to the chagrin of the royal officials. If this were permitted to happen, revenue from the sale of offices would decline at a time when expenditures were already exceeding ordinary revenue by from five to seven million livres annually.

Villeroy left no memorandums advising Luynes what to do, but we can assume with reasonable confidence that he wanted to placate the nobility by abolishing the paulette, as the king had promised to do after closing the Estates General. He may have also recalled the prediction that Bellièvre had made in 1602 that if the paulette were established, it would weaken the king's authority. The recent effort of the parlement of Paris to expand its role from making remonstrances concerning royal edicts to summoning the magnates to a meeting to instigate a general political reformation suggested that his former colleague had been an all-too-successful prognosticator. The financial situation made economies, including a reduction in pensions, necessary. If venal officials were certain to oppose the abolition of the paulette, magnates were sure to try to block financial reform that affected them adversely. There was also confusion over the duties and personnel in the various councils of the king, which had worsened during the regency. Changes that excluded a magnate or his clients would arouse their opposition. Faced with this situation, Villeroy and his colleagues adopted a typical Renaissance solution: they would hold an Assembly of Notables in which the sovereign courts and nobles would be persuaded of the necessity of reform. As good and loyal subjects, they would accept the required personal sacrifices, or at least enough public pressure could be brought to bear to make them do so.[8]

Since it was the nobility and the bureaucracy who were selected to make the sacrifices, there was no need to summon representatives from the towns or a large number of financial officials, as had been done in 1596. Villeroy evidently wanted a smaller, more manageable assembly. To guide the deliberations, he and his colleagues prepared a list of twenty propositions they wanted the notables to consider. As the members of the sovereign courts who attended outnumbered the nobles by about two to one, it is not surprising that the assembly advocated cutting pensions by three million livres but rejected a proposal to create a special itinerant court to judge complaints against the various parlements and their members. The assembly refused to endorse the abolition of the paulette, but Louis was adamant on this score.

As might have been anticipated, neither the court nor the nobility was willing to accept the proposed economies, which would cost them so dearly, and the royal officials persisted in their efforts to get the paulette renewed. No ordonnance based on the advice of the Estates General and Assembly of Notables was issued, and the deficits continued. In March 1619, to raise money, Louis abandoned all pretense of trying to redeem the domain and alienated what remained of the part that Sully had repossessed. In 1620, he reinstated the paulette—in part to ensure the loyalty of the sovereign courts during this time of troubles and in part to increase the revenue he received from the parties casuelles. The terms under which he renewed the paulette were so unfavorable to the bureaucracy, however, that the parlement of Paris refused to participate. Nevertheless, a combination of the renewal and the new offices he created for revenue purposes increased the yield from the parties casuelles to over thirteen million livres in 1620, nearly four times what it had been the year before.

In 1620, then, the situation was far less favorable to the crown than it had been in 1610 when Henry IV and Sully were still at the helm. But what of the provincial estates? Did they, like the magnates, profit from the departure of that remarkable pair to assume a more independent role, or did Villeroy, who died in December 1616, and his colleagues adhere to the policies of their former master in this regard?

THE ESTATES IN GUYENNE

The provincial estates in Guyenne had done all in their power to prevent the implementation of the decree in January 1603 establishing eight new élections in the généralité. They had turned to the sovereign courts to secure delays; they had threatened local royal officials and others favorable to the decree; they had sought the support of their sympathetic governor, the king's mistress, and other influential persons; they had offered to reimburse the élus if their offices were suppressed, but all to no avail. By 1609, the élus were established everywhere in the généralité, and on November 21 of that year, the king's council once more rejected a

financial offer in return for the suppression of the élections. So determined were the provincial leaders to defend their liberties, however, that
neither this rejection nor the death of their beloved governor in January
1610 terminated their efforts. Perhaps taking their cue from the council's
statement that the élus had been created to prevent taxes from being
levied without the king's consent and to curb other disorders, the estates
now set about discrediting the élus by showing that their fiscal administration was more reprehensible than their own.

Hardly had their petitions been rejected in November 1609 than the
deputies of the various provincial estates in Guyenne charged that the
élus were imposing unauthorized taxes to increase their own income. The
council referred the matter to the treasurers of the bureau of finances at
Bordeaux, who thereupon launched an investigation. Their findings, as
the estates had anticipated, were that the élus were at least as inefficient
and dishonest as the officials of the estates. By February 1610, the
treasurers had begun to issue ordonnances against the élus in some
seneschalsies for levying many times the amount authorized for their fees.
They went to the length of suspending the salaries of the élus in Lannes
until they presented their books for inspection, and in a letter to Sully,
they attributed the delays in collecting taxes in Guyenne to the élus'
negligence. At last the tide was turning. The élus could no longer appear
to the unbiased members of the king's council as the obvious answer to
the need for good fiscal administration.

The stage was thus set to launch a new attack on the élus. The
assassination of Henry IV provided an excellent excuse for the estates of
the seneschalsies to meet in order to send deputies to court to offer their
submission to the new king, to obtain a confirmation of their privileges,
and to seek once more to have the élections suppressed. Whether there
was a formal meeting of the estates of the généralité is not known, but
deputies from Quercy, Condomois, Lannes, Agenais, Rouergue, Armagnac,
Comminges, and Rivère-Verdun joined together on November 20, 1610,
to sign a petition in which they promised to reimburse the élus for the
loss of their offices if the council would suppress them. The élus were
useless, they argued, because the taille could easily be divided in
accordance with old cadastres. They were costly because of their salaries
and special privileges, and their activities were the source of numerous
complaints and lawsuits. Pointedly, the deputies remarked that in his
coronation oath, a king swore to maintain and conserve the privileges of
his people. Languedoc, Provence, Dauphiné, Burgundy, Brittany, and
several other provinces had continued to have their privileges and estates;

only Guyenne, whose fidelity was exceeded by none, had lost hers.

The deputies must have approached the king's council at a time when the struggle between Sully, the apostle of absolutism, and Villeroy, the apostle of appeasement, was reaching its peak. Whether their demands entered directly into this dispute, we do not know. Contemporary observers saw the conflict in terms more of personalities than of policies and have left no clues. But this much is certain: it was not until February 12, 1611, just after Sully fell from power, that the council finally suppressed the eight élections in Guyenne. By the terms of this edict, the king "perpetually and irrevocably" suppressed the élections and promised never to reestablish the élus. In return, the eight estates were to reimburse the élus for the costs of purchasing their offices, the total figure coming to 252,080 livres. Mindful of the abuses committed by the estates that had ostensibly led to the establishment of the élus in 1603, the council then issued a series of regulations designed to prevent their reoccurrence. The estates of the seneschalsies and subordinate jurisdictions were to be held annually to apportion and impose taxes designated for the king and for the authorized expenses of the estates. If this provision guaranteed the continued existence of representative assemblies, those that followed seemingly denied them effective roles. Taxes required by the king were to be levied without any "reduction, retrenchment, or delay," and no taxes were to be levied by the estates without the king's express permission. Procedures designed to ensure that the estates obeyed this last injunction were carefully spelled out. To reduce the costs of holding the estates, the number and allowances of those who were permitted to attend were limited. Syndics were to be elected for terms of one or two years only and were to have no assistants. Furthermore, they were forbidden to institute any suit without the permission of the estates.

The publication of an edict and its enforcement, however, are two different things. The third estate of Agenais habitually met several times a year, and special sessions of the estates of Rouergue, Rivière-Verdun, and probably other seneschalsies sometimes took place. More important is the question of whether the estates actually lost all control of or influence over royal taxation.

The estates of the généralité met in the summer of 1612 to deal with its affairs, and the deputies who attended the Estates General at Paris during the winter of 1614–15 prepared a cahier for each estate of the généralité to submit to the king. The cahier of the nobility included a request that the three estates (not just the third) be convoked regularly in all the seneschalsies as they were in Rouergue, Comminges, and Quercy.

No action was taken by the council on this request, but in 1616 the estates of Guyenne became active once more. During this same period, the third estate of Agenais met from one to three times a year to apportion taxes, handle matters related to the suppression of the élus, elect deputies to the Estates General of 1614, and quarrel about how the taille should be divided among the various jurisdictions in Guyenne.

A new era for the deputies of the généralité commenced in 1616, when they decided to offer the king 900,000 livres, to be collected over a two-year period, in return for suppressing some tolls on wine and several other products transported on the Garonne and Dordogne rivers. The council accepted their offer, but in the shift in the nature of the tax, Bordeaux managed to push a higher portion on the other seneschalsies than they thought justified. This led to formal and informal meetings of the estates of the généralité, appeals to the parlement of Bordeaux, and the decision to appoint two permanent agents, one of whom was to reside at court to look after the interests of the region and the other to serve in the généralité. The actions of the estates were so successful in slowing the flow of revenue to Paris that in September 1617, the crown issued a decree creating commissioners of the tailles. Agents of the estates succeeded in preventing the implementation of the decree by blocking its registration in the sovereign courts. The crown countered by taking measures to override the opposition of the courts and giving royal officials a larger role in the sessions of the estates and the imposition of taxes. When the estates of the généralité met in February–March 1619, the intendant admitted that the commissioners of the tailles had been created to provide revenue through the sale of the offices and suggested that the estates compensate his majesty for their suppression. This the estates did to the tune of 150,000 livres and a gift of 20,000 more to win the goodwill of their new governor. When the three estates of Quercy met in February 1620, they refused to vote part of the money that the king requested, and their syndics added to this injury by failing to collect all of the stipulated taxes. Exasperated, the treasurers at Bordeaux ordered that all public funds in Quercy be seized except those earmarked to support the University of Cahors and to pay the debts of the province.

Thus in the decade following the death of Henry IV, the precarious balance of power between the crown and the estates was restored. The estates had succeeded in getting the élections abolished and in blocking increases in taxation so effectively that it had become necessary for the crown to find additional revenue by creating offices, establishing new tolls, and employing other expedients in areas that lay outside the direct jurisdiction of the estates. The estates had then made financial concessions in return for the suppression of the tolls and offices, but there had been difficulties in raising the promised sums. Some of the estates, such as those of Rouergue and Quercy, were clearly disillusioned by the repeated efforts of the crown to extort money by whatever means available and had no intention of cooperating. The leaders of Agenais were more subtle in their opposition, but they were perhaps more dangerous because of that very fact.

The dissatisfaction of the crown with the estates must have been intensified when it considered the relative ease with which the two seneschalsies with élections could be taxed. Far from showing a more permissive attitude toward Bordeaux, the crown violated its autonomy by appointing its jurats as well as its mayor. The change was accompanied by a sharp decline in the frequency with which the jurats summoned the smaller towns and communities of Bordelais to assemblies during this decade. Périgord also gained nothing from the new regime. About a month after the fall of Sully, the bishop and mayor of Périgueux and a representative of the nobility petitioned the crown to revive the estates, but Marie de Medici refused their request in September 1611 on the grounds that such assemblies "make only bad resolutions that are prejudicial to the service of the king and to the good and repose of his subjects."[9] With such a contrasting situation in the same généralité, the question was becoming one of how long the rapidly maturing Louis XIII would accept the limitations the estates placed on his power when an alternate form of fiscal administration was so readily available.

THE GREAT PAYS D'ETATS

Henry IV had checked Sully's attempt to weaken the provincial estates of Languedoc shortly before his assassination, so there was relative calm when his son came to the throne. For six years the crown avoided offending the estates by asking for only the usual taxes, although it did hint, without success, that more would be welcome. The relatively mild friction that had existed between the crown and the estates worsened when the deputies assembled at Béziers on December 29, 1616. The Barbin ministry had arbitrarily raised the tax on salt without their consent, and they were also alarmed to learn that the Protestant-dominated chamber of accounts and court of aides of Montpellier were seeking royal permission to unite into a single, stronger court. The estates had not forgotten that they had had to fight to prevent the chamber of accounts from auditing their accounts during the preceding reign. The deputies therefore refused to vote even the usual taxes and dispatched a deputation to court to rectify the situation. The deputation won a promise that the chamber of accounts and the court of aides would not be united, but on April 6, less than three weeks before Concini's murder, the council refused to revoke the increase in the salt tax. The deputies responded by rejecting the crown's request for an additional 180,000 livres, but in the long run they were unable to prevent the increased tax on salt.

Henry IV had gravely threatened the estates of Burgundy by insisting that he choose the mayor of Dijon from the three candidates who received the most votes. As long as this situation prevailed, royal appointees, including the mayor, comprised half the voting strength in the chamber of the élus, the principal administrative organ in the province, which was charged with looking after the affairs of the estates during the three-year interval between sessions. Young Louis XIII directed that this procedure be followed in 1610, but Sully had been removed from office by the time elections were held in 1611, and in Louis's name the king's council abandoned the crown's claim to choose the mayor. In doing so it returned the control of the chamber to the estates.

The three estates displayed their independence in 1614 by rejecting a tax of 180,000 livres that the crown claimed that they had promised when Bresse, Bugey, and Gex were included in their généralité. Thereafter, the crown often chose to seek additional funds by going through the chamber of the élus or holding rump assemblies, but without success. In 1617, the chamber of the élus, with the governor's assistance, forced the government to withdraw its demands for a special military tax and prevented the levying of the *don gratuit* because the regular triennial meeting of the estates had not been held. When the estates did meet in 1618, they protested strongly the failure to hold a meeting in 1617 and refused to do more than vote the palty traditional don gratuit of 16,667 livres for 1617, 1618, and the three years that followed. They emerged from the first decade of the new reign stronger than they had been at its beginning.

The remaining estates in provinces in which there were no élections had been left relatively unscathed by Henry and Sully. As a result, the new regime marked less of a change in the treatment they received, although a threat that had been hanging over their heads was removed. In Provence either the three estates or the assembly of the communities met every year during the decade after Henry's death, except in 1613 and

1619. Neither of these gaps appears to have provoked concern, because they were probably caused by the absence of their governor. More important in stilling the Provençals' concern, perhaps, was the continued activity of the *procureurs du pays nés* during these long intervals between sessions. Between the estates of December 1612 and the assembly of the communities in August 1614, the procureurs met no fewer than seventeen times to perform tasks as varied as buying fruit and olives for the chancellor, inspecting the construction of a bridge, and arranging for the passage of two thousand troops through the province. The parlement at Aix became concerned about the procureurs' activities and in 1619 forbad them to summon the *procureurs du pays nés et joints*. The procureurs replied that there were three kinds of assemblies in Provence— those of the estates, those of the communities, and those of the procureurs du pays nés et joints—and that they had the right to convoke the last whenever it was necessary. Taxation, of course, did not cease in the years in which neither the estates nor the communities met, but the crown was careful to make no new demands on these occasions, and the procureurs permitted the routine taxes to be collected without argument. Only the *procureurs joints* of the clergy and nobility attended the assemblies of the communities, but there were separate assemblies of both orders and they had officials to look after their interests when they were not in session.

The first meeting of the three estates of Dauphiné that took place in the new reign was held in Valence in February 1611. Since the king asked for only the same taxes that had been voted the year before, the relations between the deputies and the crown were friendly. As had happened so often before, the third estate and the more privileged orders were the antagonists. The principal difficulty arose over the salt tax. In 1601, the estates and the crown had agreed to establish a salt tax that would yield 278,400 livres per year for ten years. Of this sum, 150,000 livres was to be applied to redeeming the royal domain, and the remainder was assigned to paying the provincial debts. By 1611, the term of the contract was drawing to a close, and the third estate was anxious to reduce the salt tax sharply and use all that was levied to support its activities. The nobles and clergy, on the other hand, wanted part of the salt tax to pay their expenses. Lesdiguiéres, the king's lieutenant general, worked diligently to secure a compromise and was finally successful.

The accord that was reached in 1611 became known as the "union of the three orders" and was frequently referred to thereafter. It did not remove the basic cause of the friction between the estates, because the problem centered on the question of whether nobles should pay the taille on the non-noble land they owned. It did, however, offer a chance for a degree of cooperation so long as the powerful and statesmanlike Lesdiguiéres was present to reconcile differences, and the crown did not revive the issue by raising the taille. The calm that prevailed was enough to enable the estates that met at Grenoble in January 1613 to agree on twenty-seven articles defining their procedures. Among them were provisions that the estates would meet "every year as has always been observed" and that in view of the union of the three orders, there would be no separate assemblies, proposals, deliberations, or delegations.

By the time the estates met in late January and early February 1616, a new problem had arisen. The salt tax that had been agreed upon in 1611 was scheduled to be reduced. Lesdiguières asked, however, that it be continued at the same level. The privileged orders protested strongly and talked of a union with the long robe. The third estate was more amenable, and in the end the tax was extended for another year with part of the proceeds assigned to support troops in the province. In May 1617, the three estates mustered enough unity to reject a royal proposal that they increase taxes in order to support the expanded military forces in the province, but they once more fell to quarreling about the distribution of the salt tax, a controversy that was still raging when the estates met in Grenoble in 1619. There deputies from the dioceses and bailiwicks joined in the deliberations of the first two orders and drew closer to the "gentlemen of the long robe," who now had their own council of five to speak for them. In the end, the salt tax was continued, and the privileged orders obtained a modest portion.

The bitter quarrel between the nobility and third estate did not abate. Soon after the deputies to the estates of 1619 had departed, the council of the nobility learned that the *lieutenant particulier* of Vienne had submitted an "insolent" petition to the parlement of Grenoble and that that body had rendered a favorable decree. The secretary of the nobility never specifically stated the nature of the petition, but it was enough to touch off talk of sending a large delegation to the king. The deputies of the nobility of the bailiwicks were assembled in July, and they were soon deputing to Lesdiguières and the parlement. Before they disbanded, they elected six gentlemen to remain in Grenoble to conserve the dignity of their order. To secure the revocation of the offending decree, a deputy was sent to court, where he spent much of 1620 trying to have the case resolved by the king's council. The union between the three orders was shattered and relations between the privileged orders and the third estate could hardly have been worse. By the close of the first decade of Louis's reign, the three estates of Dauphiné, at times it seemed almost premeditatedly, were moving toward their destruction.

With Henry's assassination, Brittany entered into a new phase. Vendôme, the governor, now in his teens and free of the restraining hand of his natural father, began to take a direct interest in the province. He presided over the estates that met in September–October 1610 and occasionally thereafter when his presence furthered his intrigues. The three estates promptly obtained the confirmation of their privileges and the suppression of a number of offices that Henry had created. They were asked to vote only the usual taxes during the first three years of Louis's reign. The nine-year tax on the retail sale of wine that the estates had established in 1609 to redeem the royal domain was retained, and they continued to give Vendôme and other influential persons gratifications to win their support.

In November 1613, Vendôme persuaded the estate to pay his guards, whom he promptly used to support Condé's rebellion. It was therefore with some embarrassment that the Bretons appeared at the estates of 1614, where Marie de Medici and her twelve-year-old son were present. To demonstrate that they had been deceived by Vendôme, they revoked their promise to support his guards and asked that he be denied the privilege of having them. In response to the request that they pay for the cost of suppressing the rebellion, they extended the wine tax that they had voted to redeem the domain for a year. They also gave Marie de Medici a special gift of 50,000 livres and elected deputies to the Estates General who were favorably disposed toward the crown.

The estates of Brittany were not convoked in the fall of 1615, and the usual taxes were collected in 1616 without consent. The atmosphere was therefore tense when the estates once again assembled in Rennes on October 23, 1616, to consider levies for the following year. In his letter to his commissioners, Louis insisted that he had intended to hold a meeting in 1615 but had not done so because a new rebellion by Condé would have made the assembly an "occasion and pretext of various designs prejudicial to our authority and to the repose of the province." Therefore he had postponed the estates and had ordered that only those taxes customarily "consented to" by the estates be collected, although he had had need of "great succor" to suppress the uprising.[10] By not having the estates, Louis thus suggested, the Bretons had been asked to pay less than if they had been held. But no such forbearance was necessary now, because the estates were once more in session. Louis's commissioners requested from 900,000 to 1.2 million livres in addition to the tax to redeem the domain and the usual levies. The estates cut this mammoth demand to 400,000 livres but agreed to continue to make payments on the domain.

Although the three estates had cooperated to the extent of offering the king part of what he had requested, they were not disposed to pass over the events of the past year in silence. In the first article of their cahier, they pointed out that annual meetings of the estates and the right to consent to taxes were two of the conditions, accepted by earlier kings, that formed the basis of the union between Brittany and the crown. "The *fouages* and other monies," they declared, "have been divided and levied on the orders of your officials in the present year without the consent of the estates . . . which is directly contrary to the rights, privileges, and liberties of Brittany." The estates then asked the king "to declare and order that henceforth no similar commissions would be expedited or levies of the *fouage* and other taxes made without the consent of the estates," which would be assembled every year without fail on September 25. Almost meekly, the king replied, "The will of the king is to hold the estates of his province of Brittany annually and to conserve and maintain their privileges in that and all other things."[11]

There is no reason to believe that the failure to issue letters of convocation in 1615 was intended as an attack on the estates. The excuse the crown offered for its inaction was almost certainly sincere. During the fall of 1615, when the estates would normally have been held, Vendôme was busy raising troops in Brittany, and he soon joined Condé in his revolt.

By the time the estates opened on October 22, 1618, the original contract to redeem the domain in nine years was about to expire, and the king asked only for the usual taxes, plus 200,000 livres to complete this task. After some debate, the estates granted his request. Once the wine tax was no longer needed to redeem the domain, the crown prodded the estates into voting a don gratuit. Considering the sixty years that elapsed between 1560 and 1620, with their bloody wars and heavy inflation, one is surprised that the crown was able to add only the don gratuit to its list of Breton taxes, especially as the amount of the don gratuit was still very much subject to negotiation.

THE OTHER ESTATES

The first decade of Louis's reign did not see a growth in the authority of the three estates of Normandy, but neither did it witness a further decline of their privileges. The estates met regularly, but the crown continued to take what taxes it wanted regardless of how much was voted. The only exception was that the estates were not convoked in the fall of 1615 to vote taxes for 1616. The explanation for this oversight lies in the disorders that attended a revolt led by the prince of Condé and the ease with which the crown could bypass the estates and order the élus to levy the desired sum. The syndic of the estates was kept informed on developments, but there is no evidence that he protested levying taxes without consent. Indeed, the crown silenced some possible opposition by ordering that those who usually served as commissioners to the estates be paid just as though the estates had been held. Since these commissioners were Norman notables, the king's generosity was in effect a bribe designed to encourage them to leave matters as they were. What is surprising is that when the three estates met in Rouen in December 1616, they offered no protest against taxes being levied that year without consent. It is interesting to note that the commissioners used the word *consent* in regard to appropriations.

The history of the remaining estates in France was relatively uneventful during the first decade of Louis's reign. As in the past, the échevins of Clermont convoked the nineteen good towns of Basse-Auvergne when the occasion seemed to warrant. From 1610 through 1620, there were twenty-two meetings, at least one in each year. In addition, there were five meetings of the six nearest towns to Clermont and one meeting of the three estates to elect deputies to the Estates General of 1614. On several occasions the inhabitants of Basse-Auvergne were called upon to pay increased taxes to support the troops required to maintain order during Condé's rebellions, but probably the most impressive development was the steady progress toward paying the provincial debt. In 1605, Basse-Auvergne had begun to liquidate it at a rate of 90,000 livres a year. By 1614, 900,000 livres had been repaid, and in December 1621, the deputies of the nineteen good towns received the happy news that they owed only 29,122 livres. Clearly, the estates handled their financial affairs far better than the crown did during these years.

Historians have assumed that the assembly of the four towns and provostships of Haute-Auvergne was suppressed during this period. This presumption has been based on a report the intendant, Jean de Mesgrigny, made in 1637 about a decree the late Henri de Noailles, lieutenant of the Haute-Pays, had obtained from the king's council at some point prior to 1620. Actually, all Mesgrigny said was that the decree forbad St. Flour and the other provost capitals to assemble the third estate without permission, hardly enough to prove the assembly's demise, and there is ample evidence that it continued to meet after 1620.

The reason for Noailles's action against the third estate probably dated back to a quarrel he had had with the town of St. Flour during the elections to the Estates General of 1614. The letters of convocation specified that the three estates were to meet at St. Flour, but Noailles directed them to convene at Aurillac, where he lay ill with the gout. St. Flour immediately sent deputies to ask him to restore the original venue. At first, Noailles refused to see them, and when he finally did, they fell to quarreling. The deputies wanted Noailles to postpone the elections until he was well enough to go to St. Flour, but he refused. They then laid plans to summon the estates to meet in St. Flour on their own authority, but fled to their homes when they learned that Noailles was planning to have them arrested. In the end, deputies were elected in both St. Flour and Aurillac. The king's council was left to decide whom to seat, and Noailles, we may suspect, was infuriated.

The nobles of Haute-Auvergne remained organized. In February 1614, they sought permission to elect a syndic to support the third estate in a quarrel with the farmers of the salt tax, and some months later they elected deputies to the Estates General.

The towns of Forez continued to assemble, and when the occasion warranted, their deputies cooperated with the syndic of the plat pays of Lyonnais and the deputy of the town of Villefranche in representing the interests of the three provinces in the government of Lyonnais. As far as can be ascertained, the small Pyrenean estates that lay within the confines of France functioned normally during the first decade of Louis's reign.

Indeed, this period can be characterized as a return to normal conditions throughout France. Following Villeroy's advice, the crown resumed the consultative traditions of the Renaissance monarchy. The élections were abolished in Guyenne, and the estates of that region resumed their traditional tax-collecting duties. Threats to the estates of Languedoc, Burgundy, and elsewhere ceased. Except for the brief Barbin ministry, the only ominous signs were in Béarn and Navarre, the two little states that were not yet incorporated into the crown of France, but even here it was religion rather than absolutism that motivated the government to take action.

THE ESTATES OF BÉARN AND NAVARRE

Henry IV had respected the privileges of Béarn and Navarre and preserved their status as independent states, but he had insisted that

Catholics be permitted to hold office and to practice their religion in a limited number of designated places. The Protestants who controlled the estates and other institutions in Béarn had protested unsuccessfully against these concessions, but they could take satisfaction in the fact that there were definite limits as to how far Henry would go to please his new co-religionists. His death, followed by the growth of Catholic strength at court, led the two Béarnais bishops and other Catholics to seek further concessions. Included were demands that the Catholic rite be celebrated in some one hundred localities where it was currently illegal, that the church property that Jeanne d'Albret had confiscated be restored, and that a Catholic be appointed to the vacant post of first president at Pau, although Henry had promised to name a Protestant. In addition, the Béarnais bishops wanted to be given precedence in the estates and the Conseil souverain.

These demands, and Sully's removal from office in January 1611, further increased the Protestants' fears, and when the three estates of Béarn met that April, they took the unusual step of naming deputies to the general assembly of the French Protestants at Saumur in order to obtain its support. Marie de Medici quickly countered by saying that if the Béarnais wanted to unite with the French churches, she would unite their country with France. The Béarnais did not take this hint and persisted in their course. Marie failed to implement her threat, but to weaken the Béarnais position, she insisted that they negotiate separately with her council rather than in conjunction with the French Huguenots.

In the years that followed, both Béarnais Catholics and Protestants sought the support of their French co-religionists. The former won the backing of the clergy in the Estates General of 1614, and the latter continued to attend French Protestant assemblies in spite of the crown's disapproval. The Protestant governor of Béarn and Navarre, the marquis of La Force, staunchly defended the privileges of the two states and the rights of his church. As a reward, he received generous grants from the Béarnais estates, but he was compelled to follow the dangerous and somewhat devious course of protesting his loyalty to the crown while simultaneously raising troops to defend his position and that of his adherents. As a result, when the determined Mangot and Barbin came to power during the ministerial revolution in the summer of 1616, they began to take steps to strengthen the crown's position.

On December 31, 1616, the new leaders of the king's council issued a decree incorporating Béarn and Navarre into the realm of France. The change was to some extent the logical outcome of the constant pleas the

Béarnais Catholics and Protestants had made to their co-religionists in France, but it nevertheless led to considerable agitation. The estates of Béarn met in a special session in February 1617, where they argued that the decree was illegal because it contradicted their privileges. Anyone who accepted the edict of union was a traitor to his country, the estates unanimously declared. They sought La Force's assistance and instructed their syndics to oppose the union by all proper means at their disposal. Predominantly Catholic Navarre, an innocent victim of the religious quarrel, also protested.

The estates of Béarn and Navarre managed to prevent the implementation of the edict of union until after the assassination of Concini in April 1617, but the assembly of the French Catholic clergy that met in Paris shortly thereafter renewed its effort to improve the situation of the Béarnais Catholics. This time their requests were delivered to the favorably disposed and determined young Louis XIII, now acting in his own right. On June 25, his council issued a decree reestablishing the Catholic rite throughout Béarn and returning to the church all the lands and revenue that Jeanne d'Albret had confiscated. The Béarnais were to retain their separate state, but their resistance was soon to jeopardize this privilege.

La Force was summoned to court to receive instructions to enforce the decree. There he vigorously defended the Béarnais position, while in Pau, the Conseil souverain refused to register it. The resulting delay led the Béarnais Catholics to submit a long petition to the king's council in August 1617, but the three estates of Béarn that met in November countered by voting unanimously against union with France and, by fifty-seven to fourteen, along strictly religious lines, against returning the former church property. La Force counseled moderation, but Rohan and other French Protestants offered their support. A deputation was dispatched to the king, and a committee of the estates met frequently in the months that followed.

The opposition to the edict returning the church property was so strong that La Force claimed that he could not enforce it, but the crown suspected that he was at the bottom of the resistance. Protestant deputies from Languedoc and Guyenne met with those of Béarn, in spite of royal orders not to do so, but soon more cautious French Huguenots were advising their Béarnais brethren to compromise. Nevertheless, the Conseil souverain steadfastly refused to register the king's decree. Royal anger at La Force grew, and his sons lost their court positions. Slowly the one-time favorite was driven from a position of at least outward compliance to the acceptance of rebellion as a desperate means to maintain his position and that of his co-religionists. The youthful Louis also despaired of implementing his will through letters and commissioners. In the summer of 1620, after easily suppressing a rebellion led by his mother, he set out for Guyenne and Béarn with an army. His initial move was probably directed only at the intransigent Protestants, but in the end his march to the south was to inaugurate a new effort to establish royal absolutism in France.

VII

France Finds a King, 1620–1624

LOUIS XIII AND HIS EPOCH

When Louis XIII began to march his army toward Béarn and Navarre in the summer of 1620, he was not yet nineteen years old. Of average height, he had inherited his father's restless energy and capacity to endure fatigue. When he accompanied his troops into battle, it was to share their dangers and hardships. He was to be the last of France's soldier kings. His tastes were simple, and frugality was as much a part of his character as it was absent from that of both of his parents. Louis stammered. To avoid embarrassment, he said little when it was not necessary. When he took a position, he spoke slowly to cloak his handicap. At times he was morose or bad tempered, and he had a sadistic streak that made him immune to the pleas of wives and kinsmen that he spare the lives of rebellious, disobedient nobles. He inherited his mother's mediocre mind. This probably accounted for a certain timidity and lack of confidence, which he hid under a cloak of aloofness and largely overcame by his determination to have a glorious reign. To be a great king, as he saw it, he had to win glory upon the battlefield, but even more important, perhaps, he had to mete out stern justice and be obeyed.[1]

These traits appeared early in his career and ought to have given warning of what to expect when he reached manhood. When the baron de Guémadeuc killed another noble and shut himself up in the château of Fougères rather than surrender to the authorities, Louis, not yet sixteen, was prepared to march at the head of an army to compel obedience. Alarmed, Guémadeuc surrendered. He had powerful friends at court and no doubt expected to escape with little or no punishment. Instead, he was sentenced to death. When his wife threw herself on her knees before Louis and pleaded for mercy, Louis dryly replied: "I owe justice to my subjects and in this instance I prefer justice to mercy."[2] Guémadeuc was beheaded.

Obedience and justice! When Louis was only sixteen, one of his secretaries of state noted these traits when he wrote a prominent noble that Louis "wants to be obeyed and is offended by those who fail him in this duty, unless it is through ignorance. If it is, he pardons freely and listens to reason very easily."[3] A year or two later, Louis wrote to his oft-estranged mother trying to explain his actions and sometimes to reproach her for her deeds. He spoke of his determination to use force "to maintain my authority and the public tranquility of my kingdom."[4] Repeatedly he used such phrases as "to reestablish royal authority," "to conserve the authority," "against my authority," "to the prejudice of my authority," and "to make my authority recognized." He also talked of "the good of my state and the glory of my reign,"[5] but he saw it as being achieved by stamping out factions, suppressing disorder, and reestablishing "public tranquility."[6] "From concord is born the repose of the mind and the tranquility of the soul; from discord comes the ruin of towns, the desolation of the countryside, and all the miseries of life."[7]

Here we see the young Louis. He longs for glory, which could best be achieved by restoring order to his kingdom for the benefit of his people. It is not surprising that he should have such a goal. Was not his father, whom he revered, already being called "the great" because he had done this very thing? Louis gave no thought to winning glory by humbling the Habsburgs. The evil genius of Richelieu had not yet directed his attention away from domestic reform. Rather he resumed the policies of the great Henry as he vaguely understood them. Less experienced than his father, yes; less intelligent, yes; but perhaps for these very reasons he was more determined and less willing to compromise.

The Protestant population had peaked during the reign of Henry IV at a little over a million adherents, and under Louis a slow but irregular decline set in, accompanied by a lessening of religious zeal.[8] Internal conflicts increased, and leadership became less effective. This situation, and a growing realization that the overwhelming majority of Frenchmen would always be Catholic, led the more lukewarm adherents of the new faith to return to the ancient church. But the most important reason for the reversal of Protestant fortunes was the rising tide of the Catholic reform movement.

If the history of the last half of the sixteenth century must be thought of largely in terms of the Protestant challenge, that of the seventeenth century must be conceived largely in terms of the Catholic revival. This was true not only in France but also in most of the rest of the European continent. This situation not only propelled the French crown toward a confrontation with its powerful Protestant minority but also became a factor in foreign policy. In the Empire, the resurgent forces of Catholicism were at length ready to assert themselves, while Spain, although weakened, prepared to renew the attempt to bring its rebellious Dutch provinces to obedience. In 1618 and 1619, while the Protestants of Béarn were resisting Louis's efforts to reestablish Catholicism in their little state, their co-religionists in Bohemia reacted even more strongly against Habsburg and Catholic pressures. They seized control of the kingdom and elected the Calvinist elector Frederick of the Palatinate king. The Austrian Habsburgs counterattacked with the aid of Spain and the German Catholic princes. Soon this conflict became involved with Spain's effort to reconquer its former Dutch provinces, and a bloody war ensued, which was to last until 1648.

At first Louis refrained from taking an active military role in the conflict and devoted his energies to strengthening his position within his own kingdom. He made great strides in this direction, especially between 1620 and 1622. Not until 1624 did he and his advisers succumb to the temptation of trying to prevent the Habsburgs from reaping the full rewards of their initial victories and seek to secure some advantage for France. They did this by making alliances with the Protestant states and attempting to cut the Spanish supply lines through the Alps to the Empire. From then until November 1630, there was a tug of war in France between those who favored domestic reform and those who opted for active participation in the European conflict. The ultimate victory of the latter was to have a profound effect on the nature of French government and society.

The growing temptation to intervene in the Thirty Years War paralleled a change in the direction of the economy. The Italian wars of the sixteenth century had been supported by an expanding economy, but now, when the French were about to challenge the Habsburgs once more, the economic upturn that had begun in the late fifteenth century came to an end. It is quite possible that on the eve of the bad harvests of 1628–30, France's population reached a peak not surpassed until well into the reign of Louis XV. The French were in no condition to engage in a major foreign war in which the size of their armies and costs of supplying each individual soldier would be far greater than when they invaded Italy in 1494.

BÉARN AND THE PROTESTANT REVOLT

The possibility that he might soon be supporting the Protestants in the Empire against their Habsburg lords probably never entered young Louis's mind in 1618, 1619, or 1620. What angered him most then was that his own Protestant subjects were as disobedient and potentially rebellious as those of his Habsburg rivals. In these circumstances, it is not surprising that after suppressing an uprising led by Marie de Medici and a number of magnates in August 1620, he marched at the head of his army to the south to restore order in Guyenne and Béarn.

Louis's stay in Béarn was brief. Within a week he compelled the Conseil souverain to register the edict restoring the property of the Catholic church, held the estates in which the bishops of Lescar and Oloron resumed their seats and were given the precedence they had once enjoyed, issued an edict uniting Béarn and Navarre to the crown of France, and created a parlement at Pau to serve Béarn, Navarre, and Soule. To further the Catholic cause, Louis created a Jesuit college, and to ensure his control over the region, he replaced the Protestant governor and the garrison of the powerful fortress of the Navarrenx with Catholics. By November 7, Louis was back in Paris. In a few decisive months, he had suppressed an uprising in northern France and restored his authority in the south, but the real test was yet to come.

Louis was received as a hero by the Catholics of Paris, but the Protestants were thoroughly alarmed. A political assembly met at La Rochelle in late December to determine what action to take. When the king ordered it to disband, it refused. Both Luynes and the more moderate Protestants wanted a peaceful solution, but the majority of the assembly at La Rochelle insisted that their co-religionists in Béarn be returned to their former position, and that Louis withdraw the troops he had left in the south. These conditions were unacceptable. Louis began to arm, and the assembly countered by taking measures to defend the Protestant faith. Unfortunately for its cause, most of the Huguenot magnates refused to participate. As Louis began to move south in the spring of 1621, the Huguenot towns in Saintonge and Guyenne, with few exceptions, opened their gates to him. Saint-Jean d'Angély resisted but was taken after nearly a month's siege. By July the royal army had reached the powerfully fortified town of Montauban. Here the Protestants defended themselves with such determination that Louis abandoned the siege in November. The following month, Luynes died of fever, and the campaign of 1621 came to an end.

In the spring of 1622, Louis resumed the war, and by July he was besieging Montpellier. Once again the royal army was unsuccessful, and peace was made in October. By its terms Louis reconfirmed the Edict of Nantes, thereby assuring the Protestants the continuation of their religious and civil liberties. In the course of the conflict, however, many of their places of security had been taken, and as a condition of peace Louis insisted that all or part of the new fortifications that had been constructed at Montpellier, Nîmes, Castres, and Millau be destroyed. Of the great Protestant strongholds, only La Rochelle and Montauban remained. Equally important was the changing attitude of the Protestant magnates. Some had remained neutral throughout the war, and Lesdiguières had actually led a royal army, although he always worked for a peace settlement. During the course of the conflict, other leading Protestant lords, including La Force, had made peace with the king in return for rich rewards. Only Rohan, the greatest and most unselfish of the Protestant leaders, had fought to the end. In less than a year and a half, Louis had gone far toward dismantling the state within a state.

It would be difficult to overestimate the significance of Louis's accomplishment. Although only about 6 percent of the French were Protestants, they were remarkably well organized in areas where they constituted a large portion of the population. Through their assemblies they commissioned officers, raised armies, voted taxes, and floated loans. Quarrels within their ranks could be bitter, but they governed the areas they controlled at least as effectively as the king did other parts of France. Their armies were not feudal levies but well-organized regiments and companies, commanded by officers who were appointed with little regard to their status in the feudal hierarchy. The Protestants not only seized royal revenues to support their troops, they increased the tax levies severalfold. Louis did not destroy this edifice. In the peace of October 1622, he even promised to continue to pay the remaining Protestant garrisons and to authorize the general political assembly to meet every three years to elect agents to represent their interests at court. What he had done, however, was to dismantle many of their fortifications and, above all, to weaken their will to resist.

Louis accomplished the latter by slowly convincing most of his Protestant subjects that they should put their trust in him rather than in their armies and fortified towns. He had shown that resistance at best brought higher taxes and at the worse suffering and death. Saint-Jean d'Angely had been stripped of its privileges, Clairac had seen its pastor and several prominent citizens hanged, Saint-Antonin and Nègrepelisse had been sacked. Decisive victory could never be theirs, because they lacked the strength to mount an offensive. They could only hope to stave off defeat at a terrible cost. As an alternative to war, Louis offered religious freedom, civil rights, and the possibility of generous rewards in return for loyal service. To implement his policy, Louis never hesitated to reconfirm the public articles of the Edict of Nantes. When he had insisted on returning the property of the Catholic church in Béarn, he had promised to compensate the Protestants by assigning them revenue from the royal domain to support their religion. The Béarnais resistance to his edict must have taxed his patience, but even after he had imposed his will at the head of an army, he had renewed this pledge, although his chronic financial difficulties prevented him from giving all that was due. Under these circumstances Lesdiguières became a Catholic in return for being made constable, and other nobles followed his example in return for lesser rewards. Even nobles who remained faithful to the reformed church often believed that not only their personal interests but those of their religion could best be served by putting their trust in their king. Often municipal leaders also came to believe that their privileges could best be preserved through loyalty to the crown. Only the boldest favored rebellion after 1622.

NEW ELECTIONS FOR GUYENNE

Louis was not content with subverting the privileges of his Protestant subjects in the south. He took advantage of the presence of his armies to renew the assault on the provincial estates and the assemblies of the towns that his father had begun nearly two decades before. In September 1621, he issued an edict reestablishing the eight élections in the généralité of Guyenne that he had suppressed in 1611. At that time, he had promised never to reestablish them, but in addition to having the estates compensate the élus for the loss of their offices, he had made conditions that included a provision that royal taxes would be levied without "any reduction, retrenchment, or delay" and that the costs incurred by the estates would be reduced.[9] However, the estates had continued to do all in their power to prevent increases in taxation and had conducted their affairs much as they had before the élections had been created in 1603. It was this failure of the estates to adhere to his conditions that Louis used to justify breaking his pledge. He also accused them of oppressing his people with their own levies and of failing to follow the prescribed safeguards to prevent fiscal dishonesty. In 1622, and again in 1627, Louis created additional élections by subdividing some of the larger ones. In the end, there were sixteen élections in Guyenne.[10]

The estates responded in their traditional way. They appealed to the sovereign courts and the bureau of finances at Bordeaux to prevent the implementation of the decrees, they sought the support of their governor and other influential persons, and above all they dispatched deputies to the king with authority to compensate him for his losses if he canceled the proposed sale of offices in the élections. The deputies began with an offer of 250,000 livres, the sum they had given to have the élections suppressed in 1611. When Louis refused to move, they increased their offer to 300,000 and ultimately to 900,000, but he never budged in his determination. Instead, he issued an edict forbidding the various estates in Guyenne to send deputies to him or his council to seek to have the élections suppressed. He overrode the parlement of Bordeaux when it refused to register the edict creating the élections unless the money the estates had paid for their suppression in 1611 was returned. When the treasurers of the bureau of finances at Bordeaux sought to levy the taille in the traditional manner in 1624, he threatened to deprive them of their offices. Never, not even in the days of Sully, had the estates been confronted by such a stone wall. Still they persisted. They gathered evidence to prove that the élus were dishonest and incompetent. The rumor was even spread among the peasants of Quercy in 1624 that the clergy, nobility, and townsmen would support them if they would take up arms to abolish the new élections, but the rebels were quickly dispersed. All was in vain. The élections remained.

But why was Louis so determined to have the élections at any cost? Why did he refuse to consider a princely offer of 900,000 livres to abolish them? He could, of course, anticipate an immediate profit from the sale of offices, and this led him to overstaff the élections, but the total amount he received was considerably less than he could have obtained by accepting the offer of the estates. Furthermore, these officers had to be paid. In Rouergue, for example, the officers in the new élection were to receive 7,025 livres plus fees annually, whereas the officers of the estates of Rouergue were paid only 2,054 livres to apportion and collect taxes and to perform many other duties. In 1625, Louis added five more offices to the élection, whose salaries came to 2,240 livres per year. Finally, in March 1627, he divided Rouergue into three élections, thereby bringing the annual payroll to 27,795 livres, thirteen times what it would have cost the estates to have performed these and other duties. Indeed, the salaries and all the expenses of the estates together had totaled only 8,204 livres around 1620.

Louis undoubtedly believed that the officials of the estates imposed unauthorized taxes. In 1623, the last year before the élus took over the tax-collection machinery, the towns and communities of Agenais were accused of levying 19,680 livres in taxes without permission, and the king's council ordered that the receiver of the tailles retain this money until all the facts could be ascertained. Even if the charge were correct, it does not prove that the officials were dishonest. Much or all of the money may have gone to pay the debts that still weighed heavily on many communities or to finance local projects. What angered Louis and his advisers was that local elected officials were levying taxes to meet local needs, which these officials determined, when in their minds the money would be better spent meeting the king's needs.

Louis also suspected the local elected officials of graft. Perhaps he even thought that they were more dishonest than his own officials, although he certainly knew that the latter were not above reproach. In 1624 he created a Chamber of Justice to uncover and punish fraud committed by his financial officials, and incidentally to encourage them to offer a large sum to call off the investigation. He also thought it necessary to order the bureau of finances at Bordeaux to launch an investigation to determine what taxes the élus had levied without permission in 1625. Those of Bordelais were especially suspect. Thus Louis ought to have seen corruption as a secondary issue when he compared tax collection by the estates with tax collection by the élus. His primary motive for issuing the edict of September 1621 must have been to control the tax-collecting machinery so that more money would flow into his coffers and less into those of the estates and towns. If these duly constituted bodies withered and died as a result, it was of little concern to him.

To insist that Louis embarked on a deliberate policy of increasing his authority in Guyenne and decreasing that of rival governing bodies is not to say that he made any direct effort to destroy the estates. An edict forbidding them to meet again under any circumstances would have created further unrest. The local leaders already felt threatened. On December 28, 1622, the outgoing *consuls* of Agen urged their successors to make every effort to prevent the abolition of the office of syndic of Agenais. As long as this post was filled, there would be someone who could act to protect the interests of the seneschalsy before the king's council and the sovereign courts without having to be empowered by the estates, which might not be permitted to assemble. In April 1628, the *consuls* of Agen persuaded the estates to empower them to act as syndics of Agenais and to borrow money in the name of the province. Since the continued existence of a municipal government in Agen appeared certain, this meant that Agenais would have a constituted body with the necessary funds to act in its interests.

The estates felt threatened, but Louis did not directly question their right to exist. It was enough to break their powers in taxation. If they continued to function for a few more years, it would do little harm. Gradually the people would come to consider their meetings a needless expense, and they would slowly die without causing the outburst that would certainly take place if he acted hastily to achieve this end. It cannot be proved that these were the thoughts in Louis's and his advisers' minds, but this is what was to happen.

The quarrel with the élus was enough, with the usual matters, to keep the third estate of Agenais busy until 1630. During this period there were one or more meetings per year. Try as they would, however, the leaders of Agenais could not find a way to ensure a permanent role for the estates under the new regime. A feeling of disillusionment and despair seems to have come over the once-proud burghers. After 1630, they assembled irregularly, with occasional gaps of four or five years between meetings, although the total extinction of the estates was not to come until several generations later. The three estates of Rouergue were equally active during the first few years, and, as far as can be ascertained, the estates in the other seneschalsies had somewhat similar experiences.

The estates of the généralité were even less fortunate than those of the seneschalsies. Further removed from the people, they enjoyed less popular support. They were also vulnerable because there was no town whose *consuls* had the right to convoke a meeting or to ask the governor to summon one. There were probably several meetings of the estates, or at least informal gatherings of the deputies of the seneschalsies between 1622 and 1624 to try to get the élections suppressed. Another attempt was made in January 1626. Thereafter, as far as can be ascertained, the estates of the généralité met only once, in February 1635. The largest representative institution in France had ceased to exist.

THE THREAT TO THE ESTATES OF LANGUEDOC

Just as Louis took advantage of his campaign in Guyenne in 1621 to impose his will on the estates, he planned a similar fate for Languedoc when he led his army there in 1622, this despite the fact that in the two preceding years the estates had been more generous than was their wont. That June he issued an edict creating fifteen élections to assume the tax-collecting role of the diocesan estates. At this point the duke of

Ventadour, and perhaps his cousin of Montmorency, intervened, and Louis was persuaded to abandon the élections. Either he was encouraged to hope that the estates would mend their ways, or else he realized that he had acted prematurely. His campaign against the Protestants in Languedoc was only beginning, and it was no time to alienate his Catholic subjects there, especially when they had the support of their powerful dukes. But Louis did not abandon his desire to curb the independence of the estates, and in July he issued an edict creating a clerk of the tailles in each diocese, town, and community in Languedoc. The diocesan clerks were to convoke the diocesan estates, take minutes of their deliberations and apportionment of the taxes, and participate in auditing the accounts. The clerks of the towns and communities were to keep an equally watchful eye on the financial activities of the urban officials.

Peace with the Huguenots had been made by the time the estates assembled at Beaucaire in November 1622. Ventadour was the senior royal official present at the opening meeting, and he prepared his address with more than usual care. After pointing to the king's great financial needs, he declared: "I cannot pass over in silence the great complaints that have been made to the king and to his court of parlement at Toulouse concerning the abuses and frauds that have been committed in the meetings of the twenty-two dioceses of this province, where they have used great gifts, gratifications, rewards, travel allowances, and other excessive expenses to crush and oppress the king's subjects. Of 100 écus that are imposed, not 10 reach his majesty's purse. . . . This disorder, gentlemen, gave grounds for the edict on the élus that was on the point of being verified and registered in the court of parlement when I made remonstrances on your behalf as you would have desired. I reiterated these remonstrances in the presence of the king, attended by the princes of his blood, cardinals, dukes, and other leading lords of his council."[11]

Ventadour's speech was generally applauded, but both his appeal for reform and the king's appeal for financial assistance fell on nearly deaf ears. Toward straightening out their own affairs, the three estates would do no more than rule that henceforth those who arrived three or more days late would not be seated. They did ask the barons and prelates to attend the estates in person at least every third year, but they coupled this plea with one that the allowances of those who came be increased. Far more serious was their refusal to vote Louis more than 200,000 livres, to be collected over a period of two years, although one of his commissioners had warned them that "they would regret not giving the king satisfaction." Instead, those present argued that taxes ought to be reduced because of the sufferings Languedoc had undergone during the rebellion. Their own unwillingness to cooperate more fully did not prevent them from asking the king to revoke the edict creating the clerks in the dioceses and towns. Ventadour, who had served Languedoc well as lieutenant general since the days of the Catholic League, fell ill near the close of the estates. He died knowing that the deputies had failed to heed his warning that they must correct abuses if they were to preserve their privileges.

When the deputies assembled in March 1624, it quickly became apparent that their principal objective would be to obtain the suppression of the edict creating the clerks in the dioceses and towns. They dispatched a deputation to the king on this matter and agreed not to disband until they had received its report. Montmorency consented to halt the sale of these offices until after the deputation had returned. Louis replied on April 18 that great sums of money had been advanced in anticipation of the execution of the edict, but that he authorized Montmorency to make proposals to the estates on the subject. Montmorency sought to soothe them by explaining that the king had not created the clerks to infringe on their privileges; rather, he needed money, and he would suppress the edict in return for 1.39 million livres. The estates rejected this proposal and after some debate reached a compromise figure of 720,000 livres. The episode reveals once more that the king's authority to create offices could infringe on the estates' right to consent to taxation.

THE OTHER PROVINCIAL ESTATES AND ASSEMBLIES

The Bretons were thought to be undertaxed. It is therefore not surprising that the crown sought a special levy of 600,000 livres when the estates met early in 1621. Only after long, bitter bargaining did the deputies consent to a tax of 450,000 livres, to be collected over a two-year period. Louis renewed his quest for a special one-year grant of 600,000 livres when the estates opened in December 1622, but in the end he had to be content with a two-year grant totaling 400,000 livres. In 1623, he adopted a new tactic; he created a bureau of finance in Brittany. Whether this was intended as the first step toward establishing élections, or whether his goal was merely to extract more money from the province cannot be ascertained, but it had the latter effect. The estates offered 450,000 livres in return for the suppression of this much-feared institution.

The Burgundians were also subjected to heavy pressure by the crown. Their practice of holding the estates every third year put the king at a disadvantage when the need arose for additional funds. He could convoke a special session of the estates, try to persuade the chamber of the élus to levy an additional sum that had not been consented to, or simply do without. By the close of September 1621, Louis's finances were no longer in a position to permit him to continue to opt for the last solution, and he ordered the Burgundian deputies to assemble at Dijon in November. Because the previous meeting had been held in the fall of 1618, and those who had attended had only voted taxes through 1621, this assembly was not significantly premature. Nevertheless, Louis preferred to consider it an extraordinary session and used this as an excuse to convoke only one clergyman and one nobleman from each bailiwick and one deputy from each of the principal towns. Presumably he hoped that a smaller assembly could be more easily persuaded to do his bidding than the full estates. At the meeting the governor, Bellegarde, and the other commissioners explained royal policy and stressed the need for money to suppress the revolt. Cajoled but not forgetful of their own interests, those present voted 300,000 livres.

The regular meeting of the estates was not held until June 1622. Once more Louis asked for a special grant of 400,000 livres, but this time he was met with a blunt refusal. The three estates protested the composition of the previous assembly. Taxes, they declared, could be voted only in a full assembly of the estates. Angered, Louis assembled the estates again in August, when they were sufficiently chastened by his indignation to offer 150,000 livres.

The meetings of the three estates of Dauphiné were more noteworthy for their quarrels with each other than with the crown. In the estates in 1621, Claude Brosse, the syndic of the villages, reopened the old question of the nature of the taille in Dauphiné and the settlement imposed by Henry IV. In spite of the "union of the three orders" achieved in 1611, which had supposedly brought an end to separate meetings of the individual estates, the nobility, including some members of the long robe, assembled apart from the third estate every few days to draft a response to Brosse's petition. Brosse has usually been depicted as the gallant and unselfish defender of the villages. Certainly he did all in his power to shift the burden of taxation from the peasants to the privileged, but in doing so he appears to have had the tacit support of the king's council, whose members realized that if the king was to get more money from Dauphiné, it would have to come from those who could best afford to pay. Not only did the council protect Brosse from physical violence and legal machinations, it also permitted him to draw a handsome annual stipend of 1,500 livres from the villages and in 1621 apparently authorized a princely gift of 30,000 écus. Not surprisingly, the villages refused to reelect Brosse as their syndic, and for a few years he was out of office.[12] In 1622, the king asked the estates for 550,000 livres to support the war effort, but instead of giving him what he wanted, those present offered their governor, Lesdiguières, 36,000 livres if he would get the new taxes suppressed. That able but greedy man refused to cooperate, probably because the royal taxes fell largely into his hands, but in the end the maximum annual revenue the royal treasury received from Dauphiné in the years 1621–24 was only 28,731 livres.

The estates of the remaining pays d'états were treated more gently. Only once did Louis seek an extraordinary contribution from Provence during these four years, and in the end he accepted the smaller grant that the estates were willing to give.

Louis continued the practice of collecting the taxes he requested of the Normans whether the estates consented to the entire sum or not. A Protestant uprising in 1621 prevented him from holding the estates to vote the levies for 1622, but the required sums were imposed anyway. The province was already so overtaxed, however, that he did not take advantage of the situation, and the amount turned over to the royal treasury actually declined somewhat during the four years. Louis also showed restraint in the taxes he imposed in Auvergne and Lyonnais, where the assemblies remained active.

The Catholic clergy strongly approved of Louis's decision to restore the church lands in Béarn and Navarre and of the war with the Protestants that followed. There was never any doubt that Louis would seek extraordinary aid from them, or that they would give generously. The only questions were how much they would offer and how the money could be raised. After some bargaining, the Assembly of the Clergy that met in 1621 offered three million livres. In return, they asked that Louis destroy La Rochelle and the other Protestant strongholds, but they did not suggest that Protestants be denied liberty of conscience. Persuasion, not force, was to be used to return them to the Catholic fold. The Catholic clergy's Protestant policy in 1621 was thus essentially the same as that adopted by Louis in 1622, and as that which Richelieu is often credited with establishing at a later date.

CONCLUSIONS

The difference in the way the crown treated the various provincial estates between 1621 and 1623 is striking. Those in Guyenne received their death blow. Others were treated roughly, yet some were handled with as much consideration as before. If the former had been the weaker estates and the latter those that were strong, the historian's task in explaining the crown's divergent policy would be simple, but the reverse was more nearly the case. The estates of Languedoc, Brittany, and Burgundy were subjected to exceptional pressure to produce more funds, while few additional demands were placed on those of Normandy and Basse-Auvergne.

There is a hypothesis that might explain the lack of consistency. In August 1619, the council of finances was divided into four groups, composed of an intendant of finances and four other councillors, each charged with dealing with a certain number of provinces. The committee of the council that administered Guyenne and Brittany was headed by the intendant, Gilles de Maupeou, a Protestant convert who had been one of Sully's most trusted lieutenants. Maupeou had served in the généralité of Guyenne from 1595 to 1597 as a financial investigator and administrator. His reaction to what he saw is not known, but the sieur de Selves, the deputy from Agenais, frequently reported to his constituents that Maupeou was the only member of the council who supported Sully in his insistence that the élections were necessary. On one occasion he wrote that Maupeou had rebuffed him as much as or more than that notoriously rude statesman.

Another group of the council was responsible for Languedoc, Provence, Auvergne, and Lyonnais. Nothing is known of the position of the intendant, Charles Duret, and at least two of the councillors, Vic and Caumartin, were moderates, but a fourth was Michel de Marillac. Marillac had been dispatched to Guyenne in 1598–99 to ensure that the taille was apportioned and collected in a fair, honest, and efficient manner. It may have been his unfavorable report that led Sully to decide to establish élections there. Soon he was to become the most determined foe the estates ever had. It is probable, therefore, that he was responsible for the decision to take advantage of the presence of a royal army in Languedoc in 1622 to issue an edict creating élections. It is also probable that his support among his fellow councillors was so lukewarm that Ventadour and other friends of the estates had little difficulty in securing its suppression. In view of the predominantly mild attitude of this group of the council, it is not surprising that the estates and assemblies in Provence, Auvergne, and Lyonnais, where there were no royal armies, escaped unscathed.

Not enough is known of the attitude of the councillors toward the estates in either of the other two groups to offer a persuasive hypothesis as to why the one that dealt with Burgundy was more severe than the one responsible for Dauphiné. Whatever the explanation of the events of these four eventful years, these facts cannot be disputed: Louis XIII had ensured that Béarn and Navarre would always be united with France in the person of the king, he had seriously weakened the power of the Protestant nobles and towns, and he had taken steps that led to the decline of the estates of the largest généralité in France. Even had he died in 1624, he would have been one of the principal architects of the absolute monarchy in France.

VIII

Richelieu and Marillac, 1624–1629

THE TWO MEN

Cardinal Richelieu entered the king's council on April 29, 1624. He owed his appointment to Marie de Medici, Bérulle, and others who had used their influence to persuade Louis to take this step despite his dislike for him, a dislike that stemmed back to the time when he had briefly served in the government during the Concini era. Once admitted to the council, Richelieu soon became its most influential member, and Michel de Marillac was named co-superintendent of finances.[1]

Too often the Richelieus have been depicted as members of the minor nobility. In fact the family was an old one. On the paternal side, the cardinal's grandmother was a Rochechouart, and on the maternal side she was the lord of three fiefs and connected with the ancient house of Feuquières. The latter lady had married a La Porte, a lawyer, member of the parlement of Paris, and himself the lord of two seigneuries. Through him the cardinal had useful connections in the sovereign courts and legal profession. At the time of his premature death in 1590 at the age of forty-two, the cardinal's father was already grand provost of France, a knight of the Order of the Holy Ghost, captain of the royal guards, and friend and companion of the king. He was clearly of the middle nobility, and had he lived a few decades longer, he might have advanced into its front ranks.

Volumes have been written about Richelieu's early career, depicting how he rose to be the king's first minister through intrigue, flattery, and dissimulation. At times he found himself in the camp of the rebels, but he also sought to avoid becoming too closely attached to any faction and to remain on good terms with everyone with influence. When the king reluctantly admitted him to his council in 1624, both the "good Frenchmen" and the "devouts" welcomed his appointment. Once in power he displayed no gratitude toward Marie de Medici, Barbin, and

others who had aided him unless it was clear that they would be his
servants. He packed the government with his creatures and insisted on
their unquestioned loyalty. In spite of his conduct, in his written
pronouncements he always took the stance of a divine right, absolute
monarchist and strictly orthodox Catholic. His Catholicism, however,
was of the sort that made salvation easy to achieve, and he was willing to
make moral compromises when it was to his advantage or that of the state
to do so. Although a product of the Catholic Reformation, in that he
wanted to eradicate abuses and bring Protestants back into the fold, he
was almost untouched by the spirituality of that great movement.

No one has ever questioned Richelieu's superb intellectual powers.
Whether the causes he lent them to profited France is another matter. His
accomplishments are all the more remarkable because he was a highly
nervous, irritable individual who suffered from poor health. Only his
indomitable will kept him at his tasks, but even he quickly recognized
that there were limits to what he could do. Because of his health, Louis
specifically directed in June 1626 that he free himself from secondary
matters in order to devote all his energies to foreign affairs and to general
concerns of great importance. Local business and individual petitions
were to be handled by other ministers and the secretaries of state. As a
result, Richelieu had little direct contact with the provincial estates.
Matters concerning them were the responsibility of the keeper of the
seals, the secretaries of state, financial officials, and other members of the
king's council. This is not to say that Richelieu was not in fact Louis's
chief minister, but it does suggest that the routine administration of the
kingdom, and to a large degree the directions domestic policy took, were
in the hands of others. Of these men, none was more important than
Michel de Marillac.

The Marillacs were an old noble family whose members had served in
the church, the robe, and the sword. Michel, a devout Catholic, had
considered entering the clergy, but the death of a relative who was a
member of the parlement of Paris led him to carry on the family tradition
there. His half brother, Louis, on the other hand, joined the military and
became a marshal of France and the husband of Catherine de Medici, a
cousin and maid of honor to the queen mother herself.

After the close of the Wars of Religion, Michel de Marillac was given
the difficult task of ensuring that taxes were apportioned and collected in
a fair, honest, and efficient manner in the généralités of Limoges and
Guyenne. It is likely that his unfavorable report caused Henry and Sully
to attack the provincial estates in Guyenne. This experience probably also

contributed to his low opinion of the estates. Marillac was also sent on missions to Brittany, Bourbonnais, Auvergne, and the Spanish frontier, but more and more he turned to religion. In 1602, he began to frequent the hotel of Madame Acarie, a noted mystic, where he became a close friend of Pierre de Bérulle, the future cardinal, and other leaders of the Catholic Reformation. He won the respect of Chancellor Bellièvre, who reportedly attempted to make him a president of the parlement of Paris, but he was greatly relieved when the post was assigned to someone else. In 1612, he was named to the king's council, and he quickly became one of the five most active members of that body. As a councillor, he witnessed the Estates General of 1614, and he was instrumental in resolving quarrels over precedence in the estates of Brittany and in the Assembly of Notables in 1617. Marillac became acquainted with Richelieu during the Estates General or the latter's first ministry. Never one to desert a friend in adversity, he and especially his brother corresponded with the future cardinal during his exile from court. In view of these friendly relations, it is not surprising that when Richelieu became chief minister, Marillac was named co-superintendent of finances.

THE EARLY YEARS

For the first few years, the two statesmen worked together without serious difficulty, although disagreements did occur. Richelieu quickly became concerned about the Austrian Habsburgs' efforts to strengthen their position in the Empire, and their Spanish cousins' attempts to regain their lost provinces in the Low Countries. Near the close of 1624, he dispatched a small army to Italy to cut the Spanish route through the Valtelline valley to Germany. At this point, Rohan led elements of the Protestant movement into rebellion. Caught between a foreign war and an internal insurrection, Richelieu prepared a memorandum for the king early in May 1625. "It seems," he wrote, "that everything now conspires to humble the pride of Spain. . . . There has never been such a splendid opportunity for the king to increase his power and clip the wings of his enemies." Nevertheless Richelieu recognized that "as long as the Huguenots have a foothold in France, the king will never be the master of the interior or capable of undertaking any glorious action abroad."[2] For the moment Richelieu was not ready to tackle either the Spanish or the Huguenots. First it was necessary to reform the kingdom. Sometime in 1625, he prepared a document that reveals that he had little conception of the administrative changes that would be necessary to transform

France into an absolute monarchy. In it, he urged that four councils be created, the most important of which was to be dominated by the magnates. The second and third councils were to deal with fiscal matters and petitions from the provinces. They were to be composed of the chancellor, the keeper of the seals, the superintendent of finances, and clergymen, nobles of the sword, and nobles of the robe in equal numbers. Since the clergymen selected were likely to be of noble extraction, the proposal, if implemented, would have greatly increased the role of the nobility in the government. The fourth council, two-thirds of whose members were to be cardinals and other prelates, was to advise the king on matters of conscience and on ecclesiastical appointments.

Among the many articles that dealt with the reformation of the church, Richelieu proposed that archbishops hold provincial councils every third year, a step that would have transformed what had been occasional meetings into a new type of representative institution common to all of France. He also advocated economies by reducing the expenses of the royal household, the size of the bureaucracy, and the salaries of government officials. The nobility was to be given a monopoly on household and military positions. Venality was to be abolished, and dishonest financial officials were to be punished. Finally, the domain was to be redeemed, so that the burden on the taxpayers could be lessened.

Many of Richelieu's suggestions were derived from the Estates General of 1614 and the Assembly of Notables of 1617. One, a proposal to establish an itinerant court to hear and judge complaints against anyone, including members of the sovereign courts, was similar to a proposal rejected by that robe-dominated assembly. Another dealt with payments *par comptant,* a method of dispensing with royal funds without going through the chamber of accounts, which enabled the king to give secret subsidies to foreign powers and to the Huguenots. Unfortunately, much of this money was diverted into the pockets of courtiers and financiers. Bellièvre had tried to solve the problem in 1596–97 by dividing revenue into two parts and allocating one to meet the contractual obligations of the crown. Richelieu, couching his statement in the form of a royal edict, approached the problem by having the king declare that "we wish to deprive ourselves of the freedom that we and our predecessors have formerly used to dispose of money by secret ways of accounting, recognizing that although the practice can be useful on many occasions . . . , the abuse is nevertheless of such consequence that we can say that it is one of the principal causes of the dissipation of our finances."[3] Then, after expressing the desire not to have to increase the tax burden on the people, Richelieu recommended measures to reduce gifts and gratifications.

Reflecting the older Renaissance attitude of making local agencies rather than the crown responsible for welfare, Richelieu made municipal and parish officials responsible for correcting the disorders in hospital administration in conjunction with the clergy. He also recommended that the poor in every town and the surrounding district be employed in public works. To administer this program, he advocated having "the deputies of the clergy, officers, mayors, and échevins . . . assemble annually to discuss and resolve the yearly cost and the means of finding funds."[4] Sums needed beyond that available for the poor from the usual sources were to be raised by taxes consented to by each locality and collected by persons elected for this purpose. Thus in 1625 Richelieu considered creating a nationwide system of periodic provincial assemblies for the clergy, increasing the responsibilities and the taxing powers of the duly constituted local bodies, augmenting the role of the nobility in the council, and placing limitations on how the king spent his revenue.

Richelieu probably hoped to begin to implement his reform program immediately after the restoration of peace in the winter of 1626, but the intrigues surrounding the marriage of Louis's younger brother, Gaston, and the related Chalais conspiracy caused a delay. The episode provided Louis with another opportunity to display his firmness by beheading one of the culprits, but the results of the affair were of far greater importance. To weaken the conspirators, Richelieu reached an accord with Condé. From this time on, Condé supported him in all his endeavors and behaved as a loyal subject of the king. In return, Richelieu gave him many lucrative assignments, including conducting the negotiations with the provincial estates after the Day of Dupes. Condé, who stood second in line to the throne, was a valuable acquisition, for he served as a counterweight to Gaston, who became involved in many conspiracies during the reign.

The Chalais conspiracy also led to a shake-up in the government. Chancellor d'Aligre displayed such weakness in dealing with the problem that Louis took the seals from him and gave them to Marillac. Since chancellors held the office for life, d'Aligre continued to enjoy the title, but Marillac performed his duties. Nicolas Lefèvre, Marillac's admirer and the author of an unpublished biography, says that the king had seriously considered giving him the seals on several occasions before Richelieu became a minister and leaves the reader to assume that he now did so on his own initiative. Richelieu's memoirs, on the other hand, present Marillac as the cardinal's choice because of his integrity and experience. Both versions are subject to suspicion; after the Day of Dupes, Richelieu and his propagandists wanted to portray Marillac as an unfaithful client, while Marillac's supporters insisted that he had long been a trusted adviser of the king and his mother and owed his position to royal favor alone. Undoubtedly Marillac was an old and valued servant, and it is possible that Louis or his mother initiated his appointment, but there is no reason to believe that Richelieu objected. At this point, his influence was so strong that he could probably have persuaded Louis not to name someone unacceptable to him to such an important post. Indeed, he secured the appointment of one of his creatures, Antoine Coiffier de Ruzé, marquis d'Effiat, as superintendent of finances in Marillac's place, and by threatening to resign, he won Louis's permission to have a guard to protect him from conspirators, such as Chalais, who sought his life.

These appointments were of greater significance than might ordinarily have been the case, because the state of Richelieu's health led him to turn over the routine administration of the government to Marillac and others. On June 9, Louis pleaded with him not to resign because of his indisposition and promised to protect him from his enemies. Several weeks later, he signed an order granting Richelieu's request to devote all of his energy to foreign affairs and to general matters of great importance. People with petitions were directed to present them to other members of the council or to the secretaries of state.

Richelieu was now in a position to act, but to implement the reforms he thought mandatory, he still had to persuade the nobility to accept the necessary economies, the wealthy to pay for the redemption of the royal domain so that the peasants could be spared, the venturesome to engage in overseas trade, and the sovereign courts to register the desired edicts, even when their own interests were at stake. To do so, Richelieu sponsored the publication of several pamphlets; then, early in October, he persuaded Louis to convoke the Assembly of Notables.

THE ASSEMBLY OF NOTABLES AND THE ORDONNANCE OF 1629

The meeting opened on December 2 in Paris. Participating were twelve prelates, ten nobles, twenty-seven members of the sovereign courts, the provost of the merchants of Paris, and a secretary. In addition, Louis's brother, Gaston, now duke of Orléans, was named president of the assembly, and the cardinal of La Valette, the duke of La Force, and Marshal Bassompierre were appointed assistant presidents. The composition of the assembly was thus quite similar to that of the one held in 1617 at Rouen, where Gaston had presided and sixteen of the same notables had served. Once more the courts had a numerical predominance, and this fact was to cause trouble in the meeting.

Louis opened the assembly with the one-sentence statement that he had called the meeting to remedy the disorders in his state, and that the keeper of the seals would make known his will. Marillac's address had been prepared after considerable conversation with other leading members of the council, including Richelieu. In it, he stressed the great expenses that the foreign wars and domestic revolts had caused since 1620. The king's ordinary annual revenue was only 16 million livres, but in spite of economies in the royal household and elsewhere, his expenses had been from 36 million to 40 million livres per year. Nevertheless, he had not increased the taille or reduced the rentes owed to his subjects or the salaries due his officers. Rather, he had sought other expedients, and he was now over 50 million livres in debt. To redress the situation, the king sought their advice. To economize further, he was considering reducing the size of the army and razing useless fortifications. To increase his income, he wanted to redeem the domain and alienated taxes. He also desired the notables' help in restoring commerce "to enrich the people and to repair the honor of France."

The notables devoted most of their time to fiscal matters and the related questions of the army, navy, and economy. The budget obviously had to be balanced, but the peasants could pay no more taxes. To increase revenue, the notables readily agreed that the domain should be reclaimed, but they were unwilling to provide a capital sum to speed the process. Instead, they chose the slower process that Sully had used of making the domain produce all the needed money for its redemption over a period of about sixteen years. Another suggested source of revenue was to increase the efficiency and honesty of the financial officials, but the notables rejected a government proposal that a permanent chamber of justice be established to uncover and punish those who were dishonest. The ordinary courts, they thought, would suffice. Absent from the government's proposals and the notables' reactions was any suggestion that new élections be created or that the role of the provincial estates and towns in taxation be diminished.

The notables were enthusiastic about Richelieu's plan to increase the wealth of France through trade. They approved the formation of trading companies as the British and Dutch had done and, more surprisingly, accepted the idea of creating a navy of forty-five vessels at a cost of 1,283,160 livres. The project was presented to them not only as a necessity to protect trade but also as an economy, for larger sums had been spent procuring ships from other sources in recent years.

Since some time would elapse before the king could receive increased revenue from the domain and trade, the immediate need was to curtail expenses. The greatest savings could be made by reducing the costs of the army and garrisons, but it was necessary to retain a large enough force to defend the frontiers and maintain order in the interior. Equally important was the need to ensure that the troops were paid, supplied, and disciplined, so that they would not add to the misery of the people by preying on the countryside. Richelieu put France's peacetime military requirements at 18,000 to 20,000 foot and 2,000 horse, about twice the size of Henry IV's standing army. The government wanted to throw the costs of this force onto the people. To make them more willing to accept the burden, it proposed that each regiment bear the name of the province that supported it and each company the name of a town. This deliberate appeal to provincial pride did not silence the concerns of the notables. In the end, the majority opted for an infantry of 17,700 men, at an annual cost of 4,674,630 livres. Of this sum, 1,590,000 livres was to come from the estates in provinces in which there were no élections, 2,058,420 livres from the ordinary revenue of the crown, and 1,028,210 livres from the towns. The notables agreed that the 2,000 horse were necessary and that they should be supported by the taillon, which would have to be increased.

The high cost of maintaining garrisons in the château-forts had long concerned the provincial estates, and the notables devoted considerable time to this problem. Some of the data they considered are revealing. After a study of the situation in Dauphiné, the parlement of Grenoble had recommended that sixty-two of the sixty-six fortified places be razed. Of the sixty-two, thirty-six belonged to the king. Twenty-one of these were garrisoned, but the remainder were unguarded. These figures suggest that an indiscriminate destruction of fortified places might weaken royal authority more than its opponents, a fact recognized at the time. On December 20, 1626, a noble wrote Richelieu that it was necessary to retain the fortifications in the interior of the kingdom in order to ensure the obedience of the people. He recalled that "in the time of the League . . . the only places that remained in the service of the king were those in which there were châteaux that were used by governors and captains who were creatures of the king to keep the people and the parlements in obedience."[5]

The notables, like the Estates General, the provincial estates, and the towns on other occasions, showed as much or more enthusiasm for the destruction of forts as the king did. The reasons they most often avowed for their positions were to avoid having to support the garrisons and to remove the risk that poorly guarded forts would become nests of thieves, but one wonders if there were not many instances in Louis's reign when towns and estates sought the destruction of forts to remove the royal presence, and occasionally they frankly said so. After all, a royal castle could be used more effectively to overawe a people without artillery than a feudal castle could be used against a royal army with artillery.

The total cost of the proposed navy, infantry, and cavalry came to 7.5 million livres, a substantial sum, but still 4.5 million less than was being spent during the current year, and not half the amount devoted to these purposes in 1625. Additional economies were nevertheless mandatory, and the notables approved reducing the costs of the royal households, cutting pensions to 2 million livres a year, and suppressing the vacant offices of constable and admiral of France.

The government was also concerned about the frequent rebellions and general disobedience to royal commands. With no difficulty, the notables were persuaded to confirm old laws against raising troops, manufacturing or owning artillery, fortifying towns and châteaux, levying taxes, and holding assemblies without the king's permission. However, when it came to a royal proposal to establish an itinerant court to judge complaints presented by the people against all persons, including the members of parlement, the notables were intractable. It would only be permissible, they declared, to have a grand jours within the jurisdiction of each parlement and staffed by officials of that court, a counterproposal that meant, in effect, that the members of a parlement would be judged only by a court composed largely of their colleagues.

As a noble, Richelieu sympathized with the problems of that class. Without difficulty he persuaded the assembly that more nobles should be admitted to the royal council and that venality of offices should be suppressed in the royal households and the army, so that positions could be awarded on the basis of "birth and merit." This was not enough for the nobles, however, for they took advantage of the meeting to present a special cahier to the king in which they asked that they be given more benefices and offices, including seats in the parlements. They also asked to engage in trade without loss of their privileges.

The officers of the sovereign courts were not to be outdone by the nobility. They too submitted a special petition, but whereas that of the nobility consisted primarily of pleading by the powerful for their less fortunate brethren, that of the parlements was largely composed of selfish requests that were often unwise, unjust, and prejudicial to royal authority. They sought the suppression of the special courts containing some Protestants that had been established under the provisions of the Edict of Nantes so that members of that religion would not have to seek justice in all-Catholic courts. They protested the royal council's assuming jurisdiction over cases in their courts, and the "new practice" of sending intendants of justice into their jurisdictions, undermining their authority. They modestly asked that they receive only small presents from litigants in their courts, in order to reduce the costs of obtaining justice, but then protested the evil practice of telling the accused the names of the witnesses against them. It is with relief that we read an altruistic article charging the élus of Guyenne with oppressing the people and asking that they not be permitted to exceed their authority.

From the first, Richelieu appears to have recognized that there were limits as to how much cooperation he could expect from an assembly in which members of the sovereign courts were so numerous. At no point did he mention the paulette, and he limited his attack on venality of office to the royal households and the military, areas that in no way affected them. If the time came to attack venality, he could always cite the recommendation of the Estates General of 1614 as justification.

Richelieu had also been silent in another area. He never hinted that new élections should be established anywhere in France, and he proposed no administrative changes that would weaken the provincial estates. We know that in his reform proposals of 1625 he had opposed venality and can therefore assume that his silence in 1626 on this score should be attributed to his desire to win the support of the sovereign courts. He had taken no position on the élections, on the other hand, in 1625, or so far as is known at any earlier time in his career. His silence can therefore be explained only by the assumption that he did not believe that they were necessary. He still sought to rule through persuasion rather than bureaucratic absolutism.

The assembly terminated on February 24, but just eight days before the final meeting, Louis issued a declaration in which he swore that he would do all that was in his power to reform his kingdom. He spoke of the need to reunite all of his subjects in the Catholic church, but promised to use "gentleness, love, patience, and good examples" as his means. Protestants were to retain all their liberties until "it pleases God to illuminate their hearts and bring them back into the bosom of his church." None of them should lend an ear to those who preached rebellion. Nobles were to have more positions in the royal households, the army, and the navy, and their children were to be given free instruction. Justice was to flourish, and trade was to be expanded. Upon "the faith and word of a king," Louis swore to reduce taxes by 3 million livres by 1632 in order to lighten the load on the people. Already he had reduced their burden for the current year by 600,000 livres. Furthermore, he was going to redeem his alienated domain, tailles, and gabelles to compensate for the loss in revenue.[6]

Louis's blueprint for the future was striking enough, but even more startling was the effort to publicize his plans. Parlements, chambers of accounts, and courts of aides throughout the kingdom were directed to register the declaration and to have it published in all the subordinate seats in their respective jurisdictions. It was printed in the *Mercure françois* and circulated as a pamphlet. Richelieu, the master of the art of propaganda, was undoubtedly the motivating force behind these moves designed to win popular support for his government and its program. There was a danger, of course, that he might not be able to fulfill his promises, but he must have been reasonably confident that he could, or he would not have publicized his ambitious plans so broadly. Success, of course, depended on maintaining foreign and domestic peace, and this would not have been too unrealistic a goal if Richelieu had restrained French ambitions and the leaders of other nations had acted sensibly, but this was too much to ask of the statesmen of that day. In July 1627, an English army under the duke of Buckingham landed near La Rochelle and prodded its much-abused citizens to revolt. Rohan once more raised an army in Languedoc, but the bulk of the Huguenot nobility and burghers were most reluctant to join his cause.

Richelieu reacted quickly to the English invasion and the new revolt. The reform program was slowed, although Marillac and others continued to work on a great ordonnance when they could find the time. An army led by Louis himself lay siege to La Rochelle, and another under Condé attempted to reduce the rebels in Languedoc. The defenders of La Rochelle fought with great determination until October 29, 1628, when they were forced to capitulate. By then all hope of new supplies reaching them from the bungling English had vanished, and nearly two-thirds of their number had perished, for the most part from starvation. Those who survived were granted their lives, religion, and property, but the town lost its fortifications and privileges. No longer would its proud burghers be able to flout the authority of the king. Instead, they were compelled to witness the installation of a Catholic bishop in their midst.

Louis now had to decide in what direction he should direct his efforts: to Germany, where the emperor had won several notable victories and appeared firmly established on the Baltic; to Italy, where the duke of Nevers's inheritance of Mantua was being challenged by the Habsburgs; to Languedoc, where the outnumbered Huguenots were still defying royal authority; or to long-overdue domestic reform. On January 13, 1629, Richelieu addressed himself to those problems in more than his usual grandiose fashion. "Now that La Rochelle is taken," he wrote, "if the king wants to make himself the most powerful monarch and the most esteemed prince in the world, he ought . . . to examine carefully and secretly with his faithful creatures" what policies he should pursue. On the domestic scene, it was first necessary to suppress the Huguenot rebellion. Interior fortifications must be raised and those on the frontier strengthened. The paulette should not be renewed when it expired in a year, and the courts "who through their pretended sovereignty daily oppose the good of the kingdom must be humbled and reduced."[7] The king must make both great and small obedient to his will. He must appoint wise and able people to the bishoprics, redeem the domain, and increase his revenue by one-half, but at the same time reduce the burden on the people. The domestic program that Richelieu had outlined several times before thus remained intact. To his presentation to the notables, he had added the suppression of the paulette and the humbling of the sovereign courts, but the former, at least, had long been on his mind. Again conspicuously absent was any mention of establishing élections or weakening the provincial estates, although Marillac was already moving in that direction.

Turning to foreign affairs, Richelieu urged that Louis assist Nevers in his claim to Mantua by raising the siege of Casal and then return to Languedoc and suppress the Huguenot revolt by July. Amazingly this proposal was actually accomplished ahead of schedule. Casal was relieved, and on June 27, the Huguenot rebellion was terminated with the peace of Alès. By its terms, the Huguenots retained their religious and civil liberties, but all their fortifications and cannon were destroyed. Their political assemblies were to cease, and their proud towns were humbled. "The roots of heresy, rebellion, disorder, and civil war, which have exhausted France for so long, are dried up," Richelieu wrote Louis. "Now all your subjects will compete with each other in rendering the obedience which is due Your Majesty."[8] A giant step toward royal absolutism had been taken. The state within a state had come to an end.

While Richelieu was devoting most of his time to foreign policy and the Huguenots, Marillac was attempting to carry on the routine administration and to prepare a great reforming ordonnance based largely on the work of the Estates General of 1614 and the Assemblies of Notables of 1617 and 1626–27. Included were numerous articles concerning the reformation of the clergy, the welfare of the sick and the poor, the maintenance of internal order and the discipline of troops, the administration of justice and finance, and the development of a navy and commerce. Repeated were old laws against printing and selling books, levying taxes, raising troops, owning cannon or large quantities of powder, fortifying towns and châteaux, and convoking assemblies without the king's permission. Useless fortifications in the interior were to be demolished, and the king announced that henceforth he would appoint the officers of his household and his army, contrary to the tradition of the grand masters of his household and the colonel of the infantry naming their subordinates. This last measure and one directing that neither the servants nor the relatives of generals or provincial governors be sent to them as intendants dealt blows to the patron-client relationship. Another article required royal officials to obtain permission before entering the service of anyone, including members of the royal family. If some articles were aimed at limiting the capacity of the nobility to revolt, many others were designed to increase their role in the government and to improve their economic position. Venality of office in the royal households and the military was again forbidden, and positions in the church, army, parlements, and royal council were reserved for them. These measures were probably an outgrowth of the ideas Richelieu expressed in 1625 and in the Assembly of Notables of 1626–27. More clearly, he was responsible for the provision permitting nobles to engage in sea trade without derogation.

The dreams of lessening the fiscal burden were not forgotten. Garrisons and pensions were to be reduced, and gifts par comptant were forbidden. The crown's promise to the notables that the domain would be soon redeemed was temporarily abandoned, but the goal of reducing the taille by 3 million livres was reiterated, and arrears in taxes prior to 1624 were canceled.

The royal officials fared less well than the nobility or the people. They won few concessions, and many articles were designed to correct their abuses. Indeed, in Marillac's and perhaps Richelieu's opinion, they were

becoming the principal obstacles to good government. Marillac announced the crown's intention to hold grand jours in the individual
provinces and to establish a permanent chamber of justice to punish
officials guilty of financial malpractices. Most serious of all, parlement
was given only two months in which to make remonstrances against
provisions in royal edicts, after which they were to be registered without
more ado.

Marillac had spent much of his career as a maître des requêtes, and he
had acquired a high opinion of the value of such officials. As a result, he
included a long article in the ordonnance greatly extending their powers
and authority. They were to be sent to the provinces annually to hear the
complaints of the people against royal officials and other persons and to
report their findings to the chancellor or keeper of the seals. They were to
inform the government of excessive salaries and presents received by
officials, to observe the levying and collection of taxes, and to correct
abuses. In the instructions Marillac actually gave to the maîtres des
requêtes, he went into more detail. They were to work quietly and to
remain on good terms with the members of the sovereign courts in order
to obtain useful information from them. But they were also to report any
abuses that they or the financial officials committed. They were to inform
the crown about the behavior of the clergy and the way governors
comported themselves. Information on local leaders, factions, and those
most loyal to the king was to be sought.

One of the most striking features of the ordonnance was the number
of articles devoted to ensuring that the military, the fiscal bureaucracy,
and the courts performed their duties without abusing the people. On
the other hand, the ordonnance contained very little concerning the duly
constituted, self-governing bodies. The failure to lash out at the provincial estates and towns should not be construed as evidence that Marillac
favored a degree of self-government. He had carefully read the cahiers
that the deputies of the Estates General of 1614 presented to the king,
but he did not incorporate the suggestion made by the nobility that they
be assembled in each province every third year to elect a syndic, or of the
third estate that the Estates General be held every tenth year and that
provincial estates, towns, and parishes be permitted to levy large sums for
their own use without having to seek royal permission. More surprising,
the suggestion Richelieu made in 1625 that archbishops hold provincial
councils every third year was ignored, although most of the cardinal's
ideas in this memorandum were incorporated. Perhaps the cardinal had
changed his mind. Perhaps he had forgotten the whole affair, and

Marillac had not seen fit to raise the issue. Marillac had decided to deal with the existing provincial estates in another fashion, and he was determined that there should be no more deliberative bodies. Also absent from the ordonnance was any mention of the paulette. Here we know that Richelieu had decided to wait for the end of the year, when the current contract expired.

Richelieu anticipated trouble with the parlement of Paris over the ordonnance. To speed registration, it was decided that the king would hold a lit de justice just before his departure for Italy. It took place on January 15, 1629, with the usual pomp reserved for such occasions. As keeper of the seals, it fell to Marillac to be the royal spokesman. He obviously devoted considerable time to doing research for his speech, and it led to a book-length study of the authority of the king and the role of parlement, which he later presented to Louis. Not until the fourteenth century, when the parlement of Paris separated from the council and became sedentary, Marillac insisted, had kings adopted the practice of having that body register their ordonnances so that they would be better observed. Since its members were important, experienced men, the king permitted them to make remonstrances when they found articles that needed to be more clearly expressed or modified. However, if a king persevered in his original opinion, parlement must proceed with the registration. It had no authority of its own, and kings could use other means to publish their decrees as they had done long ago. "The authority of the kings of France," therefore, "is independent of all other power and they render account only to God for the temporal administration of their state." If officers could judge the actions of the king, "the king is no longer king. He is under the tutelage of his officers and sovereignty is depended on them. . . . It is true, therefore, that the king alone is the judge of the justice of his actions. He is accountable for them to God alone."[9]

When Marillac had finished, President Le Jay responded for parlement. He had been involved with Condé and other magnates in their revolts during the early part of Louis's reign, but now he declared in the same vein as Marillac that the officers of parlement had no power except what the king gave them. Nevertheless, after the king's departure for Italy, the judges refused to publish the ordonnance or send it to the provinces until they had deliberated on each article and made remonstrances. In short, they decided to proceed just as though Louis had not held the lit de justice. There were some articles they did not like, but what infuriated them most was that the king had ordered that the ordonnance be registered before they had had an opportunity to make remonstrances. Even worse, Marillac had lectured them on the absolute power of the king and had denied them any intrinsic authority. On him they placed the blame for the contents of the ordonnance and the way it was presented to them. From that time on, parlement never lost an opportunity to ridicule or malign Marillac and his ordonnance, which they derisively called the Code Michau, a play on his first name.

When Marie de Medici expressed surprise on January 25 that parlement had not submitted the verified ordonnance, Le Jay was far less submissive than when he had been in the presence of the king. Parlement, he insisted "was immortal . . . it would cease to exist only with the monarchy."[10] Marillac was livid. Angrily he reported the course of events to Richelieu. Parlement should be compelled to accept the ordonnance, he urged, but neither Richelieu nor the king appears to have been overly concerned at their keeper of the seals' plight. Italy was uppermost in their minds, and Marie, who was acting as regent, allowed parlement four months to consider the ordonnance. With provocative slowness, its members proceeded with the verification. By March 16, two months after the lit de justice, they had reached the fourth article of an ordonnance that had 461. By May 12, near the end of the generous allotment of time granted by the queen mother, they were debating the tenth. Not until September 7, after the king had returned to Paris and applied direct pressure, was the Code Michau registered and published. Parlement went unpunished, but Marillac succeeded in blocking Le Jay's appointment as first president of the parlement of Paris, the duties of which office he had been performing while it was vacant.

By the close of 1629, Richelieu and Marillac were growing apart. They had shared an interest in reform and a desire to reduce the tax burden on the people, but Richelieu was increasingly ready to sacrifice these goals to his desire to humble the Habsburgs. In a meeting of the council on December 26, 1628, Marillac had joined those who opposed the decision to relieve Casal, and when Richelieu returned to court in September 1629, he blamed Marillac for the queen mother's coldness toward him. But there was more than a growing difference in priorities between the two men; there was a difference in method as well.

IX

⟨Marillac and the ⟩Provincial Estates

The crown's proposals to the Assembly of Notables for a reduction of the taille in the overtaxed provinces with élections was temporarily partially achieved, but it was to be accompanied by an increase in the taillon and in the levies on the relatively undertaxed towns and provinces with estates. As planned, pensions and payments par comptant were cut—except in 1629, when the latter were substantially increased—but significant reductions in the royal households and other nonmilitary areas were not achieved. More serious, the siege of La Rochelle, the assault on the Huguenots in Languedoc, and the intervention in Italy caused military expenses to soar. In 1628, the total outlay by the government was about 3.3 million livres more than it was in 1627, and expenses tended to increase rather than decrease thereafter. Under these circumstances it is necessary to inquire how the provincial estates fared in a government led by two such strong men as Richelieu and Marillac.[1]

THE PROVINCIAL ESTATES IN THE PAYS D'ELECTIONS

During the first six years of Richelieu's regime, there was little change in the crown's policy toward the estates in provinces in which there were also élections. Twice taxes were collected in Normandy without convoking the estates, and in the remaining years, the crown levied more taxes than the estates were willing to vote, but there were ample precedents for these actions. In Guyenne, where the élections had recently been created, the estates were clearly decaying, but elsewhere they were as active as before. The estates of Basse-Auvergne won a notable victory when the king's council ruled that no tax was to be levied to satisfy any claims against the third estate without consulting the deputies of the good towns. The consuls of St. Flour obtained royal confirmation of their right to hold assemblies that could impose 4,000 livres annually for local needs, but these victories had to be balanced against the creation of additional élections in Auvergne and Forez, probably to provide more offices to sell. It is in the provinces in which there were no élections that a new royal policy can be discerned.

THE PAYS D'ETAT AND THE ELECTIONS

Dauphiné probably suffered more from fiscal exactions in the 1620s than any other province.[2] The inhabitants were frequently called upon to supply troops as they marched across the Rhône Valley and up the Alpine passes. If they failed in this duty, the soldiers took what they wanted. Fiscal exactions were often far greater than those authorized by the crown, even though little money taken from the province ever found its way into the royal coffers in Paris. The Dauphinois were proud of their extensive privileges, but they had become so divided that they did little to protect themselves. The dispute on whether the taille was réele or personnelle divided the third estate from the privileged orders, and within the third estate, the villages were often at odds with the towns, who tried to shift more of the tax burden upon them. The crown was generally sympathetic to the third estate, in part because the suffering of the poorer people was recognized by conscientious administrators, but more so because it was necessary to make the privileged pay more taxes if the troops in transit were to be properly supported and more revenue was to flow to Paris.

In the early 1620s, the three estates managed to assemble together to argue about their differences, but the meeting at Grenoble in the fall of 1623 proved to be the last until 1627. During the intervening period, the people of Dauphiné were by no means inactive. A smaller group, referred to as the *assemblée du pays* or the assembly of the ten towns, was in effect transformed from an executive committee of the estates into an assembly that performed the duties of the estates, a role that it had usually assumed only in emergencies before. It included the commis of the clergy and the nobility and the syndic of the villages as well as the deputies of the ten towns. When the three estates finally assembled again in April 1627, a member of the third estate proposed that the king be asked to revoke all patents of nobility granted during the past sixty years. This obvious attempt to separate the old nobility from the new by appealing to the former's traditional dislike of the recent initiates into their order only served to drive the two noble factions closer together. Rumors that the crown was about to issue some edicts that threatened the liberties and privileges of the province caused the assemblée du pays that met in

October to attempt to reunite the three estates, but it was too late. From December 1627 through June 1628, one bombshell fell after another. First came edicts creating a bureau of finances, a chamber of accounts, a court of aides, and ten élections, each with twenty-nine officers. Then, having provided a complete royal fiscal structure to replace that of the estates, and new sovereign courts that weakened the parlement at Grenoble, Louis drastically altered the composition of the provincial estates.

The new assembly established by the edict of June 26, 1630, was to consist of the bishop of Grenoble, or in his absence another ecclesiastic, who was to preside, four barons, the procureur du pays, two commis of the clergy, twelve commis of the nobility, the *consuls* of the ten towns, and ten commis of the villages. The commis were to be elected by their constituents, except that five of the village commis must be royal chatelains, who could be nobles. This meant that those chosen by the third estate would approximately equal those who served by right or were elected by the privileged orders. Since the old estates had been dominated by the nobility, the new arrangement greatly increased the strength of the towns and villages. They therefore did not lift a finger to save the old estates and took no concerted action to oppose the establishment of the élections, which many saw as a move toward a more just system of taxation. The privileged sought to restore the old fiscal administration and the estates, but alone they could do nothing.

Louis justified the new financial institutions on the grounds that they would ensure that taxes would be more equally divided and that no levies would be made without his permission. The new assembly, he insisted, would reduce expenses and correct the abuses the third estate had so often complained about. Sessions were to be convoked only by order of the king, and they were normally to be limited to fifteen days. The annual costs of holding the meetings and related expenses were limited to 30,000 livres.

The hypocrisy of the crown's accusing the three estates of overburdening the people with the expenses they incurred becomes apparent when one notes that in 1621 they appropriated only 15,000 livres to pay the salaries and expenses of their officers and defray the costs of their meetings. In addition, some funds derived from the salt tax went to support the officers and activities of the clergy and nobility. In January 1626, the king's council limited the amount the estates could spend on salaries, travel, and their meetings to 30,000 livres, and this figure appears to have served as a guide for the sum allocated to support the reformed assembly of the estates. In addition to the 30,000 livres authorized by the new arrangement, however, the Dauphinois now had the burden of paying the salaries of the élus, which came to nearly 100,000 livres annually, as well as their fees. The size of the fees is difficult to determine, because it varied with the size of the tax, but the total cost of the new arrangement, exclusive of the expenditures for the bureau of finances and the new courts, must have exceeded 210,000 livres per year, seven times the sum spent by the estates. In 1621, the total amount voted by the three estates was only 166,431 livres, a smaller sum than that now assigned to the newly created élus. Collecting the crown's taxes need not have cost so much, but once the decision had been taken to establish the élections, the impoverished government could not resist creating five times as many offices as were necessary in order to profit from their sale. Furthermore, the crown found it advisable to give pensions to the "natural" leaders of dissident groups. The bishop of Grenoble, president-born of the estates, was granted 6,000 livres annually, and two of the barons who served as commis of the nobility were given 3,000 livres each.

Although the June 1630 decree of the council used the term *états* to describe the new assembly it created, the Dauphinois did not adopt the word. Rather it became known as the assemblée du pays, after the somewhat similar institution that had often met between the regular meetings of the three estates. The assembly of the ten towns also continued to be held, but neither institution was assigned the tax-consenting and administrative roles of the estates. They could only submit petitions of grievances, which were frequently ignored. For 1629, the crown demanded only 439,000 livres, but two years later the figure became 593,156 livres. The actual revenue turned over to the royal treasurer during these years jumped from 67,055 to 384,637 livres. The people of Dauphiné were exploited more than ever before.

The first two years of the Richelieu ministry were relatively uneventful in Burgundy, but when the triennial meeting of the estates opened in Dijon on September 14, 1626, there were indications that those attending sensed an approaching crisis and sought to prepare for it. To remove any doubt concerning their position, they asked Louis to confirm Henry II's declaration of May 1555 giving them and the chamber of the élus the right to handle the economic and administrative affairs of the province. To weaken royal influence in the chamber of the élus, they urged that the two members of the chamber of accounts who participated be denied the right to have a deliberative voice. The deputies of the third estate also sought to have their two élus given full votes instead of half a vote each, but the nobility and clergy were unwilling to tolerate this augmentation of the third estate's influence, although it would have strengthened the role of the estates as a whole in dealing with the representatives of the crown. The three estates asked to be convoked in May every third year and took steps to prepare a collection of documents concerning their rights and privileges. As a final precaution to ensure their independence, they took an oath to keep their deliberations secret and ordered their ushers to prevent outsiders from attending their deliberations.

The Burgundian governor, Bellegarde, reported to Richelieu that the deputies to court bearing these requests were very badly treated.[3] The next alarming event did not take place until January 1629, when on a visit to Dijon, Louis dodged a request that he make the customary pledge to preserve the town's privileges by directing that the relevant documents be shown to Marillac. Then, in spite of their efforts, the officers of the estates could not obtain permission to hold the estates that May. Marillac made difficulties about sealing the necessary letters, and the estates were not assembled until November. By then Louis had issued an edict creating ten new élections in Burgundy, to be staffed by 333 officials, whose annual salaries and fees would come to nearly 250,000 livres.

Louis justified this on the grounds that taxes were unfairly apportioned and often levied without his permission. The new élus in Guyenne, he asserted, were achieving so much success that the people of Dauphiné had asked that they be established in their province. Since the Burgundians had always been loyal subjects, he promised to continue to permit their estates to meet every third year and to elect officers to attend to their affairs between the sessions.

The estates were acutely aware that if the élections were established, their privileges would rapidly erode. They therefore dispatched a delegation to court and voted substantial sums for potential friends in high places. As a form of flattery to win his support, Richelieu, who had a right to sit in their assembly by virtue of his recent appointment as abbot of Cluny, was asked to become an officer of the estates, but he declined this honor. The king, on the other hand, was asked to be content with his usual don gratuit of 50,000 livres.

The Burgundian delegation to Paris ran into one obstacle after another. The king's council, they found, had a doctrinaire conviction that there should be fiscal uniformity in France. "Nothing opposes us so much," the mayor of Dijon wrote from Paris in mid January, "as the council's maxim that it is necessary to make all the provinces uniform."

And he wrote again on January 23: "As to the affairs of our deputation, we are only waiting for a reply from his majesty, which we will perhaps find more favorable than those of the ministers of state who are making [the élections] a general maxim for all the provinces."[4] Soon some Burgundian leaders began to believe that the money they were offering the king was not likely to be enough to persuade him to suppress the élections. If there was serious unrest in the province because of the élections, however, the king and his advisers might decide that it was wiser to accept their offer. This was especially true because Burgundy was a frontier province and France was in a struggle with the Habsburgs, who were descendants of their former dukes. They therefore began to plan disturbances in Dijon, Beaune, and perhaps other towns.

Reports of these preparations soon reached Paris, and both the mayor of Dijon and Bellegarde advised that violence would bring ruin on the town, which would be made to serve as an example for all of France. In spite of these warnings, the échevins made little effort to calm the inhabitants. Indeed, someone spread rumors that new taxes were about to be imposed on the province, including one on the sale of wine. There were apparently those who feared that the populace would not understand how serious a threat the élections would be to their liberties and their pocketbooks, and they were making sure that there were enough recognizable grievances to warrant a riot. In the evening of February 27, a crowd composed largely of grape growers marched through the streets, threw rocks at the houses of several financial officials, and threatened to kill them and burn their dwellings. The next day the demonstrators broke into several homes and did considerable damage. They again threatened royal officials, burned a portrait of the king, and, remembering the happy days when they were ruled by their dukes, some cried, "Long live the Emperor." Finally, the authorities decided that the mob was getting out of hand and ordered the militia to restore order, which it did after some bloodshed.[5]

Louis was furious when the news reached him at Fontainebleau, and on March 4 he declared that he was going to strip Dijon of all its privileges and tear down its walls. Troops were dispatched to the town, and several of the culprits were executed. In spite of this outburst, the Burgundian deputies at court still expected Louis to accept a financial offer in return for abolishing the élections, but around the middle of March their hopes were dashed. Louis rejected their offer of 1.8 million livres because, as Marillac reported to Richelieu, he insisted on establishing the élections in order to have uniformity in his kingdom. The idea may have been one that the keeper of the seals had planted in the king's mind, but it was not one to which the cardinal subscribed: "This news grieved him," Richeleau's memoirs inform us, "because he was sorry that in these times they made it difficult to satisfy this province," in which taxes were levied only with the king's permission and the estates did not overburden the people.[6]

When Louis and Marillac visited Dijon in April, the latter lectured the kneeling Burgundians on the duties of passive obedience. "To revolt against the magistrate," he declared, "is to revolt against the king himself who reigns through his officers and through the order established for the government of the towns and provinces." Then after describing the evils of rebellion, beginning with the fall of Satan, he insisted that "it is not for inferiors to examine the reasons for an order. . . . If they obey only when they find it reasonable, they no longer have a superior. The key to public tranquility and order lies in the reverence due the superior powers." The Dijon officials had committed a grievous fault by not halting the spread of sedition when it first appeared. "If you do not have the courage to expose yourself to an honorable death," he moralized, "you deserve a shameful one."[7] Because of the pleas of the duke of Bellegarde and their submission, however, the king would pardon them, but new parish officers were to be elected subject to his approval, and the municipal council was to be reduced to a mayor and six échevins, who were to be chosen by a very restrictive suffrage. Indeed, for the next six years, the king would choose the mayor from a list of three names submitted to him.

Two days after his Dijon speech, Marillac wrote to Richelieu with obvious delight that over a hundred inhabitants had pleaded on their knees with the king to pardon them. Perhaps the cardinal was less pleased. Shortly after the meeting, an English agent informed his master that "the Keeper of the Seals had displayed more ability and strength of mind in this encounter than the adherents of the Cardinal desired."[8] The latter feared, with reason, that Marillac was persuading the king to join the party of the queen mother. Whatever Richelieu's reaction to these events, one fact is clear: Louis and his imperious minister had humbled the proud Burgundians. Both capital and province had lost their most cherished liberties.

During the first three years of the Richelieu regime, the relations between the crown and the provincial estates of Provence were friendly, but their governor, the duke of Guise, was increasingly at odds with the cardinal. The two were already on bad terms when Guise refused to surrender his post of admiral of the Levant unless he were generously compensated. Richelieu, who coveted the office, had his clients do all they could to discredit Guise. Instead of behaving discreetly, Guise quarreled with the estates and the parlement. Thus when the estates entered one of the most critical periods of their history, they had a governor whom they did not trust to defend their interests, and who had little influence at court even if he chose to try to do so.

The three estates that met at Aix in May 1628 were confronted with royal demands for sharp increases in the taillon and the salt tax. Instead of giving their consent, they dispatched a deputation to court headed by Richelieu's older brother, the archbishop of Aix. This mentally unstable prelate constituted their best chance of winning the revocation of the offending taxes, and he did secure an audience with the king, who was content to turn their cahier over to a secretary. Effiat, the superintendant of finances, responded to the deputies' pleas of poverty by explaining the king's financial needs, and Marillac did little more than complete the circuit by saying that he would speak to his majesty. At this point the archbishop dashed what remained of their hopes by informing them that he could no longer be their spokesman because he was being transferred to the see of Lyons. The deputies returned to Provence, defiant but empty-handed.

The difficulties the Provençals faced multiplied in 1629–30. Poor crops led to a scarcity of food, but royal demands that they feed troops moving through the province increased. As a result, prices rose. By 1630, the cost of bread was half again as high as it had been in 1627, and the price of mutton and wine jumped forward even more rapidly. There was widespread hunger. As if this were not enough, the plague struck Digne in June 1629 and was soon decimating the population of other towns and villages. Still the crown did nothing to mitigate its demands.

When the estates opened on July 11, 1629, they were confronted with a royal demand for 1.5 million livres, and the news that the king had prepared an edict creating ten élections in Provence with 350 officers. Louis's justification for this last act was that it was intended to free his subjects from the excessive burdens caused largely by taxes levied without his permission. Shocked, the estates failed to act, as was apparently anticipated, because on July 14, Guise presented the deputies with letters from the king directing that the meeting terminate on July 16. Severely shaken by this arbitrary curtailment of their meeting, the estates decided to offer Louis 900,000 livres in lieu of the 1.5 million requested, on the condition that the edict on the élections and other offending measures were suppressed.

The deputation from the estates appeared before the king and Marillac on July 16, and that same day Marillac reported to Richelieu: "I pointed out that the élections, which they called oppressive, lightened the burden, and I offered proof of this proposition. Finally, I told them that the king could not accept these offers."[9] On July 17, the deputies reported to the estates that they had informed the king and council of their offer, but instead of being warmly treated, they had been unceremoniously dismissed. Shocked, the estates voted taxes for a number of purposes and disbanded the following day. Conspicuously absent from their levies were the 900,000 livres they had conditionally offered the king and any money for Guise's guards, company of ordonnance, or salary. Guise had appeared before the king and council with their deputies, but he either lacked credit at court or was tempted by a bribe the crown was prepared to offer in return for his cooperation in establishing the élections.[10] Whatever the reason, no significant concessions were won.

At first the officers of the estates met frequently after these events, and there were several assemblies of the communities, but their protests brought no relief. Indeed, a further blow fell when Louis announced that he was moving the court of accounts from Aix to Toulon and banning further assemblies. The province was seething with discontent when on September 19, 1630, a maître des requêtes named Druex d'Aubray entered Aix with the mission of seeing that the élections were established and the court of accounts was transferred. D'Aubray's assignment had been known for several weeks before his arrival, ample time to organize a riot, especially since Guise was conveniently absent at court. On the twentieth, the mob struck. D'Aubray escaped by scrambling over the rooftops, but his carriage was burned, and he had to leave the city.

It was one thing for the Provençals to stir up a mob, however, and another to organize a province to defend itself, or at least to give the appearance of being prepared to do so. Only by offering a display of determination could they hope that the crown would abandon its program of curbing their liberties. Already on September 15, an assembly of the nobility had appointed a committee of six to work with their syndics to prevent the implementation of the hated edicts. It was rumored that the committee was also to organize armed resistance and to raise the necessary funds by securing contributions from their fellow nobles.

On September 23, the procureurs du pays met in Aix and proceeded more discreetly. They protested the decision of the chamber of accounts to move to Toulon as the king had directed and noted in their minutes that d'Aubray had departed because of "a little noise." The vicar-general of Aix was asked to go to that frightened official to seek his favor. On October 9, the procureurs du pays nés et joints and the committee elected by the nobles met in Aix and decided that the three estates should assemble at the same time and place but in separate buildings. To meet together would be to hold the estates without royal permission, a revolutionary step they were not prepared to take. The permission of the parlement, so easily obtainable, was enough to justify an assembly of the communities, and the clergy and nobility had traditionally been relatively free to meet at the behest of their prelates and elected officers.

Meanwhile the unrest continued. A false report of Effiat's death caused a celebration in Aix. As if to make certain that he was dead, he was burned in effigy. On October 18, the parlement refused to register the edict creating the élus because their activities would destroy the liberties of the province and their salaries and fees would constitute an excessive burden on the people. The chamber of accounts was criticized for accepting the edict, remonstrances were sent to the king, and anyone who accepted the post of élu was threatened with a 10,000-livre fine.

Aix must have been tense when the three orders assembled separately a week later. The *assesseur,* who was also one of the procureurs du pays by virtue of his office, told the deputies of the communities that the purpose of the meeting was to inform them of the attempt to establish élections in the province, "which will be the most prejudicial thing not only regarding the goods, but also to the liberties, even the very lives of the inhabitants of this *pays;* for besides the fact that the edict of *élections* means the annihilation of all the usages, customs, privileges and liberties of this *pays,* it will deprive the inhabitants of the disposition of their goods."[11] After declaring that élections would turn them into "miserable slaves," he praised the parlement for its actions the week before and said that Guise had promised his support. He then charged that the chamber of accounts was being moved to Toulon because the crown believed that it would be easier to obtain the verification of unpopular edicts if that court was far from the center of the province.

On October 28, the deputies voted unanimously to send a deputation to the king to protest the edict on the élections and the transfer of the chamber of accounts to Toulon. To ensure that the individual communities defended their privileges and those of the province, the deputies directed that the archives be searched for relevant documents and that they be printed and distributed. As if suspecting that this would not be enough, they then voted taxes to purchase 4,000 muskets and 2,000 pikes. This action was taken "under the good pleasure of the king," and the official reason given was to provide the towns with the means to defend themselves from disorderly troops passing through the province, but the king's councillors could hardly fail to interpret it as a thinly veiled threat.[12] Those in Paris must be made to realize that the establishment of the élections was not worth the cost involved.

Meanwhile, conditions were deteriorating in Aix. A November visitor reported that "all the city was in arms." The nobility "had rendered these *élus* so detestable and so horrible to the populace that they had formed an opposition party, named the *cascaveù*. . . . The sedition was so violent that the homes of solid citizens were ransacked" if they were suspected of favoring the *élus*.[13] One opponent of the élus developed a contract theory of government in which the people promised obedience to their sovereign, who in return was to provide good government. "Your Majesty cannot violate the conventions under which this province was reunited to the crown of France; yes, Sire, for Your Majesty loves truth itself."[14]

Early in November, the first *consul* of Aix was driven from the city because he was suspected of favoring the establishment of the élections. Guise became angered by these excesses, but at the urging of the representatives of the estates, he agreed not to take military action and promised to help obtain the suppression of the unpopular edicts. In mid November, Guise thought that he had been spared from making the difficult decision of choosing between the court and Provence. Word reached him that Richelieu had been dismissed. Elated at this "good news," he notified the parlement and the procureurs of the estates that he was leaving at once for Paris. The procureurs rushed deputies to him to make certain that his visit to court would be on their behalf as well as in his own interest. The Day of Dupes thus found Provence still without élus but with a state of turmoil in Aix, the capital, itself that approached insurrection.

The relations between the crown and the estates of Languedoc were relatively cordial during the first year of the Richelieu regime, but they worsened after Marillac became keeper of the seals in June 1626. Louis did not ask the estates that met the following month for an additional grant, but his officials unilaterally increased the salt tax in upper Languedoc. The estates complained bitterly at this action, which they believed violated pledges that had been made to them. These "edicts and decrees of your council," they bluntly declared in their cahier, "are the most sacred and religious bonds that can be found concerning the faith and word of kings toward their subjects. They [the subjects] would be reduced to that full measure of misfortune of being able henceforth neither to hope for anything from the contracts that they had the honor to make with your majesty nor to find any security in the pledges that were given them on his behalf."[15]

When Montmorency opened the estates in February 1627, he took credit for thwarting an attempt by the crown to appropriate the tax on the sale of meat, fish, and wine called the equivalent. This was no mean victory because all the proceeds from this tax went to support provincial affairs, except for 70,000 livres assigned to the crown. Montmorency had not, however, been able to prevent the creation of offices to sell, and worst of all he had to ask the estates for 800,000 livres in the king's name, to be collected over a two-year period. After some debate, the estates granted 300,000. This was a severe blow to the crown, because it had intended to ask for an increase in the taillon as well once the 800,000 livres had been agreed upon.

The Huguenot revolt was near its height when the prince of Condé asked the estates that opened in March 1628 for over one million livres to support his army. At the request of the deputies, Montmorency interceded with Condé, who was his brother-in-law, and in the end the estates did no more than loan the king 300,000 livres. In gratitude, they voted Condé and his wife 60,000 livres and Montmorency a somewhat smaller sum. The crown was the loser, but only temporarily, for by the time the estates met in Pézenas in April 1629, the Huguenots had been nearly defeated, and Louis would soon be in Languedoc with an army. A syndic of the estates warned the deputies that the entire court was determined to destroy their rights. Nevertheless, when the information spread that Louis had ordered an increase of 200,000 livres in the taillon without the consent of the estates, it came as a shock. The estates protested, but Louis bided his time until after he had concluded the peace of Alès with the Huguenots and was free to deal with these uncooperative subjects from a position of strength. In quick succession he asked the estates for 500,000 or 600,000 écus to meet his heavy expenses, and issued edicts uniting the court of aides and the chamber of accounts at Montpellier and creating twenty-two élections in Languedoc.

The chamber of accounts had been a relatively recent creation, which had neither the power nor the prestige of comparable institutions elsewhere. Its members had long sought a union with the court of aides to strengthen their position, and in gratitude for Louis's concession, they registered the edict creating the élections without protest. Louis justified the élus by arguing that they would lighten the burden on the people by reducing illegal taxation. He neglected to mention that the salaries and perquisites of these 700 new officials would come to about 400,000 livres annually; ten times what it cost for the estates to collect taxes. The élus, of course, would bring some immediate financial advantage to the crown. It was anticipated that they would pay 4 million livres for their offices. Once they took charge of tax collection, the amount that was levied without the king's permission could be reduced. Far more important to the crown's thinking, one suspects, was that the élus could impose taxes without the consent of the estates, as they did in Normandy and elsewhere where there were élections. Furthermore, once the provincial and diocesan estates were deprived of their tax-collecting powers, they would become minor nuisances or perhaps disappear altogether.

Cardinal Richelieu had not played a direct role in establishing the élections in Dauphiné, Burgundy, and Provence. His memoirs scarcely mention the subject, and when they do, as in the case of Burgundy, it is to sympathize with the estates. But he was more vocal when he dealt with Languedoc, either because he believed that the abuses of the estates were worse there or because of his jealousy of Montmorency, whom he wished to destroy. His memoirs put it this way: "The king had long desired to establish the élus in this province to prevent the disorders that come from the abuses that the estates and dioceses committed in imposing every year on the province all that seemed good to them. This disorder had reached the point in this province, which was on the surface exempt from the tailles, that for four years it had paid three or four million livres annually. The authority of the king was scarcely known there. Levies were made in the name of the estates, and the name of the provincial governor had almost more weight than that of his majesty. He [Montmorency] favored or disfavored through this company [the estates] everyone in Languedoc who was on good or bad terms with him."[16] Having offered evidence to demonstrate the need for élections, the compiler of Richelieu's memoirs sought to add weight to his argument by declaring that "the late king who knew of these drawbacks had desired to establish élections but had not dared to do so."[17]

This unprecedented effort to justify the erection of élections suggests that Richelieu was more involved in their creation in Languedoc than elsewhere. He had been in Nîmes with the king in mid July when the edict on the élus had been prepared, and he was detained by illness at

Pézenas when the deliberations of the estates were reaching a critical phase. The estates visited him en masse on July 28, but little of consequence appears to have taken place. Three days later they voted to increase the taillon from the traditional 82,800 livres to 165,600 livres for that year only. Still the total fell far short of the 282,800 livres that Louis had ordered to be collected. More serious from his point of view, the deputies did not even bother to debate whether they would grant all or part of the additional 500,000 or 600,000 écus that he had requested.

By August 1, news from Montpellier concerning the registration of the edict on the élections had reached the estates. The seriousness of the threat caused them to expand the deputation they had already elected to carry their cahiers to the king. They further resolved that "in view of the certainty that the establishment of the élus in this province would entirely take away and destroy all the franchises and liberties that it has happily enjoyed under the just and glorious rule of our invincible monarch and the kings his predecessors for many centuries, we very expressly charge the deputies to court to speed their departure . . . in order to obtain from his unequaled justice and goodness the revocation of the edict and the continuation of the ancient order of the estates and twenty-two dioceses of the said province."[18] They were also to seek the revocation of the edict uniting the chamber of accounts and court of aides and a reduction in the sales taxes.

On August 2, the estates voted the routine taxes and gratifications, but near the close of their deliberations, a royal official appeared bearing a lettre de cachet from the king dated July 14 and a decree dated July 15 ordering the estates to disband. Louis and his advisers had anticipated that the estates would be obstinate and had prepared the letter and decree at Nîmes at the very time when they drew up the edicts creating the élections and uniting the two courts in Montpellier. The official had waited until it was obvious that the estates had no intention of voting a significant sum and then had delivered his blow.

Sick though he was, Richelieu must have approved the decision to disband the estates, but the only contemporary expression he has left covering these events is contained in a letter he wrote the king on August 5, saying, "It is impossible to describe to you his [Condé's] joy over the establishment of the élus in this province."[19] If Richelieu was reluctant to leave any direct evidence of his involvement, Marillac gleefully revealed his own position. The business of the estates was of the greatest importance, he wrote Richelieu on August 16. But then, obviously fearful that Richelieu's resolve might weaken, he added that it was wise to keep a watchful eye to assure that "*this establishment be effective and lasting and that posterity receive the fruit of your arduous and laborious travels*" (Marillac's emphasis).[20]

Marillac had every reason to be concerned over whether the government would maintain its position. Before disbanding, the estates had elected a deputation to secure the revocation of the edict creating the élections, and they were probably prepared to pay a large price. Towns and local officials flooded the council with petitions. The parlement of Toulouse refused to register the edicts on the élections and on uniting the two financial courts in Montpellier. Obstacles were placed in the way of selling the new offices, and Montmorency used his influence to defend the privileges of the people of his government. In spite of these efforts, more money flowed into the royal treasury in 1630 from Languedoc than in any previous year of Louis's reign, and all of it without the consent of the estates. In 1629, Louis had conquered his Catholic subjects in Languedoc as well as his Protestant ones, but the province was seething with discontent.

THE ESTATES IN THE PYRENEES

The crucial events in Béarn and Navarre had taken place before Richelieu joined the council. In 1620, Louis had issued an edict uniting the two states to the crown of France, and at the head of an army he had enforced earlier orders that the Protestants return the property of the Catholic church that they had confiscated. He also created a parlement with its seat at Pau to serve Béarn and Navarre and the contiguous viscounty of Soule. The estates of Navarre protested the loss of their judicial autonomy, but in 1624 Louis compelled them to accept the new arrangement, and as a conciliatory gesture he named the new court the parlement of Navarre. Between 1624 and 1630, there were few events of significance. The bishop of Lescar assumed the presidency of the estates of Béarn, which his predecessors had enjoyed before the Reformation, and the other clergymen joined the nobility to form a single house, as had been the former practice. The count of Grammont was made governor of both Béarn and Navarre. He and his descendants held this position until 1789 and were nearly as generously treated by the estates as the king. The central theme in Béarnais history was not the quarrel between the crown and the estates over the size of the annual tax but rather that between the resurgent Catholics and the Protestants, who only grudgingly surrendered their once-preferred position.

The estates in Bigorre, Foix, and the other Pyrenean lands were active. Royal exactions remained relatively constant, but the provinces were continually plagued by demands that they support the troops operating in the area. Protestant troops also proved a problem, and in 1621 and 1622 they appropriated the royal taxes in Foix.

Up until 1630, the Pyrenean estates were treated with some consideration. But once peace had been made with the defeated Huguenots in 1629, and the élus had been established in the larger provinces with estates, the crown was in a position to direct its attention to the tiny but strategically located Pyrenean provinces. When the estates of Béarn met in January 1630, there was agitation because of a report that an élection and a court of aides were about to be introduced into the viscounty. The usual deputations to court followed, and that May the estates met again to deal with the threat. Their resistance was sufficient to stave off the pending disaster until Marillac was removed from office that November.

THE ESTATES OF BRITTANY

During the Richelieu ministry, the government continued its efforts to extract more money from Brittany than earlier in the reign. In the fall of 1624, Louis asked for 600,000 livres, but he had to be content with 325,000. The following year, he repeated his request, but the estates disbanded after refusing to vote anything because their grievances had not been satisfied. Louis reassembled the estates in April 1626, and this time he finally managed to obtain 500,000 livres. Less than a month after the estates ended, Louis arrested the governor of Brittany because of his involvement in the Chalais conspiracy. To ensure his control over the province, he then went to Nantes, where, in the company of Richelieu and Marillac, he held still another meeting of the estates in July. Awed by the royal presence, the deputies increased their offer from 500,000 to 800,000 livres. Having fleeced the Bretons so successfully in 1626, Louis gave them a brief respite before asking for 1.2 or 1.3 million livres for 1628. Only after considerable haggling was he able to obtain about half that sum. The following year, the estates were slightly more generous, but their gift still fell far below the requested amount. Always the estates established conditions for their grants, and with equal certainty they voted substantial sums for influential persons at court who might mollify the royal anger at their modest gifts.

In the meantime, Richelieu was becoming increasingly interested in Brittany. He had obtained the admiralty rights to the Atlantic provinces from Montmorency in 1626 and was pressing to acquire those of Provence from Guise, but his efforts to secure full control over trade and naval matters still hinged on the authority he could exercise in Brittany. In opposition to his claims and those of Montmorency before him, the Bretons asserted that maritime affairs were a ducal right that had been transferred to the king upon the reunion with the crown and could now be exercised only by the royal governor. Already in 1624, to preserve more of their autonomy, the estates had declared that "they would recognize no one as admiral except their governor."[21] As long as they made good this pretension, Richelieu's dream of a royal navy and large trading companies could not fully mature. He badly needed Brittany's splendid ports and seafaring tradition.

Richelieu's proposal for the establishment of a trading company with extensive privileges that would be based in Brittany won some support in the estates, especially among those of the nobility who foresaw the economic advantages that would occur. However, other Breton interests, including those of the important port of Saint-Malo, were opposed. More seriously, parlement did all in its power to block Richelieu's plans because it feared the loss of part of its jurisdiction to the new admiralty courts. The impasse continued, but by the early months of 1630, it had occurred to Richelieu that since much of the Bretons' opposition to his proposals grew out of their desire that their governor exercise the admiralty rights, he could resolve many difficulties by assuming that office himself.

Soon after becoming first minister, Richelieu had begun to seek influential clients in Brittany. The head of his trading company was the brother of the powerful procureur syndic of the estates, Jean de Bruc, sieur de la Grée. Within the ranks of the unfriendly parlement of Rennes, he secured the services of Claude de Marbeuf, one of its presidents. To direct the efforts of his local clients, Richelieu dispatched his influential ally the prince of Condé to serve as the leading royal commissioner when the estates met in 1630. Condé's official instructions dealt primarily with the king's need for extraordinary financial assistance, but it is probable that Richelieu also gave directions concerning his desire that the estates ask that he be named governor.

The estates that opened on August 7, 1630, were quickly confronted with a request for a don gratuit of 1.2 million livres, but on August 13, before the debate began on the question, someone proposed that the matter of the vacant governorship be resolved by asking the king to appoint his mother to the post. The choice of the queen mother grew out of the Bretons' desire to have the most influential friend possible at court. Marie had custody of the royal domain in Brittany and for this reason had long taken an interest in Breton affairs. Often she had done favors for the Bretons, and in return they had voted her handsome presents. Richelieu's clients may have heard this proposal with alarm, but they could not offer direct opposition to it. Instead, one of them suggested that if she could not accept, they should seek the services of the cardinal, who appeared to be the second most powerful person in the entourage of the king. It was not until the sixteenth that the debate over the size of the don gratuit commenced. The estates began with an offer of 600,000 livres but in the end voted the king 900,000 and Richelieu 100,000, to be paid in seven quarters, four in 1631 and three in 1632. By spreading the tax over a period of nearly two years, the three estates in effect reduced the annual amount that they would give. On the other hand, because the seventh quarter would not end until the early fall of 1632, the crown saw no need for the estates to meet again to vote a don gratuit until the summer of that year. It was at this point and for this reason that the practice of holding biennial rather than annual meetings of the estates began.

Condé quickly reported the decision of the estates on the governorship to Richelieu, and before the end of August the Bretons received assurances that Marie de Medici had never thought of becoming governor. The governorship thus became available to Richelieu, as he had no doubt planned, but he was not appointed to the post until September 1631, after he had won his final victory over the queen mother and she had departed from the court. Thus, while élections were being established in Dauphiné, Burgundy, Provence, and Languedoc, and the Pyrenean estates were being threatened, Brittany escaped with minor changes. The Bretons owed their good fortune in part to a strong provincial loyalty, a willingness to unite to maintain their privileges, and the generosity with which they had always treated influential people. They also profited from Richelieu's interest in maritime affairs, which caused him to take the Bretons under his protection to secure their cooperation.

RESPONSIBILITIES

The crown gave as its principal excuse for creating élections in the four provinces in 1628 and 1629 the desire to lighten the burden on the people by ensuring that no taxes were levied without the king's permission, and that those that were approved were fairly apportioned. Similar excuses had been used to justify creating élections in earlier reigns, and there is no reason to doubt that they were a factor. Nevertheless,

throughout the sixteenth century, the estates quickly secured the abolition of the élections in return for reimbursing the crown for the loss of
the anticipated profits from the sale of the new offices. Thus, in 1519
Francis I created élections in Languedoc, but within a few months he
abolished them in return for 71,800 livres voted by the estates. Again, in
January 1555, Henry II created élections in Burgundy, but that August
he abolished them in return for 20,000 livres. In both instances after
issuing the edict creating the élections, the king had confirmed the
privileges of the three estates and promised not to levy any taxes without
their consent, a concession that suggests that there was no immediate
intention to undermine provincial privileges.[22] A desire for uniformity
was also expressed by Francis I. If Languedoc had élections, he stated in
his 1519 edict, tax administration there would conform with "all the
other provinces in our kingdom."[23] Dreams of uniformity appear to have
subsided after Francis's death, only to reappear in Sully in the seventeenth
century.

Another motive for creating élections was suggested in 1629. Sir
Thomas Edmondes, the newly arrived British ambassador, reported:

> The Cardinal de Richelieu, to diminish the authority of the princes and the
> greate men which are gouvernors of provinces, hath begunn another worke
> of greate importance, which is, to take away that power which the
> provinciale gouvernors did usually practise, by virtue of the privileges of the
> countries to call the Assemblies of the States, either for the leavyinge of
> monnies in the countries for the King's service, or to consult of other
> occasions: Att which time the saide gouvernors did also annually draw greate
> summes of monny from the Country, which by way of gratification was
> presented unto them, for their owne particular. But now hee hath abolished
> that custome of callinge the states by the gouvernor, and hath appointed that
> upon the issuinge of any Commissions from hence for the leavyinge of any
> Monnies in any of the provinces, the same shale be executed only by the
> Esleus of the Countri, who are the persons that are accustomed to make the
> severale taxations throughout the Countrie, and by this meanes, of making
> their authority more absolute, they doe sell the places of the saide Esleus att
> a much dearer rate, and doe cleane cutt off the profitt of the gouvernors.
> This hee hath already (as is saide) putt in execution in the provinces of
> Provence, Dauphiné, and Languedoc, and if hee can establish the like in
> Bretaigne, which will bee of greater difficulty because they are more strongly
> founded in their privileges, hee will then bee able to make the same to bee
> afterwards more easily received in the other Countries.[24]

No document specifically connects the creation of élections with a
desire on the part of the crown to weaken the governors, but it would not

be illogical to suppose that this was a factor in 1628–29 and perhaps in earlier reigns. Neither the wish to weaken the governors, the desire for uniformity, nor the urge to lighten the tax burden on the people, however, had been sufficient in the sixteenth century to stop the crown from abolishing the élections provided the estates made a reasonable offer. It is difficult to escape the conclusion, therefore, that from the time royal offices became venal to the profit of the crown until the regime of Sully, the principal reason for creating élections was to raise money from the sale of offices. Sully had created élections in Guyenne and the newly conquered provinces of Bresse, Bugey, and Gex. He was unable to erect them in the remainder of France as he had planned, but he introduced a new era when he succeeded in blocking the efforts of the estates of Guyenne to bribe the crown to abolish the élections. Shortly after he retired from office in 1611, the estates of Guyenne succeeded in having the élections removed. Then, in 1621, they were reestablished, and once more financial offers from the estates were to no avail. And now, in 1628–29, élections were thrust on four of the five great pays d'etats, and the efforts of three of them to pay to have the offending edicts annulled were rebuffed without ceremony. An administrative revolution was in the making.

Most historians have attributed changes that would have gone far toward establishing absolutism and fiscal administrative uniformity to Cardinal Richelieu. Since he was the king's chief minister, it has usually been assumed that he was responsible for all the important acts of the reign. No critical analysis or proof has been required. As far back as Sir Thomas Edmondes, the British ambassador whose report is quoted above, this has been true. But Edmondes did not embark on his mission until July 1629, when Richelieu was in Languedoc and the élections were being established there. Edmondes's lack of familiarity with the French scene is reflected by the fact that he failed to detect the growing rift between Bérulle and Richelieu and persisted until the former's death in regarding him as Richelieu's not-too-capable creature.[25] Other observers were better informed. Factual and circumstantial evidence suggest that Michel de Marillac was the principal architect of this revolutionary program. It is necessary to explore the role of these two men and also of that of Effiat, the superintendant of finances, to understand the part they each played.

There is no question that Richelieu was Louis's principal minister. Marillac, like other royal advisers, frequently deferred to him and sought his opinion before acting. Richelieu, however, had little interest in administrative routine and left many decisions to subordinates. As early as June 1626, Louis had directed that Richelieu devote his attention to general problems of great importance and that more specific matters be handled by other ministers and the secretaries of state who dealt with the various provinces.[26] As the chief judicial and administrative officer of the kingdom, Marillac was responsible for the routines of government. Thus, when Louis and Richelieu visited Dijon at the end of January 1629, the officials of the Burgundian estates decided not to raise the question of the élections that they had just learned were to be created in their province because Marillac was not present. As part of the ceremony accompanying the visit, the mayor of Dijon took an oath of fidelity to the king. In return, it was expected that Louis would take the customary pledge to respect the privileges of the town. Instead, he directed the Dijon officials to show the relevant documents to Marillac when he was available.[27] To the Burgundians, Marillac was responsible for the élections; to the king, he was equally responsible for verifying the privileges of Dijon.

Richelieu himself often gave advice rather than commands and sought advice if he felt the need. When Marillac proposed in the summer of 1630 that the Protestants of Dauphiné be stripped of many of their privileges, Richelieu found the proposals good but added that if they were implemented it might cause unrest. He then left the decision to Marillac's "good prudence."[28] In mid August of that year, Richelieu sought Marillac's advice on how to deal with the duke of Guise.[29] Even in the crucial decisions of whether there should be war or peace following the capture of Pignerol, he seemed to leave the question open. In his memoir of April 13, 1630, to the king, he outlined the advantages and disadvantages of both policies. "If the king resolves on war," he wrote, "it will be necessary to give up all thoughts of repose, economy, and reform inside the kingdom. If, on the other hand, he wants peace, it will be necessary to give up thoughts of Italy in the future."[30] In Marillac's opinion, Richelieu had judiciously pointed out the advantages and disadvantages to be gained by war and by peace, but he had not clearly stated his preference.[31] When he wrote Richelieu to this effect, the latter, who was absent from court, responded that his only desire was to follow the orders of the king as advised by his mother and those who were near him. "Being near the King one can and ought to give advice; being absent one ought to explain the state of affairs and receive orders."[32] Richelieu must have believed that the king would choose war, but if Louis's mother persuaded him otherwise, he had covered himself.

To say that Richelieu left a wide latitude to his subordinates is not to argue that he was devoid of ideas about the reformation of the kingdom. He had been a prominent member of the Estates General of 1614, and his thinking was somewhat influenced by that assembly. In the memorandums he prepared for the king in the early years of his administration, he advocated creating a nationwide system of periodic provincial assemblies of the clergy, increasing the responsibilities and the taxing powers of the towns, augmenting the role of the nobility in the king's council, and placing limitations on how the king spent his revenue. Following the Assembly of Notables, he was probably responsible for the wide publicity given to Louis's pledge to give more positions to the nobility and to provide free education for their children, to expand trade, and above all to reduce taxes by 3 million livres by 1632. Often he spoke of redeeming the domain, establishing a chamber of justice to correct financial and administrative abuses, and abolishing the sale of offices and the paulette. Conspicuously absent was any mention of the élus, the intendants, or any other new creations that have been associated with absolutism.[33] It is equally striking that in his extensive correspondence and memoirs, Richelieu makes only two references to the élections during this period. In August 1629, he reported to the king that Condé was delighted that élections had been created in Languedoc. In January 1630, in response to a letter from Marillac saying that the king had rejected an offer of 1.8 million livres in return for abolishing the élections in Burgundy, his memoirs record: "This news grieved him because he was sorry that in these times they made it difficult to satisfy this province."[34] Clearly new élections were not high on Richelieu's agenda. He was ready to take money for their abolition in Burgundy, where he thought that taxes were levied only with the king's permission and the estates did not overburden the people. In Languedoc, on the other hand, where he believed abuses were greater, he was more willing to see élus established, especially since they would weaken the powerful governor, Montmorency, of whom he was intensely jealous.

If Richelieu's role in creating élections was essentially passive, the initiative must have been taken by Marillac or Effiat. As superintendent of finances, Effiat's primary responsibility was to provide money and supplies to support an aggressive, warlike foreign and domestic policy. In this he appears to have done a good job, although his previous experience had been as much in war and diplomacy as in finance, and military distinction may have been his greatest ambition. He spent some months fighting with the army in Italy during the summer of 1630 and was made a marshal of France at the beginning of the following year.[35] Only in

Provence is there any evidence that Effiat was directly involved in creating élections. The Provençal delegates to court in the summer of 1628, prior to the edict on the élections, dealt more with Effiat than with Marillac. Their goal was to get rid of some recently created offices and to prevent increases in the taillon and the salt tax. In return, they were willing to offer a substantial sum. The crown readily agreed to abolish the offices if adequately compensated but insisted on retaining the tax increases. The deputies refused to reach an agreement on these terms because the taxes were their greatest concern, and the deputation ended in failure. Effiat was therefore already closely associated with the Provençals' troubles when news of the edict creating élections reached them in 1629. It is not surprising that a false rumor of his death the following year touched off a celebration and he was burned in effigy. Effiat undoubtedly favored creating the élections, because it meant that there would be more offices to sell, and he may well have been responsible for seeing that each élection was grossly overstaffed. There is no evidence, however, that he would not have been willing to abolish the élections in return for money. Refusal to do so is the true test of absolutism.[36]

If Effiat's career was marked by pragmatism, and he is not known to have any absolutist positions based on principle, the same cannot be said for Marillac. He had been a maître des requêtes when he had been dispatched on an investigatory mission to Guyenne in 1598, and his report probably contributed to a curtailment of the activities of the estates and the establishment of the élus there in 1603. He had been a prominent member of the king's council in 1622 with special responsibility for Languedoc when an attempt had been made to create élections there. When he prepared the great ordonnances of 1629, he accepted many of the recommendations of the Estates General of 1614, but conspicuously absent were any references to the request that the Estates General meet regularly and that provincial assemblies be created in areas where they did not exist. His absolutist theory and authoritarian ways are well established. In 1597, he lectured the parlement of Rouen on the subordination of the individual to the state, declaring, "Necessity is above the laws."[37] He prepared a book-length study of the parlement of Paris in which he demonstrated that it had no independent authority; rather, as he informed that body in 1629, "The authority of the kings of France is independent of all other power and they render account only to God for the temporal administration of the state."[38] He was furious when parlement delayed in registering the great ordonnance of 1629 even after a lit de justice and accused the judges of wanting to subject royal authority to their own. He bombarded Richelieu with letters describing their bad behavior. He even found President Le Jay's statement that the king could not overturn the fundamental laws of the kingdom "very strange."[39]

Richelieu was unperturbed by Marillac's difficulties. Indeed, he found a letter that Marillac had prepared for the queen mother to send the parlement to be framed in poorly chosen words that would have a bad effect. She should use her authority more sparingly. "The king can write this way, but it is not à propos for the queen mother to act in this fashion."[40]

Marillac was a stickler for enforcing even forgotten laws in spite of the political consequences. The lieutenant civil of Paris complained to Richelieu that Marillac had ordered him to close the gambling houses in Paris, although the law in question had long been a dead letter and these establishments were frequented by the great, including the king's brother. The parlement of Paris was furious at Marillac's insistence on enforcing the long-ignored laws against close relatives being members of that body. When a grandson of the late Chancellor Bellièvre was excluded because his father was a member, the court carried its complaints to the king and the cardinal. Being more practical than Marillac, Louis and Richelieu permitted the younger Bellièvre to take his seat so as to avoid needlessly offending parlement on what they regarded as a minor matter.[41]

With his background and temperament it is not surprising that Marillac was determined to create élections to ensure that taxes were fairly apportioned and levied only with royal approval. The establishment of élections in four of the five great pays d'etats marked the achievement of a long-sought goal for him. His letters leave no doubt on where he stood. When Louis rejected an offer from the estates of Provence of 900,000 livres in return for abolishing the élections and other concessions, Marillac informed the absent Richelieu with obvious pleasure. He was equally delighted to report that the king had turned down an offer of 1.8 million livres from the estates of Burgundy to be freed of the élections—an ill-advised decision to Richelieu's mind, as we have seen. Marillac was well aware of the temptation to suppress the élus in return for money. The offer of the estates usually equaled the income from the sale of offices. If the élections were suppressed, there would be no salaries to pay, and of course someday élections could be created again. Fiscally, suppression was the more profitable course from the crown's point of view, and it created few enemies. Hence, when Marillac expressed his pleasure at the creation of élections in Languedoc, he was careful to point out to Richelieu that they must be lasting, so that "*posterity will receive the fruit*" (Marillac's emphasis).[42] At that moment, Richelieu would probably have agreed, but he was anxious not to anger the leaders of provincial society. And Effiat, as far as we know, only thought of the money that could be raised from the sale of the offices.

It has been suggested that the élus were not the answer the absolutists sought in their effort to get control of taxation, because they were corrupt and inefficient. This turned out to be true, but around 1630 no one knew this. Indeed, the intendants' role in taxation developed almost unconsciously to meet immediate needs, and they were not so obviously superior to the élus. Colbert considered creating élections in some of the pays d'états on several occasions, as will be shown in a later chapter.

The attitudes of the three men on the issue of reform versus money are reflected in their treatment of the paulette, which was scheduled to expire on December 31, 1629. Both Richelieu and Marillac had advocated its suppression, so that offices would no longer be hereditary, but Effiat proposed that officials be frightened by the threat of nonrenewal and then offered the opportunity to continue it at a much higher rate. He hoped to double the crown's revenue from the paulette in this fashion. If he succeeded, it would be a "great coup," a somewhat skeptical Richelieu declared.[43] The money was needed for the war, but Richelieu was always anxious not to alienate officeholders more than necessary. Marillac, we can rest assured, would have opted for reform.[44]

X

The Triumph of Richelieu and Mazarin

THE DAY OF DUPES

Michel de Marillac must have had mixed feelings as he surveyed the domestic and foreign scene during the summer of 1630. The lands of the Catholic church in Béarn and Navarre had been restored to it, and the Huguenot state within a state had been destroyed. It was true that those willful heretics had been permitted to retain too many religious and civil liberties, but with their political power broken, the rising tide of Catholic reform could be counted upon to engulf them at a later date. After some difficulty, the parlements had been compelled to register his great reforming ordonnance of 1629, which was designed to restore justice and stamp out disorder in the kingdom. The judicial and financial officials had borne the brunt of his attack, but instead of submitting peaceably to sovereign authority, they continued to try to have his decrees reversed. Richelieu had shared in his desire to let the paulette die when the time came for its renewal at the close of 1629, but the expedition to Italy had led the crown to restore that instrument of making offices hereditary to the financial officials in return for sharply increased payments. The officers in parlement continued to agitate for a renewal of the paulette, but instead of expressing their gratitude when this was accorded them in June 1630, they had increased their protests because they were expected to pay at the same rate as their brethren in finance rather than the lesser amount required when the paulette was first established in 1604. Clearly the bureaucracy was far from tamed, but Marillac had reason to hope the tables would be turned once the return of peace made such financial expedients unnecessary.[1]

Furthermore, he had persuaded the king to take steps to weaken the provincial parlements. In Burgundy and Dauphiné, where the parlements had exercised some jurisdiction over indirect taxes, courts of aides had been created to assume their role and attached to the chamber of accounts. In Languedoc, the existing court of aides had been joined to the chamber of accounts at Montpellier to strengthen the position of these relatively docile courts in their dealings with the powerful parlement of Toulouse. To reduce the likelihood of the sovereign courts of a province joining forces against the crown, they had been relocated in different cities. This situation had already existed in Languedoc, where Montpellier and Toulouse had long been rival judicial-administrative capitals, but now the chamber of accounts of Burgundy had been transferred from Dijon to Autun and then to Beaune, and the chamber of accounts of Provence was being moved from Aix to Toulon. Plans were also being made to establish a court of aides for Dauphiné in Vienne.

In every instance the reorganization of the sovereign courts had preceded the creation of élections, strong evidence that Marillac and his associates regarded this as a necessary preliminary step to what appears to have been their primary objective: the destruction of the provincial estates and the replacement of their tax officials by those of the crown. It was true that the inhabitants of Burgundy, Provence, and Languedoc were doing everything legally, and sometimes illegally, in their power to prevent the élus from being appointed and from performing their duties once they were. Plans to establish élections in the Pyrenean provinces were well advanced. Thus Marillac could anticipate that within several years the new fiscal system would be functioning smoothly. All of France would be administered in the same fashion, and the provincial estates would begin to wither away in every province except Brittany, where for the moment Richelieu needed local cooperation in order to further his maritime policies.

If Marillac's passion for administrative uniformity appeared about to be satisfied, the same cannot be said of his desire for a prosperous, orderly kingdom. Poor crops had caused food prices to be nearly 50 percent higher than usual in 1630. Riots were becoming more frequent, and the privileged orders were not reticent about directing popular discontent against his reforms. If only the promised reduction in taxes could be put into effect, the suffering of the people would be mitigated, but military intervention in Italy made this impossible. Indeed, to support the army, it had been necessary to turn to expedients, including selling many times more offices in the new élections than were necessary. One wonders whether Marillac realized that the salaries and perquisites of these officials came to about ten times as much as the entire amount that the estates had levied to support their own activities. If he did, he gave no sign that he was willing to relent in order to reduce the burden on the people.

Marillac was troubled by his worsening relations with the cardinal. He and his brother had not abandoned Richelieu after the fall of Concini, and they very likely supported the efforts of Marie de Medici, Bérulle, and others to have him brought back into the government in 1624. At first Marillac and Richelieu had seemed to share the same objectives, and their disagreements had been no more frequent than one would expect of two strong-willed men. In September 1625, they had argued over whether priority should be given to intervention in Italy or to defeating the Huguenots and instituting domestic reforms. Initially, Richelieu had been successful, but he had soon reversed himself and embarked on a course acceptable to Marillac. Again in December 1628, Richelieu had placed Italy ahead of defeating the Huguenots in Languedoc and internal affairs. Again he had won, but after achieving his Italian objectives, he had once more directed his attention to France. When he returned to court in September 1629, he could point to the destruction of the Huguenot state within a state, as well as to his Italian laurels, to justify his policy. Ever anxious for glory, Louis was more than content with his services, but the queen mother, who regarded Richelieu as her creature, had been estranged by his independent actions.

Richelieu placed much of the blame for Marie de Medici's coldness on Marillac's shoulders. According to Marillac's friends, he began to try to undermine Marillac's influence with the king by questioning his integrity. In November 1629 and March 1630, Marillac sought to resign, but Louis refused to let him. Richelieu concurred in his master's decision, either because he still valued Marillac's services or because he wanted to avoid an open break. In either case, the two men could hardly have failed to have noted the growing divergence in their policies. Marillac's dedication to domestic reform continued unabated, but he must have felt that Richelieu gave only the most lukewarm support to his efforts. As early as February 1629, Marillac's collaborator, Bérulle, had written Richelieu: "It is said . . . that we are beginning an interminable war in the midst of necessities of state and the people's misery, and that under the pretext of relieving Casal, we wish to enter Milanese territory."[2] To this appeal, Marillac added, "The management of affairs obliges me to represent to you that we do many things that cause the people great suffering. . . . It seems to me that the principal glory of good government is to think of the welfare of the subjects and the good regulation of the state, which can be done only through peace."[3] He then proceeded to elaborate on Bérulle's argument that if they succeeded in raising the siege of Casal, they would be tempted to attack Milan. The Habsburgs would retaliate by invading Picardy and Champagne from their bases in Flanders and Germany. A limited operation would thus become a long and terrible war, which would be embarked upon at a time when France was seething with discontent, and neither the king nor his brother had produced an heir to perpetuate the dynasty.

It is customary to see the devout faction as advocating a hopelessly naive foreign policy predicated upon their pro-Spanish and pro-Catholic sympathies, but such sentiments were conspicuously absent from the arguments they offered to support their cause. Rather they should be credited as being farseeing statesmen who recognized that what was undertaken as a limited involvement in Italy would lead to a costly war, for which France was ill prepared. One wonders whether Richelieu would have been so insistent on embarking on a course that led to full-scale intervention in the Thirty Years War if he had foretold the future as clearly.

Casal was relieved, and France was temporarily spared the further adventures in Italy that Marillac and Bérulle feared in 1629, but the year 1630 had hardly begun before French troops were once more on their way to the peninsula. On March 29, Pignerol fell, and the plains of northwestern Italy lay open to the French army. This time there was no Huguenot rebellion in Languedoc to compel the French troops to return home. It was possible to make a choice between further aggrandizement in Italy and Marillac's program of domestic reform. Richelieu saw the issue clearly. "If the king decides for war, it will be necessary to abandon all thought of repose, economy, and reorganization within the realm," he noted in a memorandum prepared on April 13. "If on the other hand peace is desired, it will be necessary to abandon all thought of Italy."[4]

No one who knew Louis would have doubted that he would choose the road to glory. The question was whether Marillac could persuade him that more glory could be won by providing for "the welfare of the subjects and the good regulation of the State" than by foreign conquests. He could not, but Richelieu and his supporters became alarmed at Marillac's persistence. Then came Louis's serious illness in Lyons. As he began to recover, the news spread that the council was debating whether the crown should persist in its efforts to establish élections in Provence and Languedoc despite the resistance that was being encountered. The two governors, Guise and Montmorency, were suspected of being behind the disturbances, and it was predicted that they would join with the other governors "to preserve the provincial estates from which they obtain great sums each year."[5] Both nobles were described as being very close to the queen mother.

When the court began its return to Paris, Marie de Medici must have felt more confident of her position than she had in a long time. Her son had grown closer to her during his illness, and she may have extracted a promise from him to dismiss Richelieu after their arrival in the capital. Around her gathered a strange mixture of devout, authoritarian Catholics, such as Marillac, who wanted to break the power of the sovereign courts, estates, and other autonomous institutions, and libertine magnates who were bent on preserving the privileges of the provinces they governed. If the cardinal fell, there was likely to be a struggle between the two factions. In the meantime, both wings of Marie's supporters were confident that they would soon replace the Richelieu regime. It was the sudden reversal of their fortunes on November 11 that has been called the Day of Dupes.

Some of the drama of the events was captured by the November 12 report of the English agents in Paris. The day began with the agents receiving a note saying that Richelieu was disgraced. They left their lodgings and soon learned from a friend "that yesterday the Queene Mother . . . told the king at last in plain terms that she had suffered so much from the Cardinal as either she or he must needs quit the court." Thereupon the cardinal entered, and the king said to him: "I have done what I can with her (speaking of the Queen Mother and herself being present) but I cannot prevail with her. It is true, said the Queen Mother, and go your way said she to the Cardinal and let me see you no more. Thereupon the Cardinal kissed the hem of her robe and the like did Madam Comballet [Richelieu's niece] who is now retired to the Carmelites, what will become of this business you shall not fail to be informed." Then in a postscript hastily scribbled an hour later, "The king backed up Cardinal. He will not fall. Happened in Luxembourg House."[6]

Following the confrontation on the 11th, Louis set out for Versailles without giving any indication of his intentions. Richelieu, who had thought he had lost, was greatly relieved when he received a royal summons to come to Versailles. There the bond between the two men was renewed. Louis broke with his mother, and before many months she fled from France, as did her ineffectual son Gaston of Orléans.

The Marillacs also had to be dealt with. Louis, the marshal, was arrested on trumped-up charges and tried by a special commission of hand-picked judges who met in one of Richelieu's palaces. After a courageous defense, he was condemned to death by a vote of only thirteen to ten. Michel was imprisoned in Châteaudun until his death in August 1632. During his last months, while his brother was being tried and executed, Richelieu's pamphleteers launched a vitriolic attack against him, but he never offered a word in his own defense and discouraged others from doing so. Richelieu, of course, had vocal enemies, but anti-Richelieu pamphlets were generally published abroad under the aegis of the exiled Marie de Medici, and anti-Richelieu memoirs were written by libertine magnates who had little sympathy for Marillac's centralizing policies. Indeed, parts of Marillac's program were so unpopular among the magnates and bureaucrats that it is hardly surprising that they and their supporters passed over it in silence or tried to blame it on the cardinal. When Matthieu de Morgues attempted to saddle Richelieu with the responsibility for Marillac's program of breaking the power of the sovereign courts and diminishing provincial independence, Harlay de Sancy, one of Richelieu's creatures, responded with a long pamphlet. To the charge that Richelieu had humbled parlement, he declared: "The author [Morgues] is blind and does not know what he wants. Never were so many new edicts passed as in the time of Keeper of the Seals, Marillac. He sealed twenty times as many as all of his predecessors together. The last time he accompanied the king to parlement, he had so many of them to seal . . . that he forgot to seal all of them in his home and . . . hastily did so on the altar of the Sainte-Chapelle."[7] Furthermore, Sancy charged, Marillac had responded rudely to parlement's protests. His edicts should not be blamed on the cardinal, who did not mix in such affairs. The cardinal was not the first minister. Every minister was free to exercise his office. He left everything to do with justice in Marillac's hands and took no cognizance of what he did.

Marillac's potential defenders were not to be found with the queen mother and the magnates but rather among his relatives and friends, the leaders of the Catholic reformation, and the reformist element in the bureaucracy, but they remained in France where they were subject to censorship. Furthermore, Marillac had asked them to attack no one on his behalf. Hence the few attempts that were made to defend his position have remained in manuscripts. As if to explain this situation, one of the most eloquent of these defenses began with this quatrain:

> Je parriostray lorsque la viollance
> aura cessé d'opprimer l'innocence,
> et qu'en la France on aura liberté
> de pouvoir ouir et dire vérité.[8]

In the text that followed, the author was at pains to show that Marillac had not been a creature of Richelieu who had betrayed his master; rather he was an elder statesman who had rebuffed attempts to make him a president in the parlement of Paris and the keeper of seals before Richelieu had entered the council in 1624. The differences between the two men lay in the fact that

> the Cardinal desired war and feared peace in which the accustomed course of the laws, order, and justice would have deprived him of any pretext to be so thoroughly occupied, to absorb so completely the mind of the King, and to advance measures that are occasioned by the expenses of war. The Keeper of the Seals, on the other hand, desired peace and did all in his power to achieve it by sure and honorable means. He perceived the needs of the church and religion, the great misery of the people, the disorder of justice, the extraordinary measures that were daily necessary to raise money, the risks that the king incurred to his health, the frequent uprisings of the people, and the universal discontent. This is why he desired peace, contrary to the Cardinal.[9]

Notably absent from this eloquent statement was any mention of Marillac's efforts to subject the sovereign courts to the will of the king and to undermine the provincial estates. These had been unpopular measures, and his supporters passed over them in silence, just as Sully failed to mention his own similar activities in his memoirs.

THE ABANDONMENT OF ABSOLUTISM

But what of the great cardinal? After his lay rival had departed from the scene, that prince of the church continued to seek titles, benefices, and wealth. His first step was to consolidate his position. Henceforth only his creatures were to be given high positions in the government. If they betrayed him, they would be fortunate to escape with only the loss of their posts. Existing officials also quickly recognized the virtues of obedience. "The king was alarmed," Roland Mousnier wrote, "to see his captains leave him and pass into the cardinal's service. He foresaw the time when he would not be able to command obedience in his kingdom except through Richelieu and his men."[10] But he took no countermeasures because he believed that his minister, his mayor of the palace, was making him one of the greatest kings in the world.

Richelieu, like Marillac, was alarmed at the unrest throughout most of the kingdom, but he blamed it on Marillac's efforts to control the sovereign courts, curtail the independence of the bureaucracy, undermine the provincial estates, and subvert traditional popular liberties. If France was to have a foreign war, there must be peace at home. It was therefore not only necessary to saddle Marillac with the blame for the enforced registration of the Code Michau and as many of the unpopular acts of the government as possible but also to reverse the governmental revolution he had come so close to achieving by the time of his disgrace.

Richelieu himself had favored the abolition of the paulette, and he had very likely subscribed to the effort to curtail parlement's right of remonstrance, but he immediately set about placating the bureaucracy and sovereign courts. Champigny, the first president of the parlement of Paris, had died in April, and now, on November 14, just two days after Marillac had surrendered the seals, Louis appointed Le Jay to succeed him. Le Jay had been a partisan of Condé's during his revolts under the regency, and he had taken the lead in trying to prevent the registration of the Code Michau. The appointment of a man with such a record might seem strange, but it served to notify the judges that a new conciliatory policy was being inaugurated. Furthermore, Le Jay had become Richelieu's creature.

Of far greater importance was the paulette, which had expired at the close of 1629. In return for renewing it, the crown had demanded a far heavier contribution than before. The parlement had refused to permit its members to pay, and an impasse had been reached. Hardly had Marillac been dismissed and Le Jay been appointed first president than appeals were made to renew the paulette under the traditional conditions. In August 1631, the paulette was reduced to the former rate for the officers of the sovereign courts and a higher figure for lesser royal officials. Louis and Richelieu had surrendered, but in return not even the parlement of Toulouse supported Montmorency in his rebellion in 1632.

This is not to say that friction between crown and parlement ceased, but through tact, diplomacy, and a readiness to compromise, Richelieu placated the sovereign courts and the lesser bureaucracy enough to secure a degree of cooperation from them, in spite of the repeated need to create new offices and levy taxes to finance his foreign policy. In this Richelieu proved far more flexible than the king, who was ever inclined to stand on his prerogative and to insist on being obeyed absolutely. Thus Richelieu managed to avoid a Fronde, although discontent among officials, especially in the provinces, remained high.

Richelieu did not wait until the sovereign courts and bureaucracy were placated before turning to the question of the provincial estates and the élections. As if by chance, the situation in Burgundy first claimed his attention. On November 7, 1630, officials of the estates visited Bellegarde, their governor, to learn what steps they could take to get the élections abolished and the garrisons in the province removed. He suggested that a new deputation be sent to the king. The officials took his advice, and negotiations were reopened with the crown a few weeks after the Day of Dupes. On January 1, 1631, one of them wrote from Paris that conditions were ripe to obtain the revocation of the edict on the élections in return for a financial contribution. Thus in less than two months after the Day of Dupes, Richelieu had decided to quell the discontent in those pays d'états in which élections had recently been created.

The belief that the question of the élections could be resolved contributed to the Burgundian decision not to join Orléans and Bellegarde when they tried to raise a revolt in the province in March 1631. When Louis himself passed through Dijon late that month, he told the chamber of the élus that because of his great need for money, he was prepared to abolish the élections in accordance with the terms Condé would present to them. When the estates opened on May 7, a bargain was soon struck, in which Condé agreed in the king's name to suppress the élections in return for 1.6 million livres, 200,000 less than the crown had rejected before the Day of Dupes. Dijon's privileges were restored and other concessions were made. The grateful estates voted Condé 100,000 livres in recognition of his good offices, and the king was so pleased that he made him governor of Burgundy.

Louis was so angered over the September 1630 riots in Aix that at first the fall of Marillac brought no change in policy. He ordered parlement to move to Brignoles and considered transferring the seat of the seneschal to Trets. Since the court of accounts had already been transferred to Toulon, he seemed determined that Aix was to cease to be the capital of Provence. Thoroughly alarmed, the procureurs asked their governor, the duke of Guise, for permission to hold an assembly of the communities. Guise, who had remained discreetly in the background during the troubled period, thought it safest to refuse, but on December 16, the procureurs decided to assemble the procureurs nés et joints on January 7 and to notify the communities by letter of the dangerous course of events. If the *consuls* of the communities should happen to be in Aix on the seventh, they could learn more details. Guise made no apparent effort to prevent this thinly disguised meeting of the communities. By his formal refusal to permit one to take place, he hoped that he had done enough to satisfy the king.

Meanwhile a shift in royal policy was taking place in spite of Louis's reluctance to abandon his intention of punishing his insolent subjects. A deputy to court had reported on his insistence that Aix be chastised. It took a while for Richelieu to persuade the irate monarch, who was jealous of his authority, that it would be wiser to permit the Provençals to buy back their privileges. The Provençals first became aware of the new royal policy on December 23, when a *consul* of Aix was summoned to parlement and informed that this would be a good time to depute to the king to ask that the edict on the élections be revoked. The procureurs decided to take the hint. On December 30, Guise authorized the meeting but insisted that it take place at Marseilles rather than in trouble-ridden Aix. It is not known who prompted parlement to take this step, but it presumably acted on instructions from someone at court. Already, on December 21, Louis had addressed a letter to the people of the three estates of Provence telling them that he had authorized them to meet. To this welcome news the incensed monarch could not resist adding that he had placed Condé in command of an army to ensure that they rendered the obedience they owed him.

The assembly of the communities that Guise had authorized opened on January 12, 1631. The harassed duke pleaded for funds to activate his company of ordonnance, but the bulk of the session was devoted to the problem of how much to offer the king in return for abolishing the élections, and what tactics to use to ensure that he responded favorably to their request. However, on the morning of January 15, before much had been accomplished, Guise summoned the deputies to his lodging to inform them that he had received commands by an express courier from the king to disband the meeting immediately. Louis had decided that if the estates were to meet, it would not be under the questionable auspices of the duke of Guise.

The man selected to effect a reconciliation was once more the prince of Condé. His initial instructions had been to punish those guilty of subversion, restore order, and establish the élections, but on January 10, a secret directive was prepared authorizing him to abandon the élections in return for 2 million livres. Still later, on March 6, he was empowered to permit the exiled courts to return to Aix after the guilty parties had been punished.[11] When Condé opened a meeting of the estates, he offered in the king's name to revoke the edict establishing the élus in return for 2.1 million livres and an edict creating officers to audit the municipal accounts for 900,000 more. If the estates were open-handed, the sovereign courts would be reestablished at Aix at no extra charge. After some haggling, Condé accepted an offer of 1.5 million livres in return for suppressing the élus and the auditors of the municipal accounts. Although this was only half what he had originally requested and considerably less than the king had stipulated, he permitted the sovereign courts to move back to Aix. As a show of appreciation, the estates voted Condé 100,000 livres, but he magnanimously accepted only 50,000 for himself and 20,000 for the officers of his household. Guise was compensated for his services, but soon fled to Italy because he feared arrest. By fall, Marillac's grand design had been reversed and Provence was nearly back to normal.

Marillac's fall brought no immediate change in the situation in Languedoc. Richelieu was determined to break Montmorency's hold on the province. He sincerely believed that large taxes were imposed without the king's permission, and in this one place he was involved in the decision to establish the élus. Hence, to abandon the élections was to abandon his own work. About eight months were to elapse after the Day of Dupes before the cardinal, always a pragmatist, reached the conclusion that it would be wise to placate the Midi. Even then he made so few concessions in return for such a high price that the estates hesitated to accept his conditions.

During this eight-month period, the situation in Languedoc remained as unsettled as when Marillac was in office. The parlement of Toulouse and many municipal officials continued to put every obstacle in the way of the appointment of the élus and their performance of their duties. A syndic and a deputation from the estates remained continuously at court and occasionally presented specific requests to the council. Deputations from one diocesan assembly after another made their appearances, but despite a continuous Languedocian presence, negotiations were at a standstill. In 1631, as in 1630, taxes were collected without the consent of the estates.

Montmorency made a sincere effort to reconcile the differences between the cardinal and the estates, although he knew that large concessions by the latter would weaken his powers and reduce his prestige in Languedoc. For months there was no progress, but at length Montmorency brought the two sides together. Richelieu needed peace at home to have war abroad, and the deputies came to realize that if year after year passed without their meeting, the estates would die, along with their other privileges. Finally, on August 25, 1631, Montmorency's secretary announced to one of his staunchest partisans that the élus would be suppressed, although it was not until the following month that Louis issued the necessary edict. In it he expressed his desire that "Languedoc enjoy all its ancient rights, privileges, franchises, favors, and concessions,

. . . and that henceforth no levy or imposition be made without the consent of the people of the three estates."[12]

But Languedoc was expected to pay for the revival of its estates and the right to consent to taxation. Louis wanted 3,886,000 livres to compensate the élus and 200,000 more for the partisan who had purchased the right to sell the offices that were to be suppressed. Equally serious was the provision that six commissioners would be appointed in each diocese to participate with the diocesan officials in apportioning and collecting taxes. The amount that Languedoc was asked to pay in return for the suppression of its twenty-two élections was proportionally little more than Burgundy and Provence gave to get rid of theirs, but only its estates were to be denied the privilege of having their agents resume full responsibility for apportioning and collecting taxes. This and some other provisions in the September agreement were kept secret in order not to arouse opposition before Montmorency had time to return to Languedoc, convoke the estates, and persuade those who attended that it would be wise to accept the terms.

The estates, which opened in Pézenas on December 12, 1631, were so shocked to learn the terms of the agreement that they moved very slowly. Between January 30 and April 17, there were no formal sessions at all. The deputies were less troubled by the huge sum that they were expected to pay than by the role assigned to the commissioners in the dioceses and a requirement that the communities have their financial records audited by the Chamber of Accounts. When Effiat, the superintendent of finances, told the bureau of finances to divide the direct taxes for 1632 among the dioceses and to have them collected by the élus, Montmorency directed that no action be taken pending the anticipated settlement. The bureau and the élus ignored his orders, and no help came from Paris. As one event after another revealed his lack of credit at court, Montmorency felt his influence in Languedoc slipping. He was, an official reported to Richelieu, "an extremely tormented" man.

The haste of the bureau of finances had tragic consequences. On May 1, an intendant informed Richelieu that only the decision to direct the élus to collect taxes stood in the way of a settlement. The principal and unique liberty of the estates, he pointed out, was to make these levies. If this right was taken from them, he might have added, at the very moment when they were about to pay a huge sum to regain it, the negotiations of the past months would be meaningless. He urged that either a decree be sent immediately halting the levy or the estates be disbanded. Three days later, the estates, professing to believe that it was not the intention of the king that taxes be levied by his own fiscal agents, voted unanimously to direct the *consuls* of the towns to refuse to accept the commissions of the élus. They also wrote those prelates and barons of Languedoc who were absent from the estates to ask them to lend assistance in their respective dioceses. Montmorency, still loyal to the crown, urged the estates to countermand their order, but they respectfully refused. The bishops, barons, and *consuls* cooperated with the estates, and the collection of the tax was temporarily halted.

At this point a new factor entered the picture. Montmorency consented to consider the proposal of the bishop of Albi and his nephew that he raise a rebellion in Languedoc to support an invasion by the duke of Orléans. He had ample motives to take this perilous step. His great services to the crown in the siege of La Rochelle, in the Italian campaigns, and on other occasions had not been adequately rewarded. Indeed, Richelieu had forced him to abandon his office of admiral of France. His requests that positions be assigned to his clients had often been rebuffed, and the terms he had been able to win for Languedoc in the matter of the élus had been less favorable than those obtained by Burgundy and Provence. Now it appeared likely that the king was abandoning the agreement that he had helped to negotiate. Not only was he afraid that his credit was deteriorating in Languedoc, but he also felt that his honor was being tainted because he was unable to make good the promises that he had made in good faith to the estates. As early as May 12, a French agent in Brussels reported to Richelieu that Montmorency was joining the Orléanists, but neither the cardinal nor the council made significant concessions to keep him from doing so. They seemed bent on destroying Montmorency's reputation at the risk of causing a dangerous rebellion, so that he would lose his influence in Languedoc. Not surprisingly, the duke's supporters later charged both Richelieu and Effiat with following this very policy.

While Montmorency hesitated, the estates capitulated. On June 2, they accepted all the king's terms except the provision calling for the reimbursement of the partisan. Again a peaceful solution to the conflict seemed probable, but at about this time Montmorency promised to assist Orléans provided he was given sufficient time to organize Languedoc for the revolt. To win support, he informed the crown that he was indifferent to whether the new royal tax officials in the dioceses were called commissioners or élus. As he anticipated, the government preferred the latter. When the three estates learned that there would be élus in spite of the agreement that had been reached, they were furious at having been deceived again. The session of July 22 opened with a decision to send a deputation to the king to inform him of the deplorable state of the province, but before it had closed, Montmorency had persuaded those present to join him in a military effort to defend the privileges of the province and to rid France of the cardinal's influence.

Montmorency's action on July 22 had been precipitated by Orléans's decision to march through France to Languedoc two months before the appointed date. Montmorency's well-known charm had been sufficient to win the support of the deputies, but there was no time for him to raise an adequate army or persuade the bulk of the nobility and burghers to join his camp. Under such circumstances, defeat was a foregone conclusion. On September 1, he was captured when he charged the royalist infantry with only a handful of his troops. The rebellion quickly collapsed. Montmorency was tried before the parlement of Toulouse, convicted, and executed on October 30.[13]

Since the estates had voted to support the rebellion, Louis had a legitimate excuse to suppress the institution, but he did not do so. With Montmorency on the way to his execution, Richelieu saw no need to treat Languedoc differently from Burgundy and Provence. He was not wedded to any theoretical desire for absolutism or uniformity, and he had no objection to representative assemblies provided that they voted the money he needed. Hence he readily accepted the advice of the first president of the parlement of Toulouse that the estates be retained and the élus suppressed. At the same time, he took steps to ensure that the crown increased its revenue, and that taxes were no longer levied without the king's consent. To install the new regime, a meeting of the three estates was held in Béziers from October 11 to 23. Louis himself attended, as did the cardinal and a number of other dignitaries.

The provisions of the Edict of Béziers that the estates were required to approve can be divided into three groups. One group implemented the edict of September 1631 that Montmorency and the deputies of the estates had negotiated. As provided, the élus were suppressed, and other concessions were granted in return for compensation being paid to the partisan and those who had purchased offices. There was one important change, however: the six commissioners were not created in each diocese to replace the élus. This was a real victory for the estates, although the role of treasurers of the bureau of finances in the diocesan assemblies was expanded. A second group of provisions dealt with the continued refusal of the estates to vote all the money the king requested, and here the people of Languedoc were dealt a severe blow. The taillon, which the crown had been trying to get the estates to increase since the Assembly of Notables of 1627, was fixed at 282,500 livres. Other expenses that the estates had often balked at paying were also included in a permanent tax base. Gratifications were limited to 79,000 livres, of which 48,000 were assigned to the governor and the lieutenant general, a provision that made these two officials more beholden to the crown than to the estates for their stipends. Since these sums were to be spent in Languedoc, an additional million livres was to be levied annually to support the general expenses of the state.

The third group of provisions was designed to curb the expenses of the estates, diocesan assemblies, and towns by returning to the approach that Henry IV and Sully had tried in 1608. The estates were to meet each year in October for a maximum of fifteen days. Compensation for those who attended was fixed at a total of 11,160 livres and was to be paid only to the deputies of the third estate. In addition, 50,000 livres were assigned to pay the officers of the estates and to meet other expenses. The diocesan assemblies were limited to one eight-day meeting per year, and taxes for their support were fixed. Levies of from 300 to 900 livres were assigned to support each town and community depending on its size and importance. To prevent the local organs of government from spending more than provided for in the taxes assigned for their support, they were forbidden to borrow money without permission. These measures, which so crippled the estates, diocesan assemblies, and towns, undoubtedly saved the people some money, but the total amount was small when compared with the additional millions the king demanded.

On October 23, the deputies disbanded after an eventful session of only twelve days. They had had to accept a permanent tax burden that had been multiplied severalfold, as well as to raise an additional sum to compensate the élus. But the estates had not been suppressed in spite of the rebellion, the élus were gone, and the right to consent to taxes in excess of those fixed by the Edict of Béziers had not been challenged. Richelieu's triumph on the Day of Dupes had ensured their survival, because he was more interested in obtaining money for his war than in imposing a centralized, uniform system of government in France.

Only in Dauphiné did Marillac's work survive. The nobility and clergy desired to get the edict creating the élections revoked in return for compensating the élus, but the third estate was unwilling to act unless the tax base was changed. On December 21, just six weeks after the Day of Dupes, the first consul of Grenoble informed his fellow municipal officials that the nobles were going to assemble in their city on January 20 to consider what to do about the élections. Initially, the crown canceled the meeting, but at length the nobles were permitted to assemble on February 2 and on other occasions. The third estate also met, but the bitter quarrel over whether the taille was réele or personnelle, and the unwillingness of the nobility to contribute to the abolition of the élections prevented any coordinate action.[14]

By May 1632, just eighteen months after the Day of Dupes, Louis and Richelieu must have felt satisfaction as they surveyed the provincial estates. The treasury had profited immensely from the sale of offices in the élections in Dauphiné, and Burgundy, Provence, and Languedoc had paid handsomely to be rid of those officials. There had been considerable unrest in the latter provinces, but the decision to reverse Marillac's absolutist policies was restoring calm. With this example before them, the great cardinal and his royal master now decided to carry out Marillac's plan to create élections in the Pyrenean provinces and pocket the money from the sale of the new offices, but then satisfy their fiercely independent subjects by permitting them to reimburse the new élus in order to have their positions abolished. They issued edicts creating six élections in the Pyrenean provinces and a court of aides of Navarre with the appropriate number of officers. There was the anticipated response, and in September 1633, Louis, having profited from the sale of the new offices, suppressed the élections and the court of aides in return for the usual compensation. Henceforth, he declared, "the estates of our kingdom of Navarre and the provinces of Béarn, Foix, Bigorre, Nébouzan, and Marsan will enjoy the same privileges, liberties and advantages that they formerly had, notwithstanding all edicts, decrees, and regulations to the contrary."[15]

Brittany, the one remaining province that had escaped Marillac's determined efforts to establish a centralized, uniform government, was equally fortunate in its dealings with Richelieu. Perhaps the cardinal realized that he could make a quick profit there by creating élections and letting the inhabitants pay to be rid of them. There is no evidence, however, that he ever seriously considered such a plan. He needed the cooperation of the Bretons for his maritime and commercial policies; they had a troublesome reputation for independence, and also he had become their governor. Like most other magnates, he was, perhaps unconsciously, a defender of the autonomy of his government. Had Marillac triumphed in the Day of Dupes, it would have been another story. But he had not, and several years after his downfall, France, institutionally speaking, looked very much the way it had before he became keeper of the seals.

RICHELIEU AND THE PAYS D'ETATS

When Condé opened the estates of Burgundy in November 1632 with a speech stressing the great needs of the king and the duty of those present to render him "blind obedience," he seemed to be suggesting that a new era was dawning. But this was not the case. The estates continued to meet at least every third year to vote taxes, and when the need arose, there were special sessions. Because of the war, a large number of troops were stationed in the province or passed through it. Occasionally it was necessary for the chamber of the élus to take extraordinary steps to provide for their support, but the estates could and did vote the king less than he requested. In 1636, for example, they gave only 200,000 livres of the 300,000 demanded, and in 1639, with Condé's assistance, they managed to escape part of the costs of the troops in Burgundy. During the last decade of Louis's reign, the Burgundians poured considerably less money into his treasury than in the first, but these figures do not, of course, include the substantial sums they contributed to the support of resident troops during the latter period.

The Provençals proved less cooperative than the Burgundians. In November 1631, the new governor, Marshal Vitry, assembled the deputies of the communities to ask for 147,000 livres to support the army and 375,000 for the galleys. Those who came initially offered a third that amount, but after some haggling, they agreed to give a little more. Partially victorious in this instance, the Provençals nevertheless had difficulty in checking the ever-increasing fiscal demands of the crown. If other measures failed, Louis created offices to sell, and the Provençals were expected to pay the salaries of the purchasers. When the three estates met December 1632, they were informed that because of desolation and suffering in the province, the king had decided to ask for only 1.8 million livres during the next three years rather than the 3 million he had originally intended. The usual bargaining followed, and a compromise was eventually reached, in which the king took far less than he desired.

Since the grant that the estates had voted in December 1632 was to be collected over a four-year period, the king could scarcely hope to gain a large additional sum in the near future. As a result, the tension between the crown and the Provençals relaxed a little, but in February 1636, Louis asked the assembly of the communities to vote 1.2 million livres to support a naval operation to drive the Spanish from their coast. The deputies complied because their own interests were so closely involved. Although there was no clear distinction between the duties of the meetings of the three estates and those of the communities, they did point out that the former assembly should have been called upon to vote such a large sum. When Louis decided in 1639 to ask the Provençals for troop support and an additional 400,000 livres a year until the end of the war, he therefore convoked the three estates. Those present balked at voting so large a sum for an indefinite period. Only with considerable difficulty could they be persuaded to grant 600,000 livres annually for the support of the troops in Provence. They rejected the remainder of the royal requests. That November, Louis turned to the assembly of the communities with better success. Neither he nor his successors ever convoked the three estates of Provence again.

When Richelieu restored the duties of apportioning and collecting taxes to the estates of Languedoc and their dioceses in 1633, he probably thought that he ran no great risk of diminishing royal authority. As part of the agreement, taxes were to be levied annually without debate to support specific expenses within the province, and 1.05 million livres was to be turned over to the royal treasury. This was far more than Languedoc had ever contributed in the past, and Richelieu doubtless thought that it was sufficient to meet the crown's needs in the foreseeable future. However, the approaching war with the Habsburgs and the formal opening of a full-scale conflict in 1635 made it necessary for the crown to increase its demands, with the result that the quarrel over how much the estates of Languedoc would vote continued as before.

In 1633, Louis asked for 280,000 livres in addition to what had now become the automatic grant, but the estates would vote for only 50,000. In 1634, he requested a larger sum, but the estates would give him only 30,000 livres. This double refusal infuriated him. He ordered that 100,000 livres be levied to fortify Narbonne without the consent of the estates, and he created commissioners in each diocese. Because these were the very officials Richelieu had originally intended to use to replace the élus, this was an obvious threat that the crown was prepared to substitute its own tax collectors for those of the estates if more cooperation were not forthcoming. Instead of cringing, however, the estates devoted most of their efforts to protesting these violations of their privileges and refused to vote more than 50,000 livres. In 1636, Louis asked for an additional 1.2 million livres, but the estates refused to give him any of it. They did offer 900,000 to be rid once more of the commissioners.

This series of meetings shows clearly that the Edict of Béziers had not paralyzed the ability of the estates to resist taxation. Indeed, they frequently cited its provisions as a defense against the exactions of the crown. The few additional sums they had voted the king were designated for local fortifications. Languedoc poured nearly 3 million livres into the royal treasury in 1633 and again in 1634, but thereafter it contributed an average of only about 1.2 million a year during the reign. Although this figure does not include local expenses, such as the support of troops, which became increasingly onerous as the war progressed, it was sufficiently restricted to arouse the ire of the crown. In 1638, Louis gave the estates a choice of voting 1.06 million livres or having troops lodged in the province for the winter, but once more he was repulsed. In 1639, the prince of Condé presided over the estates, with no better results.

Louis had had enough. On December 10, 1639, Condé ordered that an additional 1.21 million livres be levied on the dioceses to support the troops. Since he had no tax-collecting machinery of his own, he had to use that of the estates. During the past several years, when the estates had refused to vote money for the troops, individual communities and sometimes dioceses had provided food or money to prevent looting, although by doing so they undermined the right of the estates to give consent. What Condé's order did was to generalize the system throughout the province. We do not know how effective these "illegal" taxes were. Very likely few diocesan or community officials refused to obey orders emanating from the king or his leading representatives in the province. On the other hand, unless they were threatened by troops in the immediate vicinity, most officials and taxpayers probably found excuses to procrastinate. The system was certainly most unsatisfactory to the estates and was very likely not too satisfactory to the crown. It is not surprising, therefore, that the estates adopted a new approach when they met in 1640.

In that year, Louis asked for 1.65 million livres to support troops during the winter and an additional sum for the garrison. The estates, although protesting loudly that these demands violated the Edict of Béziers, voted the former both to prevent a stronger precedent from developing for the king's levying taxes without their consent and to ensure that their tax-collecting machinery was used. This was a wise move, for their officials soon learned to provide for the troops so well that their cooperation became indispensable to the crown. When Richelieu and Louis died several years later, they left Languedoc an exploited province that had experienced illegal taxation, but the position of the three estates was intact, and their administrative system was more essential to the crown than ever before.

To test Richelieu's attitude toward the provincial estates, it is best to turn to Brittany, because it is only here that there is evidence that he followed their activities closely. His interest, of course, was derived from the fact that in 1631 he became governor of the province, a post he had sought because of his maritime and naval projects. For his overly proud and bad-tempered young cousin, Charles de La Porte, marquis de La Meilleraye, he prepared instructions in November 1634 directing how the estates should be treated. He had had La Meilleraye appointed lieutenant general in the county of Nantes and was about to use him as the principal royal commissioner in the forthcoming meeting of the estates. The estates, he explained, should have the service of the king and the welfare of the province as their sole aim. It was essential that he acquit his assignment satisfactorily, because everyone would assume that "his actions will be based on my advice and opinions. Consequently, the honor or dishonor they bring will reflect as much on me as on himself." After associating his own reputation with his advice in this fashion, Richelieu continued:

> He [La Meilleraye] will restore the estates to their ancient liberty, permitting everyone who has the right to participate to come freely in order to vote on the matters which will be proposed, without any obstacles either directly or indirectly being placed in their way.
>
> He will permit them to deliberate on their affairs as they think advisable, without interfering on behalf of anyone, but leaving them to disentangle their interests among themselves so that they will judge what the good of the province will require, provided that under this pretext nothing is done which can be disagreeable to the king.[16]

Of course, La Meilleraye was to persuade the estates to vote the king the largest sum that the province could bear in its present state. He was also to see that the right to collect the taxes was awarded to the highest bidder in an auction in which everyone was free to participate.

These instructions taxed the credulity of the careful editor of Richelieu's letters, and he was inclined to discount them. Yet one suspects that La Meilleraye paid heed to the advice that he had received when he held this and other meetings of the estates. On December 21, the day the estates of 1634 ended, one of Richelieu's correspondents referred to the fact that it had pleased the cardinal "to reestablish order and liberty" in the estates, and another pointed out that the estates had ended happily and that the highest possible price had been received for the farm "because freedom was given to everyone to bid as much as he wished." After the estates of 1636–37 had voted the don gratuit, La Meilleraye informed the king's secretary of state for Brittany that he had obtained all that he could without "extreme violence," which he had been unwilling to use. The bishop of Saint-Malo, who doubled as Richelieu's client and as a deputy to the estates, praised La Meilleraye's conduct, for it had enabled him to obtain 2 million livres from the estates "without violence on his part or regret on ours."[17]

The estates responded to this treatment by voting larger don gratuits during the Richelieu regime than ever before. In 1632, they were asked for 1.4 million livres to be collected over a two-year period. After the usual bargaining, the estates gave 1.05 million. In 1634, they were asked for 1.5 million livres and finally voted 1.2 million, plus an additional 300,000 for raising troops in Brittany. In 1636, they were asked for 2.5 million for one year and gave 2 million, to be paid in three years. In 1640, they were asked for 3 million and gave 2 million plus 400,000 for the suppression of some offices. Although the estates had always given the cardinal considerably less than he requested except in 1634, the size of the don gratuit doubled between 1632 and 1640.

How did Richelieu accomplish this miracle? Two factors are unquestionably important. First, he worked within the framework of the traditional Breton institutions and refrained from blatantly arbitrary acts. Second, he placed his clients in key positions and drew leading Bretons into his network. They, in turn, brought their own clients into his service. In addition to his cousin, La Meilleraye, Richelieu's noble clients included the baron de Pontchâteau who is reported to have brought over a hundred gentlemen with him to the estates of 1636. A number of bishops and abbots were in Richelieu's entourage. Included was Achille de Harlay, baron de Sancy, one of his leading pamphleteers and the principal compiler of his memoirs. In November 1631, Richelieu had him nominated for the bishopric of Saint-Malo so that he would have a seat in the estates and an opportunity to influence and report on Breton affairs. Even the procureur syndic of the estates was Richelieu's client. Those outside the chosen circle were as likely to court the cardinal's favor in hope of reward as to oppose his will. To encourage this hope, Richelieu made sure that his creatures received handsome rewards, and his leading henchmen at the estates gave lavish entertainments in order to draw still more deputies into his net.

If the cardinal had a way of prevailing on the deputies, the deputies in turn had their means of persuading the king's men to accept less than their master wanted and to make numerous other concessions. For Richelieu himself, the estates appropriated a princely 100,000 livres in every meeting from 1630 on. The influence of La Meilleraye was valued at 36,000 livres by 1636. Great Breton nobles like Brissac and Pontchâteau were given from 12,000 to 20,000 livres. The secretary of state for Brittany received 6,000, and there were often grants for many lesser persons, including Richelieu's physician, secretary, and guards. The estates of Brittany had always been among the most generous, but during Richelieu's regime, they became more lavish than before.

THE INTENDANTS AND THE
ESTATES IN THE PAYS D'ELECTIONS

Since the turn of the century, the pays d'élections had been the ideal of the more authoritarian and absolutist bureaucrats. They saw in uniformity a positive virtue and thought of themselves as reformers. If the élus were established everywhere in France, taxes would be apportioned more fairly, corruption would be reduced, and when a levy was made, it would go to the king, except for the funds he permitted to remain in the provinces for local expenses. The result would be more money for the king and lower taxes for his subjects. Sully had begun to put this program into effect, Louis XIII had returned to this objective when he recreated élections in Guyenne in 1621, and Marillac had made great strides in this direction before his program was abruptly reversed by the triumphant Richelieu. But the élus themselves were quickly found inadequate.

Under Sully's administration about 10 million of some 16.5 million livres of direct taxes levied went to support the central government; the remainder was used to meet local expenses. By the late 1620s and early 1630s, the gross direct taxes had climbed to from 28 to 35 million livres, of which only 7 million were available to the central government. Its share had fallen from about 60 percent to from 20 to 25 percent. A large part of the missing 75 to 80 percent was going to royal officials who had purchased the right to a percentage of the taille that was added to the basic levy as a surtax. This percentage was calculated to give the buyer a 10 percent return on his investment at the time of purchase. Since the buyer had a right to a percentage of the levy rather than a percentage of the purchase price, his return increased if the taille increased. This practice began in 1616 and was frequently used to raise money to support the warlike activities of the crown in the 1620s and early 1630s. Indirect taxes were alienated in a similar fashion. By 1634, the breaking point had been reached. The peasants could and would pay no more and the needs of the crown continued to increase. In January of that year, Louis sought to alleviate the situation by issuing an edict designed to reduce the number of persons exempt from the taille and to make the treasurers and élus more efficient. Then, in February, he reduced the huge cost of servicing the national debt by transferring the surtaxes to a rente on the Hôtel de ville of Paris. Instead of the lenders getting the 14 million livres that would have been due them from direct taxes under the old system, they received 3.5 million livres in rentes. A similar transfer took place in regard to indirect taxes. The savings to the crown were immense, but the royal tax officials who had purchased the right to most of the surtaxes were alienated.[18]

The élus had purchased or inherited their offices, and they could not be discharged without compensation unless they were convicted of a serious crime. They therefore did not necessarily have adequate qualifications for the office, and their principal incentive to gather taxes energetically prior to 1634 was that they got a percentage of all they collected. Now this incentive was removed at the very time when France was moving from an undeclared to a declared war with Spain and the needs of the treasury rapidly increased. As a corrective, instructions were issued on May 16, 1634, for the intendants in the généralités not only to inspect and report any errors or injustices committed by tax officials, but also to correct any mistakes made without delay. In the years that immediately followed, the role of the intendants increased, until the regulations of August 22, 1642, gave them primary responsibility for apportioning and collecting the taille and related taxes in the pays d'élections. The venal tax officials continued to exist, but their duties virtually ceased. A few of the ablest and most dedicated might be employed by the intendants as assistants, but as an officer corps they had been largely replaced, to their great chagrin.

Since the reign of Henry II, intendants had been sent to the provinces to investigate and report; now they became permanent administrators who resided in the provinces. For the most part they were drawn from the maîtres des requêtes and were non-venal officials directly responsible to and removable by the crown. Their emergence marked a great step forward toward a more absolutist regime. It is almost certain that Richelieu had little or nothing to do with this revolutionary change. In the rare instances when he ever mentioned the intendants, it is clear that he thought of them as occasional inspectors rather than as permanent administrators. His rival Marillac, who had served as a maître des requêtes, gave far more thought to their role. As keeper of the seals, he had corresponded with the intendants and defined their duties. Several articles in his ordonnance of 1629 dealt with their role, but there is no reason to believe that he ever saw them as resident administrators. Probably the crown drifted into using them in the latter capacity almost unconsciously and initially in the belief that their enhanced role was a temporary expedient.

In the provinces where the estates apportioned and collected taxes, the intendants continued to serve more as advisers and assistants to the governors, but in the pays d'élections, where the estates did not perform these duties, their role in determining the fate of these institutions after they were assigned tax responsibilities in 1634 can scarcely be exaggerated. On December 2, 1637, for example, Jean de Mesgrigny, intendant of Auvergne, prepared an account of the situation in that province. In Haute-Auvergne, he declared approvingly, meetings of the estates had been forbidden by the council at the request of the late sieur de Noailles, lieutenant of the king, because they were prejudicial to the interests of the crown. In Basse-Auvergne, on the other hand, the échevins of Clermont summoned the third estate three or four times annually. There were widespread complaints among the people, he continued, about the way échevins of Clermont claimed to represent the third estate. Each year 6,000 livres were levied on the people and placed in the hands of the échevins to be used in the interest of the province, but because of the costs of their deputations, gifts, and gratifications for royal officials, this was not enough, and more taxes had to be placed on the people. "The majority of the towns wish that this assembly would be abolished as it is burdensome to them because of the levies and impositions. It is by this means that the town of Clermont and her échevins oppress the remainder of the province. . . . Moreover, the said assemblies of the third estate of Basse-Auvergne are true monopolies and cabals that are prejudicial to the affairs of the king." As a result, Mesgrigny had forbidden the échevins of Clermont to assemble the third estate without the king's permission and to pretend to represent that order. Although the king's council had upheld his decree and had ordered that the 6,000 livres formerly given to the échevins be turned over to the treasury, these decisions had not been enforced. "And I consider, Monseigneur," he continued, "that it is very important for the service of the king, for the good and repose of the province and the welfare of the poor people, to abolish totally this assembly of the third estate of Basse-Auvergne as it has been abolished in Haute-Auvergne, where some people are trying to reestablish it."[19]

It is not difficult to guess where Mesgrigny obtained such an unflattering picture of the échevins of Clermont. For generations their dominant position in the assemblies of the good towns had been challenged by Riom, whose claim to importance was derived from the fact that it served as the seat of both the seneschalsy and the presidial court. The officers of these two institutions could not bear to see the elected officials of Clermont convoke the third estate whenever they wished, serve as syndics of the province, and spend the 6,000 livres collected annually in taxes on various activities that they claimed were in the interest of the province. Such powers, they thought, were regalian and should be exercised in the absence of the king only by his officials— namely, themselves. Mesgrigny may have erred when he listened too attentively to them, but he did not miss the mark by much when he spoke of the activity of the third estate of Basse-Auvergne. The nineteen good towns assembled three times in 1636, the year before he prepared his memorandum, although once or twice a year had usually sufficed earlier in the decade. On March 24, 1637, they also met, and Mesgrigny, who was then in Clermont on his mission, sent word that he would like to attend. The deputies asked him not to come because it would be contrary to ancient custom. What must have been a somewhat startled intendant responded that he had special orders from the king to attend, but that he had no intention of interfering with their privileges. The estates then sent a deputation inviting him to come. During the course of the meeting, the viscount of Polignac informed those present that he had an edict from the king's council ordering that 11,000 livres be levied to pay his guard and 12,000 to pay his salary as the king's lieutenant. He did not wish to have the order executed without first securing "the consent of the said third estate." The deputies who were present readily gave their approval with equal tact.

Even the assemblies of the four provostships of Haute-Auvergne were not as dead as Mesgrigny believed, or wanted to believe. In March 1630, the *consuls* of St. Flour had won confirmation of their right to convoke the third estate, and they proceeded to do so in 1630, 1632, and 1636. Unhappily for their pretensions, Mesgrigny was in the province on the last occasion. Perhaps he intervened to prevent deputies from Aurillac and Maurs from attending, for when a deputation from St. Flour complained to him about their absence, he forbad the meeting. The king, he claimed, wanted the towns to act individually to provide the financial assistance necessary to drive the invaders from France. Nevertheless, in 1637, and nearly every year thereafter in Louis's reign, there were one or more meetings of either individual provostships, groups of provostships, or the third estate. Royal officials did limit their activity, and perhaps it was their watchful eye that caused the *consuls* of Aurillac, Maurs, Mauriac, and St. Flour to refer to a meeting in St. Flour in late February 1643 as a conference rather than as an assembly of the third estate.

No such convenient villain as Mesgrigny can be singled out to explain the sad fate of the estates of Normandy. During the early 1630s, the estates regularly voted only part of what the crown requested, but the full amount was collected anyway. Then there were no meeting of the estates in December 1635 or 1636 to vote taxes for the following year, but substantial sums continued to be extracted from the province. When the three estates again met in January–February 1638, they raised a cry of despair. In their first article they complained about the failure to issue annual summonses and to respond to their grievances favorably. They clearly believed the estates were dying, but to their complaints the council would reply only that their governor had been too busy serving in his majesty's army to hold a meeting. In article after article that followed, the deputies described the suffering of the people with unusual fervor, and in conclusion they lamented that all that survived of their ancient privileges was the right to address complaints to the king. They did not bother to consent to any tax; to do so had become meaningless, because the crown always levied more than they were willing to give. Instead, they pleaded with the king to take only half the sum listed in the commission for holding the estates, but they were ignored as usual.

If the king's councillors had been both attentive and perceptive, they would have seen that the Normans were on the verge of revolt. Their only concern, however, was how much money they could extract from the province. They did not bother to respond to the cahiers of December 1630 and September 1631 until June 1633, and a new record was set when they delayed until April 1638 to answer the cahier of December 1634. Under such circumstances, it took only the well-founded rumor that the crown planned to establish the gabelle in Lower Normandy, and an edict creating an inspector in every town to enforce regulations on the type of dye used in the textile industry to provoke the revolt of the Nu-Pieds, one of the most serious uprisings during Louis's reign.

The estates of 1638 turned out to be the last in Louis's reign. It is impossible to determine who was responsible for this. There was certainly little reason for any officials to fear such an impotent institution. Furthermore, it cost the people no more when the estates met than when it did not, because taxes to support its activities were collected and turned over to its treasurer, and the usual gratifications continued to be paid in either case. Included were not only the governor, lieutenant general, secretary of state, and intendant but also the members of the Norman sovereign courts, who traditionally served as commissioners to the estates. Those who profited when the estates met were thus permitted to profit by an equal amount when they did not, and they were spared the trouble of attending. It seems likely, therefore, that the estates did not meet because their governor and the king's council were busy with more important matters, and influential Normans did not press for a convocation, as their interests were safeguarded.

The establishment of élections in Dauphiné did not bring to an end the activity of the various assemblies there. The crown altered the composition of the estates by reducing the number of those who could attend in order to make the meetings more manageable and to give the third estate a voice more nearly equal to those of the two privileged orders combined. In addition, assemblies of the individual estates continued to function. Dauphiné's location along the principal routes to Italy made it necessary for the inhabitants to provide supplies for the passing troops. For them to do so, the king's council continually sought means to increase the tax digest, for the overburdened peasants could pay no more. Claude Brosse, once more the syndic of the villages, charged that the reverse was taking place, because tax-exempt persons were continuing to acquire land. This led to several separate meetings of the privileged orders and the third estate, and to an edict of the king's council dated May 31, 1634, declaring that the taille was réele in Dauphiné. Existing common land was to be taxed regardless of the status of anyone who might acquire it. In addition, ecclesiastical holdings acquired after 1556 were to be added to the tax digest. Old nobles were to keep their exemptions for land acquired before 1628, but all ennoblements since 1602 were revoked and their recipients' property added to the land to be taxed.[20]

The edict of 1634 led to strong protests from the privileged and a number of meetings to prepare counterarguments. There had long been a close bond between the old and new nobility in Dauphiné. Many of the latter were members of the parlement of Grenoble or prominent in the legal profession. Surprisingly, it was the latter group that won control of the assembly and council of the nobility. The intendant, who had done much to enlarge the tax digest, complained that men "of their social position can decide among themselves all affairs concerning the nobility, send delegates to court whenever they wish, order levies in the province through *arriére bans* without royal permission, and form a general opposition in the province to the imposition of royal tailles."[21] At first the crown sought to weaken the protests by forbidding the nobles to meet and to undermine the parlement where the resistance centered by creating a *siège présidial* at Valence and a court of aides at Vienne. Then, in a final effort to resolve the dispute, the nobles were permitted to meet in the fall of 1638 to prepare arguments and to send deputies to the king's council. This led to a decree of October 1639 in which the crown, ever anxious to have the support of the privileged, made significant concessions. The taille was to continue to be réele, but nobles and officeholders who had held that status prior to 1602 were to be exempt for the property that they had acquired before 1635. For all its efforts, the crown had not done much more than ensure that there would be no further erosion of the tax base. To compensate for the financial loss, additional taxes were levied on the towns. The nobles continued to fight the arrangement, because the anoblis remained subject to the taille, and provincial assemblies continued to play a role in farming the salt tax, but the reign ended with the privileges of the province seriously undermined.[22]

Guyenne was the first province to be subjected to élections during Louis's reign, but the inhabitants remained unreconciled to the innovation. Heavy taxation led to riots and revolts, especially in 1635 and thereafter. Often the élus and other royal officials were the targets of the discontent, and a local noble sometimes provided leadership for the masses. Against this background of social unrest, the once-vibrant assemblies of Guyenne slowly perished.

The estates of the généralité were all but moribund when Richelieu came to power, although after a long period of inactivity, there was to be a final meeting in February 1635. The estates in the individual provinces fared better, for here there were often syndics or *consuls* of the capital towns to take the initiative in calling for assemblies. Between December 1631 and May 1636, the *consuls* of Agen managed to obtain permission from their governor to assemble the principal towns of Agenais on four occasions to deal with problems relating to the élus, tax farmers, and their debts. During the next five years, there were no meetings, but then between June 1641 and March 1643, the deputies of the town assembled no fewer than five times to settle a quarrel over taxation with the recently created élection of Lomagne.

The nobility and third estate of Armagnac and its seven collectes were active throughout Richelieu's regime, and their representatives participated in the apportionment of the taille, but the three estates of Rouergue, like those of Agenais, appear to have passed through periods in which they did not meet. Not enough is known about the other estates in the region to judge the degree of their activity, but there is no doubt that they sometimes met. Indeed, the towns of Bordeaux, Libourne, and Saint-Emilion dispatched a deputy to Paris in 1635 in the name of the smaller communities, as if to demonstrate that there was still a sense of unity among the towns of Bordelais. Two years later, the communes of Périgord asked that their estates, which Henry IV had discontinued forty years before, be revived, and that they be permitted to have a syndic.

The thirteen towns of Forez assembled a number of times during the reign to deal with the passage of troops, tax matters, and the additional costs caused by the creation of a new élection. The nobles met in 1628 to elect a syndic and four councillors who were to serve for three years or until replaced by new élections. There was at least one other assembly of the nobility of Forez. The third estate of Beaujolais remained active, but the plat pays of Lyonnais apparently ceased to meet because of the opposition of the town of Lyons.[23] We are left with the conclusion that in those places where Richelieu's predecessors had undermined the position of the estates, he permitted them to continue to decay. Since it was not necessary for the estates to meet periodically on tax matters where there were élections, intendants and other royal officials sometimes took steps to avoid convoking them. No evidence has been found to prove that this was a deliberate policy on the part of Richelieu or the king's council. On the other hand, in provinces that had no élections, Richelieu resumed the time-honored policy of bargaining with the estates to obtain the funds he desired. To secure his goals, he conciliated the elites, sought the assistance of his clients in the estates, gave pensions and other rewards to a few, and tried to persuade the bulk of the deputies to vote most of what was asked. Only in extreme cases where the estates repeatedly refused to cooperate, as in Languedoc in 1639, did he or his officials employ force or otherwise seriously violate the privileges of a province.

THE ASSEMBLY OF THE CLERGY AND THE GOVERNANCE OF FRANCE

Richelieu also sought to employ his persuasive techniques to obtain what he wanted from the clergy, and here, as a prince of the church, he was much more directly involved in the negotiations than with the estates. When Louis XIII undertook the expensive siege of La Rochelle, Richelieu appealed to the pope for authorization to acquire part of the goods of the French clergy. Permission was readily granted, but instead of taking the papal letter to the individual dioceses to collect the desired sum, as the nuncio desired, Richelieu insisted on seeking the consent of the Assembly of the Clergy in the customary manner. When the royal commissioner asked for 4 million livres, the assembly responded with an offer of half that amount. Richelieu was angry, Louis was threatening, and in the end the clergy were persuaded to offer 3 million livres, the very amount Richelieu had told the pope he wanted in the first place.

The launching of a full-scale war against the Habsburgs in 1635 provoked a new financial crisis. The clergy had less enthusiasm for donating their goods to kill their fellow Catholics than they had been to slaughter the Huguenots. This time the crown wanted a long-term annual grant of 600,000 livres. Considerable haggling followed, in which Richelieu sought to influence the deliberations by urging the king to treat the bishops devoted to his interest warmly but to be colder to those who were uncooperative. Only after a mixture of threats and persuasion had been applied could the assembly be persuaded to vote a little over half what the crown had originally requested. The grant was noteworthy, however, because papal permission to tax the clergy had not been sought. An important step toward establishing the independence of the Gallican church from Rome had been taken.

Richelieu attempted to persuade a group of twenty-two bishops who happened to be in Paris in December 1640 to agree to another grant in order to avoid the lengthy bargaining with the larger assembly, but he had little success. Forced to turn once more to the full Assembly of the Clergy, he took every step to ensure a compliant meeting. He chose the location of the meeting with care and sent a list of approved candidates to each electoral province. This procedure led to the selection of many loyal deputies, but there was still enough opposition to require months of negotiation.

Richelieu would have been happy to control the provinces in the traditional way—that is, he was willing to make use of the governors and their network of clients. He was no enemy of the great nobles; indeed, he aspired to become one himself. The trouble with using the governors was that most of them regarded themselves as his equals and displayed little inclination to become his creatures. When one, like Condé, was willing to cooperate, Richelieu gave him considerable authority. Condé was the true governor of Burgundy, and he and his descendants were permitted to enjoy almost complete control of Burgundian patronage. Governors who were unwilling to become part of Richelieu's network were a potential threat, and he sought to have Louis remove them when an excuse could be found or manufactured. The Montmorencies had virtually turned Languedoc into a hereditary fief. The handsome, chivalrous duke had offered to protect Richelieu from his enemies when Louis was thought to be dying in Lyons shortly before the Day of Dupes. Gratitude was not one of Richelieu's strong points, however, and he drove Montmorency into rebellion. Once he was brought to trial, Richelieu became fearful that Louis might pardon him because of his great services and those of his house. To strengthen Louis's resolve, Richelieu prepared a document belittling the Montmorencies' achievements.[24] Once the duke was beheaded, Richelieu succeeded in having first Schomberg and then his son, both faithful clients, appointed governor of Languedoc. He frightened Guise into abandoning his governorship of Provence, but had to accept Vitry in his place because Louis felt deeply in his debt. It was not until 1637 that Richelieu managed to have him replaced by a less unruly governor. The equally difficult Epernon held on to the government of Guyenne until 1638, and Montbazon, Villeroy, and Longueville served as governors of the Ile-de-France, Lyonnais, and Normandy throughout Richelieu's ministry. Clearly he could not rely solely on governors as instruments for controlling the provinces.

It has often been assumed that the intendants replaced the governors as chief administrators of the provinces, but a few intendants were actually the clients of the governors, and others served at their request.[25] Richelieu looked upon them more as inspectors than as administrators. Only permanent residents could serve his purpose. He found a solution to his problem, not in a particular institution or type of official, but in a complex network of clients and subclients, or, as it has been called, a patron-broker-client relationship.

When a governor failed to become his creature, or to a lesser extent even when he did, Richelieu sought men of importance but of somewhat lesser rank in his government to become his brokers. They might be bishops, abbots, lieutenant generals, presidents of the sovereign courts, leaders of the provincial estates, or even important municipal officials. Some were intendants but many intendants were not within his circle. Richelieu won their loyalty by the generous rewards he gave them as their patron. As his brokers they in turn became patrons of clients of lesser rank. Together they formed a vast network reaching into all the provinces, but especially those along the frontiers and in the south, where ties to Paris were more precarious. Thus the governors who had formerly served as the principal dispensers of royal patronage in their governments were largely bypassed unless they were part of Richelieu's network. Previous kings and ministers had had some broker-clients in the provinces other than the governors, but no one had ever developed such an extensive network before. Richelieu used them to provide information to such a degree that it has been thought that he had a secret service. More important, they became his agents, implementing his will through persuasion, rewards, and, occasionally, thinly veiled threats.[26]

Whenever possible, Richelieu chose his clients from among his relatives and from the relatives of those who had already become his faithful creatures. As their number did not suffice, he brought hundreds of others into his network. According to his intimate adviser Father Joseph, he chose only those "who would be faithful to him and only to him without exception and without reservation. He does not want those who serve two masters knowing full well he would not find fidelity in them."[27] He also believed that to command obedience, he must acquire wealth. His "central conviction seems to have been," Joseph Bergin has written, "that power required magnificence in order to achieve its objectives of assent and respect."[28] To this end, he acquired the greatest fortune in France, at a time when the crown was falling hopelessly into debt and peasants and workers were cruelly exploited. His income and total wealth far exceeded that of any prince of the blood or peer of the realm, and the splendor of his household far outshone the king's. To further enhance his prestige, he became a patron of the arts, and as founder of the French Academy, he was to have a profound impact on the language and literature of the people.

The greatest accomplishment of these years, the destruction of the Huguenot state within a state, should be attributed as much, or more, to Louis himself as to his chief minister. The king had begun this work before he named Richelieu to his council, and there were times when the cardinal had deflected him from his purpose by directing his attention toward Italy. Nor did Louis need his minister to tell him that he should punish rebellious nobles, for again he had begun this practice prior to the cardinal's appointment and required little encouragement to behead those who flouted his authority. It is true that royal patronage was used more effectively than ever before to secure the loyalty of the nobles, but in the process the cardinal made them his creatures rather than the king's, a situation that was not devoid of danger to the crown.

The royal army was greatly enlarged because of the war, and the assignment of intendants to the various commands probably improved logistics and discipline, but as the Fronde was soon to prove, individual units continued to be under the control of their commanders, who filled the subordinate positions with their vassals, kinsmen, clients, and friends. When a regimental commander died, Louis replaced him with his son, for, he informed Richelieu, "If I had given the regiment to someone else, it would have completely disbanded, because all the captains were *from his region and were kinsmen or friends of the deceased.*"[29] The war proved far more expensive than any conflict in the past, because the army was larger and its equipment more expensive, but no attempt was made to alter the tax structure fundamentally to provide additional revenue. The poor were exploited more than ever before, but the well-to-do continued to escape with relatively modest contributions. To tap the wealth of the bureaucracy and middle class, the crown turned to expedients, the most important of which was the creation of useless offices. The purchasers of these offices drew salaries that necessitated still higher taxes, which they themselves now escaped because of the positions they held. At times the revenue derived from offices approached and once even exceeded half the receipts of the treasury, but irreparable harm was done to the society and economy. On the whole, Louis's reign was an almost unmitigated disaster for the mass of the French people and ultimately for the monarchy itself.

Perhaps Richelieu's most original contribution, if it can be called that, was his use of propaganda and censorship. Under him, Alfred Soman has written, "the royal government for the first time began methodically to exploit the full possibilities of propaganda. Théophraste Renaudot poured out such a deluge of pamphlets as thenceforth to drown all opposing voices, except for a brief period during the Fronde. And . . . it was roughly at this time that censorship began to be centralized directly under the crown."[30]

It has long been customary to justify Richelieu's decision to abandon his ambitious plans for internal reform and economic progress by citing the need to check the rising power of the Habsburgs, but in fact Spain was already in a state of decline, and Richelieu's aggressive German policy served only to drive the princes into the arms of the emperor. In 1630, they had forced the emperor to give up Wallenstein and had refused to elect his son king of the Romans, but by 1635, French pressure had caused Catholic and Protestant German princes to unite in a national war against the invaders, and a Habsburg succession was assured. As a result of the war, France received some additional territory, but who can say whether the French would not have been left in a better position to defend their national interests if Marillac had been permitted to develop a more efficient government, and if Richelieu himself had succeeded in improving the economy and establishing a colonial empire. As late as 1630, fewer than 4,000 English and Dutch were living on the North American continent between Florida and the Arctic Ocean, and five-eights of them resided in the single colony of Virginia.[31] An empire larger than the whole of Europe still lay within France's grasp at far less cost in money and arms than the Habsburg wars. Richelieu can hardly be blamed for not fully recognizing the opportunity, but with peace in Europe, he could have done far more than he did. One of the unanswered, indeed, almost unasked, questions in history is why thousands of Spanish and English citizens flocked to the New World, but so few French paid the slightest heed to the opportunities it presented for colonization. As a result of their negligence, English was to replace French as the leading language of the Western world.

Richelieu was the most brilliant statesman of his age. One need only read his memoirs and letters to the king to realize the sharpness of his mind and the clearness of his vision. Yet it was the incompetent Stuarts and their divided people who took advantage of the continent across the Atlantic, just as it was the autocratic bureaucrat Marillac who more clearly saw France's domestic needs. Early in his career, Marillac realized two truths that Richelieu failed to grasp: first that "the glory of good government is principally to think of the welfare of the subjects and the good regulation of the state, which can be done only through peace," and second, that strong government and significant reforms must be institutionalized in order to prove lasting.[32] As Jean-H. Mariéjol observed many years ago, Richelieu was "indifferent to institutions."[33] Insistent as he was on loyalty and obedience, Richelieu was unable to construct a system that could survive six years after his death without a major revolt. It was based on personal relationships, which died with him, rather than on an institutional structure that could function long after he had departed.

MAZARIN

Cardinal Richelieu died in December 1642, and Louis XIII in May 1643. With surprising rapidity, Louis's wife, Anne of Austria, was named regent, and Jules Mazarin, a cardinal but not a priest of the church, became her principal minister. As he soon won Anne's love, he enjoyed a more secure position with regard to the throne than Richelieu had ever achieved. The problems he faced were not with rivals seeking to supplant him in the affections of his sovereign, but rather the opposition of nearly every element of French society to his policies and methods.[34]

Richelieu had been a statesman. If he was mistaken to choose foreign adventures over domestic reforms, he was at least conscious of making a choice and did so on the basis of what he took to be rational priorities. Mazarin, on the other hand, was a man of intrigue. Suave and ingratiating, he sought to govern by persuasion, flattery, and bribes. When they did not suffice, he tried to divide his opponents by lies, false promises, and appeals to their diverse interests. Few were fooled for long by his outwardly obliging conduct, and he soon became as distrusted as he was hated. He never understood the government of France and occasionally was not above boasting of this fact to escape censure for the administrative actions of his subordinates. No reform program ever emerged from his subtle brain. Indeed, his correspondence suggests that he paid little attention to domestic affairs until the Fronde, and that he then directed his efforts toward intrigues to retain his position rather than trying to alleviate the ever-increasing suffering of the French people. After that much-discussed and confused rebellion, he lapsed, in part at least, into his old indifference to domestic concerns, except those of a financial nature. All he wanted from France was money to pursue the wars he had inherited and to line his pockets. He died the richest man in France and was very likely the biggest thief who ever served a French king.

Anne and Mazarin decided to keep many of Richelieu's officials at court and in the central government, just as they continued his foreign policy. They also inherited Richelieu's provincial network of brokers and clients. Mazarin retained them also but appears to have been less attentive until the Fronde taught him a painful lesson. In Guyenne, especially, he allowed the network to deteriorate, and here the rebellion was longest-lived. Richelieu had relied on Condé to control his government of Burgundy and developed no clientage system of his own. Since Mazarin had no alliance with Condé similar to the one Richelieu had enjoyed, he had to create a clientage system quickly when Condé joined the rebels. As an Italian, he was less familiar with French provincial officials and families, and his control over the kingdom was less firm, as the Fronde was to prove.[35]

Mazarin's fiscal policies soon brought him into conflict with the sovereign courts and the bulk of the royal officials, whom he sought to exploit as he did the peasantry. By the close of 1648, Paris was on the verge of an uprising. To escape the threat, Mazarin fled with the royal family to Saint-Germain early in January of the following year, and the widespread revolt known as the Fronde broke out. To rally public opinion to his side, Mazarin issued orders convoking the Estates General. Both antagonists began to arm, but peace terms were agreed upon in March before there had been much serious fighting. The meeting of the Estates General was postponed on several occasions on one excuse or another, and it was finally abandoned in September, but only after elections had been held in at least forty-three electoral jurisdictions.

The idea that a meeting of the Estates General should be held would not die. The nobility of middle rank especially pushed for such an assembly in unauthorized meetings in Paris and in the provinces. Finally, in March 1651, when Mazarin was in exile, Anne of Austria agreed that the Estates General should meet. She chose September 8 for the opening ceremony because by then Louis XIV would have entered upon his fourteenth year, the traditional point at which the kings of France were considered to have reached their majority. Again the meeting was postponed on several occasions, the last time being on January 25, 1653. Again it was finally abandoned altogether, but during 1651, elections took place in at least sixty-four bailiwicks and comparable jurisdictions.

It is of interest to consider Mazarin's ideas concerning the Estates General and other representative institutions. In a letter to Le Tellier in July 1650, he revealed that he looked with disfavor on the efforts of the nobility to push the government into convoking the Estates General. In March 1651, he informed Lionne that "it is good to talk of convoking the Estates General if that is enough to make the duke of Orléans and the prince [of Condé] take another course; but I do not know whether I should advise that it [actually] be assembled, because assuredly the princes . . . and their friends . . . have the largest party in the governments of the kingdom . . . and will use all their industry to have deputies elected to the estates who will be dependent upon them." But then he added with admirable foresight that the "parlements will be alarmed by the estates and will believe that not only the queen but also the princes themselves want to assemble them in order to repress their authority and to find remedies for many of the enterprises that they have undertaken. Therefore, to prevent the estates from being held, the parlements will join the queen and take a position which in the present situation is favorable to the interests of their majesties."[36]

In April, when it appeared as though the Estates General might actually meet, Mazarin cautioned Lionne that it was necessary to employ intelligent persons in the provinces "in order to win the deputies who will be elected." From the opening of the Estates General, he warned, the princes would seek to obtain control over the deputies. "It is necessary to try by every means," he added, "to have a great many favors to distribute at this time because this has always been the surest way kings have had to bring the estates to do what they desire." If the Estates General met, he informed Colbert that June, "it would be necessary to employ one of the best pens in Paris . . . to reveal my zeal, my disinterest, the integrity of my actions, without invective and without attacking anyone."[37] Nowhere did Mazarin make a doctrinaire statement for or against the Estates General. He had no conception of its role as an institution. To him, it was a body composed of people who could be bribed with gifts or persuaded by propaganda. In general, he opposed permitting it to meet because he believed that most deputies would be won by the opposing forces. He was especially fearful of a plan advocated by some of his opponents to have the Estates General postpone the age when the young king reached his majority until he was eighteen. To govern during the interim, the deputies were to be asked to elect a council composed of six members of each estate plus the queen mother, Orléans, and Condé.

Mazarin's approach to the Assemblies of the Clergy was much the same as it was to the Estates General. He sought to influence the choice of the deputies who attended and of the president of the assembly once it had begun to meet. To encourage cooperation on the part of those who were present in 1645, he wrote in his notebook that he should delay awarding benefices and abbeys during the assembly in order to keep alive the hope in each individual that he would receive one. At first these tactics were successful, and the Assembly of the Clergy of 1645–46 was persuaded to vote a don gratuit of 4 million livres in addition to the now-routine annual levy of 1,292,906 livres. The clergymen who assembled in 1650 during the Fronde were far less complacent, and it was only after making various concessions that Mazarin was able to obtain a paltry don gratuit of 600,000 livres. Furthermore, the clergy granted the money to pay Louis's coronation expenses, not to support the war against their fellow Catholics of Spain. In 1656–57, they won still more concessions in return for opening their pocketbooks, but in this period of relative calm, they granted a don gratuit of 2.7 million livres and renewed the annual levy for ten more years. Perhaps Mazarin was not displeased to grant so many of the clergy's requests, for no one in France profited as much from these concessions as he did because of his entrenched position within the framework of church property and offices.

Mazarin's attitude toward the provincial estates was similar to that which he displayed toward the Assemblies of the Clergy. He accepted their existence as regularly functioning, traditional institutions without question. When he was named governor of Auvergne in 1658, he made sure that he was given authority "to convoke and assemble before him . . . the people of the church, the nobility, échevins, consuls, and inhabitants of the towns and places in the said government."[38] Nevertheless, he sought to control the provincial estates in much the same manner as he did the Assemblies of the Clergy. Often he wrote to friends of the crown asking them to attend and to display all possible zeal in the service of his majesty. He sent directives to deputies and other officials while the estates were in session, and if he thought that they performed well, he was not slow to praise them for their work. Only rarely did he find it necessary to criticize someone for failing to be present at a meeting, or for not doing everything in his power to implement the crown's program. More often he exonerated an official from any blame for failure to obtain all the king had requested. Only in a few instances when the estates persisted in giving less than the required amount did Mazarin resort to threats. In 1657 and 1659, he talked of lodging additional troops and creating élections in Languedoc, and of bringing the king in person to Brittany to see that he was obeyed. In the intervening year, the three estates of Burgundy were actually exiled to Noyes to encourage them to loosen their purse strings.

Although flattery, persuasion, and bribery were the weapons that Mazarin preferred to use in dealing with the estates, at least until near the end of his career, his subordinates often sought to curtail their activities. In a letter to Chancellor Pierre Séguier concerning a meeting of the estates of Normandy in the fall of 1643, one of their number insisted "that such assemblies and liberties are extremely prejudicial to the service of the king. It seemed to me that our intendants of justice were under cross examination for some terrible crime. In the future it will be necessary to strike a heavier blow than in the past to levy the taille. The people are now quite persuaded that it is a tyranny, and consider the tax farmers scoundrels and the commissioners or intendants infamous persons. It is necessary to try to prevent anyone from printing the cahier." In 1645, an intendant from Auvergne tried to prevent the nobility from electing a syndic to replace one who had died. In February of that same year, another royal official informed Séguier that he had never seen an assembly as bold as the estates of Languedoc, or one with "so little respect for the things proposed to them in the name of the king." A week later, one of his colleagues lectured the estates on their obstinacy in refusing to vote money destined for the troops: "My lords, the estates of Languedoc are not absolute and independent. They are subordinate to the will of the king, who reserves for himself authority over them in order to leave them their liberty when they are good and to take it away from them when they abuse it."[39]

In spite of threats and pleas, the estates of Languedoc that opened in January 1645 persisted in refusing to consent to the bulk of the desired tax. The exasperated royal officials flooded Séguier with accounts of the bad behavior of the estates. They recognized the difficulties that would result if an attempt were made to collect the desired sum without the assembly's approval, but they interpreted any opposition to the royal will as malice, conspiracy, or worse. Talk in the estates of trying to get the intendants suppressed or of excluding them from their customary gratification aroused their anger, and they obviously disapproved when the estates appropriated over 200,000 livres for gifts, although 140,000 were to go to the king's brother, who had recently been named their governor, and 34,000 were designated for his wife. They worried lest the refusal of the estates to grant the king's request and the widespread publicity given to the incident "had persuaded the people that they had some power in public affairs and that they could disobey the king with impunity on any matter." The people might think that "they have a liberty that they can even use against the one who had accorded it to them."[40] The fears of the royal officials proved justified. The estates persisted in their refusal to vote 1,550,000 livres to support the troops quartered in the province, and the crown ordered that the tax be collected anyway.

In September 1645, as the time for the next meeting of the estates of Languedoc approached, one of the crown officials reported to Séguier that the only way to ensure the province's obedience was for "his royal highness or monseigneur the prince to attend the estates." In December, he declared that he hoped for little from the estates because of the unrest in the province. Neither the governor nor the lieutenant general was giving direction to affairs, and "the bishops and barons had let themselves be led astray last year by the pressure of the people over whom they have difficulty reassuming their authority."[41] By February 1646, he was complaining at the length of the estates and the burden their expenses would place upon the people, a protest that another royal official was to repeat in 1649. In spite of these attacks, it was the estates that won the first major victory, for in return for opening their pocketbooks, the hard-pressed government revoked the Edict of Béziers in October 1649. The regulations preventing the abuses of the estates were retained, but it ceased to be necessary for estates to turn over 1.05 million livres to the royal treasury and to levy some lesser sums without giving their consent.

The estates had bargained with the crown when acting under the terms of the Edict of Béziers, but only over contributions in addition to the ones that were automatically levied; now they bargained over nearly the entire amount the king demanded. The result was that the level of the contributions initially dropped, and the crown had to make additional concessions to obtain what it did get, although the presence of troops in the province during the war continued to pose a threat to the estates. In one year prior to 1659, they refused to vote any don gratuit at all; in another, they gave 2 million livres, but their most common grant was about 600,000. Languedoc was further from being subjected than at any other time since 1629 in spite of the efforts of Mazarin and his local agents.

Troubles in Provence centered around bitter family rivalries, which were largely manifested in the struggle to control the parlement of Aix. The three estates were never convoked during the Mazarin era, and consent to taxes was given in the assembly of the communities. After 1648, the communities sought the restoration of the estates year after year without success. The baron d'Oppède, who became Mazarin's leading broker in the province and the first president of the parlement of Aix despite a rebellious past, wrote Mazarin that he was well rid of the estates, although he claimed that he could control their deliberations. Actually, neither he nor anyone else could bring the assembly of the communities, much less the three estates, to as generous a mood as the crown desired.[42]

As long as Condé remained loyal, his government of Burgundy was quiet and the estates were cooperative. Once he joined the Fronde, however, the province became divided into factions and the parlement of Dijon was filled with dissension. When the crown asked for 1.8 million livres in 1658, the estates' initial response was an offer of only 300,000, although the youthful Louis XIV was in Dijon for the meeting. After lengthy, bitter negotiations, accompanied by the transferal of the estates to Noyers, the deputies voted 1,053,000 livres, which was reluctantly accepted.[43]

Brittany became divided into rival noble factions. The parlement of Rennes threw in its lot with the anti-Mazarin forces during the Fronde, and there was considerable turmoil. The estates consistently voted much less than the requested amount, but this did not prevent the crown from increasing its demands. By 1655, the government was seeking 4 million livres over a two-year period, and the estates countered with an offer of 800,000. Only after seven weeks of negotiations was a compromise figure of 2.5 million livres reached. In 1657, Mazarin requested 3.5 million livres over a period of two years, and the estates offered 600,000. The nineteen-year-old Louis was furious, but in the end he accepted 2 million. In 1659, the bargaining was resumed. Always the estates extracted concessions in return for their generosity.

Mazarin thus got what he could from the estates through persuasion, using provincial officials, brokers, and clients as his tools. Only near the close of his life did he display a firmer hand, probably at the instigation of the emerging Louis XIV. Where the estates did not have the right to consent to taxation, Mazarin gave local officials a free hand. For the most part, they were opposed to the estates and allowed them to wither, but the duke of Longueville was permitted to hold a meeting of the estates of the fiscally all-important province of Normandy in 1655 after a twelve-year lapse. Clearly, Mazarin was neither a disciple nor an opponent of the estates. He was above all a pragmatist.

Among the officials Mazarin came to rely on most were the intendants. By the close of Richelieu's regime, they had assumed primary responsibility for tax collection in the pays d'élections, and they served as investigators, advisers, and informers in these provinces and the pays d'états. Only Brittany occasionally escaped their presence during Mazarin's earlier years. Not surprisingly, the broad authority assigned to the intendants in civil and criminal matters soon brought them into conflict with the parlements, who saw their own aspirations threatened. When the intendants assumed responsibility for tax collection, the treasurers and élus in the généralités and élections found their roles sharply curtailed, and the courts of aides felt threatened. Not surprisingly, one of the principal demands of the first Fronde, which was led by the sovereign courts, was that the intendants be recalled. The hard-pressed government gave way before this widespread demand in July 1648. Only with difficulty were the intendants preserved in six frontier provinces, and even here their financial duties were largely limited to providing support for the army. Stripped of their services, the government went bankrupt. Mazarin could only lament the intendants' absence and express his belief to his chancellor in June 1649 that their reestablishment would help furnish "new resources." Until the Fronde was defeated, it was impossible to restore the intendants; all the crown could do was to increase the number of temporary inspectors and to assign intendants to the armies. Such measures proved inadequate, and with the collapse of resistance in 1653, the intendants were reestablished in all the pays d'élections. They were also assigned important roles in Languedoc and Burgundy, but did not become permanent administrators in the remaining pays d'états until the following reign. At last the crown had non-venal officials in the provinces, who were usually appointed for limited periods of time and could be removed at will.[44]

Hardly less important were the creation of a war department and reorganization of the army, first by Sublet des Noyes and then by Michel Le Tellier. In doing so they made full use of the intendants of the army and the provincial intendants, who were often given responsibilities with the army located in their jurisdiction. These officials were responsible for the payment of the troops, supplies, and general administration. They also informed the crown on the behavior of the generals, who sometimes ignored commands from Paris. At first progress was slow, but after the Fronde ended, Le Tellier was able to move more rapidly. By the time Louis began his personal rule, he had or was soon to have a large, well-organized, loyal force at his disposal.[45]

The sovereign courts and especially the parlements were Mazarin's greatest problems. Their role in the Fronde has often been told, but after the termination of that uprising, they were no more subservient than before. In 1658, Mazarin had to threaten the parlement of Grenoble with the prospect that the king would go to Dauphiné to compel its obedience. Indeed, Lloyd Moote has argued that the judges were not totally defeated during the Fronde, and that their resistance taught Colbert a lesson. It was safer to work with the parlements and the venal royal officials than to risk rebellion by ignoring their interests.[46] There is much truth in Moote's assessment, for Louis and Colbert did not push their absolutist policies as far as they might in areas where they were likely to encounter great resistance. On the other hand, there is also considerable truth in the older view that it was the ignominies that Louis suffered during the Fronde that caused him to adopt the absolutist policies of some of his predecessors rather than the more temperate ones of his Renaissance forebears. Furthermore, the suffering and futility of the Fronde made most of the people willing to accept a more absolutist form of government than they would have before. Thus the Fronde furthered the cause of absolutism, although at the same time it caused Louis and his ministers to move more cautiously than they would otherwise have done in their dealings with their own venal officials and the nobility.

As Cardinal Mazarin lay on his deathbed, he gave Louis advice, which the young king was quick to dictate to his secretary. The church should be maintained in all its rights and privileges. Benefices should be given only to able, pious persons, who should also be Louis's loyal servants. The nobles were his right arm. They should be treated with confidence and kindness. Magistrates should be treated with respect, "but it is very important to prevent members of this profession from emancipating themselves. They should be obliged to stay within the limits of their duty and to think only of rendering impartially to all my subjects the justice that I have assigned to them."[47]

How different this was from the advice that Villeroy had given Marie de Medici nearly fifty years before. He had seen the magnates as the greatest threat, and he had paled at the thought of the Huguenots becoming their allies. The members of parlement, far from being seen as dangerous, were to be assigned the task of keeping an eye on the magnates.

Half a century of hereditary officeholding had changed all of that. To Mazarin, the adherents of the "new feudalism" were the principal sources of danger. He did suggest that Louis award the crown patronage himself, so that everyone would look to him for favors, a policy that would strengthen him in his dealings with the magnates as well as with the bureaucracy, but the change in the relative position of the two groups in regard to the crown is nevertheless striking.

XI

The Nobility

What had happened by 1661 to cause Mazarin to see in the high robe a greater threat to the monarchy than the traditional nobility? The answer to this question would seem to lie in part in the slow weakening of the vertical ties between the great nobles, the middle nobles, and the simple provincial gentlemen—that is, in a decline of the clientage system—and in part in the growing pretensions of the robe, which were all too clearly demonstrated during the Fronde.

THE DECLINE OF THE CLIENTAGE SYSTEM

Henry IV had assumed that governors would spend most of their time in their governments and that nobles in general would reside on their estates, but even before his death, great nobles had begun to acquire residences in Paris. Lured by the social and cultural attractions of the capital, and above all by the practical advantages of being near the court, their city hôtels gradually replaced their rural châteaux as their principal places of residence. Here they could best compete for royal patronage for themselves and their clients. Here marriage alliances could best be negotiated, financial transactions arranged, and legal matters resolved.

The decision of the magnates to shift the center of their lives from the country to the capital weakened their ties with the lesser nobility. Only rarely did they hunt and joust together. Only rarely were the children of simple gentlemen raised in great noble households. Once the social life of the lesser nobility had centered around ducal châteaux; now that pleasure was largely gone. Once the great noble had traveled on horseback, where he could see and be seen by his neighbors. Now he often rode in an enclosed coach drawn by four or more horses. More serious than the loss of social contact was the decline in the rewards a great noble could give his clients. With the establishment of the paulette, many royal offices had become hereditary and therefore not available to the crown or to a favorite magnate to award to would-be clients. The companies of ordonnance had once been a source of patronage for the great nobles who commanded them, but the number of these companies diminished and appointments in the troops that replaced them were less under the control of their commanders. As largely absentee governors, they had less influence on appointments than in the past. Their role as brokers between the court and the people in their governments was in part taken by the lieutenant generals and intendants who resided. Then, too, the magnates were unwilling to devote as much of their own resources to their clients. Rarely did they give land to reward faithful servants, and their households and retinues began to shrink, especially after the middle of the century. A Paris hôtel required a smaller staff than a château, and once Louis XIV moved the court to Versailles, there was no room for a duke to be accommodated with many of his gentlemen. This is not to say that clientage disappeared. It was ever present, but during the Fronde, great nobles often found that they could raise fewer troops from among their clients than they expected. Once Louis XIV personally assumed the reins of government, it is doubtful whether they could have mustered as much as a corporal's guard, even had they so desired.[1]

There had always been a conflict of interest between the high nobility, the middle nobility, and the simple untitled gentlemen. Except for the magnates, however, nobles liked to think of themselves as belonging to a single order. In their cahiers prepared during the Estates General of 1614, the deputies of the nobility sought to preserve the integrity of their order by asking that no more duchy-peerages be created and that ennoblements cease and recent ennoblements be reversed.[2] The vertical ties of the patron-client relationship were nevertheless still strong enough to bind a duke, a baron, and a gentleman together. By the Fronde, the personal bonds between the three had weakened, and the service the client gave and the rewards he received were often so meager that the material advantages of continuing the arrangement were minimal. Under these circumstances, the system showed signs of collapsing.

During the Fronde, the goal of each magnate and his allies was to control the government and its patronage, either by working with Mazarin or by replacing him with one of their own number. First, Condé and his friends assisted Mazarin in defeating the parlementary Fronde. Then, when Mazarin did not reward them adequately with power and the fruits thereof, they became the opposition and others joined the cardinal. At one point, France's two greatest generals, Condé and

Turenne, were fighting each other. Each magnate may have had a policy, but as a group they spoke with many voices.

It is the middle nobility, Jean-Marie Constant's *noblesse seconde,* that claims our attention. Its members were the leaders of provincial society. Such men might hold minor positions at court or appointments in the army, but individually they had no hope of controlling the government. Some were counts or barons, but for the most part, their titles, although not their nobility, were of recent origin. Others were prominent untitled gentlemen, the lords of a few fiefs who one day were likely to see their lands elevated into viscounties or counties by a grateful sovereign. They were of the sort who were elected to the Estates General of 1614 in bailiwick assemblies of their order. With the magnates so divided, they now sought to take the lead, to develop a policy for the good of their order and also for the people of France. They may be compared with the gentry of England, who in midcentury had replaced the lords as the leaders of government and had attempted to rule the land through the House of Commons. The middle nobility of France had no such institution at their disposal, but they attempted to create one out of the Estates General.[3]

Their first opportunity came in October 1649, when Anne of Austria and Mazarin assembled about two hundred of their number in a brief meeting to serve as a counterweight to Condé and his allies, who had demanded what they deemed as excessive rewards in return for terminating the parlementary Fronde. These nobles of middling rank proclaimed the union of the nobility and sharply criticized the granting of honorific privileges reserved for those of royal blood to dukes, peers, and members of slightly less elevated families. As these privileges had been obtained at the behest of Condé and his allies, their action constituted a mild rebuke. As the privileges granted involved such things as sitting on a stool in the presence of the queen, they may not seem of earthshaking importance to us, but opposition to them reflects these nobles' determination that one noble should not be exalted above another. To underscore this point, they signed the act of union without distinction as to rank.[4]

The meeting in 1649 provided precedence for further meetings of the nobility. In February and March 1651, nearly five hundred nobles assembled in Paris on their own initiative. Their goals were to secure a meeting of the Estates General to reform the kingdom and to win the release of Condé and several other magnates who had been imprisoned. In the latter, they were quickly successful, but the former proved more difficult, for although the Estates General was convoked, they could not be sure that the meeting would actually be held. With this well-justified fear in mind, they refused to disband until they had received a written promise that they would be convoked if the Estates General was postponed. While in session they once more affirmed the unity of their order. They also took care to separate themselves from the magnates. In 1649, they had refused access to their assembly to the magnates' clients, and the same spirit prevailed in 1651. On the other hand, they took pains to inform the gentlemen in the bailiwicks of their actions and sought to bind them to their cause.

When the promised meeting of the Estates General was again postponed, the nobility assembled in a number of bailiwicks in northern France in 1652. This time many minor nobles attended, but it was again nobles of middle rank who appear to have been in control. They offered their services to the king, but in doing so they did not hesitate to ask once more for the Estates General to correct the abuses in the kingdom. When the Estates General was again postponed, the nobles resumed their agitation. In Normandy and Orléans, they met on their own initiative four times in 1658–59 in hopes of securing the convocation of the Estates General. Their efforts ceased only when the approaching peace with Spain put the crown in a position to repress their activities. Throughout the tumultuous decade, Orléans and the other magnates, with rare exceptions, supported the nobility only when it was to their advantage to do so. The nobles' desire to curb the depredations of the soldiery, to alleviate the tax burden, to drive out dishonest fiscal officials, or to take other actions for the public good failed to elicit their firm support, and in the end Orléans even turned his back on holding the Estates General. Small wonder the mass of the nobility ceased to look to the magnates for leadership or to be willing to serve them, except in individual cases when it was profitable to do so.

The weakening of the ties among the nobility was not marked by a decline in oath taking. Indeed, written oaths appear to have become more common in the seventeenth century than before, and they tended to be longer into the bargain.[5] They were of four types. There were treaties of alliance between nobles of equal status, such as the one signed between the dukes of Vendôme and Mayenne on January 10, 1617, in which they vowed to free the youthful Louis XIII from the foreigners who had taken possession of the government. Second, there were contracts between groups of nobles, such as the acts of union in 1649, 1651, and 1652.[6] Third, there were reciprocal pledges made by a patron and a group of clients. And finally there were the pledges made between a patron and a single client. It is the last two types of pledges that are especially significant in understanding the vertical ties among the nobility. When Marie de Medici prepared to lead a revolt in 1620, she promised not to enter into separate negotiations with the crown and to protect her followers to the best of her ability. The nobles who signed the same document swore "on pain of the loss of our honor never to separate from her majesty . . . and to employ our goods and our lives to guarantee her from harm."[7] Similar reciprocal pledges were made between Marie and individual nobles. It took many more words in 1659 for two representatives of a group of nobles and the count of Harcourt to pledge to work together to secure the convocation of the Estates General.[8] Individual oaths also seem to have become longer. In 1658, a Captain Deslandes made a pledge to the powerful minister Nicolas Fouquet that in part said:

> I promise and give my fealty to My Lord the Procurator-General . . . never to belong to any but him, to whom I give myself and attach myself with the greatest attachment of which I am capable; and I promise to serve him generally against all persons without exception and to obey none but him, nor even to have any dealings with those whom he forbids me to deal with. . . . I promise him to sacrifice my life against all whom he pleases . . . without any exception whatsoever.[9]

Deslandes was to command a fort. A briefer pledge sufficed for President Maridor of the parlement of Rennes, who swore "to execute [Fouquet's] orders blindly in everything that will present itself and will concern him personally."[10] But the longer and stronger the pledge, the weaker the tie, because it was when there was some doubt that the patron required the greatest assurances.

In none of these statements did the client reserve his primary loyalty to the king as he would normally have done in the late Middle Ages. This was probably because it was assumed that a client's highest loyalty was to the king. When a great noble revolted in the seventeenth century, it was to free the king from his evil advisers, to get rid of foreign upstarts, such as Concini and Mazarin, or to reverse a misguided policy, such as the Habsburg wars, to the benefit of the king and the public good. The fiction that one was serving one's king in making war on his ministers was easy to preserve as long as the king was a minor, but it quickly faded when a king became old enough to act on his own. This fact was clearly revealed in the revolt Marie de Medici led against her son in 1620.

On paper, Marie's uprising was the most dangerous the crown faced between the Religious Wars and the Fronde, if not the Revolution itself. Into her net she drew the two illegitimate half-brothers of the king, a prince of the blood, and at least seven dukes, including Epernon, who, as colonel-general of the infantry, had filled the royal army with his clients. By the end of June 1620, she had 2,273,000 livres in her treasury and most of western France was in her hands. From this position of strength, she and her confederates hoped so to overawe the youthful Louis and his favorite, the duke of Luynes, that they would come to terms. Less imposing coalitions had been paid off by the crown more than once before. But the rebels reckoned without young Louis, who was now eighteen years of age and determined to exert his authority. He set off for Normandy, where the governor, the duke of Longueville, had joined the rebels. When the burghers of Rouen learned that the king was with the army, they threw open their gates, although Louis had a scant five hundred men. Prudent Michaut, the commander of the château of Caen, was determined to resist, but when he was convinced that the king was truly present among the besieging troops, he capitulated, saying, "I would rather die than oppose the first triumph of his arms."[11] Longueville surrendered with his army without a fight, and Normandy was in Louis's hands. He next turned toward Anjou, where Marie's army was in position at Ponts-de-Cé. Before battle was joined, the duke of Retz marched from the field with his fifteen hundred men, leaving a gap in the rebel lines. The royal army was quickly victorious, and it was Marie who had to sue for peace. The scrap of paper that Retz and others had signed pledging Marie their support meant nothing when they were confronted by a king acting in his own name. Had Louis been younger and Luynes come alone, it might have been a different story.[12]

The same lesson was repeated when Louis XIV had Fouquet arrested in 1661. Fouquet had won powerful allies and had created an elaborate network of clients, who took extravagant oaths of loyalty. Had Mazarin been in charge, they might have acted on his behalf. But Mazarin was dead and Louis was in command. None of Fouquet's clients raised a finger to save him, and the commander of the powerful fort he had built off the coast of Brittany surrendered without firing a shot.[13] Mazarin knew whereof he spoke. If Louis became his own first minister and dispensed favors himself, the great nobles would cease to rebel, and their clients would fail to follow them if they did. This is what the middle nobility wanted. In the Estates General of 1614, they had asked that "pensions, offices, or other gifts" be awarded only by the king so that they would be indebted only to him.[14] Louis felt threatened by Fouquet's powerful position and took elaborate precautions in his arrest, but he need not have worried. Once he assumed personal command, the nobility ceased to be a serious threat.

DEMOGRAPHIC FACTORS AND THE INFLATION OF HONORS

The declining threat from the nobility was not owing to demographic or economic factors. The population of France increased slowly during the first quarter of the seventeenth century, but disease, wars, and hunger caused it to fluctuate thereafter. The century ended with few more people than when it began.[15] But how did the nobility fare during this period of demographic stagnation. In pursuing this problem, it is best to consider the great nobility, the middle nobility, and the masses of plain gentlemen separately.

It is probable that a high percentage of the peerage were celibate during the seventeenth century, but this was compensated for in part by the early age of their first marriage. The median age for men was 23.8 years, somewhat less than for the population as a whole, but for women it was 18.6 years, as compared to about 25 for the typical peasant. These noblewomen who married before the age of 20 averaged a little over six children each, a contribution that must have gone far to prevent a significant demographic decline among the peerage. It was only with the dawn of the eighteenth century that the size of peer families declined sharply, despite the continuation of early marriages. Presumably it was at this point that birth control methods came into general practice.[16]

A much larger sample drawn primarily from the middle nobility reveals that around 1620, only 48 percent of men and 44 percent of women twenty-five or more years of age were married. By 1690, the percentage of married males had climbed to 54 percent and of married females to 62 percent, a figure still so low that it could not but have had a detrimental impact on the demographic pattern. The principal cause of this shortfall among women was that around 1620, 48 percent of them chose a religious vocation and 29 percent continued to do so in 1690. Only 8 or 9 percent of the men followed this path. The second half of the seventeenth century also saw a decline in life expectancy. Until near the close of the century, the average age at first marriage among this sample was about thirty-one for men and twenty-four for women, considerably higher than for the peerage, and about the same for the population as a whole. Despite their relatively late marriages when compared with the peers, these noble families produced on average nearly as many children. A decline in fecundity also set in at the turn of the century.[17]

The lower nobility were too numerous, and the surviving records are too scant, for a demographic analysis of the whole of France, but several local studies that include some members of the middle nobility are available. Of the 557 noble families in the élection of Bayeux in 1598, only 459 still resided there in 1666, the only serious decline since the close of the Hundred Years War. However, some of the missing families had moved elsewhere and had been replaced by 105 old noble families from other parts of France, bringing the total to 564 families, as opposed to 557 in 1598. The noble population had remained static even without considering newly ennobled families during the period.[18] Whether Bayeux was typical can only be ascertained after further regional studies of families, not lineages, have been done, but based on limited evidence, it seems probable that at every level, noble families reproduced or nearly reproduced themselves during the seventeenth century. Any slackening of their numbers was more than compensated for by ennoblements.

Aspiring members of the third estate could be ennobled by royal letter, by prescription, or by holding certain royal or municipal offices. It is impossible to present exact figures on the number of persons who entered the second estate by each of these methods. Even where the letters of ennoblement survive, as for Normandy, there is much confusion. All the seventeenth-century kings revoked ennoblements for the preceding years at one time or another, but sooner or later they usually relented in return for financial contributions from the individuals affected.[19] For the jurisdiction of the chamber of accounts of Paris, we have only a list through 1660 prepared before that depository was burned in the eighteenth century. It is probable that at least two-thirds of all the ennoblements by letter took place in these two jurisdictions.

Table 11.1. Ennoblements by Royal Letter

	Normandy	Paris	Total	Average per year
Henry IV (from 1600)	54	81	135	13.5
Louis XIII	111	256	367	11.1
Louis XIV (Mazarin period)	378	269	647	36.0
Louis XIV (personal reign)	422	?	?	?

SOURCES: G. d'Arundel de Condé, *Anoblissements maintenues et réhabilitations en Normandie, 1598–1790* (Paris, 1981), 89–91; id., *Dictionnaire des anoblis normands, 1600–1790* (Rouen, 1975); Ellery Schalk, "Ennoblement in France from 1350 to 1660," *Journal of Social History* 16 (1982): 101–110; and *Dictionnaire des anoblissements, extrait des registres de la Chambre des comptes depuis 1345 jusqu'en 1660*, ed. E. de Barthélemy (Paris, 1875).

NOTE: In Provence, Henry IV ennobled an average of 0.71 persons per year; Louis XIII, 0.73; and Louis XIV, 0.99 (Donna Bohanan, *Old and New Nobility in Aix-en Provence, 1600–1695* [Baton Rouge, 1992], 25).

Table 11.1 suggests that Henry IV and Louis XIII followed a rather cautious policy on ennoblements, but that Mazarin went berserk, only to have Louis XIV correct his indiscretions during his personal reign. The actual facts are more complex, because all the monarchs were willing to trade letters of ennoblement for money and support during times of trouble. Thus Henry IV limited himself to creating between 4 and 16 new nobles per year in the two jurisdictions between 1600 and 1608, but 29 commoners were elevated in 1609 as war approached and 53 in 1610 when the war and then a royal minority faced the crown. From 1619, when Louis XIII began to make his presence felt, through 1634, between 1 and 8 letters were issued annually, except in troubled 1629, when 13 were awarded. Then, with the outbreak of war in 1635, 23 letters were issued. Mazarin issued 72 in 1643 and 70 in 1644 to stabilize his regime, but thereafter he kept the numbers in the 20s until the Fronde. That revolt caused him to surpass all his predecessors by ennobling 104 commoners in 1653 and 82 in 1654. By the dawn of 1656, he had made his position secure and was at war only with enfeebled Spain. In that year and the four that followed, he elevated a total of only 48 commoners, an average of fewer than 10 a year. Louis XIV granted fewer than 8 letters a year to Normans during his long reign, and many of these were to confirm someone's nobility that had been challenged in his search for false nobles, but even Louis could unbend when his financial need was great. He issued 130 letters to Normans alone in 1697 through 1699.

A comparison of the number of letters issued at a given date with the political and financial position of the crown leaves no doubt that there was a close correlation, but nevertheless those in authority usually found it advisable to offer a less mundane reason for the rewards granted. In Normandy in the last two centuries of the old regime, 45 percent of the letters of ennoblement gave military service as the reason and 47 percent service as officials. The remainder of the letters in which a reason was offered were given to members of the bourgeoisie. Most of the officials so honored held non-ennobling positions in the bailiwicks and élections, but a few served in higher positions.[20]

The preferred method of ennoblement varied widely from one part of France to another. In the élection of Bayeux, 23 persons were ennobled by letter between 1599 and 1666, and only 10 by prescription, but the method of ennoblement of 12 more is unknown. Most likely most of them owed their advancement to prescription, so that there was less difference between the two methods than would appear. There is no known instance of ennoblement by office.[21] In the Beauce region, within a day's ride of Paris, with its vast numbers of bureaucrats, the situation was quite different. Here 17 persons were ennobled by office, 7 by perscription, and only 3 by royal letter during the seventeenth century. Of those ennobled by office, 4 each owed their advancement to posts in the sovereign courts, the bureau of finances, and the secretaryship of the king. On the whole, they were lawyers, merchants, and bourgeois of Orléans, Paris, and Chartres.[22]

The elevation of commoners to the nobility was paralleled by the erection of simple fiefs into counties, marquisates, and peerages. Of the last, there were three types of lay peerages: Capetian princes—that is, relatives of the royal family; foreign princes; and French nobles. The number of persons in the first two categories was determined by their capacity to survive biologically, as no new foreign princes were admitted to the peerage during the seventeenth century. There were ten Capetian peers in 1589 when Henry IV ascended to the throne but only six in 1715 when Louis XIV died. The number of foreign peers declined from fourteen to eleven during the same period, and their fate would have been worse had not three French nobles, who married the daughters of foreign peers without male heirs, been awarded the titles of their fathers-in-law. The great gain was by the French nobility. It comprised eleven peerages when Henry IV came to the throne and seventeen when he died in 1610. Under Louis XIII, the number increased to twenty-eight, and in the minority of Louis XIV, it rose to thirty-eight. By the time Louis XIV died in 1715 there were forty-eight.[23] As might be expected, the bulk of these creations took place in times of trouble. Twelve peerages were submitted to the parlement of Paris for registration in 1663, but six resulted from letters Mazarin had issued during the Fronde and one from a letter he had given in 1643, when he was consolidating his position. Louis felt obligated to honor the cardinal's promises. He himself issued five letters in 1663 and four more in 1665. Then, firmly established and with his debts paid, he refrained from further promotions until 1690. He created eight peerages between 1709 and 1715, but in general, he sought to preserve the social status quo, and those he elevated were of ancient families, boasting distinguished military service. Only near the close of his reign did Louis upset the social hierarchy by making his illegitimate sons princes of the blood.[24] Thus the number of nobles, both titled and untitled, grew in the seventeenth century, albeit at a very slow pace, except for lay peerages and probably other titled noblemen.

ECONOMIC FACTORS

The nobility prospered greatly during the century before the Wars of Religion because land rents and farm prices rose much more rapidly than the prices of things they bought. Those who escaped plundering armies probably held their own during the wars, and a few made large profits from service to the crown or from the wars themselves. The return of peace brought the depredations of war to an end, and with them the prospect of sudden and catastrophic losses, but the economy did not boom as it had following the Hundred Years War. The seventeenth century was an age of relative stagnation, and it was only with difficulty that the nobility as a whole made modest economic gains.

The greatest profits were made by the princes of the blood and those whom the king held in high favor. The fortunes of the former grew from an average of 1,588,000 livres in 1588–1624 to 3,000,000 in 1693–1723. Of their number, none prospered more than the princes of Condé. The first two princes had been relatively poor considering their exalted status, but Henry II de Condé decided to hitch his star to Richelieu's. From that time, wealth flowed into his coffers from royal offices and gifts and from his marriage to the Montmorency heiress. When he died in 1651, his income from his estates alone is estimated at 425,000 livres and his total worth at 14.6 million. His son, the great Condé, sided with the Fronde and then fought with the Spanish against his king. Such activities added little to his wealth, but once he returned to his allegiance, Louis showered him and his successors with offices and pensions. By the dawn of the eighteenth century, his successor's landed fortune exceeded 20 million livres, and he and his family were drawing 750,000 livres a year from the crown.[25]

The dependence of the princes on the royal largess was also reflected in the fate of the princes of Conti, the younger branch of the Condé family. When Armond de Conti died in 1666, he enjoyed a revenue of about 1.1 million livres, but as his eldest son was only five years of age, there was a sharp decline in revenue of from 300,000 to 600,000 livres per year until 1685 because of a loss of income from offices and pensions. Happily, revenue from property grew slightly during the same period, and the advisers of the young prince were able to cut expenses enough to balance the budget. With adult princes and royal favor, the Conti were able to amass a great fortune during the eighteenth century.[26] Louis XIV's brother, Philip, was almost totally dependent on him until he received the heavily indebted Orléans inheritance in 1693. Until then, Philip had an income of about 1.4 million livres, of which about 85 percent was derived from pensions and the like, and the remainder from an appanage Louis had given him. Philip and his advisers made the best of the situation by purchasing land and building canals, including one connecting the Loire to the Seine River, that brought huge profits. By the 1740s, Philip's descendants had become financially independent of the crown and the greatest landlords in France other than the king.[27]

Other peers also benefited from royal largess, but as they were not related to the king, they usually received smaller gifts than the Capetian princes. On the whole, the revenue of these dukes increased only slightly during the seventeenth century, but as a large number of gentlemen were elevated to the peerage, the newcomers tended to pull down the average. Most ducal families thus managed to improve their financial positions. The La Trémoille increased their seigneurial income from 43,670 livres in 1619 to 117,900 livres in 1709 by acquiring new fiefs.[28] The La Portes enjoyed a much more rapid increase in their fortunes, and an almost equally precipitant decline in the latter part of the century. Charles (1602–64) inherited three seigneuries from his father in 1625, and with this relatively humble beginning, he managed to acquire enough land to have the family seigneurie of La Meilleraye erected into a duchy-peerage in 1663. He owed his rise more to his close relationship to Cardinal Richelieu, and the royal favor this brought him, than to his own ability. His son, Armand Charles, married the niece of Cardinal Mazarin and brought that prelate's immense fortune, including two duchies, into the family. Armand succeeded to his father's offices, which brought him over 200,000 livres a year, as well as to his lands, which together with the Mazarin inheritance added 280,000 more. Soon after Mazarin's death, Armand lost royal favor and with it his father's offices. Large dowries for his daughters, expensive life-style, and poor management reduced a once colossal income to 78,000 livres by 1702. Even so, the family was far more wealthy than it had been when Charles began his career three-quarters of a century before.[29]

The most rapid way to wealth was to become the king's chief minister. Between 1598 and 1610, Henry IV gave Sully 2,087,000 livres in salary, pensions, and presents, and another 223,500 in revenue from abbeys, which the staunch Protestant did not scorn to take. By the latter date, Sully's fortune was over 2.2 million livres, of which 80 percent was invested in land. His fall from favor in 1611 greatly reduced his income, but he was able to leave a debt-free estate of 5.1 million livres when he died in 1641, proof that with careful management and wise investments, a noble who was out of favor could still add to his fortune in the seventeenth century.[30]

Richelieu enjoyed about six more years in royal favor than Sully and proved himself to be many times more greedy. After relatively modest beginnings, his annual revenue reached 266,000 livres by 1628, and it had passed the million mark in 1639, when nearly two-thirds of the total came from his royal offices and benefices. Only 106,920 livres were derived from land, the most important source of revenue for nobles whose hands were not in the royal trough. At Richelieu's death, he left a gross estate of about 20 million livres.[31] Mazarin's accumulation was even more rapid. He had little when he entered French service and no great fortune at the end of the Fronde. As late as June 1658, his total wealth was only 8,052,165 livres, but by his death in March 1661, he had accumulated an estate of 35,000,000, over twice as much as Richelieu left after his debts were deducted. No prince of the blood could rival his wealth, and nearly all of it came from the crown, except for the 522,600 livres annually from the numerous benefices a youthful and complacent monarch permitted him to take. No wonder a scapegoat had to be found after his death.[32] The man chosen was Nicolas Fouquet. Unlike the two cardinals, Fouquet was a wealthy man when he became involved in royal finances. In 1653, just before he became superintendant of finances, he was worth 3,411,000 livres. In the best years that followed, his annual income reached 500,000 livres, a good part of which came from the king, and by the time he was arrested in 1661, he had assets of about 15.5 million livres. His debts, however, were slightly larger, and a good part of them were money borrowed to support the crown on his own credit. Mazarin, on the other hand, had been most reluctant to risk his fortune to aid the government he headed.[33] The two princes of the church ended their lives rolling in wealth, but the layman, the least grasping of the three, spent his last years in prison.

In addition to nobles who profited from offices, pensions, and gifts from the crown, there were those who made large sums from contracts or treaties to collect indirect taxes, sell offices, and perform other services in return for an immediate payment into the always-empty treasury. Large sums could also be made by loaning money to the crown at interest rates so high that these payments were kept secret. These secret payments varied from 10.5 million livres to 66.8 million livres annually between 1625 and 1659. Much but not all of this sum went to service the royal debt.[34] About two-thirds of the financiers who performed these contractual services during the first half of the century were nobles, and four-fifths of them enjoyed that status during the last half. It is true that most of these financiers were nobles of recent origin, but what is intriguing is the number of peers and nobles of the middle rank who worked with the financiers behind the scenes or who loaned money to the king. They also often obtained rights to part of his domain and to other sources of income. When the clergy had to borrow 5.5 million livres to help pay the grant they made to Louis XIV in 1690, the nobility were the biggest lenders.[35]

It is clear that nobles who held royal offices, received pensions, or had the capital to profit from the king's needs were in a position to make large profits, but what of the typical noble who was dependent on the revenue from a fief or two, or perhaps even less, for his survival? Many were able to profit from peasant distress brought on by high taxes or crop failures to purchase their land. The process had been going on for generations and was to continue well into the eighteenth century.[36] Even if seigneurial revenue per acre was stagnant, it was possible to enjoy modest increases by getting more land. Under such circumstances, the Norman abbey of Montivilliers was able to increase its revenue $2^1/_2$ fold between 1605 and 1657, and the duchy of Estouteville and the county of Tancarville did nearly as well. But when the declining purchasing power of the livre is taken into consideration, their profits became much less impressive and the closing years of the century were a period of general decline.[37] Under such circumstances, it is not surprising that between 1619 and 1709, the revenue from the La Trémoille fiefs of Thouars declined from 20,000 to 17,000 livres, that of Talmont from 3,200 to 2,100, and that of Didonne from 5,500 to 4,500. It was fortunate for the family that it increased its revenue from several fiefs and acquired a number of new ones.[38] The nobility in Beauvaisis suffered a decline during the course of the century. On the other hand, the gentlemen of the Beauce held their own until the catastrophes of the 1690s.[39]

The above data are drawn entirely from northwestern France, and even for this region, the evidence is inconclusive. It does suggest that seigneurial revenue fluctuated, but that it more or less held its own until the last decade of the century, when there was a collapse that adversely affected nearly every element of society. It is this collapse that may have led to the poor showing of the La Trémoille fiefs between 1619 and 1709. Of greater significance, perhaps, is how the nobility fared in regard to other people. Happily there is a local study that addresses this question. The nobility of the élection of Bayeux sold 24 fiefs to commoners between 1503 and 1640, but during the same period, they bought 36 fiefs from them. In the brief span between 1597 and 1640, the proportion of the total revenue from the fiefs in the élection that went to commoners and unidentifiable persons declined from 11 to 2 percent. When a noble did go bankrupt between 1622 and 1675, it was more likely that his property would be taken over by another noble than by a commoner. Furthermore, throughout the period, old nobles fared better than new nobles.[40] Based on very limited information, it seems probable that the nobleman dependent on his landed income held or nearly held his own during the generally stagnant seventeenth century.

NOBLE CAREERS

Some nobles looked beyond their fields and pastures and sought careers in the army, the church, or the bureaucracy. The great expansion of the army during the seventeenth century provided the most obvious opportunity for nobles seeking careers. Exclusive of foreign units, the peacetime army, which under Henry IV had stood at 10,000 men, grew to twice that number by 1661, and had increased tenfold by 1683. In wartime, the number of troops greatly expanded. At its peak, Louis XIV had about 350,000 men at his disposal, of whom at least 20,000 were officers. In general, about 80 percent of the officers and 1 percent of the soldiers were nobles. When the army was expanded during a war, the commoner element swelled, but when peace came, the army became more aristocratic. To secure a more efficient army and provide career opportunities for poorer nobles, Louis XIV abolished the sale of commissions as lieutenants and lieutenant colonels and made it possible for able officers to bypass the ranks of captain and colonel, which remained venal. Thus a poor noble, and even a commoner, could rise to the rank of general at least in theory. A few did, as the career of the king's musketeer D'Artagnan proves, but money remained important, as did influence at court. The higher ranks continued to be the preserve of the upper nobility.[41]

Several local studies permit us to gain some idea of the impact the expansion of the army had on the nobility. In the élection of Bayeux, only 3 percent of fief owners were already on active military service when the ban was summoned in 1639, although the war with the Habsburgs was already four years old. Of course, some nobles had already served, and others were to serve before the war came to an end. A better view of the nobles' military role can be obtained in 1666. At this point, 57 percent of the nobility had seen no military service, and 28 percent had taken part in fewer than five campaigns or had been in the military for less than five years. Only 10 percent were hardened veterans with ten or more campaigns or years of service under their belts, still a marked improvement over 1639. In the Beauce, some nobles also seized the opportunity to have military careers. Only 6 percent of them had served in the army or the royal household during the Wars of Religion, but this number swelled to nearly 9 percent in 1600–1660, and then to 16 percent during the remainder of the century. Eldest sons were more than twice as likely to serve as their younger brothers. Ninety-four percent had chosen the cavalry during the sixteenth century, but the growing importance of the infantry caused an equal number to select that branch in the seventeenth century, and about 10 percent each chose the artillery or the navy. In both Bayeux and the Beauce, new nobles were more likely to serve than old ones, doubtless to win acceptance by the more established members of their order, and in both the highest ranks were earned by the wealthier members of the old nobility.[42] Of the 122 nobles who responded to the ban in the seneschalsy of Sarlat in 1674, only 7 were currently in the army, but 18 more had either served or had sons who had served, bringing the total to 25. Sarlat was in Guyenne, and in 1697 an intendant of Languedoc commented on how warlike its nobility was in comparison with the nobility of his province. Statistics support his observation. Of the 1,400 nobles in the intendancy of Montpellier in the early part of Louis XIV's reign, only 11.5 percent exercised the trade of arms.[43]

The church has traditionally been considered as providing career opportunities for nobles, especially younger sons, but in fact it was of limited use. There were only 115 archdioceses and dioceses in France at the beginning of the century. Conquests and partitions of dioceses added only a handful more, but the most coveted positions remained few in number. Once they had been the preserve of the old nobility, but 30 percent of Henry IV's nominations were either new nobles or commoners, and most of the twenty-two bishops whose backgrounds cannot be determined were probably of similar origins. The old nobility managed to increase its share of the appointments, especially during the personal reign of Louis XIV, but the episcopacy became largely the preserve of those with court influence, whether old noble courtiers or new nobles from the administration or the sovereign courts. Forty percent of the nominees between 1661 and 1685 were actually born in the Ile-de-France. Many dioceses became the preserve of this or that family. Louis XIV eventually did away with these dynastic arrangements and made more nominations from southern France, but during the century as a whole, the rural nobility felt that it had one more reason to be alienated from the court.[44]

There were, of course, lesser livings in the church, and there were nobles who did not scorn the position of parish priest. Nevertheless, only a small percentage of the nobility as a whole were attracted to ecclesiastical careers. Only 2.4 percent of the nobility of the Beauce entered the church during the seventeenth century. Even among the daughters of the nobility, there was a lack of enthusiasm. Only 3.1 percent entered convents during the same period.[45] Wholesale and maritime trade, mining, glassblowing, medicine, law, and so on, claimed a handful of nobles,[46] and some found employment in great noble households, but the royal administrative and judicial bureaucracies were of greater interest. In the cahiers prepared during the Estates General, nobles repeatedly attacked venality of office and sought to have certain positions reserved for their order. As late as 1615, they had asked that two positions in each parlement be assigned to them. Many offices passed from father to son, but a large number of new positions were being created that ought to have provided appointments for aspiring nobles. Nevertheless, the number of nobles in the élection of Bayeux who held office or who were engaged in such professions as law or medicine increased from 3.4 percent in 1598 to only 3.7 percent in 1639, and 6.6 percent in 1666. A slight majority of the officeholders were new nobles, many of whom may have held their positions before ennoblement. In the Beauce, the number of noble officials declined from 5.48 percent between 1600 and 1660 to 2.05 percent during the remainder of the century.[47]

The failure of the traditional nobility to take advantage of the vast number of new offices that were created must be attributed to the fact that their price began to rise rapidly under the last Valois king and soared ever higher after the creation of the paulette made them hereditary. Not until the eighteenth century did a long period of decline set in that made them a more reasonable investment for those who had the wherewithal. Only the wealthier noblesse de race could afford to purchase a position in parlement during the seventeenth century, and such fortunate individuals rarely had a desire to do so. Many members of the third estate were also excluded from the more expensive offices, and these positions were often passed on from father to son, from uncle to nephew. The eldest son normally assumed his father's office, as it was very likely the family's most valuable possession, and the younger son entered the army, once thought the more enviable career.[48] A second deterrent to the nobility's acquiring offices was the cost of education. To become a member of parlement, it was necessary to earn university degrees in the arts and law, and the price of such an education rose rapidly in the late sixteenth and early seventeenth centuries. Since the Middle Ages, too, the educational requirements for lesser judicial offices had increased. In spite of these handicaps, the non-officeholding nobility produced 15 percent of the new parlementaires in Rouen between 1619 and 1638, but they provided only 2.4 percent of the new judges in the parlement of Paris between 1653 and 1673. Positions in financial administration required less education, but they were less respectable. A few nobles took them, but the great majority of the nobility had to rely primarily on land for their incomes. They had no other careers.[49]

THE NOBILITY OF THE ROBE

There was one element of the nobility, the robe, that was defined by its careers. When the medieval monarchs began to establish bureaucracies, they naturally turned to their nobility. Nobles had been the administrators, judges, and law enforcers in their fiefs. No group was better prepared to perform similar duties on a larger scale for their king. In the parlement of Paris, where the concept of a robe nobility probably first emerged, no fewer than 58 percent of the judges between 1345 and 1454 whose origins can be identified were nobles, and another 11 percent were anoblis. Bailiffs, seneschals, provosts, and lieutenant generals were drawn overwhelmingly from their order. Only minor positions in the judiciary and administration were dominated by commoners.[50] As the sixteenth century progressed, however, the growing educational requirements and the higher costs of office gradually excluded the traditional nobility from most non-military positions in the government, and the social origins of the bureaucracy changed. The percentage of the new members of the parlement of Paris whose ancestors were noblesse de race declined. Between 1483 and 1515, little more than 10 percent of the councillors who entered the parlement of Paris were of the traditional nobility.[51] There were further declines between 1515 and the Wars of Religion, and in the two decades following 1653, only 2.4 percent of the new members had immediate antecedents who were nobles of the sword.[52] The decline was not accompanied by an influx of the bourgeoisie, however. Between 1596 and 1622, only 3.7 percent of the new members had their social origins in this class.[53] Rather the membership became almost entirely composed of the sons of members of parlement and other royal officials. Their immediate antecedents in the male line were of the robe, but many could find a few nobles of the sword among their ancestors, especially if the female line was considered.

The composition of the parlement of Paris did not change greatly during the eighteenth century. Of the 590 families who provided members between 1715 and 1771, 477 were nobles at the time they took office. The overwhelming majority of their families had been ennobled by office, but many had enjoyed noble status for generations. Indeed, 33 families could prove that their ancestors in the paternal line had been nobles in the Middle Ages,[54] an antiquity that most families of the sword could not demonstrate. Robe and sword families enjoyed the same legal status and constantly interacted with each other. The eldest sons of robe nobles usually followed in their fathers' footsteps, but younger sons sometimes opted for military careers.[55] Thus François Bluche can argue that the distinction between robe and sword was not one of class, but was determined by choice of career.[56] In his careful study of the members of the parlement of Rouen (see table 11.2), Jonathan Dewald found that most of the sons of noblemen who held no office came from old families who could trace their noble origins back to the fifteenth century. A large number of the sons of members of the sovereign courts were also nobles. Together, the two groups constituted a significant minority of the members of parlement. Between 1559 and 1588, 38 percent of those seated were nobles.

Table 11.2. The Fathers of Members of the Parlement of Rouen (%)

Date Received	Nobles Without Office	Members of Sovereign Courts	Lawyers and Lesser Officials	Bourgeois	Unknown
1539–1558	13	23	30	15	19
1559–1578	22	22	15	11	30
1579–1588	18	28	34	13	7
1589–1598	13	26	6	19	36
1599–1618	19	47	16	10	8
1619–1638	15	60	7	6	12

SOURCE: Jonathan Dewald, *The Formation of a Provincial Nobility: The Magistrates of the Parlement of Rouen, 1499–1610* (Princeton, 1980), 75–80. This table is derived from four of Dewald's tables. He provides no "unknown" column.

In southern France the distinction between the robe and the sword was still more blurred. Provence did not become a possession of the crown until the close of the Middle Ages, and when a parlement was created there in 1501, old nobles vied with others to obtain seats. "In a group of 70 parlementaire families holding office between 1629 and

1649," Sharon Kettering has found, "17, or 25 percent, were traditional or sword nobles ennobled before 1500; 34, or 48 percent, were robe nobles ennobled before 1600; 10, or 15 percent, were ennobled between 1600 and 1660; 7, or 10 percent, were non-nobles; and the rank of 2 percent is unknown."[57] Donna Bohanan's research on Aix-en-Provence reveals that of the eighty-one resident extended noble families in the seventeenth century, thirty-eight had been nobles prior to 1500. Only seven of these old noble families and six of the forty-three anoblis failed to have had members who held offices in the parlement or court of accounts of Aix. The nobility, both old and new, dominated the municipal government and civic life of Aix, and because of their powerful role in Aix, they played key roles in the provincial estates as well. The typical noble family produced both soldiers and officials, and it was not unusual for the same individual to play both roles.[58] The parlement of Rennes was the most aristocratic of all. Sixty-three percent of its members in 1668 could trace the nobility of their families back to the Middle Ages, as compared with only 28 percent of the Breton nobility as a whole. From 1671 on, virtually all the new members of this parlement were nobles.[59]

Unfortunately, there has been little research on the membership of the other parlements, but what is known suggests that they did not differ greatly from those already discussed. Around 1680, a commentator referred to the large number of members of the parlement of Grenoble who were "of old and noble extraction."[60] Here the nobility of the sword and the robe, new nobles, and old nobles, formed a union to protect their tax privileges from the legal assaults of the peasantry. Of the 127 families that furnished members to the parlement of Bordeaux during the reign of Louis XVI, 24 had nobility going back to the sixteenth century or earlier, and only 13 were commoners at the time they obtained office.[61]

The nobles of the robe in the sovereign courts had either purchased or inherited their offices, but there was another type of robe noble who acted on the king's commission to perform designated tasks. Their offices were not venal, and they were essentially administrators rather than judges. Included in their number were members of the king's council, governors, ambassadors, superintendants of finances, and intendants. They often quarreled bitterly with the judicial robe.[62] Indeed, the robe was as divided within itself as was the peerage. Not only was there a division between the judicial and administrative nobility, but within the former, parlements, chambers of accounts, and courts of aides were often at odds. Higher courts bickered with lower courts, and within the same court there were frequently bitter personal rivalries. Thus neither the robe nor the sword could present a united front against the crown.

High administrative offices ennobled just as judicial ones did. In both cases, many were nobles before they became officials. Below this level, judicial and administrative offices did not ennoble, but some of these positions were held by nobles. The social origins of the members of the presidial and bailiwick courts are not well known, but a study of the officials in the châtelet, the Parisian equivalent of these jurisdictions, is most revealing. These positions did not ennoble, but in 1661, 37 percent of the occupants were nobles and 9 percent were in the process of becoming nobles. Only 4.6 percent were the sons of merchants and 1.3 percent the sons of seigneurs. Most of the remainder were the sons of officials of one type or another.[63] The secondary courts in the provinces were presumably less aristocratic, but their membership included the children of many officials, a few of whom were nobles. Thus by the late seventeenth century, the judicial and administrative bureaucracy, which in the Middle Ages had been largely dominated by the children of the nobility, had become the preserve of the sons of officials who were themselves often nobles, and in some instances of ancient extraction.

Although the robe strongly preferred to marry the daughters of other officials, some had ancestors who were of the traditional nobility or had relatives who had opted for military careers. Although in some respects the robe was distinct, in other respects it was hopelessly intertwined with the traditional nobility. Thus it should come as no surprise that Gilles Picot, seigneur of Gouberville and Mesnil au Val, held a lieutenancy in the *eaux et forêts* as had his father before him, but that his nobility can be traced back to around 1270, when Guillaume Picot, knight, married Georgette Suhard, who brought the important fief of Russy into the family. Gouberville never engaged in military campaigns and consorted easily with what we would call nobles of the robe and of the sword. There were knights among his ancestors and relatives, but his sister married the lieutenant general of the bailiwick of Caen, who was ennobled only in 1544. Although he was a peace-loving man himself, Gouberville's brother, Louis, indulged in the violence so often attributed to the noblesse de race. Except for his penchant for recording the daily episodes of his uneventful life, Gouberville came close to being a typical French noble.[64] On the other hand, Jean Savaron, deputy of the third estate of Basse-Auvergne, pointed out to the deputies of the nobility to the Estates General of 1614 that he had borne arms for five years before serving in the courts of justice for twenty-five years.[65]

The mixture of robe and sword extended upward to the highest echelons of the nobility. The first marshal and duke of Villeroy and the first marshal and duke of Villars were members of old robe families who chose military careers. The first marshal and duke of Retz was the son of a Florentine merchant who had settled in Lyons. The dukes of Tresmes were descendants of a Paris family that had often held municipal and royal offices. The dukes of Epernon descended from a municipal official of Toulouse. Always the advancement of a robe or bourgeois family to the peerage was preceded by a shift to a military career. Other dukes had robe ancestors in the maternal line. Sully's paternal ancestors counted kings and emperors among their connections, but his maternal grandfather had been a president of the chamber of accounts. His first wife was a descendant of Louis VI, the Fat, but he chose his second wife from among the robe. The dukes of Montmorency owed their beautiful estate at Chantilly to an Orgemont bride whose great-grandfather had been chancellor of France and whose great-great-grandfather had been a bourgeois of Lagny. Sometimes the flow was in the other direction. Richard Le Pelletier was able to marry his son to a Montmorency despite the fact that his great-grandfather had been a merchant of Rouen.[66] Therefore, although there was a marked tendency for peers to intermarry, just as lesser nobles sought mates from among their social equals, enough marriages took place between persons of different status for there to be few nobles of the sword who did not have an official or even a burgher among their ancestors or relatives. Indeed, within the same generation, one brother often opted for a military career and another chose the robe, as the Marillacs had done. Or take the case of Henri de Mesmes. He was lieutenant civil of the provostship of Paris and deputy of the third estate to the Estates General of 1614. Nevertheless, he could trace his noble ancestry back to the Middle Ages. Most of the family marriages in the sixteenth century had been in the robe, but he himself married Jeanne de Monluc, widow of Charles d'Amboise, marquis of Reynel and Bussy and a deputy of the nobility at the Estates General of 1614. Jeanne was the daughter of the famous Jean de Monluc, prince of Cambrai and marshal of France. Henri de Mesmes's daughter by a later marriage became the bride of Louis de Rochechouart, duke of Vivonne, peer and marshal of France.[67]

It must always be remembered that the law did not distinguish between the robe and the sword. Most of the customs of the bailiwicks and provinces had been redacted in the first part of the sixteenth century or earlier, and they were supposed to reflect the law as it had existed in oral tradition. The law therefore preceded the emergence of the robe in the provinces and made no allowance for its existence. In fact and in law, the robe and the sword were one and the same, except insofar as they represented different choices of careers.

THE QUARREL BETWEEN THE ROBE AND SWORD

If, as has been suggested, few members of the noblesse de race followed military careers and many nobles of the robe had one or more ancestors who were of the old nobility; if intermarriages between robe and sword, although rare, were still frequent enough to ensure that most of the aristocracy had ancestors and relatives who had pursued military and bureaucratic careers; what are we to make of the much-heralded quarrel between the robe and the sword? The foremost proponent of this rivalry, Roland Mousnier, has cited literary evidence to support his position. Charles Loyseau, a magistrate and jurist who analyzed French society in a book published in 1610, thought of the nobility as those who bore arms. He relegated nobles of the robe to the third estate and never discussed simple country gentlemen who lacked military aspirations. Time and again, Mousnier has argued that old nobles referred to the robe as bourgeois.[68] This brings forth the question, how is the literary evidence to be reconciled with statistical data pointing in the opposite direction.[69]

What immediately strikes us about Mousnier's examples is that they are nearly all taken from the late sixteenth and seventeenth centuries. If we look at the preceding period, a different picture is suggested. Gaspard de Saulx, seigneur de Tavannes, marshal of France, recommended to gentlemen who lacked great wealth that they rear only one son for the army; other sons should study law or theology. To this doughty warrior, a judicial career was permissible for a gentleman.[70] His contemporary and fellow marshal Blaise de Monluc accepted the fact that many young gentlemen were studying law, although he would clearly have preferred them to have chosen a career in arms.[71] He also complained about nobles permitting so many municipal offices to fall into the hands of commoners that "we have to bow and scrape before them."[72] Municipal offices, then, were acceptable, although regrettable, and one of the principal demands of the nobility as late as the Fronde was that they be assigned more royal offices. The quarrel was never about whether nobles should hold offices; rather it was with the occupants of these offices.

There was little or no friction between the nobility and the office-holders at the beginning of the early modern period, but the increasing pretensions of the officials and the jealousy of the nobility changed the era of good feeling into an atmosphere of ever-increasing bitterness as the sixteenth century progressed. In the assembly held in Paris in 1558, the judges who attended from the parlements constituted a fourth estate, which was given precedence over the third estate. In the Estates General that met two years later, the spokesman for the nobility declared that the only true nobility was that of birth; ennoblement by office was thereby rejected. The parlement of Paris countered by attempting to amend the ordonnance based on the recommendations of the three estates (see pp. 104–106 above).

Parlement had every reason to be suspicious of any document emanating from the estates. In 1560, the nobles had urged that judicial officials be elected and that some positions in the parlements and other sovereign courts be reserved for them.[73] Perhaps nowhere did they reveal their consciousness of their separation from the nobles of the robe more than in their frequent practice of referring to themselves as "gentlemen" rather than simply as nobles, as they had usually done in the Estates General of 1484. Expressions such as *gentilshommes de robbe courte portant épée* leave no doubt that they wanted to distance themselves from the nobles of the long robe.[74] When the estates met again the following year at Pontoise, the nobility repeated the above demands, and added a new one on their own—that judicial officers serve for three-year terms rather than for life.[75] In the Estates Generals that met in 1576 and 1588, the nobles renewed their efforts to substitute the election of officers for venality and to reduce the number of officials but at the same time to reserve more positions for themselves. In all these goals, except in their desire for preferential treatment, they were joined by the other estates.[76] A significant new element was introduced by the nobility in 1576: they declared that offices did not ennoble the posterity of commoners, and that those who had been ennobled by office during the past thirty years should be returned to their common condition, a petition that they repeated in 1588. In 1614, the nobility added verbal assaults in the assembly to the petitions in their cahier.[77] Thus the line between the traditional nobility and the robe was drawn. Nobles seemingly accepted the fact that commoners holding important offices should have the privileges of the nobility, but they refused to concur in the belief that such offices ennobled their posterity.

Meanwhile, the pretensions of the robe had been growing by leaps and bounds. In 1561, the parlement of Paris based its claim to judge the ordonnance derived from the cahiers of the Estates General of 1560 on the grounds that it had not participated in the assembly, as it had in 1468 and 1484. At the request of the town council of Paris, it was still willing to elect deputies to a municipal meeting concerning the estates. Indeed, between 1535 and 1575, nearly half the town councillors were members of the sovereign courts.[78] In 1614, and probably earlier, parlement adopted the position that it would have nothing to do with the electoral process in Paris for the Estates General, on the grounds that it would judge the deputies' proposals. In 1610, Charles Loyseau published a widely read study in which he claimed that magistrates were above even the highest nobles because they had the right to command; nobles, like other people, obeyed.[79] Seven years later, the robe claimed precedence over the nobility in the Assembly of Notables, and by the Fronde, the robe's aspirations had spread to the bailiwick level. At Chartres, the pretensions of the lieutenant particular and the lieutenant criminal led to an armed conflict, and in Angoulême the lieutenant general claimed precedence over the clergy as well as the nobles.[80] The traditional nobility was more consistent in its goal—to obtain more offices. The growing pretensions of the robe made the sword nobles more arrogant, and their very arrogance contributed to the robe's pretensions. From being a single class in the fifteenth century, the nobility had become divided into separate orders by the seventeenth century.

In many ways, the division of the nobility into robe and sword is surprising. The law drew no distinction between the two; they both drew a substantial part of their incomes from the land; and if they were wealthy, they had town houses and country châteaux. Only a small percentage of the traditional nobility followed military careers, and the majority had no military experience at all. Many sons of robe nobles, on the other hand, served in the armed forces. The antiquity of some robe nobles surpassed that of many who wore the sword, and there was scarcely a member of the noblesse de race who did not have a magistrate or even a burgher among his ancestors or relatives. In the eyes of the crown, there was indeed a hierarchy among the nobility, as reflected in the amount it was willing to pay for travel expenses, but in the eleven categories established in 1601, sword and robe were completely inter-mixed. For example, captains of fifty men-at-arms, members of the privy council, and presidents of the sovereign courts were lumped together in category four and compensated at the same rate. Those in category five, which included lieutenants of one hundred men-at-arms, governors of towns, and maîtres des requêtes, received a smaller sum.[81]

It is easy to exaggerate the rivalry between the two. In the south, the differences fade. Robe and sword cooperated against peasant demands in

Dauphiné, and in 1576 the first consul of Grenoble was elected as one of the deputies of the nobility to the Estates General. In Provence, there was no clear distinction. Marseilles and Arles had the right to elect deputies to the second estate, and in 1588 the former chose a merchant to serve in this capacity.[82] Even in the north, differences were sometimes forgotten. In 1649, the nobility of the bailiwick of Troyes elected Jérôme de Mesgrigny to be their deputy to the stillborn meeting of the Estates General, although he was from a predominantly robe family. No doubt his own long military service made him acceptable, but two years later the third estate chose his brother-in-law, the lieutenant general of the bailiwick, to be its representative.[83]

A more important division was forming among the nobility that may help explain the sword's scorn of the robe. There were the dukes and peers, the high court nobility, who enjoyed large revenues from their estates, governorships, high military offices, and generous pensions. Of the 133 persons who enjoyed this dignity between 1589 and 1723, 124 were officers in the army.[84] They owned châteaux in the country and mansions in Paris but spent much of their time at court. They were not necessarily opposed to an absolute monarchy, because their goal was to control that monarchy as individuals or with their allies. Then there were the leading provincial families, the secondary nobility, the sort of people who were elected to represent their order in the Estates General. They were often knights, bailiffs, or officers in the army. They usually resided in châteaux, occasionally visited the court, and increasingly enjoyed such titles as count, viscount, or baron. They had no hope of controlling the state as factions or individuals, and therefore sought a mixed monarchy in which they, as deputies to the Estates General, would exercise a collective voice. They rarely sought judicial or administrative offices for themselves, but tried to ensure that they would be available for the lesser nobles whom they represented in the Estates General. Finally, there were the great mass of the nobility, the simple untitled gentlemen who lived in manor houses, rarely served in the military, and almost never went to court. Many were quite poor, and their standard of living was often little better than that of the peasants among whom they lived. It was they who most coveted the offices of the robe, including the minor bureaucratic positions in the provinces that did not ennoble.

The social mores of the first two groups of nobles were similar. Our conception, and indeed the conception of the people of that day, of a nobility that served with its blood and played at court is derived from them. It was these aristocrats who wrote memoirs about their military exploits and the intrigues at Versailles. It was they who scorned the robe and regarded a bureaucratic career as inferior to one in arms, although they had relatives who had chosen the former course. Even in our heavily egalitarian society, some professions are more highly regarded than others. To be a medical doctor brings more prestige than to be a dentist or a veterinarian. Yet the same person may debate as to which profession to follow, and he may have an ancestor or a relative who made a different choice. A kinsman who has achieved wealth or position is more likely to be admired than one who is a ne'er-do-well. In early modern France, where a hierarchical conception of society held sway, these natural instincts were multiplied manyfold. Fed by the ideals of chivalry, most of society respected the gallant soldier who served with his blood more than the sedentary official or the landed proprietor.

The mentality of the great nobles was thus far removed from that of the simple gentlemen. What had the Montmorencies and Rohans, or even the Bellays and the Beauffremonts, in common with the peace-loving sire de Gouberville who so carefully recorded the daily happenings of his uneventful life. To them, the Goubervilles, who made up the great majority of their order, were country bumpkins who smacked too much of the barnyard. Too often their very existence seems to have been forgotten. When the intendant of Burgundy prepared a memoir at the close of the seventeenth century to inform the dauphin on the nature of the duchy, he named only 431 noble families. Of these, 245 were nobles of the sword, 20 were nobles of the robe, and 21 were mixed, in that some of their members were in the army and others were magistrates. The families he mentioned were drawn for the most part from the nobility of the second rank. The degree of selectivity he employed is revealed by the fact that he cited so few robe families, when there were about 150 noble magistrates in Dijon alone. Only his source of information for Bresse, Bugey, and Gex was more democratic. This small area supplied 34 percent of the nobles he listed, and only here were nobles without careers and even without fiefs mentioned in significant numbers.[85] The reports prepared by the intendants of other provinces were generally even more selective. The simple gentlemen were not a part of most aristocrats' picture of what a noble was.

The middle nobility had some contact with the simple gentlemen, near whom they resided for much of the year, and also with the peers and courtiers. They had once been the connecting link between the greatest and the least members of their order, but they were becoming estranged from the magnates, who selfishly pursued their own ends and had fewer favors to grant them. In the Estates General of 1614, they requested the king that "in the future no pensions, offices, estates or other gifts be given on the intercession of the princes and seigneurs of your kingdom, in order that the obligations of those who would receive them remain entirely to Your Majesty."[86] Thus they pleaded for direct access to their king. Their goal was a mixed monarchy in which the king and the Estates General worked together. Their last great effort to achieve this end was in the 1650s, but the failure of the magnates to provide the promised support doomed them to failure. Without a Condé or an Orléans to lead them, and without a national institution, such as the English House of Commons, through which they could act, they could do nothing. The link between the peers and the country gentlemen was broken, and Mazarin on his deathbed was correct in seeing that in the future the magistrates would be the greater threat to the authority of the king.

EDUCATION

There were significant changes in the education of the upper nobility in the seventeenth century, which prepared them for court life and the battlefield, but at the same time further separated them from the mass of the nobility in the countryside. For both great and small, education began at home, as in the earlier period. Here the child learned to read and write and the rudiments of social behavior. In wealthy households, a governess and then a governor and a tutor might be employed, but in the domiciles of simple gentlemen, the mother very likely performed these tasks. Her efforts might be followed by attendance at the village or nearby small-town school for a few years. At this point, education stopped for the poorer nobility unless a rare position as page in a great noble household could be found, or an almost equally rare scholarship at a college or academy, of which there was much talk but few endowments.[87] At worst the near-universal ability to sign one's name was acquired. In the meetings of the Estates General between 1560 and 1615, only one noble, Marc de Rosmadec, seigneur de Pontcroix, deputy from Brittany in 1576, was unable to sign his name. Since he was a prominent noble, his failure is surprising. Nearly a century later, when over a hundred nobles responded to the summons of the ban in the seneschalsy of Sarlat, only a single noble had to admit to a similar disability, and this time every fiefholder was expected to be present.[88]

Some wealthy nobles provided the secondary education of their children in their homes by employing a governor and tutors, but in the seventeenth century, it became increasingly common for them to send their sons to college when they were twelve or thirteen years of age. Many towns had established colleges during the sixteenth century, but for financial reasons, they eventually surrendered them to the Jesuits and other religious orders. The Catholic and Protestant churches also founded some colleges. At first students had to find lodging in the towns, but in 1603, Henry IV cooperated with the Jesuits to establish a college at La Flèche far from any large town. It became the first Jesuit institution with dormitories, which facilitated social control over the students, to the relief of their parents. The curriculum in these colleges was heavily classical. This led many nobles to withdraw their sons before they completed the last two years of the prescribed program, when rhetoric and philosophy were stressed. At Auch, where 14.3 percent of the out-of-town students were nobles between 1598 and 1607, over 40 percent followed this course. Those who remained were presumably bound for careers in the church or the judiciary, where a classical education was more necessary. Wealthy nobles frequently supplemented their sons' educations by providing tutors to teach them history, mathematics, fortification, geography, and modern languages. At La Flèche, the most aristocratic of all the colleges, private lessons in fencing, music, dancing, and drawing were available. Here five hundred titled noblemen were reported with some exaggeration to be studying in 1607—this out of a student body of only twelve hundred.[89]

When he turned sixteen or seventeen, the wealthy young aristocrat who was interested in a military career was likely to enter one of the academies that sprang up in the seventeenth century. There, for periods of from six months to two years, he studied riding, fencing, fortification, and dancing. Perhaps a year or two of foreign travel would follow, or perhaps he would seek military experience by serving as a volunteer in the army. Every phase of this educational program occasioned great expense, attendance at one of the academies and foreign travel being the worst of all. The overwhelming majority of the nobles were thereby excluded.[90] A few with more modest means and a patron at court might secure positions for their sons as royal pages, or as members of the household guards or the king's musketeers, where they could partake of a little of the new culture that was emerging and make contacts that might further their careers.[91]

This new culture began to be taught to the sons of the high nobility in early childhood and was pursued at each stage of the educational progress described above. Part of this education was to prepare the young noble for a military career, but its more distinctive aspect was its emphasis on grace, style, decorum, and above all the French tongue. He was to acquire a mastery of the spoken language and use it with eloquence and wit. Henry IV never lost his Gascon accent, and the highly educated Montaigne confessed that his French was corrupt in pronunciation and other respects, but the courtier of Louis XIV's time was to speak and write the pure French of the French Academy founded by Richelieu.[92] The great cardinal also thought that the educational system should instill "good habits and good morals, . . . the fear of God, obedience to princes, submission to laws, respect for magistrates, love of country, and the practice of virtue, without which great states can neither maintain themselves in peace nor exist for long."[93] Such an education produced brave soldiers, accomplished courtiers, and an obedient aristocracy, but it also created a social and cultural gulf between the great noble and the country gentleman who had once served him so well.

In the north, the upbringings of nobles destined for military and judicial careers took different directions near the close of their college educations, but another pattern emerged in the south, where the distinction between robe and sword was hardly discernible. In Provence, old noble families had opted for the sovereign courts from their creation at the dawn of the sixteenth century, and new nobles followed their example. Both produced soldiers as well, and some nobles pursued both careers during the course of their lives. Here, where robe and sword, old and new nobles were most thoroughly intermixed, there was a university founded in Aix in 1409, a college in 1583, and an academy in 1611. These institutions appear to have been used equally by all types of nobles who could afford them. Members of thirty-eight old noble families earned 141 terminal degrees at the university in the seventeenth century, and members of forty-three new noble families earned 119. College and academy enrollments are not known, but as many old nobles as new nobles gave money to support the former. Both the old and new nobles participated in the municipal life and the government of Aix and the province. Legal works constituted 21 percent of the libraries of old noble families and 28 percent of the libraries of the anoblis. When it came to history and political theory, on the other hand, old nobles led by 24 percent to 18 percent. Both shared an interest in the classics and both devoted 4 percent of their libraries to books on warfare. They enjoyed, in part at least, the court culture, but one suspects that their social mores were far removed from those of the rural gentlemen who could not afford such an education.[94]

THE CHANGING SOCIAL MORES

A noble at the court of Versailles was quite different from a noble in the Catholic League a century before. The social and cultural mores of a Louis, duke of Saint-Simon, bore little resemblance to that of Henry, duke of Guise. That a pronounced change took place has recently been documented by three fine studies by Ellery Schalk, André Devyver, and Arlette Jouanna, but the authors disagree on the nature of the change and exactly when it took place. All three involve the question of how nobles perceived themselves and not reality itself. Myths can influence men's actions, but reality must also be considered. Schalk argues, for example, that until the 1590s, nobility was thought of as the profession of arms. Only after nobles felt threatened by the increasing number of anoblis did they stress birth. In actual fact, birth had been the principal legal means of defining nobility for centuries, and at no time did more than a small minority of the nobility pursue careers in arms. It is probable that a higher percentage of the nobility was in the army during the latter part of Louis XIV's reign than at any time since the Hundred Years War, but by then the three historians see blood, race, or birth as all-important.[95]

The nobility's perception of itself may have been significant, but more important was the impact of the new educational system, which stressed grace, style, decorum, and language as well as the military arts. Closely related were the books of courtesy, ritual, and ceremony that became commonplace after 1630. Their general tenor was to impose discipline and order in action and speech. "Courtesy," Orest Ranum has written, "was used to coerce the nobility into obedience, if not subservience."[96] Even dueling, which flourished in France during the last half of the sixteenth century and the first half of the seventeenth, was brought under better control, not so much by the stringent laws of the state as by the new code of behavior. "The only thing this Prince [Louis XIV] really put an end to was the practice of seconds. Gentler manners had diminished ardour for dueling," a writer observed in the late eighteenth century.[97] The new code of behavior was adopted only by the high nobility and to some extent by nobles of secondary rank. The country gentleman was largely unaffected.

A final factor that must be considered in explaining the changing social mores of the high nobility after the Fronde was the young king himself.

XII

Louis XIV

There is no evidence that Mazarin specifically recommended to Louis that he become his own first minister.[1] According to the king himself, he did, however, urge Louis to "take care that everyone is persuaded that I am the master; that one must expect favors only from me, and especially [that I] distribute them only to those who merit them by their services, by their ability, and by their attachment to my person alone."[2] By personally assuming control of royal patronage, Louis would ensure that no one minister would ever be in a position to obtain a monopoly of the clients throughout the royal national and provincial administrations, as Richelieu and to a lesser extent Mazarin had done. There could be no first minister in the sense that they had been. The magnates would no longer have the excuse of rebelling to get rid of the king's evil adviser; they could only use all their courtier charm to win a few handouts from their king. And nobles of the second rank, the sort that sat in meetings of the Estates General, could only applaud. They had asked the king to take this step in the meeting in 1614 so that any favors they might receive would be due to him alone. He was to be their only patron.[3] Of course, patronage did not entirely cease. Courtiers, governors, ministers, and generals continued to influence appointments in the areas of their responsibilities, and Louis himself was not loathe to appoint the relatives of his great servants, but he kept ultimate control in his own hands.

LOUIS XIV, COLBERT, AND THE PAYS D'ETATS

Louis had attended meetings of the council during the Mazarin years, and one may suspect that the stronger stand the crown took in dealing with the provincial estates after 1659 was owing as much to his presence as to the termination of the long war with Spain that year. Louis must

335

have learned much from this experience, and he must have discussed the nature of the post-Mazarin government with his mentor. In any event the twenty-three-year-old king was prepared to act immediately after Mazarin's death on March 9. The following day, an eyewitness reported, he summoned "the princes, dukes and ministers of state . . . to assemble in the queen mother's chamber so that he could explain to them himself that 'he had decided to take charge of the state in person and to rely on no one else' (these were his own words) and courteously discharged them from their duties, saying that 'when he had need of their good advice, he would call for it.'"[4] Thus began what Michel Antoine has called "the revolution of 1661." Louis's mother, brother, cousins, and the dukes, indeed the chancellor himself, were to be excluded from the inner circle of government. At the head of the government was to be a council of ministers, the conseil d'en-haut, composed only of Louis, Le Tellier, Lionne, and Fouquet, who was soon to be replaced by Jean Baptiste Colbert. Louis also personally presided over the councils dealing with internal affairs and finance, in which Colbert became the principal figure. Affairs of a more judicial nature were left to a council presided over by the chancellor. Prior to 1661, the chancellor had been the chief administrative officer as well as the chief judicial officer in the kingdom. Now Colbert, first as intendant of finances and later as controller general and the holder of a host of other positions, became the principal administrative officer, and the chancellor was relegated to the background. Except for the brief period after Sully's triumph over Bellièvre, there was no precedent for such a shift in responsibility. Now it was Colbert who, under Louis's supervision, determined fiscal policy and dealt with the intendants. It was Colbert who negotiated with the provincial estates. Fiscal administration had replaced justice as the driving force in the government.[5]

Louis knew that drastic reform was necessary in many areas of government, and his concept of kingship was so exalted that he never doubted his authority to institute it. "Princes," he thought, "in whom a brilliant birth and a proper upbringing usually produce only noble and magnanimous sentiments, can never entirely eradicate these good principles from their character."[6] Not so for the mass of mankind, however, for he had a very low opinion of human nature. Those who were not of princely birth were motivated by self-interest. Hence aristocratic governments were less trustworthy than monarchies: "The decisions of their councils are based exclusively on the principle of utility. The many heads who make up these bodies have no heart that can be stirred by the fire of beautiful passions . . . it is interest alone, whether private or of the estate, that guides their conduct."[7] The provincial estates suffered from the same disability, he believed. At one time, people had been less selfish, and the estates had functioned everywhere. Even in his own day, the estates fixed the contribution of the laity "in most of our provinces, and it was practiced everywhere in the honesty of the early days; for indeed, at that time the mere spirit of justice sufficed to inspire each individual to give according to his means, which would never happen today."[8]

With such ideas as these one might expect that Louis, in his omnipotent power and infinite wisdom, would have crushed the provincial estates and other popular organs of government for the benefit of his subjects, but at heart he was too much of a conservative traditionalist to do so. Nowhere in the memoirs he prepared to instruct the dauphin did he mention the élus, who had loomed so large in Sully's and Marillac's plans, or the intendants, who were becoming so important in his day. Rather, he sought to control and utilize the estates and other popular institutions. As he explained to the dauphin: "It had been the custom not merely to ask them [the estates] for large sums in order to obtain meager ones, but also to tolerate their putting conditions on everything, to promise them everything, to circumvent everything they had been promised soon thereafter under various pretexts, even to issue a great number of edicts with no other intention than to grant, or rather to sell, their revocation soon thereafter. I found this method undignified for the sovereign and unsatisfactory for the subject. I chose an entirely different one which I have always followed since, which was to ask them for precisely what I intended to obtain, to promise little, to keep my promises faithfully, hardly ever to accept conditions, but to surpass their expectations when they appealed to my justice and to my kindness." As a result of his new policy, "The *pays d'états,* which had formerly considered themselves as independent in matters of taxation, began to use their liberty only for making their submission more pleasing to me."[9]

Thus Louis would have had the dauphin believe that he inaugurated his new policy when he began his personal rule. Perhaps he took it as his goal at that time, but in fact it was only with considerable effort over a period of a decade or more that he was able to bring the estates to conform to his desires. In this work he relied heavily on the assistance of Colbert, who was an admirer of Michel de Marillac. On one occasion Colbert referred to the Code Michau as an "excellent work," and on another he spoke of Marillac's "great experience."[10] Furthermore, Colbert shared Marillac's passion for uniformity, order, and obedience. We do not know whether he contemplated creating élections in all the pays d'états, as his predecessor had done, but he certainly considered establishing them in many parts of France. In June 1661, a threat was made to establish élections in Provence when the assembly of communities refused to raise taxes. In July 1662, Colbert himself told an intendant that serious consideration was being given to abolishing the privileges of Boulonnais and creating an élection there, and the bishop of Tarbes thought it necessary in December 1663 to persuade that same minister not to subject the Pyrenean provinces to a similar fate. For a time, Colbert appears to have abandoned his plans, but on September 3, 1681, he wrote to an intendant: "I do not doubt that you have found many disorders and abuses in the estates of Bigorre, and I shall await the report that you are to send me on these abuses in order to make an account to the king. These sorts of estates in these small provinces are only opportunities to pillage the people with impunity, accustoming them to revolts and sedition. I believe that it would suit the service of the king and the welfare of the people much better to suppress them and to establish an élection."[11]

On September 11, Colbert expressed his delight to the same official that the estates had ended, and on the 24th he informed him that "the king wants you to investigate with care and secrecy what should be done to establish élections in each of these provinces and suppress these estates, which are always a heavy burden on the people and give so little aid to his majesty."[12] The intendant responded that the estates of Bigorre could be suspended and that three small jurisdictions away from the frontier could be joined to the élection of Lannes, but he recommended that the independent-minded people in the frontier provinces be left alone. Some were too poor to support élections anyway.[13] Perhaps Colbert died before the plan could be implemented, perhaps he was overruled by the king; whatever the reason, élections were not established in Bigorre or in any other pays d'états during Louis's reign.

The fact that Colbert made no concerted effort to substitute élus for the estates as his tax-collecting agencies should not be construed to mean that he or the royal officials with whom he dealt approved of the estates or trusted their officials. His letters are full of directives to intendants telling them to see that the estates levied no taxes without the king's permission and to find out how they spent the money they collected. He even wanted the chamber of justice to investigate their possible abuses, along with those of royal financial officials. Colbert praised an intendant for not permitting the communities of Languedoc to borrow money under the auspices of the estates: "You know how important it is to the king's service not to give the provincial estates more power than they already have and not to make the communities entirely dependent on them." He was irritated whenever the estates spoke of their grievances. In 1681, he wrote to the governor of Brittany that "these estates ought to give perpetual thanks and not complaints. . . . I am so accustomed to see, with regard to all the estates, continual complaints without any foundation that I do not intend to change this habit of which they complain."[14] He expressed irritation at the length of the meetings of the estates and sometimes encouraged commissioners to terminate the session, congratulating them when they did so.

Louvois shared Colbert's antipathy toward the estates and was perhaps even more willing to ride roughshod over their privileges. Nor did the pressure cease after these two ministers died. "I cannot congratulate you too much on the termination of the estates," the chancellor wrote an official who had attended those of Brittany in 1703, "that is to say, on the end of all agitations and of every sort of trouble for an honest man. I hope that you will find more tranquility and sweetness in the exercise of your natural and ordinary functions, and that all the province will feel the effects of your zeal."[15] The same complaints continued to come from the provinces. In 1688, an intendant who had investigated the estates of Quatre-Vallées, Nébouzan, and Foix reported, "It seems to me that although these provinces are well founded in the enjoyment of their privileges, [these privileges] ought not to be preserved for a longer time than the king finds it useful for the good of his service."[16] The time was favorable, he went on to say, to suppress these estates.

With so many influential enemies, one must ask how the pays d'états managed to survive. The answer, it would seem, must lie in the protection of Louis XIV himself. It is not that Louis either liked or believed in representative institutions—he held them in low esteem—but he and his predecessors had sworn to respect the privileges of these provinces, and he would not go back on his word, at least not without grave reason and ample justification.

Louis's treatment of the provinces he conquered lends further support to this interpretation. By the terms of the surrender of Arras in August 1640, no taxes were to be levied on the county of Artois without the consent of the estates, but Louis XIII and Mazarin had not adhered to this article, and the estates of that part of Artois held by the French failed to meet between 1640 and 1661. Louis XIV revived the estates in 1661 in honor of the pledge made in his father's name and convoked them periodically throughout his reign despite the deputies' vigorous resistance to his fiscal demands and their many complaints. He also permitted the less important estates of Hainaut, Lille, and Cambrésis to function after he became their sovereign. The estates of Franche-Comté and Alsace, on the other hand, were already in a state of decadence when they were joined to France, and Louis felt no obligation to use them.

That Louis was in fact much less of a revolutionary than his professed rationalism would suggest does not mean that he had any intention of permitting the estates to thwart his will. Rather than destroy these popular institutions as Marillac had sought to do, and many of his own officials would have preferred, he followed Richelieu's lead and tried to control them. There is scarcely a device used by modern prime ministers to control their parliaments that Louis and Colbert did not employ at one time or another, and some of their tactics were so dubious that politicians in our day would hesitate to employ them. When it was to their advantage, they might alter the venue at which the estates were to meet so as to have the deliberations take place in friendly surroundings. They could set Friday as the day of the opening meeting in the hope that disaffected elements would not arrive until Monday, enabling their own followers, who would be cautioned to be on time, to organize the assembly and choose the committee that examined deputies' credentials, which could exclude undesirable members. They plotted to have faithful servants preside over the estates and found ways to exclude those they did not want to attend. They ensured that loyal prelates and magnates influenced deputies from their dioceses, and they engaged in elaborate political calculations to predict how far they could persuade the majority in an assembly to go. To increase their bargaining power, they asked for more money than they needed and kept a steady stream of directives flowing to the commissioners who held the estates and their loyal followers among the deputies. From these clients they received detailed reports in return. Every deputy must have been well aware that his actions would be reported to the king, and that he would receive favor or ill will depending on how he conducted himself. Indeed, Louis's most potent means of control was to reward, or to give the hope of reward, to deputies who served him well, and to threaten or punish those who tried to thwart his will.

It was well known that for a nobleman or clergyman to obtain a royal appointment, a more lucrative benefice, or a pension, it was necessary to serve the crown loyally both in the estates and elsewhere, and Louis went far beyond his predecessors in the use of patronage. He even took steps to see that sums were available for distribution in the estates. In 1662, Colbert ordered that 9,000 livres be secretly given to selected deputies in the estates of Languedoc and then compounded the injury by obtaining the funds from the treasurer of the estates. Ten years later, he informed the intendant to that province that Louis had authorized him to give 20,000 livres to deputies of the third estate in the hope of obtaining the desired don gratuit on the first ballot (that is, if it were necessary to do so). The king did not wish the deputies to develop a habit of receiving gifts in return for doing the things he desired. The fierce provincial loyalty of the Bretons made it more costly to win their votes, or perhaps the difficulty was that so many of them attended the estates. Whatever the reason, 60,000 livres were set aside in 1663 for "the deputies who served the best in the assembly."[17]

When bribes were not sufficient, threats were often employed. When the troublesome assembly of the communities of Provence voted the king only about a fourth of what he requested in 1661, he threatened to disband it and refused to accept any of the conditions the deputies made in return for the 300,000 livres that they were willing to give. Soon Louis relented and offered to take less than he had originally demanded, but he instructed his commissioners to terminate the assembly immediately if there were any difficulties. When the assembly did not heed his warning, the deputies were sent home, and Louis arbitrarily increased the salt tax and ordered troops to Provence. Someone added the further threat that assemblies of the communities would be discontinued permanently and that élections would be established as in Dauphiné. Thoroughly frightened, the procureur du pays summoned the first consuls of the communities to approve an additional 105,000 livres. After some further negotiations, an agreement was reached. By his threats, Louis had obtained more than he otherwise would have done, but the Provençals still gave far less than was originally demanded of them.

Neither side had won. Louis's officials continued to try to strengthen his position in Provence. In 1664, they urged that a 2,000-livre pension be paid to the syndic of the nobility "who has always done his duty well in all the assemblies for the service of the king."[18] In 1666, when the newly elected municipal officials of Aix, who doubled as procureurs du pays, proved to be less friendly to the crown than their predecessors, they were removed from office, and more pliant officials were chosen in their stead. Such measures were sufficient to create a court party, but when the remaining Provençals saw themselves betrayed by their natural leaders, they united in opposition. In 1668, the first president of the parlement of

Aix, who was also a commissioner, wrote to Colbert: "I avow to you that I have never seen an assembly like this one. We have absolutely all the leaders there, . . . and those of the deputies who depend on us. Notwithstanding this, we cannot be the masters because the number of unreasonable ruffians and monsters is so great, and so united by the conformity of their tempers, that we have brought them to where they are at present only with incredible trouble, and we shall assuredly have the greatest difficulty preparing them for what remains to be done. We forget neither intrigue nor authority, neither force nor leadership, in order to lead them where necessary, and we shall follow this same course to the end."[19]

Louis had asked for 600,000 livres, but for a long time the commissioners despaired of getting the deputies to offer more than 350,000. Finally, in a session that lasted nearly three months, the deputies increased their offer to 400,000 provided certain conditions were granted. The following year the communities met from October to January but again made a conditional grant of less than the king had requested. The struggle recommenced in December 1670. When March 1671 came and the communities had offered only 200,000 livres, a third of what he had asked, Louis directed that the meeting be terminated promptly. The king, Colbert indicated, would not reply to such an offer. He wanted the amount stated in his instructions. Frightened by this threat, the deputies increased their offer to 450,000 livres, and Louis accepted, although it was still less than his original request.

By this time Louis and Colbert had had enough. Shortly before the communities began their meeting on September 30, 1671, the latter directed a commissioner to see to it that the session ended within a month. The estates made an initial offer of 200,000 livres in response to a demand for 600,000. The commissioners evidently thought that they could persuade the deputies to give 450,000, as in the preceding year, and asked Colbert if this would be sufficient. Colbert responded that the king insisted on receiving 500,000 livres. By October 30, Colbert had become impatient. He continually compared the obstinacy of the Provençals to the submissiveness of the three estates in other provinces, who quickly gave the king what he requested. By December 11, he was informing the commissioners that the king would take what he wanted without consent if the deputies did not act quickly.

The acting governor was obviously sympathetic to the Provençals' desire to escape the full weight of the proposed tax, but confronted by the insistent demands of the crown, he requested that an order terminating the assembly be sent, along with some lettres de cachet, to be used as a last resort to punish the most seditious deputies: "There is no longer any problem about bringing them to 450,000 livres, but I believe that only the present threat can terrify them, and that they will not go to 500,000 livres unless they see an order to break up the assembly."[20] Louis had letters dispatched to exile ten deputies to Normandy and Brittany, but on December 31, he agreed to accept only 450,000 livres. Colbert's letter passing on this welcome news included a threat that the king might not assemble the communities again for a long time. Meanwhile, the frightened deputies offered 500,000 livres provided certain conditions were met. The acting governor used this long-delayed act of submission as an excuse to ask not to use the lettres de cachet that had been sent, and his plea was granted.

The assembly of the communities had finally been cowed. In December 1672, it unanimously voted the king 500,000 livres with little debate. Soon Colbert could report that even the king was satisfied with the deputies' conduct, for they were voting what he required in a single deliberation. It had been so easy to get his way that Louis decided to ask for a million livres in 1676. If the deputies would not go beyond the now-customary 500,000 livres without any arguments, the king would send troops, Colbert informed the intendant on November 8. If the deputies cooperated, his majesty would accept 800,000 livres. The communities cooperated. To Louis's credit, when peace returned, he reduced his request to 800,000 livres if the deputies were troublesome and to 600,000 if they were not. The Provençals had learned their lesson. From 1672 until the end of his reign, the Sun King had frequent reason to express his satisfaction with their behavior, although as an added precaution, he deemed it wise to have the intendant attend the deliberations from 1688 to ensure that the deputies were properly servile.

Before this time the crown probably preferred assemblies of the deputies of the towns or communities to those of the three estates, because they were believed to be more pliant. Perhaps this is why Louis sought to restrict the attendance of the nobility of Artois in 1661. His policy of bribes and threats, however, changed this situation. Most of the rewards he distributed went to members of the first two estates, and royal disfavor affected their opportunities more than those of provincial lawyers and merchants. For this reason, and because they paid most of the taxes, the third estate of Provence proved more difficult to subdue than the three estates of Burgundy or Languedoc. The prince of Condé found this to be very much the case. In a detailed letter describing his negotiations with the estates of his government of Burgundy in June 1662, he concluded "that the chamber of the clergy and that of the nobility have acted marvelously well in this encounter, having made almost no difficulty about any of the things proposed to them. To tell the truth, the deputies of the third estate have caused a little more trouble; but this is pardonable in them, since they are the ones who bear almost all of the impositions."[21]

In this same letter, Condé told Colbert how he had asked the Burgundians for 1.5 million livres in extraordinary taxes over a three-year period as he had been directed, and how the estates had offered 500,000, then 600,000, then 800,000, and then 900,000. At this point, Condé feared that they would go no further, so he reduced the king's demands to 1.2 million, as he was permitted to do in his instructions. This reduction encouraged the estates to offer 1 million and then 1.05 million, which Condé accepted. In the closing sentence of his letter, he wrote: "On my return I shall bring a report on those who have cooperated best; His Majesty will see if he believes them worthy of some gratifications, as this is always done; and he will use it as he pleases."[22]

This letter reveals that in spite of the explanation Louis prepared for the dauphin describing how a king should deal with the estates, he had done everything he had said ought not to be done. In his dealings with the estates of Burgundy, he had initially asked for 300,000 livres more than he was willing to accept; the estates had begun with an offer of far less than they were willing to give, and after considerable bargaining, Condé had accepted 150,000 livres less than he had been instructed to take. To make matters worse, Louis was expected to reward, or more accurately, to pay bribes to those who had cooperated most effectively with his commissioners. This last was such an undignified proceeding that Louis never intimated to the dauphin that it had ever been done.

The crown interfered in municipal elections in Burgundy and in elections to the chamber of the élus soon after its 1662 session, but none of this prevented the same bargaining from taking place in the estates of 1665, 1668, and 1671. By 1674, however, the will of the estates had been broken, and to Louis's delight, they voted all he requested in a single deliberation. Thereafter the estates did not seriously oppose his financial requests until near the end of his reign.

Bresse, Bugey, and Gex were within the government of Burgundy, but they did not participate directly in the estates. Since all three had élections, and the king had set the size of the tax since their annexation by Henry IV, there was no conflict between the estates and the crown over a don gratuit. The three orders in each province had their individual assemblies, which met at least every third year to elect syndics and other officials to look after their interests, and in the case of the third estate, especially, to send deputies to Dijon to submit their cahiers to the governor. There were also occasional joint meetings of the three estates or of just one estate of the three provinces. The role of these estates was to present grievances to the crown and to vote taxes to support causes of local importance. True independence on the part of the estates was prevented by the fact that their governors, the princes of Condé, appointed many of the community officials and then told them how to vote in the estates. Nevertheless, these estates continued to function until the Revolution.

Initially, Louis had to bargain with the three estates of Languedoc just as he did with those of Provence and Burgundy. In January 1662, he wanted the estates of Languedoc to vote 2.5 million livres, and Colbert went to considerable length to please his master. He and the king's most devoted servants in Languedoc made arrangements for a friendly bishop to preside, found an excuse to deny a seat to an unfriendly *consul*, made sure that the first orators to speak for the clergy and the nobility advocated making a generous grant, rallied the governor's clients among the first two orders, and ensured that they and their colleagues sought to influence the members of the third estate who were dependent on them. The treasurer of the estates was directed to provide money to bribe deputies selected by the intendant, and 9,000 livres was spent in this fashion. Most, and perhaps all, of this sum was directed toward members of the third estate, for the crown tended to reward cooperative members of the other orders with pensions, perhaps because they smelled less of bribery. The syndic of Vivarais, a gentleman, had been receiving a pension for several years at the time of the estates, as had others who were present. By 1670, it had become customary to give barons with seats in the estates annual pensions of 2,250 livres, and bishops received similar rewards.

Such measures as these, coupled with the knowledge that the king would hear of those who had served him well or had tried to thwart his will, could lead only to favorable results. The first offer of the estates of 1662 was 1.2 million livres; a proposal by the *consuls* of Narbonne that it be limited to 800,000 received only five other votes. The bishops of Béziers, Mende, Viviers, Castres, and Saint-Papoul, the marquis of Castres, the governor, the intendant, and no doubt others hastened to write Colbert the good news and to tell of their contributions. The bishop of Mende proudly declared: "I have four votes in my diocese: they will serve me and are always of my opinion. There are some deputies who offer themselves to me, and I am assured that they will serve the king well. I believe that we shall leave after two or three more sessions; but in case the business is delayed, you would very much oblige me, Monsieur, if in your reply, you would put in your letter some pleasantness for the *consuls* of my diocese, and for those who follow my advice. Ask me to tell you their names so that you can favor them on the occasions that will present themselves, or give some other similar demonstration of friendship."[23]

The bishop of Saint-Papoul indulged in political arithmetic. The fifteen clergymen had voted for the 1.2 million livre tax. With one exception, the twenty-two barons or their proxies had done the same, but two of the proxies had voted in favor only after they had seen that the motion would carry. After urging that the three barons be told to correct the behavior of their proxies, the bishop pointed out that the first two estates provided thirty-six of the forty votes necessary to pass a measure. Only four votes from the third estate were therefore necessary, but nearly thirty were available because of the care that had been taken to inform them of the king's desires. Those who were familiar with the estates said that "they have never seen a first ballot similar to this one." Even the *capitoul* of Toulouse and the *consuls* of Montpellier and Carcasonne had voted in favor of the tax. Nevertheless, the bishop was doubtful whether the king could persuade the estates to vote any more. Even if only six nobles and clergymen deserted, it would take ten votes from the third estate to carry, and these votes would be difficult to find, because members of this order had to report back to their constituents.[24]

The governor and intendant, however, thought that the deputies could be persuaded to go as high as 1.5 million livres, and they were correct. From the initial preparations for the meeting until its conclusion, Colbert and his adherents had functioned like a well-organized modern political machine. Few if any of their tactics were new, but never before had they been so fully used and so well coordinated. Still there were limits as to how far even the clergy and nobility would go in betraying the interests of the people, or, as Louis XIV would have put it, in placing their trust in his benevolence. Not only had they voted him a million less than he had requested, but they had attached a number of conditions to the grant. As an added insult, they had also appointed a committee to see if he had kept the promises that he had made in return for the money voted by the preceding estates. Colbert's work was not yet done.

For eight years affairs continued in this fashion, with Colbert using the same tactics to control the estates as in 1662. By 1670, however, he was ready to institute a change in procedure that he and Louis had long desired. "I believe that I have written you," he informed the intendant in December 1670, "that this year His Majesty wants you to declare to the estates the entire sum that he desires for the don gratuit, and that it pass in a single deliberation without any long negotiations and without sending couriers [to court]. All the deputies of the estates who have been here have begged His Majesty to use this procedure."[25] Previously Colbert had told the intendant that the king would be satisfied with a don gratuit of 1.4 million livres, but the intendant asked the estates for 2.4 million, presumably to have more bargaining power. In the end he obtained exactly what the king had wanted in the first place. Still not satisfied, Colbert made a determined effort in 1672 to get the estates to vote the entire sum the king desired in single deliberation and without bargaining. No less than 20,000 livres was made available to bribe members of the third estate, and the intendant was instructed to ask for a don gratuit of 2 million livres. On December 6, the archbishop of Toulouse informed Colbert that the deputies of the first two estates were asking about their pensions. They must have been satisfied, for three days later they joined the heavily bribed third estate in unanimously voting Louis 2 million livres without debate. They did attach some conditions to the grant, but the commissioners accepted or rejected them article by article on the spot.

The estates of Languedoc had been conquered. In the years that followed, Louis told the estates what he wanted, and they quickly voted it for him. By 1676, his appetite had grown, and he asked for and received a don gratuit of 3 million livres, a grant that was repeated the following year. In spite of these increases, only two-thirds of the revenue collected was assigned to the crown, and a good part of this sum was spent supporting the military and royal officials in Languedoc. The remainder went to the officials of the crown and the estates and to other notables in Languedoc. Louis did exercise a modest amount of restraint when his needs were less, as they seemed to be in the closing months of 1678. On that occasion, he asked for and received only 2.4 million livres. Compliant though they had become, the estates did not die, because Louis found in them and their officers useful administrative instruments. Not only did they feed and lodge troops and collect taxes at less cost than the élus in other parts of France, but they also became involved, somewhat reluctantly at first, in a host of economic and commercial enterprises, including the Canal du Midi connecting the Mediterranean with the Atlantic. Nor did the estates become entirely useless to the people. Languedoc was less exploited than provinces without representative assemblies, but this enviable position was achieved at the cost of complying with the king's will and providing large gratifications to their governor, the secretary of state for Languedoc, and other influential persons.[26]

The estates of Brittany had been most uncooperative during the last years of the Mazarin regime. When the time came to meet in August 1661, the restraining hand of Mazarin had been removed, and Louis made a quick trip to Nantes to settle his account with the estates. His representatives had asked the deputies for 4 million livres before his arrival, but on September 1, the bishop of Saint-Brieuc greeted the young monarch in the name of the estates in such flattering and submissive terms that he announced that he would be content with 3 million. Cowed by his presence, the estates quickly voted this amount without debate and without conditions. Louis alluded to this meeting in his memoirs, and the success he achieved may have caused him to formulate his subsequent policy of telling the estates how much he wanted and having them vote the required sum immediately without haggling about the amount or making conditions. If they did as he desired, he would treat them justly and kindly. Some years elapsed, however, before Louis could put this policy into effect in Brittany or elsewhere.

The importance that Colbert attached to the next biennial meeting of the estates is attested by the fact that he arranged for his brother to serve as commissioner and gave him detailed instructions on how to act. Such diverse matters came under his purview as to how to prevent a quarrel over who should be president of the clergy, because such an argument might alienate some deputies and make them less disposed to conform to the king's will. Colbert also prescribed who was to be responsible for distributing 60,000 livres that Louis had provided for those who served him best in the assembly. This was not the first time such generous bribes had been made available to deputies, for a similar sum had been allocated in 1661; Louis had not relied solely on his presence to secure compliance. Nor was he yet prepared to ask the estates for as small a gift as he was willing to take, for fear that they would automatically offer a lower sum if he were not present. Hence he requested 2.5 million livres but expressed satisfaction when 2 million was voted.

In 1665, Louis asked the estates for 3 million livres and told his commissioners that 2.4 million would be the least that he would take. The initial offer of the estates was for only a million, but because the commissioners responded to the petitions of the estates favorably, they anticipated a more generous offer. However, as one of them reported to Colbert, "In an assembly as large as this one, wise men are not always the most numerous, and especially after dinner. It so happened that the deputies chose this time to have their discussion. The ecclesiastics were the only ones who were of the opinion that 200,000 livres should be added to their first offer, and the third estate, with the nobles who were most heated with wine, persisted in their opposing offers and requests."[27] Persuasion having failed, the officers of the king applied threats. The offer of the estates jumped to 1.5 million, but the commissioners still felt it necessary to ask Colbert whether the king would not take less than he had previously told them. His reply has been lost, but after further debate the crown settled for 2.2 million.

Still the crown sought ways to control the estates. It was difficult to reward all the nobles who attended, because from 150 to 300 usually did so during this period. The third estate, which paid most of the taxes, was an even greater problem. As a result, the crown made some effort to exclude its enemies. In 1667 Colbert accused the uncooperative duchess of Rohan of sending her young son to the estates with her vassals and friends, and another deputy was forbidden to attend by a lettre de cachet, but still the estates would not give the king all he desired in that year or in 1669.

Then, in 1671, a new climate manifested itself. On being informed that the king wanted 2.5 million livres, the estates voted this amount in a single deliberation and did not make it subject to royal concessions included in a formal contract. Undoubtedly the bribes and threats of the preceding decade had taught deputies that there were advantages to complying with the wishes of their sovereign, but it is difficult to believe that the appointment of the firm, but tactful, duke of Chaulnes as governor, and the winning of the duke of Rohan to the royal cause were not decisive factors. If Rohan packed the second estate with his adherents in 1671, it was to serve the king. As a reward for their obedience—and to encourage such submission in the future—Louis reduced the tax to 2.2 million livres.

Brittany seemed on the verge of being conquered, but a series of new edicts aroused the anger of the most vocal elements of the province. One edict established a chamber of justice to revoke seigneurial justices that had been usurped and to punish the offenders. Another forbad the parlement to inform the officers of the estates of the royal acts it received and to consider the officers' attempts to delay registration. This attack on the pocketbooks of the nobility and the capacity of the estates to defend the privileges of Brittany turned the estates of 1673 into an uproar. The estates offered 3 million but coupled the grant with the requirement that the offending edicts be revoked. Conditional grants, however, were unacceptable to Louis, and the estates were finally prevailed upon to give 2.6 million unconditionally, although in the process the governor had to dismiss two noble deputies from the assembly. It took an additional 2.6 million livres to obtain a promise that most of the offending edicts would be revoked.

The estates were unable to obtain the revocation of new taxes on stamped documents, tobacco, and pewter dishes. These burdens, in addition to very heavy taxes and rumors that the gabelle was to be installed, led to uprisings in the spring and summer of 1675, which were firmly and in some cases brutally suppressed. It was in this atmosphere that the estates met in November 1675 and unanimously voted the king 3 million livres without debate or conditions, in the hope that complete submission would cause him to punish the province less severely. It did not, but from that time the estates submissively gave Louis whatever he wanted, and talk of reducing the grant or making conditions was considered little short of treasonable.

At about that time, Colbert prepared a brief statement on the administration of the king's finances. Taxes in the pays d'états were handled very much as they were elsewhere in France, he recorded: "When the king gives the estates of the provinces permission to assemble, his majesty decides what he wants to ask them for; he has instructions prepared, which are sent to his commissioners, and the estates of the provinces always accord what it pleases his majesty to ask of them."[28] Uniformity, order, and obedience—these values that Colbert and his master prized so highly were close to being achieved.

The very existence of the small estates in the Pyrenees was sometimes threatened. In October 1661, an intendant reported to Colbert that he had tried to prevent the estates of Comminges from meeting for a year because the assembly would be prejudicial to the interests of the king and delay his affairs. Then, referring to all Pyrenean estates, he declared that "they have no other aim than to advertise the misery of the people and to procure some indirect advantage for everyone who attends."[29] The intendant's low opinion of the estates may have contributed to the idea current in 1663 that Colbert planned to suppress the Pyrenean estates. The bishop of Tarbes sent Colbert a strong defense of the estates near the close of that year, in which he attempted to show that it was to the crown's advantage to retain the status quo, and the matter was apparently forgotten, at least temporarily.

Nevertheless, Colbert was far too dedicated to the concept of uniformity and far too opposed to disorder to leave the estates alone for long. In 1670, he ordered that the abuses of the estates of Foix be investigated, and in 1674, he complained that the governor of Quatre-Vallées was trying to get that province released from a tax that "all the kingdom had paid almost voluntarily."[30] In 1681, he launched a secret investigation to discover what would have to be done to establish élections in the Pyrenean provinces in the généralité of Guyenne. In 1682, he told the intendant at Pau to examine the taxes levied by the estates of Béarn and Navarre to see if there were any abuses, and he repeated his instructions in more detail the following year. Even Colbert's death shortly thereafter brought no respite. In 1684, an intendant urged that a commissioner be appointed to examine the accounts and to attend the estates of Foix, since the governor was too much involved in the matter to do a satisfactory job. Four years later, another intendant argued that the estates of Quatre-Vallées, Nébouzan, and Foix should not be allowed to survive for longer than the king thought useful.

If local royal officials sent unflattering reports about the estates to Paris and occasionally abused them, the estates and their leaders sometimes deserved the treatment that they received. In 1673, during the war with neighboring Spain, the bishop of Pamiers refused even to present to the estates of Foix a royal request that 1,000 livres be voted to repair the château in the local capital. Louis repeated his order the following year, but the bishop again refused to call for a vote. Before the threats of the governor, this stout Jansenist declared that "he feared only God and sin." A loud argument and considerable confusion followed. At length, the bishop departed with a handful of followers, but the bulk of the assembly remained to give the king satisfaction.[31]

The county of Boulonnais in the northwestern corner of France had a more exposed frontier than any other province. For this reason, the inhabitants enjoyed a number of privileges, including exemption from the tailles, aides, gabelle, and other taxes. The estates could, of course, give their sovereign a present, but they do not appear to have done so regularly, and neither did they assemble periodically. There were times when Louis's financial needs drove him to try to extract a small sum, or when greedy tax farmers in neighboring provinces attempted to include the little county in their tax farms, but when this happened the three estates swung into action, and occasionally a mob called attention to their grievances. In 1656, Louis recognized the extensive privileges of the Boulonnais, but this did not stop him from seeking an annual grant of 81,740 livres shortly thereafter to support a regiment during the winter. The three estates dutifully voted the required amount for the duration of the war and appointed two nobles to apportion the sum among the subordinate jurisdictions.

Peace in 1659 did not bring the promised respite for long, however. As Louis explained to the dauphin, he decided "to take a closer look at the exemptions claimed by certain particular areas of my kingdom. . . . The Boulonnais were among these. The people there have been warlike since the war against the English and even have a kind of militia dispersed throughout the governorship, which is rather well trained and can easily be assembled when needed. Under this pretext, they had long regarded themselves as exempt from contributing in any way to the taille. I wanted to levy a very small sum there merely to make them realize that I had the power and the right to do it."[32] With this in mind, Louis decreed an annual tax of 30,000 livres in May 1661.

The three estates, which had not been consulted in advance, met to deliver a sharp protest and to seek friends to get the decision reversed. "The Boulonnais loudly proclaim that they will pay nothing," the intendant reported to Colbert. "They are preparing to defend themselves and to take up arms."[33] A minor revolt followed, which was easily suppressed. Appeals to the king continued, and several hundred rebels were sent to the galleys. Colbert dreamed of abolishing the privileges of the province and creating an élection, but calmer counsel prevailed. Boulonnais retained its privileges, and its estates continued to meet during the following century when the need arose.

LOUIS XIV AND THE ESTATES IN THE PAYS D'ELECTIONS

Louis's policy in the pays d'états had been to seek control of the estates so that he could impose whatever taxes he chose and use their bureaucracies to assist in local government. These estates, therefore, continued to be useful to him and to some extent to the people. In the pays d'élections, on the other hand, Louis already levied the taxes he desired, and his own officials collected them. The estates, where they continued to exist, had syndics to defend their interests, but few, if any, administrative officials that could be of use to the crown. As a result, Louis had nothing to gain by prolonging their existence. He was too traditionally minded, however, to alter any situation he inherited except for compelling reasons. His intendants were another matter. With few exceptions they disliked popular assemblies and sought to prevent them from meeting whenever they could find an excuse. Hence they slowly curtailed the activities of these estates until they finally ceased to exist, not because of any edict of the council but simply because they were no longer permitted to function. Thus by the start of the eighteenth century, the distinction between the pays d'états and pays d'élections that has been made so often in textbooks finally became a reality, or almost a reality, because in parts of the government of Burgundy and in the mountains of Dauphiné, the estates and the élus continued to coexist.

In 1630, Louis XIII had created the assemblée du pays to replace the estates of Dauphiné. As the voting strength of the third estate in the new institution was approximately equal to that of the nobility and clergy combined, the privileged orders were dissatisfied. Also, the assembly had the authority only to petition and not to consent to taxes. As a result, there were numerous attempts on the part of the privileged to revive the estates, especially during the Fronde. The assemblée du pays's last known meeting took place in 1664, and that of the assembly of the ten towns, which had also continued to meet after the demise of the estates, in 1673. Since the core of the assembly included the bishop of Grenoble, two hereditary commis of the nobility, and a hereditary syndic, some sort of activity may have persisted thereafter. Indeed, the intendant obtained the register of the meetings between 1661 and 1670 from the secretary in 1700. However, it is probable that the assemblies attended by the deputies of the towns had ceased before that time. The mountainous region of Dauphiné was more fortunate, for here the assemblies of the escartons continued until the Revolution.[34]

The estates of Normandy were clearly dying when Louis XIV came to the throne, although their governor, the duke of Longueville, liked to assemble them. He was largely responsible for obtaining permission for them to meet in 1655 for the first time in twelve years. The deputies seized the opportunity to ask that the estates meet annually and that taxes be reduced. In spite of the royal commissioners' favorable recommendation, the council would only promise that the estates would be summoned if it were à propos. At no point in Louis's personal rule did such an occasion ever arise, and the estates never met again. Within three years of Longueville's death in 1663, Colbert directed that funds accumulated in the treasury to pay the deputations of the estates be turned over to the crown, and the king's council formally suppressed the offices of syndic, treasurer, and clerk of the estates. The final relics of a once-proud institution were thus swept away.

The échevins of Clermont assembled the good towns of Basse-Auvergne at least once every year, with two exceptions, during the Mazarin regime, in spite of the enmity of the intendants and the jealousy of the royal officials in Riom. In 1657, the opponents of the estates won a decree from the king's council forbidding the échevins to convoke the representatives of the towns or to levy taxes to support the activities of the estates without permission. That permission was not too difficult to obtain during the Mazarin regime, but the last periodic meeting was held two weeks after his death. Thereafter, assemblies were permitted only when there was a special need, as in 1673, when three meetings took place over the question of franc-fiefs. After a long silence, what were probably their last assemblies were held in 1679 and 1680. But old traditions were slow to die. In 1749, the échevins of Clermont were still styling themselves syndics of the third estate and claiming to represent the interests of the province. In Haute-Auvergne, the good towns had been less active during the Mazarin period, and they met only in 1661, 1672, and 1693 during the personal rule of Louis XIV.

The syndics of the third estates of Forez, Lyonnais, and Beaujolais met together in 1642, and the three seneschalsies presented a joint petition to the king's council in 1650, but there does not appear to have been a true meeting of the government of Lyonnais, of which they were a part, during Louis's reign. The three seneschalsies held meetings to elect deputies to the Estates General during the Fronde, but only the third estate of Beaujolais can be proven to have met thereafter. Traces of syndics of the third estates of Beaujolais and Forez and of the nobility of the latter can be found in the eighteenth century, but for all practical purposes assemblies of the estates had nearly ceased before Louis XIV began his personal rule.[35]

As far as can be ascertained, the history of the various estates in the généralité of Guyenne followed a somewhat similar pattern. The towns of Agenais had been very active during the last two years of Louis XIII's reign, but after a meeting in October 1644, they apparently did not assemble until 1649–51, when they met twice to elect deputies to the Estates General and once for other matters. Meetings in 1654 and 1658 followed, but then there was a long silence until the crown launched an offensive against allodial property in Guyenne in the 1670s. What was probably the last meeting of the principal towns of Agenais was held on this subject in August 1679. The following month, the intendant forbad the *consuls* of Agen to hold any further assemblies or, in their capacity as syndics of Agenais, to defend any individual against the crown's attacks on allodial property. The ban on assemblies was repeated the following year, but informal consultations among the towns continued until near the close of the century.

The estates of Armagnac and its seven *collectes* proved to be the most active and longest-lived assemblies in Guyenne. The nobility and towns of the collectes and seneschalsy occasionally went several years without meeting during the Mazarin period, but when the need arose, they assembled two or three times within a twelve-month period. There was a long hiatus from the early part of Louis XIV's personal rule until 1670, when five meetings took place in twelve months. Thereafter the records are spotty, but there was apparently an assembly as late as 1698.

Scantier records for the three estates of Comminges, Quercy, and Rouergue suggest that they followed the more familiar pattern of reasonable activity under Mazarin and a marked decline in the 1660s. Then there were meetings in Comminges and Quercy in 1673 and very likely in Rouergue in 1674 to deal with the problem of the allodial property before these once-thriving institutions passed into oblivion. It is not improbable that the last meetings of the estates of Lannes, Condomois and Bazadais, and Rivière-Verdun were held at about this time on the same subject.

As in other parts of France, the principal cause of the demise of the estates in the Guyenne was the enmity of the intendants and other royal officials. It became increasingly difficult for syndics and consuls to obtain permission to meet. When it was granted, it was often stipulated that only the specific subject that had led to the request could be discussed, and the size of deputations was limited. In the winter of 1658–59, the king's council twice forbad any assemblies to be held in Guyenne without the permission of the governor or lieutenant general, and while these decrees were not directed only at the estates, they do reflect the general climate of opinion at Paris. In 1661, a cousin of Colbert's, who served as intendant of Montauban, expressed his disapproval of permission being granted for the diocese of Comminges to meet, on the grounds that it would be prejudicial to the interests of the king. He recommended that none of the estates in the region be permitted to assemble, because all they did was complain about the misery of the people and enrich those who attended.

Local jealousies often made it difficult for the estates to resist the unfriendly bureaucracy. The bishops of Cahors and the estates of Quercy had a long-standing quarrel over the extent of the former's prerogatives. The one point they could agree on was that they did not want local royal officials convoking the three estates. When one of them usurped this privilege in 1649 and 1650, the bishop refused to attend. Finally, in 1657, the king's council confirmed the bishop's right to summon the estates, but by that time the institution had already suffered heavily.

When the estates in Guyenne were given opportunities to voice their complaints, as when they prepared cahiers to take to the Estates Generals convoked during the Fronde, they did not hesitate to do so. Those who attended the meeting of the third estate of Agenais in 1649 lashed out at the intendants and asked the king to send no more of them to the provinces, because they were useless officials who imposed heavy taxes on their own authority. Equally unpopular were the officers in the élection whose suppression they sought. Mindful of the difficulty they had assembling, they asked the king to permit an annual meeting of at least the twelve principal towns.

The nobility of Périgord assembled in 1651 to elect their deputation to the Estates General, and early in the cahier that they prepared, they asked the king to restore the estates to the position they had enjoyed in the time of Louis XII before the élections were created. They also pleaded with the king to reduce the number of judicial officials and abolish venality of office. But it was to no avail. Probably none of the cahiers prepared during the Fronde ever reached the king and council for consideration, and few have survived to testify to the devotion of the leaders of Guyenne to their estates and other privileges.

At the dawn of the seventeenth century, there had been estates in about 52.4 percent of France that had given consent to taxation, and in about 8.2 percent more that had met regularly, employed a bureaucracy, voted taxes for their own purposes, and prepared remonstrances to the king. In about 12.6 percent of France, the estates had occasionally met to deal with taxes and other matters. Even in the remaining 26.8 percent, the estates had sometimes assembled to redact customs, ratify treaties, and elect deputies to the Estates General. By the time the century drew to a close, however, assemblies had totally ceased in about 68 percent of the lands that had then been a part of France. Of the remaining 32 percent, nearly 2 percent consisted of Bresse, Bugey, Gex, and the Alpine valleys of Dauphiné, where only the third estate met regularly and there was no pretense that those who assembled consented to royal taxes. Thus in only 30 percent of France did the estates continue to vote taxes, albeit under the tutelage of the crown. To the lands that were part of France around 1601 should be added several small, recently acquired provinces to the north, where there were estates, and a few much larger ones to the northeast and east, where there were none.

In spite of this startling change, Louis XIV and Colbert had for the most part continued the policies of Richelieu in regard to the estates, although the latter had at times been tempted to follow the course of Marillac. None of the estates had been officially exterminated, but the intendants and other royal officials had been permitted to stifle the weaker ones. Their goal had been to control the estates, but to do so they employed the techniques of persuasion and threats, of bribes and punishment, far more effectively than Richelieu or any of his Renaissance predecessors. Instead of planting a few clients in the estates, as was being done as early as the fifteenth century, Louis and Colbert placed all, or virtually all, the bishops and nobles who attended the estates of Languedoc on their pension list and distributed substantial sums to the deputies of the third estate. Where the number of those who could attend the estates was so large that it would be too expensive to distribute gifts to everyone, as in the case of the Breton nobility, they won great nobles like Rohan to their cause and relied on them to pack the estates with their creatures. With such measures, accompanied by numerous parliamentary devices and occasional threats, they managed from the early 1670s on to obtain from all the large provincial estates the amount they desired without debate and with few conditions attached. Since the origin of this policy dated back to the estates of Brittany in 1661, the delay in implementing it fully must be attributed to the time it took to create a strong court party in the estates and to quell the opposition. The final effort by Louis and Colbert to achieve their goal around 1672 was obviously timed to secure funds for the Dutch war.

In the process of winning control over the estates, they also captured and made use of the estates' bureaucracies. As a result, royal absolutism was extended to the pays d'états, but because it was not done by stamping out the duly constituted bodies and replacing them with institutions dependent on the crown, provincial administration ceased to be absolutist when a strong directing hand in Paris was removed. Under Louis XV, the surviving provincial estates regained their former brilliance and resumed responsibility for a large part of provincial administration.

Louis and Colbert also followed Richelieu's policy in regard to the estates in the pays d'élection. Here they inherited nearly defunct institutions, which they left to wither away. The most important causes of the decline of these estates were the dislike of intendants and other local royal officials for such assemblies and the jealousy among the members of the various estates and towns, which made cooperation in the defense of their privileges difficult.

THE FORMATION OF THE ABSOLUTE MONARCHY

The provincial estates were not the only stumbling blocks on the path to absolute monarchy. The other duly constituted bodies also had to be dealt with, the great nobility had to be tamed, and an adequate and obedient army and bureaucracy had to be formed. In a general way, Louis employed the same principles in tackling these problems as he had with the estates. This was especially true of his dealings with the assemblies of the clergy. He did his utmost to ensure the election of friendly clergymen to the meetings and of cooperative general agents, who watched after ecclesiastical interests when the assembly was not in session. Colbert dreamed of abolishing the assemblies, but there is no evidence that Louis ever contemplated doing so, and neither did he challenge the basic privileges of the clergy, at least as he interpreted them. On the other hand, he wanted the assemblies to be short and to vote all he requested without debate. If they procrastinated or haggled, he was not above using threats. As with the estates, Louis was able to impose his will only gradually. When he asked the assembly of 1660–61 for a don gratuit of 4 million livres, he was initially offered only one million. Considerable bargaining followed, in which Louis reduced his demands first to 3 million and then to 2 million plus 400,000 for his wife, but in the end he accepted a total grant of only 2 million. Nevertheless, he had won a victory of sorts; previous don gratuits had been voted to fight the Huguenots or the Habsburgs, but this grant was given in peacetime and established a precedent for the clergy's making regular contributions to the crown whether in peace or war.

In 1665, Louis again asked for 4 million livres. The clergy appointed a committee to determine how the king could best be aided, but months then passed without any action being taken on the don gratuit. At length Colbert was able to jolt the deputies into action, and they quickly offered 2.4 million livres. The archbishop of Toulouse, anticipating what Louis would like to hear, informed that monarch that "we have no example in our registers until this moment of the gift to the king being made in a single deliberation."[36] Pleased that when the clergy finally acted, they had done so with little debate, Louis accepted the offer, although it was far from the amount he had originally requested.

Threats, rewards, or the hope of rewards, coupled with interference in the elections, gradually brought the clergy more fully into line. Only through loyal service could they hope to achieve more lucrative benefices, an archdiocese, or a pension. The general agents of the clergy, upon whom so much depended when the assembly was not in session, were special objects of Louis's generosity. They usually received gratifications while they held office and often a bishopric when their five-year terms expired. In 1670, the assembly voted Louis 2.4 million livres without attaching any conditions. Content with the ease with which this had been accomplished, Louis graciously responded that he would accept only 2.2 million. In 1675, the clergy unanimously voted him 4.5 million livres, but this time Louis was at war and could not afford to reduce their gift. In neither year did he ask for a specific amount, although probably his ministers informally told the leaders of the clergy how much was needed. In this manner the Grand Monarch avoided having to haggle with his subjects.

The clergy had succumbed like the provincial estates. During Louis's long reign, they contributed 223,909,468 livres to his enterprises, a substantial sum, yet not excessive considering the wealth of the church. The size of the contribution troubled Louis but little, for as he told the dauphin, "kings are absolute lords and naturally have free and full disposition of all the goods possessed by clergymen as well as by laymen."[37] The clergy were also expected to be his obedient servants. They followed him, albeit gingerly, into a serious quarrel with the pope and less reluctantly into the persecution of the Protestants, although hitherto the majority of them had preferred conversion by persuasion rather than by force.

Whatever chance there had been for the political assembly of the Protestants to become a permanent institution comparable to the assembly of the Catholic clergy ended with their defeat in the 1620s. The national synods, however, were allowed to continue until 1659. To this assembly fell the duty of nominating six candidates, from whom the king chose two and later only one to represent Protestant interests at court. The Protestants remained loyal during the Fronde, and in return they won some concessions. Internal peace, Catholic pressure, the approaching defeat of Spain, and perhaps the growing influence of the youthful Louis XIV led to a reversal of policy in 1656. Thereafter, their limited privileges were gradually reduced. Their provincial synods were allowed to meet until 1678–79 and to make complaints to their deputy, who presented them to the king's council, but it was rare that they won a favorable response. Then came the revocation of the Edict of Nantes in

1685, and what little remained of their rights vanished before the power of the state.[38]

The members of the sovereign courts and other venal royal officials had become more serious obstacles to the absolute monarchy than the estates and the clergy, but they were subdued in a somewhat similar fashion. At first Mazarin had attempted to make them more cooperative by suggesting that he would not renew the paulette, but when he made good his threat for a brief period in 1648, he contributed heavily to causing the Fronde. With this unhappy experience in mind, he readily restored the paulette when it was about to expire in 1657, but the courts continued to cause difficulties whenever their interests or what they conceived to be the interests of the people so dictated.[39]

Louis XIV was not the sort of man to permit this situation to continue, but the question was what measures he should take to regain the authority that the sovereign courts and some of his other officials had, in his opinion, usurped. The most obvious method was to abolish the paulette and venality of office and convert the bureaucracy into subservient officials who owed their positions to him and served at his pleasure. As early as 1659, Colbert had advocated such a course, and when the paulette came up for renewal in 1665, he twice prepared memorandums urging Louis to act, but then in a third memorandum he reversed his position. Colbert may have changed his mind because Philip IV of Spain had died the month before, and Louis was preparing for a war to claim what he professed to believe was his wife's inheritance. Under such circumstances, it was not the time to anger the magistrates. He remembered that the combination of an embittered bureaucracy and a costly war had contributed so much to causing the Fronde.

Whatever Colbert's reasons for changing his mind, the results of his shift of position were momentous. The paulette was renewed for three years in 1665 and periodically thereafter throughout Louis's reign, with apparently no further thought being given to its abolition. The bureaucracy had already become and was to remain a hereditary caste, whose members could no more be removed from their offices without compensation than nobles could be deprived of their fiefs. Bound together in their closely knit sovereign courts and lesser corporations, they were to remain outside the direct control of the king. Since officials who were deprived of their positions had to be compensated, reducing the number of magistrates was difficult, and there was always the temptation to create unnecessary offices to sell. Successful merchants thus continued to be tempted to abandon their useful occupations and purchase positions that involved fewer risks and greater prestige. Bellièvre had foreseen these evils, and Marillac had struggled in vain to eliminate their cause, but now the more practical Colbert, who shared Marillac's views, abandoned the fight and preserved his position.

A hereditary bureaucracy was to be preserved just like the provincial estates and assemblies of the clergy, but as with these other institutions, Louis and Colbert sought means to impose their will. One step was to avoid arousing the officers' anger unnecessarily. The decision to retain the paulette was the most important concession in this regard, but Louis and Colbert made a number of others, such as not enforcing the minimum age requirements for serving in parlement and the stipulation against near relatives being in the same court. They checked their council's tendency to interfere excessively with cases before the sovereign courts, and for many years they limited steps by intendants that were at the expense of officials in the provinces.

A second step was to show a reasonable interest in the economic well-being of officers and to provide generous rewards for those who served them well. The minority who were troublesome, or who failed in their duty, were likely to feel Louis's heavy hand, as the parlements of Bordeaux and Rennes discovered when they were exiled to more rural surroundings. On such occasions, however, the magistrates were far less dangerous than formerly, because the great reforms that Louis instituted during the first decade of his personal rule quelled popular discontent to the point where they could not find allies among the people as easily as in the time of the Fronde. With Colbert's assistance, Louis was able to punish dishonest financial officials, bring the budget into balance, and reduce the taille, as well as implement a number of other needed changes. In the long run, many of these reforms had to be abandoned because of the wars, but they were in effect long enough for Louis to assert control over his now-isolated bureaucracy, whose members could not help but approve of much that he was doing.

The gravest threat to absolute rule had come from the sovereign courts, a situation Louis refused to tolerate. He never questioned what he regarded as their legitimate functions, but he was determined to prevent them from interfering in political affairs. He did this by virtually terminating their right to make remonstrances and checking their aspirations in other ways. He even dubbed them "superior" rather than "sovereign" courts and insisted on the right of his council to take jurisdiction over the cases before them, although he limited this practice so as not to anger the magistrates too much. So submissive did the parlement of Paris become that in 1672, at the very time the provincial estates were brought to heel, its magistrates registered six financial edicts without opposition. The following year, Louis made his last appearance in parlement until 1713.[40]

Louis and Colbert initially assigned the intendants a smaller role in their plans for the reorganization of the kingdom than one might think. Louis did not believe they were of sufficient importance for him to explain their duties when he prepared his memoirs for the instruction of the dauphin, despite the fact that he found time to enlighten his reader on why he rejected in horror his brother's proposal that his wife should be permitted to sit in a chair with a back in the presence of the queen. Louis and Colbert first thought of intendants as investigators who were assigned to large territories, generally several généralités, for a limited period of time to gather information for the council. Administration they left in the hands of the venal officials, one reason that there was so little friction between them and the crown. In short, Louis and Colbert planned to govern France much as Henry IV and Sully (or for that matter some of their Valois predecessors) had done. Only with the Dutch war in 1672, when the traditional bureaucracy failed to meet its expanded requirements, did they begin to use the intendants as administrators because of the greater efficiency that it brought.

Louis and Colbert no more intended to destroy the organs of municipal government than they did the other institutions that depended upon the people; rather they sought to control them by reducing the number of échevins and the size of the electorate, naming official candidates or otherwise tampering with the electoral process, and introducing garrisons into exposed localities, which had become established practices. But then first Colbert's reforming zeal and later Louis's need for money for his wars led to a greater decline of municipal independence than they had sought. Colbert was deeply concerned about the heavy indebtedness of the towns, an indebtedness that the intendants reported was caused by the dishonesty, fiscal irresponsibility, and selfishness of municipal officials. The *consuls* and échevins, they insisted, were exploiting the people. At first Colbert was content to try to make the towns financially solvent by having the intendants verify their debts. Only debts incurred for legitimate reasons were to be repaid, and interest rates were set at a uniform low rate of $4^1/_6$ percent. Urban officials often resisted these measures. They disliked having their accounts inspected and were themselves sometimes municipal creditors who stood to lose from the lower interest rates and possible disallowance of the debt. Long delays resulted, which so infuriated Colbert that in 1683 he got a decree issued giving the intendants and their assistants control over municipal finances. What had begun as an effort to improve the positions of the towns by getting them out of debt had ended by putting them under the tutelage of the crown. In 1667, Louis created a lieutenant general of the police in Paris and royal guards to replace the civilian militia as the police force. Soon the reform was introduced into other cities. Louis also requisitioned their artillery for use in his wars, and in so doing deprived once-powerful urban centers of the means of defending themselves.[41] Still another blow was leveled at the towns in 1692, when Louis decreed that henceforth mayors and some other municipal officials would be hereditary venal officials. His motive was to raise money for the war, and towns were permitted to purchase the privilege of continuing to elect their officials, but some of them lacked the funds to do so. France's once-proud towns, which had retained so much of their independence until the close of the sixteenth century, had finally been sacrificed upon the altar of war.

The villages were also plagued with debt and subject to heavy exactions because of Louis's wars. The crown lacked the bureaucracy to apportion and collect taxes at the village level and therefore continued the policy of using villagers to perform these duties. This ensured the survival of the corporate identity of the villages and their assemblies. These assemblies had long been important in village government and in tax collection. Like the provincial estates that collected taxes, the village assemblies were thus essential to the crown's fiscal machinery. Peasants were ruthlessly exploited, but they were permitted to keep their self-governing institutions.[42]

Louis was as prepared to accept the status and privileges of the nobility as he was those of any other social class or corporate group. During the desperate years of his later wars, he did tax them, but in other respects he left their enviable status intact. On the other hand, he had no intention of sharing power with them or permitting them to threaten the state as they had so recently done during the Fronde. Those of the highest birth were to serve as governors, ambassadors, commanders of his armies, and ornaments of his court, but they were almost completely excluded from his inner council. To win their loyalty he employed the same technique of rewarding the faithful and punishing the disobedient that he used in his dealings with others. When he announced in 1661 that he would appoint no chief minister, he meant among other things that henceforth he would dispense the crown's patronage. The high nobles became his creatures and not those of cardinals and magnates. To the roles of sovereign and feudal overlord, he added that of patron to draw the leading nobles to his side. They and his ministers often advised him on how to fill lesser positions. If their loyalty was unquestioned, he permitted them to exercise considerable influence on appointments in their governments, as is witnessed by the now-docile Condés in Burgundy, but more than ever before, the clients of his clients looked to him as their overpatron, just as they regarded him as their ultimate feudal overlord.

When there were no more army or court positions, ecclesiastical benefices, or pensions to bestow, Louis could always win a nobleman's gratitude by awarding him a higher title of nobility or some other empty honor. As he advised the dauphin: "I finished this year [1661] and began the following one with the promotion of eight prelates and sixty-three knights of the Order of the Holy Spirit, no posts having been filled since the year 1633; that is what made for the great number, but I would have wished to be able to raise still more people to this honor, finding no purer joy for a prince than to obligate deeply many persons of quality with whom he is pleased without burdening the least of his subjects. No reward costs our people less and none strikes noble hearts more than these distinctions of rank, which are virtually the first motive of all human actions, but especially of the most noble and of the greatest."[43]

Louis's numerous wars led him to increase the size of this army to 350,000 men during the course of his reign. Had this mammoth force been no more loyal than the army during the Fronde, it would not have necessarily strengthened his position at home, but with the assistance of Le Tellier and Louvois, he managed to transform the half-feudal army of his predecessors into a well-organized, disciplined force commanded by loyal officers who owed their positions directly or indirectly to him. Its very size ensured employment for nobles who sought military adventure and removed the temptation of any magnate to raise the banner of revolt. After the first decade of Louis's personal rule, only the poor were so foolish or so miserable as to challenge his authority directly. Some nobles in Auvergne might violate his laws, but they could be disciplined by magistrates from his parlement. Still others might seek the aid of foreign powers to restore or emancipate the estates of Guyenne, Dauphiné, Provence, and Languedoc, to convoke the Estates General of the kingdom, or to reinstitute the Protestant state within a state, but they posed no serious threat. Naval officers might sabotage his efforts at reform, and intellectuals might surreptitiously voice ideas critical of his regime, but open, legal, corporate resistance virtually ceased, except in the mountain fastness of the Cévennes, where the Protestants once more raised the banners of revolt as the new century dawned. Elsewhere, the rebellions that had once threatened the monarchy were no more.[44]

In addition to the army in its colorful uniforms, Louis had those who wore the long robe of his officials to help him secure obedience. Francis I had begun his reign in 1515 with at least 4,041 officers; that is, one for every 115 square kilometers, or one for every 4,700 inhabitants. In 1665, four years after he had begun his personal reign, Louis enjoyed the services of 46,047 officials; that is, one for every 10 square kilometers, or one for every 380 inhabitants. The growth is startling, and Louis also benefited from small improvements in France's transportation and communication network. Francis I and the Renaissance monarchs had ruled largely by persuasion; Louis was in a better position to add force if it was needed. Yet we must not exaggerate. Francis's officials were expected to employ assistants to help them perform their duties. By Louis's time these assistants had become royal officials, most offices had become venal, which made their holders more difficult to control, and many were useless creations to raise money through their sale. Some even took turns performing the same duties.[45]

The growth of the army and the bureaucracy had greatly increased the burdens on the French people. Still, at the end of Louis's reign, they were only paying about $7^1/2$ livres per inhabitant, less than half what their English rivals contributed. But again statistics provide a somewhat false picture. The provinces were unequally taxed, and the poor were ruthlessly exploited, while the rich escaped with modest contributions. In England the tax structure was less unjust, and banking and instruments of credit were more advanced. The French monarchy was headed for eventual bankruptcy, while the English monarchy was to become the paymaster of Europe.[46]

Although the purchasing power of the taxes the crown collected increased fivefold during the seventeenth century, Louis was able to combine censorship with propaganda to direct public opinion away from the misery of the people during the early years of his personal rule. Hardly had he been appointed to office than Colbert began to search for historians to depict Louis in a favorable light. Louis thoroughly approved of this approach, and he also brought music, literature, drama, and the arts into his service. His cultural program helped attract the high nobility to court and added to his prestige. Under these circumstances the ties between the magnates and the lesser nobility were weakened and the polarity between court and country grew. Deserted, the lesser nobility sought other means to claim consideration. During the Renaissance, the great age of the provincial estates, they had not displayed much interest in such institutions, because they relied upon their patrons to see to their needs, but now that their former protectors groveled before the Sun King at Versailles, they turned belatedly to the estates. In Brittany, from ten to thirty-one nobles had attended in the time of Charles IX, but as many as five hundred placed their names on the rolls under Louis XIV, and in 1728 attendance soared to 978. The policy of glory had other limitations. From the triumph of Henry IV, the monarch had been the focal point of French patriotism, but as disasters accumulated during the closing years of Louis's reign, patriotism shifted from being king-centered toward emphasis on the interests of the nation.[47] The long process leading toward the creation of an absolute monarchy thus reached its fruition under Louis XIV, but his very methods laid the groundwork for the separation of the king from his people, with such horrendous results in the Revolution.

XIII

Kings, Nobles, and Estates in Retrospect

In the late fourteenth and early fifteenth centuries, the vertical ties of vassalage and clientage bound the kingdom of France together. The system was fed by a substantial flow from the royal treasury. Neither the Estates General nor the provincial estates consented to the taxes that made this possible. After a promising beginning in the fourteenth century, they had been allowed to die. The system had worked well enough until the Valois princes began to quarrel over the spoils and Henry V of England renewed the Hundred Years War. The dauphin, Charles, was disinherited, but he managed to establish a precarious foothold in the southern part of the kingdom. Clearly the old system no longer worked. It was necessary to reconstitute the government on a new basis. The Renaissance monarchy was the result.

As Charles was not in a position to tax his subjects without their consent, he revived the Estates General and the estates of Languedoil, which he usually attended in person in order to persuade the deputies that he needed additional funds. Once he and the deputies had agreed on the amount of the tax, he sent commissioners to the numerous provincial and local estates, which he also revived, to give consent to their share. After Charles's armies had won some notable victories and he had become reconciled with the duke of Burgundy, ultimate success seemed assured. His newly won prestige made large assemblies unnecessary to prepare the way for the provincial estates, and he abandoned the Estates General and the estates of Languedoil. In provinces and seneschalsies where local loyalties were strong, their estates continued to consent to taxes and to perform many other duties throughout the Renaissance. Where they were weak, taxes were collected without consent and the estates were summoned less regularly. As time passed, the more active estates, including some of those in areas where consent was not given to taxes, developed bureaucracies consisting of syndics, clerks, and others to look after their interests when they were not in session and to perform various administrative duties. Consent to taxation and much of provincial administration thus became decentralized. Law followed suit. Instead of trying to develop a common law, the crown convoked the estates of the individual bailiwicks and seneschalsies to declare what the law was in their respective localities. Finally, each of the more provincially minded provinces insisted on having its own parlement and other sovereign courts. In these and other ways, France became a decentralized monarchy.

The Renaissance monarchs were strongly motivated by dynastic considerations. They fought wars to make good dynastic claims, not to achieve nationalistic objectives. Their domains increased primarily when fiefs escheated to the crown. Marriage alliances were of the utmost importance, and legality was stressed, because territorial claims and inheritances depended on the law. Charles VII had a bureaucracy, and he created a standing army, but neither was large enough or loyal enough for him to administer the kingdom or overawe the inhabitants. He also had to rely on the nobility and the bureaucracies of the estates and towns to govern. To make the system function and to enforce his will, he made full use of the vertical ties that bound the greater, middle, and lesser nobility together. These ties extended to the sovereign courts, bureaucracy, and army, and even to municipal and village governments.

The medieval state had also been dynastic, decentralized, and dependent on the vertical ties that bound society together, but it nevertheless differed from that of the Renaissance. Medieval decentralization was derived largely through the great feudal nobles and their vassals. Renaissance decentralization came mostly from newly created provincial estates and sovereign courts. In the Middle Ages, the duchy of Burgundy was ruled by its duke; in the Renaissance, it was governed by a royally appointed great noble, who acted as go-between for the crown and the notables in his jurisdiction. He was obligated to carry out royal policies, but his effectiveness depended on how well he could represent local interests at court and how much patronage he could win for his clients. It was not the individual rights of the duke of Burgundy that were stressed vis-à-vis the crown, but the collective privileges of the inhabitants of the duchy.

The Renaissance monarchs did not make a conscious alliance with any group in society, but they nevertheless depended primarily on the nobility to govern. Nobles were the key element in the vertical ties that held the country together. They officered the army, provided most of the bishops and abbots, and held many posts in the bureaucracy, from the king's council and the sovereign courts down to the lesser posts in the provinces. The third estate, whose role Thierry so stressed, made up an ever-increasing part of the bureaucracy as the Renaissance progressed, but many of its members either owed their positions to a great noble or became the clients of one. Those in the higher reaches of government often became nobles, severed their bourgeois ties, and adopted most of the social mores of the nobility. It was in their failure to recognize this fact that Thierry and Pagès made their greatest error.

Since the kings depended so heavily on the nobles to govern, it was all-important that the nobility recover from the devastating wars and plagues of the late Middle Ages. In the late fifteenth and early sixteenth centuries, the nobility was numerically reconstituted, primarily by the advancement of many members of the third estate into its ranks. Few indeed were the noble families who could date their origins back to before the Hundred Years War. Nobles also had to improve their economic position. In this they were greatly aided by the growth in the population, which led to a rise in grain prices and an increase in land rents. By use of short-term leases and sharecroppers, nobles profited fully from these circumstances, and the century before the Wars of Religion became their golden age. They also had to revitalize the vertical ties of society. The old lord-vassal relationship had become virtually useless for this purpose, so at first they turned to the indenture, and then, as internal peace seemed more assured, to oaths, and finally to little more than a general understanding. Most nobles, and the great bulk of the population as a whole, lived outside the system. Weak though the vertical ties were, they were adequate to enable the crown to give direction to society during a period when only the peasants and the urban poor suffered economic hardships and few people had any direct contact with the state except to pay taxes.

The bankruptcy of the crown and the accidental death of Henry II brought this stable situation to an end in 1559. The three kings that followed were weak, had fewer rewards to give clients, and often distributed the available gifts unfairly. At the same time the appearance of a well-organized Protestant minority and the advent of a powerful Catholic revival led to religious strife. The small army and bureaucracy and the fragile patron-client system no longer sufficed to hold the body politic together, and France was subjected to a series of eight internal wars in the four decades that followed. During this period, the kings created new nobles and granted higher titles to existing nobles in the hope of winning their loyalty, and they revived the Estates General and Assemblies of Notables in an effort to win popular support. Governors sought to maintain their positions by allying with this or that religious group. The provincial estates increased their role, but their privileges were trampled on by kings, governors, Leaguers, and Protestants, who imposed taxes without consent when their needs were desperate.

When Henry IV inherited the throne, he was faced with making a religious settlement that would be satisfactory to most Catholics and Protestants, winning the support of the nobility and the towns, and establishing his government on a firm financial basis. He accomplished the first by becoming a Catholic and issuing the Edict of Nantes. It required more subtlety to solve the second problem. The vertical ties needed to bind France together had escaped royal control. To restore the crown's position, Henry gave the magnates who supported him reasonable rewards, but he resisted such extreme demands as that he make governorships hereditary. He made peace with the individual chiefs of the Catholic League, although he realized that it would be more costly than to deal primarily with Mayenne. To have negotiated with Mayenne as the League chief would have been to recognize him as the head of a dangerous faction. Henry won the towns by recognizing their privileges and tampering with their elections when their loyalty was in doubt. The high robe had been the first group to support his cause after his conversion to Catholicism. He therefore appointed more of its members to important ecclesiastical and administrative positions than his predecessors had done. In 1600, he also recognized for the first time that high governmental positions ennobled, and in 1604, he made most offices hereditary. This last step not only pleased the robe, it also weakened the influence of the magnates in the bureaucracy and brought needed revenue into the treasury.

Bellièvre urged that the financial problem be solved by a combination of frugality and persuasion. As an old man, he recommended that Henry return to the consultative, legalistic methods of the Renaissance monarchy. In the end, however, Henry chose Sully's more brutal, absolutist, administrative approach. Sully's ordered mind rebelled against the lack of uniformity in Renaissance government. Every province and town had its distinct privileges and procedures, but to him these served only to hide graft and corruption, which reduced the king's revenue and placed additional burdens on the people. To correct these evils, he sought to create a uniform system of taxation by introducing élections where they did not yet exist. If royal tax collectors replaced those of the estates, local leaders could be prevented from levying taxes for their own purposes and the amount of corruption could be reduced. When the estates proved recalcitrant, it would be easier to tax without their consent. Sully was also an advocate of centralization. He established personal control over the nation's artillery and concentrated a large portion of it at Paris. As grand-voyer, he began to spend large sums developing a national transportation system, often over the protests of the inhabitants who were affected. He even established a toehold in the chamber of accounts at Paris and apparently contemplated subordinating the provincial chambers of accounts and the bureaux of finance to those of the capital.

Sully's goals are clearly discernible, but he was only able to begin to put his grand design into effect. He easily established élections in the tiny conquered provinces of Bresse, Bugey, and Gex, but he encountered stiff opposition in Guyenne. In the end he was successful there, but Henry refused to permit him to do likewise in the other provinces. Henry obviously approved of Sully's policies, in that they brought more money into the royal treasury, but he was also a pragmatist. His primary goal was to establish his dynasty firmly on the throne. Talk by deputies of their privileges angered him, but there is no reason to believe that he was an apostle of uniformity, centralization, or the destruction of provincial rights. To have proceeded too far in this direction would have created strong opposition, which would have put his throne in jeopardy. Hence he often restrained his overzealous minister.

Henry was assassinated in May 1610, and Sully resigned the following January, leaving Villeroy the dominant figure in the regency government. To Villeroy, the magnates were the greatest threat to the monarchy. He therefore recommended that the crown play upon their mutual jealousies to keep them divided and establish ties with the leading nobles in the provinces. Pensions and other favors should be bestowed directly on them by the king to eliminate their dependence on the magnates, thereby weakening the patron-client relationship. He also urged a return to the consultative, legalistic methods of the Renaissance monarchy. The alarmed Protestants were placated, the élections in Guyenne were abolished at the request of the estates, and the Estates General was convoked. In spite of Villeroy's conciliatory policies, there were several revolts, but on each occasion peace was bought, albeit at a heavy cost to the treasury.

By 1620, the youthful Louis XIII was prepared to take an active role in the government. He easily defeated a rebellion led by his mother, suppressed a Protestant uprising, restored Catholics to their former position in Béarn and Navarre, and united these independent states to the crown of France. Probably acting on the advice of Gilles de Maupeou, one of Sully's principal henchmen, and Michel de Marillac, a longtime apostle of uniformity and absolutism, Louis reestablished the élections in Guyenne and threatened the estates of Languedoc. He also proved himself quite capable of executing disobedient nobles. In short, he was already well on the way of achieving most of the domestic reforms usually attributed to Richelieu when the cardinal entered the government in 1624.

At first Richelieu showed some interest in domestic reforms. In 1625, he prepared a memorandum for the king in which he advocated creating a nationwide system of provincial assemblies for the clergy, increasing the taxing powers of the duly constituted local bodies, augmenting the role of the nobility in the council, and placing limitations on how the king spent his revenue. In his letters, he revealed that he opposed venality of office and hoped to abolish the paulette. He wanted to give the nobility more positions in the government, and in 1627 he had Louis publish a widely distributed document in which he promised to reduce taxes by 3 million livres by 1632. Nowhere during these early years did he mention establishing élus or threatening the provincial estates. The intendants also failed to capture his attention. It was to foreign affairs that he increasingly devoted his energies. The removal of the Huguenot threat was his one important domestic accomplishment in the last years of the decade, and this step was necessary before he could intervene forcibly in Italy. In June 1626, Louis had specifically directed that Richelieu devote all his energies to foreign affairs and general concerns of great importance. Domestic matters were to be handled by other ministers and secretaries of state, and it was to them that the deputies from the provinces were to report. In the circumstances, the direction of the government fell largely into the hands of the head of the chancellery, Michel de Marillac.

Marillac was a devout Catholic, a doctrinary absolutist, an advocate of administrative uniformity, a vigorous opponent of venality and the paulette, and a longtime enemy of the provincial estates. He was the principal author of the great ordinance of 1629 and engaged in a bitter battle with parlement to get it registered. Instead of following the example of Henry IV and Sully and tackling the provincial estates one at a time, he established élections in Burgundy, Dauphiné, Provence, and Languedoc almost simultaneously. Béarn feared that it was next on his list. Had Marillac succeeded, taxes would have been collected in the same manner throughout France, except in Britanny. The provincial estates could have been bypassed, and the king could have levied what taxes he needed without consent. Under Marillac's influence, and to Richelieu's regret, Louis rejected a generous offer from the estates of Burgundy to be rid of the élections. Only for Languedoc is there evidence that Richelieu favored élections, and there he was primarily motivated by his desire to weaken Montmorency's hold on the province.

Marillac's policies created so much opposition that immediately after his fall, Richelieu took steps to pacify the parlements and provincial estates. The paulette was renewed, and élections were abolished everywhere except in Dauphiné, where the bitterly divided estates refused to make any financial concessions. The Burgundians escaped with a smaller offer than they had made when Marillac was in office, and even Languedoc got rid of its élus after Montmorency was imprisoned. Richelieu's attitude toward the provincial estates is best revealed by his treatment of the estates of Brittany, where he was governor. There he instructed his cousin and principal commissioner to "restore the estates to their ancient liberty." Of course, the deputies were to do nothing to upset the king; that is, they were to vote an adequate sum to support his policies.

Richelieu never appreciated the importance of institutions, and he did not foresee the administrative role of the intendants, although the incompetence of the élus caused them to be assigned primary responsibility for tax collection in the pays d'élections shortly before his death. Instead, Richelieu placed his reliance on the patron-client relationship, backed up by the most effective propaganda France had yet seen. He chose his creatures from among his relatives and those who pledged their faith to him alone. Governors and other important persons who would not join his network were replaced whenever the opportunity occurred. The great wealth he acquired added further to the awe in which he was held. During the last decade of his ministry, only the king was in a position to challenge his authority.

Richelieu's reliance on clientage meant that Mazarin inherited a network of alliances that he had difficulty controlling rather than an institutional structure staffed by loyal bureaucrats. He sought to compensate by making greater use of the intendants, which so angered the parlementaires and other officials that it became one of the principal causes of the Fronde. By the time of his death, he recognized that the magistrates had replaced the magnates as the most dangerous threat to the crown.

Meanwhile, the nobility had undergone slow but significant changes. The ties that bound the magnates, the leading bailiwick families, and the great mass of the nobility together had long been weakening. After the religious wars, the magnates chose to make Paris or the court their principal place of residence, and this, along with the pattern of their education, separated them from their rural brethren. At the same time, their political objectives grew apart. A magnate's goal was to control the government alone or with a small number of allies. He was not above abandoning the interest of his clients if it was to his advantage to do so. Nobles of secondary rank, on the other hand, had no hope of controlling the government individually or in small groups. Instead, they sought to realize their aspirations through the Estates General and the provincial estates. In 1615, they specifically asked that the king award his patronage directly to them rather than going through the magnates, clear evidence that the magnates had already lost their allegiance.

A robe nobility with ever-increasing pretensions had also emerged. In the Middle Ages, many royal officials had been nobles, but as time passed more and more of the new appointees were drawn, not from the bourgeoisie, but from the sons of existing officials. As a result the traditional nobility found itself largely excluded. The judiciary, especially, became the preserve of the new officer class. Beginning in the parlement of Paris, these officials gradually developed an esprit de corps and became conscious of themselves as members of a corporation. Regardless of their origins, those in the sovereign courts and in the more important positions of the government came to be considered nobles if they held their positions long enough. The peers and nobles of the second rank, who for the most part followed careers in arms, heaped scorn on these upstarts— this despite the fact that nearly all of them had ancestors or relatives drawn from that very class. The robe responded by claiming precedence over the sword nobility on the grounds that they, as the king's represent- atives, judged the other members of society regardless of their rank. The high nobility had no interest in the type of positions held by the robe, but the vast majority of the nobility sought such offices constantly. To further confuse the situation, the robe became divided not only between those who held the higher and the lower positions in the government, but also between those who held venal offices and those who held commissions, such as the intendants. The first Fronde was largely provoked by the intendants' assuming many of the duties of the venal bureaucracy. Thus when Louis XIV began his personal rule, he found a nobility divided into numerous groups on the basis of careers, birth, rank, wealth, and social mores. This division of the nobility into many factions and interest groups made his task all the easier.

It was Louis XIV who finally achieved the absolute monarchy. The long road leading to a consolidation of monarchical power that had begun with Henry IV finally came to an end. Louis achieved this goal in part by taking control of the patronage system. Courtiers, governors, and others continued to influence appointments, but ultimate control of the vertical ties of clientage was in his hands. He also followed what Bismarck was later to call a policy of "the carrot and the stick." He assured every individual, class, order, and corporate group that he would protect and preserve their social status and economic well-being but not their political independence. If they cooperated, increased wealth and prestige would be theirs. If they did not, at best neglect and at worst exile or imprisonment would be their reward.

Louis's methods can best seen in his relations with the provincial estates. His goal was to have the deputies vote the desired amount in their first deliberation without haggling or making conditions. He achieved this objective after a decade or more of effort by giving handsome rewards to all the influential deputies and employing every parliamentary device. Where there was strong resistance, as in Provence, he was not averse to coercion. Weak estates were allowed to die, but nowhere did Louis deliberately destroy an effective assembly. He established control over a greatly enlarged army to fight his foreign enemies, but even the most stupid peer must have realized that it could be used against him if he strayed from his obedience.

Colbert may have dreamed of a centralized, uniform state, in which the élus collected taxes as the king directed, and of an obedient, non-hereditary officer corps, as Michel de Marillac had done, but either he was too wise to try to implement his desires or Louis stayed his hand. In the end, Louis took the pragmatic path followed by Henry IV and Richelieu. His methods served him well, but his successors lacked the energy or the ability to make the system work. By separating the crown and the high nobility from the people, Louis weakened the vertical ties that bound society together and contributed to the coming Revolution.

Perhaps the monarchy could have adapted to the new age that was dawning if it had taken Bellièvre's advice and reverted to the consultative policies of the Renaissance monarchy; if, as deputies to the Estates General so often advocated, it had modeled itself on the rule of Louis XII, "the father of his people." But this is one of the many "ifs" of history for which we can never know the answer.

Abbreviations

AC   Archives communales
AD   Archives départementales
AN   Archives nationales
BN, *MS* fr.   Bibliothèque nationale, manuscrits français
BN, *MS* n.a. fr.   Bibliothèque nationale, manuscrits nouvelles acquisitions
                    français
Cahiers   *Recueil des cahiers généraux des trois ordres aux Etats généraux*,
                    eds. Lalourcé and Duval (Paris, 1789), 4 vols.
HL   *Histoire générale de Languedoc,* ed. Claude de Vic and Jean
                    Vaissete (Toulouse, 1872–92), 15 vols.
Isambert   *Recueil général des anciennes lois françaises depuis l'an 420
                    jusqu'à la Révolution de 1789,* eds. François A. Isambert et al.
                    (Paris, 1821–33), 29 vols.
Major   J. R. Major, *Representative Government in Early Modern
                    France* (New Haven, 1980)
Richelieu, *Letters*   *Lettres, instructions diplomatiques et papiers d'état du Cardinal
                    de Richelieu,* ed. Denis-L.-M. Avenel (Paris, 1853–78), 8
                    vols.
Richelieu, *Papiers*   *Les Papiers de Richelieu,* ed. Pierre Grillon (Paris, 1975–)

Notes

INTRODUCTION

1.   Augustin Thierry, ed., *Recueil des monuments inédits de l'histoire du tiers état* (Paris, 1850–70), 4 vols.

2.   MSS n.a. fr. 3375–3429.

3.   Augustin Thierry, *The Formation and Progress of the Tiers Etat, or Third Estate in France*, trans. Francis B. Wells (London, 1859), 2 vols.

4.   Augustin Thierry, *Essai sur l'histoire de la formation et des progrès du tiers état* (Paris, 1853), ix.

5.   Ibid., xii.

6.   Ibid., 46, 49, 134, 49–50.

7.   Ibid., 131–32.

8.   For two accounts of Thierry's influence, see Boris Porchnev, *Les Soulèvements populaires en France de 1623 à 1648* (Paris, 1963), 34–40, and Bernard Guenée, "L'Histoire de l'état en France à la fin du moyen âge, vue par les historiens français depuis cent ans," *Revue historique* 232 (1964): 331–60.

9.   Porchnev, *Les Soulèvements*; A. D. Lublinskaya, *French Absolutism: The Crucial Phase, 1620–1629*, trans. Brian Pierce (Cambridge, 1968).

10. A. F. Pollard, *Factors in Modern History* (New York, 1907), 41.

11. Georges Pagès, "La Vénalité des offices dans l'ancienne France," *Revue historique* 169 (1932): 477–95; quotations from pp. 493, 495.

12. See J. Russell Major, *The Estates General of 1560* (Princeton, 1951); id., "The Third Estate in the Estates General of Pontoise, 1561," *Speculum* 29 (1954): 460–76; id., "The Renaissance Monarchy: A Contribution to the Periodization of History," *Emory University Quarterly* 13 (1957): 123, reprinted in *The "New Monarchies" and Representative Assemblies: Medieval Constitutionalism or Modern Absolutism?* ed. A. J. Slavin (Boston, 1964), 77–84; id., *Representative Institutions in Renaissance France, 1421–1559* (Madison, Wis., 1960); id., *The Deputies to the Estates General of Renaissance France* (Madison, Wis., 1960); and id., "The Crown and the Aristocracy in Renaissance France," *American Historical Review* 69 (1964): 631–45 (paper read at the meeting of the American Historical Association in December 1962), reprinted in *Lordship and Community in Medieval Europe*, ed. F. L. Cheyette (New York, 1968), 240–54.

13. See J. Russell Major, "Henry IV and Guyenne: A Study Concerning the Origins of Royal Absolutism," *French Historical Studies* 4 (1966): 363–83, reprinted in *State and Society in Seventeenth-Century France*, ed. Raymond Kierstead (New York, 1975), 2–24; id., *Bellièvre, Sully, and the Assembly of Notables of 1596*, Transactions of the American Philosophical Society, 64 (1974); and id., *Representative Government in Early Modern France* (New Haven, 1980), henceforth cited as "Major."

14. See J. Russell Major, "Noble Income, Inflation, and the Wars of Religion in France," *American Historical Review* 86 (1981): 21–48; id., "Bastard Feudalism and the Kiss: Changing Social Mores in Late Medieval and Early Modern France," *Journal of Interdisciplinary History* 17 (1987): 509–35; and id., "The Revolt of 1620: A Study of Ties of Fidelity," *French Historical Studies* 14 (1986): 391–408. These and some of my other essays are collected in *The Monarchy, the Estates and the Aristocracy in Renaissance France* (London, 1988).

15. James B. Wood, *The Nobility of the Election of Bayeux, 1463–1666* (Princeton, 1980); Jean-Marie Constant, *Nobles et paysans en Beauce aux XVIème et XVIIème siècles* (Lille, 1981); Amanda Eurich, *The Economics of Power: The Private Finances of the House of Foix-Navarre-Albret, 1517–1610* (Kirksville, Mo., 1994); William A. Weary, "Royal Policy and Patronage in Renaissance France: The Monarchy and the House of La Trémoille" (Ph.D diss., Yale University, 1972).

16. Françoise Autrand, *Naissance d'un grand corps de l'état: Les Gens du Parlement de Paris, 1345–1454* (Paris, 1981); Donna Bohanan, *Old and New Nobility in Aix-en-Provence, 1600–1695* (Baton Rouge, 1992); Jonathan DeWald, *The Formation of a Provincial Nobility: The Magistrates of the Parlement of Rouen, 1499–1610* (Princeton, 1980).

17. J. H. M. Salmon, "Storm over the Noblesse," *Journal of Modern History* 53 (1981): 242–57.

18. P. S. Lewis has published his most important articles in *Essays in Later Medieval French History* (London, 1985); Robert Harding, *Anatomy of a Power Elite: The Provincial Governors of Early Modern France* (New Haven, 1978); *Hommage à Roland Mousnier: Clientèles et fidélités en Europe à l'époque moderne*, ed. Yves Durand (Paris, 1981); Sharon Kettering, *Patrons, Brokers, and Clients in Seventeenth-Century France* (New York, 1986).

19. Arlette Jouanna, *Ordre social: Mythes et hiérarchies dans la France du XVIe siècle* (Paris, 1977); Ellery Schalk, *From Valor to Pedigree: Ideas of Nobility in France in the Sixteenth and Seventeenth Centuries* (Princeton, 1986); Kristen Neuschel, *Word of Honor: Interpreting Noble Culture in Sixteenth-Century France* (Ithaca, N.Y., 1989); Mack P. Holt, *The Duke of Anjou and the Politique Struggle during the Wars of Religion* (Cambridge, 1986); Mark Motley, *Becoming an Aristocrat: The Education of the Court Nobility, 1580–1715* (Princeton, 1990); Arlette Jouanna, *Le Devoir de révolte; La Noblesse française et la gestation de l'état moderne* (Paris, 1989); Jean-Marie Constant, *Les Guises, 1559–1661* (Paris, 1984), and *Les Conjurateurs* (Paris, 1987).

20. Roland Mousnier, "La Participation des gouvernés à l'activité des gouvernants

dans la France du XVIIe et du XVIIIe siècles," *Schweizer Beiträge zur Allgemeinen Geschichte* 20 (1962–63): 200–29.

21. Albert N. Hamscher, *The Parlement of Paris after the Fronde, 1653–1673* (Pittsburgh, 1976), and *The Conseil privé and the Parlements in the Age of Louis XIV: A Study in French Absolutism* (Philadelphia, 1987).

22. William Beik, *Absolutism and Society in Seventeenth-Century France* (Cambridge, 1985).

23. Roger Mettam, *Power and Faction in Louis XIV's France* (Oxford, 1988).

24. Thomas S. Kuhn, *The Structure of Scientific Revolutions,* 2d ed. (Chicago, 1970).

25. Roland Mousnier, *The Institutions of France under the Absolute Monarchy, 1598– 1789,* trans. Arthur Goldhammer (Chicago, 1984), 2: 683.

I. THE ESTABLISHMENT OF THE RENAISSANCE MONARCHY

1. Malcolm G. A. Vale, *Charles VII* (Berkeley and Los Angeles, 1974), esp. 3–12, 45–69, 229, plate 1. See also Roger G. Little, *The Parlement of Poitiers: War, Government and Politics in France, 1418–1436* (London, 1984), 58n, 94–123, 140, 210–14.

2. For this section, see Major, 10–45.

3. *Ordonnances des rois de France de la troisième race,* ed. Denis F. Secousse et al. (Paris, 1769), 9: 86–90.

4. Harry A. Miskimin, *Money and Power in Fifteenth-Century France* (New Haven, 1984), 54–59.

5. *Ordonnances,* 14: 139–45.

6. Ibid., 270–75.

7. Paul M. Kendall, *Louis XI* (New York, 1971), 128.

8. Helmut G. Koenigsberger, *Estates and Revolutions* (Ithaca, N.Y., 1971), 51–52.

9. *Ordonnances,* 15: 502.

10. Ibid., 17: 293.

11. Ibid., 18: 167.

12. J. R. Major, *Representative Institutions in Renaissance France* (Madison, Wis., 1960), 54–58. Recent works on the Estates General of 1468 include P. S. Lewis, "The Estates of Tours," in his *Essays in Later Medieval French History* (London, 1985), 139–49; Neithard Bulst, "The Deputies at the French Estates General of 1468 and 1484: A Prosopographical Approach," *Medieval Prosopography* 4 (1984): 65–79; and "Louis XI et les états généraux de 1468," in *La France de la fin du XVe siècle,* ed. Bernard Chevalier and Philippe Contamine (Paris, 1985), 91–104.

13. Martin Wolfe, *The Fiscal System of Renaissance France* (New Haven, 1972), 52.

14. Neithard Bulst has argued in "Deputies at the French Estates General of 1468 and 1484," 65–79, and "Vers les états modernes: Le Tiers Etat aux états généraux de Tours en 1484," in *Représentation et vouloir politiques autour des états-généraux de*

1614, ed. Roger Chartier and Denis Richet (Paris, 1982), 11–23, that the Beaujeus introduced the new procedure because bailiwick assemblies would be more likely to elect royal officials than municipal officials to represent the third estate. This actually happened because the governing oligarchies in the bailiwick capitals were frequently unpopular in the smaller communities. However, it is by no means clear that the Beaujeus controlled the king's council. There is no hint that the Orléanist faction or the great nobles led by Bourbon objected to the new procedure. It is probable that it was acceptable to all concerned. For over a century there had been complaints about the costs of deputations, and there had been instances of bailiwicks and other jurisdictions electing deputies under the earlier procedure to save expenses. Bailiwick elections reduced the number of deputies and made all the inhabitants responsible for paying their expenses. Earlier towns, chapters, and individuals who were summoned had had to pay, a very heavy burden except for the most wealthy. A few large cities continued to elect deputies to the Estates General after 1484 as part of bailiwick delegations, and Paris, Marseilles, and Arles won the right to have their own deputations. It is probable that the decision in 1482 to have the three estates of the bailiwicks ratify the treaty of Arras in the name of the three estates of France provided a useful precedent for the new procedure. It should be added that the new procedure reduced the ability of the crown to determine the composition of the first two estates, since bailiwick elections replaced direct summons. For elections by bailiwicks and comparable jurisdictions before 1484, see my *Representative Institutions,* 66–68; and for the ratification of the treaty of Arras and the Estates General itself, see 58–116.

15. Recent studies on the Estates General of 1484 include J.-L. Gazzaniga, "Les Etats généraux de Tours en 1484 et les affaires de l'église," *Revue historique de droit français et étranger* 62 (1984): 31–45; and J. Krynen, "Réflexions sur les idées politiques aux états généraux de Tours de 1484," ibid., 183–204.

16. For this section, see Major, 45–48.

17. P. S. Lewis, *Later Medieval France* (New York, 1968), 343.

18. *Chronique de Mathieu d'Escouchy,* ed G. du Fresne de Beaucourt (Paris, 1864), 3: 75.

19. Philippe de Commynes, *Mémoires,* ed. J. Calmette (Paris, 1925), 2: 219.

20. *Lettres de Louis XI, roi de France,* ed. Joseph Vaësen (Paris, 1895), 5: 136.

21. Jehan Masselin, *Journal des états généraux de France tenus à Tours en 1484 sous le règne de Charles VIII,* ed. A. Bernier (Paris, 1835), 419–21.

22. For this section, see Major, 49–51.

2. THE FLOWERING OF THE RENAISSANCE MONARCHY

1. For this section, see Major, 51–57.

2. Louis Caillet, *Les Ducs de Bourbonnais et la ville de Lyon* (Moulins, 1912), 61–72. Sarah Hanley, *The Lit de Justice of the Kings of France* (Princeton, 1983), 42–47. Major, *Representative Institutions in Renaissance France* (Madison, Wis., 1960), 117–25.

3.   Amable Floquet, *Histoire du Parlement de Normandie* (Rouen, 1840), 1: 325–26.

4.   Jean-J. Clamageran, *Histoire de l'impôt en France* (Paris, 1868), 2: 101.

5.   R. J. Knecht, *Francis I* (Cambridge, 1982), 51–65; Major, *Representative Institutions,* 128, 130–31.

6.   Major, *Representative Institutions,* 130–40. Hanley, *Lit de Justice,* 48–85.

7.   BN, MS n.a. fr. 7678, fols. 195–99v.

8.   James E. Brink, "The Estates of Languedoc, 1515–1560" (Ph.D. diss., University of Washington, 1974), 76, 66.

9.   Roger Doucet, *Etude sur le gouvernement de François Ier dans ses rapports avec le Parlement de Paris* (Paris, 1921), 1: 349.

10.   For the reforms of Henry II, see Michel Antoine, "Institutions françaises en Italie sous le règne de Henri II: Gouverneurs et intendants, 1547–1559," *Mélanges de l'Ecole française de Rome: Moyen Age Temps Modernes* 94 (1982), pt. 2: 759–818; "Genèse de l'institution des intendants," *Journal des Savants* (1982): 283–317; and *Le Dur Métier de roi* (Paris, 1986), 31–60. For Henry's reign, see Frederic J. Baumgartner, *Henry II* (Durham, 1988); and Ivan Cloulas, *Henri II* (Paris, 1985).

11.   Federico Chabod, "Was There a Renaissance State?" in *The Development of the Modern State,* ed. Heinz Lubasz (New York, 1964), 40.

12.   Roland Mousnier, *Le Conseil du roi de Louis XII à la Révolution* (Paris, 1970), 17–20. See also Pierre Chaunu's calculations in *Histoire économique et sociale de la France,* ed. F. Braudel and E. Labrousse (Paris, 1977), 1: 35–37.

13.   Bernard Chevalier, "The *bonnes villes* and the King's Council in Fifteenth-Century France," in *The Crown and Local Communities in England and France in the Fifteenth Century,* ed. J. R. L. Highfield and R. Jeffs (Gloucester, 1981), 120–22.

14.   Bernard Guenée, "Espace et état dans la France du bas moyen âge," *Annales: Economies, sociétés, civilisations* 23 (1968): 751–52. Robert-Henri Bautier, "Recherches sur les routes de l'Europe médiévale," *Bulletin philologique et historique (jusqu'à 1610) du Comité des travaux historiques et scientifiques* (1960): 102 n. 2.

15.   Chaunu, *Histoire économique,* 1: 37–39. Major, *Representative Institutions,* 9–10.

16.   I have dealt briefly with these assemblies in *The Deputies to the Estates General in Renaissance France* (Madison, Wis., 1960).

17.   For the remainder of this section, see Major, 59–159, and esp. 160–77. Recent works on the provincial estates during this period include René Souriac, *Le Comté de Comminges au milieu du XVIe siècle* (Paris, 1977); Albert Rigaudière, *Saint-Flour, ville d'Auvergne au bas moyen âge* (Paris, 1982), esp. 2: 588–649; *Recherches sur les états généraux et les états provinciaux de la France médiévale: Actes du 110e Congrès national des sociétés savantes, Montpellier, 1985, section d'histoire médiévale et de philologie* (Paris, 1986), vol. 3; C. T. Allmand, *Lancastrian Normandy, 1415–1450* (Oxford, 1983), esp. 171–86; Michel Duval, "Les Premiers Procureurs syndics des états de Bretagne, 1534–1636," in *Actes du 111e Congrès national des sociétés savantes, Poitiers*

1986, Section d'histoire moderne et contemporaine (Paris, 1987), 1, pt. 1: 7–25; *Documents sur les trois états du pays et comté de Forez,* ed. Etienne Fournial and Jean-Pierre Gutton (Saint-Etienne, 1987–89), 2 vols.; and P. S. Lewis, "Breton Estates," in his *Essays in Later Medieval French History* (London, 1985), 127–38.

18.   *HL,* 12: 493.

19.   J. R. Major, "Popular Initiative in Renaissance France," in *Aspects of the Renaissance,* ed. Archibald R. Lewis (Austin, 1967), 36–37.

20.   Henri Prentout, *Les Etats provinciaux de Normandie* (Caen, 1925), 2: 513. Henri Gilles, *Les Etats de Languedoc au XVe siècle* (Toulouse, 1965), 279–80. Barthélemy Pocquet, *Histoire de Bretagne* (Rennes, 1913), 5: 75.

21.   *Dictionnaire d'histoire et de géographie ecclésiastiques,* vol. 13 (Paris, 1956), 381.

22.   D. Oppetit-Perné, "La Vicomté de Turenne à la fin du XVe siècle: Essai d'histoire économique," in *Positions de thèses, Ecole nationale des Chartes* 1971: 141.

23.   Henri Drouot, *Mayenne et la Bourgogne* (Paris, 1937), 1: 94, 100.

24.   Roger Doucet, *Les Institutions de la France au XVIe siècle* (Paris, 1948), 1: 339, 350, 357.

25.   Bernard Chevalier, "The Policy of Louis XI towards the *bonnes villes*: The Case of Tours," in *The Recovery of France in the Fifteenth Century,* ed. P. S. Lewis (London, 1971), 276.

26.   Doucet, *Les Institutions,* 1: 362.

27.   G. Tholin, "La Ville d'Agen pendant les guerres de religion du XVIe siècle," *Revue de l'Agenais* 20 (1893): 199. Bernard Chevalier, "L'Etat et les bonnes villes en France au temps de leur accord parfait (1450–1550)," in *La Ville, la bourgeoisie et la genèse de l'état moderne (XIIe–XVIIIe siècles),* ed. Neithard Bulst and Jean-Philippe Genet (Paris, 1988), 85. François Lebrun, *Histoire d'Angers* (Toulouse, 1975), 39–81.

28.   For this section, see Major, 177–87. Quentin Skinner, *The Foundations of Modern Political Thought* (Cambridge, 1978), esp. 2: 113–23, 239–348.

29.   Niccolò Machiavelli, *The Prince,* trans. L. Ricci and rev. E. R. P. Vincent (New York, 1950), chs. 18–20.

30.   Erasmus, *The Education of a Christian Prince,* trans. Lester K. Born (New York, 1936), 179–80.

31.   *Recueil des instructions données aux ambassadeurs et ministres de France depuis les traités de Westphalie jusqu'à la Révolution française,* ed. J. J. Jusserand (Paris, 1929), 24: 35.

32.   Ibid., 35.

33.   *Pièces originales,* 1: 76–99. J. Russell Major, *The Estates General of 1560* (Princeton, 1951), 31–36.

34.   Major, *Estates General of 1560,* 36–37.

35.   Alfred F. Pollard, *Henry VIII* (London, 1905), 258.

36.   Julian H. Franklin, *Jean Bodin and the Rise of Absolutist Theory* (Cambridge, 1973), 7.

37. Ibid., 21.

38. Louis Le Caron, *Responses et décisions du droict françois* (Paris, 1612), unpaginated frontmatter.

39. Jean Combes, *Traité des tailles et autres charges* (Paris, 1584), esp. fols. 6–16.

40. Jean Hennequin, *Le Guidon général des finances* (Paris, 1585), fols. 78–78v.

41. René-Laurent La Barre, *Formulaire des esleuz* (Rouen, 1622), 76–77. Pertinent extracts have been reprinted in *Cahiers des états de Normandie sous les régnes de Louis XIII et de Louis XIV,* ed. Charles de Robillard de Beaurepaire (Rouen, 1877), 3: 429–35.

42. Jehan Masselin, *Journal des états généraux de France tenus à Tours en 1484,* ed. A. Bernier (Paris, 1835), 146–51. I quote the abridged translation of John S. C. Bridge, *A History of France from the Death of Louis XI* (Oxford, 1921), 1: 77–80, with minor changes.

43. Gerard F. Denault, "The Legitimation of the Parlement of Paris and the Estates General of France, 1560–1614" (Ph.D. diss., Washington University, 1975), 500.

44. François Hotman, *Francogallia,* ed. R. E. Giesey and J. H. M. Salmon (Cambridge, 1972), 155.

45. Pierre de Saint-Julien de Balleure, *De l'origine des Bourgongnons et antiquité des estats de Bourgongne* (Paris, 1581), 64.

46. Léonce Raffin, *Saint-Julien de Balleure* (Paris, 1926), 80.

47. *Histoire de la Normandie,* ed. Michel de Boüard (Toulouse, 1970), 271.

48. AD, Aveyron, C 1902.

49. Jean Savaron, *Les Origines de Clermont, ville capitale d'Auvergne* (Clermont, 1607), 254–55.

50. Alexandre Thomas, *Une Province sous Louis XIV: Situation politique et administrative de la Bourgogne, de 1661 à 1715* (Paris, 1844), 39.

51. Alain Destrée, *La Basse Navarre et ses institutions de 1620 à la Révolution* (Saragossa, 1955), 410.

52. *Loix municipales et économiques de Languedoc,* ed. Jean Albisson (Montpellier, 1780), 1: 316, 322.

3. THE LATE MEDIEVAL-RENAISSANCE NOBILITY

1. Marie-Thérèse Caron, *La Noblesse dans le duché de Bourgogne, 1315–1477* (Lille, 1987), 33–62. Jacques Mourier, "Nobilitas, quid est? Un Procès à Tain-l'Hermitage en 1408," *Bibliothèque de l'Ecole des Chartes* 142 (1984): 262–64. Edouard Perroy has also stressed the noble way of life more than birth. See his "Social Mobility among the French Noblesse in the Later Middle Ages," *Past and Present* 21 (1962): 25–38.

2. *La Noblesse au moyen âge, XIe–XVe siècles: Essais à la mémoire de Robert Boutruche,* ed. Philippe Contamine (Paris, 1976), 26–31; Georges Duby, *The Chivalrous Society,* trans. C. Postan (Berkeley, 1977), 59–80, 94–111; and Maurice Keen, *Chivalry* (New Haven, 1984), 143–61. For an excellent review of recent

studies, see T. N. Bisson, "Nobility and Family in Medieval France," *French Historical Studies* 16 (1990): 597–615.

3.   Henri Dubois, "La Dépression (XIVᵉ et XVᵉ siècles)," in *Histoire de la population française*, ed. Jacques Dupâquier (Paris, 1988), 1: 313–66, 515. Hugues Neveux, "Déclin et reprise: La Fluctuation biséculaire, 1330–1560," in *Histoire de la France rurale*, ed. Georges Duby and Armand Wallon (Tours, 1975), vol. 2, esp. 72–75. Guy Bois, *The Crisis of Feudalism* (Cambridge, 1984), 65–67. Emmanuel Le Roy Ladurie's estimates are more conservative. See his "Les Masses profondes: La Paysannerie," in *Histoire économique et sociale de la France*, ed. Fernand Braudel and Ernest Labrousse (Paris, 1977), 1, pt. 2: 487–99.

4.   J. R. Major, "Noble Income, Inflation, and the Wars of Religion in France," *American Historical Review* 86 (1981): 22–23. Neveux, "Déclin et réprise," 77–87.

5.   Major, "Noble Income," 22. Major, 28. P. S. Lewis, *Later Medieval France* (London, 1968), 212–37.

6.   John Bell Henneman, *Royal Taxation in Fourteenth-Century France: The Captivity and Ransom of John II, 1356–1370* (Philadelphia, 1976), 274–83, 298–311. Major, 20–23, 29, 38–39. Françoise Autrand, *Naissance d'un grand corps de l'état: Les Gens du parlement de Paris, 1345–1454* (Paris, 1981), 210–43.

7.   For this and the following paragraphs on clientage, see J. Russell Major, "'Bastard Feudalism' and the Kiss: Changing Social Mores in Late Medieval and Early Modern France," *Journal of Interdisciplinary History* 17 (1987): 509–35.

8.   Lewis, *Later Medieval France*, 198.

9.   Michael Nordberg, *Les Ducs et la royauté: Etudes sur la rivalité des ducs d'Orléans et de Bourgogne, 1392–1407* (Uppsala, 1964), 156–84. P. S. Lewis, "Decayed and Non-Feudalism in Later Medieval France," *Bulletin of the Institute of Historical Research* 37 (1964): 158–60. C. A. J. Armstrong, "Had the Burgundian Government a Policy for the Nobility?" *Britain and the Netherlands* 2 (1964): 22–24. For the Bourbons, see André Leguai, *Les Ducs de Bourbon pendant la crise monarchique du XVᵉ siècle* (Paris, 1962), 34–36.

10.   Bryce D. Lyon, *From Fief to Indenture* (New York, 1972), 7–9, 167.

11.   *Comptes généraux de l'état Bourguignon entre 1416 et 1420*, ed. Michel Mollat (Paris, 1965), pt. 1, 310.

12.   Ibid., pt. 1, 22–37, 155–64, 290–310; pt. 2, 96–102, 322–33, 713–19; pt. 3, 175–94, 501–23. B.-A. Pocquet du Haut-Jussé, "Les Pensionnaires fieffés des ducs de Bourgogne de 1352 à 1419," *Mémoires de la société pour l'histoire du droit et des institutions des anciens pays bourguignons comtois et romands* 8 (1942): 127–50.

13.   Lewis, "Decayed and Non-Feudalism," 178–79, 183–84; and "Of Breton *Alliances* and Other Matters," in *War, Literature, and Politics in the Late Middle Ages*, ed. C. T. Allmand (Liverpool, 1976), 140.

14.   AN, P.I, no. 347; P.II, no. 168; P.III, nos. 150, 250. For a detailed inventory, see *Hommages rendus à la Chambre de France: Chambre des comptes de Paris, Série P,*

ed. Léon Mirot (Paris, 1982), 1: 106–107. Another fief-rente passed from Geoffri de Senlis, bourgeois of Beaumont-sur-Oise, through to his great-grandson, Jacques Roussel, who did homage in 1508 for a fief of ten livres per year derived from a toll bridge over the Oise River. AN, P.V, no. 192.

15. AN, P.VII, nos. 80, 81; P.V, no. 254; P.VII, no. 110; P.XVI, no. 300.

16. Charles Du Moulin, *Omnia Quae Extant Opera* (Paris, 1681), 1: 129–30. Sir Edward Coke, *The First Part of the Institutes of the Laws of England; or, a Commentary upon Littleton* (London, ed. of 1794), vol. 1, section 87.

17. Gaspard Thaumas de la Thaumassière, *Nouveaux commentaires sur les coutumes générales des pays et duché de Berri* (Bourges, ed. of 1701), 136.

18. Jean Gallet, "Fidélité et féodalité: Quelques aspects de la fidélité des vassaux en Bretagne au XVIIᵉ siècle," in *Hommage à Roland Mousnier: Clientèles et fidélités en Europe à l'époque moderne,* ed. Yves Durand (Paris, 1981), 118.

19. Lewis, "Decayed and Non-Feudalism," 157–84.

20. *Archives historiques du département de la Gironde* 8 (1866): 296–97.

21. Honoré Bonet, *The Tree of Battles,* ed. C. W. Coopland (Cambridge, Mass., 1949), 122, 131, 132.

22. P. S. Lewis, "Of Breton *Alliances,*" 122–43.

23. Malcolm Vale, *War and Chivalry* (Athens, Ga., 1981), pp. 33–62. Keen, *Chivalry,* 179–99. Armstrong, "Had the Burgundian Government a Policy for the Nobility?" 25–28. Louis XI created the Order of St. Michael primarily for political purposes. D'Arcy Jonathan Dacre Boulton, *The Knights of the Crown* (New York, 1987), 427–47. Philippe Contamine, "Sur l'ordre de Saint-Michel au temps de Louis XI et de Charles VIII," *Bulletin de la Société nationale des antiquaires de France* (1976): 212–36.

24. Neveux, "Déclin et reprise," 2: 89–107. Le Roy Ladurie, "Les Masses profondes," vol. 1, pt. 2: 555–60.

25. P. Desportes, "La Population de Reims au XVᵉ siècle d'après un dénombrement de 1422," *Le Moyen Age* 72 (1966): 501. Jacques Rossiaud, "Prostitution, Youth, and Society in the Towns of Southeastern France in the Fifteenth Century," in *Deviants and the Abandoned in French Society,* ed. Robert Forster and Orest Ranum (Baltimore, 1978), 9. The median age of brides in Jumièges, Normandy c. 1550 was also about 20 years. Bois, *Crisis of Feudalism,* p. 370.

26. Neveux, "Déclin et reprise," 2: 101.

27. Jacques Houdaille, "La Noblesse française avant 1600," *Population* 45 (1990): 1070–75. T. H. Hollingsworth, "A Demographic Study of the British Ducal Families," in *Population in History,* ed. D. V. Glass and D. E. C. Eversley (London, 1965), 358–59, 364–65, 367, 377.

28. Edouard Baratier, *La Démographie provençale du XIIIᵉ au XVIᵉ siècle* (Paris, 1961), 88–89.

29. Perroy, "Social Mobility," 31.

30. James B. Wood, *The Nobility of the Election of Bayeux, 1463–1666* (Princeton, 1980), 48–51.

31. In his careful study, Etienne Dravasa cites few instances of derogation. See his *"Vivre noblement": Recherches sur la dérogeance de noblesse du XIVe au XVIe siècles* (Bordeaux, 1965). For the Beauce, see Jean-Marie Constant, *Nobles et paysans en Beauce aux XVIème et XVIIème siècles* (Lille, 1981), 38, 44bis, table 13.

32. Jean-Marie Constant, "Quelques problèmes de mobilité sociale et de vie matérielle chez les gentilshommes de Beauce aux XVIe et XVIIe siècles," *Acta Poloniae Historica* 36 (1977): 85.

33. Monique Cubells, "A propos des usurpations de noblesse en Provence sous l'ancien régime," *Provence historique* 20 (1970): 249.

34. Jean Meyer, *La Noblesse bretonne au XVIIIe siècle* (Paris, 1966), 1: 57.

35. *Histoire de la Savoie*, ed. Paul Guichonnet (Toulouse, 1973), 216.

36. R. H. Lucas, "Ennoblement in Late Medieval France," *Medieval Studies* 39 (1977): 247–51. Ellery Schalk, "Ennoblement in France from 1350 to 1660," *Journal of Social History* 16 (Winter 1982): 101–10. Godet de Soudé, "Dictionnaire des anoblissements: Extrait des registres de la Chambre des Comptes depuis 1345 jusqu'en 1660," *Revue historique nobiliaire et biographique: Recueil de mémoires documents* (1875): 252–74, 301–18. Wood, *Nobility*, 64–66.

37. Lucas, "Ennoblement," 243–50. Jean-Richard Bloch, *L'Anoblissement en France au temps de François Ier* (Paris, 1934), 27–61.

38. François Bluche and Pierre Durye, *L'Anoblissement par charges avant 1789* (La Roche-sur-Yon, 1962), 1: 23–24.

39. Ibid., 1: 40–45; 2: 35–39. Bloch, *Anoblissement*, 75–101.

40. Constant, *Nobles et paysans en Beauce*, 45–61.

41. Cubells, "A propos des usurpations," 249.

42. Wood, *Nobility*, 64.

43. D'Arcy Jonathan Dacre Boulton, "Dominical Titles of Dignity in France, 1223–1515" (Ph.D. diss., University of Pennsylvania, 1978), 184–87, 200, 222–26, 257–60.

44. Ibid., 457–60, 549–50.

45. Jean-Pierre Labatut, *Les Ducs et pairs de France au XVIIe siècle* (Paris, 1972), 57–61.

46. Roger Doucet, *Les Institutions de la France au XVIe siècle* (Paris, 1948), 2: 463.

47. Except as otherwise indicated, this section is taken from J. Russell Major, "Noble Income, Inflation, and the Wars of Religion in France," *American Historical Review* 86 (1981): 21–48. I am indebted to the *American Historical Review* for permission to reproduce portions of this article here.

48. For an exceptionally lively and detailed study of the Albret, see Susan Amanda Eurich, "Anatomy of a Fortune: The House of Foix-Navarre-Albret, 1517–1610" (Ph.D. diss., Emory University, 1988). For sources of Albret income, see p. 67.

49. E. H. Phelps Brown and Sheila V. Hopkins, "Wage-Rates and Prices: Evidence for Population Pressure in the Sixteenth Century," *Economica*, n.s., 24 (1957): 289–306. The authors' source for France is not reliable, but their study shows so much correlation between wage and price movements in France, southern England, and Alsace that their estimates for France are probably fairly close to being correct. Using a base of 1451–75 = 100, they found that in 1601–20 the indices are as indicated in Table N.1.

Correlation between Wage and Price Movements in France,
Southern England, and Alsace, 1601–1620

Index of	Alsace	Southern England	France
Prices of foodstuffs	517	555	729
Prices of some industrial products	294	265	335
Builders' wage rates	150	200	268

NOTE: 1451–75 = 100.

50. Eurich, "Anatomy," 98–210.

51. William A. Weary, "Royal Policy and Patronage in Renaissance France: The Monarchy and the House of La Trémoille" (Ph.D. diss., Yale University, 1972), 33–58, 82, 204–16, 226–33, and "The House of La Trémoille, Fifteenth through Eighteenth Centuries: Change and Adaptation in a French Noble Family," *Journal of Modern History* 49 (1977): "demand article."

52. Mark Greengrass, "Property and Politics in Sixteenth-Century France: The Landed Fortune of Constable Anne de Montmorency," *French History* 2 (1988): 371–98.

53. Ibid., 396–97.

54. Michèle Conchon, "Un Budget seigneurial aux XVᵉ et XVIᵉ siècles: Les Comptes de la baronnie de Sully-sur-Loire, 1479–1549," in *Positions des thèses, Ecole nationale des Chartes* 1981: 63–64. Bois, *Crisis of Feudalism,* 363, 359, 253, 257–59. André Plaisse, *La Baronnie du Neubourg* (Paris, 1961), 225, 326, 339–43, 372–73, 539, 551. Jacques Bottin, *Seigneurs et paysans dans l'ouest du pays de Caux, 1540–1650* (Paris, 1983), 185–87. Jonathan Dewald, *The Formation of a Provincial Nobility: The Magistrates of the Parlement of Rouen, 1499–1610* (Princeton, 1980), 201–19.

55. Guy Fourquin, *Les Campagnes de la région parisienne à la fin du moyen âge* (Paris, 1964), 482. Jean Jacquart, *La Crise rurale en Ile-de-France, 1550–1670* (Paris, 1974), 217.

56. Bernard Chevalier, *Tours, ville royale, 1356–1520* (Louvain and Paris, 1975), 462–63.

57. Wood, *Nobility,* 145–47.

58. Constant, *Nobles et paysons en Beauce,* 104–30.

59. Ibid., 127.

60. Dewald, *Formation of a Provincial Nobility,* 171–73, 176. Philip Benedict, "Civil War and Natural Disaster in Northern France," in *The European Crisis of the 1590's,* ed. Peter Clark (London, 1985), 96–98. Neveux, "Déclin et réprise," 130–31. Jean Gallet, *La Seigneurie bretonne, 1450–1680* (Paris, 1983), 311–41.

61. René Souriac, *Le Comté de Comminges au milieu du XVIe siècle* (Paris, 1977), 131–35.

62. Denis Crouzet, "Recherches sur la crise de l'aristocratie en France au XVIème siècle: Les Dettes de la maison de Nevers," *Histoire économie et société* 1 (1982), 7–50. Robert R. Harding, *Anatomy of a Power Elite: The Provincial Governors of Early Modern France* (New Haven, 1978), 143–49. Simple neglect could also be a problem. The lords of the important Breton seigneurie of Largouët were too occupied with court life and war to take advantage of their opportunities, and their revenue increased from 1250 Breton livres in 1493 to only 1558 livres in 1577, far from enough to compensate for inflation. Gallet, *Seigneurie bretonne,* 390.

63. Weary, "Royal Policy," 37, 197–98.

64. Harding, *Anatomy,* 160.

65. Contamine, "The French Nobility and the War," in *The Hundred Years War,* ed. K. Fowler (London, 1971), 150. Ralph E. Giesey, "Rules of Inheritance and Strategies of Mobility in Prerevolutionary France," *American Historical Review* 82 (1977): 271–89.

66. Xavier Martin, *Le Principe d'égalité dans les successions roturières en Anjou et dans le Maine* (Paris, 1972), 29–31. Joan Thirsk, "The European Debate on Customs of Inheritance, 1500–1700," in *Family and Inheritance: Rural Society in Western Europe, 1200–1800,* ed. Jack Goody et al. (Cambridge, 1976), 177–91.

67. Jacques Poumarède, *Les Successions dans le sud-ouest de la France au moyen âge* (Paris, 1972), 84–91, 182–217. Jacques Lafon, *Régimes matrimoniaux et mutations sociales: Les Epoux bordelais, 1450–1550* (Paris, 1972), 52–55. J. P. Cooper, "Patterns of Inheritance and Settlement by Great Landowners from the Fifteenth to the Eighteenth Centuries," in *Family and Inheritance,* ed. Jack Goody et al. (Cambridge, 1976), 252–58.

68. Ibid., 258–76. Paul Ourliac and J. de Malafosse, *Histoire du droit privé* (Paris, 1968), 3: 472–73, 527–35.

69. Ibid., 2: 403–20.

70. *Documents inédits sur Philippe de Commynes,* ed. Charles Fierville (Paris, 1881), 51.

71. Lucien Romier, *La Carrière d'un favori: Jacques d'Albon de Saint-André, maréchal de France, 1512–1562* (Paris, 1909), 245. Isambert, 13: 469–71, 14: 391. Hubert Jedin, *Crisis and Closure of the Council of Trent,* trans. N. D. Smith (London, 1967), 141–45.

72. Vale, *War and Chivalry,* 100–146, 184.

73. Philippe Contamine, *War in the Middle Ages,* trans. Michael Jones (Oxford, 1984), 193–207. For the development of the bastion, see J. R. Hale, "The Early

Development of the Bastion: An Italian Chronology, c. 1440–c. 1534," in *Europe in the Later Middle Ages*, ed. J. R. Hale, J. R. L. Highfield, and B. Smalley (Evanston, Ill., 1965), 466–94.

74. Philippe Contamine, *Guerre, état et société à la fin du moyen âge* (Paris, 1972), 278–319, 399–434.

75. Major, "'Bastard Feudalism,'" 509–35. AN, P XVII, no. 61. Philippe Contamine, *La France au XIVe et XVe siècles: Hommes, mentalités, guerre et paix* (London, 1981), 12: 212–36. P. Jeulin, "L'Hommage de la Bretagne en droit et dans les faits," *Annales de Bretagne* 41 (1934): 457.

76. Major, "'Bastard Feudalism,'" 531–32.

77. M. J. Baudel, *Notes pour servir a' l'histoire des états provinciaux du Quercy* (Cahors, 1881), 8. For examples of noble alliances and oaths, see Henri Stein, *Charles de France: Frère de Louis XI* (Paris, 1919), 622, 633–34, 695–96, 700–701.

78. *Procédures politiques du règne de Louis XII*, ed. René-Alphonse-Marie de Maulde-la-Clavière (Paris, 1885), 3–7, 26, 36, 55, 79, 82–83, 88–89, 96–97, 129–34, 144–46, 155–56, 161, 243–47, 251–52, 738. For an account of the trial, see John S. C. Bridge, *A History of France from the Death of Louis XI* (Oxford, 1929), 3: 225–43.

79. J. R. Major, *The Deputies to the Estates General in Renaissance France* (Madison, Wis., 1960), 144. Isambert, 13: 26–28; 14: 1–3. *Cahiers*, 1: 324.

80. Harding, *Anatomy of a Power Elite*, 21–45. Mikhaël Harsgor, *Recherches sur le personnel du conseil du roi sous Charles VIII et Louis XII* (Lille, 1980), 4: 2680–2712.

81. Katherine Fedden, *Manor Life in Old France* (New York, 1933), 131–43. *Un Sire de Gouberville*, ed. A. Tollemer (Paris, ed. of 1972), 411–28.

82. Elizabeth Teall, "The Myth of Royal Centralization and the Reality of the Neighborhood: The Journals of the Sire de Gouberville," in *Social Groups and Religious Ideas in the Sixteenth Century*, ed. Miriam Usher Chrisman and Otto Gründler (Kalamazoo, Mich., 1978), 1–11.

83. Ferdinand Lot, *Recherches sur les effectifs des armées françaises des guerres d'Italie aux guerres de religion, 1494–1562* (Paris, 1962), 21. Contamine, *Guerre, état et société*, esp. 296–97, 454–56, 465, 476; and "French Nobility and the War," 139. Contamine does not estimate the number of pages who were nobles. I have put the figure at 30 percent.

84. Wood, *Nobility*, 81–98. Jean-Marie Constant, "Les Barons français pendant les guerres de religion," in *Quatrième centenaire de la bataille de Coutras* (Pau, 1989), 53–55, and *Nobles et paysans*, 158–89.

85. Marilyn M. Edelstein, "Les Origines sociales de l'episcopat sous Louis XII et François Ier," *Revue d'histoire moderne et contemporaine* 24 (1977): 239–47.

86. Michel Péronnet, "Pouvoir monarchique et épiscopat: Le Roi et les évêques députés nés des Etats de Languedoc à l'epoque moderne," *Parliaments, Estates and Representation* 3 (1983): 117.

87. Constant, *Nobles et paysans*, 158bis, 159bis, 188–89.

88. Autrand, *Naissance d'un grand corps,* 168, 177–267.

89. Constant, *Nobles et paysans,* 159bis.

90. Jacques Verger, "Noblesse et savoir: Etudiants nobles aux universités d'Avignon, Cahors, Montpellier et Toulouse (fin du XIVe siècle)," in *La Noblesse au moyen âge, XIe–XVe siécles: Essais à la mémoire de Robert Boutruche,* ed. Philippe Contamine (Paris, 1976), 289–313. Autrand, *Naissance d'un grand corps,* 168, 444.

91. Michel Rouche, *Histoire générale de l'enseignement de l'éducation en France,* vol. 1, *Des origines à la Renaissance* (Paris, 1981), 562–89. Pierre Charbonnier, *Guillaume de Murol: Un Petit Seigneur auvergnat au début du XVe siècle* (Clermont-Ferrand, 1973), 47–62.

92. Bernard Guenée, *Tribunaux et gens de justice dans le bailliage de Senlis à la fin du moyen âge* (Paris, 1963), 185–202, 417–45, 532–34. Dewald, *The Formation of a Provincial Nobility,* 22–31, 130–37. L. W. Brockliss, "Patterns of Attendance at the University of Paris, 1400–1800," *Historical Journal* 21 (1978): 531–33.

93. François Lebrun, Marc Venard, and Jean Quéniart, *Histoire générale de l'enseignement et de l'éducation en France,* vol. 2, *De Gutenberg aux lumières* (Paris, 1981), 173–382. Constant, *Nobles et paysans,* 474–79. Natalie Z. Davis, "Sixteenth-Century French Arithmetics on the Business Life," *Journal of the History of Ideas* 21 (1960): 25-27. Weary, "Royal Policy," 56–76, 226–33. Major, "Noble Income," 21–48. Elizabeth Salmon Teall, "The Public Mind of the *noblesse d'épée,* 1484–1589" (Ph.D. diss., Radcliffe College, 1959), 381–462. John David Nordhaus, *"Arma et litterae:* The Education of the *noblesse de race* in Sixteenth-Century France" (Ph.D. diss., Columbia University, 1974), 97–242.

94. Autrand, *Naissance d'un grand corps,* 168, 177-267. For a correction to Autrand's thesis, see Christopher Stocker, *"Parti,* Clientage, and Lineage in the Fifteenth-Century *parlement* of Paris," *Proceedings of the Annual Meeting of the Western Society for French History* 13 (1986): 10–20.

95. Bloch, *Anoblissement,* 59–60.

96. Bluche and Durye, *Anoblissement,* 2: 11–25.

97. Jehan Masselin, *Journal des états généraux de France tenus à Tours en 1484 sous le règne de Charles VIII,* ed. A. Bernier (Paris, 1835), esp. 668, 683, 695.

98. *HL,* 11: 119–23; 12: 327–35. Claude de Seyssel, *La Monarchie de France,* ed. Jacques Poujol (Paris, 1961), 135.

99. Christopher W. Stocker, "Offices and Officers in the Parlement of Paris, 1483–1515" (Ph.D. diss., Cornell University, 1965), 232–38, 346–53. Dewald, *Formation of a Provincial Nobility,* 73–80.

100. AN, X[1a] 1587, fol. 2v. AD, Côte d'Or, C 3469. J. R. Major, *Representative Institutions in Renaissance France* (Madison, Wis., 1960), 144–47, 176.

101. André Devyver, *La Sang épuré: Les Préjugés de race chez les gentilshommes français de l'ancien régime* (Brussels, 1973), 7.

102. *Cahiers,* 1: 68–275, and esp. 253. BN, MS fr. 4763, fols. 88–106v.

103. J. R. Major, "The Third Estate in the Estates General of Pontoise, 1561," *Speculum* 29 (1954): 460–67.

4. THE WARS OF RELIGION

1. See Major, 205–7. For recent and only partially successful efforts to rehabilitate Henry III, see Jacqueline Boucher, *Société et mentalités autour de Henri III* (Lyons, 1981), 4 vols., and Pierre Chevallier, *Henri III* (Paris, 1985).

2. Denis Crouzet, "Royalty, Nobility and Religion: Research on the War in Italy," *Proceedings of the Annual Meeting of the Western Society for French History* 18 (1991): 11.

3. This section is based on Robert R. Harding, *Anatomy of a Power Elite: The Provincial Governors of Early Modern France* (New Haven, 1978), 46–107; Sharon Kettering, "Clientage during the French Wars of Religion," *Sixteenth-Century Journal* 20 (1989): 221–39; Elie Barnavi, "Fidèles et partisans dans la Ligue parisienne, 1585–1594," in *Hommage à Roland Mousnier: Clientèles et fidélités en Europe à l'époque moderne*, ed. Yves Durand (Paris, 1981), 139–52; and Kristen B. Neuschel, *Word of Honor: Interpreting Noble Culture in Sixteenth-Century France* (Ithaca, N.Y., 1989). Mark Greengrass, "Noble Affinities in Early Modern France: The Case of Henri I de Montmorency, Constable of France," *European History Quarterly* 16 (1986): 275–311, presents a more favorable view of clientage loyalty, but he bases his account on correspondence rather than actual behavior in war. Also, Montmorency's clients were less tempted to desert because he was a successful leader who stood in high royal favor during much of the period Greengrass considers. For the inadequacies of the royal army, see James B. Wood, "The Royal Army during the Early Wars of Religion, 1559–1576," in *Society and Institutions in Early Modern France*, ed. Mack P. Holt (Athens, Ga., 1991), 1–35.

4. Harding, *Anatomy of a Power Elite*, 82.

5. Ibid., 80–84, 256 n. 124.

6. Isambert, 15: 361–62. For Henry III's policies, see especially Chevallier, *Henri III*, and Boucher, *Société et mentalités*.

7. J. R. Major, "The Crown and the Aristocracy in Renaissance France," *American Historical Review* 69 (1964): 637.

8. *HL*, 13: 633–43. Harding, *Anatomy of a Power Elite*, 57–58.

9. *Preuves de la maison de Polignac*, ed. Antoine Jacotin (Paris, 1899), 3: 56. See also ibid., 98–99 for another League oath.

10. Neuschel, *Word of Honor*, 38–68. Jean de Viguerie, "Contribution à l'histoire de la fidélité: Note sur le serment en France à l'epoque des guerres de religion," *Annales de Bretagne et des pays de l'ouest* 82 (1975): 294.

11. See the exellent study of Arlette Jouanna, *Le Devoir de révolte: La Noblesse française et la gestation de l'état moderne* (Paris, 1989); and Jean-Marie Constant, *Les Guises* (Paris, 1984).

12. Paul van Dyke, "The Estates of Pontoise," *English Historical Review* 28 (1913): 493–95. Georges Picot, *Histoire des états généraux,* 2d. ed. (Paris, 2nd ed., 1888), 2: 216–26. *Cahiers,* 1: 69, 447. Henri Tartière, *Etats généraux de Pontoise cahier du tiers état* (Mont-de-Marsan, 1867), art. 4. BN, MS fr. 4763, fols. 90v, 96, 101, 106.

13. *Cahiers,* vol. 2, clergy, arts. 240, 429, 433; nobles, arts. 175, 244; third estate, arts. 11, 119, 333–36. Picot, *Histoire des états généraux,* 3: 87–95, 285–88.

14. *Cahiers,* vol. 3, clergy, arts. 136, 221; nobles, arts. 100, 161, 164, 233; third estate, arts. 223, 224. Picot, *Histoire des états généraux,* 4: 44–53.

15. For the provincial estates, see Major, 207–53.

16. Claude Michaud, "Finances et guerres de religion en France," *Revue de histoire moderne et contemporaine* 28 (1981): 572–96. Pierre Chaunu, "L'Etat," in *Histoire économique et sociale de la France,* ed. Fernand Braudel and Ernest Labrousse (Paris, 1977), 1: pt. 1: 166–78.

17. Daniel Hickey, *The Coming of French Absolutism: The Struggle for Tax Reform in the Province of Dauphiné, 1540–1640* (Toronto, 1986), 33–47.

18. *Registres des délibérations du bureau de la ville de Paris,* ed. Alexandre Tuetey (Paris, 1892), 5: 444–45.

19. Yves Durand, "Les Républiques urbaines en France à la fin du XVIᵉ siècle," *Société d'histoire et d'archéologie de l'arrondissement de Saint-Malo* (1990), 205–44.

20. For Rouen and the various interpretations of who became Protestants, see Philip Benedict, *Rouen during the Wars of Religion* (Cambridge, 1981), 71–94. See also Mack P. Holt, "Wine, Community and the Reformation in Sixteenth-Century Burgundy," *Past and Present* 138 (1993): 58–93; and Mark Greengrass, *The French Reformation* (Oxford, 1987), 42–62.

21. J. R. Major, *The Deputies to the Estates General in Renaissance France* (Madison, Wis., 1960), 10–11. *Catalogue des actes de Henri II* (Paris, 1979–86), 1: 398–400, 2: 266, 301. Isambert, 13: 34–35. Roger Chartier and Hugues Neveux, "La Ville dominante et soumise," in *Histoire de la France urbaine,* ed. Georges Duby (Paris, 1981), 3: 161–63.

22. Henri Drouot, *Mayenne et la Bourgogne* (Paris, 1937), 1: 43–55, 339–43. Elie Barnavi, *Le Parti de Dieu* (Brussels, 1980), 25–53. Benedict, *Rouen,* 181–89. Robert Harding, "Revolution and Reform in the Holy League: Angers, Rennes, Nantes," *Journal of Modern History* 53 (1981): 379–416.

23. Robert Descimon, "Qui étaient les Seize?" *Mémoires de la Fédération des sociétés historiques et archéologiques de Paris et de l'Ile-de-France* 34 (1983): 8–300. Elie Barnavi and Robert Descimon, *La Sainte Ligue, le juge et la potence: L'Assassinat du président Brisson* (Paris, 1985). For a penetrating review of these and other works, see Barbara Diefendorf, "The Catholic League: Social Crisis or Apocalypse Now?" *French Historical Studies* 15 (1987): 332–44.

24. John H. M. Salmon, *Society in Crisis: France in the Sixteenth Century* (New York, 1975), 253–57. Arthur Le Moyne de La Borderie, *Histoire de Bretagne* (Rennes, 1913), 5: 157–60. A. Prudhomme, *Histoire de Grenoble* (Grenoble, 1888), 416.

25. *Histoire de Bordeaux,* ed. Robert Boutruche (Bordeaux, 1966), 4: 310.

26. Jean Jacquart, "Immobilisme et catastrophes, 1560–1660," in *Histoire de la France rurale,* ed. Georges Duby and Armand Wallon (Paris, 1975), 2: 282–300. Major, *Deputies,* 124–28; and Major, 163–64. Hickey, *Coming of French Absolutism,* 33–100.

27. Emmanuel Le Roy Ladurie, "Les Masses profondes: La Paysannerie," in *Histoire économique et sociale de la France,* ed. Fernand Braudel and Ernest Labrousse (Paris, 1977), 1, pt. 2: 719–26.

28. J. R. Major, "Noble Income, Inflation, and the Wars of Religion in France," *American Historical Review* 86 (1981): 27–35.

29. Susan Amanda Eurich, "Anatomy of a Fortune: The House of Foix-Navarre-Albret, 1517–1610" (Ph.D. diss., Emory University, 1988), 13–46.

30. Mark Greengrass, "Property and Politics in Sixteenth-Century France: The Landed Fortune of Constable Anne de Montmorency," *French History* 2 (1988): 374–75. Jonathan Dewald, *Pont-St.-Pierre, 1398–1789: Lordship, Community, and Capitalism in Early Modern France* (Berkeley and Los Angeles, 1987), 233–35. Jacques Bottin, *Seigneurs et paysans dans l'ouest du pays de Caux, 1540–1650* (Paris, 1983), 185–219. Jean-Marie Constant, *Nobles et paysans en Beauce aux XVIème et XVIIème siècles* (Lille, 1981), 114–17.

31. Philip T. Hoffman, "Taxes and Agrarian Life in Early Modern France: Land Sales, 1550–1730," *Journal of Economic History* 46 (1986): 37–55. Hickey, *Coming of French Absolutism,* 123–37. Le Roy Ladurie, "Masses profondes," 1, pt. 2: 699–712, 786–99. N. Becquart, "Les Aliénations du temporel ecclésiastique au diocèse de Périgueux de 1563 à 1585," *Annales du Midi* 86 (1974): 325–33. Claude Michaud, "Redistribution foncière en rentière en 1569: Les Aliénations du temporel ecclésiastique dans quatre diocèses du centre de la France," *Revue historique* 267 (1982): 305–56.

32. Harding, *Anatomy of a Power Elite,* 135–42. Isabelle Aristide, *La Fortune de Sully* (Paris, 1990), 30. Major, "Noble Income," 42–43.

33. Constant, *Nobles,* 159bis.

34. Eurich, "Anatomy," 114–18, 162–202.

35. Harding, *Anatomy of a Power Elite,* 143–49, 228–30. Denis Crouzet, "Recherches sur la crise de l'aristocratie en France au XVIème siècle: Les Dettes de la maison de Nevers," *Histoire économie et société* 1 (1982): 7–50.

36. Harding, *Anatomy of a Power Elite,* 154–59.

37. Constant, *Nobles,* tables 27, 30, 31. James B. Wood, *The Nobility of the Election of Bayeux, 1463–1666* (Princeton, 1980), 145–49.

5. HENRY IV

1. See J. R. Major, *Bellièvre, Sully, and the Assembly of Notables of 1596* (Philadelphia, 1964); or Major, 260–66. James B. Collins, *The Fiscal Limits of Absolutism* (Berkeley and Los Angeles, 1988), 55–80.

2.   R. Charlier-Meniolle, *L'Assemblée des Notables tenue à Rouen en 1596* (Paris, 1911), 19.

3.   The idea of such a division of tax revenue had been suggested by the Chamber of Accounts in 1588, but it had gotten nowhere. Richard Bonney, *The King's Debts: Finance and Politics in France* (Oxford, 1981), 27.

4.   David Buisseret, *Sully* (London, 1968), 46.

5.   For this section, see Major, 266–94.

6.   *Recueil des lettres missives de Henri IV,* ed. Berger de Xivrey (Paris, 1848), 4: 343.

7.   The Selves correspondence is located at AC, Agen, CC 111, CC 120, and CC 123.

8.   Major, 295–305.

9.   Ibid., 306–48. For Dauphiné, see also Daniel Hickey, *The Coming of French Absolutism: The Struggle for Tax Reform in the Province of Dauphiné, 1540–1640* (Toronto, 1986), 70–160, and the review of this book by Vital Chomel in *Cahiers d'histoire* 33 (1988): 71–81.

10.   BN, MS fr. 15,911, fol. 84.

11.   P. Beaune, "Henri IV aux députés des états de Bourgogne, 1608," *Le Cabinet historique* 6 (1860), pt. 1: 122–25.

12.   For this section, see Major, 348–55.

13.   Ibid., 355–74. For Forez, see also *Documents sur les trois états du pays et comté de Forez,* ed. Etienne Fournial and Jean-Pierre Gutton (Saint-Etienne, 1989), 2: 5–17, 179–237.

14.   *Cahiers des états de Normandie sous le règne de Henri IV,* ed. Charles de Robillard de Beaurepaire (Rouen, 1882), 2: 160.

15.   *Lettres de Henri IV,* 3: 206–7.

16.   Selves to Agen, AC, Agen, CC. 123, no. 13. See also no. 2.

17.   *An Historical View of the Negociations between the Courts of England, France, and Brussels from the Year 1592 to 1617,* ed. Thomas Birch (London, 1749), 487.

18.   For this section, see Major, 380–87.

19.   Annette Finley-Croswhite, "Henry IV and the Towns: Royal Authority and Municipal Autonomy, 1589–1610" (Ph.D. diss., Emory University, 1990), 124. This discussion of the towns is indebted to her study.

20.   Ibid., 346–57.

21.   *Histoire de Lyon et du Lyonnais,* ed. André Latreille (Toulouse, 1975), 197. Christopher Stocker, "Henry IV and the Echevinage of Orleans" (paper read at the meeting of the Society for French Historical Studies in El Paso, 1992), 2.

22.   Finley-Croswhite, "Henry IV," 135.

23.   Ibid., 150.

24.   *Notes et documents pour servir à l'histoire de Lyon sous le règne d'Henri IV, 1594–1610,* ed. Antoine Péricaud (Lyon, 1845), 174–75.

25. *Collection des procès-verbaux des Assemblées-générales du Clergé de France* (Paris, 1767), 1: 740, 741. Sully could be polite when he wanted to, as he demonstrated in his early years in office, when he showed deference to his senior colleagues. D. Buisseret and B. Barbiche, "Lettres inédites de Sully à Henry IV et à Villeroy," *Annuaire-bulletin de la Société de l'histoire de France, années 1974–1975,* 87.

26. Edouard Maugis, *Histoire du parlement de Paris* (Paris, 1914), 2: 255.

27. Albert Chamberland, *Le Conflit de 1597 entre Henri IV et le parlement de Paris* (Paris, 1904), 35.

28. In addition to Maugis and Chamberland, see Sarah Hanley, *The Lit de Justice of the Kings of France* (Princeton, 1983), 223–30; and J. H. Shennan, *The Parlement of Paris* (London, 1968), 222–41.

29. Bernard Barbiche, *Sully* (Paris, 1978), 65–76. Buisseret, *Sully,* 91–95.

30. Julian H. Franklin, *Jean Bodin and the Rise of Absolutist Theory* (Cambridge, 1973), 38. For this section I am indebted to William F. Church, *Constitutional Thought in Sixteenth-Century France* (Cambridge, Mass., 1941), 194–242; *Jean Bodin: Proceedings of the International Conference on Bodin in Munich,* ed. Horst Denzer (Munich, 1973), 151–397; Donald R. Kelley, *Foundations of Modern Historical Scholarship* (New York, 1970); and Quentin Skinner, *The Foundations of Modern Political Thought* (Cambridge, 1978), vol. 2. See also Major, 177–87, 256–58.

31. Jean Bodin, *Les Six Livres de la république* (Paris, ed. of 1583), bk. 1, ch. 8, p. 122.

32. Ibid., bk. 2, ch. 1, p. 266.

33. Ibid., bk. 1, ch. 8, p. 141.

34. Ibid., bk. 3, ch. 7, p. 500.

35. Ibid., bk. 1, ch. 8, p. 140.

36. I have used the translation of Kenneth D. McRae in his edition of Knolles's translation of Jean Bodin, *The Six Bookes of a Commonweale* (Cambridge, Mass., 1962), A 71–72.

37. Church, *Constitutional Thought,* 194–271, 303–35. L. W. B. Brockliss, *French Higher Education in the Seventeenth and Eighteenth Centuries* (Oxford, 1987), 444–58.

38. Ralph E. Giesey, *The Royal Funeral Ceremony in Renaissance France* (Geneva, 1960), 177–92.

39. Mark L. Cummings, "The Long Robe and the Scepter: A Quantitative Study of the Parlement of Paris and the Monarchy in the Early Seventeenth Century" (Ph.D. diss., University of Colorado, 1974), 166.

40. These figures are derived from Michel C. Péronnet, *Les Evêques de l'ancienne France* (Lille, 1977), 2: 1440.

41. François Bluche and Pierre Durye, *L'Anoblissement par charges avant 1789* (Paris, 1962), 2: 15.

42. *Lettres de Henri IV,* 4: 110–11, 385.

43. Major, *Bellièvre,* 19, 29.

44. Hyacynthe de Fourmont, *Histoire de la chambre des comptes de Bretagne* (Paris, 1854), 148.

45. *The Political Testament of Cardinal Richelieu,* trans. Henry B. King (Madison, Wis., 1961), 28–29.

46. For the debate concerning the creation of the paulette, see Roland Mousnier, *La Vénalité des offices sous Henri IV et Louis XIII,* 2d ed. (Paris, 1971), 579–605; James B. Collins, *The Fiscal Limits of Absolutism* (Berkeley and Los Angeles, 1988), 80–87; Major, *Bellièvre,* 29–30. It is true that the surviving documents on the discussions in the council concerning the paulette do not mention the patron-client relationship, but Henry and Sully may have kept this motive a secret in order not to anger the magnates.

47. Major, 261, 370.

48. J.-P. Brancourt, "La Monarchie et les châteaux du XVIᵉ au XVIIIᵉ siècle," *XVIIᵉ Siècle* 118 (1978): 25–28.

49. Robert R. Harding, *Anatomy of a Power Elite* (New Haven, 1978), 171–99.

50. For the remainder of the chapter, see Major, 391–96.

51. Buisseret, *Sully,* 153.

6. THE REPRIEVE, 1610–1620

1. For this section, see Major, 397–449.

2. Salvo Mastellone, *La Reggenza di Maria de' Medici* (Florence, 1962), 229.

3. Ibid., 233.

4. Jack A. Clarke, *Huguenot Warrior: The Life and Times of Henri de Rohan, 1579–1638* (The Hague, 1966), 52.

5. Roland Mousnier, *The Assassination of Henry IV,* trans. J. Spencer (New York, 1973), 382.

6. *Cahiers,* 4: 432–33.

7. Ibid., 192.

8. Richard Bonney disagrees with the key role I have given Villeroy in the decision to summon the Assembly of Notables (Major, 410–12; Bonney, *The King's Debts: Finance and Politics in France, 1589–1661* [Oxford, 1981], 96 n. 4). Paul Phelypeaux de Pontchartrain, a mature, well-informed secretary of state, assigned Luynes no part in preparing for the meeting, but stressed the role of Villeroy and other councillors. François Duval, marquis de Fontenay-Mareuil, a 23-year-old army officer, gives Luynes a larger part, but nevertheless says that he "was advised" to call the assembly. The inexperienced Luynes could have persuaded Louis not to hold the meeting, but the initiative to do so almost certainly lay with trusted advisers like Villeroy, who had dealt with assemblies and estates in the past and favored their use when the situation warranted. See "Mémoires de P. Phelypeaux de Pontchartrain," 396, and "Mémoires

de Fontenay-Mareuil," in *Nouvelle collection des mémoires pour servir à l'histoire de France*, 2d ser., vol. 5, ed. Joseph Michaud and Jean-J.-F. Poujoulat (Paris, 1837), 126–27.

9. H. de Montégut, "Les Etats de Périgord," *Bulletin de la société historique et archéologique du Périgord* 4 (1887): 90.

10. AD, Ille-et-Vilaine, C 2649, 10–11.

11. Ibid., 137–38.

7. FRANCE FINDS A KING, 1620–1624

1. For this chapter, see Major, 450–86. A. Lloyd Moote, *Louis XIII, The Just* (Berkeley and Los Angeles, 1989) confirms my judgment that Louis was a strong king capable of acting on his own initiative.

2. Louis Batiffol, *Le Roi Louis XIII à vingt ans* (Paris, 1910), 177.

3. *Journal de ma vie: Mémoires du maréchal de Bassompierre*, ed. Audoin de La Cropte de Chantérac (Paris, 1873), 2: 417.

4. E. Griselle, "Louis XIII et sa mère," *Revue historique* 105 (1910): 308.

5. Ibid., 310, 312, 315, 322; ibid. 106 (1911): 299, 303.

6. Ibid., 105: 308, 320; ibid., 106: 299, 303.

7. Ibid., 106: 299.

8. Philip Benedict, "La Population réformée française de 1600 à 1685," *Annales: Economies, sociétés, civilisations* 42 (1987): 1433–65.

9. AC, Agen, CC 143.

10. Yves-Marie Bercé, *Histoire des Croquants* (Geneva, 1974), 88–89, 436–38. Bercé suggests that one of Louis's motives in creating the élections was to install Catholic officers. He does not, however, demonstrate that the officers of the estates in Guyenne were Protestants. Indeed, there were few Protestants in some of the areas where the élections were established. For an opinion concurring with mine, see Maurice Bordes, "De la création des élections en Guyenne et Gascogne," *Annales du Midi* 98 (1986): 259.

11. *Mercure françois* 8 (1622): 877–78.

12. Daniel Hickey, *The Coming of French Absolutism: The Struggle for Tax Reform in the Province of Dauphiné, 1540–1640* (Toronto, 1986), 145–49.

8. RICHELIEU AND MARILLAC, 1624–1629

1. For this chapter, see Major, 487–518. On the families and early careers of Richelieu and Marillac, see Joseph Bergin, *The Rise of Richelieu* (New Haven, 1991), and Donald A. Bailey, "The Family and Early Career of Michel de Marillac (1560–1632)," in *Society and Institutions in Early Modern France*, ed. Mack P. Holt (Athens, Ga., 1991), 170–89.

2. Richelieu, *Papiers,* 1: 181, 183, 185.

3. Ibid., 262.

4. Ibid., 266.

5. Jeanne Petit, *L'Assemblée des Notables de 1626–1627* (Paris, 1936), 156 n. 163.

6. *Mercure françois* 12 (1627): 34–39.

7. Richelieu, *Papiers,* 4: 24–25.

8. Jack A. Clarke, *Huguenot Warrior: The Life and Times of Henri de Rohan, 1579–1638* (The Hague, 1966), 179.

9. *Mercure françois* 15 (1629): 17, 20.

10. *Pièces originales,* 8: 464.

9. MARILLAC AND THE PROVINCIAL ESTATES

1. For this chapter, see Major, 519–67.

2. On Dauphiné, see also René Favier, "Les Assemblées du Dauphiné après la suspension des états en 1628," *Cahiers d'histoire* 24 (1979): 59–69; and Daniel Hickey, *The Coming of French Absolutism: The Struggle for Tax Reform in the Province of Dauphiné, 1540–1640* (Toronto, 1986), 147–78.

3. Richelieu, *Papiers,* 1: 498.

4. *Correspondance de la mairie de Dijon,* ed. Joseph Garnier (Dijon, 1870), 3: 222, 224.

5. For a good recent account of the riot, see James R. Farr, *Hands of Honor: Artisans and Their World in Dijon, 1550–1650* (Ithaca, N.Y., 1988), 201–10. Farr seems unaware that both the mayor of Dijon and Bellegarde heard rumors that a riot was planned and warned the échevins against such an action. Richelieu was with the army in Italy and had nothing to do with the actions of the crown. For Marillac's letters informing him on the course of events, see Richelieu, *Papiers,* 5: 51–54, 232–34, 238–39.

6. "Mémoires de Cardinal de Richelieu," *Nouvelle collection des mémoires pour servir à l'histoire de France,* 2d. ser., vol. 8, ed. Joseph F. Michaud and Jean-J.-F. Poujoulat (Paris, 1836–39), 149.

7. *Mercure françois* 16 (1630): 157, 160, 162.

8. Augier to Dorchester, April 29, 1630. Public Record Office, S.P. 78/86, fols. 257–58.

9. Richelieu, *Papiers,* 4: 478–79.

10. On bribing Guise, see ibid., 479, 704–705 n. 2.

11. Jonathan L. Pearl, "Guise and Provence: Political Conflict in the Epoch of Richelieu" (Ph.D. diss., Northwestern University, 1968), 202.

12. AD, Bouches-du-Rhône, C 16, fols. 63–65, 67v–69.

13. Pearl, "Guise," 204.

14. Ibid., 205.

15. Paul Gachon, *Les Etats de Languedoc et l'édit de Béziers, 1632* (Paris, 1887), 40.

16. *Mémoires du Cardinal de Richelieu,* ed. Robert Lavollée (Paris, 1929), 9: 302.

17. Ibid., 303.

18. AD, Hérault, *procès-verbal* of the estates of April–August 1629.

19. Richelieu, *Papiers,* 4: 512.

20. Ibid., 544.

21. L.-A. Boiteux, *Richelieu, grand maître de la navigation et du commerce en France* (Paris, 1955), 144.

22. James E. Brink, "The Estates of Languedoc: 1515–1560" (Ph.D. diss., University of Washington, 1974), 74–80. *Recueil des édits, déclarations, lettres-patentes, arrêts du conseil . . . concernant l'administration des états de Bourgogne* (Dijon, 1787), 2: 59–62, 68–79.

23. *Ordonnances des rois de France, règne de François I* (Paris, 1916), 2: 525. In the preamble to an edict of November 1542, Francis stated that it was "very useful in the administration of the public weal, even in monarchies, to make statutes and establish laws and ordonnances, which are general for all subjects, without any diversity, division, or particularity" (Isambert, 12: 790).

24. Edmondes to Dorchester, Public Record Office. S.P. 78/84, fols. 275–77.

25. Ibid., fols. 181, 325.

26. Richelieu, *Papiers,* 1: 368.

27. AD, Cote d'Or, C 3079, fols. 43v–44, 50v–51, 55. *Correspondance de la mairie de Dijon,* 3: lii–lvii, 185–202.

28. Richelieu, *Papiers,* 5: 491–92.

29. Ibid., 519–20.

30. Ibid., 212.

31. Ibid., 232–34.

32. Ibid., 249.

33. Richelieu, *Papiers,* 1: 113–22, 244–45, 248–69, 586. *Mercure françois,* 12 (1627): 34–39.

34. *Mémoires de Cardinal de Richelieu,* 2nd. ser., vol. 8, 149. Richelieu, *Papiers,* 4: 512; 5: 51.

35. Richelieu, *Papiers,* 4: 680, 739–40; but Condé was critical of Effiat, ibid., 412–14. Richard Bonney is quite favorable; see his *The King's Debts: Finance and Politics in France* (Oxford, 1981), 139–47.

36. AD, Bouches-du-Rhône, C 15, fols. 162–63v, 179–81. Peiresc did associate Effiat with the élections, but he had no way of knowing what happened in the king's council. See *Lettres de Peiresc,* ed. Philippe Tamizey de Larroque (Paris, 1890), 2: 263. René Pillorget, *Les Mouvements insurrectionnels de Provence entre 1596 et 1715* (Paris, 1975), 317–54.

37. Amable Floquet, *Histoire du parlement de Normandie* (Rouen, 1841), 4: 122.

38. *Mercure françois* 15 (1629): 17.

39. Richelieu, *Papiers,* 4: 21–22, 54, 67, 75–76, 80, 86–87, 90–91, 104–105, 112, 212–13, 215–16, 565.

40. Ibid., 102.

41. Ibid., 3: 382, 388; 4: 17–18, 86–87.

42. Ibid., 4: 478–79, 543–45; 5: 51–54.

43. Ibid., 5: 193.

44. Richard Bonney attributes the effort to create élections to Effiat because "Marillac favoured temporization and conciliation, while D'Effiat was more authoritarian" (*Political Change in France under Richelieu and Mazarin, 1624–1661* [Oxford, 1978], 350). Effiat may have been a good finance minister, but neither here nor in *King's Debts*, 139–46, does Bonney offer any evidence that he was especially authoritarian. Conversely, there is no doubt about Marillac's absolutist attitude. The final proof is that the crown reversed the policy of creating élections immediately after Marillac's fall, although Effiat continued to be superintendant of finances. As indicated in chapter 10, Richelieu can be connected with creating élections only in Languedoc, and once he got rid of Montmorency, he was willing to abandon them there on reasonable terms.

10. THE TRIUMPH OF RICHELIEU AND MAZARIN

1. For this chapter, see Major, 568–630.

2. Richelieu, *Papiers,* 5: 111. William F. Church, *Richelieu and Reason of State* (Princeton, 1972), p. 201.

3. Georges Pagès, "Autour du 'Grand Orage.' Richelieu et Marillac: Deux politiques," *Revue historique* 179 (1937): 66. For a recent account of the rivalry, see Pierre Chevallier, *Louis XIII* (Paris, 1979), 359–407.

4. Pagès, "Autour," 85, and Church, *Richelieu,* 203–4.

5. Augier to Dorchester from Lyons, Oct. 8/18, 1630, Public Record Office, S.P. 78/87, fols. 322–25.

6. Augier and de Vic to Dorchester from Paris, Public Record Office, S.P. 78/87, fol. 376. For a detailed account of the events and many documents, see Pierre Chevallier, "La Véritable Journée des dupes," *Mémoires de la Société académique de l'Aube* 108 (1974–77): 193–253.

7. Achille de Harlay de Sancy, *Response au libelle intitulé: Très-humble, très-véritable, et très-importante remonstrance au roy* (n.p., 1632), 70.

8. "Apologie pour le sieur de Marillac, garde de sceaux de France, contre ung libelle diffamatoire, publié soubz le tiltre d'Entretiens des Champs Elisées." BN, MSS fr. 5183, 17, 485, 17, 486, 18, 461.

9. Church, *Richelieu,* 223.

10. Roland Mousnier, "French Institutions and Society, 1610–1661," in *The New Cambridge Modern History,* ed. J. P. Cooper (Cambridge, 1970), 4: 493.

11. Richelieu, *Papiers,* 6: 11–15, 23–24, 140–42. This volume contains many letters concerning Guise and Provence.

12. Jean Albisson, ed., *Lois municipales et économiques de Languedoc* (Montpellier, 1780), 1: 287.

13. For an explanation of Montmorency's actions, see Arlette Jouanna, *Le Devoir de révolte* (Paris, 1989), 239–41, and Jean-Marie Constant, *Les Conjurateurs* (Paris, 1987), 64–78.

14. Richelieu, *Papiers,* 5: 72; 6: 15–16, 27, 74.

15. A copy of the edict is in the Bibliothèque nationale, F 46,977; quotation on p. 5.

16. Richelieu, *Lettres,* 7: 728–29.

17. Archives du Ministère des affaires étrangères: Mémoires et documents: France, MS 1504, fol. 153; MS 1505, fols. 94, 100, 382.

18. James B. Collins, *Fiscal Limits of Absolutism* (Berkeley, 1988), esp. 98–107, 111, 141. Isambert, 16: 389–406.

19. *Lettres et mémoires adressés au Chancelier Séguier, 1633–1649,* ed. Roland Mousnier (Paris, 1964), 2: 1136–38.

20. Daniel Hickey, *The Coming of French Absolutism: The Struggle for Tax Reform in the Province of Dauphiné, 1540–1640* (Toronto, 1986), 166–73.

21. Ibid., 169.

22. Ibid., 170–74. Major, 614–17. René Favier, "Les Assemblées du Dauphiné après la suspension des états en 1628," *Cahiers d'histoire* 24 (1979): 62–63.

23. *Documents sur les trois états du pays et comté de Forez,* ed. Etienne Fournial and Jean-Pierre Gutton (Saint-Etienne, 1989), 2: 261–324. Jean-Pierre Gutton, "Les Etats de Lyonnais," in *L'Europe, l'Alsace et la France: Problèmes interieures et relations internationales à l'époque moderne,* ed. Jean Bérenger et al. (Colmar, 1980), 156, 159.

24. Richelieu, *Lettres,* 4: 355–59.

25. Robert Harding, *Anatomy of a Power Elite* (New Haven, 1978), 179–212.

26. Sharon Kettering, *Patrons, Brokers, and Clients in Seventeenth-Century France* (New York, 1986), 9, 142–43, 157–61.

27. Maximin Deloche, *La Maison du Cardinal de Richelieu* (Paris, 1912), 370.

28. Joseph Bergin, *Cardinal Richelieu: Power and the Pursuit of Wealth* (New Haven, 1985), 6.

29. Georges Pagès, *La Monarchie d'ancien régime en France,* 4th ed. (Paris, 1946), 95. Pagès's emphasis.

30. Alfred Soman, "Press, Pulpit, and Censorship in France before Richelieu," *Proceedings of the American Philosophical Society* 120 (1976): 463.

31. R. C. Simmons, *The American Colonies from Settlement to Independence* (New York, 1976), 24.

32. Pagès, "Autour," 66.

33. Jean-H. Mariéjol, *Histoire de France,* ed. E. Lavisse (Paris, 1911), 6, pt. 2: 410.

34. For the relation between Anne and Mazarin, see Ruth Kleinman, *Anne of Austria* (Columbus, 1985), 166–73, 226–32. Georges Dethan, *Mazarin un homme de*

paix à l'âge baroque, 1602–1661 (Paris, 1981), paints a more favorable picture of Mazarin than I have.

35. Kettering, *Patrons, Brokers, and Clients,* 161–67.

36. *Lettres du Cardinal Mazarin pendant son ministère,* ed. A. Chéruel (Paris, 1887), 4: 73–74.

37. Ibid., 127, 269. For other comments by Mazarin on the Estates General, see 144, 151, 159–61, 260–61, 264–65, 280, 285, 339, 356, 509–10.

38. R. Mousnier, "Note sur les rapports entre les gouverneurs de provinces et les intendants dans la première moitié du XVIIe siècle," *Revue historique* 228 (1962): 347.

39. *Lettres . . . au Séguier, 1633–1649,* ed. Mousnier (Paris, 1964), 1: 604–5; 2: 725–26. *Lettres et mémoires adressés au Chancelier P. Séguier, 1633–1649,* ed. A. D. Lublinskaya (Moscow, 1966), 115, 116.

40. Ibid., 129. For the meetings of the estates during this period, see William Beik, *Absolutism and Society in Seventeenth-Century France* (Cambridge, 1985), esp. 133–36, 202–14, and John Miller, "Les Etats de Languedoc pendant la Fronde," *Annales du Midi* 95 (1983): 43–65.

41. *Lettres . . . au Séguier,* ed. Lublinskaya, 156, 163–64. For an account of how the crown tried to control the nobility through bribery and intimidation and the response of the estates, see Arlette Jouanna, "Le Pouvoir royal et les barons des états de Languedoc," *Parliaments, Estates and Representation* 4 (1984): 37–43.

42. Sharon Kettering, *Judicial Politics and Urban Revolt in Seventeenth-Century France* (Princeton, 1978), 64–65, 298–336. René Pillorget has almost nothing to say about the assembly of the communities during the Fronde, but has a long account of its activities thereafter, thereby revealing its minor role in the Fronde but its central position in Provençal life in more normal times. See his *Les Mouvements insurrectionnels de Provence entre 1596 et 1715* (Paris, 1975), 617, 660, 688, 691, and 708–862 passim.

43. J. Garnier has published a detailed summary of the estates of 1658 in *Inventaire-sommaire des archives départementales antérieures à 1790, Côte-d'Or, série C* (Dijon, 1886), 3: 25–26.

44. Richard Bonney, *Political Change in France under Richelieu and Mazarin, 1624–1661* (Oxford, 1978), 29–75, 163–213, 238–58.

45. Ibid., 259–83. Douglas Clark Baxter, *Servants of the Sword: French Intendants of the Army, 1630–70* (Urbana, Ill., 1976).

46. A. Lloyd Moote, *The Revolt of the Judges: The Parlement of Paris and the Fronde, 1643–1652* (Princeton, 1971), 373–76.

47. *Lettres, instructions et mémoires de Colbert,* ed. Pierre Clément (Paris, 1861), 1: 535.

II. THE NOBILITY

1.   Sharon Kettering, "The Decline of Great Noble Clientage during the Reign of Louis XIV," *Canadian Journal of History* 24 (1989): 157–77.

2.   Jean-Dominique Lassaigne, *Les Assemblées de la noblesse de France aux XVIIe et XVIIIe siècles* (Paris, 1965), 59–60.

3.   J.-M. Constant, "Un Groupe socio-politique stratégique dans la France de la première moitié du XVIIe siècle: La Noblesse seconde," in *L'Etat et les aristocraties,* ed. Philippe Contamine (Paris, 1989), 279–304; and "La Troisième Fronde: Les Gentilshommes et les libertés nobiliaires," *XVIIe Siècle* 145 (1984): 341–54.

4.   For these assemblées, see Constant, "Troisième Fronde"; Lassaigne, *Assemblées;* and Arlette Jouanna, *Le Devoir de révolte* (Paris, 1989), 262–78, 362–67.

5.   For background to these paragraphs, see Jouanna, *Devoir,* 368–84; and J. R. Major, "The Revolt of 1620: A Study of Ties of Fidelity," *French Historical Studies* 14 (1986): 391–408.

6.   The acts of union are published in Lassaigne, *Assemblées,* 177–82, 187–98, 206–207.

7.   Major, "Revolt of 1620," 395. For the full text of this and other pledges, see 407–408.

8.   Lassaigne, *Assemblées,* 226–28.

9.   Marc Bloch, *Feudal Society,* trans. L. A. Manyon (Chicago, 1968), 450. For the full text, see *Lettres, instructions et mémoires de Colbert,* ed. Pierre Clément (Paris, 1863), 2: xxx.

10.   *Lettres . . . de Colbert,* ed. Clément, 2: xxx.

11.   Eusèbe Pavie, *La Guerre entre Louis XIII et Marie de Médicis, 1619–1620* (Angers, 1899), 288.

12.   Major, "Revolt of 1620," 391–408.

13.   *Lettres . . . de Colbert,* 2: i–xlvi. Inès Murat, *Colbert,* trans. R. F. Cook and J. Van Asselt (Charlottesville, Va., 1984), 35–71. Daniel Dessert, *Fouquet* (Paris, 1987), rehabilitates the fallen minister.

14.   *Cahiers,* 4: 192.

15.   *Histoire de la population française,* ed. Jacques Dupâquier (Paris, 1988), 2: 151–53, 197–209.

16.   Claude Lévy and Louis Henry, "Ducs et pairs sous l'ancien régime: Caractéristiques démographiques d'une caste," *Population* 15 (1960): 807–30.

17.   Jacques Houdaille, "La Noblesse française, 1600–1900," *Population* 44 (1989): 501–13.

18.   James B. Wood, *The Nobility of the Election of Bayeux, 1463–1666* (Princeton, 1980), 50, 55.

19.   G. d'Arundel de Condé, *Anoblissements maintenues et réhabilitations en Normandie, 1598–1790* (Paris, 1981), 89–91.

20. Arundel de Condé, *Anoblissements,* 117.

21. Wood, *Nobility,* 58–65.

22. Jean-Marie Constant, *Nobles et paysans en Beauce aux XVIᵉᵐᵉ et XVIIᵉᵐᵉ siècles* (Lille, 1981), 46ᵇⁱˢ, 67–67ᵗᵉʳ.

23. Jean-Pierre Labatut, *Les Ducs et pairs de France au XVIIᵉ siècle* (Paris, 1972), 66–74.

24. Roger Mettam, *Power and Faction in Louis XIV's France* (Oxford, 1988), 197–203.

25. Labatut, *Ducs,* 248, 258–60. Daniel Roche, "Aperçus sur la fortune et les revenus des princes de Condé à l'aube du 18ᵉ siècle," *Revue d'histoire moderne et contemporaine* 14 (1967): 217–43.

26. François-Charles Mougel, "La Fortune des princes de Bourbon-Conty: Revenus et gestion, 1655–1791," *Revue d'histoire moderne et contemporaine* 18 (1971): 30–49.

27. Nancy N. Barker, "Philippe d'Orléans, frère unique du roi: Founder of the Family Fortune," *French Historical Studies* 13 (1983): 145–71.

28. Labatut, *Ducs,* 248, 267.

29. Jacques Peret, "Seigneurs et seigneuries en Gâtine poitevine: Le Duché de La Meilleraye XVIIᵉ–XVIIIᵉ siècles," *Mémoires de la société des antiquaires de l'Ouest,* 4th ser., 13 (1974–76): 1–40.

30. Isabelle Aristide, *La Fortune de Sully* (Paris, 1990), 43, 91–95.

31. Joseph Bergin, *Cardinal Richelieu: Power and the Pursuit of Wealth* (New Haven, 1985), 248, 255.

32. Daniel Dessert, "Pouvoir et finance au XVIIᵉ siècle: La Fortune du Cardinal Mazarin," *Revue d'histoire moderne et contemporaine* 23 (1976): 161–81.

33. Dessert, *Fouquet,* 152, 161–62, 348–50.

34. Richard Bonney, "The Secret Expenses of Richelieu and Mazarin, 1624–1661," *English Historical Review* 91 (1976): 825–36.

35. Françoise Bayard, *Le Monde des financiers au XVIIᵉ siècle* (Paris, 1988), 438. Daniel Dessert, *Argent, pouvoir et société au grand siècle* (Paris, 1984), 87, 91–94, 349–78. C. Michaud, "Notariat et sociologie de la rente à Paris au XVIIᵉ siècle: L'Emprunt du clergé de 1690," *Annales: Economies, sociétés, civilisations* 32 (1977): 1154–87.

36. Philip T. Hoffman, "Taxes and Agrarian Life in Early Modern France: Land Sales, 1550–1730," *Journal of Economic History* 46 (1986): 37–55.

37. Jacques Bottin, *Seigneurs et paysans dans l'ouest du pays de Caux, 1540–1650* (Paris, 1983), 239–44, 301–305, annex D, graphs 28–40.

38. Labatut, *Ducs,* 267.

39. Pierre Goubert, *Beauvais et le Beauvaisis de 1600 à 1730* (Paris, 1960), vol. 1, 206–22. Constant, *Nobles et paysans,* 114–27.

40. Wood, *Nobility,* 120–55.

41. André Corvisier, *Armies and Societies in Europe, 1494–1789,* trans. A. T. Siddall (Bloomington, Ind., 1979), 46, 49, 54, 100–103; id., *Louvois* (Paris, 1983), 341, 514–18; and id., *L'Armée française de la fin du XVIIe siècle au ministère de Choiseul* (Paris, 1964), 1: 483.

42. Wood, *Nobility,* 83, 89, 93, 96. Constant, *Nobles et paysans,* 159bis–60bis, 173bis, 175bis. Ninety-three percent of the dukes and peers had military careers in the seventeenth century, Labatut, *Ducs,* 182.

43. "Procès-verbal et pièces relatives à la convocation du ban de la noblesse de la sénéchaussée de Sarlat," *Archives historiques du département de la Gironde* 18 (1878): 260–315. *L'Intendance de Languedoc à la fin du XVIIe siècle,* ed. Françoise Moreil (Paris, 1985), 163. Anne Blanchard, "Les Officiers militaires en Languedoc: Montpellier durant le règne de Louis XIV," in *Actes du 103e Congrès national des sociétés savantes, Nancy-Metz, 1978* (Paris, 1979), 1: 65.

44. Michel C. Péronnet, *Les Evêques de l'ancienne France* (Lille, 1977), 1: 502–54, 697–715; 2: 1440–45.

45. Constant, *Nobles et paysans,* 158bis–159bis.

46. For the crown's efforts to encourage nobles to engage in maritime trade and the relative lack of success, see Guy Richard, "Un Aspect particulier de la politique économique et sociale de la monarchie au XVIIe siècle: Richelieu, Colbert, la noblesse et le commerce," *XVIIe siècle* 49 (1960): 11–41.

47. Wood, *Nobility,* 74–77. Constant, *Nobles et paysans,* 158–59bis.

48. Roland Mousnier, *La Vénalité des offices sous Henri IV et Louis XIII,* 2d ed. (Paris, 1971), 356–69; and id., *The Institutions of France under the Absolute Monarchy, 1598–1789,* trans. A. Goldhammer (Chicago, 1984), 2: 341–44. Jonathan Dewald, *The Formation of a Provincial Nobility: The Magistrates of the Parlement of Rouen, 1499–1610* (Princeton, 1980), 138–45, 333–39.

49. Ibid., 22–29, 78–79, 133–37. Albert N. Hamscher, *The Parlement of Paris after the Fronde, 1653–1673* (Pittsburgh, 1976), 42.

50. Françoise Autrand, *Naissance d'un grand corps de l'état: Les Gens du Parlement de Paris, 1345–1454* (Paris, 1981), 168. Etienne Dravasa, *"Vivre noblement": Recherches sur la dérogeance de noblesse du XIVe au XVIe siècles* (Bordeaux, 1965), 133.

51. Autrand, *Naissance,* 444. Christopher Stocker, "Offices and Officers in the Parlement of Paris, 1483–1515" (Ph.D. diss., Cornell University, 1965), 232–38, 346–54. Edouard Maugis, *Histoire du parlement de Paris de l'avenement des rois Valois à le mort d'Henri IV* (Paris, 1916), 3: 148–215.

52. Hamscher, *Parlement of Paris,* 42.

53. Mark L. Cummings, "The Long Robe and the Scepter: A Quantitative Study of the Parlement of Paris and the French Monarchy in the Early Seventeenth Century" (Ph.D. diss., University of Colorado, 1974), 104. See also his "The Social Impact of the Paulette: The Case of the Parlement of Paris," *Canadian Journal of History* 15 (1980): 329–54.

54. François Bluche, *Les Magistrats du Parlement de Paris au XVIIIe siècle, 1715–1771* (Paris, 1960), 88–96.

55. Mousnier, *Institutions of France,* 1: 204.

56. Bluche, *Magistrats,* 303–86.

57. Sharon Kettering, *Judicial Politics and Urban Revolt in Seventeenth-Century France: The Parlement of Aix, 1629–1659* (Princeton, 1978), 216.

58. Donna Bohanan, "The Sword as the Robe in Seventeenth-Century Provence and Brittany," in *Society and Institutions in Early Modern France,* ed. Mack P. Holt (Athens, Ga., 1991), 53. See also her *Old and New Nobility in Aix-en Provence, 1600–1695* (Baton Rouge, 1992), esp. 82–85, 140–45.

59. Jean Meyer, *La Noblesse bretonne au XVIIIe siècle* (Paris, 1966), 2: 957. Mousnier, *Institutions of France,* 2: 324.

60. Jean Egret, *Le Parlement de Dauphiné et les affaires publiques dans la deuxième moitié du XVIIIe siècle* (Grenoble, 1942), 1: 20.

61. William Doyle, *The Parlement of Bordeaux and the End of the Old Regime 1771–1790* (London, 1974), 18–20.

62. Mousnier, *Institutions of France,* 2: 60–79, 583–633.

63. Ibid., 351.

64. For documents concerning the Gouberville family, see Auguste de Blangy, *Généalogie des sires de Russy, de Gouberville et du Mesnil au Val* (Caen, 1887). Michel Devèze, *La Vie de la forêt française au XVIe siècle* (Paris, 1961), 2: 157–60, contains an account of Gouberville as a forest official. Here and in ibid., 1: 284–85, he points out that nobles sought to be forest officials.

65. Georges Picot, *Histoire des états généraux,* 2d ed. (Paris, 1888), 4: 191.

66. Labatut, *Ducs,* esp. 98–142, 184–94. Léon Mirot, *Les d'Orgemont* (Paris, 1913); Roland Mousnier, *Etat et société sous François Ier et pendant le gouvernement personnel de Louis XIV* (Paris: Les Cours de Sorbonne, n.d.), 212–13.

67. J. R. Major, *The Deputies to the Estates General in Renaissance France* (Madison, Wis., 1960), 135. For some other examples of members of the same family following both military and bureaucratic careers, see Dewald, *Formation of a Provincial Nobility,* 102–3.

68. Roland Mousnier, *Social Hierarchies, 1450 to the Present,* trans. Peter Evans (New York, 1973), 67–89; *Institutions of France,* 1: 4–16, 547; *Vénalité des offices,* 529–41; and id., J.-P. Labatut, and Yves Durand, eds., *Problèmes de stratification sociale: Deux cahiers de la noblesse pour les états généraux de 1649–1651* (Paris, 1965), 25–43. Charles Loyseau, *Livre des ordres et simples dignitez,* in *Les Oeuvres* (Paris, 1660), esp. chs. 4–5.

69. For a penetrating review article concerning this question, see J. H. M. Salmon, "Storm over the Noblesse," *Journal of Modern History* 53 (1981): 242–57. I am indebted to him for his comments on an unpublished article on this subject.

70. "Mémoires de Gaspard de Saulx, seigneur de Tavannes," *Nouvelle collection des mémoires pour servir à l'histoire de France*, 1st ser., vol. 8, ed. Joseph F. Michaud and Jean-J.-F. Poujoulat (Paris 1838), 55.

71. Dewald, *Formation of a Provincial Nobility*, 16.

72. Davis Bitton, *The French Nobility in Crisis, 1560–1640* (Stanford, 1969), 43.

73. *Cahiers*, 1: 73–74, 155, 159–60, 198–99, 249, 253.

74. Ibid., 253.

75. BN, MS fr. 4763, fols. 88–106v.

76. *Cahiers*, 2: 136, 147, 149, 151, 161, 163; 3: 103–106, 136–37, 166–67. Picot, *Histoire des états généraux*, 2: 265–73, 280–85; 3: 179–86, 206–207.

77. *Cahiers*, 2: 134; 3: 136–37; 4: 188–89, 194–95, 197, 205–209. Mousnier, *Institutions of France*, 2: 221–23.

78. Barbara B. Diefendorf, *Paris City Councillors in the Sixteenth Century* (Princeton, 1983), 44. J. R. Major, "The Third Estate in the Estates General of Pontoise," *Speculum* 29 (1954): 469.

79. Mousnier, *Institutions of France*, 1: 13–16.

80. Major, *Deputies*, 54–55, 68–69.

81. Bernard Barbiche, "La Hiérarchie des dignités et des charges au début du dix-septième siècle d'après l'état des taxes des voyages du 25 août 1601," *XVIIᵉ Siècle* 157 (1987): 360.

82. Manfred Orlea, *La Noblesse aux états généraux de 1576 et de 1588* (Paris, 1980), 114–15. Major, *Deputies*, 112–13. Bohanan, *Old and New Nobility*.

83. Mousnier, Labatut, and Durand, eds., *Problèmes de stratification sociale*, 115–20. A misprint gives the date of Mesgrigny's election to the Estates General as 1614.

84. Labatut, *Ducs*, 175.

85. Daniel Ligou, ed., *L'Intendance de Bourgogne à la fin du XVIIᵉ siècle* (Paris, 1988), 127–33, 198–204, 225–27, 250–51, 257–63, 274–77, 284–86, 291, 304–12, 329–37, 352–55, 362–65, 371–74, 386–91, 399–403, 418–23, 431–42, 474–77, 498–513, 545–58, 570–73.

86. *Cahiers*, 4: 192.

87. Mark Motley, *Becoming a French Aristocrat: The Education of the Court Nobility, 1580–1715* (Princeton, 1990), 18–67.

88. *Cahiers*, 2: 182. "Procès-verbal et pièces relatives à la convocation du ban de la noblesse de la sénéchaussée de Sarlat," *Archives historiques du département de la Gironde* 18 (1878): 286.

89. George Huppert, *Public Schools in Renaissance France* (Urbana, Ill., 1984). François Lebrun, Marc Venard, and Jean Quéniart, *Histoire générale de l'enseignement et de l'éducation en France*, vol. 2, *De Gutenberg aux lumières* (Paris, 1981), 315–67. Willem Frijhoff and Dominique Julia, *Ecole et société dans la France d'ancien régime*

(Paris, 1975), esp. 14, 60. Roger Chartier, Dominique Julia, and Marie-Madeleine Compère, *L'Education en France du XVIe au XVIIIe siècle* (Paris, 1976), 147–99.

90. Motley, *Becoming a French Aristocrat*, 123–68. Ellery Schalk, *From Valor to Pedigree: Ideas of Nobility in France in the Sixteenth and Seventeenth Centuries* (Princeton, 1986), 174–201.

91. Motley, *Becoming a French Aristocrat*, 169–208.

92. Ibid., esp. 70–79. Montaigne, *Essais*, ch. 17.

93. Chartier, Julia, and Compère, *Education*, 183.

94. Donna Bohanan, "The Education of Nobles in Seventeenth-Century Aix-en-Provence," *Journal of Social History* 20 (1986–87): 757–64. The academy at Aix received some funds from the estates of Provence and therefore enrolled some less wealthy students including commoners. See also Bohanan's *Old and New Nobility*, 120–32. Schalk, *From Valor to Pedigree*, 188–89.

95. Schalk, *From Valor to Pedigree*, 188–89. André Devyver, *Le Sang épuré: Les Préjugés de race chez les gentilshommes français de l'ancien régime, 1560–1720* (Brussels, 1973). Arlette Jouanna, *Ordre social: Mythes et hiérarchies dans la France du XVIe siècle* (Paris, 1977).

96. Orest Ranum, "Courtesy, Absolutism, and the Rise of the French State, 1630–1660," *Journal of Modern History* 52 (1980): 450.

97. François Bellacois, *The Duel: Its Rise and Fall in Early Modern France*, trans. Trista Selous (New Haven, 1990), 178.

12. LOUIS XIV

1. For this chapter, see Major, 630–72.

2. *Lettres, instructions et mémoires de Colbert*, ed. Pierre Clément (Paris, 1861), 1: 535.

3. *Cahiers*, 4: 192.

4. François Bluche, *Louis XIV*, trans. Mark Greengrass (Oxford, 1990), 95.

5. Michel Antoine, "Colbert et la révolution de 1661," in *Un Nouveau Colbert*, ed. Roland Mousnier (Paris, 1985), 99–109. Bluche, *Louis XIV*, 95–100, 104–108. Roland Mousnier, *The Institutions of France under the Absolute Monarchy*, trans. Arthur Goldhammer (Chicago, 1979), 2: 151–59.

6. Louis XIV, *Mémoires for the Instruction of the Dauphin*, trans. Paul Sonnino (New York, 1970), 196.

7. Ibid.

8. Ibid., 166.

9. Ibid., 86–87.

10. *Lettres de Colbert*, 6: 366, 381.

11. *Correspondance administrative sous le règne de Louis XIV*, ed. G. B. Depping (Paris, 1852), 3: 284.

12. Ibid., 1: 627.

13. Richard Bonney, "Was There a Bourbon Style of Government?" in *From Valois to Bourbon*, ed. Keith Cameron (Exeter, 1989), 164–65.

14. *Lettres de Colbert*, 4: 138 n. 1, 147.

15. *Correspondance administrative*, 1: 558.

16. *Correspondance des contrôleurs généraux des finances avec les intendants des provinces*, ed. A. M. de Boislisle (Paris, 1874), 1: no. 531.

17. *Lettres de Colbert*, 4: 18.

18. *Correspondance administrative*, 1: 334, 340–42.

19. Ibid., 376.

20. Ibid., 397.

21. Ibid., 430–31. For a recent account that centers on the eighteenth century and shows that the nobility played a more important role than previously thought, see Fr.-X. Emmanuelli, "Pour une réhabilitation de la histoire politique régionale: L'Example de l'assemblée des communautés de Provence, 1660–1786," *Revue historique de droit français et étranger*, 4th ser., 59 (1981): 431–50.

22. *Correspondance administrative*, 1: 431.

23. Ibid., 67.

24. Ibid., 72–75.

25. *Lettres de Colbert*, 4: 51.

26. For an excellent study with a somewhat different emphasis, see William Beik, *Absolutism and Society in Seventeenth-Century France: State Power and Provincial Aristocracy in Languedoc* (Cambridge, 1985), esp. 258–70.

27. *Correspondance administrative*, 1: 488.

28. *Lettres de Colbert*, 2: 84.

29. *Correspondance administrative*, 1: 619.

30. *Lettres de Colbert*, 2: 337.

31. Germain Arnaud, *Mémoire sur les états de Foix, 1608–1789* (Toulouse, 1904), 78–81. For examples of the tyranny of earlier governors, see ibid., 74–78. For an account of the estates and other events in the Pyrennes, see J. H. M. Salmon, "The Audijos Revolt: Provincial Liberties and Institutional Rivalries under Louis XIV," *European History Quarterly* 14 (1984): 119–49.

32. Louis XIV, *Mémoires*, trans. Sonnino, 111.

33. P. Héliot, "La Guerre dite de Lustucru et les privilèges du Boulonnais," *Revue du Nord* 21 (1935): 286.

34. R. Favier, "Les Assemblées du Dauphiné après la suspension des états en 1628," *Cahiers d'histoire* 24 (1979): 59–69. For the escartons, a term used for the jurisdictions in the mountains, see Harriet G. Rosenberg, *A Negotiated World: Three Centuries of Change in a French Alpine Valley* (Toronto, 1988), 39–74.

35. Jean-Pierre Gutton, "Les Etats de Lyonnais, XVe–XVIIe siècles," in *L'Europe, l'Alsace et la France: Problèmes interieures et relations internationales à l'époque moderne*,

ed. Jean Bérenger et al. (Colmar, 1986), 158 and n. 56. *Documents sur les trois états du pays et comté de Forez,* ed. Etienne Fournial and Jean-Pierre Gutton (Saint-Etienne, 1989), 2: 16, 325–53.

36.   Pierre Blet, *Le Clergé de France et la monarchie* (Rome, 1959), 2: 286. For Colbert's attitude towards the assemblies, see Louis Serbat, *Les Assemblées du clergé de France: Origines, organisation, développement, 1561–1615* (Paris, 1906), 355.

37.   Louis XIV, *Mémoires,* trans. Sonnino, 165.

38.   Solange Deyon, *Du loyalisme au refus: Les Protestants français et leur député général entre la Fronde et la revocation* (Lille, 1976).

39.   My treatment of Louis's relations with the magistrates is derived largely from Albert N. Hamscher, *The Parlement of Paris after the Fronde, 1653–1673* (Pittsburgh, 1976); and *The Conseil privé and the Parlements in the Age of Louis XIV: A Study in French Absolutism* (Philadelphia, 1987).

40.   Sarah Hanley, *The Lit de Justice of the Kings of France* (Princeton, 1983), 327.

41.   Philip Benedict, "French Cities from the Sixteenth Century to the Revolution: An Overview," in his *Cities and Social Change in Early Modern France* (London, 1989), 33–36.

42.   Hilton L. Root, *Peasants and King in Burgundy: Agrarian Foundations of French Absolutism* (Berkeley and Los Angeles, 1987).

43.   Louis XIV, *Mémoires,* trans. Sonnino, 79–80.

44.   For an account of the disorders, see Roger Mettam, *Power and Faction in Louis XIV's France* (Oxford, 1988), 309–22.

45.   Roland Mousnier, *Le Conseil du roi de Louis XII à la Révolution* (Paris, 1970), 17–20.

46.   Jean Meyer, *Le Poids de l'état* (Paris, 1983), 63, 138–43.

47.   Pierre Chaunu, "L'Etat," in *Histoire économique et sociale de la France* (Paris, 1977), 1, pt. 1: 47. Orest Ranum, *Artisans of Glory* (Chapel Hill, N.C., 1980), 169–77. Armand Rebillon, *Les Etats de Bretagne de 1661 à 1789* (Paris, 1932), 94–96. William F. Church, "France," in *National Consciousness, History, and Political Culture in Early-Modern Europe,* ed. Orest Ranum (Baltimore, 1975), 43–66.

Bibliography

This book deals primarily with the relations between the French crown and the provincial estates and with the role the nobility played as the dominant order in society. For a survey of the archival and printed material on the estates, see my "French Representative Assemblies: Research Opportunities and Research Published," Studies in Medieval and Renaissance History 1 (1964): 183–219; reprinted in The Monarchy, the Estates, and the Aristocracy in Renaissance France (London, 1988). For more specific information on the material I have used on the estates, see the bibliography in my Representative Government in Early Modern France (New Haven, 1980), cited as "Major" in the notes to this book.

To understand the political and administrative history of this period, it is necessary to consider the viewpoints of both Paris and the provinces. With this in mind, I explored six depositories in or near Paris and the diplomatic correspondence concerning France in the Public Record Office in London. I have also made use of material found in approximately twenty departmental and thirty-five communal archives, including those deposited in departmental archives. Among the Paris depositories, I found the decrees of the king's council, for the most part located in the Archives nationales, series E; the Richelieu papers, housed in the Archives des Affaires étrangères; and the correspondence of Bellièvre and other statesmen in the Bibliothèque nationale to be of great value.

Archival material for the study of the French nobility is scattered throughout nearly all the Parisian and departmental depositories, and much remains in private hands. I have only sampled the vast collection of some four thousand cahiers and cartons relating to the finances of the house of Foix-Navarre-Albret in the Archives départementales, Pyrénées atlantique, and the massive collection of homages deposited in series P of the Archives nationales. Therefore, my debt to other historians for their published documents and studies concerning the nobility is especially great.

PRIMARY SOURCES

Albisson, Jean, ed. *Loixs municipales et économiques de Languedoc.* 7 vols. Montpellier, 1780.

Barthélemy, E. de. *Dictionnaire des anoblissements, extrait des registres de la Chambre des comptes depuis 1345 jusqu'en 1660.* Paris, 1875.

Bassompierre, *Journal de ma vie: Mémoires du maréchal de Bassompierre.* Edited by Audoin de La Cropte de Chantérac. 4 vols. Paris, 1870–77.

Birch, Thomas, ed. *An Historical View of the Negociations between the Courts of England, France, and Brussels from the Year 1592 to 1617*. London, 1749.

Bodin, Jean. *Les Six Livres de la république*. Paris, ed. of 1583. Kenneth D. McRae has edited Richard Knolles's translation of 1606 entitled *The Six Bookes of a Commonweale*. Cambridge, Mass., 1962.

Boislisle, A. M. de, ed. *Correspondance des contrôleurs généraux des finances avec les intendants des provinces*. 3 vols. Paris, 1874–97.

Bonet, Honoré, *The Tree of Battles*. Edited by C. W. Coopland. Cambridge, Mass., 1949.

Buisseret, D., and B. Barbiche, eds. "Lettres inédites de Sully à Henri IV et à Villeroy." *Annuaire-bulletin de la Société de l'histoire de France, années 1974–1975*, 81–117.

Catalogue des actes de Henri II. 3 vols. to date. Paris, 1979–.

Coke, Sir Edward. *The First Part of the Institutes of the Laws of England; or, a Commentary upon Littleton*. London, ed. of 1794.

Colbert, Jean-Baptiste. *Lettres, instructions et mémoires de Colbert*. Edited by Pierre Clément. 7 vols. Paris, 1861–73.

Collection des procès-verbaux des Assemblées-générales du Clergé de France. 9 vols. Paris, 1767–80.

Combes, Jean, *Traité des tailles et autres charges*. Paris, 1584.

Commynes, Philippe de. *Mémoires*. Edited by J. Calmette. 3 vols. Paris, 1924–25.

Depping, G. B., ed. *Correspondance administrative sous le règne de Louis XIV*. 4 vols. Paris, 1850–55.

Du Moulin, Charles. *Omnia Quae Extant Opera*. Paris, 1681.

Durand, Yves, ed. "Cahiers de doléances de la noblesse des gouvernements d'Orléanais, Normandie et Bretagne pour les états généraux de 1614." *Enquêtes et documents* 1 (1971): 53–134.

———. *Cahiers de doléances du bailliage de Troyes pour les états généraux de 1614*. Paris, 1966.

Erasmus, Desiderius. *The Education of a Christian Prince*. Translated by Lester K. Born. New York, 1936.

Escouchy, Mathieu d'. *Chronique*. Edited by G. du Fresne de Beaucourt. 3 vols. Paris, 1863–64.

Fierville, Charles, ed. *Documents inédits sur Philippe de Commynes*. Paris, 1881.

Fontenay-Mareuil, François Duval, marquis de. "Mémoires de Fontenay-Mareuil." In *Nouvelle collection des mémoires pour servir à l'histoire de France*, 2d ser., vol. 5. Edited by Joseph Michaud and Jean-J.-F. Poujoulat. Paris, 1837.

Fournial, Etienne, and Jean-Pierre Gutton, eds. *Documents sur les trois états du pays et comté de Forez*. 2 vols. Saint-Etienne, 1987–89.

Garnier, Joseph, ed. *Correspondance de la mairie de Dijon*. 3 vols. Dijon, 1868–70.

————. *Inventaire-sommaire des archives départementales antérieures à 1790, Côte-d'Or, sér. C.* vols. 3–4. Dijon, 1886–90.

Harlay de Sancy, Achille de. *Response au libelle intitulé: Très-humble, très-véritable, et très-importants remonstrance au roy.* N.p., 1632.

Hennequin, Jean, *Le Guidon général des finances.* Paris, 1585.

Henri IV. *Recueil des lettres missives de Henri IV.* Edited by Berger de Xivrey. 9 vols. Paris, 1843–76.

Hotman, François, *Francogallia.* Edited by R. E. Giesey and J. H. M. Salmon. Cambridge, 1972.

Jacotin, Antoine, ed. *Preuves de la maison de Polignac.* 5 vols. Paris, 1898–1906.

Jusserand, J. J., ed. *Recueil des instructions données aux ambassadeurs et ministres de France depuis les traités de Westphalie jusqu'à la Révolution française.* Vol. 24. Paris, 1929.

La Barre, René-Laurent. *Formulaire des esleuz.* Rouen, 1622.

Le Caron, Louis. *Responses et décisions du droict françois.* Paris, 1612.

Ligou, Daniel, ed. *L'Intendance de Bourgogne à la fin du XVIIe siècle.* Paris, 1988.

Louis XI. *Lettres de Louis XI, roi de France.* Edited by Joseph Vaësen and Etienne Charavay. 11 vols. Paris, 1883–1909.

Louis XIV. *Louis XIV King of France and of Navarre: Mémoires for the Instruction of the Dauphin.* Translated by Paul Sonnino. New York, 1970.

Loyseau, Charles. *Livre des ordres et simples dignitez.* In *Les Oeuvres.* Paris, 1660.

Lublinskaya, A. D., ed. *Lettres et mémoires adressés au Chancelier P. Séguier, 1633–1649.* Moscow, 1966.

Machiavelli, Niccolò. *The Prince.* Translated by L. Ricci. Revised by E. R. P. Vincent. New York, 1930.

Masselin, Jehan. *Journal des états généraux de France tenus à Tours en 1484 sous le règne de Charles VII.* Edited by A. Bernier. Paris, 1835.

Maulde-la-Claviére, René-Alphonse-Marie de, ed. *Procédures politiques du règne de Louis XII.* Paris, 1885.

Mazarin, Jules. *Lettres du Cardinal Mazarin pendant son ministère.* Edited by A. Chéruel. 9 vols. Paris, 1872–1906.

Mercure françois. 25 vols. Paris, 1613–48.

Mirot, Léon, and Jean-Pierre Babelon, eds. *Hommages rendus à la Chambre de France: Chambre des comptes de Paris, Série P.* 3 vols. Paris, 1982–85.

Mollat, Michel, ed. *Comptes généraux de l'état Bourguignon entre 1416 et 1420.* Parts 1–3. Paris, 1965–76.

Moreil, Françoise, ed. *L'Intendance de Languedoc à la fin du XVIIe siécle.* Paris, 1985.

Mousnier, Roland, ed. *Lettres et mémoires adressés au Chancelier Séguier, 1633–1649.* 2 vols. Paris, 1964.

Mousnier, Roland, J. P. Labatut, and Yves Durand, eds. *Problèmes de stratification sociale: Deux cahiers de la noblesse pour les états généraux de 1649–1651*. Paris, 1965.

Ordonnances des rois de France de la troisième race. 21 vols. Paris, 1723–1849.

Ordonnances des rois de France, règne de François I. 9 vols. to date. Paris, 1902–.

Peiresc, Nicolas Claude Fabri de. *Lettres de Peiresc*. Edited by Philippe Tamizey de Larroque. 7 vols. Paris, 1888–98.

Péricaud, Antoine, ed. *Notes et documents pour servir à l'histoire de Lyon sous le règne d'Henri IV, 1594–1610*. Lyons, 1845.

"Procès-verbal et pièces relatives à la convocation du ban de la noblesse de la sénéchaussée de Sarlat." *Archives historiques du département de la Gironde* 18 (1878): 260–318.

Recueil des cahiers généraux des trois ordres aux états généraux. Edited by Lalource and Duval. 4 vols. Paris, 1789.

Recueil des édits, déclarations, lettres-patentes, arrêts du conseil . . . concernant l'administration des états de Bourgogne. 2 vols. Dijon, 1784–87.

Recueil général des anciennes lois françaises depuis l'an 420 jusqu'à la Révolution de 1789. Edited by François A. Isambert et al. 29 vols. Paris 1821–33.

Richelieu, Armand Jean du Plessis, cardinal de. *Lettres, instructions diplomatiques et papiers d'état du Cardinal de Richelieu*. Edited by Denis-L.-M. Avenel. 8 vols. Paris, 1853–78.

———. "Mémoires du Cardinal de Richelieu." In *Nouvelle collection des mémoires pour servir à l'histoire de France*, 2d ser., vol. 8. Ed. Joseph Michaud and Jean-J.-F. Poujoulat. Paris, 1838.

———. *Mémoires du Cardinal de Richelieu*. Edited by Horric de Beaucaire, Roger Gaucheron, Emile Dermenghem, and Robert Lavollée. 10 vols. Paris, 1907–31.

———. *Les Papiers de Richelieu*. Edited by Pierre Grillon. 6 vols. to date. Paris, 1975–.

———. *The Political Testament of Cardinal Richelieu*. Translated by Henry B. King. Madison, Wis., 1961.

Robillard de Beaurepaire, Charles de, ed. *Cahiers des états de Normandie sous le règne de Henri IV*. 2 vols. Rouen, 1880–82.

Saint-Julien de Balleure, Pierre de. *De l'origine des Bourgongnons et antiquité des estats de Bourgongne*. Paris, 1581.

Saulx, Gaspard de, seigneur de Tavannes. "Mémoires de Gaspard de Saulx, seigneur de Tavannes." In *Nouvelle collection des mémoires pour servir à l'histoire de France*, 1st ser., vol. 8. Edited by Joseph F. Michaud and Jean-J.-F. Poujoulat. Paris 1838.

Savaron, Jean. *Les Origines de Clermont, ville capitale d'Auvergne*. Clermont, 1607.

Seyssel, Claude de. *La Monarchie de France*. Edited by Jacques Poujol. Paris, 1961.

Tartière, Henri. *Etats généraux de Pontoise: Cahier du tiers état.* Mont-de-Marsan, 1967.

Thaumas de la Thaumassière, Gaspard. *Nouveaux commentaires sur les coutumes générales des pays et duché de Berri.* Bourges, ed. of 1701.

Thierry, Augustin, ed. *Recueil des monuments inédits de l'histoire du tiers état.* 4 vols. Paris, 1850–70.

Tollemer, A., ed. *Un Sire de Gouberville.* Paris, ed. of 1972.

Tuetey, Alexandre, ed. *Registres des délibérations du bureau de la ville de Paris.* Vol. 5. Paris, 1892.

Vic, Claude de, and Jean Vaissete. *Histoire générale de Languedoc.* 15 vols. Toulouse, 1872–92.

SECONDARY WORKS

GENERAL

Allmand, C. T. *Lancastrian Normandy, 1415–1450.* Oxford, 1983.

Antoine, Michel. "Colbert et la révolution de 1661." In *Un Nouveau Colbert,* edited by Roland Mousnier, 99–109. Paris, 1985.

———. *Le Dur Métier de roi.* Paris, 1986.

———. "Genèse de l'institution des intendants." *Journal des Savants,* 1982: 283–317.

Aristide, Isabelle. *La Fortune de Sully.* Paris, 1990.

Bailey, Donald A. "The Family and Early Career of Michel de Marillac (1560–1632)." In *Society and Institutions in Early Modern France,* edited by Mack P. Holt, 170–89. Athens, Ga., 1991.

Baratier, Edouard. *La Démographie provençale du XIIIe au XVIe siècle.* Paris, 1971.

Barbiche, Bernard. "La Hiérarchie des dignités et des charges au début du dix-septième siècle d'après l'état des taxes des voyages du 25 août 1601." *XVIIe Siècle* 157 (1987): 359–70.

———. *Sully.* Paris, 1978.

Barnavi, Elie. "Fidèles et partisans dans la Ligue parisienne, 1585–1594." In *Hommage à Roland Mousnier: Clientèles et fidélités en Europe à l'époque moderne,* edited by Yves Durand, 139–52. Paris, 1981.

———. *Le Parti de Dieu.* Brussels, 1980.

Barnavi, Elie, and Robert Descimon. *La Sainte Ligue, le juge et la potence: L'Assassinat du président Brisson.* Paris, 1985.

Baumgartner, Frederic J. *Henry II.* Durham, N.C., 1988.

———. *Change and Continuity in the French Episcopate: The Bishops and the Wars of Religion, 1547–1610.* Durham, N.C., 1986.

Bautier, Robert-Henri. "Recherches sur les routes de l'Europe médiévale." *Bulletin philologique et historique (jusqu'à 1610) du Comité des travaux historiques et scientifiques,* 1960, 1: 99–143.

Baxter, Douglas Clark. *Servants of the Sword: French Intendants of the Army, 1630–1670.* Urbana, Ill., 1976.

Bayard, Françoise. *Le Monde des financiers au XVIIe siècle.* Paris, 1988.

Becquart, N. "Les Aliénations du temporel ecclésiastique au diocèse de Périgueux de 1563 à 1585." *Annales du Midi* 86 (1974): 325–33.

Beik, William. *Absolutism and Society in Seventeenth-Century France.* Cambridge, 1985.

Benedict, Philip. "Civil War and Natural Disaster in Northern France." In *The European Crisis of the 1590's,* edited by Peter Clark, 84–105. London, 1985.

———. "French Cities from the Sixteenth Century to the Revolution: An Overview." In id., *Cities and Social Change in Early Modern France,* 7–78. London, 1989.

———. "La Population réformée française de 1600 à 1685." *Annales: Economies, sociétés, civilisations* 42 (1987): 1433–65.

———. *Rouen during the Wars of Religion.* Cambridge, 1981.

Bercé, Yves-Marie. *Histoire des Croquants.* Geneva, 1974.

Bergin, Joseph. *Cardinal Richelieu: Power and the Pursuit of Wealth.* New Haven, 1985.

———. *The Rise of Richelieu.* New Haven, 1991.

Bergin, Joseph, and Laurence Brockliss, eds. *Richelieu and His Age.* Oxford, 1992.

Blanchard, Anne. "Les Officiers militaires en Languedoc: Montpellier durant le règne de Louis XIV." In *Actes du 103e Congrès national des sociétés savantes, Nancy-Metz, 1978,* 1: 65–77. Paris, 1979.

Bloch, Marc. *Les Caractères originaux de l'histoire rurale française.* 2d ed. 2 vols. Paris, 1955.

Bluche, François. *Louis XIV.* Translated by Mark Greengrass. Oxford, 1990.

———. *Les Magistrats du Parlement de Paris au XVIIIe siècle, 1715–1771.* Paris, 1960.

Bluche, François, and Pierre Durye. *L'Anoblissement par charges avant 1789.* 2 vols. La Roche-sur-Yon, 1962.

Boiteux, L.-A. *Richelieu, grand maître de la navigation et du commerce en France.* Paris, 1955.

Bonney, Richard. *The King's Debts: Finance and Politics in France, 1589–1661.* Oxford, 1981.

———. *Political Change in France under Richelieu and Mazarin, 1624–1661.* Oxford, 1978.

———. "The Secret Expenses of Richelieu and Mazarin, 1624–1661." *English Historical Review* 91 (1976): 825–36.

———. "Was There a Bourbon Style of Government?" In *From Valois to Bourbon: Dynasty, State and Society in Early Modern France,* ed. Keith Cameron, 161–77. Exeter, 1989.

Bordes, Maurice. "De la création des élections en Guyenne et Gascogne." *Annales du Midi* 98 (1986): 257–65.

Boüard, Michel de, ed. *Histoire de la Normandie*. Toulouse, 1970.

Boucher, Jacqueline. *Société et mentalités autour de Henri III*. 4 vols. Lyons, 1981.

Boutruche, Robert, ed. *Histoire de Bordeaux*. Vol. 4. Bordeaux, 1966.

Brancourt, J.-P. "La Monarchie et les châteaux du XVIe au XVIIIe siècle." *XVIIe Siècle* 118 (1978): 25–36.

Braudel, F., and E. Labrousse, eds. *Histoire économique et sociale de la France*. 4 vols. Paris, 1970–82.

Bridge, John S. C. *A History of France from the Death of Louis XI*. 5 vols. Oxford, 1921–36.

Brockliss, L. W. *French Higher Education in the Seventeenth and Eighteenth Centuries*. Oxford, 1987.

———. "Patterns of Attendance at the University of Paris, 1400–1800." *Historical Journal* 21 (1978): 503–41.

Brown, E. H. Phelps, and Sheila V. Hopkins. "Wage-Rates and Prices: Evidence for Population Pressure in the Sixteenth Century." *Economica*, n.s., 24 (1957): 289–306.

Buisseret, David. *Sully*. London, 1968.

Chabod, Federico. "Was There a Renaissance State?" In *The Development of the Modern State*, edited by Heinz Lubasz, 26–42. New York, 1964.

Chamberland, Albert. *Le Conflit de 1597 entre Henri IV et le parlement de Paris*. Paris, 1904.

Chartier, Roger, Dominique Julia, and Marie-Madeleine Compère. *L'Education en France du XVIe au XVIIIe siécle*. Paris, 1976.

Chartier, Roger, and Hugues Neveux. "La Ville dominante et soumise." In *Histoire de la France urbaine*, edited by Georges Duby, 3: 16–385. Paris 1981.

Chaunu, Pierre. "L'Etat." In *Histoire économique et sociale de la France*, edited by Fernand Braudel and Ernest Labrousse, 1, pt. 1: 9–228. Paris, 1977.

Chevalier, Bernard. "The *bonnes villes* and the King's Council in Fifteenth-Century France." In *The Crown and Local Communities in England and France in the Fifteenth Century*, edited by J. R. L. Highfield and R. Jeffs, 110–28. Gloucester, 1981.

———. "L'Etat et les bonnes villes en France au temps de leur accord perfait (1450–1550)." In *La Ville, la bourgeoisie et la genèse de l'état moderne (XIIe–XVIIIe siècles)*, edited by Neithard Bulst and Jean-Philippe Genet, 71–85. Paris, 1988.

———. "The Policy of Louis XI towards the *bonnes villes*: The Case of Tours." In *The Recovery of France in the Fifteenth Century*, edited by P. S. Lewis, 265–93. London, 1971.

———. *Tours, ville royale, 1356–1520*. Louvain and Paris, 1975.

Chevallier, Pierre. *Henri III.* Paris, 1985.

———. *Louis XIII.* Paris, 1979.

———. "La Véritable Journée des dupes." *Mémoires de la Société académique de l'Aube* 108 (1974–77): 193–253.

Church, William F. *Constitutional Thought in Sixteenth-Century France.* Cambridge, Mass., 1941.

———. "France." In *National Consciousness, History, and Political Culture in Early-Modern Europe,* edited by Orest Ranum, 43–66. Baltimore, 1975.

———. *Richelieu and Reason of State.* Princeton, 1972.

Clamageran, Jean-J. *Histoire de l'impôt en France.* 3 vols. Paris, 1867–76.

Clarke, Jack A. *Huguenot Warrior: The Life and Times of Henri de Rohan, 1579–1638.* The Hague, 1966.

Cloulas, Ivan. *Henri II.* Paris, 1985.

Collins, James B. *Fiscal Limits of Absolutism.* Berkeley and Los Angeles, 1988.

Contamine, Philippe. *La France au XIVe et XVe siècles: Hommes, mentalités, guerre et paix.* London, 1981.

———. *Guerre, état et société à la fin du moyen âge.* Paris, 1972.

———. *War in the Middle Ages.* Translated by Michael Jones. Oxford, 1984.

Cooper, J. P. "Patterns of Inheritance and Settlement by Great Landowners from the Fifteenth to the Eighteenth Centuries." In *Family and Inheritance,* edited by Jack Goody, Joan Thirsk, and E. P. Thompson, 192–327. Cambridge, 1976.

Corvisier, André. *L'Armée française de la fin du XVIIe siècle au ministère de Choiseul.* 2 vols. Paris, 1964.

———. *Armies and Societies in Europe, 1494–1789.* Translated by A. T. Siddall. Bloomington, Ind., 1979.

———. *Louvois.* Paris, 1983.

Cummings, Mark L. "The Long Robe and the Scepter: A Quantitative Study of the Parlement of Paris and the French Monarchy in the Early Seventeenth Century." Ph.D. diss., University of Colorado, 1974.

———. "The Social Impact of the Paulette: The Case of the Parlement of Paris." *Canadian Journal of History* 15 (1980): 329–54.

Davis, Natalie Z. "Sixteenth-Century French Arithmetics on the Business Life." *Journal of the History of Ideas* 21 (1960): 18–48.

Denault, Gerard F. "The Legitimation of the Parlement of Paris and the Estates General of France, 1560–1614." Ph.D. diss., Washington University, 1975.

Denzer, Horst, ed. *Jean Bodin: Proceedings of the International Conference on Bodin in Munich.* Munich, 1973.

Descimon, Robert. "Qui étaient les Seize?" *Mémoires de la Fédération des sociétés historiques et archéologiques de Paris et de l'Ile-de-France* 34 (1983): 1–300.

Desportes, P. "La Population de Reims au XVe siècle d'après un dénombrement de 1422." *Le Moyen Age* 72 (1966): 463–509.

Dessert, Daniel. *Argent, pouvoir et société au grand siècle.* Paris, 1984.

———. *Fouquet.* Paris, 1987.

———. "Pouvoir et finance au XVIIe siècle: La Fortune du Cardinal Mazarin." *Revue d'histoire moderne et contemporaine* 23 (1976): 161–81.

Dethan, Georges. *Mazarin un homme de paix à l'âge baroque, 1602–1661.* Paris, 1981.

Devèze, Michel. *La Vie de la forêt française au XVIe siècle.* 2 vols. Paris, 1961.

Deyon, Solange. *Du loyalisme au refus: Les Protestants français et leur député général entre la Fronde et la revocation.* Lille, 1976.

Diefendorf, Barbara. "The Catholic League: Social Crisis or Apocalypse Now?" *French Historical Studies* 15 (1987): 332–44.

Doucet, Roger. *Etude sur le gouvernement de François Ier dans ses rapports avec le Parlement de Paris.* 2 vols. Paris, 1921.

———. *Les Institutions de la France au XVIe siècle.* 2 vols. Paris, 1948.

Doyle, William. *The Parlement of Bordeaux and the End of the Old Regime, 1771–1790.* London, 1974.

Drouot, Henri. *Mayenne et la Bourgogne.* 2 vols. Paris, 1937.

Duby, Georges, ed. *Histoire de la France urbaine.* 5 vols. Paris, 1980–85.

Duby, Georges, and Armand Wallon, eds. *Histoire de la France rurale.* Vol. 2. Tours, 1975.

Dupâquier, Jacques, ed. *Histoire de la population française.* Vols. 1 and 2. Paris, 1988.

Dupont-Ferrier, Gustave. *La Formation de l'état français et l'unité française.* 3d ed. Paris, 1946.

———. *Les Officiers royaux des bailliages et sénéchaussées et les institutions monarchiques locales en France à la fin du moyen âge.* Paris, 1902.

Durand, Yves. "Les Républiques urbaines en France à la fin du XVIe siècle." *Annales de la Société d'histoire et d'archéologie de l'arrondissement de Saint-Malo,* 1990: 205–44.

———, ed. *Hommage à Roland Mousnier: Clientèles et fidélités en Europe à la époque moderne.* Paris, 1981.

Edelstein, Marilyn M. "Les Origines sociales de l'episcopat sous Louis XII et François Ier." *Revue d'histoire moderne et contemporaine* 24 (1977): 239–47.

Farr, James R. *Hands of Honor: Artisans and Their World in Dijon, 1550–1650.* Ithaca, N.Y., 1988.

Finley-Croswhite, Annette. "Henry IV and the Towns: Royal Authority and Municipal Autonomy, 1589–1610." Ph.D. diss., Emory University, 1990.

Floquet, Amable. *Histoire du parlement de Normandie.* 7 vols. Rouen, 1840–42.

Fourmont, Hyacynthe de. *Histoire de la chambre des comptes de Bretagne.* Paris, 1854.

Fourquin, Guy. *Les Campagnes de la région parisienne à la fin du moyen âge.* Paris, 1964.

Franklin, Julian H. *Jean Bodin and the Rise of Absolutist Theory.* Cambridge, 1973.

Frijhoff, Willem, and Dominique Julia. *Ecole et société dans la France d'ancien régime.* Paris, 1975.

Giesey, Ralph E. *The Royal Funeral Ceremony in Renaissance France.* Geneva, 1960.

————. "Rules of Inheritance and Strategies of Mobility in Prerevolutionary France." *American Historical Review* 82 (1977): 271–89.

Goubert, Pierre. *Beauvais et le Beauvaisis de 1600 à 1730.* 2 vols. Paris, 1960.

Greengrass, Mark. *The French Reformation.* Oxford, 1987.

Griselle, E. "Louis XIII et sa mère." *Revue historique* 105 (1910): 302–31; 106 (1911): 83–100, 295–308.

Guenée, Bernard. "Espace et état dans la France du bas moyen âge." *Annales: Economies, sociétés, civilisations* 23 (1968): 744–58.

————. "L'Histoire de l'état en France à la fin du moyen âge, vue par les historiens français depuis cent ans." *Revue historique* 232 (1964): 331–60.

————. *Tribunaux et gens de justice dans le bailliage de Senlis à la fin du moyen âge.* Paris, 1963.

Guichonnet, Paul, ed., *Histoire de la Savoie.* Toulouse, 1973.

Hale, J. R. "The Early Development of the Bastion: An Italian Chronology, c. 1440–c. 1534." In *Europe in the Later Middle Ages,* edited by J. R. Hale, J. R. L. Highfield and B. Smalley, 466–94. Evanston, Ill., 1965.

Hamscher, Albert N. *The Conseil privé and the Parlements in the Age of Louis XIV: A Study in French Absolutism.* Philadelphia, 1987.

————. *The Parlement of Paris after the Fronde, 1653–1673.* Pittsburgh, 1976.

Hanley, Sarah. *The Lit de Justice of the Kings of France.* Princeton, 1983.

Harding, Robert, "Revolution and Reform in the Holy League: Angers, Rennes, Nantes." *Journal of Modern History* 53 (1981): 379–416.

Harsgor, Mikhaël. *Recherches sur le personnel du conseil du roi sous Charles VIII et Louis XII.* 4 vols. Lille, 1980.

Héliot, P. "La Guerre dite de Lustucru et les privilèges du Boulonnais." *Revue du Nord* 21 (1935): 265–318.

Henneman, John Bell. *Royal Taxation in Fourteenth-Century France: The Captivity and Ransom of John II, 1356–1370.* Philadelphia, 1976.

Hickey, Daniel. *The Coming of French Absolutism: The Struggle for Tax Reform in the Province of Dauphiné, 1540–1640.* Toronto, 1986.

Hoffman, Philip T. "Taxes and Agrarian Life in Early Modern France: Land Sales, 1550–1730." *Journal of Economic History* 46 (1986): 37–55.

Holt, Mack P. "Wine, Community and the Reformation in Sixteenth-Century Burgundy." *Past and Present* 138 (1993): 58–93.

———, ed. *Society and Institutions in Early Modern France.* Athens, Ga., 1991.

Huppert, George. *Public Schools in Renaissance France.* Urbana, 1984.

Jacquart, Jean. *La Crise rurale en Ile-de-France, 1550–1670.* Paris, 1974.

———. "Immobilisme et catastrophes, 1560–1660." In *Histoire de la France rurale,* vol 2, edited by Georges Duby and Armand Wallon, 175–353. Paris, 1975.

Jedin, Hubert. *Crisis and Closure of the Council of Trent.* Translated by N. D. Smith. London, 1967.

Jouanna, Arlette. *Ordre social: Mythes et hiérarchies dans la France du XVIᵉ siècle.* Paris, 1977.

Kelley, Donald R. *Foundations of Modern Historical Scholarship.* New York, 1970.

Kendall, Paul M. *Louis XI.* New York, 1971.

Kettering, Sharon. *Judicial Politics and Urban Revolt in Seventeenth-Century France: The Parlement of Aix, 1629–1659.* Princeton, 1978.

Kleinman, Ruth. *Anne of Austria.* Columbus, 1985.

Knecht, R. J. *Francis I.* Cambridge, 1982.

———. *Richelieu.* London, 1991.

Kuhn, Thomas S. *The Structure of Scientific Revolutions.* 2d ed. Chicago, 1970.

Lafon, Jacques. *Régimes matrimoniaux et mutations sociales: Les Epoux bordelais, 1450–1550.* Paris, 1972.

Latreille, André, ed. *Histoire de Lyon et du Lyonnais.* Toulouse, 1975.

Lebrun, François. *Histoire d'Angers.* Toulouse, 1975.

Lebrun, François, Marc Venard, and Jean Quéniart. *Histoire générale de l'enseignement et de l'éducation en France.* Vol. 2, *De Gutenberg aux lumières.* Paris, 1981.

Le Moyne de La Borderie, Arthur. *Histoire de Bretagne.* Vols. 5–6. Rennes, 1913–14.

Le Roy Ladurie, Emmanuel. "Les Masses profondes: La Paysannerie." In *Histoire économique et sociale de la France,* edited by Fernand Braudel and Ernest Labrousse, 1, pt. 2: 481–865. Paris, 1977.

Lewis, P. S. *Later Medieval France.* New York, 1968.

Little, Roger G. *The Parlement of Poitiers: War, Government and Politics in France, 1418–1436.* London, 1984.

Lot, Ferdinand. *Recherches sur les effectifs des armées françaises des guerres d'Italie aux guerres de religion, 1492–1562.* Paris, 1962.

Lublinskaya, A. D. *French Absolutism: The Crucial Phase, 1620–1629.* Translated by Brian Pierce. Cambridge, 1968.

Major, J. Russell. "Popular Initiative in Renaissance France." In *Aspects of the Renaissance,* edited by A. R. Lewis, 27–41. Austin, 1967.

————. "The Renaissance Monarchy: A Contribution to the Periodization of History." *Emory University Quarterly* 13 (1957): 112–24. Reprinted in *The "New Monarchies" and Representative Assemblies: Medieval Constitutionalism or Modern Absolutism?* edited by A. J. Slavin. Boston, 1964.

————. "The Renaissance Monarchy As Seen by Erasmus, More, Seyssel, and Machiavelli." In *Action and Conviction in Early Modern Europe: Essays in Memory of E. H. Harbison,* edited by T. K. Rabb and J. E. Siegel, 17–31. Princeton, 1969.

Mariéjol, Jean-H. *Histoire de France.* Vol. 6, pt. 2. Ed. E. Lavisse. Paris, 1911.

Martin, Xavier. *Le Principe d'égalité dans les successions roturierès en Anjou et dans le Maine.* Paris, 1972.

Mastellone, Salvo. *La Reggenza di Maria de' Medici.* Florence, 1962.

Maugis, Edouard. *Histoire du parlement de Paris.* 3 vols. Paris, 1914–16.

Mettam, Roger. *Power and Faction in Louis XIV's France.* Oxford, 1988.

Meyer, Jean. *Le Poids de l'état.* Paris, 1983.

Michaud, Claude. "Finances et guerres de religion en France." *Revue de histoire moderne et contemporaine* 28 (1981): 572–96.

————. "Notariat et sociologie de la rente à Paris au XVIIᵉ siècle: L'Emprunt du clergé de 1690." *Annales: Economies, sociétés, civilisations* 32 (1977): 1154–87.

————. "Redistribution foncière en rentière en 1569: Les Aliénations du temporel ecclésiastique dans quatre diocèses du centre de la France." *Revue historique* 267 (1982): 305–56.

Mirot, Léon. *Les d'Orgemont.* Paris, 1913.

Miskimin, Harry A. *Money and Power in Fifteenth-Century France.* New Haven, 1984.

Moote, A. Lloyd. *The Revolt of the Judges: The Parlement of Paris and the Fronde, 1643–1652.* Princeton, 1971.

Mousnier, Roland. *The Assassination of Henry IV.* Translated by J. Spencer. New York, 1973.

————. *Le Conseil du roi de Louis XII à la Révolution.* Paris, 1970.

————. *Etat et société sous François Iᵉʳ et pendant le gouvernement personnel de Louis XIV.* Paris: Les Cours de Sorbonne, n.d.

————. "French Institutions and Society, 1610–1661." In *The New Cambridge Modern History,* vol. 4, edited by J. P. Cooper, 474–502. Cambridge, 1970.

————. *The Institutions of France under the Absolute Monarchy, 1598–1789.* Translated by Arthur Goldhammer. 2 vols. Chicago, 1979–84.

————. "Note sur les rapports entre les gouverneurs de provinces et les intendants dans la première moitié du XVIIᵉ siècle." *Revue historique* 228 (1962): 339–50.

————. "La Participation des gouvernés à l'activité des gouvernants dans la France du XVIIᵉ et du XVIIIᵉ siècles." *Schweizer Beiträge zur Allgemeinen Geschichte* 20 (1962–63): 200–229.

————. *Social Hierarchies, 1450 to the Present.* Translated by Peter Evans. New York, 1973.

————. *La Vénalité des offices sous Henri IV et Louis XIII.* Rouen, 1945. 2d ed. Paris, 1971.

Murat, Inès. *Colbert.* Translated by R. F. Cook and J. Van Asselt. Charlottesville, Va., 1984.

Ourliac, Paul, and J. de Malafosse. *Histoire du droit privé.* 3 vols. Paris, 1961–68.

Pagès, Georges. "Autour du 'Grand Orage.' Richelieu et Marillac: Deux politiques." *Revue historique* 179 (1937): 63–97.

————. *La Monarchie d'ancien régime en France.* 4th ed. Paris, 1946.

————. "La Vénalité des offices dans l'ancienne France." *Revue historique* 169 (1932):477–95.

Parker, David. *The Making of French Absolutism.* London, 1983.

Pavie, Eusèbe. *La Guerre entre Louis XIII et Marie de Médicis, 1619–1620.* Angers, 1899.

Pearl, Jonathan L. "Guise and Provence: Political Conflict in the Epoch of Richelieu." Ph.D. diss., Northwestern University, 1968.

Peronnet, Michel C. *Les Evêques de l'ancienne France.* 2 vols. Lille, 1977.

Pillorget, René. *Les Mouvements insurrectionnels de Provence entre 1596 et 1715.* Paris, 1975.

Pollard, A. F. *Factors in Modern History.* New York, 1907.

Porchnev, Boris. *Les Soulèvements populaires en France de 1623 à 1648.* Paris, 1963.

Poumarède, Jacques. *Les Successions dans le sud-ouest de la France au moyen âge.* Paris, 1972.

Prudhomme, A. *Histoire de Grenoble.* Grenoble, 1888.

Ranum, Orest. *Artisans of Glory.* Chapel Hill, N.C., 1980.

————. "Courtesy, Absolutism, and the Rise of the French State, 1630–1660." *Journal of Modern History* 52 (1980): 426–51.

————. *Richelieu and the Councillors of Louis XIII.* Oxford, 1963.

Rigaudière, Albert. *Saint-Flour, ville d'Auvergne au bas moyen âge.* 2 vols. Paris, 1982.

Root, Hilton L. *Peasants and King in Burgundy: Agrarian Foundations of French Absolutism.* Berkeley and Los Angeles, 1987.

Rosenberg, Harriet G. *A Negotiated World: Three Centuries of Change in a French Alpine Valley.* Toronto, 1988.

Rossiaud, Jacques. "Prostitution, Youth, and Society in the Towns of Southeastern France in the Fifteenth Century." In *Deviants and the Abandoned in French Society,* edited by Robert Forster and Orest Ranum, 1–46. Baltimore, 1978.

Rouche, Michel. *Histoire générale de l'enseignement de l'éducation en France.* Vol. 1, *Des origines à la Renaissance.* Paris, 1981.

Salmon, J. H. M. *Society in Crisis: France in the Sixteenth Century.* New York, 1975.

Shennan, J. H. *The Parlement of Paris.* London, 1968.

Simmons, R. C. *The American Colonies from Settlement to Independence.* New York, 1976.

Skinner, Quentin. *The Foundations of Modern Political Thought.* 2 vols. Cambridge, 1978.

Soman, A. "Press, Pulpit, and Censorship in France before Richelieu." *Proceedings of the American Philosophical Society* 120 (1976): 439–63.

Stocker, Christopher. "Henry IV and the Echevinage of Orleans." Paper read at the meeting of the Society for French Historical Studies in El Paso, 1992.

Thirsk, Joan. "The European Debate on Customs of Inheritance, 1500–1700." In *Family and Inheritance: Rural Society in Western Europe, 1200–1800,* edited by Jack Goody, Joan Thirsk, and E. P. Thompson, 177–91. Cambridge, 1976.

Tholin, G. "La Ville d'Agen pendant les guerres de religion du XVIᵉ siècle." *Revue de l'Agenais* 20 (1893): 52–67, 177–206.

Thomas, Alexandre. *Une Province sous Louis XIV: Situation politique et administrative de la Bourgogne, de 1661 à 1715.* Paris, 1844.

Vale, Malcolm G. A. *Charles VII.* Berkeley and Los Angeles, 1974.

Wolfe, Martin. *The Fiscal System of Renaissance France.* New Haven, 1972.

Wood, James B. "The Royal Army during the Early Wars of Religion, 1559–1576." In *Society and Institutions in Early Modern France,* edited by Mack P. Holt, 1–35. Athens, Ga., 1991.

THE NOBILITY

Armstrong, C. A. J. "Had the Burgundian Government a Policy for the Nobility?" *Britain and the Netherlands* 2 (1964): 9–32.

Arundel de Condé, G. d'. *Anoblissements maintenues et réhabilitations en Normandie, 1598–1790.* Paris, 1981.

———. *Dictionnaire des anoblis normands, 1600–1790.* Rouen, 1975.

Autrand, Françoise. *Naissance d'un grand corps de l'état: Les Gens du Parlement de Paris, 1345–1454.* Paris, 1981.

Barker, Nancy N. "Philippe d'Orléans, frère unique du roi: Founder of the Family Fortune." *French Historical Studies* 13 (1983): 145–71.

Batiffol, Louis. *Le Roi Louis XIII à vingt ans.* Paris, 1910.

Bellacois, François. *The Duel: Its Rise and Fall in Early Modern France.* Translated by Trista Selous. New Haven, 1990.

Bisson, Thomas N. "Nobility and Family in Medieval France." *French Historical Studies* 16 (1990): 597–615.

Bitton, Davis. *The French Nobility in Crisis, 1560–1640.* Stanford, 1969.

Blangy, Auguste de. *Généalogie des sires de Russy, de Gouberville et du Mesnil au Val.* Caen, 1887.

Bloch, Jean-Richard. *L'Anoblissement en France au temps de François Ier* . Paris, 1934.

Bloch, Marc. *Feudal Society.* Translated by L. A. Manyon. Chicago, 1968.

Bluche, François, and Pierre Durye. *L'Anoblissement par charges avant 1789.* 2 vols. La Roche-sur-Yon, 1962.

Bohanan, Donna. "The Education of Nobles in Seventeenth-Century Aix-en-Provence." *Journal of Social History* 20 (1986–87): 757–64.

———. *Old and New Nobility in Aix-en-Provence, 1600–1695.* Baton Rouge, 1992.

———. "The Sword as the Robe in Seventeenth-Century Provence and Brittany." In *Society and Institutions in Early Modern France,* edited by Mack P. Holt, 51–62. Athens, Ga., 1991.

Bois, Guy. *The Crisis of Feudalism.* Cambridge, 1984.

Bottin, Jacques. *Seigneurs et paysans dans l'ouest du pays de Caux, 1540–1650.* Paris, 1983.

Boulton, D'Arcy Jonathan Dacre. "Dominical Titles of Dignity in France, 1223–1515." Ph.D. diss., University of Pennsylvania, 1978.

———. *The Knights of the Crown.* New York, 1987.

Brink, James E. "The Estates of Languedoc, 1515–1560." Ph.D. diss., University of Washington, 1974.

Caillet, Louis. *Les Ducs de Bourbonnais et la ville de Lyon.* Moulins, 1912.

Caron, Marie-Thérèse. *La Noblesse dans le duché de Bourgogne, 1315–1477.* Lille, 1987.

Charbonnier, Pierre. *Guillaume de Murol: Un Petit Seigneur auvergnat au début du XVe siècle.* Clermont-Ferrand, 1973.

Conchon, Michèle. "Une Budget seigneurial aux XVe et XVIe siècles: Les Comptes de la baronnie de Sully-sur-Loire, 1479–1549." *Positions des thèses, Ecole nationale des Chartes,* 1981: 51–64.

Constant, Jean-Marie. "Les Barons français pendant les guerres de religion." In *Quatrième centenaire de la bataille de Coutras,* 49–62. Pau, 1989.

———. *Les Conjurateurs.* Paris, 1987.

———. "Un Groupe socio-politique stratégique dans la France de la première moitié du XVIIe siècle: La Noblesse seconde." In *L'Etat et les aristocraties,* edited by Philippe Contamine, 279–304. Paris, 1989.

———. *Les Guises.* Paris, 1984.

———. *Nobles et paysans en Beauce aux XVIème et XVIIème siècles.* Lille, 1981.

———. "Quelques problèmes de mobilité sociale et de vie matérielle chez les gentilshommes de Beauce aux XVIe et XVIIe siècles." *Acta Poloniae Historica* 36 (1977): 83–94.

———. "La Troisième Fronde: Les Gentilshommes et les libertés nobiliaires." *XVIIe Siècle* 145 (1984): 341–54.

Contamine, Philippe. "The French Nobility and the War." In *The Hundred Years War,* edited by K. Fowler, 135–62. London, 1971.

―――. "Sur l'ordre de Saint-Michel au temps de Louis XI et de Charles VIII." *Bulletin de la Société nationale des antiquaires de France* 1976: 212–36.

―――, ed. *L'Etat et les aristocraties.* Paris, 1989.

―――. *La Noblesse au moyen âge, XIe–XVe siècles: Essais à la mémoire de Robert Boutruche.* Paris, 1976.

Crouzet, Denis. "Recherches sur la crise de l'aristocratie en France au XVIème siècle: Les Dettes de la maison de Nevers." *Histoire économie et société* 1 (1982): 7–50.

―――. "Royalty, Nobility and Religion: Research on the War in Italy." *Proceedings of the Annual Meeting of the Western Society for French History* 18 (1991): 1–14.

Cubells, Monique. "A propos des usurpations de noblesse en Provence sous l'ancien régime." *Provence historique* 20 (1970): 224–301.

Deloche, Maximin. *La Maison du Cardinal de Richelieu.* Paris, 1912.

Devyver, André. *Le Sang épuré: Les Préjugés de race chez les gentilshommes français de l'ancien régime, 1560–1720.* Brussels, 1973.

Dewald, Jonathan. *The Formation of a Provincial Nobility: The Magistrates of the Parlement of Rouen, 1499–1610.* Princeton, 1980.

―――. *Pont-St.-Pierre, 1398–1789: Lordship, Community, and Capitalism in Early Modern France.* Berkeley and Los Angeles, 1987.

Dravasa, Etienne. *"Vivre noblement": Recherches sur la dérogeance de noblesse du XIVe au XVIe siècles.* Bordeaux, 1965.

Duby, Georges. *The Chivalrous Society.* Translated by C. Postan. Berkeley and Los Angeles, 1977.

Egret, Jean. *Le Parlement de Dauphinè et les affaires publiques dans la deuxième moitié du XVIIIe siècle.* 2 vols. Grenoble, 1942.

Eurich, Amanda. *The Economics of Power: The Private Finances of the House of Foix-Navarre-Albret, 1517–1610.* Kirksville, Mo., 1994.

Fedden, Katherine. *Manor Life in Old France.* New York, 1933.

Gachon, Paul. *Les Etats de Languedoc et l'édit de Béziers, 1632.* Paris, 1887.

Gallet, Jean. "Fidélité et féodalité: Quelques aspects de la fidélité des vassaux en Bretagne au XVIIe siècle." In *Hommage à Roland Mousnier: Clientèles et fidélités en Europe à l'époque moderne,* edited by Yves Durand, 105–22. Paris, 1981.

―――. *La Seigneurie bretonne, 1450–1680.* Paris, 1983.

Greengrass, Mark. "Noble Affinities in Early Modern France: The Case of Henri I de Montmorency, Constable of France." *European History Quarterly* 16 (1986): 275–311.

―――. "Property and Politics in Sixteenth-Century France: The Landed Fortune of Constable Anne de Montmorency." *French History* 2 (1988): 371–98.

Harding, Robert. *Anatomy of a Power Elite: The Provincial Governors of Early Modern France*. New Haven, 1978.

Hollingsworth, T. H. "A Demographic Study of the British Ducal Families." In *Population in History*, edited by D. V. Glass and D. E. C. Eversley. London, 1965.

Holt, Mack P. *The Duke of Anjou and the Politique Struggle during the Wars of Religion*. Cambridge, 1986.

Hommage à Roland Mousnier: Clientèles et fidélités en Europe à l'époque moderne. Edited by Yves Durand. Paris, 1981.

Houdaille, Jacques. "La Noblesse française avant 1600." *Population* 45 (1990): 1070–75.

———. "La Noblesse française, 1600–1900." *Population* 44 (1989): 501–14.

Jeulin, P. "L'Hommage de la Bretagne en droit et dans les faits." *Annales de Bretagne* 41 (1934): 380–473.

Jouanna, Arlette. *Le Devoir de révolte: La Noblesse française et la gestation de l'état moderne*. Paris, 1989.

———. *Ordre social: Mythes et hiérarchies dans la France du XVIᵉ siècle*. Paris, 1977.

Keen, Maurice. *Chivalry*. New Haven, 1984.

Kettering, Sharon. "Clientage during the French Wars of Religion." *Sixteenth-Century Journal* 20 (1989): 221–39.

———. "The Decline of Great Noble Clientage during the Reign of Louis XIV." *Canadian Journal of History* 24 (1989): 157–77.

———. *Patrons, Brokers, and Clients in Seventeenth-Century France*. New York, 1986.

Labatut, Jean-Pierre. *Les Ducs et pairs de France au XVIIᵉ siècle*. Paris, 1972.

Lassaigne, Jean-Dominique. *Les Assemblées de la noblesse de France aux XVIIᵉ et XVIIIᵉ siècles*. Paris, 1965.

Leguai, André. *Les Ducs de Bourbon pendant la crise monarchique du XVᵉ siècle*. Paris, 1962.

Lévy, Claude, and Louis Henry. "Ducs et pairs sous l'ancien régime: Caractéristiques démographiques d'une caste." *Population* 15 (1960): 807–30.

Lewis, P. S. "Decayed and Non-Feudalism in Later Medieval France." *Bulletin of the Institute of Historical Research* 37 (1964): 157–84.

———. *Essays in Later Medieval French History*. London, 1985.

———. "Of Breton *Alliances* and Other Matters." In *War, Literature, and Politics in the Late Middle Ages*, edited by C. T. Allmand, 122–43. Liverpool, 1976.

Lucas, R. H. "Ennoblement in Late Medieval France." *Medieval Studies* 39 (1977): 239–60.

Lyon, Bryce D. *From Fief to Indenture*. New York, 1972.

Major, J. Russell. "'Bastard Feudalism' and the Kiss: Changing Social Mores In Late Medieval and Early Modern France." *Journal of Interdisciplinary History* 17 (1987): 509–35.

———. "The Crown and the Aristocracy in Renaissance France." *American Historical Review* 69 (1964): 631–45. Reprinted in *Lordship and Community in Medieval Europe,* edited by F. L. Cheyette. New York, 1968.

———. "Noble Income, Inflation, and the Wars of Religion in France." *American Historical Review* 86 (1981): 21–48.

———. "The Revolt of 1620: A Study of Ties of Fidelity." *French Historical Studies* 14 (1986): 391–408.

Meyer, Jean. *La Noblesse bretonne au XVIIIe siècle.* 2 vols. Paris, 1966.

Moote, A. Lloyd. *Louis XIII, The Just.* Berkeley and Los Angeles, 1989.

Motley, Mark. *Becoming a French Aristocrat: The Education of the Court Nobility, 1580–1715.* Princeton, 1990.

Mougel, François-Charles. "La Fortune des princes de Bourbon-Conty: Revenus et gestion, 1655–1791." *Revue d'histoire moderne et contemporaine* 18 (1971): 30–49.

Mourier, Jacques. "Nobilitas, quid est? Un Procès à Tain-l'Hermitage en 1408." *Bibliothèque de L'Ecole des Chartres* 142 (1984): 255–69.

Neuschel, Kristen. *Word of Honor: Interpreting Noble Culture in Sixteenth-Century France.* Ithaca, N.Y., 1989.

Norberg, Michael. *Les Ducs et la royauté: Etudes sur la rivalité des ducs d'Orléans et de Bourgogne, 1392–1407.* Uppsala, 1964.

Nordhaus, John David. "*Arma et litterae:* The Education of the *noblesse de race* in Sixteenth-Century France." Ph.D. diss., Columbia University, 1974.

Oppetit-Perné, D. "La Vicomté de Turenne à la fin du XVe siècle: Essai d'histoire économique." *Positions de thèses, Ecole nationale des Chartes* 1971: 137–42.

Orlea, Manfred. *La Noblesse aux états généraux de 1576 et de 1588.* Paris, 1980.

Peret, Jacques. "Seigneurs et seigneuries en Gâtine poitevine: Le Duché de La Meilleraye XVIIe–XVIIIe siècles." *Mémoires de la société des antiquaires de l'Ouest,* 4th ser., 13 (1974–76): 1–269.

Perroy, Edouard. "Social Mobility among the French Noblesse in the Later Middle Ages." *Past and Present* 21 (1962): 25–38.

Plaisse, André. *La Baronnie du Neubourg.* Paris, 1961.

Pocquet du Haut-Jussé, B.-A. "Les Pensionnaires fieffés des ducs de Bourgogne de 1352 à 1419." *Mémoires de la société pour l'histoire du droit et des institutions des anciens pays bourguignons comtois et romands* 8 (1942): 127–50.

Raffin, Léonce. *Saint-Julien de Balleure.* Paris, 1926.

Roche, Daniel. "Aperçus sur le fortune et les revenus des princes de Condé à l'aube du 18e siècle." *Revue d'histoire moderne et contemporaine* 14 (1967): 217–43.

Romier, Lucien. *La Carrière d'un favori: Jacques d'Albon de Saint-André, maréchal de France, 1512–1562.* Paris, 1909.

Salmon, J. H. M. "Storm over the Noblesse." *Journal of Modern History* 53 (1981): 242–57.

Schalk, Ellery. "Ennoblement in France from 1350 to 1660." *Journal of Social History* 16 (Winter 1982): 101–10.

———. *From Valor to Pedigree: Ideas of Nobility in France in the Sixteenth and Seventeenth Centuries.* Princeton, 1986.

Soudé, Godet de. "Dictionnaire des anoblissements: Extrait des registres de la Chambre des Comptes depuis 1345 jusqu'en 1660." *Revue historique nobiliaire et biographique: Recueil de mémoires documents* 1875: 252–74, 301–18.

Stocker, Christopher. "Offices and Officers in the Parlement of Paris, 1483–1515." Ph.D. diss., Cornell University, 1965.

———. "*Parti*, Clientage, and Lineage in the Fifteenth-Century *parlement* of Paris." *Proceedings of the Annual Meeting of the Western Society for French History* 13 (1986): 10–20.

Teall, Elizabeth Salmon. "The Myth of Royal Centralization and the Reality of the Neighborhood: The Journals of the Sire de Gouberville." In *Social Groups and Religious Ideas in the Sixteenth Century,* edited by Miriam Usher Chrisman and Otto Gründler, 1–11. Kalamazoo, Mich., 1978.

———. "The Public Mind of the *noblesse d'épée,* 1484–1589." Ph.D. diss., Radcliffe College, 1974.

Vale, Malcolm G. A. *War and Chivalry.* Athens, Ga., 1981.

Verger, Jacques. "Noblesse et savoir: Etudiants nobles aux universités d'Avignon, Cahors, Montpellier et Toulouse (fin du XIVᵉ siècle)." In *La Noblesse au moyen âge, XIᵉ–XVᵉ siècles: Essais à la mémoire de Robert Boutruche,* edited by Philippe Contamine, 289–313. Paris, 1976.

Viguerie, Jean de. "Contribution à l'histoire de la fidélité: Note sur le serment en France à l'époque des guerres de religion." *Annales de Bretagne et des pays de l'ouest* 82 (1975): 291–95.

Weary, William A. "The House of La Trémoille, Fifteenth through Eighteenth Centuries: Change and Adaptation in a French Noble Family." *Journal of Modern History* 49 (1977), demand article.

———. "Royal Policy and Patronage in Renaissance France: The Monarchy and the House of La Trémoille." Ph.D diss., Yale University, 1972.

Wood, James B. *The Nobility of the Election of Bayeux, 1463–1666.* Princeton, 1980.

THE ESTATES AND ASSEMBLIES

Arnaud, Germain, *Mémoire sur les états de Foix, 1608–1789.* Toulouse, 1904.

Beaune, P. "Henri IV aux députés des états de Bourgogne, 1608." *Le Cabinet historique* 6, pt. 1 (1860): 122–25.

Blet, Pierre. *Les Assemblées du clergé et Louis XIV de 1670 à 1693.* Rome, 1972.

———. *Le Clergé de France et la monarchie: Etude sur les Assemblées générales du clergé de 1615 à 1666.* 2 vols. Rome, 1959.

Bulst, Neithard. "The Deputies at the French Estates General of 1468 and 1484: A Prosopographical Approach." *Medieval Prosopography* 4 (1984): 65–79.

———. "Louis XI et les états généraux de 1468." In *La France de la fin du XVe siècle,* edited by Bernard Chevalier and Philippe Contamine, 91–104. Paris, 1985.

———. "Vers les états modernes: Le Tiers Etat aux états généraux de Tours en 1484." In *Représentation et vouloir politiques autour des états-généraux de 1614,* edited by Roger Chartier and Denis Richet, 11–23. Paris, 1982.

Charlier-Meniolle, R. *L'Assemblée des Notables tenue à Rouen en 1596.* Paris, 1911.

Chartier, Roger, and Denis Richet, eds. *Répresentation et vouloir politiques autour des états généraux de 1614.* Paris, 1982.

Destrée, Alain. *La Basse Navarre et ses institutions de 1620 à la Révolution.* Saragossa, 1955.

Duval, Michel. "Les Premiers Procureurs syndics des états de Bretagne, 1534–1636." In *Actes du 111e Congrès national des sociétés savantes, Poitiers 1986, Section d'histoire moderne et contemporaine,* 1, pt. 1: 7–25. Paris, 1987.

Emmanuelli, Fr.-X. "Pour une réhabilitation de la histoire politique régionale: L'Example de l'assemblée des communautés de Provence, 1660–1786." *Revue historique de droit français et étranger,* 4th ser., 59 (1981): 431–50.

Favier, René. "Les Assemblées du Dauphiné après la suspension des états en 1628," *Cahiers d'histoire* 24 (1979): 59–69.

Gazzaniga, J.-L. "Les Etats généraux de Tours en 1484 et les affaires de l'église." *Revue historique de droit français et étranger* 62 (1984): 31–45.

Gutton, Jean-Pierre. "Les Etats de Lyonnais." In *L'Europe, l'Alsace et la France: Problèmes interieures et relations internationales à l'époque moderne,* edited by Jean Bérenger et al., 151–61. Colmar, 1986.

Hayden, J. Michael. *France and the Estates General of 1614.* Cambridge, 1974.

Koenigsberger, Helmut G. *Estates and Revolutions.* Ithaca, N.Y., 1971.

Krynen, J. "Réflexions sur les idées politiques aux états généraux de Tours de 1484." *Revue historique de droit français et étranger* 62 (1984): 183–204.

Major, J. Russell. *Bellièvre, Sully, and the Assembly of Notables of 1596.* Transactions of the American Philosophical Society, 64 (1974).

———. *The Estates General of 1560.* Princeton, 1951.

———. *The Deputies to the Estates General in Renaissance France.* Madison, Wis., 1960.

———. "Henry IV and Guyenne: A Study Concerning the Origins of Royal Absolutism." *French Historical Studies* 4 (1966): 363–83. Reprinted in *State and*

Society in Seventeenth-Century France, edited by Raymond Kierstead. New York, 1975.

————. *The Monarchy, the Estates, and the Aristocracy in Renaissance France.* London, 1988.

————. *Representative Institutions in Renaissance France, 1421–1559.* Madison, Wis., 1960.

————. "The Third Estate in the Estates General of Pontoise, 1561." *Speculum* 29 (1954): 460–76.

Miller, John. "Les Etats de Languedoc pendant la Fronde." *Annales du Midi* 95 (1983): 43–65.

Montégut, H. de. "Les Etats de Périgord." *Bulletin de la société historique et archéologique du Périgord* 4 (1887): 87–91.

Péronnet, Michel. "Pouvoir monarchique et épiscopat: Le Roi et les évêques députés nés des Etats de Languedoc à l'epoque moderne." *Parliaments, Estates and Representation* 3 (1983): 115–21.

Petit, Jeanne. *L'Assemblée des Notables de 1626–1627.* Paris, 1936.

Picot, Georges. *Histoire des états généraux.* 2d ed. 5 vols. Paris, 1888.

Prentout, Henri. *Les Etats provinciaux de Normandie.* 3 vols. Caen, 1925–27.

Rebillon, Armand. *Les Etats de Bretagne de 1661 à 1789.* Paris, 1932.

Recherches sur les états généraux et les états provinciaux de la France médièvale: Actes du 110e Congrès national des sociétés savantes, Montpellier, 1985, section d'histoire médièvale et de philologie. Vol. 3. Paris, 1986.

Salmon, J. H. M. "The Audijos Revolt: Provincial Liberties and Institutional Rivalries under Louis XIV." *European History Quarterly* 14(1984): 119–49.

Serbat, Louis. *Les Assemblées du clergé de France: Origines, organisation, développement, 1561–1615.* Paris, 1906.

Souriac, René. *Le Comté de Comminges au milieu du XVIe siècle.* Paris, 1977.

Terrell, Joseph M. *A History of the Estates of Poitou.* The Hague, 1968.

Thierry, Augustin. *Essai sur l'histoire de la formation et des progrès du tiers état.* Paris, 1853. Translated by Francis B. Wells as *The Formation and Progress of the Tiers Etat, or Third Estate in France.* 2 vols. London, 1859.

Index

Abbeville, 162
Absolutism. *See* Monarchy,
    absolute
Acarie, Madame, 222
Agen, 137, 212–13, 288
Agenais: estates of, 35, 36,
    37, 38, 141, 192, 194;
    government of, 212–13;
    taille in, 85; town
    meetings in, 115, 288,
    354–55
Agriculture: and French
    nobility, 75–86
Aides, court of. *See* Court of
    aides
Aix: under Louis XIII, 269–
    71; under Louis XIV,
    341–42; nobility in, 323;
    parlement of, 122, 148,
    196, 300; university in,
    333. *See also* Provence
Albisson, Jean, 56
Albret, Amanieu VII d', 88
Albret, Catherine d', 81
Albret, Charles d', 67
Albret, Henri II d': fiefs of,
    76–78, 81; fortification
    of, 91
Albret, Jeanne d', 81, 123,
    127, 157, 202, 203
Albret family: fiefs of, 76–
    81, 83; income of, 125,
    127
Almain, Jacques, 171
Alsace, estates of, 340
Amboise, Charles d', 325
Amboise, Conspiracy of,
    108
Amiens, 134, 162

Angoulême, 328
Angoulême, Francis, count
    of, 94
Angoulême, Marguerite d',
    102
Angoumois, estates of, 35
Anjou, René of, 68
Anjou: estates of, 9;
    inheritance law of, 87
Anne of Austria: as regent,
    294, 295–96, 306
Anne of Brittany, 94
Antoine, Michel, 336
Aquitaine, 20
Argenton, Antoine d', 89
Arles, 34, 149, 329
Armagnac, Jean, count of,
    93
Armagnac: estates of, 288,
    355; fiefs of, 76, 77–78,
    81; during Wars of
    Religion, 124–25
Armor, 90–91
Army: as career option for
    nobles, 97–98, 318–19;
    in France during
    Renaissance, 33; under
    Louis XIII, 227–28, 292–
    93; under Louis XIV,
    364–65; under Mazarin,
    301–2; standing, 91–92.
    See also Indenture
Arras, surrender of, 339
Artillery, 178–79
Artois, estates of, 14, 343
Assemblies: tradition of, 5–
    6. *See also* Estates,
    provincial; Estates
    Generals

Assemblies of the Clergy,
    116–17, 164, 165, 217;
    and Mazarin, 297–98;
    and Richelieu, 289–90
Assembly of Notables, 112,
    133, 167, 174, 189–90,
    223, 328, 369; of 1626–
    27, 225–30, 232
Auch, 89, 332
Autrand, Françoise, xix, 103
Autun: bishop of, 152;
    estates of, 34
Auvergne: Catholics in, 111;
    élections in, 237; estates
    of, 11, 53, 115, 284–85;
    nobility of, 79; taxation
    of, 217. *See also* Basse-
    Auvergne, estates of;
    Haute-Auvergne, estates
    of
Auxerre, estates of, 34
Auzan, 83
Avignon, university of, 100

Barbin, Claude, 188, 194,
    202, 220–21
Bar-sur-Seine, estates of, 34
Basin, Thomas, 17
Bas-Limousin, estates of, 35
Basse-Auvergne, estates of,
    36, 158–59, 200, 236,
    284, 354
Basse-Marche, estates of, 35
Bassompierre, Marshal, 226
Bauffrement, Claude de, 54
Bayeux, nobility in, 70, 73,
    128, 311, 312, 317–18,
    319, 320
Bazadais, estates of, 355

Béarn: administration of, 40; and Albret family, 76–77, 79, 80, 81, 123; Catholics in, 202–3, 207, 208, 210, 217; estates of, 35, 39, 201–4; fiefs of, 125; and Henry IV, 155–57; under Louis XIII, 208, 210, 250–51, 276

Beauce: nobility of, 70–71, 73, 84, 98, 99, 127, 128, 312–13, 317, 319, 320; noble income in, 125

Beaujeu, Anne de, 23, 53

Beaujeu, Pierre de, 23, 53

Beaujolais, estates of, 35, 160, 289, 354

Beauvais-Nangis, Nicolas de Brichanteau de, 98

Beik, William, xix–xx

Bellay, Joachim du, 102

Bellegarde, Governor, 216, 240, 241, 242, 268, 269

Bellièvre, Pomponne de, 131–34, 139, 150, 161, 163, 164, 174, 189, 222, 223, 259, 361, 370, 375

Bergin, Joseph, 292

Berry, estates of, 9

Bérulle, Pierre de (cardinal), 220, 222, 255, 263

Béza, Theodore, 55

Béziers, Edict of, 274–75, 278–79, 299

Bigorre: estates of, 250–51, 338; fiefs in, 75, 155, 157

Biron, duke of, 152–53, 176; conspiracy of, 175, 179

Bismarck, Otto von, 375

Black Death, 6; impact of on population, 59, 69

Bloch, Marc, xviii

Blois: Estates General at, 112, 114; sire de Gouberville at, 96–97; ordonnance of, 90

Bluche, François, 322

Bodin, Jean, 169–71

Bohanan, Donna, xix, 323

Bologna, Concordat of, 26, 98

Bonet, Honoré, 67

Bonne, François de, 126

Bordeaux, 136, 161, 191, 211; fiefs of, 77; inheritance law of, 88; parlement of, 11–12, 21, 122, 136, 323, 361; taxation of, 14, 193

Boulonnais, 338, 351–52

Bourbon, house of: during Wars of Religion, 109, 124–25

Bourbonnais, estates of, 11

Bresse: élections in, 255, 371; estates of, 142–43, 160, 195; under Louis XIV, 344–45, 356; nobility in, 330

Brittany: army of, 178; during Colbert ministry, 339; dukes of, 94; estates of, 37, 39, 40, 42, 55, 115, 154–55, 160–61, 191, 198–99; indentures in, 68; under Louis XIV, 343, 348–50, 357; nobility in, 323, 331; parlement of, 34; during Richelieu ministry, 251–53, 276, 279–82; taxation of, 154–55, 198–99, 215

Brosse, Claude, 150–51, 216–17, 287

Buckingham, duke of, 230

Bugey: élections in, 255, 371; estates of, 142–43, 160, 195; under Louis XIV, 344–45, 356; nobility in, 330

Burgundy: administration of, 20, 38, 368; courts of aides in, 261–62; élections in, 254, 256, 257, 259, 276; élus of, 115; estates of, 21–22, 24, 35, 37, 40, 42, 53, 55, 115, 152–54, 179, 191, 195, 201, 277; intendants of, 301; lay peerage of, 74; under Louis XIV, 343–44; nobility in, 330; during Richelieu ministry, 239–

42, 268–69, 290; taxation of, 105, 152–54, 160, 215–16, 240–41

Cahors: bishops of, 355; university of, 100, 193

Calvinism: in Renaissance France, 107–8. See also Protestants

Capetian princes, 313, 315

Carcassonne, parlement of, 122

Casal, 231, 263–64

Castres, 209

Catherine (sister of Henry IV), 157

Catholic League, 119–22; and Henry IV, 161–62, 172, 370

Catholic reformation, 221, 222, 223, 266

Catholics: in Béarn, 202–3; and Henry IV, 130, 156–57, 161, 164–66, 172, 370; under Louis XIII, 206–7, 229–30, 261; under Louis XIV, 359; and Richelieu, 221; during Wars of Religion, 111, 119–22

Caumartin, 218

Caux region, 125

Chabod, Federico, 32

Chalais conspiracy, 224, 225, 251

Chamber of accounts, 5, 194–95, 247–48; of Burgundy, 153, 262; in Languedoc, 145, 272; in Provence, 244–45, 262

Champagne, estates of, 9, 33

Champigny, President, 268

Chantilly, 82

Charles V, 4, 6–7, 17, 33, 37, 60, 101; army of, 91; nobility under, 71, 72, 74

Charles V (emperor), 94

Charles VI, 4, 7, 9, 17, 60, 71

Charles VII, 3–4, 13, 15–16, 20–21, 22, 23, 28, 59; army of, 33, 91–92,

367; as dauphin, 8; and estates, 8–9, 18, 34, 36, 37; and Estates General, 8, 367; nobility under, 74; taxation under, 8–12, 17, 37, 44, 368

Charles VIII, 23, 37, 53; army of, 97; and Marshal Gié, 94; nobility under, 74, 93

Charles IX, 86, 95, 107, 108; and municipal governments, 118; taxation under, 115

Charles the Bold, 15, 21

Charolais, estates of, 34

Chartres, 328

Chasseneuz, Barthélemy de, 51

Châteauneuf-de-Mazenc, 123

Châtellerault, assembly at, 166

Chaulnes, duke of, 349

Chevalier, Bernard, 46

Childeric, 54

Chivalric orders, 68

Church: as career option for nobility, 98, 100, 319–20

Clairac, 209

Claude (daughter of Louis XII), 26, 94

Clément, Jacques, 130

Clergy: and Louis XIII, 203; and Richelieu, 289–90; and Sully, 164–65, 166. See also Assemblies of the Clergy; Church

Clermont-en-Beauvaisis: échevins of, 284–85, 354; estates of, 51–52, 159, 200

Code Michau, 235, 268, 337

Colbert, Jean Baptiste, 260, 296, 302; as minister to Louis XIV, 336, 337–52, 353–57, 358–63, 375

Coligny, Admiral, 107

Colleges, 332

Comballet, Madame, 265

Combes, Jean, 52

Comminges, 143;

administration of, 38; estates of, 35, 38, 350, 355; taille in, 85

Commynes, Philippe de, 9, 13, 17–18, 102

Concini, Concino, 188, 195, 263, 308

Concordat of Bologna, 25

Condé, Henri II, prince of, 147, 182, 183, 184, 188, 189, 200, 224, 247, 252, 253, 257, 269, 270–71, 277, 279, 290, 295, 296, 300, 305–6, 314

Condé, Louis I, prince of, 107–8, 111, 112

Condé, Louis II, prince of, 314, 343–44

Condomois: estates of, 36, 355; taille in, 85

Constant, Jean-Marie, xix, 84, 306

Conti, Armond de, 314

Coriolis, president of parlement of Aix, 148

Court of aides, 5, 14; of Burgundy, 261–62; of Dauphiné, 261–62; of Montpellier, 194

Crossbows, 90, 91

Crouzet, Denis, 108

Crussol, count of, 111

Cujas, Jacques, 41

d'Albret. See Albret

d'Aligre, Chancellor, 224

Damville, 82

Damville, Henri de. See Montmorency, Henri I de

D'Artagnan, 318

D'Aubray, Druex, 244

Dauphiné: assemblée du pays, 239, 353; assemblies in, 122, 356; court of aides in, 261–62; élections in, 253, 275–76, 287; estates of, 34, 37, 39–40, 41, 55, 149–52, 191, 196; fortifications in, 227; under Louis XIII, 237–39; nobility in, 58–59, 126, 177, 287, 329;

Protestants in, 114–15; taxation in, 85, 117, 138, 149–52, 216–17, 287

Day of Dupes, 224, 225, 246, 261–67

De la Roche-Flavin, Bernard, 51

Deslandes, Captain, 308

Déville-lès-Rouen, 83

Devyver, André, 105, 334

DeWald, Jonathan, xix, 322

Digne, 243

Dijon, 152, 162, 163; and Louis XIII, 269; marriage in, 69; nobility in, 330; parlement of, 56, 105, 131; sovereign court at, 122. See also Burgundy

Doucet, Roger, 28–29, 42–43

Drouot, Henri, 42, 120

Dueling, 179–80

Du Moulin, Charles, 65

Duplessis-Mornay, Philippe, 102

Dupont-Ferrier, Gustave, xv–xvi, xvii

Durefort, Gailhard de, 67

Duret, Charles, 218

Edmondes, Sir Thomas, 254, 255

Education, of nobility, 100–102, 321, 331–34

Edward III, 4

Effiat, Antone Coiffier de Ruzé, 225, 243, 245; as superintendent of finances, 257–59, 260, 272, 273

Élections: abolition of, 191–92, 268–78, 371, 373; creation of, 137–43, 210–14, 237–60, 370–71, 372–73; under Henry IV, 158–61; under Louis XIII, 236–37, 282–89; under Louis XIV, 352–58. See also Élus; names of individual jurisdictions

Élus, 6–7, 11, 12, 13, 14, 41, 135; become royal appointees, 7. See also

Élus *(continued)*
  Names of individual
  jurisdictions
Entails, 88–89
Epernon, duke of, 109, 111,
  177, 178, 291, 325
Estates, provincial: of
  Anjou, 9; of Agenais, 35,
  36, 37, 38, 141; of
  Angoumois, 35; of Artois,
  14; of Autun, 34; of
  Auvergne, 11, 53, 115,
  284–85; of Auxerre, 34;
  of Bar-sur-Seine, 34; of
  Bas-Limousin, 35; of
  Basse-Auvergne, 36, 158–
  59, 200; of Basse-Marche,
  35; of Béarn, 39, 201–4;
  of Berry, 9; of
  Bourbonnais, 11; of
  Bresse, 142–43, 160, 195;
  of Brittany, 37, 39, 40,
  42, 55, 115, 154–55,
  191, 198–99, 251–53; of
  Bugey, 142–43, 160, 195;
  of Burgundy, 21–22, 24,
  35, 37, 40, 42, 53, 55,
  115, 152–54, 191, 201,
  277, 300; of Champagne,
  9, 33; of Charolais, 34; of
  Clermont-en-Beauvaisis,
  51–52, 200; of
  Comminges, 35, 38, 350;
  of Condomois, 36; of
  Dauphiné, 34, 37, 39–
  40, 41, 55, 149–52, 191,
  196, 287; of Forez, 11; of
  Gex, 142–43, 160, 195;
  of Guyenne, 11–12, 14,
  21, 30, 34–35, 36, 115,
  135–42, 166, 190–94; of
  Haute-Auvergne, 36,
  200–201; of Haute-
  Marche, 35; of Ile-de-
  France, 9, 33; of Haut-
  Limousin, 35; of La
  Marche, 11; of
  Languedoc, 6, 10, 18, 20,
  21, 34, 36, 41, 104, 116,
  143–47, 191, 201; of
  Languedoil, 6–7, 8, 17,
  368; of Lannes, 14; of
  Loire Valley, 33; and
  Louis XIII, 210–19; and

Louis XIV, 339–52; of
  Lyonnais, 9, 90; of
  Mâconnais, 34; of Maine,
  9; and Marillac, 236–60;
  and Mazarin, 297–301;
  and monarchy, 193–94;
  of Moulins, 23; of
  Navarre, 40, 56, 202–3;
  of Normandy, 11, 12, 34,
  37, 49, 53, 115, 141,
  158, 199–200, 286–87,
  298; of Orléanais, 9; of
  Orléans, 114; of Périgord,
  11, 14, 35, 38, 141–42,
  160, 194; of Picardy, 9,
  33; of Poitou, 9, 35; of
  Pontoise, 31, 106, 113; of
  Provence, 37, 148–49,
  191, 195, 277–78, 300;
  of Quercy, 38, 41, 193,
  194; and Richelieu, 236–
  60; of Rouergue, 38, 57,
  192, 194, 211, 213, 288;
  of Saintonge, 9, 35; of
  Somme, 14; and Sully,
  136–55, 160–61, 181–
  82; of Touraine, 9
Estates Generals, 6–9; of
  1468, 14, 94–95; of
  1484, 15–16, 94–95,
  327; of 1560, xviii, 105,
  113, 327; of 1561, 114;
  of 1576, 327; of 1588,
  179, 327; of 1614, 184–
  90, 192, 193, 200, 202,
  222, 223, 232, 233, 257,
  258, 309, 331, 335; and
  Anne of Austria, 295–97,
  306–7; under Charles
  VII, 33–35, 36–37, 41,
  367; under Charles VIII,
  37; composition of, 35;
  and Francis I, 28, 41–42;
  functions of, 40–41;
  under Henry II, 41; and
  Louise of Savoy, 26;
  under Marie de Medici,
  184–90, 198; and
  monarchy, 49–50, 112–
  17, 170; nobility in, 327–
  28, 329; role of in
  taxation, 17, 31, 36, 44,
  52, 116
Eurich, Amanda, xix

Evident necessity, doctrine
  of, 18–19

Ferrebouc, Pierre, 64
Feudalism: rise of, 5–6. *See
  also* Indenture
Fézenzaguet, viscounty of,
  78
Fief-rente, 61, 62–63, 64
Flanders, lay peerage of, 74
Flavigny, parlement of, 122
Foix, Gaston IV, count of,
  63
Foix: estates of, 339, 351;
  under Henry IV, 155;
  under Louis XIII, 250–51
Foix, house of. *See* Albret
  family
Forez: élections in, 237;
  estates of, 11, 201, 289,
  354; nobility of, 70;
  royalists in, 159
Fouquet, Jean, 3
Fouquet, Nicolas, 308, 309–
  10, 316, 336
Franche-Comté, estates of,
  340
Francis I, xxi, 35, 365; and
  élections, 254; and
  estates, 36–37; and fief-
  rente, 64; nobility under,
  82, 98, 104; taxation
  under, 25, 26–28, 30, 44,
  45
Francis II, 95, 107, 108
Franklin, Julian, 51, 169
Frederick of the Palatinate,
  207
Fresnes, Forget de, 139, 140
Fronde, 47, 295, 301, 302,
  305, 359, 360, 363, 374

Gabelle, 25, 30, 35
Gaston IV, count of Foix,
  63
General Council of the
  Holy Union, 121
Gex: élections in, 255, 371;
  estates of, 142–43, 160,
  195; under Louis XIV,
  344–45, 356; nobility in,
  330
Gié, Marshal, treason trial
  of, 93–94

Gigors, 123
Gilles, Henri, 42
Gorgias, Michel, 64
Gouberville, Gilles Picot, sire de, 79, 96–97, 324
Grammont, count of, 250
Grée, Jean de Bruc, sieur de la, 252
Greengrass, Mark, 83
Grenoble, 21, 149–50, 329; parlement of, 117, 122, 151, 227, 323. See also Dauphiné
Guémadeuc, baron de, 205–6
Guise, Charles, duke of, 148, 176, 242–43, 244, 251, 256, 264–65, 269, 270, 291
Guise, François, duke of, 108
Guise, Henri, duke of, 109, 113, 116, 120
Guise, dukes of, 96; during Wars of Religion, 108–12
Guyenne: demise of estates, 355–56; élections in, 190–92, 255, 282, 288, 371, 372; élus in, 41, 137–42, 190–92, 210–13, 229; estates of, 11–12, 14, 21, 30, 34–35, 36, 115, 135–42, 143, 160, 166, 190–94; governor of, 126; under Louis XIII, 210–13, 354–55; parlement of, 21; Protestants in, 188; taxation of, 221, 236, 288
Guymier, Cosme, 51

Habsburgs, 155, 207, 208, 222, 231, 235; war against, 264, 278, 290, 293–94, 308, 318
Hamscher, Albert N., xix
Harcourt, count of, 308
Harding, Robert, xix
Haute-Auvergne, estates of, 36, 176, 200–201, 284, 285, 354
Haute-Marche, estates of, 35

Haut-Limousin, estates of, 35
Hautot-sur-Dieppe, 83
Hennequin, Jean, 52
Henry II (France), 29, 95, 239; death of, 107, 369; and élections, 254; and municipal government, 120; nobility under, 72, 82; taxation under, 29–30, 45
Henry III (France), 19, 50, 54, 107; death of, 130; taxation under, 116; during Wars of Religion, 109–10, 112
Henry IV (France), 85, 88, 123, 332, 333; and absolutism, 168–69, 180; army of, 178–79, 318; relations with Catholics, 130, 156–57, 161, 164–66, 172, 370; and clientage, 175–78; death of, 181, 371; on dueling, 179–80; financial problems of, 130–35; and estates in Guyenne, 135–42, 143; and hereditary lands, 155–61; nobility under, 172–74, 304, 312, 313, 319; and Protestants, 130, 156–57, 161, 165, 370; and provincial estates, 142–55, 158–61, 180; Sully as adviser to, 131, 134–35, 136–42, 143, 144–45, 146, 154–55, 157, 160, 161, 172, 175, 177, 178, 194, 282, 370–71; Sully's wealth from, 315–16; taxation under, 135–41, 142–55, 370–71; and towns, 161–68
Henry V (England), 4, 7, 34, 367
Henry VIII (England), 25, 50
Henry of Navarre, 81, 127. See also Henry IV (France)
Higounet, Charles, 42
Holt, Mack, xix, 119

Homosexuality, 65
Hotman, François, 54–56
Huguenots: assemblies of, 121; under Louis XIII, 231, 236, 247, 261, 263, 292, 372; taxation by, 116
Hundred Years War, 19, 33, 68, 367; impact of on population, 59; vassals in, 62

Ile-de-France, 26–27, 291, 319; estates of, 9, 33
Indenture, 61–68; advantages of, 62–63; as distinguished from fief-rente, 61, 64–65; terms of, 66–67
Inheritance laws, 86–90
Intendants, 29, 283–84, 291, 292, 301, 362, 372
Isabella of Bavaria, 4
Italy, France's involvement in, 263–64

Jean V, duke of Brittany, 71
Jeannin, President, 153, 172, 181
Joan of Arc, 3
John II, 6, 26; nobility under, 68, 71, 74
John, duke of Brittany, 63
John the Fearless, 4, 7, 62
Joly, Claude, 55
Joseph, Father, 292
Jouanna, Arlette, xix, 334
Joyeuse, Anne de, 109
Judicial office, as career option for nobles, 98–99, 101–2, 323–24
Justinian, 87

Kersaliou, Raoul de, 63
Kettering, Sharon, xix, 323
Kneeling, 66
Kuhn, Thomas S., xx

La Barre, René-Laurent, 52–53
La Flèche, 332
La Force, Jacques Nompar de Caumont, duke of, 156, 203–4, 209, 226

La Marche, estates of, 11
La Meilleraye, Armand Charles de La Porte, marquis de, 315
La Meilleraye, Charles de La Porte, marquis de, 280–81, 315
Languedoc: administration of, 36, 38, 338–39; court of aides in, 262; élections in, 254, 258, 259–60, 264, 276; élus in, 41, 273–74; intendants in, 301; under Louis XIII, 213–15, 271–75, 372; Protestants in, 110, 114–15, 188, 214; during Richelieu ministry, 246–50, 273, 290–91; taille in, 85; taxation of, 9, 18, 138, 144–46, 160, 278, 279
Languedoc, estates of, 6, 10, 18, 20, 21, 34, 36, 41, 104, 116, 143–47, 191, 201, 272, 298–99; administration of, 38; composition of, 35; and Louis XIV, 341, 345–48, 357; Protestants in, 111
Languedoil, estates of, 6–7, 8, 17, 368
Lannes, 338; élus in, 12; estates of, 14, 355
La Noue, François de, 45
La Rochelle, 35, 118, 217, 230–31, 236, 273, 289; assembly at, 208; nobility in, 72
La Trémoille, François de, 82, 86, 102
La Trémoille, Georges de, 66–67, 81–82
La Trémoille family, 81–82, 83, 315, 317
Lauwart, Pierre, 63
La Valette, cardinal of, 226
La Valette, Jean Louis de Nogaret de, 109
Lebrun, François, 46
Le Caron, Louis, 52
Lefèvre, Nicolas, 224
Le Jay, President, 234, 235, 259, 268

Le Pelletier, Richard, 325
Lescar, bishop of, 250
Lesdiguières, duke of, 126, 152, 177, 196, 197, 209, 210
Le Tellier, François-Michel, Marquis de Louvois, 336
Le Tellier, Michel, 296, 301–2
Lettre de retenue, 61
Lévis family, 100
Lewis, P. S., xix
L'Hôpital, Michel de, 31, 50, 114, 167
Limoges, 162, 221
Limousin, fiefs of, 76, 77
Lionne, Hugues de, 296, 336
Littleton, Thomas, 65
Livron, 123
Loire Valley, estates of, 33
Longueville, duke of, 291, 309
Louis, duke of Orléans, 4, 62, 63
Louis VI, 325
Louis XI, 12–15, 21–22, 68; army of, 92; and estates, 14, 37; and Marshal Gié, 94; nobility under, 72, 93, 103; taxation under, 14–16, 18–19, 44–45, 48–49, 71
Louis XII, 23–26, 74, 375; and Marshal Gié, 94; nobility under, 98
Louis XIII, 184, 307, 371–72; absolutism of, 204, 219; army of, 227–28, 292–93; and Assembly of Notables, 190, 225–30; relations with Brittany, 251–53; relations with Burgundy, 240, 241–42; and Catholic clergy, 203; death of, 294; early years of, 205–7, 309; and Guyenne élections, 210–13; illness of, 264; and Languedoc, 213–15; and Marillac, 221–22, 224–25, 232–35; nobility under, 312, 313; and Protestant revolt, 208–10;

and provincial estates, 194, 217–19; and Pyrenean estates, 250–51; religious freedom under, 209–10; and Richelieu, 222–25, 230, 231–35, 265; taxation under, 196, 210–13, 215–17, 282–89
Louis XIV, xix, xx, xxi, 56, 182, 296, 301; as absolute monarch, 358–66, 375; army of, 318; Colbert as adviser to, 336, 337–52, 353–57, 358–63; nobility under, 72, 312, 313, 314–15, 317, 319–20, 363, 374–75; Protestants under, 359; and provincial estates, 339–52; taxation under, 365–66
Louise of Savoy, 26
Louis Philippe, xiv
Louvois, François-Michel Le Tellier, marquis de, 336
Loyseau, Charles, 326
Lublinskaya, A. D., xvi
Lusignan, Guy de, 128
Lusignan, Louis de, 128
Luxembourg, Waleran de, 63
Luynes, Charles d'Albret, seigneur de, 188, 189, 208, 309
Lyonnais, 35, 160, 201, 289, 291; estates of, 9, 90, 354; taxation of, 217
Lyons, 9, 289; estates of, 35; and Henry IV, 161–62; land ownership in, 84; Protestants in, 119

Machiavelli, Niccolò, 47–48
Mâconnais, estates of, 34
Maine, estates of, 9
Major, John, 171
Mangot, Claude, 188, 202
Mantua, 231
Marbeuf, Claude de, 252
Marguerite of Valois, 81
Maridor, President, 308
Mariéjol, Jean-H., 294
Marillac, Charles de, 49–50
Marillac, Louis de, 221, 266

Marillac, Michel de, 136, 143, 218, 220, 337, 357, 361, 375; as administrator, 255–56, 257, 259–60, 261–63, 264, 293, 294; and estates of Burgundy, 240, 241–42; and estates of Languedoc, 246, 249–50; and estates of Provence, 243, 244; as minister under Louis XIII, 221–22, 224–25, 231, 232–35, 372–73; and ordonnance of 1629, 232–35, 283; relationship with Richelieu, 263; reversal of fortune, 265–68, 271, 276

Marriage patterns, 69–70, 310

Marseilles, 34, 118, 149, 162, 329

Matignon, governor of Guyenne, 126

Maupeou, Gilles de, 139, 174, 218, 372

Mayenne, duke of, 121, 173–74, 307, 370

Mazarin, Jules, cardinal, 48, 305–6, 308, 348, 354, 373; death of, 336; and Estates General, 295–97; as minister to Anne of Austria, 294–303; as minister to Louis XIV, 335, 360; and nobility, 313, 315, 316; and provincial estates, 297–301; wealth of, 316

Medici, Catherine de, 107; as regent, 108–9; taxation under, 116

Medici, Lorenzo de, 18

Medici, Marie de, 208, 252–53, 308–9; and Béarn, 202; and Estates General, 184–90, 198; and Marillac, 263; and nobility, 308; and ordonnance of 1629, 232–35; and provincial estates, 194; and Richelieu, 220–21, 265,

266; Villeroy as adviser to, 181–84, 185, 188–90, 302–3

Mende, bishop of, 346

Mercoeur, 154, 176

Mesgrigny, Jean de, 200–201, 284–85

Mesgrigny, Jérôme de, 329

Mesmes, Henri de, 325

Mettam, Roger, xx

Mézières, Philippe de, 68

Military. See Army; Indenture

Millau, 209

Monarchy, absolute, xxi; and the Fronde, 302; under Louis XIII, 204, 219; under Louis XIV, 358–66, 375; tendency toward, 168–71

Monarchy, Renaissance, 367–75; administration of, 32–47; decentralization of, 19–22, 368; and Estates Generals, 112–17; and growth of self-government, 47–50; under Louis XII, 24–25; and nobility, 57–58, 368–69; perceptions of, 47–56; inherent weakness of, xx–xxi

Monluc, Blaise de, 326

Monluc, Jean de, 325

Monluc, Jeanne de, 325

Montaigne, 333

Montauban, 208

Montbazon, Governor, 291

Montesquieu, 89

Montgomery, count of, 123

Montmorency, Anne de, 40, 82–83, 102, 125, 144, 145, 146–47

Montmorency, Guillaume de, 82

Montmorency, Henri I de, 144–47

Montmorency, Henri II de, 93, 214, 215, 247, 248, 251, 252, 257, 264–65, 268, 271–72, 273–74, 290–91, 373

Montmorency family, 82–83, 96, 147, 325

Montpellier, 209, 249, 262; court of aides of, 194; university of, 100

Montpensier, duke of, 176

Moote, Lloyd, 302

More, Thomas, 48

Moret, countess of, 141

Morgues, Matthieu de, 266

Mornay, Philippe du Plessis, 55

Motley, Mark, xix

Moulins: Assembly of Notables at, 112; estates of, 23

Mousnier, Roland, xvii, xix, xx, 32, 267, 326

Municipal governments, 34–40, 326; activities of, 46–47; under Louis XIV, 362–63. See also Towns

Murol, Guillaume de, 79, 100

Nantes, 162; sovereign court at, 122

Nantes, Edict of, 156, 165–66, 167, 229, 370; and Louis XIII, 209, 210; revocation of, 359–60

Narbonne, 278

Navarre: Albret family in, 76, 77, 81; estates of, 40, 56, 202–4; and Henry IV, 157; and Louis XIII, 208, 217, 250, 261

Navarrenx, fortification at, 91, 208

Nébouzan, estates of, 339, 351

Nègrepelisse, 209

Nérac, barony of, 125

Netz, Nicolas de, 140–41

Neubourg, 83

Neuschel, Kristen, xix, 112

Nevers, dukes of, 50, 85–86, 231; income of, 128

Nîmes, 209

Noailles, Henri de, 200–201, 284

Noailles family, 100

Nobility: agricultural

Nobility *(continued)*
   income of, 75–86; and
   the army, 90–92, 97,
   118–19, 318–19; careers
   of, 96–100, 318–21;
   changes in, 374; defined,
   58–59; demographic
   changes, 69–75, 172,
   310–13; economic status
   of, 59–60, 314–18, 369;
   education of, 100–102,
   321, 331–34; in Estates
   Generals, 113–14;
   government officials as,
   99; income of, 123–29,
   314–18; inheritance laws
   for, 86–90; kings'
   dependence upon, 57–58,
   368–69; land holdings of,
   85–86; lay peers, 74–75,
   313; under Louis XIV,
   72, 312, 313, 314–15,
   317, 319–20, 363–64;
   marriage patterns of, 69–
   70, 89–90, 310; means of
   achieving, 71–74, 311–
   13; under Marie de
   Medici, 185–86, 187;
   and patron-client
   relationship, 93–96, 187–
   88, 304–10; robe versus
   sword, 103–6, 172–73,
   321–31, 374; role of in
   French history, xviii–xix,
   xxi; social mores of, 329–
   31, 334; taxation of, 60–
   61; during Wars of
   Religion, 108–12, 123–
   29. *See also* Indenture
Normandy: administration
   of, 21, 38, 291; estates of,
   11, 12, 34, 37, 49, 53,
   115, 141, 158, 199–200,
   286–87, 298; under
   Louis XIV, 343, 353;
   nobility of, 71, 83, 307,
   312; taxation of, 9, 115,
   158, 236
Noyes, Sublet des, 301

Oppède, baron d', 300
Oppetit-Perné, Danielle, 42
Ordonnance of 1629, 232–
   35, 258, 283

Orléanais, estates of, 9
Orléans, 162; and Anne of
   Brittany, 94; entailed
   estates in, 89; estates of,
   114; nobility of, 307;
   ordonnance of, 95
Orléans, Charles d', 101
Orléans, Gaston, duke of,
   224, 225–26, 265
Orléans, Louis duke of, 63
Orléans, Philip of, 314–15
Ornano, Alfonso d', 126,
   137–38, 140, 179
Outre-Seine, taxation of, 9

Pagès, Georges, xvii, 369
Pamiers, bishop of, 351
Pancarte, 164, 167
Paris, 162; Catholic League
   in, 122; Estates General
   of, 112–13; inheritance
   law in, 87; nobility in,
   84, 176–77; parlement
   of, 20, 26, 99, 103, 104,
   106, 167, 188, 234–35,
   259, 321, 322, 327;
   University of, 171
Parlements, 5; of Aix, 122,
   148, 196, 300; of
   Bordeaux, 21, 26, 323,
   361; in Brittany, 34; of
   Burgundy, 22; in
   Dauphiné, 21; of Dijon,
   56, 105; of Grenoble,
   117, 122, 151, 227, 323;
   nobility in, 322–23; of
   Paris, 20, 26, 99, 103,
   104, 106, 167, 188, 234–
   35, 259, 321, 322, 327;
   of Pau, 208; of Rennes,
   122, 308, 323, 361; of
   Rouen, 26, 105, 258,
   321, 322; of Toulouse,
   20, 136, 262, 268, 271,
   274
Pau, parlement at, 208
Paulette, 174, 175–76, 177,
   185–86, 188, 189, 190,
   261, 268, 304, 360
Peasants, taxation of, 125–
   26
Pension, 63–64
Pension à vie, 63
Pension à volenté, 63

Perche: inheritance law in,
   87
Périgord, 176, 289;
   administration of, 38, 40;
   élus in, 12; estates of, 11,
   14, 35, 38, 141–42, 160,
   194, 356; fiefs of, 76, 77
Périgueux, 126, 194
Perron, Cardinal, 186
Pertuis, parlement of, 122
Philibert, Emmanuel, 142
Philip II (Spain), 107, 128
Philip IV, 4; nobility under,
   74
Philip VI, 4; nobility under,
   74
Philip the Good of
   Burgundy, 4, 5, 8, 63, 68
Picardy, estates of, 9, 33
Picot, Guillaume, 324
Picot, Louis, 324
Plague. *See* Black Death
Plessis, Armand du. *See*
   Richelieu, Armand du
   Plessis (Cardinal)
Pocquet, Barthélemy, 42
Poissy, contract of, 31
Poitiers, 9, 162; inheritance
   law in, 87; parlement of,
   20
Poitou, estates of, 9, 35
Polignac, viscount of, 285
Politiques, 119–20
Pollard, A. F., xvi–xvii
Polybius, 52
Ponchâteau, baron de, 281–
   82
Pontcroix, Marc de
   Rosmadec, seigneur de,
   331
Pontoise, estates of, 31, 106,
   113
Pont-St.-Pierre, barony of,
   125
Porchnev, Boris, xvi
Pot, Philipe, 53
Prentout, Henri, 42
Property law, 86–89
Protestants: in Béarn, 202–
   3; and Henry IV, 130,
   156–57, 161, 165, 166;
   in Languedoc, 110, 111;
   under Louis XIII, 206,
   208–10, 229, 230, 256;

under Louis XIV, 359;
and Marie de Medici,
183; and split with
Catholics, 119
Provence: administration of,
34, 40; assemblies of,
115; élections in, 258,
259, 264, 276, 338;
estates of, 37, 148–49,
191, 195, 277–78, 300;
under Louis XIII, 242–
46, 269–71; under Louis
XIV, 341–43; nobility of,
70, 73, 322–23;
parlement of, 322–23;
taille in, 85; taxation in,
39, 138, 148
Provincial estates. *See*
Estates, provincial
Pyrenean provinces, 250–
51, 276; under Louis
XIV, 338, 350–51

Quatre-Vallés, estates of,
339, 351
Quercy, 211; administration
of, 38; estates of, 38, 41,
193, 194, 355; nobility
of, 93

Rais, Gilles de, 66–67
Ranum, Orest, 334
Rennes, parlement of, 122,
308, 323
Retrait lignager, 89
Retz, duke of, 309, 325
Rheims: marriage in, 69
Richelieu, Armand du
Plessis (Cardinal), xvii,
xviii, 147, 175, 220–21,
315; and Assembly of
Notables, 226–29; and
clergy, 289–90; death of,
294; and élections, 254–
55, 257; German policy,
293; as minister under
Louis XIII, 222–25, 230,
231–35, 255–60, 261–
67, 293–95, 372; and
provincial estates, 288–
89, 290–91, 357, 372,
373; and provincial
unrest, 267–76; relations

with Brittany, 251–53,
276, 279–82; relations
with Burgundy, 239–40,
268–69, 290; relations
with Languedoc, 246–50,
273, 278, 290–91;
relations with Provence,
242–46; wealth of, 316
Rivière-Verdun, estates of,
192, 355
Rochechouart family, 100
Rochefort, Jacques de Silly,
count of, 105
Rohan, duchess of, 349
Rohan, duke of, 184, 203,
209, 222, 230, 349, 357
Romans, parlement of, 122
Rouen, 112; Assembly of
Notables in, 133;
parlement of, 26, 105,
321, 322; Protestants in,
119
Rouergue: estates of, 38, 57,
192, 194, 211, 213, 288,
355; fiefs of, 76; taxation
of, 9, 136

Saint-Antonin, 209
Saint-Benôit, Jean de, 64
Saint-Brieuc, bishop of, 348
Sainte-Foy, assembly at, 166
Sainte-Menehould, treaty of,
184
Saint-Esprit, 109–10
Saint-Flour, 200–201, 236–
37, 285
Saint-Germain: Assembly of
Notables at, 112
Saint-Jean d'Angély, 208,
209
Saint-Julien, Pierre, 55–56
Saint-Malo, 252; bishop of,
281
Saint Michael, Order of, 68,
93, 109
Saintonge, estates of, 9, 35
Saint-Papoul, bishop of, 346
Saint-Paul-Trois-Châteaux,
123
Salmon, John, xix
Salt tax. *See* Gabelle
Sancy, Achille de Harlay,
baron de, 133, 266, 281

Sarlat, 319
Saulx-Tavannes, Gaspard de,
86, 98, 126, 326
Savaron, Jean, 56, 324
Savoy, 13, 142; nobility of,
71
Schalk, Ellery, xix, 334
Séguier, Pierre, 298
Selves, Julien de
Camberfore, sieur de,
137–41, 143, 144–45,
218
Seyssel, Claude de, 48, 51,
104
Sillery, Brulart de, 139, 150,
181
Silly, Jacques de. *See*
Rochefort, Jacques de
Silly, count of
Soman, Alfred, 293
Somme, estates of, 14
Souvert, Jean de, 153
Sovereign courts, 117–22,
262; under Louis XIV,
361–62; nobility in, 323–
24
Sovereignty, 169
Suhard, Georgette, 324
Sully, Maximilian de
Béthune, duke of, 191,
255, 325; as adviser to
Henry IV, 131, 134–35,
136–42, 143, 144–45,
146, 154–55, 157, 160,
161, 172, 175, 177, 178,
194, 282, 370–71; and
artillery, 178–79; and
clergy, 164–65, 166; and
Marie de Medici, 181–
82, 192; and municipal
governments, 163; and
sovereign courts, 168;
wealth of, 315–16
Sully-sur-Loire, 83

Taille. *See* Taxation
Taillon, 30
Tancarville, 83
Tarbes, bishop of, 338,
350–51
Taxation: under Catherine
de Medici, 115; under
Charles VII, 8–12, 17;

Taxation *(continued)*
under Charles IX, 115;
and Estates Generals, 17,
31, 36, 37, 44, 52, 116;
under Francis I, 25, 26–
28, 43–44; under Henry
II, 29–30; under Henry
III, 116; under Henry IV,
135–41, 142–55, 370–
71; under Louis XI, 14–
16, 18–19, 43, 48–49;
under Louis XIII, 196,
210–13, 215–17, 282–
83; under Louis XIV,
365–66; of nobility, 60–
61; of peasants, 125–26;
statistics on, 43–44. *See
also* Élections; Élus
Tax collectors. *See* Élus
Terride, baron of, 123, 127
Thaumassière, Gaspard
Thaumas de la, 65
Thierry, Augustin, xiii–xvi,
xvii, xviii, 57, 369
Thirty Years War, France's
involvement in, 207, 264
Tholin, Georges, 46
Thou, Jacques-Auguste de,
176
Toulon, 245–46

Toulouse: archbishop of,
358; fiefs of, 77; and
Henry II, 120; nobility
in, 72, 79; parlement of,
20, 136, 262, 268, 271,
274; Protestants in, 119;
sovereign court at, 122;
university of, 100
Touraine, estates of, 9
Tours: Estates General of,
14–16, 94–95; nobility
of, 84; parlement at, 122
Towns: Catholics versus
Protestants in, 119;
financial problems of,
123; and Henry IV, 161–
68; during Wars of
Religion, 117–23. *See also*
Municipal governments
Trent, Council of, 90
Troyes, 162, 163, 329;
treaty of, 26
Turenne, General, 306

Vendôme, César, duke of,
198, 199, 307
Ventadour, duke of, 144,
145, 146, 214–15
Versailles, 305
Vic, 218

Villars, seigneur de, 173
Villefranche, 201
Villeroy, Nicolas de
Neufville de, 172, 201,
291, 325; as adviser to
Louis XIII, 188–90, 192;
as adviser to Marie de
Medici, 181–84, 185,
188–90, 302–3, 371
Villiers, 82
Vitry, Marshal, 277, 291
Vivonne, Louis de
Rochechouart, duke of,
325

Wars of Religion, xxi, 16,
32, 45, 81, 83, 86, 106;
impact of on noble
income, 123–29; kings
and nobles during, 108–
12, 319; taxation during,
151; towns during, 117–
23
Weapons, 90–91
Weary, William A., xix, 81
Wills. *See* Inheritance laws
Wolfe, Martin, 15
Wood, James B., xix